SCHOOL PROGRAM • TEACHER EDITION

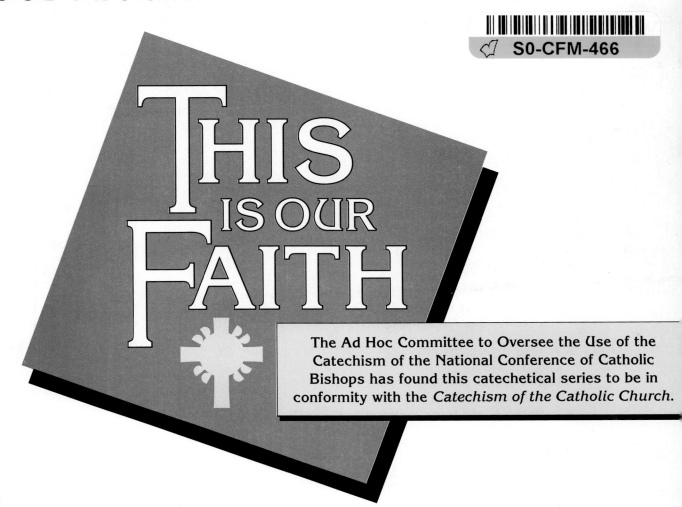

THIS IS OUR FAITH

The Ad Hoc Committee to Oversee the Use of the Catechism of the National Conference of Catholic Bishops has found this catechetical series to be in conformity with the *Catechism of the Catholic Church.*

Series Authors: Janaan Manternach
Carl J. Pfeifer

Teacher Edition Authors: Kate Sweeney Ristow **Sister Carolyn Puccio, C.S.J.**
Dolores Ready **Ana Maria Bencomo Cape**

Susan G. Keys **Barbara Carol Vasiloff**
Maureen Shaughnessy, S.C. Mary Mescher
Paula Lenz

Student Edition Authors: Jo'Ann Chiarani **Maureen Gallagher**
Joan R. DeMerchant **Jean Marie Weber**

SILVER BURDETT GINN
PARSIPPANY, NJ

Contents . . . .

Consultants
Linda Blanchette, Anita Bridge, Fred Brown, Rod Brownfield, Sister Mary Michael Burns, S.C., Patricia Burns, Bernadine Carroll, Mary Ellen Cocks, Sister Peggy Conlon, R.S.M., Mary Ann Crowley, Pamela Danni, Sister Jamesetta DeFelice, O.S.U., Sister Mary Elizabeth Duke, S.N.D., Mary M. Gibbons, Yolanda Gremillion, Sister Angela Hallahan, C.H.F., Alice J. Heard, Sister Michele O'Connoll, P.B.V.M., Sister Angela O'Mahoney, P.B.V.M., Sister Ruthann O'Mara, S.S.J., Sandra Okulicz-Hulme, Judy Papandria, Rachel Pasano, Sallie Ann Phelan, Sister Geraldine M. Rogers, S.S.J., Mary Lou Schlosser, Patricia Ann Sibilia, Margaret E. Skelly, Lisa Ann Sorlie, Sister Victorine Stoltz, O.S.B., Sister Nancy Jean Turner, S.H.C.J., Christine Ward, Judith Reidel Weber, Kay White, Elizabeth M. Williams, Catherine R. Wolf, Florence Bambrick Yarney, Kathryn K. Zapcic

Advisory Board
Rev. Louis J. Cameli, Philip J. Cunningham, Sister Clare E. Fitzgerald, William J. Freburger, Greer G. Gordon, Sister Veronica R. Grover, S.H.C.J., Rev. Thomas Guarino, Rev. Robert E. Harahan, Rev. Eugene LaVerdieré, S.S.S., Rev. Frank J. McNulty, Rev. Msgr. John J. Strynkowski

National Catechetical Advisor
Kathleen Hendricks

Nihil Obstat
Kathleen Flanagan, S.C., Ph.D., Censor Librorum
Ellen Joyce, S.C., Ph.D., Censor Librorum

Imprimatur
✠ Most Reverend Frank J. Rodimer, Bishop of Paterson

The *nihil obstat* and *imprimatur* are official declarations that a book or pamphlet is free of doctrinal and moral error. No implication is contained therein that those who have granted the *nihil obstat* and *imprimatur* agree with the contents, opinions, or statements expressed.

Dear Catholic School Teacher,

The teaching of religion is an important responsibility for all Catholic School teachers. We commend you for assuming this responsibility and are proud to be your partner in sharing the Catholic faith with children.

We are especially pleased to announce that the National Conference of Catholic Bishops' Ad Hoc Committee to Oversee the Use of the Catechism has found this new edition of *This Is Our Faith* to be in conformity with the *Catechism of the Catholic Church*. This means that *This Is Our Faith* has a breadth and depth of content wherein the presentation of Catholic doctrine is authentic and therefore suitable for catechetical instruction.

This sharing of faith includes many dimensions: the instruction in doctrine, Scripture, and morality; the experience of prayer and liturgy; the building of a value system; the ability to relate teaching to life; the knowledge of the rich heritage we share in time, place, and people; and the profound respect for and love of the Catholic Church. *This Is Our Faith* addresses each of these dimensions.

We take our responsibility to Catholic education seriously and once again we have consulted you, the classroom teacher, at every step along the way of the development of this revision. The next few pages will give you an overview of the new *This Is Our Faith*. We know that you will find in this program everything that a publisher can provide to support you in your important work.

Your commitment to Catholic education and to the children whom you teach is one that we share. This program has been created to be the best for you and for your class. It is to you that we dedicate this edition of *This Is Our Faith*.

Sincerely,

Raymond T. Latour
Vice President & Director
Religion Division

Content is important to Catholic Identity.

What content is included?

THIS IS OUR FAITH is a developmental program, based on Scripture and rooted in the teachings of the *Catechism of the Catholic Church*. While the content for each year centers on one particular theme, strands on Church, Sacraments, Trinity, and Morality are interwoven throughout the program. The presentation of doctrine has been increased in each chapter of this new edition.

Plus—chapter reviews and **expanded unit reviews** help you to evaluate student progress as you teach!!

The chart to the right outlines the doctrinal content of Grade 3.

TRINITY — THREE PERSONS ONE GOD

CREATOR/FATHER
God is our creator.
The Father takes care of us and is always faithful to us.
God loves us like a loving parent.
God is Father, Son, and Holy Spirit.

JESUS
Jesus is always with us and is our best friend.
Jesus lived, died, and rose to new life.
Jesus is with us as a community of his followers, the Church.
Jesus began his new Church on earth.
Jesus came to bring us God's word.
Jesus' life was a life of prayer.
Jesus spent his life serving people in need.

THE BIBLE
The Bible is organized into books, chapters and verses.
The Bible contains information about God and prayer.
The psalms were prayers that Jesus liked to pray.

PRAYERS AND PRECEPTS
Sign of the Cross
The Lord's Prayer
Hail Mary
Glory Be to the Father
Morning Prayer
Evening Prayer
Grace Before Meals
Grace After Meals
Prayer of Sorrow
Apostles' Creed
Prayer to the Holy Spirit
Prayers and precepts of the Church are used in lessons throughout the texts. Selected traditional prayers and precepts also appear in a special end-of-text section designed to encourage their memorization.

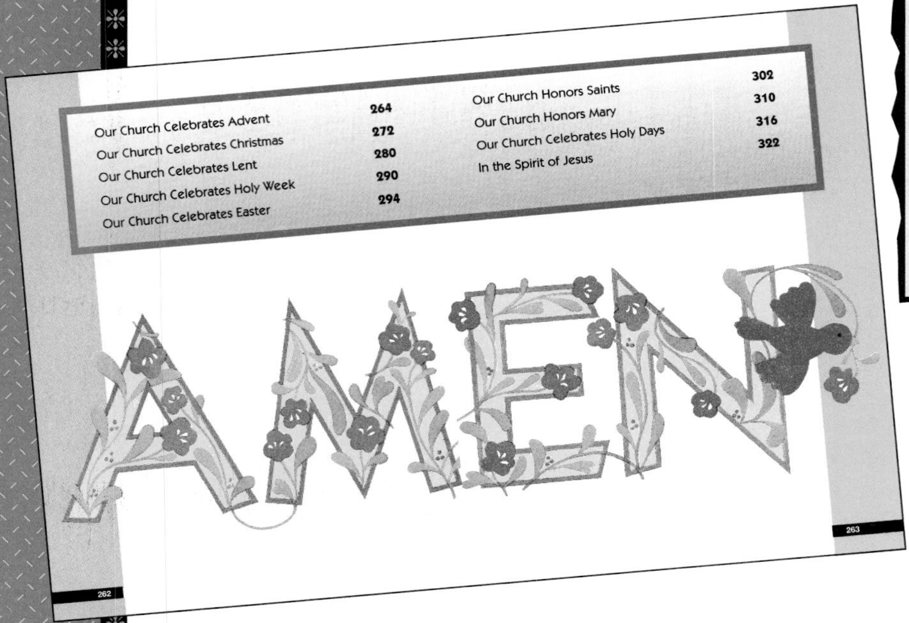

263

262

Our Amen Section of Saints, Feasts and Seasons is still conveniently located in the back of the student book and has been expanded just as you requested. Every year your students will have the opportunity to celebrate the holy seasons of Advent, Lent, Christmas, and Easter in addition to other special feasts.

THE HOLY SPIRIT

The Holy Spirit is always with us as our helper and guide.

The Holy Spirit draws Jesus' followers together as brothers and sisters in one Christian family.

The Holy Spirit came to the disciples on Pentecost.

The Holy Spirit is with us to help us pray.

The Holy Spirit inspires us to live a Christian life.

The Holy Spirit gives life to the Church on earth.

SACRAMENTS

Baptism, Confirmation, and Eucharist are the sacraments of initiation into the Church.

In Confirmation, we are sealed with the gift of the Holy Spirit.

Reconciliation and Anointing of the Sick are sacraments of healing.

Anointing of the Sick brings us healing and peace.

Matrimony and Holy Orders are sacraments of vocation.

Holy Orders is a sacrament of special service and commitment to the Church.

About the Mass

About Reconciliation

A complete lesson reviewing the basics of these sacraments.

CHURCH

The Catholic Church is the worldwide Christian community that recognizes the pope and bishops as its leaders and that celebrates the seven sacraments.

The first Christians were followers of Jesus and formed the earliest Christian communities.

The Catholic Church is one, holy, catholic, and apostolic.

The Church welcomes new members by celebrating the sacraments of initiation.

The Church continues Jesus' ministries of community building, preaching the word, worship, and service.

The Church works for love, justice, and peace.

MORALITY

We must serve people in need, as Jesus did.

The commandments show us ways of loving God and others and help us live good lives.

Jesus sums up the commandments for us in his commandment to love.

We show care and concern by living the works of mercy.

RELIGIOUS VOCABULARY

Anointing	Confirmation	Immersion	Parables	Saints
Anointing the Sick	Corporal	Initiation	Parish	Savior
Apostles' Creed	crux gemmata	Jesse Tree	Pastor	Scribes
Apostolic	Deacon	Justice	Pentecost	Scriptures
Ash Wednesday	Diocese	Lector	Pope	Sin
Baptism	Doctor	Liturgy	Praise	Spiritual
Baptismal Font	Easter Vigil	Liturgy of the Hours	Prayer	Stations of the Cross
Baptismal Pool	Epistles	Marks of the Church	Prophet	Synagogue
Bishop	Eucharist	Matrimony	Psalms	Tomb
Blackrobes	Faith	Mercy	Reconciliation	Triduum
Blessed Trinity	Faithful	Ministry	Respect	Trinity
Calvary	Gospel	Ministry of Community Building	Resurrection	Trust
Catholic	Grace	Ministry of Service	Reverence	Twelve Apostles
Catholic Church	Great Commandment	Ministry of the Word	Ritual	Vocation
Catholics	Healing	Ministry of Worship	Rosary	Witness
Christ	Heaven	Mission	Sabbath	Worship
Christians	Holy	Missionaries	Sacraments	
Communion of Saints	Holy Orders	Myrrh		
Commandments	Holy Week			

Our Catholic Heritage, a special doctrinal section organized according to the four pillars of the *Catechism of the Catholic Church,* is included in each grade-level student book to provide you with the opportunity and resources necessary to teach and review basic Catholic teachings every year.

OUR CATHOLIC HERITAGE

What Catholics Believe		How Catholics Live	
About the Bible	328	About the Beatitudes	342
About the Trinity	330	About the Commandments	343
About the Catholic Church	331	About Sin and Grace	344
About Mary and the Saints	332	About Vocations	345
About Life Everlasting	332	About Missionaries	347
How Catholics Worship		How Catholics Pray	
About the Sacraments	333	About Kinds of Prayer	348
About the Mass	336	Stations of the Cross	349
About Reconciliation	340	About The Lord's Prayer	353

What about prayer?

THIS IS OUR FAITH emphasizes prayer in all forms from traditional to spontaneous, from music to meditation, from the spoken word and formal liturgical prayer to the psalms and prayers of the heart. Children learn not only prayers, but how to pray alone, in a small group, within the classroom or school or in the church assembly. **Among other resources within THIS IS OUR FAITH, you will find the following:**

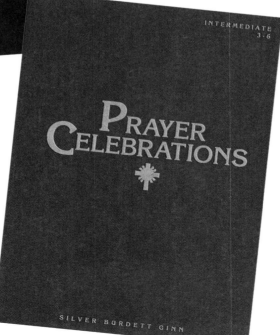

Praying a Litany of Saints

On the Feast of All Saints, we hear a joyful prayer that tells us that we, the living children of God, are united with all holy men and women, even those who have died. The priest prays that all Christians may come to share with the saints "all the joys of our Father's house." Today, we pray a Litany of Saints, a prayer that asks the saints in heaven to pray for us. We ask for their help as we continue to grow in holiness.

We want to live as your children. Lord, have mercy.
Lord, have mercy.
We want to live as Jesus taught us. Christ, have mercy.
Christ, have mercy.
We want to grow in holiness. Lord, have mercy.
Lord, have mercy.
Holy Mary, Mother of God, **pray for us.**
Michael, Gabriel, and all holy angels of God, **pray for us.**
John the Baptizer and all holy prophets, **pray for us.**
St. Joseph, **pray for us.**
Matthew, Mark, Luke, and John, **pray for us.**

_____, **pray for us.**

_____, **pray for us.**

_____, **pray for us.**

All you holy men and women, **hear our prayer.**

30 Prayer

▲ **Prayer pages** in each chapter of the student book provide instruction on and an experience of prayer each week.

▲
Prayers for Every Day is a wonderful resource for you. In it you will find prayers for every day of the year, as well as additional prayers to be said during special times and seasons.

▲
Prayer Celebrations are resource books full of complete grade-level-specific prayer services ready to use with your class. Everything is done for you. All you need to do is read the special preparation page, duplicate the master sheet, and begin the celebration!

What about Sunday?

This brand-new supplemental program helps prepare children to better understand the Sunday readings. It provides ways to help children participate more fully in the Sunday liturgy—a need expressed by many teachers. Here's how to do it!

Each week, perhaps on Friday, distribute the student leaflets for Sunday. Then together, listen to the Word of God and follow the specific activities that will help the Word take on real meaning for children. They will be ready to listen and pray on Sunday!

This is indeed a true liturgical-year program! Each leaflet is brand-new and developed for each liturgical cycle!

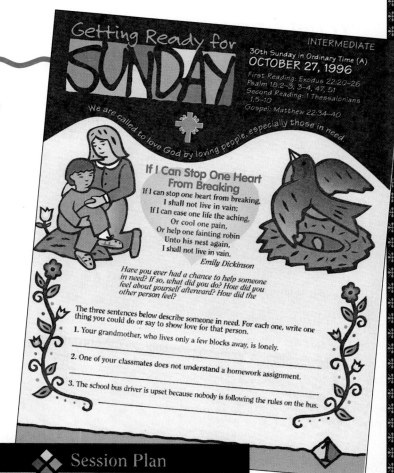

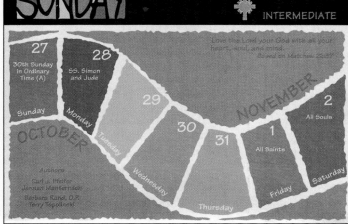

Background for the Teacher and a session outline are clearly and simply presented on each teacher folder—which also provides a handy storage unit for the student leaflets.

THIS IS OUR FAITH has always provided the best in Teacher Editions.

What's new in this one?

Chapter Organizers keep you on target and make planning quick and easy.

All content is correlated with the *Catechism of the Catholic Church*

19 Our Church Worships God

Objectives

To help the students
- Understand what it means to praise God.
- Recognize how the Church continues Jesus' ministry of worship.
- Identify different forms of the ministry of worship.
- Develop an attitude of praise.
- Pray a prayer of praise for the ministry of worship and review the chapter.

Correlation to the *Catechism of the Catholic Church*
Paragraphs
2623, 2624, 2625, 2633, 2639, 2641, 2701, 2742

Plan Ahead

Chapter Outline

	Step 1 Learning About Our Lives	Step 2 Learning About Our Faith	Step 3 Learning How to Live Our Faith
Day 1	■ Introduce the chapter. ■ Identify reasons for praising God. ■ Discuss questions. *ABOUT 18 MINUTES*	■ Read a psalm of praise. ■ Memorize the vocabulary. *ABOUT 8 MINUTES*	■ Examine our actions and attitudes. *ABOUT 4 MINUTES*
Day 2	■ Write about prayer. ■ Learn the vocabulary. *ABOUT 7 MINUTES*	■ Read the story. ■ Learn about the ministry of worship. ■ Review the vocabulary. *ABOUT 18 MINUTES*	■ Discuss participation at Mass. *ABOUT 5 MINUTES*
Day 3	■ Discuss liturgical roles. *ABOUT 4 MINUTES*	■ Identify ministers of worship. *ABOUT 8 MINUTES*	■ Complete a writing activity. ■ Research Scripture. ■ Pray together. *ABOUT 18 MINUTES*
Day 4	■ Review the chapter. *ABOUT 5 MINUTES*	■ Read a Scripture story. ■ Read the text. *ABOUT 9 MINUTES*	■ Make a bulletin board. ■ Learn a sign-language prayer. *ABOUT 16 MINUTES*
Day 5	**Prayer** Prepare for prayer; pray for the ministers of worship. **Review** Unscramble words; review the chapter; pray with the scriptural verse.		

	Preparing Your Class	Materials Needed
Day 1	Read through the lesson plan for this session. Be prepared to share some of your own experiences of praising God.	■ chalkboard
Day 2	Read through the lesson plan for this session. To prepare for the discussion in Step 3, consider whether your actions and attitudes help or hinder the prayer of others.	■ chalkboard ■ pencils or pens ■ writing paper
Day 3	Read through the lesson plan for this session. Try to discover the names of people in your parish who perform the various ministries listed on page 237.	■ chalkboard ■ pencils or pens ■ Bibles ■ paper
Day 4	Think of an example of discouragement in your own life to share with the students in Step 1. Practice the sign-language gestures.	■ pencils or pens ■ colored construction paper ■ scissors, tape, yarn ■ crayons or markers
Day 5	Read through the lesson plan for this session. Prepare an environment for prayer in the classroom. Decide how you will carry out the blessing ritual.	■ colored paper streamers ■ pencils or pens

Additional Resources

As you plan this chapter, consider using the following materials from The Resourceful Teacher Package.

- *Classroom Activity Sheets 19 and 19a*
- *Family Activity Sheets 19 and 19a*
- *Chapter 19 Test*
- *Prayers for Every Day*
- *Projects: Grade 3*

You may also wish to refer to the following Big Books.
- *We Celebrate the Sacraments,* page 7
- *We Celebrate the Mass,* pages 2, 3, and 21

In preparing the students for the Sunday readings, you may wish to use Silver Burdett Ginn's *Getting Ready for Sunday* student and teacher materials.

Chapter Organizer 231b

231a Chapter Organizer

Also in each chapter you will find special feature boxes, giving you additional tips where you need them.

Focus On
provides background information for you on specific topics.

Curriculum Connection
helps you tie in what is being taught in Religion with other content areas.

Enriching the Lesson
includes extras—additional ideas to expand and enrich the lesson.

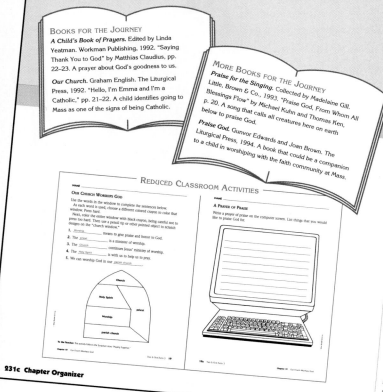

BOOKS FOR THE JOURNEY

A Child's Book of Prayers. Edited by Linda Yeatman. Workman Publishing, 1992. "Saying Thank You to God" by Matthias Claudius, pp. 22–23. A prayer about God's goodness to us.

Our Church. Graham English. The Liturgical Press, 1992. "Hello, I'm Emma and I'm a Catholic," pp. 21–22. A child identifies going to Mass as one of the signs of being Catholic.

MORE BOOKS FOR THE JOURNEY

Praise for the Singing. Collected by Madelaine Gill. Little, Brown & Co., 1993. "Praise God, From Whom All Blessings Flow" by Michael Kuhn and Thomas Ken, p. 20. A song that calls all creatures here on earth below to praise God.

Praise God. Gunvor Edwards and Joan Brown. The Liturgical Press, 1994. A book that could be a companion to a child in worshiping with the faith community at Mass.

REDUCED CLASSROOM ACTIVITIES

OUR CHURCH WORSHIPS GOD

Use the words in the window to complete the sentences below. As each word is used, choose a different colored crayon to color that window. Press hard.

Next, color the entire window with black crayon, being careful not to press too hard. Then use a pencil tip or other pointed object to scratch designs on the "church window."

1. _____ Worship _____ means to give praise and honor to God.
2. The _____ priest _____ is a leader of worship.
3. The _____ Church _____ continues Jesus' ministry of worship.
4. The _____ Holy Spirit _____ is with us to help us to pray.
5. We can worship God in our _____ parish church _____.

A PRAYER OF PRAISE

Write a prayer of praise on the computer screen. List things that you would like to praise God for.

231c Chapter Organizer

Background for the Teacher

THE EXPERIENCE OF PRAYER

Some of the students in your group have a rich experience of prayer. Their families pray together often and they participate weekly in the Sunday liturgy. Other students may have little experience with prayer. Their families may not pray and may seldom attend Mass. Most of the students' experience is probably somewhere between these two extremes.

This chapter explores with the students the experience of prayer. It is important for them to share something of their own prayer experiences. This sharing provides an opportunity for the students to become more aware of what they think and feel about God in their lives.

FOLLOWING JESUS' EXAMPLE

Against the backdrop of the students' own experiences of prayer, this chapter considers how all Catholics are called to take an active part in the Church's worship. We have seen earlier in the year that Jesus prayed often. He offers us a model of prayer. In this chapter, students will learn that after Jesus' resurrection his followers continued to pray together. They worshiped God in the Temple and in their homes. Their experiences were communal and private, formal and informal. Recognizing Jesus' closeness to God in prayer and his dedication to people in need led the early Church to

describe him as a priest, that is, as a mediator between God and humanity. Jesus' life was one of building bridges between people and God. Jesus was an intercessor for humankind with God. This came to be seen as Christ's priesthood.

All Christians share in the priesthood of Christ by reason of their Baptism and Confirmation. Some members of the Church share in the priesthood of Christ in a special way through ordination. They are the bishops, priests, and deacons of the Church. Ordained priestly service is meant to encourage and support the priesthood of all the baptized, many of whom serve the Catholic community in the ministry of worship.

We hope the students will come to understand that worship is at the center of the Church's life of faith. They will come to understand that as members of the Church, we are all called to pray and to participate in Catholic worship.

Chapter Organizer **231d**

Background for teachers provides excellent information for you on what is to be taught as well as insights into how to teach it.

 *Cultural Awareness*

 **Teaching Tips**

Cultural Awareness
gives you needed information to aid students in their appreciation of other cultures.

Teaching Tips
provides just what you need—an extra idea, project, or help - just when you need it.

These new features plus our new size and easier to use format, along with our proven method of teaching—our three-step lesson plan—and a complete lesson every day makes this the best teacher edition ever!

You've always had great additional teacher resources.

What's new in this edition?

We've already told you about the *new* **Prayer Celebrations Book**, the *new* **Prayers for Every Day**, and the *new* **Getting Ready for Sunday** program.

Here's more!

► **Project Books**
One per grade give ideas and opportunities to enhance and expand learning.

▲ **Saints and Other Holy People**
provide excellent role models for students.

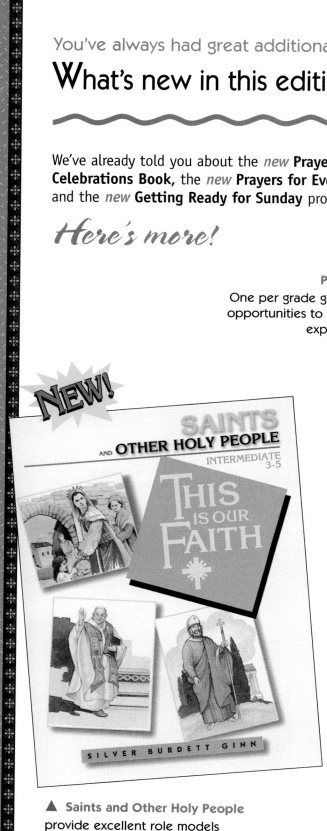

► **Saints Cards**
(32 of 6 Saints for each year)
Take-home cards for
each child to treasure.

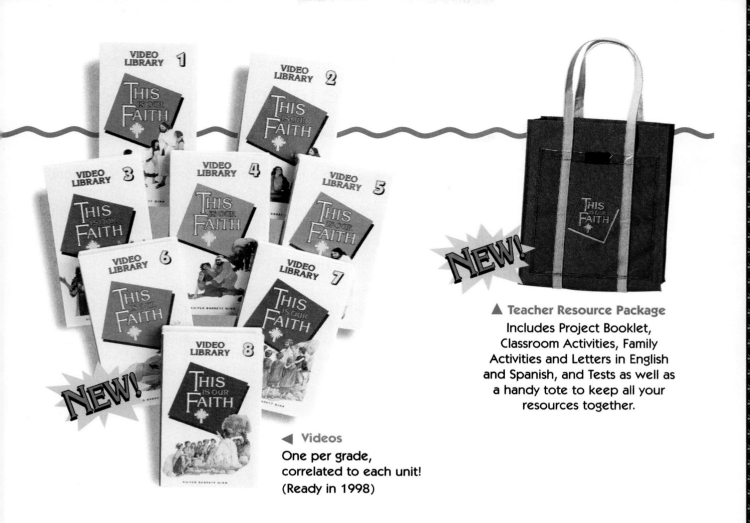

Videos
One per grade,
correlated to each unit!
(Ready in 1998)

NEW!

▲ **Teacher Resource Package**
Includes Project Booklet,
Classroom Activities, Family
Activities and Letters in English
and Spanish, and Tests as well as
a handy tote to keep all your
resources together.

Familiar Resources Designed Especially for the 1998 Edition!

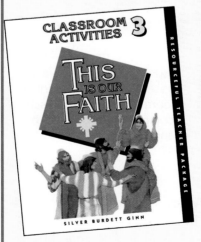

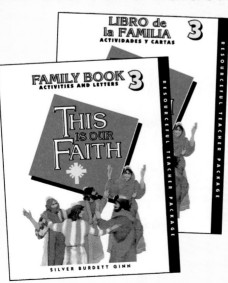

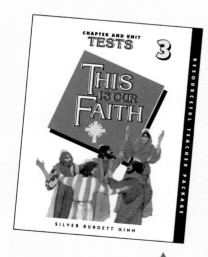

▲ **Classroom Activities**
two sheets for every chapter!

▲ **Family Activities and Letters**
(in English and in Spanish)
Ready to duplicate and send home!

▲ **Tests**
Both Chapter and Unit

And, as your students would say,

"What does This Is Our Faith have to do with real life?"

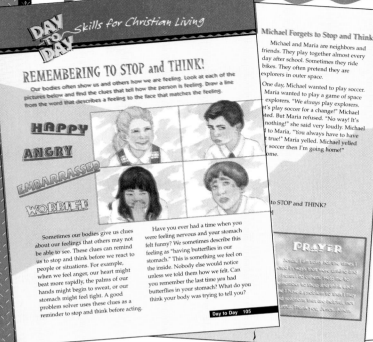

DAY TO DAY — Skills for Christian Living

REMEMBERING TO STOP and THINK!

Our bodies often show us and others how we are feeling. Look at each of the pictures below and find the clues that tell how the person is feeling. Draw a line from the word that describes a feeling to the face that matches the feeling.

HAPPY
ANGRY
EMBARRASSED
WORRIED

Sometimes our bodies give us clues about our feelings that others may not be able to see. These clues can remind us to stop and think before we react to people or situations. For example, when we feel anger, our heart might beat more rapidly, the palms of our hands might begin to sweat, or our stomach might feel tight. A good problem solver uses these clues as a reminder to stop and think before acting.

Have you ever had a time when you were feeling nervous and your stomach felt funny? We sometimes describe this feeling as "having butterflies in our stomach." This is something we feel on the inside. Nobody else would notice unless we told them how we felt. Can you remember the last time you had butterflies in your stomach? What do you think your body was trying to tell you?

Day to Day 105

Michael Forgets to Stop and Think

Michael and Maria are neighbors and friends. They play together almost every day after school. Sometimes they ride bikes. They often pretend they are explorers in outer space.

One day, Michael wanted to play soccer. Maria wanted to play a game of space explorers. "We *always* play explorers. [Le]t's play soccer for a change!" Michael [insis]ted. But Maria refused. "No way! It's [nothing!" she said very loudly. Michael [   ] to Maria, "You always have to have [it   ] true!" Maria yelled. Michael yelled [   ] soccer then I'm going home!" [   ]ome.

to STOP and THINK?

PRAYER

Living our faith goes well beyond the classroom experience into the everyday challenges and opportunities faced by each of our children every day. Each class begins with a life experience and ends with an integration of what has been learned into the child's life.

◀ **Day to Day: Skills for Christian Living**
At the end of each unit, two pages focus on the development of personal and moral skills in a sensitive and constructive way consistent with our Gospel values and Christian life. This is an infinitely practical feature that will help the faith and life to emerge as one.

I,
_____
will work hard this year
to understand what it means
TO BE
a Catholic Christian,
TO BELONG
to God's special family,
and
TO BELIEVE
as a member of
the Catholic Church.

◀ For each grade-level the gatefold invites students to journey together as a school community through faith and life!

This Is Our Faith provides a complete and comprehensive coverage of Doctrine, Scripture, Morality, Prayer and Review, all taught in age-appropriate and proven ways.

Including all of the resources you've used and loved—and many new ones that you've wanted.

Written with you in mind and backed by the very best service in publishing for Catholic schools.

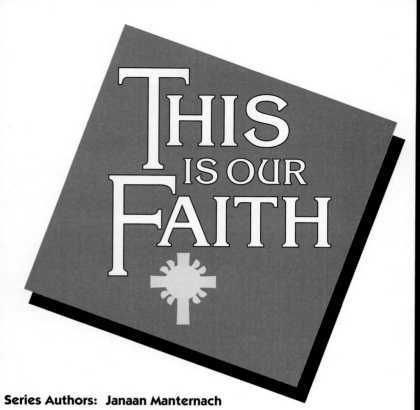

THIS IS OUR FAITH

Series Authors: **Janaan Manternach**
Carl J. Pfeifer

Authors: **Jo'Ann Chiarani**
Joan R. DeMerchant
Maureen Gallagher
Jean Marie Weber

Contributing authors: **Sister Carolyn Puccio, C.S.J.**
Kate Sweeney Ristow

SILVER BURDETT GINN
PARSIPPANY, NJ

THIS IS OUR FAITH
SCHOOL PROGRAM

Contributing authors: James Bitney, Sister Cecilia Maureen Cromwell, I.H.M., Patricia Frevert, Robert M. Hamma, Mary Lou Ihrig, Paula A. Lenz, Judene Leon, Yvette Nelson, Sister Arlene Pomije, C.S.J., Sister Carolyn Puccio, C.S.J., Anna Ready, Kate Sweeney Ristow, Sister Mary Agnes Ryan, I.H.M., Sister Maureen Shaughnessy, S.C., Brother Michael Sheerin, F.M.S., Barbara Carol Vasiloff

Opening Doors: A Take-Home Magazine: Peter H.M. Demkovitz, Janie Gustafson, Margaret Savitskas

Day to Day: Skills for Christian Living: Susan G. Keys

Advisory Board:

Rev. Louis J. Cameli

Philip J. Cunningham

Sister Clare E. Fitzgerald

William J. Freburger

Greer G. Gordon

Sister Veronica R. Grover, S.H.C.J.

Rev. Thomas Guarino

Rev. Robert E. Harahan

Kathleen Hendricks

Rev. Eugene LaVerdieré, S.S.S.

Rev. Frank J. McNulty

Rev. Msgr. John J. Strynkowski

Consultants: Linda Blanchette, Anita Bridge, Fred Brown, Rod Brownfield, Sister Mary Michael Burns, S.C., Patricia Burns, Bernadine Carroll, Mary Ellen Cocks, Sister Peggy Conlon, R.S.M., Mary Ann Crowley, Pamela Danni, Sister Jamesetta DeFelice, O.S.U., Sister Mary Elizabeth Duke, S.N.D., Mary M. Gibbons, Yolando Gremillion, Sister Angela Hallahan, C.H.F., Alice J. Heard, Sister Michele O'Connoll, P.B.V.M., Sister Angela O'Mahoney, P.B.V.M., Sister Ruthann O'Mara, S.S.J., Sandra Okulicz-Hulme, Judy Papandria, Rachel Pasano, Sallie Ann Phelan, Sister Geraldine M. Rogers, S.S.J., Mary Lou Schlosser, Patricia Ann Sibilia, Margaret E. Skelly, Lisa Ann Sorlie, Sister Victorine Stoltz, O.S.B., Sister Nancy Jean Turner, S.H.C.J., Christine Ward, Judith Reidel Weber, Kay White, Elizabeth M. Williams, Catherine R. Wolf, Florence Bambrick Yarney, Kathryn K. Zapcic

Nihil Obstat

Kathleen Flanagan, S.C., Ph.D.
Censor Librorum

Ellen Joyce, S.C., Ph.D.
Censor Librorum

Imprimatur

✠ Most Rev. Frank J. Rodimer
   Bishop of Paterson

November 22, 1996

The *nihil obstat* and *imprimatur* are official declarations that a book or pamphlet is free of doctrinal and moral error. No implication is contained therein that those who have granted the *nihil obstat* and *imprimatur* agree with the contents, opinions, or statements expressed.

ACKNOWLEDGMENTS

Excerpts from *The New American Bible* © 1970 by the Confraternity of Christian Doctrine are used by permission of the copyright owner.

Excerpts from *The New American Bible with Revised New Testament* © 1986, 1970 by the Confraternity of Christian Doctrine, Washington, D.C. 20017. Used with permission. All rights reserved.

All adaptations of Scripture are based on *The New American Bible with Revised New Testament*.

Excerpts from the English translation of *Rite of Baptism for Children* © 1969, International Committee on English in the Liturgy, Inc. (ICEL); the English translation of psalm responses from the *Lectionary for Mass* © 1969, ICEL; excerpts from the English translation of *The Roman Missal* © 1973, ICEL; excerpts from the English translation of *Rite of Penance* © 1974, ICEL; excerpts from the English translation of *Rite of Confirmation*, Second Edition © 1975, ICEL; excerpts from the English translation of *Pastoral Care of the Sick: Rites of Anointing and Viaticum* © 1982, ICEL. All rights reserved.

Excerpt from the *Lectionary for Masses with Children* Copyright ©1991, United States Catholic Conference, Washington, D.C. Used with permission.

Excerpts from an article by Sr. Thea Bowman, F.S.P.A. in *Lead Me, Guide Me: The African American Catholic Hymnal* published by G.I.A. Publications, Inc. are reprinted by permission.

Contents

Catechism of the Catholic Church

Since its publication in June 1994, the English translation of the *Catechism of the Catholic Church* has enjoyed a wide readership among Catholics throughout the United States. Parents and teachers will want to know how the chapter themes in THIS IS OUR FAITH relate to the content of the *Catechism*.

As a service, we have included a Catechism Reference Box at the beginning of each chapter in the Teacher Edition. We suggest that, in preparing to teach the chapter, teachers first read the section "Background for the Teacher." For additional enrichment, you may wish to refer to the paragraphs in the *Catechism* that are indicated in the Reference Box.

Although the *Catechism of the Catholic Church* is not the only source of enrichment regarding doctrine, it can be most helpful in broadening our understanding of faith. We are encouraged to use it as a reference in our ongoing study of our Catholic tradition.

1

The students at this age probably have learned most of the prayers on these pages. You may want to review these prayers by discussing the meaning of each line of every prayer and the meaning of each prayer in our daily lives.

Introducing the Prayers

Ask the students to look at the prayers on pages 2–6. The prayers are placed here as an easy-to-find reference for the students. Some of the prayers appear in both English and Spanish. You might use one or more of these prayers to open and close each class session. Challenge the students to commit these prayers to memory and to pray them often. Suggest that they pray one or more of these prayers each night before falling asleep. Ask the students to suggest other times when they might say the prayers on this page.

Let Us Pray

The Lord's Prayer

Our Father, who art in heaven,
  hallowed be thy name;
thy kingdom come;
thy will be done on earth
  as it is in heaven.
Give us this day our daily bread;
and forgive us our trespasses
  as we forgive those
  who trespass against us;
and lead us not into temptation,
  but deliver us from evil.
Amen.

Padre Nuestro

Padre nuestro, que estás en el cielo,
  santificado sea tu nombre;
venga a nosotros tu reino;
hágase tu voluntad en la tierra
  como en el cielo.
Danos hoy nuestro pan de cada día;
perdona nuestras ofensas,
  como también nosotros
    perdonamos
  a los que nos ofenden;
no nos dejes caer en la tentación,
  y líbranos del mal.
Amén.

Sign of the Cross

In the name of the Father,
  and of the Son,
  and of the Holy Spirit.
Amen.

Señal de la Cruz

En el nombre del Padre
  y del Hijo
  y del Espíritu Santo.
Amén.

Hail Mary

Hail Mary, full of grace,
    the Lord is with you.
Blessed are you among women,
    and blessed is the fruit
    of your womb, Jesus.
Holy Mary, Mother of God,
    pray for us sinners, now,
    and at the hour of our death.
Amen.

Ave María

Dios te salve, María, llena eres
    de gracia,
    el Señor es contigo.
Bendita tú eres entre todas las
    mujeres,
    y bendito es el fruto
    de tu vientre, Jesús.
Santa María, Madre de Dios,
    ruega por nosotros, pecadores,
    ahora y en la hora de nuestra
       muerte.
Amén.

Glory Be to the Father

Glory be to the Father,
    and to the Son,
    and to the Holy Spirit.
As it was in the beginning,
    is now, and ever shall be,
    world without end.
Amen.

Gloria al Padre

Gloria al Padre,
    y al Hijo,
    y al Espíritu Santo.
Como era en el principio,
    ahora y siempre,
    por los siglos de los siglos.
Amén.

Let Us Pray

Morning Prayer

My God, I offer you today,
all that I think and do and say,
and ask for your blessing
as you lead me in your ways.
Amen.

Evening Prayer

My God, before I sleep tonight
I want to thank you
for being with me today.
As I close my eyes to rest,
keep me in your loving care.
Amen.

Grace Before Meals

Bless us, O Lord,
and these your gifts,
which we are about to receive
from your goodness,
through Christ our Lord.
Amen.

Grace After Meals

We give thanks, O God,
for these and all your gifts,
which we have received
through Christ our Lord.
Amen.

Prayer of Sorrow

My God,
I am sorry for my sins with all my heart.
In choosing to do wrong
and failing to do good,
I have sinned against you
whom I should love above all things.
I firmly intend, with your help,
to do penance,
to sin no more,
and to avoid whatever leads me to sin.

Revised Rite of Penance

Apostles' Creed

I believe in God, the Father almighty,
    creator of heaven and earth.

I believe in Jesus Christ, his only Son, our Lord.
    He was conceived by the power of the Holy Spirit
        and born of the Virgin Mary.
    He suffered under Pontius Pilate,
        was crucified, died, and was buried.
    He descended to the dead.
    On the third day he rose again.
    He ascended into heaven,
        and is seated at the right hand of the Father.
    He will come again to judge the living and the dead.

I believe in the Holy Spirit,
    the holy catholic Church,
    the communion of saints,
    the forgiveness of sins,
    the resurrection of the body
    and life everlasting. Amen.

Let Us Pray

Prayer to the Holy Spirit
Come, Holy Spirit,
   fill the hearts of your faithful,
   and kindle in them
   the fire of your love.
Send forth your Spirit, O Lord,
   and they shall be created.
And you shall renew
   the face of the earth.
Amen.

Beginning the Journey

Introductory Lesson

Objectives

To help the students
- Get acquainted with one another.
- Desire to learn more about the Catholic Church.
- Dedicate themselves to the journey of faith.

Lesson Outline

- Welcome the students.
- Introduce the student text.
- Complete the writing and drawing activities.
- Pray together.
- Make a commitment to the faith journey.
- Conclude the session.

Plan Ahead

Arrange materials for making name tags on a large table where all the students can work together.

Prepare a special area in your room for prayer. Cover a table or desk with a cloth and place a Bible and candle on the cloth. You might also add flowers to decorate the table or desk.

Materials Needed

- construction paper, scissors, and several one-hole punchers
- an 18" piece of yarn for each student
- crayons or felt-tip markers
- pens or pencils
- a Bible
- a candle and matches
- flowers (optional)
- *Parent Preview Magazine*

Background for the Teacher

Becoming a Community

You and your students are about to embark on a very special journey. Together, you will begin to explore what makes the Catholic Church unique. The students will learn more about what it means to be members of the Church community.

The introductory session will help the students begin to think of themselves as a special community within the Church. As they get acquainted, they will discover common interests and experiences. We hope they will begin to appreciate their unique talents and gifts which can help your group become a community.

The process of forming a community does not happen instantly. It takes time, effort, and nurturing. Some of your students may already know one another; other students may be new to your school or to your class of students. It is important that you encourage the students to talk to one another, to share their experiences, and to engage in activities together. It is also important that *you* share some of your own experiences with the group. Recall how throughout his public ministry Jesus focused on building up and teaching the small community of disciples he had called to journey with him. He called the disciples to be one with him—a family and a community bonded by love, respect, and faith.

Professing Our Faith

During this session, the students will have a special opportunity to make a personal commitment to grow in their faith and to learn what it means to be a member of God's family. In the prayer service they will be introduced to the Apostles' Creed, which summarizes our Catholic beliefs. During the year, the students will come to understand what our creed means and how we live out our beliefs as Catholics. As they grow in understanding, they will, with the help of the Spirit, proudly embrace the faith to which they are called.

Starting the Year Right

A successful year begins long before your students arrive for the first session. To help you succeed, The Resourceful Teacher section of this book, beginning on page 365, includes

■ notes on catechesis, faith, the role of the teacher, the *National Catechetical Directory,* and the *Catechism of the Catholic Church*

■ a profile of the third-grade child

■ tips on creating a healthy classroom environment

■ suggestions for helping the students develop social skills

■ tips on good planning strategies

■ ideas on using learning activities

■ suggestions for assessing learning

■ ideas for using prayer within the sessions

■ tips on involving the community

Refer to The Resourceful Teacher section before planning your first session and whenever you need help throughout the year.

Beginning the Journey

We are growing up as God's children. We meet new people in God's family. We learn about new places.

Here are some things I would like to do with my class this year.

_____

_____

Here are my drawings of some of God's special people and places that I like best. As I begin my third-grade journey, I remember what these people and places mean to me.

Here are some things about Jesus and the Church that I want to find out about this year.

_____

_____

Each time we meet together this year, we will learn more about what it means to be members of the Catholic Church.

7

Welcoming the Students

If you have not already done so, welcome the students to your class and introduce yourself. Have the students introduce themselves to one another. Call attention to the materials for making name tags. Direct each student to write his or her name in the center of a sheet of construction paper. Invite the students to draw pictures around their names that tell something about themselves. Suggest that they draw pictures of their families, favorite foods, activities they enjoy, or what they want to be when they grow up. As the students work, talk with them individually about their drawings. When they have finished, have them punch two holes at the top of the paper and thread the yarn through the holes, knotting it and making a large enough loop so that the name tag can be worn around the neck. Invite the students to share their drawings with the group.

Introducing the Student Text

Distribute the student texts and invite the students to comment as they look through them. Review the Contents page with the students. Point out the special features in the back of the book that can help them learn about special feasts and seasons of the Church year, the Bible, sacraments, prayers, and beliefs of the Church. If you have not already done so, also point out the Let Us Pray pages at the front of the book.

Completing an Activity

Instruct the students to open their books to page 7. Read aloud the lesson title together. Then ask a volunteer to read the first paragraph aloud. Clarify that, as God's children, we are all part of one family. Direct the students to complete the activities. Encourage them to share their responses.

Tell the students that Jesus wants them to know all about him and to grow closer to him. Help them understand that in the third grade they will learn about the Catholic Church and how the Church can help them to know and follow Jesus more closely.

Praying Together

Gather the students around the prayer table. Have them bring their books and markers with them. Light the candle as a sign that Jesus is with us.

Have the students turn to page 8. Invite them to make the Sign of the Cross with you. Read the opening invitation and encourage them to respond enthusiastically "We will."

Read aloud the next paragraph. Explain that the words *commitment* and *covenant* both mean "a promise." Suggest that the students use their best handwriting to sign the covenant. Have each student, individually, say "I" and his or her name. Then recite the rest of the covenant together.

Read aloud the next paragraph on page 8. Read together the Apostles' Creed on page 5.

Ask the students to read with you slowly the closing prayer on page 8. Explain that this prayer is used at a special ceremony of welcome in the Catholic Church.

Concluding the Session

Tell your group how happy you are that they have begun this year's journey with you. Remind them of their commitment to learn more about being Catholic Christians, belonging to God's family, and being believing members of the Catholic community. Remember to send home with the students the *Parent Preview Magazine* from the student text.

Prayer for the Journey

Leader: As members of the Church, we are on a special journey. Jesus is our leader. The Holy Spirit is our helper and guide. Friends and followers of Jesus all over the world are traveling with us on our journey. Will you join me on this special journey?

All: We will.

Leader: As a sign of our commitment—our promise— to journey together, let us sign our names on the covenant inside the front cover of our books. Now let's read together what we will do on our journey as Christians.

Leader: Almost since the beginning, Jesus' followers have had a special way of saying what they believe as Christians. We call this our creed. Our parents and friends said a creed for us at our Baptism. We can say a creed together now. We will learn more about what our creed means as we journey through this year together.

All: *This is our faith. This is the faith of the Church. We are proud to profess our faith in Christ Jesus our Lord. Amen.*

- based on the bishop's proclamation in the *Rite of Confirmation*

8

Enriching the Lesson

Make a journey poster with the students. Take a Polaroid photograph of them. Glue the photograph to the center of the poster and ask the students to think of a caption, such as "Our Journey of Faith." Invite all the students to sign or print their names on the poster.

THIS IS OUR FAITH

A Preview of Grade 3

SILVER BURDETT GINN • SCHOOL PROGRAM

OPENING DOORS
A Take-Home Magazine

We hope you will join us . . .

A Profile of the Third-Grade Child

As parent or guardian, you will want to relate to your maturing third grader in the most effective way possible. As an eight-year-old child begins moving toward independence, he or she needs the love, approval, guidance, and reinforcement of a supportive family. Your child is changing in many ways.

- Curious about life, nature, and people, many third graders prefer to learn from their own observations.

- Mastering the ability to read and to reason, they can be more exciting and challenging to teach.

- An increased social sense places great emphasis on friendships and increases a third grader's willingness to share. It also makes them more self-conscious about being criticized in front of their friends.

Third graders learn best when they

- have guidelines and rules to follow.
- are assigned simple tasks that allow for success and build self-esteem.
- can trust significant adults who care for them.
- know that their feelings are accepted.

Taking Time Take the time this week to talk to your third grader about his or her daily responsibilities at home and at school. Be sure that your expectations are reasonable. Express to your child the confidence you have that he or she can meet those expectations.

4

A Preview of Grade 3

The purpose of the *Parent Preview Magazine* is to introduce the parents of your students to THIS IS OUR FAITH, Grade 3. This preview invites the family to join their child on this year's journey of faith, while providing a brief summary of the material taught in Grade 3. Special emphasis is given to describing *Opening Doors: A Take-Home Magazine,* as well as to profiling the third-grade child.

Sending the Magazine Home

At the end of the first session, help the students carefully remove the *Parent Preview Magazine* from their texts. Explain to the students that this preview magazine will introduce their families to THIS IS OUR FAITH, Grade 3. Demonstrate how to fold the magazine. Encourage the students to bring the magazine home and to share it with their families.

for an adventure that will give you and your third grader a closer look at the life of the Church. As your child promises, in faith, to seek a greater understanding of the Church this year, you are invited aboard as the most important guide in your child's faith life and as a cojourneyer who learns alongside of your young companion.

This Year in Grade 3

The focus of Grade 3 is the Church and the kind of community the Church is called to be. The mission, the message, the prayer, and the actions of God's special family will be explored.

In Unit 1 your child will learn about the community of Jesus'

friends and will consider some of the joys and challenges of living as one, holy, catholic, and apostolic Church. Your third grader will look at these priorities of the early Christian communities and will come to understand how they continue to guide the people of God today.

OPENING DOORS is a take-home magazine you can look forward to receiving each time your child completes a unit of THIS IS OUR FAITH. It is our hope that the features of each magazine will help to open the doors of faith and story-sharing in your home as you and your child grow together in faith.

A Closer Look

includes an adult-level reflection on the theme of the unit with a focus on the Mass and family pages for you to enjoy with your child.

Being Catholic

highlights something special about our American Catholic heritage.

Growing Closer

suggests activities to help you and your family integrate your faith into everyday life.

And also...

Looking Ahead

previews the next unit of THIS IS OUR FAITH.

UNIT 1

A Marked Community

Why would you want to belong to a group like this?

Introducing the UNIT

Invite the students to study the photograph and tell a story about it. Read aloud the question and invite the students to respond. Help them appreciate everyone's need to belong.

Vocabulary

Christians
Scriptures
twelve apostles
parish
Catholic Church
holy
saints
catholic
respect
gospel
marks of the Church
apostolic
faith
witness
missionaries

Unit Aim

To help the students understand and appreciate the four marks of the Church—that it is one, holy, catholic, and apostolic.

Doctrinal Summaries

CHAPTER 1
One of the marks, or signs, of the Catholic Church is that it is one, or united. The Holy Spirit draws Jesus' followers together as brothers and sisters in one Christian family.

CHAPTER 2
One of the marks, or signs, of the Catholic Church is that it is holy. Being holy means to be close to God and to do his work in the world. It means loving God and caring about all people.

CHAPTER 3
One of the marks, or signs, of the Catholic Church is that it is catholic. Jesus wants his people, the Church, to welcome and to include people of all kinds, just as he does.

CHAPTER 4
One of the marks, or signs, of the Catholic Church is that it is apostolic. It is founded on the teachings of Jesus and his apostles. We are called to be apostolic by sharing what we have learned from the apostles and from other Catholics.

Note:
As you prepare this unit, you may wish to refer to the reference section, *Our Catholic Heritage*, beginning on page 327.

Additional resources for Unit 1 include a Unit Test and a Family Letter as well as a video and selections from THIS IS OUR FAITH Music Program. You might also find it helpful to preview *Saints and Other Holy People* and *Prayer Celebrations* for possibilities to enhance the unit.

11

Our Church Is One

Objectives

To help the students

- Recognize the importance of working together.
- Learn that unity is a mark of the Catholic Church.
- Understand that the Catholic Church is a special community.
- Desire to work for unity in their families and parish.
- Compose and pray petitions for unity and review the chapter.

Chapter Outline

	Step 1 Learning About Our Lives	**Step 2** Learning About Our Faith	**Step 3** Learning How to Live Our Faith
Day 1	■ Introduce the chapter. ■ Read and discuss a story. *ABOUT 10 MINUTES*	■ Read and discuss the text. *ABOUT 10 MINUTES*	■ Write a unity prayer. *ABOUT 10 MINUTES*
Day 2	■ Talk about groups. *ABOUT 8 MINUTES*	■ Read about the early Church. ■ Learn the vocabulary and doctrine. *ABOUT 7 MINUTES*	■ Write about group unity. ■ Complete a prayer. *ABOUT 15 MINUTES*
Day 3	■ Write about parish spirit. *ABOUT 5 MINUTES*	■ Read about the Catholic Church. *ABOUT 20 MINUTES*	■ Complete a checklist. *ABOUT 5 MINUTES*
Day 4	■ Discuss family unity. ■ Write about qualities of teamwork. *ABOUT 10 MINUTES*	■ Consider Jesus' presence. *ABOUT 5 MINUTES*	■ Learn about Catholic unity. ■ Discuss the photographs. *ABOUT 15 MINUTES*
Day 5	**Prayer** Write a prayer of petition; prepare for prayer; pray for unity. **Review** Review the chapter; pray with the scriptural verse.		

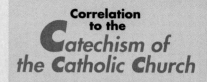
Plan Ahead

	Preparing Your Class	**Materials Needed**
Day 1	Read through the lesson plan for this class session. Think about groups or teams the students might belong to.	■ lined paper ■ pencils or pens
Day 2	Read through the lesson plan for this class session.	■ pencils or pens
Day 3	Read through the lesson plan for this session. On index cards, write actions that Catholics perform in their parishes and schools.	■ index cards ■ pencils or pens
Day 4	Read through the lesson plan.	■ parish bulletins ■ pencils or pens
Day 5	Prepare an environment for prayer in the classroom. Review this week's sessions to prepare for the chapter review.	■ Bible, candle, tablecloth ■ 1" × 4" strips of colored construction paper ■ drawing paper ■ stapler, crayons, or markers

Additional Resources

As you plan this chapter, consider using the following materials from The Resourceful Teacher Package.

■ *Classroom Activity Sheets 1* and *1a*

■ *Family Activity Sheets 1* and *1a*

■ *Chapter 1 Test*

■ *Prayers for Every Day*

■ *Projects: Grade 3*

You may also wish to refer to the following Big Books.

■ *We Celebrate God's Word,* page 22

■ *We Celebrate the Mass,* pages 11, 18–19

In preparing the students for the Sunday readings, you may wish to use Silver Burdett Ginn's *Getting Ready for Sunday* student and teacher materials.

BOOKS FOR THE JOURNEY

The Keeping Quilt. Patricia Polacco. Simon & Schuster, 1988. The keeping quilt serves as a wonderful symbol to preserve the love and faith of one family.

Stone Soup. Marcia Brown. Macmillan, 1986. Unity grows when some soldiers get everyone in the village to contribute to a pot of soup.

MORE BOOKS FOR THE JOURNEY

Christians. John Drane. Lion Publishing, 1994. "A World of Christians," Chapter 1. This section of the book answers questions on what a Christian is, what a church is, where Christians live, and how many Christians there are in the world.

The Glassmakers of Gurven. Marlys Boddy. Abingdon Press, 1988. Three glassmakers learn how important it is to work together and how beautiful the results can be.

REDUCED CLASSROOM ACTIVITIES

NAME _____

OUR CHURCH IS ONE

As a team, choose four of the slogans below that speak to you most about team spirit. Talk about the slogans with the others in your group and discuss what they mean. On the T-shirt, write your team's idea of encouraging words. Color the T-shirt and cut the picture out. Display it with those of the other teams from your class.

Keep going!	Thanks for doing your part!
Good try!	Let's do our best!
We made it!	Let's pull together!
Be on our team!	That's OK!

To the Teacher: Use this activity after the story "Surprising Teamwork."

NAME _____

UNITY

You're the songwriter for the music group Unity. Your hits are wildly popular and your fans are begging for more. The radio stations are looking for a song about how third graders today are like the early Christians. You decide to start with the tune of the familiar song "Row, Row, Row Your Boat." Here are the words.

Row, row, row your boat
Gently down the stream;
Merrily, merrily, merrily, merrily,
Life is but a dream.

By changing a few words, you could write just the song they're looking for. Use some of the words in the music notes to fill in the blanks below. The results will describe things the early Christians did that third graders do today.

_____, _____, _____ together,

This is what we do;

When we _____ and _____ together,

God is with us, too.

Now write another verse to go with the first.

_____

_____

_____

_____

Congratulations! It's a hit!

To the Teacher: This activity, which follows the story "The First Christians Live as One," stresses the parallel between third-grade disciples and the early Christians. Divide the class into small groups.

Background for the Teacher

THE MARK OF UNITY

The marks of the Church—that it is one, holy, catholic, and apostolic—are traditional ways of describing the Catholic community. They are signs that identify the Church. Today, the marks of the Church are also seen as gifts bestowed upon the Church by the Lord, gifts that the community of believers must strive to realize ever more fully.

In the first chapter, we consider the mark of oneness, or unity. We are one community when we celebrate the Eucharist. We are one when together we affirm our belief in "one Lord, one faith, one baptism; one God and Father of all" (Ephesians 4:5–6). As members of the Church, we are one when we work to become a community of deeper faith, hope, and love. The Holy Spirit is the principle of this unity, while all those who live in response to the promptings of the Spirit demonstrate this unity in a visible way.

Jesus is the center of our unity. The earliest Christians recognized this unity and based their communal life on their belief in Jesus as their Lord and Savior. They met to listen to the teachings of the twelve apostles and to pray together. They shared all they had so that none of them would be in need.

UNITY TODAY

As members of the Church today, we are called to be ever more fully one through the Holy Spirit. As the early Christians did, we believe in Jesus as Lord and celebrate our oneness around his table in the Eucharist. We seek to use our diverse talents and gifts to continue the work of Jesus in our time. This is our common goal and mission.

As members of the Catholic community, we also strive for unity with other Christian churches in today's world. Third graders may not yet be ready to deal with this larger concept of unity. However, we can help them understand the unity of working toward a common goal. The first session begins by discussing the goals and qualities of a team and then relates this to the mission of the Church.

Christian unity is a long-term goal that can be realized only after years of self-discipline. In various ways on different grade levels of THIS IS OUR FAITH, students will be reminded of this goal and will learn to recognize and celebrate its fulfillment along the way. Our task for the third-grade level is to begin to shape attitudes and behavior that promote unity. An important part of this task is to be model members of a united community of faith.

DAY 1
MORALITY

Objective

This lesson helps the students recognize the importance of working together.

Step 1/INTRODUCTION

Learning About Our Lives

Introducing the Chapter

Invite a volunteer to read the chapter title and focus question aloud. Ask the students to define the word *united*. Invite them to share experiences about how a group or team becomes more united. Explain that becoming one as a group or a team is not easy and that it takes time and effort to achieve unity.

Reading a Story

Tell the class that they are going to read about a team that discovered how to become more united. Have a volunteer read aloud "Surprising Teamwork." Ask the following questions.

■ Why did Jillian think the Bobcats weren't winning? (*They were hogging the ball.*)

■ What did Coach Pam say was the only way to win? (*By passing the ball, talking to each other, and playing together*)

■ Why were the Bobcats successful? (*They worked and played together as a team.*)

Discussing the Story

Discuss the following questions with the students. Stress that people must cooperate with one another to work together successfully.

■ What qualities make a good leader? (*Possible answers may include: responsibility, honesty, understanding, patience, and caring.*)

■ What are some ways that leaders and followers can work together? (*Possible answers may include: cooperating, respecting one another, being honest, sharing ideas, taking one's responsibility seriously, and being patient.*)

■ Why do you think it is important to work together? (*Answers will vary.*)

■ Think of your favorite organization or professional sports team. Why do you think the group is successful? (*Answers will vary.*)

12

Our Church Is One

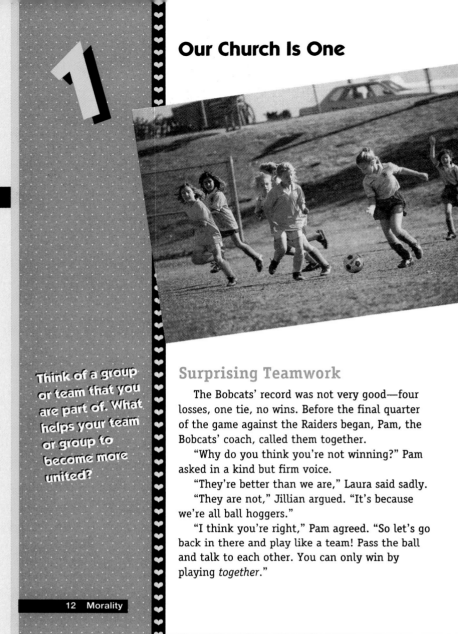

Think of a group or team that you are part of. What helps your team or group to become more united?

Surprising Teamwork

The Bobcats' record was not very good—four losses, one tie, no wins. Before the final quarter of the game against the Raiders began, Pam, the Bobcats' coach, called them together.

"Why do you think you're not winning?" Pam asked in a kind but firm voice.

"They're better than we are," Laura said sadly.

"They are not," Jillian argued. "It's because we're all ball hoggers."

"I think you're right," Pam agreed. "So let's go back in there and play like a team! Pass the ball and talk to each other. You can only win by playing *together*."

12   Morality

 **CURRICULUM CONNECTION**

Physical Education   You may wish to have the class play one of their favorite sports or games that involves teams. Encourage the students to focus on working together as a team while they play. Afterward, ask them to name specific things members of each team did to help their team. Help the class appreciate that all members must do their part to contribute to a team's success.

 **Teaching Tips**

It is important for children to learn to distinguish between good and bad leaders. When discussing the qualities of a leader, point out that the ability to lead does not necessarily mean that a particular person *should* lead. Whether or not a person can be considered a good leader depends on how he or she uses that ability.

Then, for the first time all season, it happened. The Bobcats started working together. They talked out loud to one another, "I've got it!" "You take it, Andra!" "Over here!" "Pass it to Laura!" "Keep going!" "Megan, watch out behind you!" They actually passed well a few times.

In the last minute, Erica had the ball in the clear. Jillian ran just behind her, shouting out encouragement. The goalie was all there was between them and the goal.

Erica kicked hard. The goalie blocked the ball and fell down, and the ball rolled free. Erica passed it to Jillian. Jillian scored the winning goal!

"We did it!" "We won!" "What a team!"

Pam was delighted. "You won because you learned to play together as a team," she told them. "Now you can beat the Cubs next week."

Christian Teamwork

We learned that the Bobcats really wanted to work together. Once they knew that they each had a job to do, they were able to become united and to work as a team.

The early **Christians** also worked as a team. They knew that Jesus wanted them to be united. It was not easy. They had to work toward unity. They prayed, as Jesus prayed, that they might become one with the help of the Holy Spirit.

Vocabulary

Christians: The worldwide community of people who believe that Jesus is the Son of God

Morality 13

Cultural Awareness

Invite the students to name similarities they share with each other (skin, hair, and eye color; height; gender; backgrounds; interests; and so on). You might ask questions such as, "Do we all weigh the same?" or "Do we all have the same hobbies and interests?" Discuss how accepting and respecting differences can help make your class a better "team." Emphasize the importance of respect during the discussion itself. Students will learn more about respect in Chapter 3.

Teaching Tips

Students in the third grade may not have experience in composing prayers. You may want to prepare beforehand several examples of different kinds of prayer: litanies, prayers of petition, prayers of blessing, and so forth. Keep copies of these examples, and hand them out to the class when needed to help them with prayer-writing assignments.

 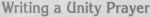
Learning About Our Faith

Reading and Discussing the Text

Introduce "Christian Teamwork" by discussing the definition of *Christians* on page 13. Read "Christian Teamwork" with the class. Invite the students to suggest why it was not easy for the early Christians to be united. Elicit from the students that the early Christians had relied on Jesus for leadership and guidance. When Jesus returned to his Father in heaven, they had to learn to rely on one another. Emphasize that the early Christians prayed for the coming of the Holy Spirit, whom Jesus had promised to send.

Step 3/CONCLUSION

Learning How to Live Our Faith

Writing a Unity Prayer

Invite the students to think about the difficulties the early Christians might have experienced as they tried to become united. Remind the class that Jesus' followers prayed for unity. Distribute lined paper and pencils. Ask the students to write a short prayer that the early Christians could have prayed, asking Jesus to help them become one. When the students have finished, encourage them to read their prayers aloud.

Objective

This lesson helps the students learn that unity is a mark of the Catholic Church.

Step 1/INTRODUCTION

Learning About Our Lives

Talking About Groups

Encourage the students to talk about the different groups to which they belong. Ask them to discuss why they joined these groups and what their purpose is. Tell the class that in this lesson, they will learn about another group to which they belong—the Catholic Church.

Step 2/DEVELOPMENT

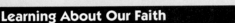
Learning About Our Faith

Reading About the Early Church

Explain that the people who first followed Jesus' example after his death and resurrection became a united group, the Church. They included the apostles, who were chosen by Jesus to teach and lead the early Church, the many men and women who believed in Jesus as their Savior. Direct the students to turn to page 14 in their books. Have volunteers read aloud "The First Christians Live as One." Use the following questions to discuss the story.

■ Where did the first Christians meet and gather? (*At the Temple in Jerusalem and in their homes*)

■ What did the Christians do when they met together? (*Read the Scriptures; listened to the teachings of the apostles; prayed, ate, and shared whatever was needed*)

■ How did Jesus want his friends and followers to live? (*In harmony*)

■ What did Jesus promise? (*To send the Holy Spirit to help them be united*)

■ How did sharing meals help the first Christians? (*In sharing food, they felt united with Jesus and with one another.*)

The First Christians Live as One

The first Christians met together every day at the Temple in Jerusalem. They also gathered daily in their homes—men, women, and children; some rich, some poor. They were people of many nationalities, races, and languages.

They read the **Scriptures**, the written word of God. They listened to the teachings of the **twelve apostles**, those chosen by Jesus to teach and lead his friends and followers. The apostles told them that Jesus wanted them to live in harmony and that Jesus promised to send the Holy Spirit to help them become united.

As they prayed together and ate together, they remembered Jesus and experienced his presence with them. Sharing meals helped them feel united with one another as well as with Jesus.

They shared all they had with one another. Those who had much shared with those who had less. Because they shared all their possessions, there was no needy person among them.

Based on Acts 2:42–47; 4:32–37

Cultural Awareness

You may want to explain to the students that although the people who met in Jerusalem were mostly Jews, there were first-century Christians of many nationalities, races, and languages. Discuss how this tradition continues today in your parish or diocese. Using your most recent parish or diocesan census, or the *Catholic Almanac,* you may want to give the students concrete statistics about the rich diversity of our Church today.

CURRICULUM CONNECTION

Map Skills While discussing the lifestyle of the early Christians, you might want to display a map of the Mediterranean area. Point out the places where Christianity began to flourish in the first century, including Jerusalem and Palestine. Then identify places like Antioch in Syria, Corinth in Greece, Alexandria in Northern Africa, and Rome in Italy. Explain that the Mediterranean Sea made it possible for people to travel easily about their world and spread the teachings of Jesus.

We Are a Team

As Catholics, we are part of the team of Jesus' followers. As followers of Jesus, we are called to work and pray for unity among all believers. The Holy Spirit can help us each to do our part.

Activity

Think of the Bobcats, what the apostles taught the early Christians, and of your own experiences in groups. Write in the figures below some of the things that you believe could help a group of people to become united. Then complete the prayer below.

Dear God,
I belong to a very special team. I am a follower of Jesus. I know that to be a member of Jesus' team I must work for unity. I know that I already_____

_____.

With the help of the Holy Spirit, I will try to_____

_____.

Help me to show that I am truly a member of this very special team. Amen.

Vocabulary

Scriptures: the written word of God

twelve apostles: those chosen by Jesus to teach and lead his friends and followers

♥♥♥♥♥♥♥♥♥♥♥

We Believe

One of the marks, or signs, of the Catholic Church is that it is one, or united. The Holy Spirit draws Jesus' followers together as brothers and sisters in one Christian family.

Doctrine   15

Teaching Tips

Some students may be familiar with the word *disciples,* which is defined in the Grade 2 student text as "persons who live and love as Jesus did." The *twelve apostles* are sometimes referred to as the *twelve disciples.* The word *apostle* means "one who is sent on a mission." Given the context in which we use the words *apostle* and *disciple* in the Grade 3 student text, the word *apostle* is used to refer only to one of the twelve whom Jesus originally chose. The term *disciple* is used to refer to all followers of Jesus.

Learning the Vocabulary and Doctrine

Direct the students' attention to the Vocabulary words on page 15. Review the definitions with them.

Then ask a volunteer to read the We Believe statement. Explain that this is the doctrinal summary of the lesson, a statement about what we believe as Catholics. Encourage the students to remember these important sections in each chapter.

Step 3/CONCLUSION

Learning How to Live Our Faith

Writing About Group Unity

Ask a volunteer to read "We Are a Team" on page 15. Then have the students complete the activity, using one-word responses, if possible. Invite them to share their responses.

Completing a Prayer

Allow time for the students to complete the prayer on this page. Encourage the students to write some things they are already doing to promote unity as Christians and resolutions for the things that they would like to try to begin doing. (*Possible answers may include: care, practice, learn, help, share, cooperate, be responsible, work together, show spirit, love others, and be a friend.*) Affirm the students for the things they are already doing.

When they have finished, gather the students in a circle. Pray the first part of the prayer aloud. Then have the students read their written responses. Conclude by reading the last sentence aloud together.

DAY 3
DOCTRINE

Objective

This lesson helps the students understand that the Catholic Church is a special community.

Step 1/INTRODUCTION

Learning About Our Lives

Writing About Parish Spirit

Read "Our Parish Community" on page 16. As the word *parish* is presented, refer to the definition in the Vocabulary box on page 17. Have the students recall the prayer about working for unity that they wrote on Day 2.

Direct the students to write the name of their parish on the lines provided. Read aloud the suggestions for what they, as individuals, can do to show parish spirit. Invite them to offer additional ideas. List their suggestions on the chalkboard. Have the students choose one of the ideas and write it in their texts. Emphasize that we have many opportunities to share our parish spirit.

or . . .

Before class, prepare index cards on which you have written ways of showing parish spirit, such as *praying together at Mass, playing a game at the parish picnic, singing in the choir, planting flowers on the parish grounds, or collecting food for the poor.* Invite volunteers to select a card and pantomime the action they have drawn. Tell them that they may choose other students to help them pantomime the action.

16   Doctrine

Our Parish Community

We can show our team spirit in our **parish** community, where we come together in unity to pray and share stories of our faith. Our Catholic school is an important part of our parish community. We do many things here that show we are part of the parish community. We celebrate school Masses and pray in our classrooms. We talk to one another about what it means for us to be Catholic. We show love for one another and for people who do not even belong to our community. The more we become a team that works and prays together, the more our parish becomes a community.

Activity

As an individual within your parish community, how can you show your team spirit as a member of the team of Jesus' followers?

I belong to the community of ____name of parish____

_____.

These are some things I can do in my parish community that show that I am part of the parish team.

I can share the sign of peace at Mass.

I can greet people who walk into church with me.

_____

_____.

Focus on

Parishes   Catholic Church jurisdictions are known as dioceses. Each diocese is divided into parishes led by a pastor or a pastoral team. Parishes are usually territorial and have clearly defined boundaries. As the Catholic population in an area grows, new parishes are formed from parts of existing ones. If the Catholic population is reduced in number, two or more parishes may be combined. Thus it is not unusual to find some rural parishes that cover several towns and some urban parishes that include only a few city blocks.

A United Community

The **Catholic Church** is the Christian community which celebrates the seven sacraments and recognizes the pope and bishops as its leaders. We are united with all Catholics and with those in our parish community when we celebrate the Eucharist.

Our parish is made up of many different kinds of people and families. There are young people and old people, married people and single people. There are people of all races and cultures, from many different places, and of different abilities.

Our parish is made up of children who attend Catholic school and those who attend public school. As members of the Catholic community, we become more united with the help of the Holy Spirit. When Christians are united, they encourage one another to love as Jesus did.

Activity

Our parish family can do many things together to show that we are a united community. What is your parish doing that shows people working, praying, and learning together?

Put a check mark next to each item that shows a way the members of your parish community work, pray, or learn together.

____ We come together to pray and share the Eucharist at Mass.

____ We share the school building and classrooms for our religion classes.

____ We have special Masses for children.

____ We prepare to receive the sacraments.

____ We participate in special athletic events.

____ We help to recycle.

____ We support and help with special parish events.

> ## Vocabulary
>
> **parish:** a special community where followers of Jesus come together to pray and share stories of our faith
>
> **Catholic Church:** the Christian community which celebrates the seven sacraments and recognizes the pope and bishops as its leaders
>
> ❤❤❤❤❤❤❤❤❤❤❤

Doctrine 17

 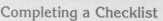
Learning About Our Faith

Reading About the Catholic Church

Ask volunteers to read aloud "A United Community" on page 17. Direct attention to the Vocabulary box as the *Catholic Church* is introduced and encourage the students to memorize the definition. Use the questions below to guide discussion.

- How many sacraments does the Catholic Church celebrate? (*Seven*)
- Whom does the Catholic Church recognize as its leaders? (*The pope and bishops*)
- What happens when we celebrate the Eucharist? (*We are united with all Catholics and with our parish community.*)
- How does the Holy Spirit help our community? (*By helping us to become more united*)
- What happens when Christians are united? (*We encourage one another to love as Jesus did.*)

Step 3/CONCLUSION

Learning How to Live Our Faith

Completing a Checklist

Invite the students to identify a variety of parish events in which parishioners work together as a community. Then have them complete the activity on page 17. Afterward, poll the class to determine which activities they participate in the most.

DAY 4
MORALITY

Objective
This lesson helps the students desire to work for unity in their families and parish.

Step 1/INTRODUCTION

Learning About Our Lives

Discussing Family Unity
Call on volunteers to read "Unity at Home" on page 18. Explain that each of us is part of more than one team. Emphasize that we are called to be in harmony in each community or team we are a part of—whether that be a sports team, our families, or the Church. Encourage the students to suggest ways we can bring harmony and unity to our families.

Writing About Qualities of Teamwork
Briefly discuss with students the qualities that make good leaders and followers. Then explain the directions for the activity on page 18. After the students have completed the two statements, invite them to share their responses. Ask the students to provide examples of times when they have been good leaders or good followers.

Step 2/DEVELOPMENT

Learning About Our Faith

Considering Jesus' Presence
As you read "The Unity of Families," emphasize Jesus' presence in the lives of our families and in the life of the Church. Explain that the word *nourish* means "to feed." Our Catholic community is nourished by Jesus' body and blood in the Eucharist. Ask the students to name other traditions, customs, or prayers that help them experience their parish communities and the entire universal Church as *family*.

Unity at Home
Earlier in this chapter, the Bobcats discovered that teamwork takes both leaders and followers. The twelve apostles were good leaders as they taught the early Christian communities. They also prayed to be good followers of Jesus. Just as the Bobcats and early Christians worked to become teams, so must our own families. Working as a team, we can often complete our tasks more easily and quickly.

Activity
Do you remember what makes good leaders and followers? Think about your team of family members as well as your team of schoolmates. As you complete the following statements, include some of the qualities that you have that make each statement true.

I am a good leader because _____.

I am a good follower because _____.

The Unity of Families
Jesus was part of a family, the Holy Family. He worked, prayed, and played with Mary, his mother, and with Joseph. They were united in their love and care for one another.

Jesus is with us in our own families, too. We know through our own experiences that no two families are alike. They may be large or small. They may have both a mother and a father or perhaps a single parent. No matter what our family is like, Jesus is with us and wants us to love and care for one another.

Families come together as Jesus' community, the Church. They gather in times of trouble as well as in times of rejoicing to praise God. They share traditions, customs, blessings, and prayers which nourish the members of a parish family.

18   Morality

 **Teaching Tips**

As you discuss families in Step 2, be especially sensitive to those students who may have recently experienced a divorce or a death in the family. Assure them that Jesus cares deeply for them and their families and that, over time, they will experience the kind of peace that only Jesus can give as they learn and grow through the changes in their lives. Be available to listen to and support those students who may need some special attention at this time.

 **Focus on**

Church Unity The *Catechism of the Catholic Church* states that "The Church is one: she acknowledges one Lord, confesses one faith, is born of one Baptism, forms only one Body, is given life by the one Spirit, for the sake of one hope (cf. Eph 4:3–5), at whose fulfillment all divisions will be overcome." (#866)

18

Growing in Unity

Jesus calls us to follow the example of unity found among the first Christians. What are some ways Jesus' followers can grow in unity today?

As Catholics, we answer Jesus' call to unity by helping our parishes grow into better communities. Wherever we live in the world, Catholics of different cultures are still united. This unity is shown in our love for Jesus.

- We are all members of the family of Jesus.

- We belong to a united community.

- We celebrate a variety of family and parish customs and practices.

- We participate within our parishes to help people in need.

- We pray and share in the Eucharist.

- We gather together each week.

- We read the Bible and share stories of Jesus with others.

Morality 19

Learning About Catholic Unity

Read the first paragraph of "Growing in Unity" on page 19. Have the students name ways Catholics today can grow in unity. (*Possible answers include: reaching out to newcomers, respecting and accepting others, praying for unity, and making an effort to love and care for others.*)

Have volunteers read the remaining text. Emphasize that the greatest uniting force among Christians is our love for Jesus.

Discussing the Photographs

Direct attention to the three photographs. Ask the students to discuss how the activities in the photographs can help to create or strengthen unity. Guide the class to see that many people in the parish community contribute to the Church's unity. Help the students name priests and other leaders in the parish. Use a parish bulletin to help students identify opportunities to become more involved in parish life.

Teaching Tips

Be aware that some of your students may absorb information most effectively through visual learning. Whenever possible, incorporate into your teaching the photographs or illustrations in the student text to help facilitate the learning process for these individuals.

DAY 5
PRAYER/REVIEW

Objective

This lesson helps the students compose and pray petitions for unity.

Writing a Prayer of Petition

Read "Praying for Unity" with the students and explain the directions for the prayer-writing activity. Have the students work in pairs to compose their petitions. As they write, guide the class to focus on the specific environments mentioned in which unity can grow. Tell them that they will have the opportunity to pray their petitions during the prayer celebration. They can take turns reading their petitions at the appropriate times.

Preparing for Prayer

Prepare an area in the classroom for prayer. Cover a desk or a table with a cloth and place a Bible and candle on it. The area should be large enough for the students to gather around comfortably in a circle. If your class is large enough, you may need to form more than one circle.

Give out 1" × 4" strips of colored construction paper and crayons. Invite the students to write one quality or gift they have that contributes to class unity. Direct each student to staple the paper end to end to form a link that joins his or her link to those of the other students to make a chain. Display the chain on the prayer table during the prayer celebration.

You may want to choose one of the following music selections to use in this prayer experience: "We Are Many Parts" (GIA) or "They'll Know We Are Christians" (FEL).

Praying for Unity

Invite the students to pray for unity using the petitions they have written. You may want to have all the students prayerfully read the first two sentences of the prayer. Then have a volunteer read each statement that begins, "Holy Spirit, we pray for unity . . . ," followed by the reading of the students' petitions at the appropriate times. Then invite the entire class to pray the last line of the prayer together.

Praying for Unity

Fill in the blanks to complete this prayer of petition for unity.

Lord, we thank you for the example of the first Christians. May your Holy Spirit help us to follow their example at all times and in all the communities to which we belong.

Holy Spirit, we pray for unity in our religion class.

Help us _____.

Holy Spirit, we pray for unity in our school.

Help us _____.

Holy Spirit, we pray for unity in our parish family.

Help us _____.

Holy Spirit, we pray for unity in our homes.

Help us _____.

Holy Spirit, help us encourage one another to live as Jesus wants us to live. Amen.

20 Prayer

🍎 Teaching Tips

One of the most effective ways to create an atmosphere that is conducive to meditative prayer is to use instrumental music. By playing music that is composed for quiet listening or for prayer, such as Gregorian chant or psalms, you can introduce a time for prayer. You may want to consult with your parish music director for specific suggestions and resources. The music will provide an excellent background for quiet reflection and for reading meditative passages or prayers.

Chapter Review

Write next to each picture words or phrases that describe how the group represented by the picture can show its unity. You may use any word or phrase more than once. *Answers will vary.*

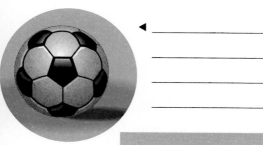

◄ _____
_____
_____

_____ ►
_____
_____
_____

▲ _____
_____
_____

Fill in the answers to the first two questions.

1. What did the twelve apostles teach the first

   Christians? <u>to live in harmony; to be united</u>

   _____

2. What did the first Christians do to grow in

   unity? <u>They met together, listened to the teachings</u>

   <u>of the apostles, prayed and ate together, and</u>

   <u>shared all they had with one another.</u>

3. Talk about how your school can grow in unity this year.

> **Jesus prays, "Father, may they be one as we are one."**
> **Based on John 17:22**

Enriching the Lesson

Ask the students to create skits based on the Scripture art on page 14. Allow time for practice. Have each group present its skit.

CURRICULUM CONNECTION

Art Distribute drawing paper and crayons or markers. Invite the students to draw a picture that illustrates one of the statements about Catholic unity on page 19 of the text. As the students work, move about the room, talking with them individually about their drawings.

Reviewing the Chapter

Explain the directions for the activity on page 21. Have the students work independently to complete it. When they have finished, invite students to share their answers aloud. (*Possible answers for Soccer Team include: teamwork, practice, play together, cooperate, and pass the ball. Possible answers for Parish include: share stories of Jesus, pray together, care, learn, love one another, help people in need, and work together. Possible answers for Family include: listen, love one another, cooperate, work together, care for each other.*)

Direct students to write the answers to the first two review questions on the lines provided in the text. Be supportive of each child who participates in the discussion of the third question.

Praying with the Scriptural Verse

Read the verse from Scripture at the bottom of the page. Help the students appreciate that Jesus wants us to love one another as he and his Father love each other.

Invite the students to reflect silently on what they can do to build unity in the class or in the school and grow closer to Jesus. Conclude with this prayer.

"Thank you, Lord, for the Church. We are united as one community of faith as we listen to your word in Scripture. We are one as we celebrate the Eucharist together. Help us to share what we have with others." Invite the students to respond, "Amen."

21

2 Our Church Is Holy

Objectives ~~~~~

To help the students

■ Define the meaning of the word *holy*.

■ Learn that the second mark of the Church is that it is holy.

■ Understand how the saints responded to Jesus' call to holiness.

■ Want to grow closer to God in prayer.

■ Ask the saints' help in growing in holiness and to review the chapter.

Chapter Outline ~~~~~

	Step 1 Learning About Our Lives	Step 2 Learning About Our Faith	Step 3 Learning How to Live Our Faith
Day 1	■ Introduce the chapter. ■ Read and discuss the story. *ABOUT 5 MINUTES*	■ Discuss holiness. ■ Learn the vocabulary. *ABOUT 12 MINUTES*	■ Recall favorite ways of praying. *ABOUT 13 MINUTES*
Day 2	■ Recognize God's presence. *ABOUT 7 MINUTES*	■ Read the Scripture story. ■ Discuss holiness. ■ Review the doctrine. *ABOUT 8 MINUTES*	■ Complete an activity. *ABOUT 15 MINUTES*
Day 3	■ Conduct an opinion poll. *ABOUT 10 MINUTES*	■ Read the text. ■ Learn the vocabulary word. *ABOUT 10 MINUTES*	■ Draw acts of holiness. ■ Research saints. *ABOUT 10 MINUTES*
Day 4	■ Consider The Lord's Prayer. *ABOUT 10 MINUTES*	■ Decode Bible messages. *ABOUT 10 MINUTES*	■ Complete an acrostic. ■ Make a holiness bulletin board. *ABOUT 10 MINUTES*
Day 5	**Prayer** Prepare for prayer; read the text; pray a litany of saints. **Review** Complete a matching activity; review the chapter; learn the scriptural verse.		

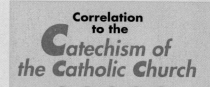
Plan Ahead

	Preparing Your Class	**Materials Needed**
Day 1	Read through the lesson plan for this class session. Be prepared to share with the students your favorite ways of praying.	■ drawing paper ■ crayons ■ pencils or pens
Day 2	Read through the lesson plan for this class session. Think of practical ways the students can show care for another person.	■ pencils or pens
Day 3	Before class, write the statements from page 26 on the chalkboard. Prepare a saint paper-doll pattern and a photocopy for each student.	■ books on the lives of the saints ■ chalkboard, posterboard, or newsprint ■ art paper, lined paper ■ paper dolls, fabric, yarn, cotton
Day 4	Read through the lesson plan. Clear a bulletin board for the students' displays.	■ magazines, scissors ■ drawing paper, markers ■ pencils or pens
Day 5	Prepare an environment for prayer in the classroom. Make sure the students' reports and saint figures are ready for presentation.	■ Bible, candle, tablecloth ■ student reports and saint figures ■ music for prayer celebration ■ pencils or pens

Additional Resources

As you plan this chapter, consider using the following materials from The Resourceful Teacher Package.

■ *Classroom Activity Sheets 2* and *2a*

■ *Family Activity Sheets 2* and *2a*

■ *Chapter 2 Test*

■ *Prayers for Every Day*

■ *Projects: Grade 3*

You may also wish to refer to the following Big Book.

■ *We Celebrate God's Word*, pages 12 and 23

In preparing the students for the Sunday readings, you may wish to use Silver Burdett Ginn's *Getting Ready for Sunday* student and teacher materials.

BOOKS FOR THE JOURNEY

An Artist. M.B. Goffstein. Harper & Row, 1980. A story that simply says that we can be like God in the things we do.

A Child's Book of Prayers. Edited by Linda Yeatman. Workman Publishing, 1992. "O Thou Great Chief," prayer of an African schoolgirl; "Lord, Teach a Little Child to Pray," by Jane Taylor. Prayers in which a closeness to God is expressed.

MORE BOOKS FOR THE JOURNEY

Sunshine Home. Eve Bunting. Clarion Books, 1994. A story of a boy who does something about his grandmother's sadness that helps the whole family.

Praise for the Singing. Collected by Madelaine Gill. Little, Brown & Co., 1993. "Sing Hosanna," pp. 12–13, traditional. A song identifying the things we need in our hearts for holiness.

REDUCED CLASSROOM ACTIVITIES

NAME _____

OUR CHURCH IS HOLY

Write the prayer "I know you're with me, God" in each box below and then cut along the heavy black lines. Tape each card to the place mentioned to help you find God anywhere.

Close to God		
On my pillow	On the doorknob	In my bedroom
On the refrigerator	On my desk	In my pocket

To the Teacher: This activity follows the story "Close to God."

NAME _____

PLACES TO BE HOLY

Unscramble the letters on each sign. Write the words correctly on the lines provided. Circle the places where you can be close to God.

1. plyagrndou 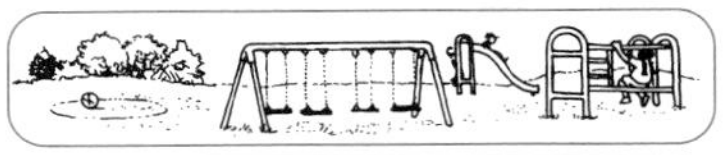
2. doohrobhgien 
3. ehom 
4. cruhch 
5. scholo

1. playground
2. neighborhood
3. home
4. church
5. school

To the Teacher: This activity will help students understand that they can be close to God in many different places.

Background for the Teacher

THE MARK OF HOLINESS

The second traditional mark, or sign, of Christ's Church is that it is called to be holy. The Holy Spirit calls all baptized members of the Catholic community to a life of holiness. This holiness is most evident when we love God, live moral lives, and work for justice and peace.

In the Old Testament, God is often called the Holy One. God's people call themselves a holy people because of their special bond with God. The Church continues this belief in God, who is infinitely perfect and holy. The Church believes that God calls each of us to holiness, or oneness with him, through the grace of Baptism.

The Church also teaches that Jesus Christ is holy. Jesus showed the world a special love for God and for others. In turn, Jesus calls all men and women to imitate his holiness. We do this by developing a life of prayer, celebrating the sacraments, and striving to live a life that demonstrates concern for the needs of others. We have the saints as outstanding examples of people who took seriously this call to holiness.

THE CHALLENGE TO BE HOLY

As members of the Catholic Church, we are to live as a community that is a living sign of God and Jesus. The Church has been sanctified by Christ and continues to be guided by the Holy Spirit. The Church has received an important mission from Jesus to proclaim the gospel, to baptize, and to call all men and women to holiness. The *National Catechetical Directory* states: "Pilgrim and sinful people that they are, the members of the Church nevertheless give visible evidence of God's holiness through acts of repentance and conversion, and through striving daily for holiness" (No. 72). Other signs of the Catholic community's holiness are its prayer and sacramental life and its visible commitment to issues of justice and peace. In this chapter on holiness as a mark of the Church, we have defined *holy* as being close to God, loving God and others, and doing God's work in the world. In other words, while holiness is first and foremost a gift given by God, holiness also involves our personal response to this gift.

DAY 1
DOCTRINE

Objective

This lesson helps the students define the meaning of the word *holy*.

Step 1/INTRODUCTION

Learning About Our Lives

Introducing the Chapter

Read aloud the chapter-focus questions and invite the students' responses. Affirm the examples the students offer and tell the class that in this chapter they will learn how Jesus helps us to grow in holiness.

Reading and Discussing the Story

Ask one or more volunteers to read aloud the story "Close to God" on pages 22 and 23. Then ask the students to consider the questions under Discuss on page 23. Encourage everyone to offer an answer or an opinion.

or . . .

Use a guided meditation to help the students recall an experience of feeling close to God. Invite them to close their eyes as they concentrate on breathing in and out, slowly and deeply. Read the following paragraph to the class, pausing briefly after each sentence.

"Remember a time when you felt that God was with you. . . . Picture where you were at that moment. . . . How did you know that God was with you? . . . Take a few moments to thank God for being with you. . . . Tell God that you want to learn what it means to be holy. . . ."

Ask the students to open their eyes. Encourage them to comment on the meditation experience.

Our Church Is Holy

2

Did you ever do anything that you thought was a holy thing to do? What was it?

22 Doctrine

Close to God

Diego loved to play soccer from the time his father coached him at home in Bolivia. One Saturday in his new home in Washington, Diego wanted to play soccer, but none of his friends could come to play with him. So he went to sit down under a tree in his backyard. This was his favorite place to go to be alone. It was quiet and peaceful.

His thoughts drifted back to Bolivia. Diego remembered the words his grandmother said to him every time he left the house. "*Vaya con Dios,*" she would say. "Go with God." In good times and in bad times, she would say, "God is always with us." And she believed this with all her heart. For a few minutes, Diego had a feeling that God was there with him, just as his grandmother had said.

"Diego! Let's play soccer!" his friend Alex shouted. "I can come out now."

Cultural Awareness

Review the meanings of the Spanish words used in "Close to God." You may wish to introduce other Spanish words and phrases to the students, such as: *hola* ("hello"); *hasta luego* ("goodbye" or "see you later"); *buenos días* ("good morning"); *buenas tardes* ("good afternoon"); *buenas noches* ("good night"); *¿Qué tal?* ("How's it going?"); *Bien, gracias.* ("Fine, thank you."); *Dios* ("God"); *Espíritu Santo* ("Holy Spirit"); and *iglesia* ("church").

Focus on

Meditation Meditation is one of the oldest forms of prayer and is practiced in almost every religion. The basis of meditative prayer is that the less we are aware of our bodies and material concerns, the more our minds and hearts can be completely turned toward God. Suggested meditation techniques are aimed at helping people to be relaxed and focused on their desire to listen and talk to God. By becoming detached from our material concerns, we are more likely to be led by the Spirit to deeper communication with God.

22

Just then Diego remembered that his mother had asked him to take the morning paper over to Clara, an elderly neighbor, so that she could read it, too.

"Alex," he answered, "I forgot to do something for Mom. I'll be back in a minute!" He ran back to his house to get the paper.

When he gave it to Clara, she smiled at him. "*Gracias,*" she said. "Thanks." As he turned to leave, she added, "*Vaya con Dios!*"

Discuss

1. When and where did Diego feel closest to God?
2. Have you ever felt especially close to God? When? Where?

Holiness Is . . .

The first Christians were **holy** people. Like Jesus, they were close to God and cared about others. They followed the ways that Jesus taught.

Like the first Christians, the Church today is also called to be holy. We pray together at home and in our parishes. We share things and help one another. To be holy is to be close to God, to love God and others, and to do his work in the world.

Vocabulary

holy: being close to God, loving God and others, and doing his work in the world

♥ ♥ ♥ ♥ ♥ ♥ ♥ ♥ ♥ ♥ ♥ ♥

Doctrine 23

Step 2/DEVELOPMENT

Learning About Our Faith

Discussing Holiness

Read "Holiness Is . . ." on page 23 with the students. Ask what the first Christians did that showed they were holy people. (*They cared about others; they followed Jesus' teachings.*)

Learning the Vocabulary

Direct the students' attention to the Vocabulary word on page 23. Ask a student to read aloud the definition for the word *holy*. Have the class repeat the definition. Check the students' understanding of the word by asking them to use it in a sentence.

Step 3/CONCLUSION

Learning How to Live Our Faith

Recalling Favorite Ways of Praying

Explain to the students that prayer is one important way of being close to God, expressing our love for God and others, and helping us to know how God wants us to work in the world. Encourage the students to describe their favorite prayers and ways of praying. Share some of your own favorite ways of praying. Ask the students to explain how such ways of praying help them to grow in holiness. Emphasize that people who are close to God talk to God and listen to him in prayer.

Objective

This lesson helps the students learn that the second mark of the Church is that it is holy.

Step 1/INTRODUCTION

Learning About Our Lives

Recognizing God's Presence

Ask the students the following questions to help them assess how aware they are of God's presence in different settings and situations.

- Do you feel God's presence more on a sunny day or a rainy day?

- Do you feel closer to God when you are alone or when you are with your friends?

- Do you feel that God is with you more in church than when you are in your room?

As the students respond, ask them to explain their reasons for feeling the way they do. Emphasize that God is always with us, wherever we are. Explain that Jesus invites us to grow closer to God by being aware of God's presence in our lives.

Step 2/DEVELOPMENT

Learning About Our Faith

Reading the Scripture Story

Introduce the Scripture story by explaining to the students that one of the ways we try to understand how to grow closer to God is to learn about how others have been close to God. Help the students to understand that the first followers of Jesus tried to be holy as Jesus was holy. We remember their example today as we seek to be holy.

Ask the students to turn to "A Holy People" on pages 24 and 25. Have volunteers read it aloud to the class. Review the main parts of the story by asking the following questions.

- Where and when did Jesus seem close to God? (*In the Temple; with other people, especially the sick and poor; when caring for others*)

- Where did the early Christians pray? (*In the Temple and at home*)

A Holy People

The Christians in Jerusalem knew how much Jesus had loved the Temple. So every day, they prayed together in the Temple.

"I used to come here often with Jesus," one of them told his friends. "God seemed to be close to us here."

Later, the Christians went back to the house where they met each day. They sat down to eat. After the meal, one of them spoke up.

"Jesus also seemed to bring God close when he was with people in their homes or in the marketplace. And he seemed to bring God's presence near when he was with the sick and the poor."

24 Scripture

Focus on

Temples and Synagogues In the early days of Christianity, the Temple in Jerusalem was considered to be the most important sanctuary in Israel and was primarily a place of worship. Synagogues, such as the one Jesus visited early in his ministry, served as places of meeting and study. Today, both words are used to designate places of meeting, study, and worship. Most Reform and some Conservative Jews refer to their meeting places as *temples*, while Orthodox Jews use the word *synagogue*.

"Jesus, the Son of God, wants us all to become sons and daughters of God," one of the women added. "He calls us to listen to God's word and to do God's work in the world. Jesus taught us to love our neighbor and to care about anyone who is in need. That's how *we* can be holy, like Jesus."

The group was silent for a moment. Barnabas placed a sack of money on the table. "I just sold my farm," he said. "I will share the money with anyone who is in need."

Like Barnabas, everyone shared whatever they had. They gave praise and thanks for God's goodness. They took bread and wine, blessed them, and shared them in memory of Jesus.

Based on Acts 2:42–47; 4:32–37, 5:11–16

Activity

Find times and places in the story when the first Christians were close to God. List some of them below. Then make a list of the times and places when we are closest to God today.

The first Christians were close to God when _____

_____

_____

_____ .

The Church today is close to God when _____

_____

_____

_____ .

We Believe

One of the marks, or signs, of the Catholic Church is that it is holy. Being holy means to be close to God and to do his work in the world. It means loving God and caring about all people.

Doctrine 25

- What did the early Christians do to be close to God? (*They shared everything in common, praised and thanked God, and celebrated the Eucharist together.*)
- Do you think people today would do what Barnabas did? Why or why not? (*Answers will vary.*)

Discussing Holiness

Help the students understand that they can grow closer to God by taking time to pay attention to God, by praying, by meditating, or by reading Scripture. Ask the students to think of one way that they pay attention to God. Then discuss with students that another way they can grow closer to God is by growing closer to and caring for one another. Have them suggest one specific way they can show care for another person at home or school. Ask the students to explain how their actions help them to become holier. Emphasize that when we follow Jesus' example of caring for others, we are growing in holiness.

Reviewing the Doctrine

Ask the students to read aloud the We Believe statement. Emphasize that holiness is the second of the four marks of the Church. Ask the students if they can remember the first mark of the Church, which they studied in the previous chapter. (*Our Church is one, or united.*)

Step 3/CONCLUSION

Learning How to Live Our Faith

Completing an Activity

Read aloud the directions for the activity on page 25. Have the students complete the activity. Then invite them to read their responses aloud.

Objective

This lesson helps the students understand how the saints responded to Jesus' call to holiness.

Step 1/INTRODUCTION

Learning About Our Lives

Conducting an Opinion Poll

Read aloud the directions for the activity on page 26. To get the students to think more deeply about holiness, give them time to complete the opinion poll. Have them do this individually before comparing answers. Write the statements on the chalkboard. Have one student read the statements aloud while another student counts the raised hands for each category and records the number of responses next to each statement. Seeing the results in this way gives the students a chance to find out how the class feels and how their individual responses compare with those of the rest of the group. Elicit the students' responses to the results of the poll.

Step 2/DEVELOPMENT

Learning About Our Faith

Reading the Text

Read through "A Holy Church" with the students. Use the following questions to guide the discussion.

- How do we, the Church, show our love for God? (*By praying and celebrating the sacraments, by helping and being kind to others, by helping people in need*)

- What do we remember when we celebrate the Eucharist? (*That the Father showed great love for us by sending Jesus to die for us*)

- What do we call the holy men and women that the Church honors? (*saints*)

Learning the Vocabulary Word

Direct attention to the Vocabulary box on page 27. Have the students read and learn the definition of the word *saints*.

26

Activity

People take opinion polls to find out what others think or feel about something. Here is an opinion poll about holiness. Now that you have learned more about what it means to be holy, take the poll yourself. Put a ✔ in the box that best fits your opinion of holiness. Answers will vary.

Opinion Poll	Agree	Disagree	Not Sure
1. People who are holy never have fun.			
2. Hardly anyone is a really holy person.			
3. A holy person cares about others.			
4. A person can become holy by doing ordinary things.			
5. God wants *me* to be a holy person.			
6. Anyone can become a holy person.			

A Holy Church

Jesus' family, the Church, grows closer to God each day and truly cares about all people. We show that we love God when we pray and celebrate the sacraments. Each time we celebrate the Eucharist, we are united with Jesus and the Church. We remember that God our Father, out of love for us, sent Jesus to save us.

The Church also shows love for God by helping and being kind to others. The whole Church throughout the world works together to help people in need, people in our own communities as well as people around the world.

The Church is holy because the people who belong to this community of believers are holy people. On the Feast of All Saints, we pray, "Father, all-powerful and ever-living God, today we rejoice in the holy men and women of every time and place." The holy men and women we honor are called **saints**.

CURRICULUM CONNECTION

Mathematics After conducting the opinion poll on page 26, show the students how the results can be displayed in a pie chart. Ask for volunteers to draw six large circles on the chalkboard. Number the circles to correspond with the items in the poll. Then, by drawing lines from the center to the outside of each circle, divide each circle into three segments, illustrating the number of students who responded "agree," "disagree," and "not sure" to each question.

Activity

Write a sentence or draw a picture that tells about something you are doing or have already done that shows you are growing as a holy person.

I Am Holy, Too

Jesus calls us to be holy. The lives of the saints give us many examples of how Christians have answered this call throughout the history of the Church. As you answer Jesus' call to holiness, you, too, could be a saint.

Vocabulary

saints: holy men and women who are honored by the Church because they showed in extraordinary ways that they loved God and others unselfishly

♥♥♥♥♥♥♥♥♥♥♥

 **Teaching Tips**

The students may think that they can't live up to the example of the saints' seemingly perfect lives. Help the students understand that the saints were human beings who responded to God's love. Like us, they relied on the help of Jesus and the Holy Spirit. Emphasize that we are all called to holiness and that each of us has the potential to be a saint.

Enriching the Lesson

Distribute lined paper to the students and ask them to think of someone they know whom they consider holy. Have the students consider the following questions as they write about the person they have chosen.

- How does this person show that he or she is close to God?
- How does this person show love and care for others?
- How can this person help you to be holy?
- Suppose this person did something that hurt someone. Would he or she still be holy?

Learning How to Live Our Faith

Drawing Acts of Holiness

Read aloud the directions at the top of page 27 and have the students complete the activity in the space provided. Ask for volunteers to share their pictures or sentences with the group.

Researching Saints

Ask for a volunteer to read aloud "I Am Holy, Too" on page 27.

Provide books on the saints for the students to research and write a brief report on their name saint or another saint of their choice. Make an 11" × 17" paper-doll pattern and run it off on heavy paper for each student. Supply art paper, fabric, yarn, cotton, trim, and other materials for the students to "dress" their saints in appropriate costumes. The costumes can reflect the saints' occupations, religious orders, or some other distinctive feature. When the students have finished, have them put their saint figures aside for use in the prayer service on Day 5.

Objective

This lesson helps the students want to grow closer to God in prayer.

Step 1/INTRODUCTION

Learning About Our Lives

Considering The Lord's Prayer

Read aloud "Close to God in Prayer" on page 28. Then use the following to review the meaning of The Lord's Prayer. You may also want to teach the students the American Sign Language gestures for "Hallowed be thy name."

Our Father, who art in heaven, hallowed be thy name: We call God "Father" and say that God's name is holy.

Thy kingdom come: We pray that God's kingdom of love will come in all its fullness.

Thy will be done on earth as it is in heaven: We trust and cooperate with God's plans for our lives and for the life of the Church.

Give us this day our daily bread: We know that everything comes from God. We pray that everyone will have what they need to live happy lives.

Forgive us our trespasses as we forgive those who trespass against us: We say we are sorry for our sins and promise to forgive others.

Lead us not into temptation, but deliver us from evil: We ask God to protect us when we are tempted and to help us make good choices.

HALLOWED   BE

THY   NAME

28

Close to God in Prayer

Jesus taught his first followers to pray to God as "Father." We are all God's children. When we pray The Lord's Prayer, also called the Our Father, we pray as sons and daughters of God. In Matthew 6:8b, Jesus says, "Your Father knows what you need before you ask him." Likewise, parents often know what their children need before their children ask. What do we, God's children, ask for when we pray the Our Father?

Activity

Look up Matthew 7:7 in your Bibles. Then decode the Bible words in the following activity to discover three simple things you can do if you want to get closer to God in prayer.

a =   e =   n =   s =

c =   k =   o =

1. "<u>A</u> <u>s</u> <u>k</u> and it will be given to you." Name one thing God can give to you.

_____

2. "<u>S</u> <u>e</u> <u>e</u> <u>k</u> and you will find." Name one special place where you can always find God.

_____

3. "<u>K</u> <u>n</u> <u>o</u> <u>c</u> <u>k</u> and the door will be opened to you." Write one thing you could talk to God about the next time you pray.

_____

🍎 Teaching Tips

Use the reference to Matthew 7:7 as an opportunity for students to practice their Bible skills. Distribute Bibles to the students and ask them to locate the passage. As they do this, assist those who may be having difficulty. Additional Bible skills can be reviewed by using "About the Bible" on page 328 in the Our Catholic Heritage section of the student text.

Activity

The Holy Spirit is guiding us to live as holy people. Use the letters in the word *holiness* to tell what growing in holiness means to you. Two are done for you.

_____ *H* _____

_____ *O* _____

_____ Ca *L* ling God "Father" _____

_____ *I* _____

_____ *N* _____

_____ Loving oth *E* rs _____

_____ *S* _____

_____ *S* _____

CURRICULUM CONNECTION

Spelling As the students complete the activity on page 29, check to see if any of them are having difficulty with spelling. You might go around the classroom and provide any necessary help or write the difficult words on the chalkboard.

Focus on

The Lord's Prayer The *Catechism of the Catholic Church* quotes Tertullian, a Father of the early Church, who called The Lord's Prayer "the summary of the whole gospel" (#2761). Saint Thomas Aquinas called it "the most perfect of prayers" (# 2763). It is called The Lord's Prayer "because it comes to us from the Lord Jesus, the master and model of our prayer." (# 2775)

Step 2/DEVELOPMENT

Learning About Our Faith

Decoding Bible Messages

Explain the directions for the activity on page 28. First have the students read the passage from Matthew in their Bibles, and then have them complete the activity.

Allow time for the students to share their responses. Ask them to think of gestures for the words *ask, seek,* and *knock.* Remind the students to think of these words whenever they want to feel closer to God. Stress that God is always with us.

Step 3/CONCLUSION

Learning How to Live Our Faith

Completing an Acrostic

Ask a volunteer to read the directions for the activity on page 29. Have the students work in pairs to complete the activity. Afterward, encourage them to read their ideas aloud. Emphasize that the Holy Spirit guides us, as individuals and as a Church, to grow in holiness.

Making a Holiness Bulletin Board

Distribute magazines, drawing paper, markers, and scissors. Invite the students to make a bulletin board display promoting growth in holiness. Divide the class into groups and assign tasks to each group: finding pictures which show people acting with care; creating captions; writing poems about holiness; and so on. As the students work, move about the room and comment on their work.

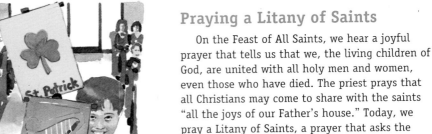

PRAYER/REVIEW

Objective

This lesson helps the students ask the saints' help in growing in holiness.

Preparing for Prayer

Invite students to introduce to the class the saints they researched on Day 3 by reading their reports and displaying their saint figures. Have the class choose three saints they want to include in the litany and write their names in the spaces provided in the text.

Plan a procession of saints around the class or in the sanctuary. Have the students carry their saint figures as they process. Choose music for the procession, such as "The Family of God" (GIA) or "This Is Holy Ground" (Birdwing Music).

Reading the Text

Read the first paragraph on page 30 with the class. Clarify the meaning of the phrase "all the joys of our Father's house" by explaining that the saints share never-ending happiness in heaven with God. Stress that the saints are an example to us; they show us how to love God and follow Jesus. Remind the class that we are *all* called to holiness.

Praying a Litany of Saints

Pray the litany with the students. Tell the students that the leader will read the words that appear in light print and that they are to read together the words that appear in bold print. Consider adding to the litany the saint names of the students in your class. Conclude by praying together The Lord's Prayer.

Praying a Litany of Saints

On the Feast of All Saints, we hear a joyful prayer that tells us that we, the living children of God, are united with all holy men and women, even those who have died. The priest prays that all Christians may come to share with the saints "all the joys of our Father's house." Today, we pray a Litany of Saints, a prayer that asks the saints in heaven to pray for us. We ask for their help as we continue to grow in holiness.

We want to live as your children. Lord, have mercy.
Lord, have mercy.
We want to live as Jesus taught us. Christ, have mercy.
Christ, have mercy.
We want to grow in holiness. Lord, have mercy.
Lord, have mercy.
Holy Mary, Mother of God, **pray for us.**
Michael, Gabriel, and all holy angels of God, **pray for us.**
John the Baptizer and all holy prophets, **pray for us.**
St. Joseph, **pray for us.**
Matthew, Mark, Luke, and John, **pray for us.**

_____, **pray for us.**

_____, **pray for us.**

_____, **pray for us.**

All you holy men and women, **hear our prayer.**

30 Prayer

Focus on

Litanies A litany is a prayer in which the leader reads a series of petitions or invocations and the congregation responds with a set phrase, such as "Pray for us." The litany of the saints used in this lesson is modeled after the longer Litany of the Saints, which is part of the Liturgy of Baptism recited during the Easter Vigil. Other official litanies of the Church include the Kyrie Eleison, the Agnus Dei (Lamb of God), and the solemn orations of Good Friday.

Chapter Review

Match each word in Column 2 with its definition in Column 1. Write the correct number from Column 1 on the line next to the word in Column 2.

Column 1

1. Being close to God
2. Promises that God answers prayer
3. Holy men and women we honor at a special feast
4. Helps us grow in holiness
5. What we can call God when we pray

Column 2

__3__ saints

__2__ Jesus

__4__ Holy Spirit

__5__ Father

__1__ holy

Fill in the answers to the first two questions.

1. What does it mean to be holy? It means being
   close to God, loving God and others, and doing
   God's work in the world.

2. How did the first Christians show they were
   holy? They showed they were holy by praying
   together, staying close to God, and sharing what
   they had with people in need.

You are called
to be a holy
people.
**Based on
1 Corinthians 1:2**

3. Talk about people today who show us what we can do to become holy.

Review 31

Completing a Matching Activity

Explain the directions for the matching activity on page 31. When the students have finished, check their answers by dividing the class into two sides. Have one side read aloud the definition from Column 1 and have the other side read the correct word from Column 2.

Reviewing the Chapter

Take time to go through the review questions. Direct the students to write the answer to each question on the lines provided in the text. Encourage all the students to participate in the discussion question.

Learning the Scriptural Verse

Direct the students' attention to the verse from Scripture at the bottom of the page and have the students read it aloud. Affirm their efforts to grow in holiness through this week's lessons by telling them that they are holy people, both together and individually. Encourage them to continue to respond to God's call to holiness each and every day.

Enriching the Lesson

Introduce the story of your parish patron saint or another saint the students may enjoy learning about. After reading or telling the students about the saint, identify how the person was close to God in both prayer and action.

Teaching Tips

As you lead the class in discussing the third question at the end of the chapter review, you may want to have ready a list of people to use as examples of those who display holiness today. The list might include teachers, priests, deacons, religious sisters and brothers, or other spiritual leaders.

3 Our Church Is Catholic

Objectives ∼∼∼∼

To help the students

- Recognize the importance of welcoming people who are different.
- Learn the meaning of the word *catholic* as a mark of the Church.
- Desire to welcome, accept, and be open to all people.
- Respect the variety of cultures within the Church.
- Pray for respect and openness and review the chapter.

Chapter Outline ∼∼∼∼∼∼∼∼∼

	Step 1 **Learning About Our Lives**	**Step 2** **Learning About Our Faith**	**Step 3** **Learning How to Live Our Faith**
Day 1	■ Introduce the chapter. ■ Read and discuss a story. ■ Complete the story. *ABOUT 12 MINUTES*	■ Read and discuss a Scripture story. *ABOUT 8 MINUTES*	■ Read and discuss a poem. ■ Compare stories. *ABOUT 10 MINUTES*
Day 2	■ Talk about strangers. *ABOUT 3 MINUTES*	■ Study the illustration. ■ Read and discuss the story. ■ Talk about being Catholic. ■ Review vocabulary and doctrine. *ABOUT 10 MINUTES*	■ Discuss ignorance. *ABOUT 17 MINUTES*
Day 3	■ Research newspapers. *ABOUT 10 MINUTES*	■ Read the text. ■ Study the photographs. *ABOUT 10 MINUTES*	■ Pray together. ■ Complete an activity. *ABOUT 10 MINUTES*
Day 4	■ Learn about respect. ■ Write about ethnic customs. *ABOUT 12 MINUTES*	■ Read about Archbishop Romero. *ABOUT 13 MINUTES*	■ Choose a class project. *ABOUT 5 MINUTES*
Day 5	**Prayer** Prepare for prayer; pray a litany of petition. **Review** Complete a crossword puzzle; review the chapter; reflect on the scriptural verse.		

Correlation to the

Catechism of the Catholic Church

Paragraphs
**830, 831, 832, 833, 834,
835, 836, 837, 838, 839,
840, 841, 842, 843, 844,
845, 846, 847, 848, 849,
850, 851, 852, 853, 854,
855, 856, 868, 1202**

Plan Ahead

	Preparing Your Class	**Materials Needed**
Day 1	Read through the lesson plan for this class session. Practice reading the poem about welcoming.	■ pencils or pens
Day 2	Read through the lesson plan for this class session.	■ pencils or pens
Day 3	Read through the lesson plan for this session. Collect newspapers for use in Step 1.	■ newspapers ■ pencils or pens
Day 4	Read through the lesson plan. Be prepared to share with the students a family tradition.	■ pencils or pens
Day 5	Plan the prayer experience. Prepare an environment for prayer in the classroom. Review this week's sessions to prepare for the chapter review.	■ Bible, candle, tablecloth ■ construction paper ■ tape or stapler ■ pencils or pens

Additional Resources

As you plan this chapter, consider using the following materials from The Resourceful Teacher Package.

■ *Classroom Activity Sheets 3* and *3a*

■ *Family Activity Sheets 3* and *3a*

■ *Chapter 3 Test*

■ *Prayers for Every Day*

■ *Projects: Grade 3*

You may also wish to refer to the following Big Books.

■ *We Celebrate God's Word,* pages 9 and 14

■ *We Celebrate the Mass,* page 18

In preparing the students for the Sunday readings, you may wish to use Silver Burdett Ginn's *Getting Ready for Sunday* student and teacher materials.

BOOKS FOR THE JOURNEY

Crow Boy. Taro Yashima. Puffin, 1976. The story of a child who was finally welcomed by a caring teacher after enduring years of unkindness.

The Hundred Dresses. Eleanor Estes. Harcourt Brace Jovanovich, 1974. A child at a new school is misjudged and treated meanly by her classmates.

MORE BOOKS FOR THE JOURNEY

The Ugly Duckling. Hans Christian Andersen. Translated by R.P. Keigwin. Scribner's, 1965. A duckling suffers greatly because he is different.

Christians. John Drane. Lion Publishing, 1994. "Roman Catholics," Chapter 11. Some pertinent facts about the Catholic Church.

REDUCED CLASSROOM ACTIVITIES

NAME _____

OUR CHURCH IS CATHOLIC

Think about what it would be like to write to a Catholic pen pal in another country. First choose a country anywhere in the world. Then follow the suggested outline below.

Name of country

_____

Dear _____ ,

I am writing to you from _____ .

The name of my parish is _____ . What's the name of your parish? In Religion class today, we talked about _____

_____

My favorite Scripture story is _____

_____ .

What's yours? What do you enjoy the most about your parish church? Are you involved in any activities in your parish community? My favorite event is our annual parish picnic. Please write soon and tell me all about yourself.

Sincerely,

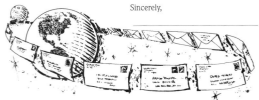

To the Teacher: This activity will help students develop an interest in the experiences and backgrounds of others.

Chapter 3 Our Church Is Catholic   THIS IS OUR FAITH 3   **3**

NAME _____

LEARNING TO LOVE ALL

Look at the scene below. What do you think the two children are saying to each other? Write their words in the speech balloons.

Spirit of Love, Open our hearts to accept all people

I wonder if I will eat alone again today.

To the Teacher: This activity will encourage students to put their faith into action.

3a THIS IS OUR FAITH 3   **Chapter 3** Our Church Is Catholic

THE CATHOLIC MARK

The third traditional mark of the Church is its catholicity. The Holy Spirit calls the Church to be catholic. The meaning of *catholic* is "open to the whole world." We retain the word today as the Church continually seeks to embrace all people.

Jesus sought to reach a wide range of people with his teaching. He aided everyone who asked for his help, including foreigners and those who were marginalized or oppressed. He welcomed all people to fellowship with himself and with the Father. Jesus expected those who followed him in this world to be equally concerned and open to all people. His command was to teach *all* nations.

People from different lands listened to the disciples at Pentecost and understood the message of Jesus in their own languages. The preaching of the disciples attracted many Gentiles who sought to turn their lives around and be baptized. The early Christian community decided that all who accepted Jesus as Lord and Savior were to be welcomed into the Church. The Church was open to all people who expressed their belief in Jesus as Lord and who were open to learning more about Jesus and his Church.

THE CHALLENGE TO BE OPEN

As Catholics, we are called to open ourselves and our communities to welcome and accept those who may be different from us in color, race, nationality, ability, or culture. Your students may well be aware of differences among people in their neighborhoods, their parishes, and their schools. Students at this age may have already heard and been influenced by the prejudices of the adults in their world. So, indeed, the challenge may be great!

As a teacher, your own openness to all the students in the class is perhaps their first lesson in what the word *catholic* means. The students look to you as an example. Seek to be open to all the young people. Help them to recognize that living, learning, and praying with people who are different from them can be an enriching experience. At the same time, be careful not to focus on the differences.

DAY 1
MORALITY/SCRIPTURE

Objective
This lesson helps the students recognize the importance of welcoming people who are different.

Step 1/INTRODUCTION

Learning About Our Lives

Introducing the Chapter
Read aloud the chapter title and focus question. As the students respond, affirm them for the ways they are open to and accepting of others. Use the questions below to discuss what it feels like when people are not welcoming of others.

- Have you ever moved to a different home? How difficult was it to make new friends?
- Have you ever felt ignored when you wanted to be part of a group? What was that like?
- Have you ever felt lonely? When? Where?

Help the class recognize that there are times when we have all experienced being new to a group or situation. You may want to share an experience of your own to highlight how universal this experience is.

or...
Ask the students to discuss how they and their friends are alike. Help them see how much they have in common with their friends. Discuss the differences they notice between themselves and their friends: likes and dislikes, physical characteristics, and different talents. Ask the students how they would feel if others would not play with them because of such differences. Explain that in Chapter 3 they will learn how Jesus wants us to treat people who may be different from us.

Reading and Discussing a Story
Ask volunteers to read aloud "A Different World" on page 32. Encourage them to use expressive voices for the dialogue. Then talk about the different reactions Mike and June had to Nishi. Ask the students what they think Nishi wanted most.

32

Our Church Is Catholic

In what ways are you open to and accepting of others?

A Different World

Nishi stood at the edge of the playground. She felt all tight inside.

She watched the boys and girls playing. She listened to their shouts and laughter. "I wonder what they are saying," she thought.

Nishi started to cry. She thought about her homeland, Japan, on the other side of the world. "I wish I were back home," she thought to herself as she wiped away a tear.

June saw Nishi standing at the edge of the playground. "Mike, look at that girl. She's crying. Do you think she's lonely? Maybe she would like to play."

"Leave her alone," Mike answered. "She's not like us. She looks different and sounds different."

"She is too like us!" June insisted. "She is!"

Nishi saw Mike and June looking at her. She knew they were talking about her. She turned around sadly and began to walk away.

32 Morality

★ ★ ★ ★
Enriching the Lesson
★ ★ ★

As an introductory activity, you might have the students stand in a circle and hold hands. Ask four or five volunteers to stand outside the circle and tell them that it is their job to try to join the circle. Give them a minute or two to accomplish this. Some may attempt to break into the circle, while some others may simply ask if they can join the circle. Afterward, ask each of the volunteers how it felt to be on the outside trying to get in. Ask the rest of the class how it felt to see some of their classmates being left out.

Activity

Write your own ending to the story.

_____

_____

_____

_____

Sometimes I'd like
   To welcome someone
Who's by herself
   Not having fun.
But deep inside
   I am afraid
That I will lose
   The friends I've made.

Jesus and Zacchaeus

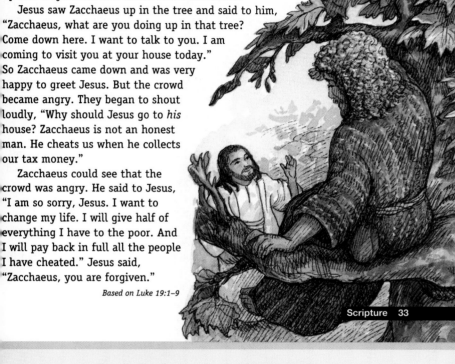

As Jesus and his disciples walked along a road in Jericho, a crowd of people gathered around them. The people were anxious to see Jesus. They had heard about all the good things he was doing. Zacchaeus, who was a very short man, wanted to see Jesus, too. So he climbed up into a sycamore tree to see above the crowd.

Jesus saw Zacchaeus up in the tree and said to him, "Zacchaeus, what are you doing up in that tree? Come down here. I want to talk to you. I am coming to visit you at your house today." So Zacchaeus came down and was very happy to greet Jesus. But the crowd became angry. They began to shout loudly, "Why should Jesus go to _his_ house? Zacchaeus is not an honest man. He cheats us when he collects our tax money."

Zacchaeus could see that the crowd was angry. He said to Jesus, "I am so sorry, Jesus. I want to change my life. I will give half of everything I have to the poor. And I will pay back in full all the people I have cheated." Jesus said, "Zacchaeus, you are forgiven."

Based on Luke 19:1–9

Scripture 33

Focus on

Tax Collectors In the time of Jesus, the method of collecting taxes was somewhat different from today. The emperor assessed each governor a certain amount. Then the governor instructed his collectors to bring in twice the assessment, keeping half for his territory and himself. Tax collectors then set about collecting double their quota, to provide a profit for themselves. They were not, therefore, looked upon as honest people. Those who resented being ruled by Rome also resented the emperor's tax collectors.

🌐 Cultural Awareness

Have the group identify how Nishi was different from the other children. (_Answers may include: the color of Nishi's skin, her facial features, or simply the fact that she was someone new._) Ask the following questions: Is it fair to judge people by the way they look or speak? Emphasize that we all want to be accepted by others and that Jesus wants us to learn how to make all people feel welcome.

Completing the Story

Have the students write their own endings for the story in the space provided on page 33. Ask for volunteers to share their endings to the story with the rest of the class. You will be able to tell much about how well the students understand the meaning of the story by listening to the ways in which they conclude it.

Step 2/DEVELOPMENT

Learning About Our Faith ✚

Reading and Discussing a Scripture Story

Read through "Jesus and Zacchaeus" with the class. Ask the following questions.

- Why did the people want to see Jesus? (_They had heard about all the good things he was doing._)
- How did Jesus show that he accepted Zacchaeus? (_Jesus told Zacchaeus that he wanted to talk to him and go to his house._)
- Why did the crowd become angry? (_They did not want Jesus to visit the house of Zacchaeus. They thought Zacchaeus was a dishonest man._)

Step 3/CONCLUSION

Learning How to Live Our Faith ✠

Reading and Discussing a Poem

Have the entire class read aloud the poem on page 33 and decide who in the story about Nishi might be speaking these words. (_June_) Help the students appreciate that sometimes we must overcome our fears and make special efforts to reach out to those who may be feeling alone or afraid.

Comparing Stories

Help the students recognize that Nishi and Zacchaeus were the same in that people were not kind to them. People disliked them because they didn't know them well. Ask the following questions.

- How did Zacchaeus respond to Jesus' welcoming him? (_He said that he had changed his life and that he gave money to the poor and paid back those he had cheated._)
- How do you think Nishi would respond to people accepting her? (_Answers will vary._)

33

DAY 2
SCRIPTURE/DOCTRINE

Objective
This lesson helps the students learn the meaning of the word *catholic* as a mark of the Church.

Step 1/INTRODUCTION

Learning About Our Lives

Talking About Strangers
Ask the students to discuss what they have learned from their parents or other adults about talking to strangers. Elicit that they have been taught not to talk to people they do not know, not to get into a stranger's car, and not to go anywhere alone with a stranger. Then ask them how this rule might apply to a new student in school, like Nishi.

Step 2/DEVELOPMENT

Learning About Our Faith

Studying the Illustration
Invite the students to look at the illustration on pages 34 and 35 and comment on what seems to be happening. Make sure that the students understand that they are looking at a group of first-century Christians and that the people are having a serious discussion.

Reading and Discussing the Story
Tell the students that in the story "Open to All" they will learn more about what is happening in the picture. Call on volunteers to read the story aloud. Use the following questions for discussion.

- Whom did Judith and David say Jesus helped? (*A Greek woman, a Roman servant, and a Samaritan*)

- What do you think Susanna was feeling when she made her last remark? (*Answers may include: frightened and angry.*)

- Who did Judith say would help them accept people who were different from them? (*The Holy Spirit*)

- What is the main point of the story? (*Answers may include: that Jesus welcomed all people and that we should do the same.*)

34

Open to All

One evening a group of Christians met in the home of Judith and David in Jerusalem. They ate, sang, and prayed together, as they did every day. They remembered some of the people whom Jesus had helped.

"Jesus once welcomed a Greek woman and healed her sick daughter," Judith said. "And he healed the servant of a Roman."

"He even talked and ate with Samaritans," David added.

"And remember when the Holy Spirit first came?" added Susanna. "People from all over the world were in Jerusalem. Each of them understood the words of the apostles, even though they spoke different languages."

"Jesus taught that all people are sons and daughters of God," said David. "So we are all brothers and sisters."

"You may be right," Susanna answered, "but it is not easy for me to accept people who are different from me."

34 Scripture

Teaching Tips

Be aware that some students will use what they have been taught about strangers as an excuse for not being kind to others and for not including new students in their circle of friends. You may need to help them distinguish safe circumstances from unsafe ones. Tell them that Jesus would not want them to take foolish risks in their attempts to live as his followers.

"The Holy Spirit will help us be open to everyone," Judith assured her.

Based on Matthew 8:5–13; Mark 7:24–30; John 4:4–43; Acts 2:1–13; Galatians 3:26–28

What Being Catholic Means

The first Christians learned from one another that, to be like Jesus, they must welcome everyone who sincerely wanted to belong to their communities. This is what it means to be **catholic**. The word *catholic* means "to be open to the whole world." The Holy Spirit helps us to include persons of all colors, races, ages, and abilities in our lives and in our Church rather than ignore them. The Holy Spirit helps us to accept rather than reject them. This is how we live as daughters and sons of God.

Vocabulary

catholic: open to and accepting of people everywhere

❤ ❤ ❤ ❤ ❤ ❤ ❤ ❤ ❤ ❤ ❤

We Believe

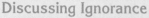

One of the marks, or signs, of the Church is that it is catholic. Jesus wants his people, the Church, to welcome and to include people of all kinds, just as he does.

Doctrine 35

Enriching the Lesson

Invite the students to dramatize the story "Open to All." Suggest that they add to the story a new character who refuses to welcome people from other countries to the Church. Have the students respond to this person.

Focus on

Samaritans The Samaritans mentioned in the story "Open to All" were from Samaria, a land north of Jerusalem. The Samaritans of the first century were a strict Jewish sect whom the general Jewish population did not recognize as Jews. There were major differences in the religious customs of the two groups. As the early Church (including many Jewish Christians) grew and spread throughout the earth, its members had to struggle as they learned what it meant to be open to all. We face this same struggle today.

Talking About Being Catholic

Read "What Being Catholic Means" with the class. Explain that the early Christians had many questions about whether to accept all people into the Church. The Holy Spirit slowly led them to realize that Jesus preached forgiveness and love for all and called his followers to welcome and accept all people who sought to believe in him.

Reviewing the Vocabulary and Doctrine

Direct the students' attention to the Vocabulary word on page 35. Read the definition with them. Then ask a volunteer to read aloud the We Believe statement. Encourage the students to remember this central part of the chapter.

Step 3/CONCLUSION

Learning How to Live Our Faith

Discussing Ignorance

Ask the students if they know what *ignorance* means. Explain that it means "not knowing." To *ignore* someone is to act as if we do not know them. Note that ignorance sometimes prevents people from accepting others whom they do not know. Explain that we might be afraid to accept people who look, speak, or act differently than we do because we do not know or understand them. Emphasize that Jesus calls us to include, rather than exclude, others, and to accept, rather than reject, others.

or...

Have the students create skits in which they welcome the following people: a third grader who uses a wheelchair; an elderly neighbor; and a classmate who doesn't speak English very well. Use the students' skits to discuss the meaning of *ignorance*.

DAY 3
DOCTRINE

Objective

This lesson helps the students desire to welcome, accept, and be open to all people.

Step 1/INTRODUCTION

Learning About Our Lives

Researching Newspapers

Divide the class into groups of three or four students each. Distribute several newspapers to each group. Have the students look through the papers for pictures and articles that discuss people of different cultures around the world. When they have finished, invite one person from each group to explain what his or her group found and what it told them about people in another part of the world. Discuss with the class some reasons that learning about other lands and peoples is important. Help the students appreciate that we all belong to the one human family, no matter where we live.

Step 2/DEVELOPMENT

Learning About Our Faith

Reading the Text

Instruct the students to turn to page 36 in their texts. Call on volunteers to read aloud "United Yet Different." Reinforce that the third mark of the Church is that it is "catholic." Help the students to identify the variety of ways that Mass is celebrated in their parishes. Invite them to share any experiences they have had with other cultures that have been especially interesting and meaningful for them.

Studying the Photographs

Direct the students' attention to the photographs on page 36. Help the students identify ways in which the people and/or actions in the photographs are different from those in your parish. Then ask the students to identify any similarities.

36

United Yet Different

The Church is one, holy, and catholic. We learned that to be catholic means to be open to people of all kinds. No matter where we live, what we look like, or who we are, the Church is called to welcome us. From the very beginning of the Church, Jesus wanted the Church to be a united community that would include all people and nations.

As Catholics, we welcome and accept people who are different from us in many ways. We are united, but we are not alike in all ways. We share the same belief in Jesus when we celebrate the Eucharist, but we celebrate in a variety of ways. We all sing songs at Mass, but we may sing in different languages. And even when we sing in the same language, we sing many different kinds of songs. Catholics may be different from one another in many ways. Can you think of some other ways that Catholics are different from one another, even though they are united?

Holy Communion in the Byzantine Rite

Easter in Guatemala

36   Doctrine

Cultural Awareness

In the Catholic Church there are more than twenty Rites, or distinct traditions. The same Catholic faith is expressed in different liturgies, hierarchies, and spiritualities. Although it is the largest, the Latin or Roman Rite is just one of these Rites. Some of the Rites of the Catholic Church are referred to as Byzantine Rites because these Rites originated in the Eastern Christianity of the Byzantine Empire. Eastern Rite Catholics are not members of the Orthodox Churches. They are Catholics in union with Rome, just as Latin Rite Catholics are.

Learning to Love All

We who call ourselves Catholics are called to welcome, accept, respect, and be open to all people.

The Catholic Church today is blessed with the special gifts of people of many nations, races, and abilities. Here are some of our brothers and sisters around the world and a prayer to help us all become more open to and accepting of others.

Spirit of Love,
open our hearts to accept
all people. Give us the strength
we need to be gentle with those
who seem different from us.
Guide all that we think, do,
and say, as we learn to love
everyone, just as Jesus does.
Amen.

Activity

Describe one way that you can put this prayer into practice. Try to be specific.

Possible answers include: being friendly to others, or

being kind to people who are treated unfairly because

they are different.

Doctrine 37

Praying Together

Ask a volunteer to read "Learning to Love All" on page 37. Emphasize that our Church community is a sign of Jesus to the world. When we welcome, accept, respect, and are open to all people, we are showing others how Jesus loves all people.

Have the students form a circle and pray the Spirit of Love prayer aloud. Tell them that this prayer asks the Holy Spirit to help them follow Jesus' example.

Completing an Activity

Read the directions for the activity. Have the students write their responses. Allow time for them to share what they have written. Praise them for their ideas and encourage them to look for opportunities and ways to accept and welcome others.

Focus on

The Unity of the Church The *Catechism of the Catholic Church* says that the many cultures within the Church encompass a "rich variety" and that this heritage, "unified in a common effort, shows all the more resplendently the catholicity of the undivided Church." (# 835) Help the students appreciate that our differences make the Church stronger and help us to learn from one another.

CURRICULUM CONNECTION

Geography Ask students to identify each race or group of people shown on page 37. (*African American, Asian American, Latin American or Hispanic, Native American, and European American*). Have the students use a globe or map to find the many possible countries of origin of these people. Stress that since we are all children of God, we are all brothers and sisters, regardless of our color, nation, language, appearance, or abilities.

Objective

This lesson helps the students respect the variety of cultures within the Church.

Step 1/INTRODUCTION

Learning About Our Lives

Learning About Respect

Read "Respecting Differences" on page 38 with the students. As the word *respect* is introduced, refer to the Vocabulary box on page 39. Have the students read the definition aloud. Invite the students to tell about situations in their own lives in which they have been taught to treat others with respect.

Writing About Ethnic Customs

Explain the directions for the activity on page 38. Allow the students sufficient time to write about their family traditions. Afterward, encourage the students to share their "differences" with the class.

Step 2/DEVELOPMENT

Learning About Our Faith

Reading About Archbishop Romero

Introduce the story by locating El Salvador on a globe. Tell the students that they are going to read a true story about an event that happened in El Salvador in 1980. Then call on volunteers to read aloud "When There Is No Respect . . ." on page 39. Ask the following questions.

- What message did Archbishop Romero try to bring to the people of El Salvador? (*Jesus' message of unity*)
- Why were most of the people of El Salvador poor? (*A few rich families had all the power and money.*)
- What did the rich families do to the priests who were helping the poor? (*Killed them or put them in jail*)
- What happened to Archbishop Romero? (*He was killed for trying to help the poor.*)
- Why was Archbishop Romero so popular with the poor people of El Salvador? (*He spoke out against violence and called for people to respect one another's rights.*)

38

Respecting Differences

As members of Jesus' family, the Church, we **respect** the many ways that Catholics around the world pray and celebrate their faith. As brothers and sisters in faith, we believe that our various cultures and customs help to make the Catholic Church a family that truly welcomes everyone. We are happy to see and respect differences among people in our own parishes as well as around the world.

Easter blessing of food in Ukraine

Activity

Think about some of the special ways that your family celebrates holidays and family celebrations. You may want to find out something new about the religious customs in the countries that your family or ancestors come from. Think of some ways you might share one of these with your class or with your parish. On the lines below, write about one prayer or custom. Then share it with your class.

First Communion in Guatemala

Cultural Awareness

In discussing the ways Catholics are different, yet united, mention some specific examples such as the following. In some farming communities, people bring crops to Mass for the Preparation of the Altar and the Gifts. In Native American communities, drums play an important role in celebrations of Mass. The sounds of the drums are reminiscent of a human heart beating and remind the community of the gift of life, the life that we all share, which comes from God.

Enriching the Lesson

Invite the students to role-play a panel discussion about respecting differences. The panel members could be Archbishop Romero, Nishi, a woman who works in a homeless shelter, a blind teenager, an immigrant to our country, and Jesus. As the teacher, you may want to serve as moderator and have the students who are not on the panel ask questions of the panel members about how we can grow in respect for one another.

When There Is No Respect . . .

Throughout the Church's history, there have been many people who worked hard to bring Jesus' message of unity to all peoples. Oscar Romero, who became the Archbishop of San Salvador in 1977, tried to bring this message to the people of El Salvador.

Most of the people in El Salvador were very poor. A few rich families were in power over the poor families and anyone who tried to help them. Archbishop Romero listened and learned about the problems of the poor people. Having money and power was so important to the rich families that they began to kill or put in jail the priests who were helping the poor. On his radio program, Archbishop Romero began to speak out against this violence. He wanted people to respect each others' rights.

Soon Archbishop Romero became so popular with the poor people that his own life was in danger. The powerful people wanted to kill him because they disagreed with what he was doing. But he did not stop speaking out. He believed that the Church needed him to speak up for the rights of the poor. He believed this was a very important part of being a Catholic Christian. So he continued his work with the poor and continued speaking out for them until March 24, 1980. On that day, he was shot and killed for trying to help the poor people of his country.

Activity

As a group, choose one of the following things to do this year that will help you appreciate the gifts of Catholics different from you.

- Write to a Catholic pen pal in another country.

- Learn a Catholic prayer in a language not your own.

- Put in a class album pictures and articles about Catholics around the world.

Vocabulary

respect: to act with care toward someone or something

♥ ♥ ♥ ♥ ♥ ♥ ♥ ♥ ♥ ♥ ♥

Morality 39

Choosing a Class Project

Read the directions for the activity on page 39 with the class. As the students consider the options for learning about the cultures of other Catholics, emphasize that reaching out to others helps us to remember that Jesus came to bring good news to all the people of the world. Note that Spanish translations of several prayers are found on pages 2 and 3 of the student text.

or . . .

Give the students the following case study: *The Chavez family is coming to Chicago from El Salvador next summer. They are being sponsored by the people of St. Luke's Parish. Mr. and Mrs. Chavez and their three children speak no English.* Ask the students to brainstorm about different ways the people of St. Luke's can reach out to the Chavez family and which parish ministries might work together to help the family in their new country.

Teaching Tips

For additional information about Archbishop Romero, you might enjoy reading *Archbishop Oscar Romero: A Shepherd's Diary* (Translated by Irene B. Hodgson. St. Anthony Messenger Press, 1993). Share some highlights with your students.

Enriching the Lesson

Help your students use an on-line computer to find Catholic pen pals in other countries with whom they can correspond. The following example on the World Wide Web is entitled "My Catholic E-Pal Project": www.serve.com/crc/epal.htm

DAY 5
PRAYER/REVIEW

Objective

This lesson helps the students pray for respect and openness.

Preparing for Prayer

Read the first paragraph on page 40 with the students. Explain that one way we can grow in respect for the gifts people from other cultures bring to the Church is to pray for openness and a spirit of welcome.

Have students work in pairs to trace a partner's handprint on construction paper and cut it out. Invite them to write on the hand five ways they can show respect, acceptance, welcome, and love for others. Tell them that they will be invited to offer their handprints during the prayer celebration.

Select music for the prayer service, such as "He's Got the Whole World in His Hands." Then choose students to read the petitions during the prayer service.

Praying a Litany of Petition

Begin the prayer celebration by having the students greet one another with the Sign of Peace. Then invite the assigned students to read the petitions and lead everyone in the response, "Lord, help us to welcome the strangers among us." After each response, have several pairs of students prayerfully present their handprints by displaying them around the prayer table or on a bulletin board, using tape or a stapler. Conclude by asking the students to pray the last paragraph on page 40 together. You may also want to include the Spirit of Love prayer from page 37 in this prayer time.

40

Praying a Litany of Petition

We pray, as Jesus did, that all Christians will be united as they learn to respect one another. We pray that all people will feel welcome in our parish communities. We pray that we can learn to be truly *catholic*.

Let us pray.

For each person in our class, that each of us will know that we are part of the family of God, we pray,
Lord, help us to welcome the strangers among us.

For all the teachers and students of our school, that we will show respect for one another in all that we say and do, we pray,
Lord, help us to welcome the strangers among us.

For our parish family, that we may always be united in our love for Jesus, we pray,
Lord, help us to welcome the strangers among us.

For the people in our community and throughout the world who are not loved as they should be, just because they are different, we pray,
Lord, help us to welcome the strangers among us.

For all those who work toward unity by teaching people ways to respect one another, we pray,
Lord, help us to welcome the strangers among us.

God of all nations, help us to be truly *catholic*. Teach us to be open to people who are different from us. Help us learn to accept them, welcome them, and love them. We pray this in Jesus' name. Amen.

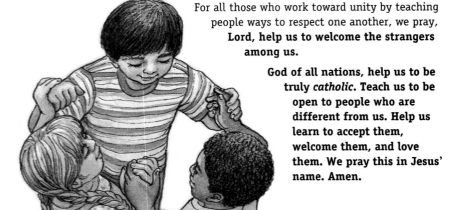

40 Prayer

CURRICULUM CONNECTION

Language Arts Ask a volunteer to read aloud the poem from page 33. Then invite the class to compose a short poem about being Catholic. Brainstorm some words to use in the class poem and then write the poem on the chalkboard, inviting all the students' responses. An unrhymed haiku might be easier for the class than a rhymed poem. The form of a haiku consists of three lines of five, seven, and five syllables, respectively.

Chapter Review

Use the clues below to fill in the crossword puzzle.

Down

1. A man whom Jesus welcomed

2. Open and accepting of people everywhere

3. The archbishop who helped the poor people of San Salvador

Across

4. The first Christians learned to _____ and accept people who were different from them.

5. To act with care toward someone or something

6. The Holy _____ helps us to accept all people.

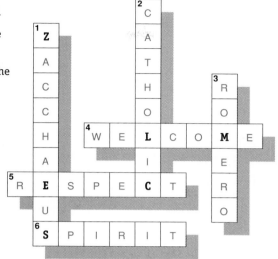

Fill in the answers to the first two questions.

1. What does *catholic* mean? It means to be open to and accepting of people everywhere.

2. Why does the Church welcome all kinds of people? because Jesus wants us to welcome and include all people, just as he does

Jesus says, "I was a stranger and you welcomed me." Based on Matthew 25:35b

3. Talk about one thing your class can do to help others feel more welcome in your parish.

Cultural Awareness

Plan a cultural heritage celebration with your class. Ask each child to contribute a food item, decoration, or special song or poem that expresses his or her background. You might have the students make flags that represent the countries their families originally came from. Have them use an encyclopedia to learn the color and design of the flags of these countries. Encourage the students to affirm one another's efforts.

Completing a Crossword Puzzle

Have the students read the clues and fill in the blanks to complete the crossword puzzle on page 41. When they have finished, check their answers.

Reviewing the Chapter

Take time to go through the questions at the bottom of the page. Direct the students to write their answers to each question on the lines provided in the text. After having the students share their responses, answer any questions they may have about what they learned in Chapter 3. Encourage all to participate in the discussion question.

Reflecting on the Scriptural Verse

Draw the students' attention to the scriptural verse on page 41. Explain that this verse is from the teaching of Jesus found in Matthew 25:31–40. Stress that Jesus taught that what we do for others, we do for Jesus himself. Tie this to the theme of this week's chapter by explaining that when we welcome others, we welcome Jesus.

Our Church Is Apostolic

Objectives ~~~~~~

To help the students

■ Learn that the fourth mark of the Catholic Church is that it is apostolic.

■ Recognize that we are all called to share the gospel.

■ Appreciate that our faith grows as we share Jesus' good news.

■ Understand that Jesus calls us to be witnesses.

■ Meditate about Jesus and review the chapter.

Chapter Outline ~~~~~~

	Step 1 Learning About Our Lives	**Step 2** Learning About Our Faith	**Step 3** Learning How to Live Our Faith
Day 1	■ Introduce the chapter. ■ Read and discuss a story. *ABOUT 10 MINUTES*	■ Read and discuss the text. ■ Learn the vocabulary and doctrine. *ABOUT 15 MINUTES*	■ Write about being apostolic. *ABOUT 5 MINUTES*
Day 2	■ Identify "good news" people. *ABOUT 5 MINUTES*	■ Read and discuss the text. ■ Discuss the stories. *ABOUT 15 MINUTES*	■ Complete a writing activity. *ABOUT 10 MINUTES*
Day 3	■ Study the photographs. ■ Learn sign language. *ABOUT 5 MINUTES*	■ Read the text. ■ Write a poem. ■ Learn the vocabulary. *ABOUT 15 MINUTES*	■ Pray together. *ABOUT 10 MINUTES*
Day 4	■ Pretend to be reporters. *ABOUT 10 MINUTES*	■ Read the text. ■ Discuss the text. *ABOUT 10 MINUTES*	■ Help others to learn about Jesus. ■ Create slogans. *ABOUT 10 MINUTES*
Day 5	**Prayer** Prepare for prayer; pray a Jesus meditation. **Review** Fill in the blanks; review the chapter; reflect on the scriptural verse.		

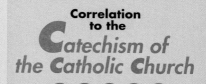

Correlation to the
Catechism of the Catholic Church

Paragraphs
**77, 642, 765, 811, 812,
857, 858, 859, 860, 861,
862, 863, 864, 865, 869**

Plan Ahead

	Preparing Your Class	**Materials Needed**
Day 1	Read through the lesson plan for this class session. Recall an experience from your own life to share in Step 1.	■ lined paper ■ pencils or pens
Day 2	Read through the lesson plan for this class session.	■ crayons or markers ■ pencils or pens
Day 3	Read through the lesson plan for this session. Practice the sign-language gestures in Step 1.	■ lined paper ■ 9" × 12" sheets of construction paper ■ pencils or pens
Day 4	Read through the lesson plan. Collect enough newspapers and periodicals for the number of small groups you will have in the class.	■ diocesan newspapers, Catholic periodicals ■ parish bulletins ■ 3" × 18" strips of construction paper
Day 5	Plan the prayer experience. Prepare an environment for prayer in the classroom. Review this week's sessions to prepare for the chapter review.	■ Bible, candle, tablecloth ■ music for prayer meditation ■ crayons or felt-tip markers ■ drawing paper ■ pencils or pens

Additional Resources

As you plan this chapter, consider using the following materials from The Resourceful Teacher Package.

■ *Classroom Activity Sheets 4 and 4a*

■ *Family Activity Sheets 4 and 4a*

■ *Chapter 4 Test*

■ *Prayers for Every Day*

■ *Projects: Grade 3*

You may also wish to refer to the following Big Books.

■ *We Celebrate the Sacraments,* page 12

■ *We Celebrate the Mass,* pages 5, 7–8

In preparing the students for the Sunday readings, you may wish to use Silver Burdett Ginn's *Getting Ready for Sunday* student and teacher materials.

BOOKS FOR THE JOURNEY

Happy Birthday, Grampie. Susan Pearson. Dial Books, 1987. The story of a child who shares the good news of her love for her grandfather.

Praise for the Singing. Collected by Madelaine Gill. Little, Brown & Co., 1993. "I Sing a Song of the Saints of God," pp. 42–43, by Lesbia Scott and John H. Hopkins. A song about people who, by their exemplary lives, have shared and lived the good news of Jesus.

MORE BOOKS FOR THE JOURNEY

Where the Sidewalk Ends. Shel Silverstein. Harper & Row, 1974. "No Difference," p. 81. A poem that playfully suggests that while differences are real, we're all the same where it really counts.

Fish Is Fish. Leo Lionni. Pantheon, 1970. A fish learns about many things from a frog who saves him and helps him to be happy.

REDUCED CLASSROOM ACTIVITIES

NAME _____

OUR CHURCH IS APOSTOLIC

Reread the story "Sharing the Good News of Jesus" in your book. Then complete the TV interview by writing Philip's answers.

Reporter: Philip, what happened today as you were walking in the desert?

Philip: _____
_____

Reporter: What did you tell the man from Ethiopia about Jesus?

Philip: _____
_____
_____
_____

Reporter: What happened after you told the man about Jesus?

Philip: _____
_____
_____

To the Teacher: This activity follows the Scripture story "Sharing the Good News of Jesus."

Chapter 4 Our Church Is Apostolic THIS IS OUR FAITH 3 **4**

NAME _____

SPREADING THE GOOD NEWS

Follow each set of directions.

1. Design a bumper sticker to remind people about Jesus' love for us. Cut it out and put it on your bike or another special place.

2. On the banner, write a message about the good news the apostles shared. Hang it at school or home.

To the Teacher: This activity will help students understand the term *apostolic* as "sharing what we have learned from the apostles and from other Catholics."

4a THIS IS OUR FAITH 3 Chapter 4 Our Church Is Apostolic

41c Chapter Organizer

THE APOSTOLIC MARK

The fourth mark, or sign, of the Church is that it is apostolic. The term *apostolic* refers to the apostles, the chosen followers of Jesus. It also refers to the mission the apostles received from Jesus to spread the gospel message to the ends of the earth.

Jesus drew to himself a large number of disciples. These men and women followed Jesus throughout the land of Galilee and the city of Jerusalem, witnessing his miracles and listening to his preaching. From these followers, Jesus chose twelve who were to become his closest companions. They have been referred to traditionally as the twelve apostles or, simply, "the twelve."

The twelve apostles enjoyed a unique experience with Jesus because of their close relationship to him. The early Christians presumed that the apostles knew Jesus and his teachings best. The words of the apostles had special authority. Today, we still listen to and respect the teachings of the twelve apostles. That is what we mean when we say that one of the marks of the Church is that it is apostolic.

THE MISSION OF THE CHURCH

We are also faithful to the mission Jesus entrusted to the apostles to make disciples of all the nations. The Church, like the apostles, is called to go out and spread the good news of Jesus. The Church does this by teaching and preaching as well as by giving examples of Christian living and action. The bishops of the Church continue the apostolic office through their leadership.

We should encourage the third graders to be willing to share with others what they know and love about Jesus and his teachings. This apostolic activity can be carried out in the parish community. There may be parish projects or service activities in which your students might become involved within the religious education program. It may be possible to enlist the aid of parents or guardians for such projects. Their presence would be a wonderful model of service to the students.

In this chapter the students will learn what the term *apostolic* means. They will be encouraged to respect the teachings of Jesus and the apostles and to put those teachings into practice today.

Objective

This lesson helps the students learn that the fourth mark of the Catholic Church is that it is apostolic.

Step 1/INTRODUCTION

Learning About Our Lives

Introducing the Chapter

Direct attention to the chapter-focus statement. Encourage each of the students to participate in the discussion. To get them started, you may want to share an experience from your own life. After the students have each had an opportunity to share their stories, explain that when we have good news, we usually want to share it with others.

Reading and Discussing a Story

Ask volunteers to read aloud "A Fascinating Cross" on pages 42 and 43. Then discuss the following questions.

- How was Angela spending the year? (*Working as a volunteer teacher in El Salvador*)

- What made the cross that Angela sent different? (*It is brightly colored and has pictures of people painted on it.*)

- Why did the people of El Salvador put pictures on the cross? (*To show the things they do every day*)

- What do the pictures help the people remember? (*That Jesus is always with them*)

- What did the people of El Salvador teach Angela? (*What it really means to be a Christian*)

- How do you think Angela's understanding of the word *catholic* influenced her work in El Salvador? (*Answers will vary.*)

or...

Assemble props (a box, a cross from El Salvador, and a folded note) for a dramatic reading of the story, and place them on a table in the front of the room. Select three students to read the parts of Harry's mom, Harry, and Molly. You can act as narrator as necessary. Have the readers come to the front of the room

42

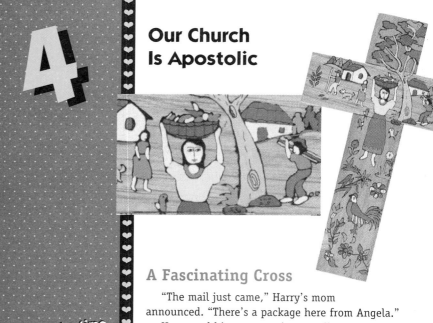

4. Our Church Is Apostolic

Tell about a time you were so excited about something that you could not wait to tell your friends all about it.

A Fascinating Cross

"The mail just came," Harry's mom announced. "There's a package here from Angela."

Harry and his younger sister, Molly, ran down the stairs eagerly. Their big sister, Angela, was spending a year in El Salvador as a volunteer teacher.

Their mom quickly opened the package.

"What is it?" Molly asked.

"It looks like a cross," Harry answered. "But it's not like any cross I've ever seen."

Their mom held it up. They examined it carefully. It was made of wood and had brightly painted pictures of people on it.

"That looks like a boy carrying firewood," Molly observed, pointing at one of the paintings.

"Is that a woman carrying a basket of fruit on her head?" asked Harry.

"It sure is," Mom said. "And that looks like a man working in a garden."

"And there's the family dog," Molly noticed.

42 Doctrine

★ Enriching the Lesson ★

Religious art usually tells us something about the culture in which it is crafted. You may want to ask the students to bring in any crosses or religious art that they have seen at home, particularly pieces that have been in the family for a long time. You can also look in your library for examples of religious art from different countries. Discuss with the children what the artist may be telling us about his or her faith through each piece of artwork.

Focus on

Church as Apostolic The *Catechism of the Catholic Church* states that "The whole Church is apostolic, in that she remains, through the successors of St. Peter and the other apostles, in communion of faith and life with her origin: and in that she is 'sent out' into the whole world. All members of the Church share in this Mission, though in various ways." (#863)

Then Mom unfolded a note, which was also in the package. "Harry, would you like to read the note from Angela for us?"

Harry read it clearly. "Hi, Mom! Hi, Molly and Harry! I hope you like this cross. It says so much about the faith of the people here. They put pictures on the cross that show the things they do every day. This reminds them that Jesus is with them all the time. I've learned so much from them about what it really means to be a Christian. I miss you all and love you very much. I wish you were here! Angela."

"Let's hang the cross in the living room," Mom said. "It can remind us of Angela and that Jesus is with us here at home and wherever we go."

Telling Others About Jesus

Because we are all different and come from different backgrounds, we learn about Jesus and come to know him in a variety of ways. The apostles lived at the same time as Jesus did. They spent much time with him and so learned about him firsthand. He was their teacher. They told others about Jesus and taught the early Christians how to live as Jesus wanted them to. They spread the good news of Jesus' love for all people by the way they lived and by what they said. We call this good news the **gospel.** Today we learn about Jesus from other Catholics. We learn about the gospel at home, during Mass, and in religion class.

We cannot see or speak to Jesus the way the apostles and early Christians did, but we can still know Jesus and be close to him through our own daily experiences.

We have already learned about three **marks of the Church**—that it is one, holy, and catholic. The fourth mark of the Church is that it is **apostolic.** This means that our Catholic Christian beliefs and ways of living are based on the teachings of Jesus and his apostles. We find these teachings in the Bible.

Vocabulary

gospel: the good news of Jesus' love for all people

marks of the Church: signs of the Church that show it is one, holy, catholic, and apostolic

apostolic: founded on and faithful to the teachings of Jesus and his apostles

♥♥♥♥♥♥♥♥♥♥♥♥

We Believe

One of the marks, or signs, of the Catholic Church is that it is apostolic. It is founded on the teachings of Jesus and his apostles. We are called to be apostolic by sharing what we have learned from the apostles and from other Catholics.

Doctrine 43

Teaching Tips

Some children, like some adults, may find it difficult to believe that Jesus loves them. Their capacity to do so is closely related to their experiences of being loved by others, especially their own parents. Be prepared to respond to students who may ask the question: "Why should I believe that Jesus loves *me*?" Be aware that the students can only share with others what they themselves have known and experienced.

Cultural Awareness

Together, examine a cross from El Salvador. You may be able to purchase one at a religious goods store, or you can order one from Tree of Life Imports, P.O. Box 4215, Hammond, IN 46324. Stress that while life is hard in El Salvador, the people still have joy and hope because they know Jesus is with them. The bright colors show that the people's faith in Jesus is alive and strong.

---

with their books and read aloud "A Fascinating Cross," using the props mentioned in the story. Then discuss the questions.

Step 2/DEVELOPMENT

Learning About Our Faith

Reading and Discussing the Text

Read with the class "Telling Others About Jesus" on page 43. Ask the following questions.

- What did the apostles do? (*Spread the good news of Jesus' love for all people by their teaching and example*)

- What is the fourth mark of the Church? (*That the Church is apostolic*)

- What does it mean when we say that the Church is apostolic? (*That our Catholic beliefs and way of living are based on the teachings of Jesus and the apostles*)

Learning the Vocabulary and Doctrine

Direct the students' attention to the Vocabulary box. Have the students read the words and definitions together. Then have a volunteer read the We Believe statement aloud. Emphasize the importance of these words. Ask the students if they have any questions.

Step 3/CONCLUSION

Learning How to Live Our Faith

Writing About Being Apostolic

Tell the students that since nobody today can see or talk to Jesus in the same way that the apostles did, it is important for those of us who know Jesus and are close to him to share his love with others. We can help others to see and hear that Jesus lives in the world today, especially through the words and actions of his followers. Ask the students to think about what they can do this week to tell someone whom they love what they know and love about Jesus. Distribute lined paper and allow ample time for the students to write down their responses in a brief composition or a single paragraph.

DAY 2

SCRIPTURE

Objective

This lesson helps the students recognize that we are all called to share the gospel.

Step 1/INTRODUCTION

Learning About Our Lives

Identifying "Good News" People

Ask the students if they know how they became Catholics. Help them recall that they became Catholics through the sacrament of Baptism. Have the students name people in their lives who have shared the gospel with them and taught them that Jesus loves them. Help them appreciate that many of them have learned about Jesus' love for them through their parents' love and the love of others who have shared Jesus with them.

Step 2/DEVELOPMENT

Learning About Our Faith

Reading and Discussing the Text

Turn to "Sharing the Good News of Jesus" on pages 44 and 45. Call on volunteers to read the story aloud. Ask the following questions.

- Who had sent Philip to share the good news of Jesus? (*God*)

- What was the man from Ethiopia reading? (*The Scriptures*)

- What did Philip say about Jesus? (*Jesus was a great teacher who brought God's love to people, especially the poor. God sent Jesus to show us how to live. Jesus rose to new life after his enemies killed him. Jesus loves us and asks us to be his followers and friends.*)

- What did the Ethiopian do as a result of hearing about Jesus? (*He asked Philip to baptize him.*)

Sharing the Good News of Jesus

Philip was sent out by God to share the good news about Jesus. As Philip was walking along a road, a carriage pulled by two large horses began to pass him. He looked up and saw an important man from the country of Ethiopia.

As the carriage passed by, Philip heard the man reading the Scriptures out loud. Philip was very surprised that this man knew about the word of God.

Philip ran and caught up with the carriage. He called out to the man inside, "Do you understand what you are reading?"

"How can I?" the man answered. "Come up and explain it to me." The man invited Philip to sit down beside him.

Philip jumped up into the carriage. Then the man read a few sentences from the Scriptures.

"Please tell me what these words are saying," he said.

"Christians believe they are about Jesus the Christ," Philip explained. "Jesus was a great teacher. He brought God's love to people, especially the poor. God sent him to show us the way to live. His enemies killed him, but God raised him to new life. Jesus loves *you*, too. You can be his follower and friend."

The man was excited. He believed in Jesus. He wanted to become a Christian.

44 Scripture

Teaching Tips

Remind the students of the strong desire of the first Christians to live as Jesus had taught them. They wanted others to know Jesus and love him as they did. They came to realize that they must be open to sharing the message of Jesus with the whole world, as Jesus called them to.

"There's water right here," the man told Philip as they came near to some water. "Could I be baptized?"

Philip and the man jumped down from the carriage. Philip baptized him. Then the man from Ethiopia went happily on his way.

Based on Acts 8:26–38

Activity

We are sometimes called to share the gospel with people who have never even heard of Jesus. Sometimes we share with people who have beliefs that are different from ours. It is especially important at these times to share the gospel by the way we live.

Can you think of some things you could do, rather than say, to show others that you are a Catholic Christian? Draw or write your ideas here.

Scripture 45

Discussing the Stories

Discuss with the students how there are many ways to share our faith as Christians. Point out to them how the people of El Salvador were different from Angela, yet they shared their faith with her in ways that were special to her. In turn, she shared with the members of her family, who each experienced Jesus in different ways. Likewise, Philip and the man from Ethiopia experienced God in different ways. Yet Philip, who was one of the twelve apostles, was able to share with this man what he had learned from Jesus firsthand. The people of El Salvador, Angela, and Philip all found ways to share the good news with people they cared about. Emphasize that although we all experience God and Jesus in different ways, we can still share our beliefs and feelings with others. We can also be encouraged by the good news that others share with us about their experiences of God and Jesus.

Step 3/CONCLUSION

Learning How to Live Our Faith

Completing a Writing Activity

Read the directions for the activity on page 45. Explain that we can be apostolic, not only by using words, but also through our caring actions towards others. Stress that actions often speak louder than words. Talk about what this means. Have the students suggest ways they can demonstrate their faith in Jesus without using words. Then invite them to write or draw in the space provided specific actions they can perform. When they have finished, encourage them to share with the class the actions they chose. Help them understand that we can *say* that we are Christians, but it is our *actions* that show others that we mean what we say.

★ Enriching the Lesson ★

Discuss some of the different images that people have of God and Jesus. For example, some people think of God as a father and Jesus as a miracle worker. Then talk about specific opportunities to share the good news with people who may not be familiar with the goodness of God that most of us know through the goodness of others. For example, what could the students say or do to share Jesus' love with a child in their neighborhood whose parents never bring him or her to church?

Focus on

Sharing with Respect When we as Catholics answer Jesus' call to share his love with others, we need to be careful to respect the person with whom we are sharing. We need to keep in mind that even within the one Church, which is *united, uniformity* is not always necessary or desired. We cannot expect people to agree completely with our Catholic Christian ways and teachings, but we can still share those teachings in meaningful ways that can truly be experienced as "good news" by all.

DAY 3
DOCTRINE

Objective

This lesson helps the students appreciate that our faith grows as we share Jesus' good news.

Step 1/INTRODUCTION

Learning About Our Lives

Studying the Photographs

Ask a volunteer to read the first paragraph on page 46. Ask the following questions.

■ What does Jesus tell the apostles to do in Mark 16:15? (*To share the good news with everyone in the world*)

■ What does having *faith* mean? (*Believing that Jesus loves us*)

Ask volunteers to describe what is happening in each photograph. Help the students see that each picture shows people being apostolic. Remind them that being apostolic involves sharing the good news that comes to us from the apostles.

Learning Sign Language

Point out the picture that shows the teacher using sign language. Explain that hearing-impaired people and those who cannot speak sometimes use sign language to communicate. Using the diagrams below, teach the class to sign *Jesus loves you*. Practice the gestures and encourage the students to share their sign-language message with a parent or sibling.

Activity

When we share the gospel with others, we can help the Church to grow. This is what Jesus told the apostles to do. In Mark 16:15, we read that Jesus told them to go into the whole world to share the good news with everyone. When we share the good news, our **faith** can grow stronger. And we also help others to have faith. Part of what it means to have faith is to believe the good news that Jesus loves us.

Look at each of the following pictures. Read about the way in which each picture shows someone spreading the good news of Jesus' love. What do you see in each picture that also shows that the Church is united, holy, and catholic?

▲ Taping a TV Mass for people who are too old or sick to go to Mass at their parishes

Teaching a hearing impaired child to say "I love you" in sign language ▼

Going halfway around the world to tell people about God's love for them ▼

46   Doctrine

★ Enriching the Lesson ★

An easy way to acquaint students with sign language is to copy the sign-language alphabet from an encyclopedia or dictionary, and distribute copies to the class. Ask if any of the students are familiar with sign language and can help their classmates learn to spell out their names. If there are no volunteers, work with the students to practice spelling out their names.

To the Ends of the Earth

The twelve apostles were sent to spread the gospel message to everyone. Just as crowds of people often gathered to hear Jesus when he taught, the apostles often taught many people about Jesus. Since they were among his closest friends, the apostles knew Jesus best. So people really listened to them. Today, we pray that we will have the courage to share the good news, too.

Jesus, you asked the apostles to go and teach all nations. You asked them to baptize all people in your name. Help us today to be like the apostles. Show us the ways that we can share the good news with one person or with many, with people who are near to us, and with people who are far away. We pray in Jesus' name. Amen.

Vocabulary

faith: the belief that Jesus loves us and our response to God's call

Doctrine 47

Learning About Our Faith

Reading the Text

Read with the students "To the Ends of the Earth" on page 47. Emphasize that the good news of Jesus has spread to every corner of the earth because of the faith of his friends and followers.

Writing a Poem

Distribute sheets of lined paper, and invite the students to work in small groups to write a four-line poem titled "To the Ends of the Earth." For the first line, have them write about Jesus' good news. For the second line, have them write about the apostles' work. For the third line, have them write about one way the Church is apostolic. For the fourth line, have the students write about their own call today to share the good news. Emphasize that the poems do not need to rhyme. Afterward, invite each group to share its poem.

Learning the Vocabulary

Direct the students' attention to the Vocabulary box on page 47. Have the students read and learn the definition for the word *faith*. Emphasize that faith includes both believing and responding.

Learning How to Live Our Faith

Praying Together

Ask the students to stand for prayer. Use an echo format to pray the prayer at the bottom of the page. Read one phrase at a time aloud to the students. Then have them repeat it prayerfully.

 Teaching Tips

Some students may not feel confident about sharing their faith with others. Other students may actually be more confident than many adults. It may help those who lack confidence to tell them that there are many simple ways that they can share their faith, such as telling a friend who is visiting their home something about a special crucifix or other religious symbol that their family displays. Or they might ask their friends if they display similar items in their own homes that show something about the faith of their families.

Enriching the Lesson

Invite the students to create a picture story about sharing their faith in Jesus through words and actions. Distribute 9" × 12" sheets of construction paper. Direct the students to fold their sheets of paper twice so that each student has four squares or "frames" on the page for his or her story. Then ask the students to write a caption for each frame.

Objective

This lesson helps the students understand that Jesus calls us to be witnesses.

Step 1/INTRODUCTION

Learning About Our Lives

Pretending to Be Reporters

Read the directions for the activity on page 48. To assist the students in completing this activity, supply them with recent copies of your diocesan newspaper, Catholic periodicals, your parish bulletin, and the Religion section of magazines and local newspapers. Direct the students to use these materials to gather information and then to use their own words in composing their own newspaper columns. Allow sufficient time for the students to complete this activity. When they have finished, invite them to share their front-page stories in small groups. As the students discuss their articles, move from group to group, praising the students for their work.

Step 2/DEVELOPMENT

Learning About Our Faith

Reading the Text

Call on volunteers to read aloud "Witnesses for Jesus" on page 49. As the vocabulary words are introduced, refer to the Vocabulary box. Have the students read and learn the definitions. Encourage the students to use each of the vocabulary words in a sentence to check their understanding.

Discussing the Text

Discuss the following questions.

■ How can we be witnesses? (*By sharing what we know about Jesus and living in the way Jesus wants us to live*)

■ What do missionaries do? (*Serve God and the Church as teachers and healthcare workers; help people to live better lives*)

■ Why is it important for Christians to live faithfully according to the Church's teachings? (*Because others will see that Christians are faithful and loving people*)

48

Activity

Pretend you are a reporter for *The Apostolic Times*. Use newspapers, magazines, and your own interviews to report on the apostolic activities of the Church today. Print your front-page story below.

THE APOSTOLIC TIMES

| Vol. 21 - No. 19 | Friday, April 15 | 30 cents |

CURRICULUM CONNECTION

Language Arts The writing assignment on page 48 can be used to teach or review language arts skills or to introduce basic journalism concepts. You may want to emphasize verbs that describe apostolic activities. Or you may want to teach the students to use the five *w*'s—who, what, where, when, and why—to help them focus their research and writing.

Witnesses for Jesus

Each of us is called to be a **witness**. We are called to share what we know about Jesus and to live in the ways that Jesus wants us to. Today, our Church leaders remind us that the witness of our lives is very important. When we live faithfully according to the Church's teachings, others will see that Catholics are faithful and loving people.

The apostles traveled long distances through all kinds of weather to spread the gospel to everyone. Like the apostles, many **missionaries** are sent out to spread the gospel throughout the world today. Missionaries, both men and women, often serve God and the Church as teachers and as healthcare workers. They also help people in many lands to live better lives.

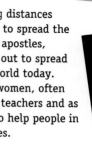

Activity

Jesus promised that all who believe in him can do great things with the help of the Holy Spirit. Even though you are not traveling throughout the world, you can still help people to learn about Jesus and to live better lives. What are some ways that you can help?

_____

_____

_____

_____

_____

Vocabulary

witness: one who shares what he or she knows about Jesus and lives in the ways that Jesus wants us to live

missionaries: people who are sent out to spread the gospel throughout the world

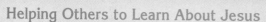

Learning How to Live Our Faith

Helping Others to Learn About Jesus

Explain the directions for the activity on page 49 and encourage the students to complete this activity with enthusiasm and confidence that they can indeed do great things. You may want them to work in pairs to encourage one another. Then invite the students to share their responses with the class. Affirm all their responses, and emphasize that their apostolic efforts make them missionaries-at-home.

Creating Slogans

Ask the students to think about some reasons that some people might not want to live as Catholic Christians or that some Catholics seldom go to Mass. Then invite the students to create slogans that invite these people to take a second look at how the Church's message about Jesus is truly "good news." Distribute strips of construction paper for the students to write their slogans on.

Focus on

Evangelii Nuntiandi In Pope Paul VI's apostolic exhortation, "On Evangelization in the Modern World," paragraph 21 stresses the importance of the "witness of life" and the "wordless witness." This kind of witness "is already a silent proclamation of the Good News and a very powerful and effective one" that can cause non-Christians to be attracted to the Christian way of life and lead them to ask meaningful questions about the Christian faith.

Teaching Tips

You may want to contact one or two missionary groups to help the students learn more about the groups' efforts. The organizations below will be delighted to hear from you and your students.

Maryknoll Educational Resources, Maryknoll, NY 10545

Mission Education Office, Columban Fathers, St. Columbans, NE 68056

Objective

This lesson helps the students meditate about Jesus.

Preparing for Prayer

As part of this prayer experience, you may want to use a water ritual to help the students recall their Baptisms. If you do this, remind the students that their call to live as Christians began with their Baptisms. Then explain that in order to share Jesus with others, we need to take the time to think about our own relationship with Jesus and what he means to us. Tell the students that today's prayer will help them to do this. Then read aloud the first paragraph on page 50.

Praying a Jesus Meditation

Using blessed water, sign the students' foreheads with water and the Sign of the Cross. Or have them come forward individually and bless themselves. Play soft instrumental music during the blessing.

While the music is still playing, invite the students to relax and to breath deeply and slowly as you begin the meditation. Dim or turn off the classroom lights during the meditation. If permissible, light a candle and have the students focus on the flame. Or invite them to close their eyes.

Read the meditation on page 50 very slowly. Pause after each question to allow time for the students to think about and experience Jesus' presence with them.

Conclude the prayer experience by having the students pray together the prayer on page 47.

Afterward, invite the students to share with the class their experiences of the meditation. Encourage them to share what they said to Jesus and how they believe Jesus responded. Affirm those that shared by telling them this is a first step in telling their friends what it is like to know Jesus.

Praying a Jesus Meditation

Our prayer today is a Jesus meditation. In this prayer of meditation, we will recall a story about Jesus from the Bible and imagine that we are there in the same place as Jesus.

Close your eyes and listen as your teacher tells the story. After each question, take some time to think about possible answers. Think about what it would be like to meet Jesus, face to face.

Jesus is entering the town of Jericho. He is walking slowly. What does he look like? What is he wearing? Many people are coming to walk with him. They know that he has just helped a blind man to see for the first time in his life. Everyone is very excited and happy that Jesus has come to their town. They all want to get closer to Jesus. Some people are pushing and shoving to get close enough to see his face. Can you see his face? Can you hear what he is saying to the crowd? Is he inviting them to come closer? You have just made your way through the crowd and are close enough for Jesus to hear your voice. Do you have something you would like to say to Jesus? Do you have a question that you think Jesus could answer for you? He is leaning toward you because he knows you want to say something. What do you say? How does he respond? What will you tell your friends about what it was like to meet Jesus?

50 Prayer

Teaching Tips

You may find the use of meditation in your classroom to be an effective means of "drawing religion out of" your students. Help them understand that meditation is a form of prayer that requires quiet, receptive listening as well as focused attention.

Chapter Review

missionaries
witness
apostolic
apostles   mark
gospel   faith

Use the words in the art to complete the sentences.

The fourth _____mark_____ of the Church is that it is _____apostolic_____ . This means that it is based on the teachings of the _____apostles_____ . Jesus sent out the apostles to be _____missionaries_____ . They spread the _____gospel_____ , the good news of Jesus' love for all people, throughout the world. Like the apostles, we are each called to be a _____witness_____ . We are called to share what we know about Jesus and to live in the ways that Jesus wants us to. When we tell others about Jesus' love for them, we help them to have ____faith____ .

Fill in the answers to the first two questions.

1. What is the meaning of *apostolic*? _It means_
   based on the teachings of Jesus and his apostles.
   _____

2. How did the apostles share the good news of Jesus? _The apostles shared the good news of_
   Jesus by the way they lived and by what they said.
   They shared the teachings of Jesus with others.

3. Talk about ways that *you* can share the good news of Jesus.

Jesus says, "Go into the whole world and share the good news with everyone."
Based on Mark 16:15

Filling in the Blanks

Direct attention to the first exercise on page 51. Explain the directions and have the students work independently to complete the exercise. When they have finished, check their understanding of the major concepts presented in this chapter by reading aloud the sentences and having the students orally supply the missing words.

Reviewing the Chapter

Take time to go through the remaining review questions. Direct the students to write the answer to each question on the lines provided in the text. Encourage all to participate in the discussion question. Be supportive of each student who responds.

Reflecting on the Scriptural Verse

Together, read aloud the verse from Scripture at the bottom of the page. Remind the class that we can share the good news by what we say and by what we do. Recall that Jesus has asked us to share the good news with everyone. Emphasize that when we do these things, we are being apostolic.

★ Enriching the Lesson ★

In order to have a better understanding of the Scripture quotes at the end of each chapter, students can be encouraged to look up the complete passage from which the quote is taken. The quote on page 51 comes from the Gospel of Mark in the section about Jesus' appearances after the resurrection. You might recall with the students that, after his death and resurrection, Jesus appeared to his disciples many times to encourage and instruct them.

CURRICULUM CONNECTION

Art Have the students make Salvadoran crosses, using pieces of balsa wood, yarn, enamel paints, and paintbrushes. Show them how to place one piece of wood across another and then wrap the yarn diagonally around the crossbars, crisscrossing until the cross is secure. Have the students decorate the crosses with signs of creation, life, and Jesus.

51

Using the Unit Organizer

Completing a graphic organizer such as a chart or table can help students to organize the information that has been presented in the unit. Organizers can enable students to visualize their thinking and recognize relationships among ideas. This will give students the opportunity to understand more completely the material they have been studying.

Explain the directions for the activity on page 52. Have the students work independently to complete it. Afterward, invite the students to compare their ideas on how the Church shows that it is one, holy, catholic, and apostolic.

Looking Back: Self-Assessment

The critical reflection questions below give the students an opportunity to sharpen their thinking skills. The questions can be used as a class discussion or independent writing activity.

- What did you learn in this unit that you think you will always remember?

- Which was your favorite Scripture story in this unit? What did you like most about it?

- Which activity in this unit did you most enjoy? Why?

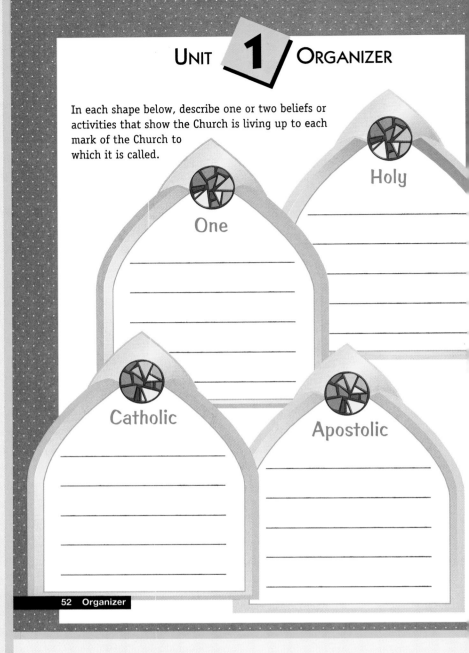

UNIT 1 ORGANIZER

In each shape below, describe one or two beliefs or activities that show the Church is living up to each mark of the Church to which it is called.

One

Holy

Catholic

Apostolic

UNIT 1 REVIEW

Use the words hidden in the puzzle to complete these sentences.

1. The first Christians _____shared_____ everything they owned.

2. One of the places the first Christians met each day was at the
   _____Temple_____ .

3. The Scriptures are the written _____word_____ of God.

4. *Holy* means being close to _____God_____ .

5. Welcoming and accepting all _____people_____ is an important part of being catholic.

6. We can _____tell_____ others about the good news of Jesus.

7. People noticed how much the first Christians _____loved_____ one another.

8. *Catholic* means _____open_____ to people everywhere.

9. Holy men and women are called _____saints_____ .

10. To share what you know about Jesus is to be a _____witness_____ .

```
X  A  S  A  I  N  T  S
R  T  H  T  E  L  L  M
E  E  A  T  S  G  O  D
W  M  R  W  O  R  V  Q
O  P  E  O  P  L  E  G
R  L  D  R  E  A  D  J
O  E  N  D  N  G  R  E
B  W  I  T  N  E  S  S
```

Reviewing the Unit

The purpose of the unit review is to reinforce concepts presented in the preceding four chapters and to check the students' understanding. After explaining the directions, give the students sufficient time to complete the two-page review. Answer any questions they may have.

Testing

After the students have completed the unit review, you may wish to distribute copies of the Unit 1 Test from the Unit Tests booklet in The Resourceful Teacher Package.

Optional Unit Project

Gather some missionary magazines that show a variety of people from different cultures at worship and engaged in tasks to improve the quality of life. Ask the students to look at the pictures in the magazines and to select one to represent each of the four marks, or signs, of the Church. Then mount and paste each of these four pictures on separate sheets of paper. At the top of each sheet, write the title of each chapter in Unit 1, such as "Our Church Is One." You might also choose to have the students mount the pictures on one large poster and title it "The Marks of the Church."

UNIT **1** REVIEW

Fill in the blanks using the name of one of the four marks of the Church to complete each sentence.

1. _____Holy_____ means being close to God, loving God and others, and doing God's work in the world.

2. A prayer for unity that Jesus prayed is, "Father, may they be

   _____one_____ as we are one."

3. Our Church is called _____apostolic_____ because it is based on the teachings of the apostles.

4. People who are open to and accepting of anyone from anywhere in the

   world, just as Jesus is, are called _____catholic_____ .

Match the words in Column A with the definitions in Column B.

Column A	Column B
1. Christians	_3_ a special community of Jesus' followers who pray together and share stories of faith
2. respect	_5_ one who shares about Jesus and lives in his ways
3. parish	_1_ the worldwide community of people who believe that Jesus is the Son of God
4. gospel	_2_ to act with care toward someone
5. witness	_4_ the good news of Jesus' love for all people

54 **Review**

54

WHAT'S a PROBLEM and HOW DO I SOLVE IT?

It is not always easy getting along with friends and members of the family. A disagreement between people is called a *problem*. Problems between people can cause hurt or upset feelings. And the people who cause the problems often hurt as much as the people whose feelings they have hurt. Thinking before acting, thinking of many possible solutions, and choosing a solution that shows you are a follower of Jesus are important parts of being a good problem solver.

STEPS TO PROBLEM SOLVING

One:	Stop and think.
Two:	Name the problem.
Three:	Clarify the goal.
Four:	Identify possible solutions.
Five:	Identify possible consequences.
Six:	Try the best solution.

Activity Jason's Problem

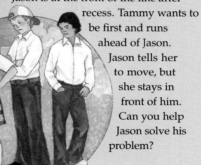

Jason is at the front of the line after recess. Tammy wants to be first and runs ahead of Jason. Jason tells her to move, but she stays in front of him. Can you help Jason solve his problem?

Circle the best response.

1. How is Jason feeling?

   (a) mad   (b) happy   (c) shy

2. What is Jason's problem?

   (a) He wants a longer recess.

   (b) Tammy cut in front of him.

   (c) Tammy won't be his friend.

3. What should Jason do next?

   (a) Tell the teacher.

   (b) Stop and think.

   (c) Push Tammy out of the way.

4. What do you think Jason would like to see happen?

   (a) Jason wants to be first in line.

   (b) Jason wants Tammy to be first.

   (c) Jason wants Tammy to say that she is sorry.

Day to Day   55

Introducing Day to Day: Skills for Christian Living

The five lessons of this feature focus on the process for solving interpersonal problems. The lessons emphasize thinking before acting, identifying possible solutions and consequences, communication skills, and what to do when feeling lonely or left out. Students are encouraged to recognize certain feelings as signals for using their problem-solving skills. Each lesson emphasizes the importance of choosing solutions that are in line with being a follower of Jesus.

Objective

This lesson helps the students identify problems in the context of interpersonal relationships and understand the steps to effective problem solving.

Introducing the Lesson

Begin the lesson by asking the students to define the word *problem*. Then invite the students to open their books to page 55 and to read with you the opening paragraph. Use examples to help them distinguish between interpersonal problems (problems that happen between people) and other problems that don't involve interactions with people.

Ask for volunteers to share experiences of times when they may have had problems getting along with others. Encourage them to share how they felt and what they did. Ask them what they think it means to choose solutions that show you are a follower of Jesus. (*Followers of Jesus should choose solutions that are helpful, kind, and selfless; not hurtful, mean, or selfish.*)

Reading About Problem Solving

Ask six volunteers to read aloud "Steps to Problem Solving." Use the following questions to help the students reflect on the six steps.

■ Why do you think it is important to stop and think when trying to solve a problem? (*If we react quickly we might not choose the best*

Lesson continues on page 56.

55

solution. *Acting impulsively can sometimes get us into more trouble.*)

- Why do you think it is important when solving a problem to be clear about what the problem really is? Why is it important to ask ourselves about our goal? (*Being clear about the problem and our goal assures that our solution fits the problem.*)

- Why is it important to think of more than one solution? (*Thinking of several possibilities gives us more options, especially if we try a solution and it doesn't work.*)

- What is a consequence? (*A consequence is what happens after a solution is tried.*)

Completing the Activity

Direct the students' attention to "Jason's Problem." Explain the directions for the activity on page 55 and have the students complete the activity independently. After they have finished, discuss their answers to the questions.

Identifying Possible Solutions

Tell the students that an important characteristic of being a good problem solver is the ability to generate many solutions for a single problem. Read aloud the directions for the activity at the top of page 56. Encourage students to think creatively as they work on this activity.

Ask a volunteer to read the paragraph following the activity. Help the students evaluate the solutions they have identified. Ask the students to decide whether or not their solutions would help Jason reach his goal in ways that are helpful to others.

Following Jesus

Read with the class "Following Jesus" at the bottom of page 56. Ask the class why they think Jesus tells us that to love God and to love others are the greatest commandments of all. Invite them to identify loving actions.

Concluding the Lesson

End the lesson by reading the prayer with the class. Allow time for the students to include individual petitions.

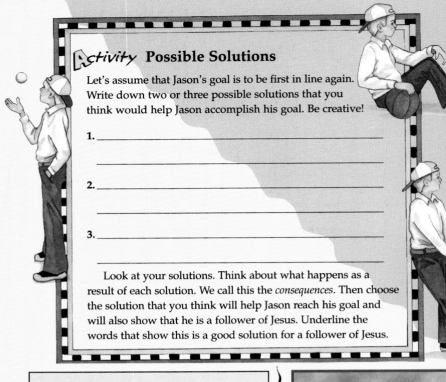

Activity Possible Solutions

Let's assume that Jason's goal is to be first in line again. Write down two or three possible solutions that you think would help Jason accomplish his goal. Be creative!

1. _____

_____

2. _____

_____

3. _____

_____

Look at your solutions. Think about what happens as a result of each solution. We call this the *consequences*. Then choose the solution that you think will help Jason reach his goal and will also show that he is a follower of Jesus. Underline the words that show this is a good solution for a follower of Jesus.

Following Jesus

As followers of Jesus, we need to think about what Jesus taught when we are trying to solve a problem. Remember that Jesus taught us to love our neighbor. One way we can do this is by acting with kindness even when others have been unkind or hurtful to us. Jesus tells us in Mark 12:28–33 that to love God and to love others are the two greatest commandments of all. Remembering this can help us solve many problems.

PRAYER

Jesus, help me choose solutions that show I am your follower. Each time I am making a choice, help me remember your greatest commandments. Help me love my neighbor as I love myself. And help me forgive others when they have hurt me. Amen.

OPENING DOORS
A Take-Home Magazine™

Growing Closer

This Week at Sacred Heart Parish

MON. - RCIA Catechist Mtg.
TUE. - Social Concerns Committee
WED. - Parent Night
SAT. - Fall Harvest Festival

TAKE SOME TIME with your family to talk about what makes you a family. Discover again the unique talents and personalities that make up your family as well as those interests and concerns you all share in common. Be grateful for the great gift your family is to you!

READ ALOUD WITH YOUR FAMILY parts of the Sunday parish bulletin. Look for items that encourage members to get to know each other better, to reach out to those in need, to teach, or to become more united in some way. Consider as a family how you might participate in one of these activities.

Answers to page 5: Gathering, welcomes, worship, celebrate, unity

Looking Ahead

THIS IS OUR FAITH, Grade 3, deals with a variety of traditional Catholic teachings. Unit 2 will focus on the most basic affirmation of our creeds. Your child will learn that these creeds focus our minds and hearts on God—Father, Son, and Holy Spirit. The unit will stress that our faith is, above all, a personal relationship with God.

8

© Silver Burdett Ginn Inc.

Opening Doors ～～

A Take-Home Magazine

The five removable, family-directed supplements entitled *Opening Doors: A Take-Home Magazine* provide you, the teacher, with a unique opportunity to involve parents or guardians more fully in their child's religion classes. Each magazine will include the following features.

A Closer Look

An adult-level reflection on the theme of the unit with a focus on the Mass and family pages based on the same material

Being Catholic

An article highlighting a particular aspect of our American Catholic heritage

Growing Closer

Suggested activities to help the family integrate faith into everyday life

Looking Ahead

A preview of the next unit of THIS IS OUR FAITH, Grade 3

Sending the Magazine Home

As you complete Unit 1 with your class, assist the students in carefully removing *Opening Doors: A Take-Home Magazine* (two pages) from their texts by separating the pages from the book along the perforations. Demonstrate how to fold the two pages to form an eight-page booklet.

When the magazines are folded, take time to explain each section of the magazine to the students. Allow the students to ask any questions they may have. Ask the students to take the magazine home and encourage their families to read it with them and to participate in the suggested activities. You may wish to attach a letter of your own, encouraging the family to use the magazine each time their child brings it home.

Follow the same procedure in sending home the remaining magazines for Units 2, 3, 4, and 5.

Called to Worship

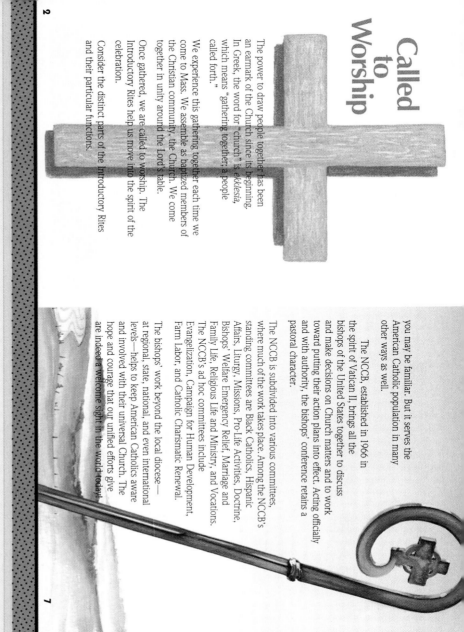

The power to draw people together has been an earmark of the Church since its beginning. In Greek, the word for "church" is *ekklesia*, which means "gathering together, a people called forth."

We experience this gathering together each time we come to Mass. We assemble as baptized members of the Christian community, the Church. We come together in unity around the Lord's table.

Once gathered, we are called to worship. The Introductory Rites help us move into the spirit of the celebration.

Consider the distinct parts of the Introductory Rites and their particular functions.

you may be familiar. But it serves the American Catholic population in many other ways as well.

The NCCB, established in 1966 in the spirit of Vatican II, brings all the bishops of the United States together to discuss and make decisions on Church matters and to work toward putting their action plans into effect. Acting officially and with authority, the bishops' conference retains a pastoral character.

The NCCB is subdivided into various committees, where much of the work takes place. Among the NCCB's standing committees are Black Catholics, Hispanic Affairs, Liturgy, Missions, Pro-Life Activities, Doctrine, Bishops' Welfare Emergency Relief, Marriage and Family Life, Religious Life and Ministry, and Vocations. The NCCB's ad hoc committees include Evangelization, Campaign for Human Development, Farm Labor, and Catholic Charismatic Renewal.

The bishops' work beyond the local diocese—at regional, state, national, and even international levels—helps to keep American Catholics aware and involved with their universal Church. The hope and courage that our unified efforts give are indeed a welcome sight in the world today.

The music and the words of the Gathering Song welcome us and invite us to participate in the celebration.

In the Greeting, the priest and the assembly greet one another and acknowledge the Lord's presence.

In the Penitential Rite, we recognize sin in our lives and humbly accept God's mercy.

In the Gloria, a prayer of praise, we applaud God's goodness.

In the Opening Prayer, we pray a prayer that expresses the theme of the celebration.

We have been gathered and we have been forgiven. We have been greeted and we have begun to pray. Now we, the assembly, are ready to be strengthened by God's word and nourished by the Eucharist.

Our American Shepherds

As Your Third Grader is learning about how the Church is organized into dioceses, he or she is learning about how bishops serve the Church. As "shepherd" of his diocese, a bishop has a very big responsibility. Locally, a bishop oversees all the parishes of his diocese as teacher, pastoral guide, and administrator. In addition, each bishop tends to the needs of Catholics throughout the country by his participation in the national bishops' conference.

At one time or another, you have probably heard of the National Conference of Catholic Bishops (NCCB). Along with its service agency, the United States Catholic Conference (USCC), the NCCB has produced and published many statements and documents with which

The Christian Family

Spend some time with your child discovering one important part of the Mass that speaks to us of our identity as Catholics. The term catholic means "open to all." The Gathering Rite welcomes us into the celebration regardless of age, race, or nationality and reminds us of the unity we share in Jesus, who is our reason for coming together around the eucharistic table. Read the following with your child.

Every family is made up of different kinds of people. Some family members are older and some are younger. Some work and some go to school. Some like sports and some enjoy music and art. Yet all these different kinds of people make up one family.

The Christian family is made up of many different ages, colors, and talents. Some members are old and some are young. Some are African American and

4

some are Asian. Some are teachers and some are students. Yet all of these different kinds of people belong to the one family of Jesus.

The Gathering Rite is the first part of the Mass that brings us together as the family of Jesus. We remember that we are different people yet members of one family. We have come together to celebrate our unity and to celebrate Jesus, our Brother and Friend, who makes us one.

Unscramble the words below. Use those words to complete a sentence that tells about the Gathering Rite.

rethnigaG   miweecso   shpiowr   atebrleec   yuint

The _____ Rite _____ all people to _____ God and to _____ our _____ in Jesus.

The next time you go to Mass, look around at the people gathered there. Notice how many different kinds of people make up the family of Jesus in your parish. Thank Jesus for bringing his family together to celebrate the Eucharist.

5

UNIT 2

A Believing Community

What are some things you really believe in?

To help the students understand and appreciate some central ideas of our Catholic faith: our beliefs about God the Father, Jesus his Son, and the Holy Spirit.

Doctrinal Summaries

CHAPTER 5

God is our creator. We call God "Father." God takes care of us like a loving parent. God is always faithful to us.

CHAPTER 6

Jesus, the Son of God, is always with us. He rose from death to new life. He is our friend forever.

CHAPTER 7

Jesus gives the community of believers, the Church, the gift of the Holy Spirit to be with us as our helper and guide. The Holy Spirit gives us courage and power to do things we never thought we could do.

CHAPTER 8

The creeds of the Catholic Church summarize our beliefs.

Note:

As you prepare this unit, you may wish to refer to the reference section, *Our Catholic Heritage,* beginning on page 327.

Additional resources for Unit 2 include a Unit Test and a Family Letter as well as a video and selections from the THIS IS OUR FAITH Music Program. You might also find it helpful to preview *Saints and Other Holy People* and *Prayer Celebrations* for possibilities to enhance the unit.

Introducing the UNIT

Ask the students to describe what is happening in the photograph. Note the Statue of Liberty image and discuss what it represents. Read aloud the focus question. Elicit responses, which may include: *fun, friends, freedom, family, God, love,* and *peace.* Tell the students that in Unit 2 they will examine what the Catholic Church believes.

Vocabulary

trust
faithful
Trinity
resurrection
Pentecost
Apostles' Creed

5 Our Church Believes in God the Father

Objectives 〜〜〜

To help the students

- Recognize that God is faithful.
- Learn Jesus' teachings about the Father's care for us.
- Get to know God more fully in the three Persons of the Trinity.
- Desire to imitate God's faithfulness.
- Celebrate their learning about God's faithfulness and review the chapter.

Chapter Outline 〜〜〜〜〜

	Step 1 **Learning About Our Lives**	Step 2 **Learning About Our Faith**	Step 3 **Learning How to Live Our Faith**
Day 1	■ Introduce the chapter. ■ Read and discuss a story. *ABOUT 12 MINUTES*	■ Learn about trust. ■ Review the doctrine. *ABOUT 8 MINUTES*	■ Identify fears. ■ Pray together. *ABOUT 10 MINUTES*
Day 2	■ Talk about experiences. *ABOUT 5 MINUTES*	■ Read and discuss a Scripture story. *ABOUT 10 MINUTES*	■ Write a prayer. ■ Pray together. *ABOUT 15 MINUTES*
Day 3	■ Review what it means to be holy. *ABOUT 5 MINUTES*	■ Decode a Scripture passage. ■ Learn about the Trinity. ■ Learn the vocabulary. *ABOUT 12 MINUTES*	■ Complete an activity. ■ Pray the Sign of the Cross. *ABOUT 13 MINUTES*
Day 4	■ Recall God's faithfulness. *ABOUT 8 MINUTES*	■ Read about God's faithfulness. ■ Read about our own faithfulness. *ABOUT 10 MINUTES*	■ Complete a word gram. *ABOUT 12 MINUTES*
Day 5	**Prayer** Complete an activity; prepare for prayer; pray together. **Review** Unscramble words; summarize the chapter; pray with the scriptural verse.		

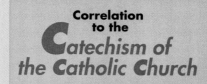
Plan Ahead

	Preparing Your Class	**Materials Needed**
Day 1	Read through the lesson plan for this class session. Think about your own fears.	■ pencils or pens
Day 2	Read through the lesson plan for this class session.	■ chalkboard ■ pencils or pens
Day 3	Read through the lesson plan for this class session. Review the definition of the word *holy*.	■ crayons ■ pencils or pens
Day 4	Review the definitions of the words *faithful* and *trust*. Review the story of Maria on pages 62–63 and the Scripture story on pages 64–65.	■ pencils or pens
Day 5	Prepare an environment for prayer in the classroom. Review this week's sessions to prepare for the chapter review. Practice the sign-language gestures on page 70.	■ crayons or markers ■ art paper, scissors, and tape ■ posterboard ■ pencils or pens

Additional Resources

As you plan this chapter, consider using the following materials from The Resourceful Teacher Package.

■ *Classroom Activity Sheets 5* and *5a*

■ *Family Activity Sheets 5* and *5a*

■ *Chapter 5 Test*

■ *Prayers for Every Day*

■ *Projects: Grade 3*

You may also wish to refer to the following Big Books.

■ *We Celebrate the Sacraments,* page 8

■ *We Celebrate God's Word,* page 11

■ *We Celebrate the Mass,* page 17

In preparing the students for the Sunday readings, you may wish to use Silver Burdett Ginn's *Getting Ready for Sunday* student and teacher materials.

BOOKS FOR THE JOURNEY

A Child's Book of Prayers. Edited by Linda Yeatman. Stewart, Tabori, and Chang 1992. "Lord Jesus, Take My Hand" by Sister Mary Raphael, p. 19. A prayer in which a child expresses a belief in Jesus' loving presence.

Festival of Freedom. Retold by Maida Silverman. Simon & Schuster, 1988. The story of Passover and God's faithfulness is joyously retold. Directions for a Seder are included.

MORE BOOKS FOR THE JOURNEY

I Never Told: And Other Poems. Myra Cohn Livingston. Macmillan Children's Books Group, 1992. "I Never Told," p. 11. A poem that describes the faithfulness of a child to his friend.

Praise for the Singing. Collected by Madelaine Gill. Little, Brown & Co., 1993. "The First Song of Isaiah," p. 36. A song expressing trust and faithfulness.

REDUCED CLASSROOM ACTIVITIES

NAME _____

OUR CHURCH BELIEVES IN GOD THE FATHER

You are writing a play with a friend that will be made into an after-school TV special. It's a story about how one person was counting on another but was afraid the other person wouldn't come through. The story can be real or made up. Think of names for the two characters. The narrator will help you tell your story. Complete the play on the lines below and on page 5a.

Counting On Someone

Narrator: Welcome to today's After-School Special. Our story is about

_____ and _____ . It's about being faithful.

_____ is trusting and depending on _____ .
(Character 1)   *(Character 2)*

_____ : "I'm trusting and depending on you
(Character 1)

to _____ ."

_____ : "You can trust me to _____
(Character 2)

_____ because I care about you."

To the Teacher: This page and page 5a can be used as an additional activity for the chapter.

Chapter 5 Our Church Believes in God the Father   THIS IS OUR FAITH 3 **5**

NAME _____

Narrator: Later it looks as if _____ isn't going to
                                        (Character 2)
come through as promised.

_____ : "I'm worried because _____
(Character 1)

_____ ."

_____ : "I hope _____ isn't worrying.
(Character 2)   *(Character 1)*
I'm planning to do what I said I'd do, but

_____ ."

Narrator: But _____ didn't have to worry because
                        (Character 1)

_____ was faithful as promised.
(Character 2)

_____ : "_____, I'm so glad you
(Character 1)   *(Character 2)*
came through for me when you _____ ."

_____ : "I'm faithful to you. That means _____
(Character 2)

_____ ."

Narrator: _____ realizes that _____ is
              (Character 1)   *(Character 2)*
faithful, just as God is.

_____ : "Now I understand how God is faithful."
(Character 1)

_____ : "Yes, _____
(Character 2)

_____ ."

5a THIS IS OUR FAITH 3   **Chapter 5** Our Church Believes in God the Father

Background for the Teacher

THE FAITHFULNESS OF GOD

A major theme of the Old Testament is the faithfulness of God. Few characteristics of God are cited as frequently in the Scriptures as his faithfulness. Although there are many episodes of infidelity on the part of God's people, his love for them is steadfast. Psalm 22:25 reassures us that God does not turn away from us when we are unfaithful. Rather, God hears us in our time of need.

God's faithfulness is symbolized in many ways in the Scriptures: by the sure rising of the sun, the unwavering presence of the moon, the resolute firmness of the hills, the fidelity of a loving spouse, the love of a mother for her child, and the constancy of a caring father.

Jesus teaches about the undying faithfulness of God. He speaks of a caring Father who is willing to welcome all who seek forgiveness. The story of the Prodigal Son is a good example of Jesus' teaching about God's fidelity.

CATHOLIC BELIEF IN GOD

While the fidelity of God is not explicitly stated in the Church's creeds, the theme serves as a valuable backdrop for understanding the creeds. The creeds proclaim God as Father, as creator, and as almighty. These proclamations imply a God whose love and care are constant. God is always faithful, no matter how unfaithful we may be. His fidelity is what underlies the loving covenant between God and us.

This chapter cannot summarize all the Church's beliefs about God. However, the basic concept of fidelity is especially meaningful as a theme because it is at the core of our relationship with God. Reliability is important to an eight- or nine-year-old in his or her relationships. The third-grade student is a stranger to neither fidelity nor disappointments in relationships. He or she has been a part of friendships that have come and gone. What is new at this level is a growing appreciation of faithfulness as an integral part of our relationships with one another and with God.

Objective

This lesson helps the students recognize that God is faithful.

Step 1/INTRODUCTION

Learning About Our Lives

Introducing the Chapter

Have a volunteer read aloud the chapter title and focus question. Encourage the students to share their own examples of people who have shown their dependability and trustworthiness. Tell the students that in this session they will learn about someone on whom they can always depend.

Reading and Discussing a Story

Call on volunteers to read aloud the story "Worries and Fears," which begins on page 62. Help the students recognize the source of Maria's fears.

Discuss with the class the questions on page 63. Emphasize that Maria's grandfather assured Maria of her mother's love. Lead the students to appreciate that Maria needed to remember and trust in her mother's love and care for her.

5 Our Church Believes in God the Father

How do people show you that you can depend on them and trust them, no matter what?

Worries and Fears

Maria was worried. Her mom was away on a business trip. It was a scary feeling, like getting lost at a parade and not remembering the way home. "A hug from Mommy would be the best thing in the world right now," she thought. Maria tried not to let her grandfather know how much she missed her mother.

It had been two days since Maria's mom had left. She had not called. Maria knew where she had gone. The country her mom was visiting seemed so far away. Maria's worries and fears grew. Many questions raced through her mind. "Why hasn't she called me yet?" "Has she forgotten me?" "Doesn't she love me?" "Is Mommy O.K.?"

Maria's grandfather sensed her concern. "Tell me what's wrong, Maria," he said gently.

Teaching Tips

Be aware that the story "Worries and Fears" may have a strong impact on students who have experienced the loss of a loved one through death, divorce, or abandonment. Be especially sensitive to the feelings that might surface during the reading and discussion.

Focus on

The Creed According the *Catechism of the Catholic Church* "Our profession of faith begins with God, for God is the First and the Last, the beginning and the end of everything. The Credo begins with God the Father, for the Father is the first divine person of the Most Holy Trinity; our Creed begins with the creation of heaven and earth, for creation is the beginning and the foundation of all God's works." (#198)

"Why doesn't Mommy call me? She usually does. Maybe she's hurt. Or maybe she's just too busy." Tears came to Maria's eyes.

Her grandfather put his arms around her. "You're scared and worried," he said. "Your mother has not forgotten you. I know how much she loves you. I'm sure she'll call soon."

Maria wiped her eyes and tried to smile, but her heart still felt sad.

Suddenly the phone rang. Grandfather answered it and then held out the phone to Maria. "It's your mom!" he said.

Maria's mom explained everything. She couldn't call sooner because a storm had cut all telephone lines in the area where she was working. She was fine and would be home in two days. Then they would spend a week of vacation together.

Discuss

1. How would you feel if you were Maria?

2. How did Maria's grandfather help her?

3. What more could you say to help Maria?

Learning to Trust

Jesus taught that whenever we feel alone or afraid, we should remember that God is always with us and cares for us very much. He teaches that God is our loving creator, who cares for all of creation and will never forget us. Just as Maria knew deep down inside that her mother really loved her, we can **trust** that God really loves us, too. Even though God may seem very far away at times, we can trust and believe in his love for us. We can trust and depend upon God as we can trust and depend upon a loving parent.

Vocabulary

trust: to have faith in God's love for us and to believe that he is always with us

★ ★ ★ ★ ★ ★ ★ ★ ★ ★ ★ ★

We Believe

God is our creator. We call God "Father." God takes care of us like a loving parent. God is always faithful to us.

Doctrine 63

Enriching the Lesson

Have the students form pairs to take a trust walk. Give each pair a blindfold to cover one partner's eyes. Tell those who are not blindfolded to carefully lead their partners around the room. Emphasize that the guiding partners are responsible for the safety of the blindfolded partners and that it is important to keep them from running into objects or other people. Then have them switch roles. Afterward, talk with the class about how they felt when being led. Discuss whether or not they began to trust and rely on their partners during this experience.

Learning About Our Faith

Learning About Trust

Have a student read "Learning to Trust" on page 63. As the word *trust* is introduced, direct attention to the Vocabulary box. Read the definition several times to help the students remember it. Stress that we can always trust and depend on God.

Reviewing the Doctrine

Read with the class the We Believe statement. Explain that we can begin to understand something about trusting God from the people in our lives whom we love, trust, and depend on. Emphasize the importance of learning the We Believe statements throughout the year.

Step 3/CONCLUSION

Learning How to Live Our Faith

Identifying Fears

Ask the students to name an antonym (a word that means the opposite of) for the word *trust.* (*Possible answers include* doubt *and* fear.) Invite the students to think of times when they experienced doubt or fear. Ask for volunteers to share their experiences and to tell how God could help them to face or overcome these feelings.

Praying Together

Have the students identify the people in their lives who help them know and understand that they can trust God. After each name is offered, have the students respond, "Loving Father, thank you for giving us these signs of your love."

Objective

This lesson helps the students learn Jesus' teachings about the Father's care for us.

Step 1/INTRODUCTION

Learning About Our Lives

Talking About Experiences

Invite the students to describe a time when they needed to be reassured that someone loved and cared for them. Help the students understand that although loving and caring words and actions do not always solve a problem or make it go away they are a source of help and support to us as we experience difficulties in life.

or...

Suggest that the students talk about an experience in which they were called on to reassure a friend or sibling that they valued, loved, or cared about this person.

Step 2/DEVELOPMENT

Learning About Our Faith

Reading a Scripture Story

Direct attention to the Vocabulary box on page 65. Read the definition to the class. Tell the students that in today's Scripture story Jesus teaches that God is always faithful and is always with us. Ask volunteers to take turns reading aloud "God Is Faithful" on pages 64 and 65 as the other students follow along in their texts.

God Is Faithful

One day, Jesus was talking to a large crowd of people. Many of the people had worries and fears. Some worried about money, about having enough food to eat, and about having decent clothes to wear. They wondered if God had forgotten them. Some even began to doubt that God really cared about them.

"Aren't five sparrows sold for just a few pennies?" Jesus asked. "Yet not one of them is forgotten by God. You are worth more than a flock of sparrows!" The people began to feel better as Jesus talked.

Then Jesus pointed to some birds flying above the trees. "Look at the birds," Jesus told them. "God feeds them. God cares for every one of them. How much more important to God are you than the birds! God will never forget you. God is totally **faithful**."

64 Scripture

Focus on

The Selling of Sparrows It was common at the time Jesus lived to sell sparrows (or other small birds) in the marketplace. Since the birds were sold for a very small sum of money, people who were poor could buy them for food. Jesus refers to the sparrows in the Scripture story from Luke as a symbol of something that has relatively little value and yet is cared for and provided for by God.

Enriching the Lesson

Bring into class pictures, slides, or videos that illustrate the beauty of God's creation. Have the students describe places they have been where they could see the beauty of nature. Then read the Scripture story beginning on page 64.

Then Jesus pointed to the flowers that covered the hills. "Look at the lilies," he told the crowd. "If the Father clothes them in such beauty, how much more will he care for you? Stop worrying. Do not be afraid. Trust that God loves you."

Based on Luke 12

Activity

One way to show that we trust God is to bring our concerns and our fears to the Father in prayer. Think about the last time you prayed to God when you were concerned or afraid. Write a prayer to thank God for being faithful to you. Or list some concerns or fears that you could bring to God the next time you pray.

_____

_____

_____

Vocabulary

faithful: someone who is always with us and always caring; someone who is to be trusted and depended upon

★ ★ ★ ★ ★ ★ ★ ★ ★ ★ ★

Scripture 65

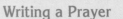
Discussing the Story

Use the following questions to guide discussion.

■ According to Jesus, how does God care for creation? (*By feeding the birds and clothing the lilies*)

■ How does God show care for you? (*Answers will vary.*)

■ What does Jesus encourage the crowd to do in this story? (*To stop worrying and put their trust in God*)

■ How do you think the people felt when they heard these words of Jesus? (*Answers will vary.*)

Help the students understand why Jesus told this story. Emphasize that Jesus wanted his followers to know that God will never forget about any one of us, even for a moment. Stress that Jesus was reassuring his followers of God's love and faithfulness.

Step 3/CONCLUSION

Learning How to Live Our Faith

Writing a Prayer

Read the directions for the activity on page 65 and have the students complete the activity independently. As the students work, move about the room, offering suggestions and helping with spelling.

Praying Together

Gather the students around you and invite volunteers to read aloud the thanksgiving prayers that they wrote. Conclude the lesson by praying, "God, you are our Creator. We trust you because we believe that you take care of us and that you are always faithful to us. Amen."

Objective

This lesson helps the students understand that we can get to know God more fully in the three Persons of the Trinity.

Step 1/INTRODUCTION

Learning About Our Lives

Reviewing What it Means to Be Holy

Recall with the class the definition of the word *holy,* which the students learned in Chapter 2. Elicit from them that being holy means being close to God, loving God and others, and doing his work in the world. Invite them to name various ways they can grow closer to God. Lead them to recognize that prayer, sharing our time and possessions with others, and helping others are all ways of growing closer to God.

Step 2/DEVELOPMENT

Learning About Our Faith

Decoding a Scripture Passage

Introduce the puzzle activity by reading aloud the first two sentences of "Calling God 'Our Father'" on page 66. Emphasize that Jesus invites all people to live as children of God. Then direct the students to decode the Scripture verse. Afterward, have the students use Bibles to check their answers. Then invite them to read aloud together the correct solution to the puzzle.

Calling God "Our Father"

Jesus taught us that when we pray, we can come to God as children and call God "Father," just as Jesus did. We believe that God loves and knows each of us, just as a mother and a father love and know their own children. Decode the Bible words below (Matthew 6:8b) to discover one more thing Jesus taught about God, our Father.

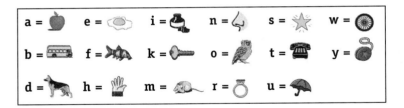

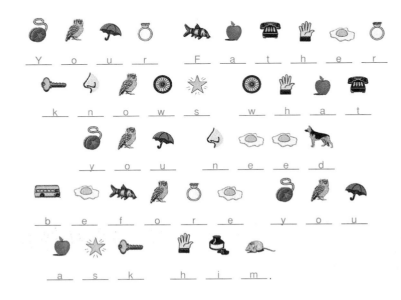

Your Father knows what you need before you ask him.

Cultural Awareness

Often people who speak more than one language express the fact that it is more meaningful to them to pray in their first language. If there are students in your class whose first language is not English, try to provide opportunities for them to pray the prayers in their native language. You may wish to give students whose first language is English a chance to learn a prayer in another language by having them learn the Sign of the Cross in Spanish (see page 2 of the pupil text).

Getting to Know Who God Is

We know that Jesus was very close to God, his Father. Jesus often reminded the people he taught that they could be close to God, too. Jesus promised to send the Holy Spirit to be with us always and to guide and teach us. Whenever we make the Sign of the Cross, we remember that we know God as three distinct Persons: God the Father, God the Son, and God the Holy Spirit. We call this one God in three Persons the **Trinity**.

Jesus told his friends, "I still have many things to tell you, but you will not understand them now. When the Holy Spirit comes, the Spirit will guide you and help you understand." (Based on John 16:12–13). Getting to know God more fully, through the three Persons of the Trinity, will take time. We will grow closer to God as we come to know God as Father, Son, and Holy Spirit.

Vocabulary

Trinity: the one God whom we know as three distinct Persons: God the Father, God the Son, and God the Holy Spirit

★ ★ ★ ★ ★ ★ ★ ★ ★ ★ ★ ★

Activity

Write a story or draw a picture of something you can do to grow closer to God.

Doctrine 67

Focus on

The Almighty God Students may be curious as to how God can know what we need before we ask. Explain that through Jesus' teachings and the experiences of God's people since creation, people came to believe that God knows and sees all things. We sum up these beliefs by saying that God is *almighty*. God can do all things. God created everything.

Enriching the Lesson

Have the students make Trinity mobiles, using yarn, tag board, hole punchers, and crayons. Give the students 15" dowels or cardboard rolls. Have them use tag board to make and decorate a symbol for each person in the Trinity. Demonstrate how to punch a hole in the symbols, thread yarn through each, and tie the symbols to the dowel.

Learning About the Trinity

Read with the class "Getting to Know Who God Is" on page 67. Discuss the reading by asking the following questions.

- Whom did Jesus promise to send to be with us always? (*The Holy Spirit*)
- What do we call the one God in three Persons? (*The Trinity*)
- Who are the three Persons of God? (*God the Father, God the Son, and God the Holy Spirit*)
- Who is God the Son? (*Jesus*)
- What did Jesus say the Holy Spirit would do? (*Guide Jesus' friends and help them understand the things Jesus wanted to tell them*)

Learning the Vocabulary

Point out the Vocabulary box on page 67 and have the students learn the definition of the word *Trinity*. Emphasize that understanding how God can be three persons and still be one God is difficult. Explain that we know God the Father as Creator; we know Jesus as God the Son, our Savior; and we have learned that God the Holy Spirit is our helper and guide.

Step 3/CONCLUSION

Learning How to Live Our Faith

Completing an Activity

Explain the directions for the activity. Allow time for the students to complete the activity. Afterward, invite volunteers to share their creations with the group.

Praying the Sign of the Cross

Conclude the lesson by having the students think quietly about the Trinity. Then invite them to name the persons in the Trinity as they prayerfully make the Sign of the Cross.

DAY 4
DOCTRINE/MORALITY

Objective
This lesson helps the students desire to imitate God's faithfulness.

Step 1/INTRODUCTION

Learning About Our Lives

Recalling God's Faithfulness
To recall what the students have learned about God's faithfulness, ask them to define the words *faithful* (someone who is always with us and always caring; someone who is to be trusted and depended upon) and *trust* (to have faith in God's love for us and to believe that he is always with us). Recall the story of Maria and her mother and how Maria feared that she could not always depend on her mother. Ask a volunteer to retell the Scripture story from Day 2. Recall the images of faithfulness that Jesus used in the story (lilies blooming, birds feeding).

Step 2/DEVELOPMENT

Learning About Our Faith

Reading About God's Faithfulness
Have several students take turns reading aloud "Faithful in Many Ways" on page 68. Use the following questions to guide discussion.

- How are we faithful to God? (*When we trust that God is with us and caring for us*)

- Where do we see God's faithfulness? (*In the care of our families and friends*)

- What do we believe about God when we remember all the ways that people have cared for us? (*That God was caring for us through these special people*)

- Through whom does God care for us? (*Friends, families, teachers, pastors, parish leaders, and even people we do not know*)

Faithful in Many Ways

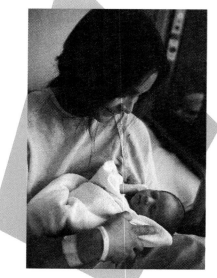

We are called to believe that God is faithful to us. *We* are faithful when we trust that God is with us and caring for us wherever we are. We can see God's faithfulness to us in the care that our families and friends show us.

When we were babies, people who loved and cared for us helped us to do many things we could not do for ourselves. They fed us, bathed us, and dressed us. When we remember all the ways that our mothers and fathers, our aunts and uncles, our grandparents, godparents, and others cared for us, we believe that God was caring for us through these special people in our lives.

As children we have often known God's love in the kind actions and words of our friends. Whenever someone has helped us or cared for us in any way, God was caring for us. God cares for us through our friends, our families, our teachers, our pastors, and our parish leaders. God can even care for us through someone we do not know. For example, families sometimes lose everything they have in a fire, a hurricane, or another kind of disaster. People whom these families do not know—people from all over the world—may send them food, clothing, and money.

68 Doctrine

CURRICULUM CONNECTION

Social Studies You may wish to have the students put together their own family history albums to help them understand how members of their families have cared for them. Have the students interview their parents, grandparents, older siblings, or other relatives who cared for the students when they were younger. The students can then write about or draw pictures of these experiences. Encourage them to bring pictures from home that show them as babies or as small children.

We Are Faithful, Too!

Just as we can know God's faithfulness through the kindness of others, others can know God's faithfulness through *our* kindness. One way we can show that we are thankful to God for being faithful to us is by our kind words and actions toward others. When we live as God wants us to live and help others to see his love, we can all grow closer to him. The way we speak and act toward others is an important part of our relationship with God. We can also show that we are faithful by praying and by celebrating the Eucharist.

Activity

Write sentences below to tell about some ways that you can be a faithful person. Begin each sentence with a different letter of the word *faithful*. Some sentences have been done for you.

F eed a hungry person. _____

A _____

I _____

T _____

H elp a friend. _____

F _____

U _____

L _____

Reading About Our Own Faithfulness

Read through "We Are Faithful, Too!" on page 69 with the class. Emphasize that Jesus showed his faithfulness to his Father by doing what God asked of him. Tell the students that they, too, can show their faithfulness by living as God asks. Ask the students to explain how they are being faithful when they are doing the following things. Invite them to suggest additional ways of being faithful.

- Telling the truth.
- Praying for the homeless.
- Helping with chores at home.
- Picking up trash in the park.

Step 3/CONCLUSION

Learning How to Live Our Faith

Completing a Word Gram

Read the directions for the activity on page 69. Have the students work in small groups to complete this activity. When finished, invite one member from each group to read aloud their list. Praise the students for their creativity in thinking of the different ways that they can be faithful and caring. Emphasize how important their cooperation was in this effort.

CURRICULUM CONNECTION

Language Arts Suggest to the students that in completing the activity on page 69 they may want to try to create a poem with rhyming lines. Once they have written the sentences beginning with each letter of *faithful*, they can reword the idea of the sentence so that it has some poetic rhythm and rhymes with the line before or after it. Sometimes this works better when two students exchange their work and edit each other's sentences.

Enriching the Lesson

Have the students work in the same small groups with which they prepared the word grams, now to create "faithfulness skits." In the skits, have them show third graders responding to a situation with kind words and actions. Suggest they use one of the ideas from their word grams. After allowing time for practice, have the groups perform their skits for the class.

PRAYER/REVIEW

Objective

This lesson helps the students celebrate their learning about God's faithfulness.

Completing an Activity

Read aloud the directions at the top of page 70 and the quotation from Isaiah at the bottom of the page. Help students as they independently fill in names. Then encourage the students to decorate the banner.

Preparing for Prayer

Direct attention to the sign-language diagrams on page 70. Demonstrate each gesture, one at a time. Encourage the students to imitate each gesture as they recite the word it represents. Practice several times with the students until they are able to pray and gesture with ease.

If your students have difficulty with the sign-language gestures, you may wish to simplify the signing by using only two or three of the gestures.

Select a volunteer to read aloud the Scripture story from Day 2 as part of your prayer service.

Make a poster titled "God Is Faithful." In the center of the poster, draw a triangle to represent the Trinity. Label the corners *God the Father, God the Son,* and *God the Holy Spirit.* Have the students cut small hearts from art paper and write their names on them.

Praying Together

Begin the prayer service with the Sign of the Cross. Follow with the reading of the Scripture from Day 2. Then call the students forward to tape their paper hearts to the poster. Tell them that this is one way to show God that they trust in his love for them. Remind them that they can know this love through the three Persons of the Trinity. Conclude by leading the students in the prayer using the gestures they have learned.

Praying with Sign Language

Read the words from Isaiah 49. They remind us of God's faithfulness to us. On one of the hands in the picture, write your name. Remember that God will never forget *you!* On the other hand, write the name of someone you love and trust. Thank God for that person. Then pray the prayer below, using sign language, to express your trust in God.

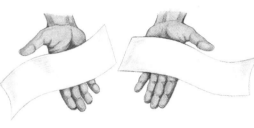

"I will not forget you...I have written your name on the palms of my hands"
Isaiah 49:15:76

God

I place

Leader: When I am lonely or afraid,

All: God, I place my life in your hands.

Leader: When I am worried or upset,

All: God, I place my life in your hands.

Leader: When I am happy or excited,

All: God, I place my life in your hands.

Leader: God, we trust in your goodness and love. We thank you in the name of Jesus.

All: Amen.

my   life   in your   hands

Teaching Tips

As you prepare to teach the sign-language gestures to your students, you may find it helpful to practice in front of a mirror to check yourself for accuracy. Learn each sign separately, then put the signs together with the words. Practice several times until you can perform the gestures confidently and without looking at the book. Also, be aware that the sign-language diagrams shown in the pupil text are drawn as mirror images. In other words, match your motions to those made in the drawings as if you were looking at them in a mirror.

CURRICULUM CONNECTION

Music Look through resources you have available in your parish and school to find hymns about the Trinity that would be suitable for use in the prayer celebrations of this unit. Possible selections might include: "Father, We Adore You," by Terrye Coelho (Maranatha! Music); "All Praise and Glad Thanksgiving," by Melvin Farrell, SS (OCP); "Praise God, From Whom All Blessings Flow," by Thomas Ken and Louis Bourgeois (OCP); "Our God Is a God of Love," by Carey Landry (NALR).

Chapter Review

CHAPTER REVIEW

Unscramble the word that follows each sentence. Then use the words to complete the sentences.

1. Jesus taught us that God will _____always_____ be with us.

   lwasay

2. As Catholics, we believe that God is _____faithful_____.

   luifathf

3. We can come to God as children and call God _____Father_____.

   erFtha

4. We can ___trust___ that God will always love us and be with us.

   ustrt

5. The _____Trinity_____ is one God in three Persons.

   yintrTi

Fill in the answers to the first two questions.

1. What does *faithful* mean? _Someone who is_ _faithful is always with us and always caring. The_ _word *faithful* also describes someone we can trust_ _and depend upon._

2. Why did Jesus tell the story of the birds and lilies? _to remind us that God, our Father, takes_ _care of us and is always faithful to us_

God says, "Can a mother forget her baby or not care about her child? I will never forget you."
Based on Isaiah 49:15

3. Talk about ways we can show our faith in God.

Unscrambling Words

Explain the directions for the scramble activity on page 71. Have the students complete it independently. When all have finished, check the students' answers by having them read aloud the sentences together.

Summarizing the Chapter

Direct the students' attention to the next two questions. Have the students write their answers to each question on the lines provided in the text. Afterward, invite volunteers to read aloud their responses. Answer any questions the students may have about what they have learned in Chapter 5. Encourage everyone to participate in the discussion of the third question.

Praying with the Scriptural Verse

With the class, read aloud the verse from Scripture at the bottom of the page. Discuss some ways a mother is faithful to her baby or her child.

Help the students understand and appreciate that God loves and cares for us and will never abandon or forget us. Invite the students to ask God to comfort anyone who feels abandoned or forgotten.

Enriching the Lesson

Ask the students to write letters to God indicating how they will be faithful to another person for a specific period of time agreed upon by the class. Have them seal the letters in envelopes with their names written on the outside. Then collect the envelopes. At the end of the time period, return the envelopes. Have the students reread their promises and consider their own faithfulness.

6 Our Church Believes in Jesus Christ

Objectives

To help the students

- Explore a story of friendship from the Old Testament.
- Understand the ways Jesus shows he is our friend.
- Learn what it means to be a true friend and follower of Jesus.
- Identify different ways of getting to know Jesus.
- Meditate with the Jesus prayer and review the chapter.

Chapter Outline

	Step 1 Learning About Our Lives	**Step 2** Learning About Our Faith	**Step 3** Learning How to Live Our Faith
Day 1	■ Introduce the chapter. ■ Discuss the poem. *ABOUT 12 MINUTES*	■ Read a Scripture story. ■ Discuss the questions. *ABOUT 10 MINUTES*	■ Write about growing in friendship. *ABOUT 8 MINUTES*
Day 2	■ Talk about loss. *ABOUT 5 MINUTES*	■ Read and discuss a story. ■ Learn about Jesus. ■ Review the vocabulary and doctrine. *ABOUT 10 MINUTES*	■ Respond to Jesus' invitation. *ABOUT 15 MINUTES*
Day 3	■ Write a dialogue. *ABOUT 10 MINUTES*	■ Read about Jesus' example. *ABOUT 12 MINUTES*	■ Complete a checklist. ■ Pray together. *ABOUT 8 MINUTES*
Day 4	■ Write about friendship. *ABOUT 10 MINUTES*	■ Read and discuss the text. *ABOUT 10 MINUTES*	■ Write about Jesus. *ABOUT 10 MINUTES*

Day 5   **Prayer**   Learn the Jesus prayer; prepare for prayer; pray the Jesus prayer.
                Review   Complete a crossword puzzle; answer the review questions; pray with the scriptural verse.

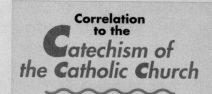
Plan Ahead ～～～～～～

	Preparing Your Class	**Materials Needed**	**Additional Resources**
Day 1	Read through the lesson plan for this class session. Think about things best friends do for one another.	■ chalkboard ■ writing paper ■ pencils or pens	As you plan this chapter, consider using the following materials from The Resourceful Teacher Package. ■ *Classroom Activity Sheets 6 and 6a* ■ *Family Activity Sheets 6 and 6a* ■ *Chapter 6 Test* ■ *Prayers for Every Day* ■ *Projects: Grade 3*
Day 2	Read through the lesson plan for this class session.	■ writing paper ■ pencils or pens	
Day 3	Read through the lesson plan for this class session. Consider possible dialogue for the Step 1 activity.	■ pencils or pens	You may also wish to refer to the following Big Book. ■ *We Celebrate God's Word,* pages 10, 12, and 19
Day 4	Read through the lesson plan for this class session. Be prepared to talk about your friendship with Jesus in Step 3.	■ writing paper ■ pencils or pens	In preparing the students for the Sunday readings, you may wish to use Silver Burdett Ginn's *Getting Ready for Sunday* student and teacher materials.
Day 5	Choose a prayer environment in which to conduct the meditation. Practice reading the Jesus prayer on page 80.	■ table with Bible and candle ■ pencils or pens	

BOOKS FOR THE JOURNEY

A Bridge to Terebithia. Katherine Paterson. HarperCollins, 1987. A story about a special friendship between two children.

The Fishermen's Surprise. Alyce Bergey. Concordia, 1967. A poetic version of the Scripture story in which Jesus and his apostles enjoy breakfast together on the beach.

MORE BOOKS FOR THE JOURNEY

The Golden Carp. Lynette Dyer Vuong. Lothrop, Lee & Shepard, 1993. "A Friend's Affection," pp. 13–28. A story of someone who thinks he is betrayed but in the end discovers how faithful and loyal his friend really is.

The Trip. Ezra Jack Keats. Greenwillow Books, 1978. A child moves with his family, misses his friends, imagines he's back with them, and then is able to make new friends.

REDUCED CLASSROOM ACTIVITIES

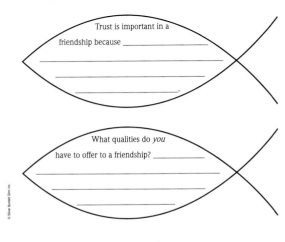

NAME _____

OUR CHURCH BELIEVES IN JESUS CHRIST

Having Jesus as our best friend means we can always trust him. In the early days of the Church, friends of Jesus used a secret symbol to identify themselves. This symbol helped them to communicate with one another and to recognize those they could trust. The symbol was that of a fish, which stood for Jesus.

On the lines below, describe why trust is an important quality in a friendship.

Trust is important in a friendship because _____
_____
_____.

What qualities do *you* have to offer to a friendship? _____
_____
_____

To the Teacher: This activity can be used to reinforce the concepts presented in Chapter 6.

Chapter 6 Our Church Believes in Jesus Christ   THIS IS OUR FAITH 3 **6**

NAME _____

JESUS TEACHES US ABOUT FRIENDSHIP

Finish the letter to a friend on the lines below. Decorate the border around the letter. Then fill in the two envelope labels. Cut out the labels and glue them to an envelope. Have someone in your family help you address the envelope.

Dear _____,

Today in Religion class we talked about how Jesus is our friend.

Jesus is very special to me because _____.

You are a special friend too because _____
_____.

Love,

_____

From:

To:
_____
_____

To the Teacher: This activity will draw on the students' experiences of friendship to deepen their understanding of their friendship with Jesus. Decide whether you or the families will mail the letters.

6a THIS IS OUR FAITH 3   **Chapter 6** Our Church Believes in Jesus Christ

71c Chapter Organizer

THE FRIENDS OF JESUS

We know from the Gospels that friendship was an important part of Jesus' life. We think of people who were friends of Jesus, such as Lazarus, Mary and Martha, Peter and John. Jesus drew to himself many followers, both men and women, with whom he sustained friendships.

Some of Jesus' friends were with him from the start of his ministry in Galilee to its earthly culmination at Calvary. Among his most faithful followers, some of the women became the first witnesses to his resurrection. Jesus' most faithful followers also included men. The twelve apostles had a special friendship with Jesus. They were chosen by Jesus to guide the early Church. At the Last Supper, Jesus repeatedly called his apostles his friends. Among the twelve, Peter, James, and John seem to have been especially close to Jesus. Jesus also embraced the children of his time, even when other adults would have kept them at a comfortable distance. (See Mark 10:13–16.)

OUR FRIENDSHIP WITH JESUS

The creeds of the Church do not speak of Jesus in terms of friendship with us. However, for the third grader, friendship with Jesus is the starting point for one's relationship with the Father and for beginning to sense the possibility of closeness with our transcendent God.

This chapter helps the students focus on the idea that at the center of a life of faith is a relationship, or friendship, with Jesus. An understanding of our human friendships can lead to a better understanding of how we can be friends with Jesus. Thinking about our relationships with others can help us appreciate Jesus and what he can mean in our lives.

The *National Catechetical Directory* says: "Because people are capable of continual development, so are their relationships with God. Essentially, development in faith is the process by which one's relationship with the Father becomes more like Jesus': it means becoming more Christlike." (#173)

Objective

This lesson helps the students explore a story of friendship from the Old Testament.

Step 1/INTRODUCTION

Learning About Our Lives

Introducing the Chapter

Ask a volunteer to read aloud the chapter-focus questions on page 72. Discuss each question separately. Help the students understand and appreciate that the way a person treats us, responds to us, and speaks with us indicates whether or not that person is a friend. Use the students' responses to the second question to make a list on the chalkboard of the things best friends do for one another. Tell the class that in this chapter Jesus invites us to enjoy friendship with him.

Discussing the Poem

Ask two students to read the poem on page 72, alternating lines. Ask the following questions.

■ What do you like about the poem? (*Answers will vary.*)

■ What does the poem tell you about friendship? (*That it means enjoying, sharing, and trusting each other*)

■ What does it mean to trust someone? (*Answers will vary.*)

or...

Ask the students to work in small groups to create "friendship want ads." In their ads, have the students list desirable qualities they look for in friends as well as qualities they have to offer to friendships.

6 Our Church Believes in Jesus Christ

How can you know that someone is your friend? What do you and your best friend do for each other?

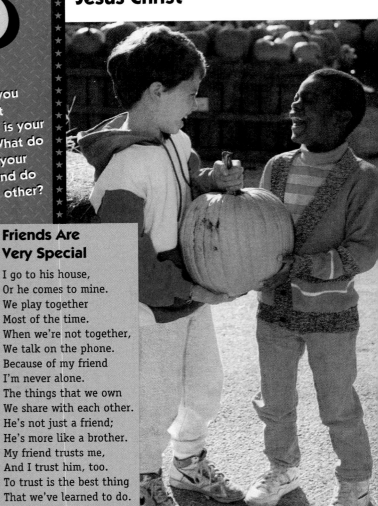

Friends Are Very Special

I go to his house,
Or he comes to mine.
We play together
Most of the time.
When we're not together,
We talk on the phone.
Because of my friend
I'm never alone.
The things that we own
We share with each other.
He's not just a friend;
He's more like a brother.
My friend trusts me,
And I trust him, too.
To trust is the best thing
That we've learned to do.

72 Scripture

🍎 Teaching Tips

As children grow, their concept of friendship usually undergoes a number of changes. In Kindergarten, anyone who plays with them or is in their class is their friend. By second grade, children begin to identify fewer people as their friends, depending on what they do together. In grade three, groups begin to be more exclusive. Boys and girls seldom mix, and children look for things in common with their friends. Ask the students to list the names of their friends now and when they were in Kindergarten. Compare lists and discuss.

Friends Forever

David was a young shepherd boy who believed he could fight the Philistine giant named Goliath and win! Goliath had insulted David's people, the Israelites. David's people were frightened. But David had so much faith and trust in God that he asked King Saul to let him fight Goliath all by himself.

Using only a slingshot, David killed Goliath. Saul was very impressed. Saul took David into his home as his own son. Saul's son Jonathan became David's best friend. Jonathan and David grew to love each other as brothers.

Saul asked David to lead many battles, and David won them all. This made Saul very happy, but only for a short time. David became very popular with the people. This made Saul jealous and angry. Saul wanted to destroy David, so he sent him into battle after battle, hoping that David would be killed. But David always won because the Lord was with him.

One day, Saul told Jonathan of his plan to kill David. Jonathan warned David about Saul's plans. Jonathan and David made secret plans to keep David safe.

Soon the day came when Saul planned to kill David. David knew that he had to leave. Jonathan and David were very sad, but they knew that they would keep their promise to be friends forever.

Based on 1 Samuel 17–20

Discuss

1. What helped David to be so brave in his battle with Goliath?

2. How did Jonathan help save David's life?

3. In what ways have you shown that you trusted a friend?

CURRICULUM CONNECTION

Art Distribute drawing paper and crayons. Have the students draw Jonathan and David's story in four scenes: David defeating Goliath; David and Jonathan in Saul's house; Jonathan warning David about Saul's plan; David and Jonathan saying goodbye. Have the students caption their stories by completing this sentence: "Jonathan and David were good friends because . . . ."

Enriching the Lesson

Students may be interested in learning more about the story of Jonathan and David and their plan to protect David from Saul. If time permits, read more details about this plan in 1 Samuel 20:11–42.

Step 2/DEVELOPMENT

Learning About Our Faith

Reading a Scripture Story

Introduce the story by telling the students that they are going to read a story from the Old Testament, the first part of the Bible. Explain that in this part of the Bible we learn about the wonderful things God did for people before Jesus was born. Then read with the class "Friends Forever" on page 73.

Discussing the Questions

Have the students answer the questions at the bottom of page 73. In discussing the first question, help the students recognize that David was victorious because he put his faith and trust in God. Ask the students what they think would have happened to Jonathan if Saul had learned of Jonathan and David's plan to keep David safe. In discussing the last question, encourage the students to give examples of times they placed their trust in a close friend.

Step 3/CONCLUSION

Learning How to Live Our Faith

Writing About Growing in Friendship

Distribute writing paper and ask the students to think quietly about the friendship between Jonathan and David. Then ask them what they can learn from Jonathan and David about being a friend. Direct the students to write two things each of them can do to be a better friend. Afterward, have them read aloud their responses.

73

DAY 2
SCRIPTURE/DOCTRINE

Objective

This lesson helps the students understand the ways Jesus shows he is our friend.

Step 1/INTRODUCTION

Learning About Our Lives

Talking About Loss

Recall with the students their discussion of friendship on Day 1. Explore the students' experiences of losing a close friend by asking the following questions.

- Have you ever had to say goodbye to a friend who was moving away or transferring to another school?

- Have you ever lost a friend because of an argument?

- How did you feel when these things happened?

- Are you still friends with the person who moved away? How do you stay in touch?

- Have you ever made up with a friend with whom you argued? How did you feel when you became friends again?

Step 2/DEVELOPMENT

Learning About Our Faith

Reading and Discussing a Story

Introduce the Scripture story on pages 74 and 75 by telling the class that it took place shortly after the death and resurrection of Jesus. Some of Jesus' followers were fishing. They were sad about losing their friend Jesus. Ask volunteers to read aloud "Jesus and His Friends." Review the story by asking the following questions.

- Who is standing on the shore? (*Jesus*)

- How did Peter get to the shore? (*He jumped into the lake and swam to shore.*)

- Why do you think Peter acted as he did? Would you have done the same as Peter? Why or why not? (*Answers will vary.*)

Jesus and His Friends

The sun was rising over the lake. Jesus' friends rowed their boat toward shore. They were sad. It was just a few days after Jesus' death. They really missed their friend Jesus.

"Did you catch any fish?" a man called out from the misty shore. "No," they answered.

"Throw the net over the right side of the boat," the man told them with great confidence.

They dropped the net into the dark waters. It filled with fish. Then John recognized the man on the shore. "It is the Lord!" he shouted.

Peter, one of the twelve apostles, was so excited to see Jesus that he dove in and swam ashore. John and the others rowed the boat in with the net full of fish. They, too, were eager to be with Jesus again.

As they secured the boat, they saw a charcoal fire with some fish on it and bread.

74 Scripture

Teaching Tips

Third graders may wonder how Jesus rose from the dead or if he looked different after the resurrection. While it is difficult to fully explain this concept, you can note that the Gospels tell us the disciples recognized Jesus when they saw him. Even in the story about the two disciples on the road to Emmaus, the disciples eventually recognize who Jesus is, if not by his appearance then by his actions. What is most important for the students to believe is that Jesus rose from the dead and was with his friends again.

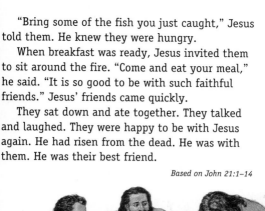

"Bring some of the fish you just caught," Jesus told them. He knew they were hungry.

When breakfast was ready, Jesus invited them to sit around the fire. "Come and eat your meal," he said. "It is so good to be with such faithful friends." Jesus' friends came quickly.

They sat down and ate together. They talked and laughed. They were happy to be with Jesus again. He had risen from the dead. He was with them. He was their best friend.

Based on John 21:1–14

Jesus, the Son of God

The apostles loved Jesus very much. He had done so much for them. He was their friend and their teacher. He loved them and taught them to love one another. Before Jesus suffered and died for them, he promised to be with them always and to send the Holy Spirit. After his **resurrection**, when he rose from death to new life, Jesus kept his promise.

Jesus, the Son of God, is always with us, too. He is our best friend, and he loves us very much. He shares in our sadness and our joys. Jesus gives us himself in the Eucharist. He teaches us how to live and how to love.

Vocabulary

resurrection: Jesus' rising from death to new life

★ ★ ★ ★ ★ ★ ★ ★ ★ ★ ★ ★

We Believe

Jesus, the Son of God, is always with us. He rose from death to new life. He is our friend forever.

Doctrine 75

Learning About Jesus

Read through "Jesus, the Son of God" on page 75. Reinforce the importance of this section by rereading the last paragraph aloud together. Discuss what we mean when we say that Jesus "rose from death to new life." Help the students recall that Jesus died on the cross and was buried. On the third day, through the power of God's love, Jesus rose from the dead. Explain that at that time Jesus was given new life.

Reviewing the Vocabulary and Doctrine

Direct attention to the Vocabulary box on page 75. Stress that Jesus' resurrection made it possible for him to be alive and with us always. Then read aloud the We Believe statement. Encourage the students to remember these important words.

Step 3/CONCLUSION

Learning How to Live Our Faith

Responding to Jesus' Invitation

Discuss with the students how they act when people say they want to be friends with them. Ask the following question: *How can you respond to Jesus' invitation to friendship with him?* Then have the students work in small groups to compose letters telling Jesus that they want to be his friend and how they will show they are friends of Jesus.

Fishermen Among the very first apostles called by Jesus were men who were fishermen by profession. Peter, Andrew, James, and John all worked in this major industry in the area around the Sea of Galilee. Far from being simple laborers, they would have had to be accomplished businessmen in order to compete successfully with the many other fishing businesses in and around Galilee. Their intelligence and experience of hard work and endurance were great assets to them as they spread the teachings of Jesus after the resurrection.

CURRICULUM CONNECTION

Geography Tell the students that the Sea of Tiberias is properly known as the Sea of Galilee. Explain that a large city called Tiberias was built on the western shore of the Sea of Galilee. Some people called that side of the sea the Sea of Tiberias. Have the students turn to page 329 in their books and use their map skills to find the Sea of Galilee.

Objective

This lesson helps the students learn what it means to be a true friend and follower of Jesus.

Step 1/INTRODUCTION

Learning About Our Lives

Writing a Dialogue

Ask the students to examine the illustrations on page 76. Start in the upper left-hand panel and call on students to discuss the questions below with respect to each picture.

- What is happening in the picture?
- What do you believe the people are thinking?
- What words describe what the people in the picture appear to be feeling?

After discussing each picture, ask the students to write dialogue in each space. Afterward, allow time for sharing.

or...

Discuss why friends like to talk to one another. Ask volunteers to choose partners and come to the front of the room to act out brief dialogues that friends might have together. You may want to supply index cards on which you have written possible dialogue topics, such as a bad test score, a TV show, what to do after school, a school event, and so forth.

Activity

Look at the pictures. Write in each space what you think one friend is saying to the other.

76 Morality

Cultural Awareness

Note that the children pictured on page 76 are friends who are of various countries and races. Discuss how being friends with someone whose language or traditions are different from one's own can enrich the friendship. Stress that friendship does not depend on a person's color or race. Have the students discuss what they might learn from a friend who is from another culture. Help them appreciate that they might learn about another culture's food, customs, and celebrations.

Christian Friendship in Action

In John 15:14, Jesus says, "You are my friends if you do what I command you." We are called to be a friend to Jesus and to others. We can show others that we are friends of Jesus by trying to follow Jesus' example and teachings. To be the kind of friend that Jesus is, we can listen to our friends when they are sad and we can be happy when they are happy. When we share both our joys and our sadness with one another, we share Christian friendship.

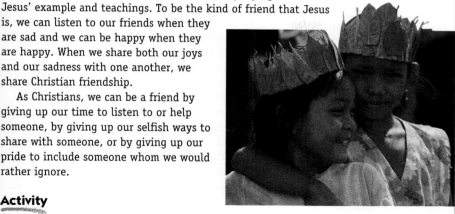

As Christians, we can be a friend by giving up our time to listen to or help someone, by giving up our selfish ways to share with someone, or by giving up our pride to include someone whom we would rather ignore.

Activity

When we follow Jesus' example of doing good things for others, we are reaching out in Christian friendship. Place an **X** beside each statement that shows what it means to be a true friend and follower of Jesus.

__X__ I can offer to rake leaves, mow the lawn, or shovel snow for my neighbors.

__X__ I can invite someone new to my house.

__X__ I can ask a new boy or girl to join our game.

_____ I can decide not to take time to comfort others when they are sad or hurting.

__X__ I can help someone with his or her work.

_____ I can ignore someone who wants to play in our game.

__X__ I can share my lunch or snack with someone who forgot to bring lunch or with someone who is hungry.

_____ I can walk away from people who need my help.

Focus on

Jesus as a Friend Jesus' calling his apostles friends (John 15:14) is but one of the references found in the New Testament regarding Jesus and friendship. In Matthew and Luke's Gospels, he was derided by the Pharisees as being a "friend of tax collectors and sinners." Jesus' special friendship with Lazarus, Mary, and Martha is depicted in John's Gospel, as is his affection for the "beloved disciple." In John 15:13, Jesus declares that the greatest love one can show is to give one's life for a friend.

Step 2/DEVELOPMENT

Learning About Our Faith

Reading About Jesus' Example

Call on volunteers to take turns reading aloud "Christian Friendship in Action" on page 77. Then ask these questions.

- How can we show others that we are friends of Jesus? (*By trying to follow Jesus' example and teaching*)

- How can we be the kind of friend that Jesus is? (*By listening to our friends when they are sad and by being happy when they are happy*)

- What are some other ways we can be a friend to others? (*By giving up our time, our selfish ways, and our pride*)

Explain to the students that *pride* means "thinking we are better than others or too important to spend time with others."

Step 3/CONCLUSION

Learning How to Live Our Faith

Completing a Checklist

Explain the directions to the activity on page 77 and have the students complete it independently. When all have finished, go through each item on the list with the class. Have the students raise their hands to indicate whether or not they checked the box you are discussing. Invite the students to give their reasons for checking or not checking each of the statements. Encourage the students to name other ways by which they can put their friendship with Jesus into action.

Praying Together

Invite the students to bow their heads as you pray, "Loving Jesus, help us to remember that you want to be our best friend. Help us, also, to learn how to be good friends to others. Amen."

Objective

This lesson helps the students identify different ways of getting to know Jesus.

Step 1/INTRODUCTION

Learning About Our Lives

Writing About Friendship

Ask the students to pretend that someone they like very much but have not seen for a long time is coming to visit them. It could be a relative who lives in a different city or a friend who has moved far away. Distribute writing paper and have the students write their answers to the following questions.

- Are you glad to see this person? Why?
- How do you show that you are happy to be with the person?
- What is special about your friendship with this person?

Then engage the students in a discussion about their answers to the three questions. Encourage everyone to participate by sharing about a special friend.

or . . .

Have the students "introduce" their best friends to the rest of the class as if this person were present. Have them stand in turn and say, "I would like you to meet my friend _____." Have each student tell one or two facts about the friend and something that the two like to do together.

Step 2/DEVELOPMENT

Learning About Our Faith

Reading and Discussing the Text

Read "Getting to Know Jesus" on page 78 with the class. Then direct attention to the Discuss questions on page 79. Help the students appreciate that the different ways they can learn about Jesus include reading Bible stories about him and listening to other people talk about him. In discussing the second question, emphasize that knowing Jesus as a personal friend means being close to Jesus. As you

Getting to Know Jesus

When we think about our closest friends, we often think about the time we spend together and the fun things we do. We talk to some of them on the telephone. We write letters to friends who live far away. We tell our best friends what is happening in our lives and how we feel about things. And if we were introducing our best friend to someone for the first time, we would have so many wonderful things to say.

Some people know many things about Jesus because they have read Bible stories about him. Or they may have heard other people talk about Jesus. Christians often talk to Jesus when they pray. Christians believe that Jesus is with them all the time. Christians know that to follow Jesus means not only to act like Jesus but also to walk with Jesus every day of their lives. Christians know Jesus as a close friend who is faithful to them.

Jesus said, "I am the way and the truth and the life. No one comes to the Father except through me. If you know me, then you will also know my Father" (John 14:6–7). We can grow closer to God by growing closer to Jesus. And we can grow closer to Jesus by sharing in a special friendship with him.

78   Doctrine

CURRICULUM CONNECTION

Language Arts Invite the students to work with you to create a class poem about Jesus as their friend. If the students have a hard time finding rhymes, use a haiku format—an unrhymed three-line verse which originated in Japan. The three lines are composed of 5, 7, and 5 syllables respectively. The first line might be "My best friend, Jesus."

Discuss

1. What are some ways that we can learn about Jesus, our friend?

2. What do you think it means to follow Jesus?

3. How can knowing Jesus as a friend help us to pray?

Activity

Jesus is our friend. Good friends know each other. They like to be together and talk together.

We can get to know Jesus better as we read or listen to the Scriptures. We can also listen to Jesus speak to us when we pray. We also share with Jesus our own joys and concerns. What do you know and like about Jesus?

WALKING WITH JESUS

What I like most about Jesus is _____.

My favorite story about Jesus is _____.

The words of Jesus I like best are _____.

When I am with Jesus, I can pray the words _____.

Doctrine   79

discuss the third question, lead the students to recognize that when we pray to Jesus as a personal friend, we can share our real feelings, sorrows, joys, hopes, and experiences, just as we would with a best friend. Emphasize that we can talk to Jesus using our own words and that Jesus understands and listens to us as carefully as a best friend does.

Step 3/CONCLUSION

Learning How to Live Our Faith

Writing About Jesus

Ask a volunteer to read the introduction and directions for the activity on page 79. Emphasize that there are no right or wrong answers to the questions. Rather, this exercise is designed to help the students think about their friendships with Jesus. Invite the students to share their written responses to each question.

Objective

This lesson helps the students meditate with the Jesus prayer.

Learning the Jesus Prayer

Read "Praying the Jesus Prayer" on page 80 with the class to familiarize the students with this method of meditation. Explain to the class that during the prayer service you will read the directions to them as they meditate on the Jesus prayer with their eyes closed.

Preparing for Prayer

Plan to meditate with the students in a large carpeted area. Consider using the church sanctuary or perhaps one of the parish meeting rooms for your prayer. Invite the students to sit cross-legged or to stretch out on the floor. Have them sit an arms' distance from their closest neighbor. This enables each of them to have his or her own space.

As preparation for the Jesus meditation, retell the story "Jesus and His Friends" from Day 2.

You might also use the Scripture used on Day 3 (John 15) or the verse from Day 4 (John 14).

Praying the Jesus Prayer

Lead the students through the Jesus prayer meditation, speaking softly and slowly.

Conclude the prayer by asking the students to open their eyes and having them repeat after you the prayer at the bottom of page 80.

80   Prayer

Praying the Jesus Prayer

The Jesus Prayer is a prayer of meditation. In a prayer of meditation, we think about and pay very close attention to someone or something. In the Jesus Prayer, we think about Jesus, believing that he is with us. We will say the name Jesus several times to help us leave all our other thoughts and feelings behind so that we can think for a few moments only about Jesus. We will pray with our hearts and our minds. The only word we will say is the name Jesus. Let us begin to pray.

Sit quietly. Choose a place in the classroom to focus on during this prayer. Or you may close your eyes if this helps. Place your hands in your lap, with your palms facing up. Think about Jesus placing his hands in yours and asking you to walk closely beside him. Think about the love that you feel for Jesus. Think about the love that Jesus wants to show you.

Breathe slowly and deeply. Be aware of each breath you take. As you inhale, feel Jesus' love coming into your heart. As you exhale, softly say the name Jesus. Inhale again. Then exhale. Know that Jesus is with you.

As you continue to breathe slowly and deeply, silently answer these questions. *Who is Jesus? What do I believe about Jesus? How do I feel about my friendship with Jesus?*

End your prayer by saying, "Jesus, thank you for being my friend. Amen."

Focus on

Forms of Prayer   Help the students understand that there are many forms of prayer. Most of the students are familiar with formal prayers like the Our Father and the Hail Mary, which are traditional prayers taken from Scripture and passed on through the centuries. Other forms of prayer such as petitions, blessings, and prayers of thanksgiving are spoken or sung on particular occasions. Repetitive prayers like the Rosary and quiet meditative prayer are meant to help us focus our thoughts on God and listen for the inspiration of the Holy Spirit.

CURRICULUM CONNECTION

Music   You may wish to play recorded instrumental music softly in the background to help set the atmosphere for the meditation. Appropriate selections might include "Song of Michael," "A Styling of Ave Verum," or "Come Breath of Life." These pieces by Patrick Loomis can be found in the THIS IS OUR FAITH Music Program.

Chapter Review

Use the clues below to fill in the crossword puzzle.

Down

1. Friends of Jesus live according to his example and _____.
3. One of the twelve apostles who was fishing when he met Jesus again
4. Another one of the twelve apostles
6. He killed Goliath with a slingshot and became Jonathan's best friend.

Across

2. Jesus' friends try to follow his _____ of doing good things for others.
5. Jesus is the _____ of God.
7. He was a true friend to David.
8. Jesus' rising from death to new life

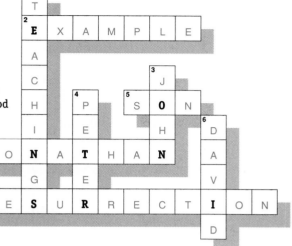

Fill in the answers to the first two questions.

1. What does *resurrection* mean? <u>Resurrection</u>

   <u>means Jesus' rising from death to new life.</u>

2. How does Jesus show us that he is our friend?

   <u>by always being with us, by loving us enough to die</u>

   <u>for us, by sharing our sadness and joys, and by</u>

   <u>giving himself to us in the Eucharist</u>

3. Talk about how you can become a better friend of Jesus.

Jesus says, "You are my friends."
Based on John 15:14

Completing a Crossword Puzzle

Have the students work independently to complete the crossword puzzle at the top of page 81. When all have finished, have them read each of the clues aloud together to check answers.

Answering the Review Questions

Have the students write their answers to the next two questions on the lines provided in the text. Then invite volunteers to read their responses aloud. Answer any questions the students may have about what they have learned in Chapter 6.

Encourage everyone to participate in the discussion question. Emphasize that we can become closer to Jesus through prayer and by following Jesus' example and teachings.

Praying with the Scriptural Verse

Direct attention to the verse from Scripture at the bottom of the page. After reading the verse with them, ask the students to think about their friendship with Jesus. Ask them to silently answer these questions: *Who is Jesus? What do I believe about Jesus? How do I feel about my friendship with Jesus?*

★ Enriching the Lesson ★

Divide the class into small groups and assign each group a scene from the story from Day 2. Scenes can include deciding to go fishing, fishing from the boat, seeing Jesus, coming to shore, preparing the breakfast, and eating and talking with Jesus. Decide with the class whether they want to dramatize their scenes or illustrate them on posterboard.

81

7 Our Church Believes in the Holy Spirit

Objectives

To help the students

- Recognize Jesus' promise to send the Holy Spirit.
- Learn the story of Pentecost.
- Understand that the Holy Spirit is our helper and guide.
- Be open to the Holy Spirit's guidance.
- Pray a Native American giveaway prayer and review the chapter.

Chapter Outline

	Step 1 Learning About Our Lives	**Step 2** Learning About Our Faith	**Step 3** Learning How to Live Our Faith
Day 1	■ Review the unit. ■ Introduce the chapter. ■ Read the story. *ABOUT 14 MINUTES*	■ Read about Jesus' promise. *ABOUT 8 MINUTES*	■ Recall biblical promises. *ABOUT 8 MINUTES*
Day 2	■ Talk about the Holy Spirit. *ABOUT 5 MINUTES*	■ Read and discuss the Scripture story. ■ Learn about Pentecost. *ABOUT 17 MINUTES*	■ Talk about birthdays. *ABOUT 8 MINUTES*
Day 3	■ Review the chapter. *ABOUT 5 MINUTES*	■ Read the text. ■ Consider decisions. ■ Learn the doctrine. *ABOUT 15 MINUTES*	■ Complete a checklist. *ABOUT 10 MINUTES*
Day 4	■ Write about the Holy Spirit. *ABOUT 5 MINUTES*	■ Read the text. ■ Read about the Holy Spirit. *ABOUT 13 MINUTES*	■ Compose a prayer. *ABOUT 12 MINUTES*
Day 5	**Prayer** Write giveaway prayers; pray a Native American prayer. **Review** Complete a matching activity; review the chapter; pray with the scriptural verse.		

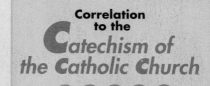

Correlation to the **Catechism of the Catholic Church**

Paragraphs
152, 243, 683, 684, 686, 688, 2670

Plan Ahead

	Preparing Your Class	**Materials Needed**
Day 1	Read through the lesson plan for this class session. Write the review sentences from Step 1 on the chalkboard.	■ pencils or pens
Day 2	Read through the lesson plan for this class session.	■ pencils or pens
Day 3	Read through the lesson plan for this class session. Think of examples of situations that require courage.	■ pencils or pens
Day 4	Read over the lesson plan for this class session.	■ writing paper ■ pencils or pens
Day 5	Prepare an environment for prayer in the classroom. Review this week's sessions to prepare for the chapter review.	■ slips of paper ■ bowl ■ pencils or pens

Additional Resources

As you plan this chapter, consider using the following materials from The Resourceful Teacher Package.

■ *Classroom Activity Sheets* 7 and 7a

■ *Family Activity Sheets* 7 and 7a

■ *Chapter 7 Test*

■ *Prayers for Every Day*

■ *Projects: Grade 3*

You may also wish to refer to the following Big Books.

■ *We Celebrate the Sacraments*, pages 10–12

■ *We Celebrate God's Word*, page 21

In preparing the students for the Sunday readings, you may wish to use Silver Burdett Ginn's *Getting Ready for Sunday* student and teacher materials.

BOOKS FOR THE JOURNEY

The Art Lesson. Tomie dePaola. G.P. Putnam's Sons, 1988. The story of a child who loves to draw, wants to be an artist, and becomes one.

Earth Prayers. Edited by Elizabeth Roberts. HarperCollins, 1991. "Grandfather Great Spirit," Sioux Prayer, p. 184; "O Great Spirit of the North" by Diann Neu, pp. 192–193. Prayers in which the Spirit is called upon to carry thoughts and prayers to God.

MORE BOOKS FOR THE JOURNEY

Experience Jesus Today. Charles Singer and Albert Hari. OCP Publications, 1993. "Pentecost," pp. 224–227. The story of Pentecost with a prayer to the Holy Spirit and suggestions for experiencing Jesus today.

The Selfish Giant. Oscar Wilde. Viking Penguin, 1991. A giant realizes how selfish he is and chooses to open his closed garden to children again.

REDUCED CLASSROOM ACTIVITIES

NAME _____

OUR CHURCH BELIEVES IN THE HOLY SPIRIT

You had an exciting dream last night! You were exploring and found two secret messages carved on a big rock. You still remember what they looked like, but you woke up before you could decode them. Do that now. Then say the words from both messages with your whole class.

(1)

The H _o_ ly Sp _i_ r _i_ t g _i_ v _e_ s us th _e_ power to do th _i_ ngs we n _e_ v _e_ r thought w _e_ could.

(2)

P _e_ n _t_ e c _o_ s _t_ is the day on which Jesus' disciples received the Holy Spirit.

To the Teacher: This activity will reinforce the Vocabulary and We Believe boxes in the chapter. Choral reading of the two messages will enhance the lesson.

Chapter 7 Our Church Believes in the Holy Spirit   THIS IS OUR FAITH 3   **7**

NAME _____

THE HOLY SPIRIT IS OUR STRENGTH

Read the statements below and circle th the response that does not belong. Talk classmates about how you chose your ar

1. These are the things that happened o
   a. The disciples spoke in different lar
   b. There was a noise like a strong wi
   c. Tongues of fire blazed above each
   d. The disciples went fishing for the

2. When the disciples were filled with t Pentecost, these things happened.
   a. They could now do what they had been afraid to do.
   b. They were angry and confused.
   c. They were full of peace and joy.
   d. They went out to tell the people about Jesus.

3. Pentecost means this.
   a. The birthday of the Church
   b. Fifty days after Passover
   c. Jesus' birthday
   d. The day on which Jesus' disciples received the Holy Spirit

4. This is what the Holy Spirit can do for us today.
   a. Cause us to act rudely to somebody
   b. Help us do hard things
   c. Help us understand that Jesus is our friend
   d. Help us realize that our peace and joy come from God

To the Teacher: This activity will help students apply the information in the story "Filled with the Spirit."

7a   THIS IS OUR FAITH 3   *Chapter 7* Our Church Believes in the Holy Spirit

THE PRESENCE OF THE HOLY SPIRIT

The presence of Christ continues in the world through the power of the Holy Spirit. Jesus promised that the Spirit of truth would remain with his followers. While God's presence and power are evident in many ways, the Holy Spirit is present in a special way in the Church. The Spirit unites us, guides us, and helps us to be the people of God.

The disciples of Jesus were hesitant, even afraid, to speak openly about Jesus after his death on the cross. Then the Holy Spirit filled them and transformed the disciples into courageous heralds of the good news of Jesus. They spoke openly and with conviction. Their efforts, with the help of the Holy Spirit, spread the preaching of Jesus to distant lands throughout the world.

The early Church experienced the Holy Spirit in many ways. The presence of the Holy Spirit guided and empowered the people to live their lives in imitation of Jesus. The members of the Church were encouraged to recognize and use wisely the gifts of the Spirit that are described in Isaiah 11:1–9: wisdom, understanding, knowledge, fortitude, counsel, piety, and fear of the Lord. In the epistles of the New Testament and in the Acts of the Apostles, we read about how the first Christians used these gifts.

SIGNS OF THE SPIRIT

The signs used by the Church to symbolize the Spirit's presence may help the third graders better understand the gifts of the Holy Spirit. The original Greek word for *spirit* means "wind" or "breath." In this lesson the signs of wind and breath as well as the sign of fire are introduced to the students. These signs are found in the story of Pentecost (Acts 2).

Third graders can be encouraged by the promise of the Holy Spirit in many situations. They may be challenged by difficulties with school work or with friendships. They may feel that they are not always meeting other people's expectations of them or even their own expectations. They may be experiencing a situation in which they are challenged to be emotionally strong. In all these situations, the students need to be assured that the Holy Spirit can help them to endure and rise to meet, and even surpass, the challenge. "Everything is possible to one who has faith" (Mark 9:23b).

Objective

This lesson helps the students recognize Jesus' promise to send the Holy Spirit.

Step 1/INTRODUCTION

Learning About Our Lives

Reviewing the Unit

Remind the students of the unit title, "A Believing Community." To help the students review what they have learned so far in this unit, write the sentences below on the chalkboard. Substitute blanks for the words in parentheses. Ask the students to complete each statement.

God is our (creator). We call God (Father). God takes care of us like a loving (parent). God is always (faithful) to us.

Jesus, the (Son) of God is always with us. He rose from death to (new life). We call Jesus' rising the (resurrection). Jesus is our (friend) forever.

Introducing the Chapter

Read aloud the chapter-focus question and invite the students' responses. Ask them to share experiences of being helped to do something they really wanted to do.

Reading the Story

Read the story "Allison's Dream" with the class. Then invite the students to respond to the Discuss questions on page 83. As you discuss these questions with the students, help them appreciate the effects of Allison's inner power, her determination and courage, and Miss Burke's encouragement.

When you are not sure you can do something that you very much want to do, who or what helps you most?

Our Church Believes in the Holy Spirit

Allison's Dream

Allison often dreamed of being a dancer. But when she woke up each morning, she could still feel some pain in her right leg. "I'll never be able to dance," she would say softly.

Allison had been in a car accident when she was six. Her leg had been badly hurt. She walked with a limp.

Miss Burke knew how much Allison wanted to be a dancer. She also knew how hard it would be for Allison to dance well. But she believed Allison had the inner power to make her dream come true.

Day after day, Miss Burke would say, "You can do it, Allison. I know you can. Let's try this move. Watch closely how I do it. Then do the same move as best you can."

Focus on

Jesus' Promise The *Cathechism of the Catholic Church* states that "Before his Passover, Jesus announced the sending of 'another Paraclete' (Advocate), the Holy Spirit. At work since creation, having previously 'spoken through the prophets,' the Spirit will now be with and in the disciples, to teach them and guide them 'into all the truth.' The Holy Spirit is thus revealed as another divine person with Jesus and the Father." (#243)

Allison slowly began to believe in herself. "I can do it," she began to tell herself as she tried each new step. But sometimes she would lose control and fall. Sometimes it was so hard that she wanted to give up.

Months went by. Miss Burke coached Allison every afternoon. "You *are* a dancer," Miss Burke would say. "Never doubt your dream. You can do it!"

At the end of the year, the dance studio had a program for parents. Allison's dad sat in the front row. Miss Burke watched the dance from the side of the stage. Allison had only a small part in the dance, but she danced her part well.

When she came out to take a bow, everyone stood up and cheered. They knew how hard she had worked to reach her dream. She truly was a dancer!

Discuss

1. Why did Allison's dream to be a dancer seem impossible at times?

2. What helped Allison to keep on trying?

3. What dreams do you have that will take courage to work toward?

The Disciples' Fears

Like Allison, Jesus' disciples thought they would never be able to do something that they were encouraged to do. Jesus had told his disciples to tell others about him. But after Jesus was arrested, the disciples were afraid. They did not dare tell people about Jesus. They had seen what happened to Jesus. He was beaten and crucified. They feared this would also happen to them.

The disciples remembered that Jesus had promised to send the Holy Spirit to give them the power to do things they never thought they could do. Confused and afraid, the disciples gathered together in a house to pray.

Doctrine 83

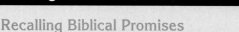

Enriching the Lesson

Give each student a large star cut from yellow construction paper. On the star, invite the students to draw a personal dream they have for themselves. Then have them write what they will need to do to achieve this dream. Afterward, allow time for sharing. Affirm the students' dreams and encourage them to work hard to achieve them.

Teaching Tips

Emphasize to the students the importance of discipline and perseverance in making any dream come true. Remind them that although Allison thought that she would never be able to dance she accomplished her goal through hard work and practice over a long period of time. Olympic sports figures and accomplished musicians are examples of people who devote years of time and energy to accomplishing their goals.

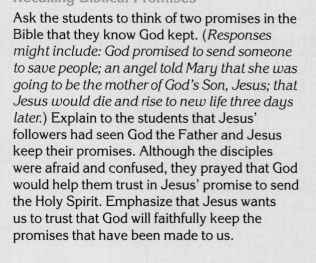

Step 2/DEVELOPMENT

Learning About Our Faith

Reading About Jesus' Promise

Ask a volunteer to read aloud "The Disciples' Fears" on page 83. Discuss the following questions.

- What did Jesus want his disciples to do? (*Tell others about him*)

- Why were the disciples afraid? (*They had seen what happened to Jesus; they were afraid that they would be arrested, beaten, and crucified.*)

- What did Jesus promise to do? (*To send the Holy Spirit to give them the power to do the things they never thought they could do*)

- What did the disciples do? (*They gathered together in a house to pray.*)

Step 3/CONCLUSION

Learning How to Live Our Faith

Recalling Biblical Promises

Ask the students to think of two promises in the Bible that they know God kept. (*Responses might include: God promised to send someone to save people; an angel told Mary that she was going to be the mother of God's Son, Jesus; that Jesus would die and rise to new life three days later.*) Explain to the students that Jesus' followers had seen God the Father and Jesus keep their promises. Although the disciples were afraid and confused, they prayed that God would help them trust in Jesus' promise to send the Holy Spirit. Emphasize that Jesus wants us to trust that God will faithfully keep the promises that have been made to us.

Objective

This lesson helps the students learn the story of Pentecost.

Step 1/INTRODUCTION

Learning About Our Lives

Talking About the Holy Spirit

Ask the students to identify what they know about the Holy Spirit. (*Responses may include: we receive the Holy Spirit at Baptism; the Holy Spirit is our helper and guide; the Holy Spirit is the third Person of the Trinity; Jesus promised to send the Holy Spirit to be with us always.*) Then discuss with the class what the disciples knew about the Holy Spirit. Lead them to the recognition that the disciples knew nothing about the Holy Spirit other than the fact that Jesus had promised to send the Holy Spirit to help them.

Step 2/DEVELOPMENT

Learning About Our Faith

Reading and Discussing the Scripture Story

Read "Filled with the Spirit" on pages 84 and 85 with the students. Review the main points of the story by asking the following questions.

- What sound did the disciples hear? (*A noise like a strong wind*)
- What did the disciples see? (*Tongues of fire above each disciple*)
- What new feelings did the disciples experience? (*A new strength inside them, joy, and peace*)
- Why did they feel this way? (*They were filled with the Holy Spirit.*)
- Who was Peter? (*One of the twelve apostles*)
- What did Peter do at Pentecost? (*He spoke to the whole crowd about Jesus.*)
- What did Peter say about Jesus? (*Jesus cared for everyone, especially the poor and suffering. Jesus died and rose again.*)
- What did Peter call on people to do? (*To believe in Jesus, change their lives, and be baptized*)

Filled with the Spirit

Suddenly, all over the house, there was a noise like a strong wind. It seemed as if tongues of fire blazed above each of the disciples. They were filled with the Holy Spirit. They began at once to talk and praise God in different languages.

The disciples felt a new strength inside them. They were full of joy and peace. Now they could do what they had been afraid to do. They opened the doors of the house and went out to tell the people about Jesus.

A large crowd of people from many different countries listened. They were amazed at what they heard and that each one heard the disciples speaking the language of his or her own country. Then Peter stood up and spoke to the whole crowd.

84 Scripture

The Pentecost Story Many Scripture scholars see a connection between the Pentecost story in Acts and the Genesis story of the Tower of Babel (Genesis 11). In Genesis, the people are divided, consumed with selfishness, and, as a result, unable to communicate. Through the Holy Spirit, the apostles in the Pentecost story are united, proclaiming the Gospel with one voice, yet everyone understands them regardless of their language. The Pentecost event, in effect, overturns the evil described in the story of Babel.

"I want to tell you about Jesus," Peter said. "Jesus went about doing good for everyone. He cared especially for the poor and suffering. Jesus loved people so much that he willingly died for them. But after he was buried, God raised him up. Believe in Jesus. Change your lives. Be baptized, and you, too, will receive the gift of the Holy Spirit."

Many people were excited after they heard Peter's words. More than three thousand people were baptized that day and became followers of Jesus.

Based on Acts 2:1–41

The Day of Pentecost

The day Jesus' first disciples received the Holy Spirit is called **Pentecost**. The Spirit changed their sadness into joy and their fear into hope. The Spirit filled them with new life and gave them courage to share Jesus with others. This new life filled all the people who believed in Jesus, and the community of believers began to meet together to share this new life. Pentecost marked the beginning of the life of the Church. This is why Pentecost is sometimes called the birthday of the Church.

Vocabulary

Pentecost: the birthday of the Church; the day on which Jesus' first disciples received the gift of the Holy Spirit

★ ★ ★ ★ ★ ★ ★ ★ ★ ★ ★ ★

Scripture 85

Focus on

Pentecost The large crowd that assembled to hear Peter on the first Pentecost had come to Jerusalem to celebrate a festival called the Feast of Weeks, which commemorated God's giving the Law to Moses. This festival was held fifty days after Passover. *Pentecost* means "fiftieth."

Learning About Pentecost

Read "The Day of Pentecost" with the students. Then point out the word *Pentecost* in the Vocabulary box on page 85. Have the students read and learn the definition. Explain that the disciples were filled with the Holy Spirit on Pentecost. The Spirit strengthened and encouraged the disciples to fulfill the mission they had received from Jesus to make disciples of all nations.

Step 3/CONCLUSION

Learning How to Live Our Faith

Talking About Birthdays

Focus on Pentecost as the birthday of the Church. Invite the students to discuss why and how we celebrate birthdays. Help them appreciate that birthdays are an opportunity to affirm our love for people and express how much we value them. Discuss the following questions.

■ What could you say to people such as your parents, siblings, or close friends on their birthdays to let them know how you feel about them?

■ What would you like people to say to *you* on your birthday?

■ How can we celebrate the birthday of the Church?

DAY 3
DOCTRINE

Objective

This lesson helps the students understand that the Holy Spirit is our helper and guide.

Step 1/INTRODUCTION

Learning About Our Lives

Reviewing the Chapter

Review what the students have studied thus far in Chapter 7 by asking the following questions.

- Whom did Jesus promise to send to the disciples? (*The Holy Spirit*)
- When did the disciples receive the Holy Spirit? (*On Pentecost*)
- With what did the Holy Spirit fill the disciples? (*A new strength, joy, peace, and hope*)
- Why do we call Pentecost the birthday of the Church? (*Because it brought the community of believers together to begin the Church*)

Step 2/DEVELOPMENT

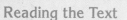

Learning About Our Faith

Reading the Text

Read with the class "The Spirit Gives Us Courage" on page 86. Discuss why living as followers of Jesus sometimes requires courage. Help the students understand that it is not always easy to do what we know is right. Also lead the students to the recognition that we may sometimes be tempted to ignore or avoid a situation when Jesus is asking us to stand up for something or someone.

Give the students the following example: *You see a classmate being teased on the playground by other students. Your classmate is crying as the other students call him or her names.* Explore the choices the students have in this situation. (*To join in the teasing; to ignore or walk away from the teasing; to speak up for and defend the classmate; to get an adult to help the classmate*) Have the students discuss these choices and decide which one would require the most courage.

86

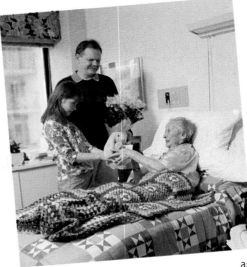

The Spirit Gives Us Courage

The Holy Spirit continues to give life to the Church and to each of us today. As our helper and guide, the Spirit gives each of us the power to do things we never thought we could do. Just as the disciples were given the courage to tell others about Jesus, we are also given the courage to live as friends and followers of Jesus.

Following Jesus in all that we do and say is not always easy. When we stop to think about the decisions we must make, we can ask the Holy Spirit to guide us in making the best decisions. Sometimes we know what the best decision is, but we do not have the courage to make that decision. For example, we know that Jesus wants us to make choices that show we care for others. But we may consider choosing to act differently or not at all.

Discuss

1. Have you ever made a decision to do something that would give someone the message that you did not care about that person? What happened?

2. What is the most courageous decision you have ever made?

3. Who or what helped you make that decision?

Teaching Tips

Sometimes you may find it necessary to repeat a lesson, part of a lesson, or key words and phrases. This is natural when working with children. Try to present the material in a different way each time you repeat it. Be particularly sensitive to those students who may have hearing impairments. They may need directions or lesson material repeated often.

Spirit-Filled Decisions

When we pray, we can ask the Holy Spirit to guide the decisions that we make each day as we try to live as Catholic Christians. We can pray at the beginning of each day for such guidance. This helps to remind us that the Spirit is always with us, all day long. This helps us to make the most caring choices throughout each day.

Activity

Place an **X** before each sentence below that shows that the Holy Spirit is guiding someone to make a caring choice. Then read the sentences again. Circle three of the caring choices that are the hardest for you to make.

_____ "I promised not to tell this to anyone, but I'll tell you anyway."

__X__ "I can help with that, Mom."

_____ "No, I'm too busy watching television."

_____ "It's not my turn. I did it yesterday."

__X__ "That's okay. I'll take out the garbage."

_____ "Figure it out yourself."

__X__ "I can teach you how to do that."

_____ "I don't care. I want to play here."

__X__ "I can play in my room if you want to rest."

__X__ "I'll play that game with you."

_____ "I don't want to. It's boring."

__X__ "I'm sorry I said that."

_____ "Give me that. It's mine."

We Believe

Jesus gives the Church —the community of believers—the gift of the Holy Spirit to be with us as our helper and guide. The Holy Spirit gives us courage and power to do difficult things and to share Jesus with others.

Doctrine 87

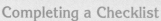

★ ★ ★ Enriching the Lesson ★

Have the students make wind socks for the Day 5 prayer, using paper-towel rolls, white art paper, yarn, red crepe paper, tape, and crayons. Have them draw designs on the white paper and then tape the paper to the roll to cover it. Cut streamers from crepe paper and tape them to one end of the roll. Staple a yarn loop to the other end of the roll.

Considering Decisions

Direct attention to the Discuss questions at the bottom of page 86. Invite the students to respond to these questions in small groups of three or four and then report back to the class.

Use the photo on page 86 as an example of a situation that might require courage. Tell the students that many people are not comfortable visiting sick or elderly people in a hospital or nursing home. Invite the students to share similar experiences of their own. Ask them who or what could help give someone courage in this situation. Suggest that the person's love and caring for an elderly relative may be all that is needed to give the person the courage to visit. Sometimes a parent can help by talking about what to expect during the visit or by joining the person for the visit.

Learning the Doctrine

Have a volunteer read aloud the We Believe statement on page 87. Ask the students if there are any questions about the meaning of what they have read. Encourage the students to remember this section once they have understood the meaning.

Step 3/CONCLUSION

Learning How to Live Our Faith

Completing a Checklist

Read aloud "Spirit-Filled Decisions" on page 87. Emphasize the importance of prayer in seeking the help and guidance of the Holy Spirit. Explain the directions for the activity. Allow time for the students to complete the checklist and to circle the three hardest choices. Discuss the students' choices. Then take a poll of the hardest choices.

Objective

This lesson helps the students be open to the Holy Spirit's guidance.

Step 1/INTRODUCTION

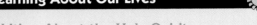

Learning About Our Lives

Writing About the Holy Spirit

Encourage the students to think about ways the Holy Spirit helps or guides them. Distribute writing paper and ask the students to complete the following sentence: *I believe the Holy Spirit is with me when . . . .* Then ask for volunteers to share their responses with the rest of the class.

Step 2/DEVELOPMENT

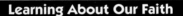

Learning About Our Faith

Reading the Text

Call on volunteers to read aloud "Signs of the Spirit" on page 88. Ask the students to recall why wind and fire are two signs of the Spirit. (*On Pentecost, the disciples heard the sound of a strong wind; tongues of fire appeared over each of the disciples.*)

Invite the students to close their eyes and imagine the Spirit as wind, carrying their thoughts, worries, joys, and prayers to God. Then invite the students to imagine the Holy Spirit as a warm, glowing fire. Ask them to picture themselves being surrounded by the warmth of God's love.

Invite a student to read aloud the prayer on page 88 that begins, "We give away our thanks." Explain that this is an example of a giveaway prayer.

Signs of the Spirit

We are called to open our hearts to receive the Holy Spirit as our helper and guide in living as followers of Jesus.

Signs are used to remind us of the Holy Spirit's activity in our lives. One sign used by the Church is wind, or breath. It reminds us that the Holy Spirit fills us with life. Another sign, fire, reminds us that the Holy Spirit fills us with the warmth of God's love.

Native Americans also believe that wind, or breath, gives life. They believe that the wind carries our thoughts and prayers to God. They say special prayers called "giveaway" prayers to give thanks for all the blessings of nature.

Black Elk's vision of the blooming sacred tree of life

We give away our thanks
to the sun
For sending light
to help our food grow.
We give away our thanks
to the seas
For giving away their waters
to refresh us.

88   Prayer

Cultural Awareness

The illustration at the top of page 88 was inspired by the vision of a Lakota Indian named Black Elk, who lived from 1863 to 1950. In Black Elk's vision, all people live in unity with one another and with the forces of nature. The black road of life and all its difficulties crosses the red road of life's goodness at the roots of the tree of life. Watering the tree of life brings harmony to the earth and all its peoples.

Images of the Spirit

As the Third Person of the Trinity, the Holy Spirit has always been with us. In the Bible, the Holy Spirit is made known to us in many ways—as a helper, as a guide, in wind, and in fire. We can also read about the Spirit at Jesus' baptism. "After all the people had been baptized and Jesus also had been baptized and was praying, heaven was opened and the holy Spirit descended upon him in bodily form like a dove. And a voice came from heaven, 'You are my beloved Son; with you I am well pleased'" (Luke 3:21–22). We sometimes see a dove on a banner or on other decorations in our churches, especially on Pentecost Sunday. A dove is often used as a symbol for the Holy Spirit. We may also see this image of the Spirit at a Baptism.

In the story of Pentecost the Holy Spirit is described as a "strong wind" and as "tongues of fire." This is why many parishes show a flame of fire on parish bulletins or banners on special occasions.

In the Bible, the Holy Spirit has many names as well as images. In John 14:26, Jesus called the Holy Spirit our "Advocate," which means one who comforts or gives courage. The Holy Spirit would comfort the disciples when Jesus died and give them courage.

Activity

Write a prayer to the Holy Spirit. Ask the Holy Spirit to show you more signs of the Spirit that can help you live as a friend and follower of Jesus.

Come, Holy Spirit. Fill me with new life.

Spirit of Love, help me to _____.

Spirit of Joy, help me to _____.

Spirit of Peace, help me to _____.

Help me to find my hidden powers, make good choices, and make God's dreams for the world come true through me. Amen.

Scripture 89

Reading About the Holy Spirit

Read through "Images of the Spirit" on page 89 with the class. Use the following questions to guide discussion.

■ How did God make the Spirit known at Jesus' baptism? (*In the form of a dove*)

■ What are some names of the Holy Spirit? (*Helper, guide, advocate, comforter, Third Person of the Trinity*)

Explain to the students that just as the Spirit comforted the disciples when they missed Jesus, the Spirit will comfort us when we are troubled. Just as the Holy Spirit continued to teach the disciples how to live as Jesus taught, the Spirit will also help us know how to live as followers of Jesus.

Step 3/CONCLUSION

Learning How to Live Our Faith

Composing a Prayer

Explain the directions for the prayer-writing activity and have the students work independently to complete it. When the students have finished, encourage them to share their prayers with the group.

Focus on

Signs of the Spirit Two signs of the Spirit—wind and fire—have an important place in the Jewish community's relationship with God. In the Creation story, we read about two references to wind or breath (Genesis 1:2b and Genesis 2:7). Fire also represented God's presence, in the call of Moses (Exodus 3:2) and in the Israelites' passage to freedom (Exodus 13:21).

DAY 5

PRAYER / REVIEW

Objective

This lesson helps the students pray a Native American giveaway prayer.

Writing Giveaway Prayers

Read aloud the first paragraph on page 90. Then divide the class into cooperative groups to write their giveaway prayers as outlined on the page. Instruct the groups to agree on a prayerful gesture to accompany each line in their prayers. After the groups write their prayers, have them practice their gestures. Then ask each group to choose one representative to read aloud the group's prayers during the prayer service.

Praying a Native American Prayer

If you had the students make wind socks on Day 3, begin the prayer with a procession around the classroom. Then have each group present its giveaway prayer of thanks to the wind with accompanying gestures. Next, have each group present its giveaway prayer of thanks to fire and so on. When each group has presented all of its giveaway prayers, invite the whole class to join together in praying the last line on page 90.

or...

Have the students write a giveaway prayer of thanks for each student in the class. For example, "We give away our thanks to the Holy Spirit for Susan, who is always kind and caring." You may want to use the fruits of the Holy Spirit listed in Galatians 5:22–23 to describe a good quality in each person. To be sure that each student's name is used, you may want to prepare slips of paper with the students' names on them. Then distribute the slips of paper to the students and ask them to write a prayer for the person named.

Praying a Native American Prayer

The Holy Spirit can be seen and known in so many ways. We pray today that the Holy Spirit will continue to fill our lives and our world. With our Native American brothers and sisters, we pray our own "giveaway" prayer to give thanks for the many signs of the Spirit that help to make our faith stronger. Write your own prayers of thanks to the Holy Spirit.

We give away our thanks for the wind because _____

_____

We give away our thanks for fire because _____

_____.

We give away our thanks to the Holy Spirit for helping us when _____

_____.

We give away our thanks to the Holy Spirit for guiding us when _____

_____.

We give away our thanks to the Holy Spirit for giving us courage when

_____.

We give away our thanks to the Holy Spirit for always being with us. Amen.

90   Prayer

Fruits of the Spirit The qualities mentioned in Galatians 5:22–23 are love, joy, peace, patience, kindness, generosity, faithfulness, gentleness, and self-control. Paul describes these characteristics as being opposed to the "works of the flesh" and as being made manifest when one's life is guided by the Holy Spirit. Tell the students that the fruits of the Holy Spirit are signs that the Spirit works in and through us and helps us to be all that God calls us to be.

Cultural Awareness

Have the children think of creative, prayerful gestures (such as dance movements) or banners for the Native American giveaway prayers. Emphasize that Native Americans are very aware of God's presence in nature.

Chapter Review

Before each definition in Column A, write the letter of the word from Column B.

Column A

<u>d</u> **1.** The Third Person of the Trinity

<u>b</u> **2.** The birthday of the Church

<u>g</u> **3.** Two ways the Holy Spirit is with us today

<u>e</u> **4.** What the disciples were doing when the Holy Spirit came

<u>a</u> **5.** The image of the Holy Spirit at Jesus' baptism

<u>f</u> **6.** A Native American prayer of thanks

<u>c</u> **7.** Images of the Holy Spirit at Pentecost

Column B

a. dove

b. Pentecost

c. wind and fire

d. Holy Spirit

e. praying

f. giveaway prayer

g. helper and guide

Fill in the answers to the first two questions.

1. What is Pentecost? <u>Pentecost is the birthday of</u> <u>the Church; the day on which Jesus' first disciples</u> <u>received the gift of the Holy Spirit.</u>

2. How does the Holy Spirit help us today? <u>The</u> <u>Holy Spirit gives us life, guides us, and gives us the</u> <u>power and courage to do difficult things.</u>

3. Talk about some signs of the Spirit that you see and appreciate in one another.

The Spirit of Christ lives in you.
Based on Romans 8:9–10

Enriching the Lesson

Distribute writing paper to the students. Ask them to imagine that they are with the apostles and disciples at Pentecost. Have them write eyewitness reports about what they see and hear. Ask the students each to include in their reports one message about Jesus that they would like to share with others.

Completing a Matching Activity

Explain the directions for the matching activity on page 91 and have the students complete it independently. When the students are finished, check their comprehension by reading aloud the statements in column A and having students call out the correct answers.

Reviewing the Chapter

Take time to go through the next three questions. Direct the students to write answers to the first two questions on the lines provided in the text. Afterward, call on volunteers to read aloud their responses. For the discussion question, encourage the students to affirm one another.

Praying with the Scriptural Verse

Read the quotation from Scripture at the bottom of the page. Help the students understand that we first receive the Holy Spirit at Baptism. Emphasize that at Baptism, the Spirit joins us to Jesus and, through Jesus, makes us God's special sons and daughters.

8 Our Church Has Creeds

Objectives

To help the students

- Recognize that the Christian community stands for the same things that Jesus taught and lived.
- Understand that the Apostles' Creed summarizes what Catholics believe.
- Learn the meaning of the Apostles' Creed.
- Identify different creeds of the Catholic Church.
- Celebrate their belief in the Trinity and review the chapter.

Chapter Outline

	Step 1 — Learning About Our Lives	Step 2 — Learning About Our Faith	Step 3 — Learning How to Live Our Faith
Day 1	■ Introduce the chapter. ■ Read the story. ■ Complete an activity. *ABOUT 16 MINUTES*	■ Discuss Jesus' followers. *ABOUT 7 MINUTES*	■ Respond as a follower of Jesus. *ABOUT 7 MINUTES*
Day 2	■ Review Day 1. *ABOUT 3 MINUTES*	■ Read a story. ■ Learn the Apostles' Creed. ■ Learn the vocabulary and doctrine. *ABOUT 20 MINUTES*	■ Discuss the Sign of the Cross. *ABOUT 7 MINUTES*
Day 3	■ Pray the Apostles' Creed. *ABOUT 3 MINUTES*	■ Learn Catholic beliefs. ■ Read about the Trinity. ■ Discuss a symbol of the Trinity. *ABOUT 19 MINUTES*	■ Discuss faith in action. *ABOUT 8 MINUTES*
Day 4	■ Discuss beliefs. *ABOUT 5 MINUTES*	■ Read the text. *ABOUT 8 MINUTES*	■ Write belief statements. *ABOUT 17 MINUTES*
Day 5	**Prayer** Create posters; prepare to pray; pray a blessing. **Review** Name the Persons of the Trinity; list beliefs; review learning; pray with the scriptural verse.		

Plan Ahead

	Preparing Your Class	Materials Needed
Day 1	Read through the lesson plan for this session.	■ pencils or pens
Day 2	Read through the lesson plan for this session. Be prepared to check that the students properly make the Sign of the Cross in Step 3.	■ pencils or pens
Day 3	Read through the lesson plan for this session.	■ pencils or pens
Day 4	Read through the lesson plan for this session.	■ pencils or pens
Day 5	Prepare an environment for prayer in the classroom. Plan how you will conduct the prayer service. Review this week's sessions to prepare for the chapter review.	■ table with Bible and candle ■ crayons or markers ■ posterboard ■ pencils or pens

Correlation to the Catechism of the Catholic Church

Paragraphs **185–197, 199, 242**

Additional Resources

As you plan this chapter, consider using the following materials from The Resourceful Teacher Package.

■ *Classroom Activity Sheets 8* and *8a*
■ *Family Activity Sheets 8* and *8a*
■ *Chapter 8 Test*
■ *Prayers for Every Day*
■ *Projects: Grade 3*

You may also wish to refer to the following Big Books.

■ *We Celebrate the Sacraments,* page 4
■ *We Celebrate God's Word,* page 22
■ *We Celebrate the Mass,* pages 3, 10

In preparing the students for the Sunday readings, you may wish to use Silver Burdett Ginn's *Getting Ready for Sunday* student and teacher materials.

Chapter Organizer 91b

BOOKS FOR THE JOURNEY

Experience Jesus Today. Charles Singer and Albert Hari. OCP Publications, 1993. "We Believe," p. 119. A prayer in which beliefs are expressed in easily understandable language.

God Is in the Mountain. Ezra Jack Keats. Henry Holt & Co., 1994. A book that encourages children to seek out similarities in the beliefs of others and to celebrate what is universal about them all.

MORE BOOKS FOR THE JOURNEY

Praise God. Gunvor Edwards and Joan Brown. Liturgical Press, 1994. "We Believe," p. 30. A prayer in which some of our beliefs are expressed.

In God's Name. Sandy Eisenberg-Sasso. Jewish Lights Publications, 1994. A book expressing ways of understanding God, believing in God, and naming God.

REDUCED CLASSROOM ACTIVITIES

NAME _____

OUR CHURCH HAS CREEDS

Fill in the missing words from the Apostles' Creed. Color the border and cut along the heavy black lines. Put the creed in a place where you will see and read it often.

I believe in __God__,
   the Father almighty,
   __creator__ of heaven and earth.
I believe in __Jesus Christ__,
   his only __Son__, our
   Lord.
He was conceived by the power of the
   Holy Spirit and born of the Virgin
   __Mary__.
He suffered under __Pontius__
   __Pilate__, was crucified, died,
   and was buried.
He descended to the dead.
On the __third__ day he rose again.
He __ascended__ into heaven, and is
   seated at the right hand of the Father.
He will come again to judge the living and
   the dead.
I believe in the __Holy Spirit__,
the holy __catholic__ Church,
the __communion__ of saints,
the __forgiveness__ of sins,
the __resurrection__ of the body,
and life everlasting. Amen.

© Silver Burdett Ginn Inc.

To the Teacher: This activity follows "The Apostles' Creed."

Chapter 8 Our Church Has Creeds

THIS IS OUR FAITH 3 **8**

NAME _____

WE BELIEVE IN GOD THE FATHER, SON, AND HOLY SPIRIT

We believe the Father is God. We believe the Son is God. We believe the Holy Spirit is God. Together they make the Trinity. *Trinity* means "three in one." The pictures below show water that is liquid, frozen, and steam. The things pictured are all water, but in three different forms. Think of something in your world that reminds you of the Father, Son, and Spirit and draw it in the box. Use your drawing to tell your family about how God is Three in One.

© Silver Burdett Ginn Inc.

To the Teacher: Display "three-in-one" pictures in a special place in your school after a class discussion of this activity.

8a THIS IS OUR FAITH 3

Chapter 8 Our Church Has Creeds

EXPRESSIONS OF FAITH

Since the Church's early days (nearly two thousand years ago), its members have met together to share and strengthen their faith. The very earliest expressions of faith, such as the Sign of the Cross, come out of this experience. The earliest Christians lived their lives "in the name of the Father, and of the Son, and of the Holy Spirit."

Over a period of time, formal statements of belief, called creeds, began to be used to say explicitly what the Church community believed. These beliefs were part of the living faith of the community, especially as the believers gathered to celebrate the Eucharist. Over time, such creeds came to be written down, taught, and shared for others to use. The Apostles' Creed is one such formulation of faith.

At other times, the leaders and members of the Church have found it necessary to gather together to counteract heresies or misconceptions about the Church's beliefs about Jesus. These gatherings of the Church, which we call councils, sometimes set forth the members' conclusions in formal statements.

OUR CATHOLIC CREEDS

In these lessons, the students learn that creeds are part of our heritage as Catholic Christians. Generations of believers in Jesus have held these statements of our beliefs to be important. People have lived and died for the beliefs these creeds express. As the *National Catechetical Directory* states, "Catechesis must . . . recognize creedal statements and doctrinal formulas as indispensable instruments for handing on the faith." (#45)

These lessons also stress the importance of being able to personally state what each one of us believes. The students will have an opportunity to express in a personal creed how they understand the gift of faith that is given to them. This activity can help them to appreciate more fully the value, importance, and meaning of the creeds of the Church.

DAY 1
MORALITY/SCRIPTURE

Objective

This lesson helps the students recognize that the Christian community stands for the same things that Jesus taught and lived.

Step 1/INTRODUCTION

Learning About Our Lives

Introducing the Chapter

Invite the students to share their responses to the first chapter-focus question. Then discuss the origin of their beliefs. Help the students appreciate that their beliefs come from what is important to them and what they learn from parents, teachers, and the faith community.

Reading the Story

Read with the class "We C.A.N. Make a Difference." Use these questions to discuss the story.

- Why did Suzie and Elisa decide to start a club? (*To improve the environment*)
- What did the club name show? (*That the girls believed they could make a difference by taking action now*)
- What kinds of activities would the club have? (*Recycling, planting, cleaning up trash*)
- Why did the girls write the C.A.N. Plus Club creed? (*To list what the club stood for*)

8

Our Church Has Creeds

What are three things you strongly believe in? Where do these beliefs come from?

We C.A.N. Make a Difference

Suzie and Elisa were excited. They had decided to start a club to improve the environment. They were now working out their plans at Elisa's house.

"Whom could we invite into our club?" Suzie asked.

"We could start with Sylvia, Pat, and Lois," Elisa suggested. "And maybe Luke and Chang. Then others will *want* to join our club."

"But what will we call ourselves?" asked Suzie.

"Let's name ourselves the Cougars, after our school mascot!" said Elisa.

"How about the C.A.N. Plus Club? The letters can stand for 'Cougars Act Now.' And our name would show that we *can* make a difference by taking action now."

"And that recycling *cans* is only the first step."

"We could put up signs telling people why recycling is so important."

"And help people learn what other things to put aside for recycling."

"How about planting trees and flowers?"

"And sweeping up trash."

Suzie and Elisa named many other projects.

92 Morality

Focus on

Life-giving Faith The *Catechism of the Catholic Church* states that "As on the day of our Baptism, when our whole life was entrusted to the 'standard of teaching,' let us embrace the Creed of our life-giving faith. To say the Credo with faith is to enter into communion with God, Father, Son, and Holy Spirit, and also with the whole Church which transmits the faith to us and in whose midst we believe." (#197)

92

"Let's go and write down all that the C.A.N. Plus Club stands for before we forget," Suzie suggested.

They spent the rest of the evening printing out their club's creed very neatly. "Now we can invite others to join our club," Suzie said. "Tomorrow we'll start!"

Activity

Think about the groups you belong to and the activities you most enjoy. What do your activities tell about the kind of person you are and what you stand for?

A group I belong to is _____.

One of my favorite activities is _____.

My favorite activities show that I am _____.

Jesus' Followers Knew What They Stood For

Jesus' followers knew what they stood for—the same things that Jesus taught and lived. Jesus told his disciples, "This is how all will know that you are my disciples, if you have love for one another" (John 13:35). Jesus told his followers that the most important sign of the Christian community is the love that Christians show for one another.

Scripture 93

Scripture 93

Teaching Tips

Tell the students that the name Suzie and Elisa chose for their club is called an acronym, because each letter of the name stands for a word. Ask the students why they think the girls added "Plus" to the name of their club? (*The word* Plus *indicates things that they can encourage people to do to improve their environment in addition to recycling cans, such as planting trees and flowers and sweeping up trash.*)

Enriching the Lesson

Have the students form cooperative groups. Tell them that each group has the responsibility to create an organization that will make the students' neighborhood, school, or world a better place. Have each group decide on its organization's name and purpose. Then have each group write a creed for its organization, clearly stating its beliefs.

Completing an Activity

Have the students complete the sentences about their participation in groups and activities. Help the students recognize that their activities show their interests and what they think is important.

Step 2/DEVELOPMENT

Learning About Our Faith

Discussing Jesus' Followers

Remind the students that the Cougars wrote a creed, a statement of their beliefs, to express what they stood for. Then call on a volunteer to read aloud "Jesus' Followers Knew What They Stood For" on page 93. Ask the following questions.

■ What did Jesus' followers stand for? (*The same things Jesus taught and lived*)

■ What did Jesus say was the most important mark of the Christian community? (*The love Christians show for one another*)

Step 3/CONCLUSION

Learning How to Live Our Faith

Responding as a Follower of Jesus

Direct attention to the verse from John's Gospel in the paragraph on page 93: "This is how all will know that you are my disciples, if you have love for one another" (John 13:35). Invite the students to discuss how they respond, as baptized members of the Church, to this command by asking the following questions.

■ What are some ways by which you show your love for others?

■ When and where do your words and actions give others a definite sign that you are a follower of Jesus?

Objective

This lesson helps the students understand that the Apostles' Creed summarizes what Catholics believe.

Step 1/INTRODUCTION

Learning About Our Lives

Reviewing Day 1

Ask the following questions.

- What is a creed? (*A statement of beliefs*)
- What does a creed say about a group, organization, or club? (*What the group believes in; what it stands for; its purpose*)

Tell the students that in today's lesson they will learn about some of the creeds of the Catholic Church.

Step 2/DEVELOPMENT

Learning About Our Faith

Reading a Story

Ask the students to recall what they learned about Pentecost in the previous chapter. Help them recall that the Holy Spirit filled the followers of Jesus with joy and peace. The early Christians were then able to go out and teach the good news of salvation that comes to all through Jesus Christ. Explain that Jesus' disciples spread his word to places far away from where Jesus grew up and preached. One of these places was the great city of Rome, which is the setting for the story "The Apostles' Creed." The first followers of Jesus have died, but their teachings live on. Call on volunteers to read aloud the story on page 94.

94

The Apostles' Creed

It is several hundred years after Pentecost. In the great city of Rome, a group of Christians are meeting in someone's home. They pray together and read from the Scriptures.

"It is so good for us to come together like this," Timothy says. "Our faith grows stronger each time we meet."

"We must never forget all that we have come to understand," Paula urges. "Let's renew our faith now before we go home."

Quietly but confidently, they said their creed.

94 Doctrine

Focus on

Rome Along with the cities of Constantinople, Alexandria, Antioch, and Jerusalem, Rome became one of the early centers of Christianity. Rome gradually became the center of Christianity in the western part of the Roman Empire, while Constantinople became the center of Christianity in the eastern part of the Roman Empire. The bishop of Rome was referred to as the pope while the bishops of the other cities were referred to as patriarchs. Eventually, the pope was seen as the head of Christianity in the western part of the Roman Empire.

I believe in God, the Father almighty,
   creator of heaven and earth.
I believe in Jesus Christ, his only Son,
   our Lord.
He was conceived by the power of the
   Holy Spirit and born of the Virgin Mary.
He suffered under Pontius Pilate,
   was crucified, died, and was buried.
He descended to the dead.
On the third day he rose again.
He ascended into heaven, and is seated at
   the right hand of the Father.
He will come again to judge the living and
   the dead.
I believe in the Holy Spirit,
   the holy catholic Church,
   the communion of saints,
   the forgiveness of sins,
   the resurrection of the body,
   and life everlasting. Amen.

Catholics and many other Christians still use that ancient creed to express their beliefs. We call it the **Apostles' Creed** because it sums up the teachings that go back to Jesus' apostles. The Nicene Creed is a longer creed that we say at Sunday Mass.

Vocabulary

Apostles' Creed: a summary of what Catholics and many other Christians believe

★ ★ ★ ★ ★ ★ ★ ★ ★ ★ ★ ★

We Believe

The creeds of the Catholic Church summarize our beliefs.

Doctrine 95

Teaching Tips

Because we say the Nicene Creed during Mass each week, it can be confusing to the students to learn a new creed. Pray the Apostles' Creed often in class to help the students remember the words. You can also write the creed on a transparency sheet, leaving blanks for significant words. Show the creed on an overhead projector and have the students supply the missing words.

Learning the Apostles' Creed

Have the students recite together the Apostles' Creed on page 95. Explain each of the lines to the class.

or . . .

Divide the Apostles' Creed into sections. Have the students work in small groups to draw pictures that illustrate the sections of the creed. When they are finished, tape or staple their drawings together to make a "filmstrip." Using a large box that has slits, make a "viewer" through which the drawings can be pulled. Have the students recite the Apostles' Creed as they view the filmstrip.

Learning the Vocabulary and Doctrine

Have the students read silently the Vocabulary and We Believe boxes. Answer any questions the students may have. Encourage them to remember these two sections.

Step 3/CONCLUSION

Learning How to Live Our Faith

Discussing the Sign of the Cross

Discuss with the students that some people also call the Sign of the Cross a creed. Explain that the words we say when we make this sign express our belief in the Father, the Son, and the Holy Spirit. Ask the students to name three different times when they make the Sign of the Cross. (*Possible answers include blessing oneself with holy water when entering the sanctuary; at the beginning and end of prayers at home; and at the beginning and end of Mass.*) Encourage the students to pray the Sign of the Cross frequently.

DAY 3
DOCTRINE

Objective

This lesson helps the students learn the meaning of the Apostles' Creed.

Step 1/INTRODUCTION

Learning About Our Lives

Praying the Apostles' Creed

To review the teachings of the Church that go back to the time of Jesus' Apostles, have the students stand and pray together the Apostles' Creed. Reinforce that these ancient words sum up our Catholic beliefs.

Step 2/DEVELOPMENT

Learning About Our Faith

Learning Catholic Beliefs

Direct attention to "Understanding Our Creeds" on page 96. Explain that the reading is a summary of the basic beliefs that are found in the Apostles' Creed. The summary is expressed as five statements, all beginning with the words *We believe.*

It is helpful for the students to see the exact place in the Apostles' Creed that each of the statements summarizes. Assign the reading of each "We believe" statement to a different volunteer. After each statement has been read, have the other students refer to the Apostles' Creed on page 95 and find the place where that basic belief is also expressed. Have them underline the words in the Apostles' Creed.

Understanding Our Creeds

We are called to remember our beliefs, to think about what they mean, and to be faithful to them in the way we live.

The community prays a creed during Baptism, Confirmation, and during Mass. Our creeds sum up our beliefs as Catholic Christians.

■ We believe in God the Father, who loves us without limit. God creates all things. Creation is a gift from God to us.

■ We believe in God's Son, Jesus Christ, who loves us like a brother and friend. Jesus lived and died for us. He rose to new life so we might live more fully.

■ We believe in the Holy Spirit. The Spirit is our helper and guide. The Spirit helps us love one another.

■ We believe in the Catholic Church as a community of God's people.

■ We believe we will rise from death to new life. We believe we will live with Jesus forever.

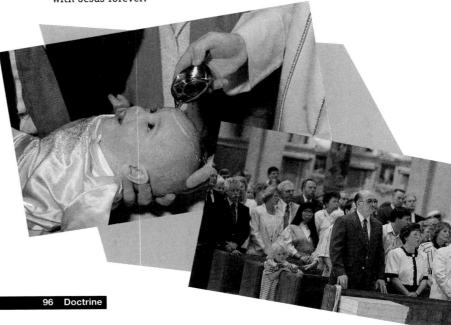

96   Doctrine

CURRICULUM CONNECTION

Social Studies Ask the students what ideas they think would be included in a national creed for the United States. You might have them look at the Pledge of Allegiance or the opening of the Declaration of Independence to help them name values and beliefs that Americans hold in common. Write their answers on the chalkboard.

The Trinity in Our Creeds

Our belief in the Trinity is an important part of all of our creeds. Each creed begins by stating our belief in God the Father, the First Person of the Trinity. We can remember that this is the first part of each creed because God the Father is the creator of all things, and creation was the beginning of all of God's wonderful works.

The second part of each creed states our belief in Jesus, the Second Person of the Trinity. We believe that Jesus is God. We believe that Jesus is both divine and human. When we say that Jesus is human, we are saying that he is like us. When we say that Jesus is divine, we are saying that he is God. This is what makes Jesus different from all other teachers and leaders who bring God's love to us.

The third part of each creed states our belief in the Holy Spirit, the Third Person of the Trinity. We believe that the Holy Spirit is the one whom Jesus promised would be with us always. We believe that the Holy Spirit is God, who is alive in the Church today and in the hearts of all believers.

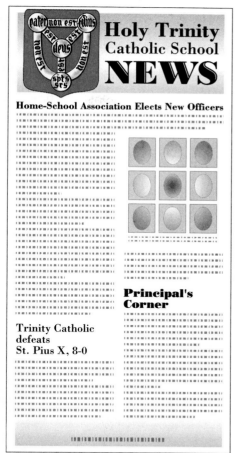

Holy Trinity Catholic School NEWS

Home-School Association Elects New Officers

Principal's Corner

Trinity Catholic defeats St. Pius X, 8-0

Doctrine 97

Teaching Tips

In discussing life everlasting in the Creed, encourage the students to share their beliefs about life after death. Recall what they have learned about heaven in previous grades. Stress that although we do not know what heaven will be like we believe that in heaven we will have new life and live happily with God and all who have tried to follow Jesus.

Reading About the Trinity

Read through "The Trinity in Our Creeds" with the class. Explain to the class that another way of saying that Jesus is both divine and human is to say that Jesus is both God and man.

Discussing a Symbol of the Trinity

Draw the students' attention to the symbol that appears on page 97. Explain that this is an early expression of the doctrine of the Blessed Trinity: three distinct Persons, yet each Person is God. The Latin text can be translated as follows.

> The Father is not the Son; the Son is not the Spirit; the Spirit is not the Father.
>
> The Father is God; the Son is God; the Spirit is God.

Step 3/CONCLUSION

Learning How to Live Our Faith

Discussing Faith in Action

Remind the students that just as we are called to show our love for Jesus by our love for one another, we are also called to show our belief in God the Father, Jesus his Son, and the Holy Spirit through our actions. Discuss what actions might result from our belief that God loves us and creates all things and gives them to us as gifts. *(Responses might include: We praise God in prayer, we thank God, we take care of the gifts God has given us; and so on.)* Repeat this procedure for Jesus and the Holy Spirit.

DAY 4
DOCTRINE

Objective

This lesson helps the students identify different creeds of the Catholic Church.

Step 1/INTRODUCTION

Learning About Our Lives

Discussing Beliefs

Ask the students to identify things that they believe without any doubt. (*Responses might include: The sun will rise each day, caterpillars turn into butterflies, seeds become flowers, that the students are loved, and so on.*) Then remind the students that the only people who actually saw Jesus during his life and after his resurrection were the people who lived during Jesus' time. As the years passed and the Church spread throughout the world, many people came to believe in Jesus without having physical proof that he had lived, died, and risen from the dead. They came to believe in Jesus through the stories they heard, the love that Christians showed for one another, and the teachings they learned. Emphasize that we, too, are called to believe in Jesus without seeing him.

Step 2/DEVELOPMENT

Learning About Our Faith

Reading the Text

Call on volunteers to take turns reading aloud "One Faith, Many Creeds," beginning on page 98. Discuss the questions below.

■ What do our creeds express? (*Our belief in the three Persons of the Trinity, in the Church, and in eternal life*)

■ When do we renew our baptismal promises? (*At baptismal ceremonies, at the Easter Vigil, and at Easter Sunday Mass*)

■ Why does the Nicene Creed begin with the word *We*? (*As a reminder that we are united in our faith with our parish families and Christians throughout the world*)

■ Why does the Apostles' Creed begin with the word *I*? (*As a reminder that our faith comes from within our hearts as individuals*)

98

One Faith, Many Creeds

Throughout history we have come together to share our faith. Creeds are important because they express what we believe as a Church community. The Church uses different creeds at different times, but each creed expresses our belief in the Three Persons of the Trinity, in the Church, and in eternal life.

There are several different creeds. Each time we celebrate Baptism, or remember the promises made at Baptism, we use a form called the baptismal creed, or Renewal of Baptismal Promises. We also use this form at the Easter Vigil and at the Easter Sunday Mass because we renew our baptismal promises at these celebrations. We believe that Baptism celebrates the beginning of

our faith. When we were baptized, our parents and godparents were asked questions that began with the words, "Do you believe?" As they answered "I do" to each question, they expressed their own faith. We also express our faith each time we answer these questions by saying, "I do."

The Nicene Creed is the creed that we usually say at Mass. It lists the primary beliefs of our faith as people of God and as members of the Catholic Church. Each statement of faith begins with the words "*We* believe." This reminds us that we are united in our faith with our parish families and with Catholics throughout the world.

98 Doctrine

★ Enriching the Lesson ★

Locate a resource in your parish that contains the Apostles' Creed, the Nicene Creed, and the Sign of the Cross. Have the students examine the Nicene Creed. Direct them to compare this creed with the Apostles' Creed and with the Sign of the Cross. Have the students make a list of those things that are similar in the three creeds.

Focus on

The Nicene Creed The Nicene Creed takes its name from the Council of Nicaea, an ecumenical meeting of Catholic bishops from around the world held in A.D. 325. The Council was called by Constantine the Great to settle a dispute about Jesus' humanity and divinity. False teachers had been preaching that Jesus was not equal to God. The Nicene Creed brought unity to the Church's beliefs.

The Apostles' Creed, based on the teachings of the apostles, is often used in Masses for children. In this shorter creed, we begin each statement of faith with the words, "*I believe.*" This reminds us that our faith comes from within the heart of each believer.

Activity

Use your own words to complete the sentences.

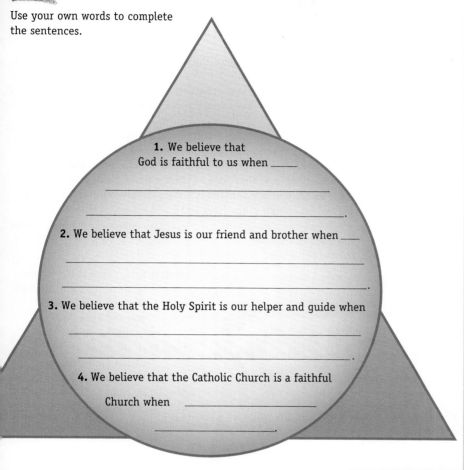

1. We believe that God is faithful to us when _____

_____

_____ .

2. We believe that Jesus is our friend and brother when _____

_____

_____ .

3. We believe that the Holy Spirit is our helper and guide when

_____

_____ .

4. We believe that the Catholic Church is a faithful

Church when _____

_____ .

Learning How to Live Our Faith

Writing Belief Statements

Explain the directions for the activity on page 99 and have the students work independently to complete it. When the students are finished, invite them to read their answers aloud. Help the students understand that as they learn more about their faith and try to grow closer to God, their belief in the Father's faithfulness, in Jesus' friendship, and in the Spirit's help will increase.

Enriching the Lesson

Use the students' responses to the activity on page 99 to compose a class creed. This creed can express the students' collective beliefs in the Father, the Son, the Spirit, and the Church in the students' own words. Write the creed on the chalkboard or on posterboard. Throughout the year, encourage the students to add to the creed new things they have learned.

Teaching Tips

Point out to the students the activity art on page 99. Explain that the three sides of the triangle represent the three distinct Persons of the Trinity and their unique qualities. The circle represents the unity of the Trinity, emphasizing their oneness.

Objective

This lesson helps the students celebrate their belief in the Trinity.

Creating Posters

Have the students work in small groups to create posters about the five sections of the creed. Assign one of the following sections of the creed to each group: God the Father, Jesus Christ, the Holy Spirit, the Church, and eternal life. Encourage the students to use drawings, words, and symbols to express their beliefs related to the section of the creed to which they have been assigned.

Preparing to Pray

Prepare an area in the classroom for prayer. Cover a desk or a table with a cloth and place a Bible and candle on it. Choose students to take the roles of leader and readers. Also divide the class into two groups for the final blessing. Allow time for the students to prepare themselves to participate in the prayer service by silently reading over their parts.

Praying a Blessing

Pray with the class the prayer found on page 100. Have the students present their posters after the reading from 2 Corinthians. For the blessing at the end of the prayer service, have the two groups of students face each other. Show the students how to raise their arms to extend a blessing to the opposite group.

Praying a Blessing

Leader: Let us pray in the name of the Father, Son, and Holy Spirit. (All make the Sign of the Cross.)
All: Amen.
Reader 1: God the Father almighty, who created heaven and earth,
All: We praise you, O God.
Reader 2: Jesus Christ, our Lord, who was conceived by the Holy Spirit, suffered and died for us, has risen, and will come again,
All: We praise you, O God.
Reader 3: Holy Spirit, who gives life to the Church and courage to all believers,
All: We praise you, O God.
Leader: Lord God, we worship you as Father, Son, and Holy Spirit. We pray that you will always keep your Church strong in faith.
All: Amen.
Leader: A reading from the second letter of Paul to the Corinthians: Goodbye, my friends. Listen to all I have said. Live peacefully with one another. Encourage one another. Show the world that you are a community of love. Greet one another warmly. I will pray for you, that the grace of our Lord Jesus Christ, the love of God the Father, and the fellowship of the Holy Spirit will always be with all of you.

(Based on 2 Corinthians 13:11–13)

The word of the Lord.
All: Thanks be to God.

100 Prayer

Leader: Let us extend our hands in blessing to one another.
Group 1: May our Lord bless you and keep you faithful always.
Group 2: In the name of the Father, Son, and Holy Spirit. Amen.
Group 2: May our Lord bless you and keep you faithful always.
Group 1: In the name of the Father, Son, and Holy Spirit. Amen.

Focus on

Trinitarian Blessings When we call upon God to bless the Church community, we most often use the Trinitarian form of blessing, mentioning each of the Divine Persons, to remind us of the many-faceted actions of God in our lives.

Chapter Review

Draw a line from each Person of the Trinity in Column A to the matching phrase in Column B.

Column A   **Column B**

God the Father   came at Pentecost

Jesus   sent Jesus to save us

The Holy Spirit   rose from the dead

List four things you say you believe in when you say the Apostles' Creed.

1._____

2._____

3._____

4._____

Fill in the answers to the first two questions.

1. What is the Apostles' Creed? _a summary of what_

   Catholics and many other Christians believe

   _____

2. What are some other creeds of the Church?

   Nicene Creed; baptismal creed

   _____

3. Talk about which parts of the creeds you would like to learn more about.

Remain faithful to what you believe.
Based on 2 Timothy 3:14

★ ★ ★ ★ ★ Enriching the Lesson ★

Distribute 2" × 6" strips of tag board and fine-line markers. Have the students make bookmarks by neatly printing the Apostles' Creed on the tag board. Cover the bookmarks with clear adhesive paper. Explain that people preparing for Baptism (catechumens) are given the creed during a ritual. Plan to give the bookmarks to catechumens for this ritual.

Naming the Persons of the Trinity

Read the directions for the first activity on page 101 and have the students complete it. Afterward, call on volunteers to read the correct answers.

Listing Beliefs

Have the students complete the second activity. Ask for volunteers to share their responses.

Reviewing Learning

Have the students write answers to the first two review questions on the lines provided. Be supportive of everyone who participates in the discussion question.

Praying with the Scriptural Verse

Ask a volunteer to read the verse from Scripture at the bottom of the page. Help the students become more aware that we show our faithfulness to our beliefs by the way we live. Invite the students to suggest concrete ways we can live according to the beliefs stated in the creeds of the Catholic Church. With the class, pray for the courage and commitment to act on each suggestion.

End-of-unit pages include a Unit Organizer; Unit Review; Day to Day: Skills for Christian Living; and *Opening Doors: A Take-Home Magazine.*

Completing a Semantic Map

Explain the directions for completing the chart on page 102. Encourage the students to list in each section what they believe about that Person of the Trinity and what they learned about the Persons of the Trinity in Unit 2. When all are finished, encourage the students to compare their maps with one another's.

Looking Back: Self-Assessment

The critical reflection questions below give the students an opportunity to sharpen their thinking skills. The questions can be used for a class discussion or for an independent writing activity.

■ Which Scripture quotation in this unit do you think you will always remember?

■ Which picture in this unit did you like best?

■ What did you like about it?

■ Which story in this unit did you most enjoy? Why?

UNIT **2** ORGANIZER

Define *creed* on the lines in the scroll. Complete the chart by describing the beliefs you profess about the Father, Jesus, and the Holy Spirit.

CREED

GOD

102 Organizer

102

UNIT 2 REVIEW

Place an X before each true sentence. Correct any false sentences by rewriting them.

1. _____ Jesus taught that birds are more important to God than people are.

2. __X__ God the Father is always faithful to us.

3. __X__ Creeds summarize the beliefs of the Church.

4. _____ The day the disciples received the Holy Spirit is called Christmas Day.

5. __X__ The resurrection of Jesus is his rising from death to new life.

Place an X before each statement that expresses a Catholic belief.

1. __X__ God loves me.

2. _____ I have to be grown up before I can be a friend of Jesus.

3. __X__ The Holy Spirit gives life to the Church and to me.

4. __X__ I will rise from death to new life.

5. _____ The Apostles' Creed lists the names of the twelve apostles.

6. __X__ Jesus will come again.

7. __X__ I can depend upon God.

8. _____ Jesus is human only, not divine.

9. _____ The dove is an image of Jesus in the Bible.

10. __X__ The Holy Spirit gives us courage.

Reviewing the Unit

The purpose of the Unit Review is to reinforce concepts presented in the preceding four chapters and to check the students' understanding. After explaining the directions, give the students sufficient time to complete the two-page review. Answer any questions the students may have.

In the first activity on page 103, the students should rewrite the first and fourth statements to read as follows.

1. *Jesus taught that people are more important to God than birds are.*

4. *The day the disciples received the Holy Spirit is called Pentecost.*

Testing

After the students have completed the Unit Review, you may wish to distribute copies of the Unit 2 Test from the Unit Tests booklet in The Resourceful Teacher Package.

Optional Unit Project

Have the students make "We Believe" booklets. Give each student two sheets of 9" × 12" white drawing paper and direct the students to fold the papers in half to make booklets. Have the students title the cover page "We Believe." The first five inside pages can be titled, "God the Father," "Jesus Christ," "Holy Spirit," "The Catholic Church," and "Eternal Life." Have each student write a sentence or two about each of the topics and then decorate the pages. On the inside back cover, the students may write the words of the Apostles' Creed, the Nicene Creed, or the Sign of the Cross.

Circle the correct letter to complete each sentence.

1. Jesus promised to send the Holy Spirit to _____ and guide us.
   (a) frighten   (b) help   (c) believe

2. Jesus taught that God, our Father, _____ us.
   (a) cares for   (b) forgets   (c) is afraid of

3. Jesus, the _____ of God, is always with us.
   (a) Father   (b) Son   (c) Holy Spirit

4. _____ is called the birthday of the Church.
   (a) Easter   (b) Christmas   (c) Pentecost

5. I believe in God, the Father _____ , creator of heaven and earth.
   (a) almighty   (b) priest   (c) sometimes

Find the words about the Holy Spirit that are hidden in the puzzle below. The first letter of each word is given.

```
P E N T E C O S T
A H E L P E R X O
T R U S E A S Y N
I O O P A W I N G
E A R L C I H U U
N O W G E N T L E
T H E I R D R L S
R O O F I R E E W
E A T T G U I D E
```

P entecost

H elper

G entle

F ire

G uide

P atient

G ift

P eace

W ind

T ongues

REMEMBERING TO STOP and THINK!

Our bodies often show us and others how we are feeling. Look at each of the pictures below and find the clues that tell how the person is feeling. Draw a line from the word that describes a feeling to the face that matches the feeling.

HAPPY

ANGRY

EMBARRASSED

WORRIED

Sometimes our bodies give us clues about our feelings that others may not be able to see. These clues can remind us to stop and think before we react to people or situations. For example, when we feel anger, our heart might beat more rapidly, the palms of our hands might begin to sweat, or our stomach might feel tight. A good problem solver uses these clues as a reminder to stop and think before acting.

Have you ever had a time when you were feeling nervous and your stomach felt funny? We sometimes describe this feeling as "having butterflies in our stomach." This is something we feel on the inside. Nobody else would notice unless we told them how we felt. Can you remember the last time *you* had butterflies in your stomach? What do you think your body was trying to tell you?

Objective

This lesson helps the students understand the importance of stopping to think when faced with a problem and how body clues can be signals for remembering this step.

Introducing the Lesson

Review with the students the problem-solving steps introduced in the lesson on pages 55–56. Tell the students that today's lesson is about remembering to stop and think when faced with a problem. Ask students why it might be difficult to remember this step.

Reading About Body Clues

Read the paragraph at the top of page 105 in the student text. Have the students complete the matching activity. Then invite each student to compare answers with a partner.

Ask for volunteers to read aloud the paragraphs at the bottom of the page. Ask if anyone can remember a time when they experienced "butterflies" or any of the other body signals mentioned. Encourage students to watch for these body signs as ways of remembering to stop and think.

Lesson continues on page 106.

105

Reading and Discussing the Text

Read with the students "Michael Forgets to Stop and Think" at the top of page 106. Then discuss the questions following the story. (*1. The problem is that Maria disagrees with what Michael wants to play. 2. Michael's goal is to get Maria to agree to play soccer. 3. Michael needed to stop and think at the point where he first began to feel upset or irritated with Maria. 4. Answers will vary. Explain that Michael and Maria might have been able to work out a solution to their problem and have an enjoyable time together.*)

Following Jesus

Read with the class "Following Jesus" at the bottom of page 106. Help the students understand that disagreeing with a friend isn't wrong. However, how we try to solve the disagreement can be helpful or hurtful, depending on the solution we choose. Emphasize that, as followers of Jesus, we are called to find helpful solutions.

Concluding the Lesson

Ask each student to sit quietly and think of a time when he or she acted in a way that was unkind or hurtful to another. Assure the students that Jesus forgives us and can help us to find good solutions to our problems. Then invite the students to pray with you the prayer at the bottom of the page.

106

Michael Forgets to Stop and Think

Michael and Maria are neighbors and friends. They play together almost every day after school. Sometimes they ride bikes. They often pretend they are explorers in outer space.

One day, Michael wanted to play soccer. Maria wanted to play a game of space explorers. "We *always* play explorers. Let's play soccer for a change!" Michael suggested. But Maria refused. "No way! It's explorers or nothing!" she said very loudly. Michael got mad and said to Maria, "You always have to have your way!" "That's not true!" Maria yelled. Michael yelled back to her, "It *is* true, and if you won't play soccer then I'm going home!" Michael called Maria a baby and stomped home.

Discuss

1. What is Michael's problem?
2. What is Michael's goal?
3. At what point in the story did Michael need to STOP and THINK?
4. How might the story have changed if Michael had remembered to STOP and THINK?

Following Jesus

Jesus calls us to be his friend and to be friends with one another. We may often disagree with others, but Jesus wants us to find helpful, not hurtful, ways to handle these disagreements. By remembering to STOP and THINK, we give ourselves more time to find the best solutions.

PRAYER

Jesus, I am sorry for the times I acted in ways that were unkind and hurtful to others. Help me to remember to stop and think each time I have a problem so that I may find solutions that are helpful, not hurtful. Thank you, Jesus. Amen.

OPENING DOORS
A Take-Home Magazine™

THIS IS OUR FAITH

Growing Closer

COMPOSE A FAMILY CREED. Ask each person to write on a sheet of paper three things he or she believes in most. Then on a posterboard, print what each one believes under the words *We Believe*. Hang your family creed in a special place.

THINK ABOUT YOUR FAMILY'S FAITHFULNESS. How are you present to your family? Do you try to spend time together? Do you stay in touch with family members who live far away or are confined to their homes? Do you pray for one another? How can you better show your unending love for your family?

Looking Ahead

Unit 3 will help your child learn about the many ways we, as Catholics, worship. The unit will focus first on praying and on the many different kinds of prayer known and practiced by Catholics. Then your child will learn that the most unique characteristic of Catholic worship is the community celebration of the seven sacraments.

8

© Silver Burdett Ginn Inc.

Opening Doors ~~~

Sending the Magazine Home

As you complete Unit 2 with your class, assist the students in carefully removing *Opening Doors: A Take-Home Magazine* (two pages) from their texts by separating the pages from the book along the perforations. Demonstrate how to fold the two pages to form an eight-page booklet.

When the magazines are folded, take time to explain each section of the magazine to the students. Allow the students to ask any questions they may have. Ask the students to take the magazine home and to encourage their families to read it with them and to participate in the suggested activities. You may wish to attach a letter of your own, encouraging the family to use the magazine each time their child brings it home.

CLAIMING THE
PROMISES OF BAPTISM

When adults were baptized in the early Christian communities of the first century, they were immersed three times. Each time, they were asked, "Do you believe?" With their first response of "yes," they were baptized in the name of the Father; with their second response, in the name of the Son; and with their third response, in the name of the Holy Spirit.

The baptismal questions beginning with "Do you believe" are used in the Easter Vigil and the Easter Sunday Mass in the Church today. The questions asked by the priest and our responses of "I do" form what we call the baptismal creed, or the Renewal of Baptismal Promises.

Each time we recite the creed, in any form, we make a statement of our faith, which began at our Baptism. The promises of Baptism are not only those that parents and godparents make to help a child live as a follower of Jesus. As significant as those promises are, one of the most noteworthy promises of the sacrament of Baptism is the promise of eternal life that *God* makes to the child or adult being baptized! Through our baptismal faith, which we affirm in our lives and in our worship, we *inherit* eternal life with God.

In the First Letter of Peter in the New Testament, we read that in Baptism, God "gave us a new birth to a living hope . . . to an inheritance . . . kept in heaven for you who by the power of God are safeguarded through faith" (1 Peter 1:3–5). A special practice used in the ceremony of Baptism for several centuries signified this blessing of Baptism. A drink of milk and honey was offered to newly baptized persons to remind them of God's promise to the Hebrew people in the

The **Apostles' Creed,** based on the teachings of the Apostles, also originated as a baptismal creed in the second century. The text of this creed first appeared in a handbook of Christian doctrine written in the eighth century. Today, it is used in Protestant liturgy and in the Roman Catholic rite. In the Roman rite, it is used specifically for the sacrament of Baptism and in Masses for children.

The Apostles' Creed describes Jesus as God's only Son and then recounts the events of his conception, birth, passion, death, resurrection, ascension, and second coming. The Nicene Creed, crucial in the fight against Arianism, includes a further description of Jesus that emphasizes his divinity.

In the shorter Apostles' Creed we say, "*I believe,*" which reminds us that faith comes from within the heart of each believer. In the Nicene Creed we say, "*We believe.*" This creed not only affirms the faith of our parish families but also joins these local faith communities together with the whole people of God who have shared a living tradition for nearly two thousand years!

desert that they would inherit "a land flowing with milk and honey" (Exodus 13:5). As people of God, the Church claims this same promise of salvation today.

John baptizing in the Jordan River

Like the Apostles' Creed and the Nicene Creed, the baptismal creed summarizes our belief that God is love. This love reaches out to all the people of God's creation, who are born of that love. It is revealed to us in the gift of the Incarnation and in the nearness of the Holy Spirit. Indeed, our God is faithful and lovingly fulfills all promises.

The Creeds

Each Sunday, Catholics recite the Nicene Creed at Mass. You may have memorized this creed, but how much do you really know about this statement of faith?

In the second and third centuries, adults preparing to join the Christian community were given a creed that summarized all that Christians believed. As the basis for their instruction, this creed was recited by the catechumens as their own profession of faith immediately before they were baptized. In the fourth century, the Church formalized this creed to make a statement against Arianism, a teaching that denied that Christ was divine. We have come to know this formal statement of Christian faith as the **Nicene Creed,** which developed from the Council of Nicaea (325 A.D.) and the First Council of Constantinople (381 A.D.). Today, this creed is a part of the eucharistic liturgy in all Catholic Churches.

6

Our Faithful God

The faithfulness of our God is the basis of the creeds we profess as Catholic Christians. The Nicene Creed we say at Mass lists all of the basic beliefs of our faith. Read the pages of this magazine with your child. Enjoy the activity together.

What does it mean to be faithful? One of the best examples of faithfulness is the love our parents or guardians show us every day. No matter what we say or, do, our parents continue to love us and provide for us.

At Mass we say the Nicene Creed. This creed, or statement of beliefs, reminds us of God's faithful love for us, the Church. When we recite the creed, we remember how God is always with us, day by day and year by year. We recall that God cares for us and has done many great things for us.

We believe that God has been faithful in times long ago. We know God's faithfulness to us now. We trust that God will be with us always, even until the end of time. We are proud to declare these beliefs together as members of the Catholic Church. We are grateful for God's loving care that will never end!

Identify all the true and false statements below. Then try to make the false statements true. Ask other members of your family to try them, too.

1. We believe in three Gods.
2. We believe in God's Son, Jesus, who lived, died, and rose to new life for us.
3. We believe that God did not send us a helper and guide.
4. We believe that the Church does not welcome most people.
5. We believe that we will live with Jesus forever.

When you go to Church, say the Nicene Creed aloud with the rest of the community. Think about what each part of the creed means to you. Thank God for being faithful!

4

5

are some of your favorite times and places to talk to God?

Unit Aim

To help the students understand and appreciate what prayer is and what the sacraments of initiation, healing, and vocation mean to Catholics.

Doctrinal Summaries

CHAPTER 9
God calls believers to pray. The Scriptures tell many stories of Jesus praying, both alone and with others. Jesus gives us the Holy Spirit to help us pray.

CHAPTER 10
The Church celebrates three sacraments of initiation: Baptism, Confirmation, and Eucharist. The Church welcomes new members through these sacraments.

CHAPTER 11
The Church brings Jesus' forgiveness and healing through the sacraments of healing. These sacraments are Anointing of the Sick and Reconciliation.

CHAPTER 12
Everyone has a God-given vocation. All vocations are important. The Church celebrates two vocations with sacraments: Holy Orders and Matrimony.

Note:
As you prepare this unit, you may wish to refer to the reference section, *Our Catholic Heritage,* beginning on page 327.

Additional resources for Unit 1 include a Unit Test and a Family Letter as well as a video and selections from the THIS IS OUR FAITH Music Program. You might also find it helpful to preview *Saints and Other Holy People* and *Prayer Celebrations* for possibilities to enhance the unit.

Introducing the UNIT

Call attention to the photograph on page 111 and read aloud the unit title. Invite comments on how the girl is praying and what she might be saying to God. Have the students discuss the unit-focus question with partners. Poll the students to determine when and where they usually pray. Emphasize that in Unit 3 they will learn more about how members of the Church community pray, both privately and publicly.

Vocabulary

prayer	baptismal pool
sacraments	immersion
psalms	healing
synagogue	Anointing of
liturgy	the Sick
Liturgy of the	anointing
Hours	sin
initiation	vocation
Easter Vigil	Holy Orders
baptismal font	Matrimony

9 Our Church Prays

Objectives

To help the students

- Understand that prayer helps us respond in faith to God's love for us.
- Become better acquainted with how Jesus prayed.
- Learn about the Church's official prayers.
- Appreciate that prayer brings us closer to God.
- Celebrate by praying with the psalms and review the chapter.

Chapter Outline

	Step 1 Learning About Our Lives	Step 2 Learning About Our Faith	Step 3 Learning How to Live Our Faith
Day 1	■ Introduce the chapter. ■ Study the illustration. ■ Read a poem. *ABOUT 10 MINUTES*	■ Read about ways of praying. ■ Learn about types of prayer. ■ Study the photograph. ■ Learn the vocabulary. *ABOUT 17 MINUTES*	■ Pray in silence. *ABOUT 3 MINUTES*
Day 2	■ Reflect on personal prayer. *ABOUT 5 MINUTES*	■ Read the story. ■ Explore the psalms. *ABOUT 14 MINUTES*	■ Write a psalm. *ABOUT 11 MINUTES*
Day 3	■ Write daily prayers. *ABOUT 15 MINUTES*	■ Read about the Church's prayer. ■ Learn the vocabulary. *ABOUT 10 MINUTES*	■ Pray with light. *ABOUT 5 MINUTES*
Day 4	■ Name ways of communicating. *ABOUT 8 MINUTES*	■ Read the text. ■ Learn the doctrine. *ABOUT 10 MINUTES*	■ Complete a checklist. *ABOUT 12 MINUTES*
Day 5	**Prayer** Identify the wonders of creation; prepare for prayer. **Review** Identify prayer types; complete the review; pray with the scriptural verse.		

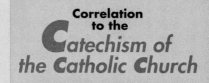

**Correlation
to the
Catechism of
the Catholic Church**

Paragraphs
**1342, 2567, 2607, 2623,
2624, 2625, 2644**

Plan Ahead

	Preparing Your Class	**Materials Needed**	**Additional Resources**

Additional Resources

As you plan this chapter, consider using the following materials from The Resourceful Teacher Package.

Day 1

Read through the lesson plan. Think about your own experiences of praying alone and with others. List the five types of prayer from Step 2 on the chalkboard.

■ chalkboard
■ pencils or pens

■ *Classroom Activity Sheets 9* and *9a*

■ *Family Activity Sheets 9* and *9a*

Day 2

Read through the lesson plan for this class session.

■ pencils or pens

■ *Chapter 9 Test*

■ *Prayers for Every Day*

■ *Projects: Grade 3*

Day 3

Read through the lesson plan for this class session. Prepare an area for prayer in the classroom.

■ pencils or pens
■ candle and matches

You may also wish to refer to the following Big Books.

■ *We Celebrate the Sacraments,* pages 2 and 3

■ *We Celebrate God's Word,* pages 12 and 23

Day 4

Read through the lesson plan for this class session.

■ pens or pencils

■ *We Celebrate the Mass,* pages 4, 11, and 17

In preparing the students for the Sunday readings, you may wish to use Silver Burdett Ginn's *Getting Ready for Sunday* student and teacher materials.

Day 5

Prepare an environment for prayer in the classroom. Review this week's sessions to prepare for the chapter review.

■ chalkboard
■ pencils or pens

BOOKS FOR THE JOURNEY

Sunday's Children. James Bitney. Resource Publications, 1986. "Morning Prayer," "Table Prayer," and "Evening Prayer." Delightful versions of morning, evening, and mealtime prayers.

Yussel's Prayer. Barbara Cohen. Lothrop, 1981. Reveals that a child's simple prayer is powerful because it comes from his heart.

MORE BOOKS FOR THE JOURNEY

Experience Jesus Today. Charles Singer and Albert Hari. OCP Publications, 1993. "Jesus' Prayer," p. 83. Information on how Jesus learned to pray and how prayer was an important part of his life.

REDUCED CLASSROOM ACTIVITIES

NAME _____

OUR CHURCH PRAYS

Read each story on pages 9 and 9a. On the line next to each picture, write which type of prayer the child might pray (praise, petition, sorrow, thanksgiving). Then write the words you think the child in the picture could pray.

sorrow
(Type of prayer)

" _____
_____
_____
_____ "

You upset your friend at recess because you fought with him. You want to tell God you're sorry.

thanksgiving
(Type of prayer)

" _____
_____
_____
_____ "

You just came back from a field trip to the zoo. You want to thank God for a wonderful time.

To the Teacher: The activity on this page and page 9a reviews four different types of prayer: praise, petition, sorrow, and thanksgiving.

© Silver Burdett Ginn Inc.

Chapter 9   Our Church Prays   THIS IS OUR FAITH 3   **9**

NAME _____

petition
(Type of prayer)

" _____
_____
_____
_____ "

You lost your library book and it's due tomorrow. You're afraid you won't find it in time. You want God to help you.

praise
(Type of prayer)

" _____
_____
_____
_____ "

You enjoy looking at the ocean and swimming in it. You want to praise God for this great gift.

To the Teacher: This activity is continued from the previous page.

© Silver Burdett Ginn Inc.

9a   THIS IS OUR FAITH 3   Chapter 9   Our Church Prays

FAITH AND PRAYER

Prayer becomes an important part of our experience of life as we grow in our awareness of God and his love for us. As a community of faith, we often pray together, especially to give thanks to God for the gift of Jesus. We also respond to God in a variety of ways in our personal prayer experiences. Our prayers, offered individually and as a community, are an important part of our response as Catholics to God's love for us.

Our model for becoming a person of prayer is Jesus. As a young boy, Jesus learned to pray the psalms and the other Jewish prayers that were part of the life of his faith community. Jesus followed the prayer traditions of his people. The Gospels give us a number of examples of Jesus praying. We gain the impression that he prayed often, in a variety of ways, and in a variety of places. He not only prayed in public, but he also frequently went off by himself to pray.

Today, both individually and as a community of faith, we respond to God through prayers of petition, thanksgiving, contrition, and adoration. Our prayers express our faith. We become more Christlike as a Church when we are prayerful people. The *National Catechetical Directory* says: "The Church is a worshiping community . . . . Worship creates, expresses, and fulfills the Church." (No. 112)

CHILDREN AND PRAYER

Children first experience prayer when they are with praying people, especially members of their own families. The next most important point of contact with prayer is the experience of the worshiping community in the parish at Sunday Mass. Religion class also gives children the opportunity to experience prayer in a variety of ways. We all pass on the tradition and value of prayer to our children.

In this chapter, discussion of the various kinds of prayer and times to pray will help the students begin to sense that prayer is a way of life. They will learn that prayer can be part of the rhythm of each day, a very natural expression of our faith in God. Giving praise and thanks to God, expressing our needs, and asking forgiveness are at the heart of our relationship with God.

Day 1
Prayer

Objective

This lesson helps the students understand that prayer helps us respond in faith to God's love for us.

Step 1/INTRODUCTION

Learning About Our Lives

Introducing the Chapter

Ask for a volunteer to read aloud the chapter title and focus statement. Invite several students to share experiences of praying with others. Help the students appreciate that praying with others is as important and meaningful as praying alone. Have the students discuss why they pray. (*Their responses may include: to thank God, to ask God's help, to show love for God, or to talk with God.*)

Studying the Illustration

Direct attention to the illustration on page 112. After allowing time for the students to study the picture, ask the following questions.

■ What is happening in the picture? (*The girl is teaching her younger brother to pray.*)

■ Why is the girl kneeling? (*Out of reverence for God*)

■ What do you believe the girl might be thinking and feeling?

■ What do you think her brother might be feeling?

Reading a Poem

Have students take turns reading aloud the three stanzas of the poem on page 112. Invite the students to reread the poem silently and circle the different ways in which they pray. Or you might ask questions such as *Do you pray by yourself? Do you talk with God?* and so on.

Step 2/DEVELOPMENT

Learning About Our Faith

Reading About Ways of Praying

Ask volunteers to read aloud "Many Ways to Pray" on page 113. Recall with the class that the definition they learned for *prayer* in Grade 1 was "talking and listening to God." Emphasize

112

---

9 Our Church Prays

We show faith, our trust in God, by praying alone and with others. Tell about a special time you prayed with others.

Prayer

Sometimes when I am by myself,
I talk with God in prayer.
It feels so good inside to know
That God is always there.

God speaks to me in silence,
And that begins my prayer.
I know God always listens
To the thoughts I want to share.

I also pray with others,
Using words, and signs, and songs,
That help us celebrate the Church
To which we all belong.

112   Prayer

Cultural Awareness

Prayer is an important part of every religious sect or denomination. For some, there are large community celebrations, like those held by Native Americans of the Southwest that involve music and dance. For others, like the Quakers and Buddhist monks, prayer is an internal matter, carried out in silence. All religious prayer has as its objective a close relationship with God and a better understanding of our relationships with one another.

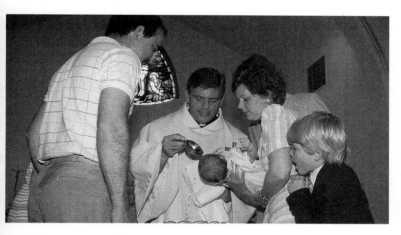

Many Ways to Pray

When we talk and listen to God, either alone or in a parish community, we are praying. Our **prayer** expresses our trust in God, as individuals and as a community of believers. Our words, our songs, and our gestures all help us to respond in faith to God's love for us. They are all part of our prayer.

We sometimes begin our prayer in silence. Sometimes when we are quiet, we can hear God speaking to us in our hearts. We sometimes pray like this in our parish churches before a Mass begins. God also speaks to us in the Scriptures we hear at Mass and when we read the Scriptures at home.

Each time we gather to celebrate the **sacraments**, we are praying in many ways. We listen to God's word and we talk to God in prayer. We know that the sacraments are special celebrations of Jesus' love for us and signs of his presence with us now. We hear about and experience Jesus' love and presence through the words, songs, and gestures of the celebrations. Can you think of some things you hear, say, or do at Mass that help you to know Jesus' love for you?

Vocabulary

prayer: listening and talking to God through our words, our songs, and our gestures

sacraments: special celebrations of the Church that show Jesus' love for us and are signs of his presence with us now

---

Focus on

Sacraments In explaining sacraments to students, emphasize that they are part of the liturgy, or official public prayers of the Church. In the sacraments we encounter Christ in unique ways, particular to specific times or needs in our lives. The sacraments provide unique opportunities for us to unite ourselves with Christ and the work of the coming kingdom.

Enriching the Lesson

Have the students use drawing paper and crayons to illustrate prayer experiences they have participated in that have special meaning for them. These might include a Christmas pageant, First Communion, a family Mass, and so on. Discuss why these celebrations are important. Emphasize that God calls us to celebrate our faith together as a community.

---

that we can pray alone or with others, any time and any place.

Learning About Types of Prayer

Introduce the five basic types of prayer by writing the words *prayers of praise* on the chalkboard. Ask the students what this prayer expresses (*Our adoration of God*). Do the same with the four other types of prayer, helping the students understand what we express in these prayers: prayers of thanksgiving (*Our gratitude to God*); prayers of sorrow (*Expressing sorrow to God for sins*); prayers of petition (*Seeking God's help in times of need*); and prayers of faith (*Expressing belief and trust in God*).

Studying the Photograph

Have the students identify what is taking place in the photograph. Remind them that Baptism is one of the sacraments. Ask the students to explain what the priest, parents, and godparents are praying for. Elicit from the class that they are asking for God's blessing on the child and for God's help as they share faith and try to be good examples to the child. Point out that sacraments do not just *include* prayers, they *are* prayers.

Learning the Vocabulary

Direct attention to the Vocabulary section and read aloud the definitions for the words *prayer* and *sacraments*.

Step 3/CONCLUSION

Learning How to Live Our Faith

Praying in Silence

Invite the students to close their eyes as you read aloud the second stanza of the poem on page 112. Ask them to take a moment to invite God to speak to them in the silence of their hearts. Conclude by having the students pray: "Speak to me, Lord. I want to hear your word."

DAY 2
SCRIPTURE

Objective

This lesson helps the students become better acquainted with how Jesus prayed.

Step 1/INTRODUCTION

Learning About Our Lives

Reflecting on Personal Prayer

Ask the students to think about the last twenty-four hours in their lives as they answer the following questions: *Did you take the time to pray this morning? Did you thank God for your food in blessings prayed before or after meals? Did you pray before you went to bed last night? What prayers have you said alone or with others today? How have you included God or Jesus in your life today?* Help the students recognize that we are called to listen to and talk to God throughout the day.

Step 2/DEVELOPMENT

Learning About Our Faith

Reading the Story

Explain that Jesus prayed in a variety of ways and in various places. Recall that Jesus is our best example of what it means to be a prayerful person who is close to God.

Have students take turns reading aloud the story "Jesus Prayed" on page 114. As the words *psalms* and *synagogue* are introduced, refer the students to the Vocabulary section on page 115 and have them learn the definitions. Then ask the following questions.

- When did Jesus pray? (*Every morning, afternoon, and evening; at meals*)
- Who taught Jesus to pray? (*Mary and Joseph*)
- What are the psalms? (*Songs of prayer from the Old Testament*)
- Where did Jesus pray? (*At home, in the synagogue, outdoors*)
- What did prayer mean for Jesus? (*Listening to and talking to God*)

Jesus Prayed

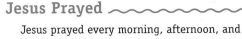

Jesus prayed every morning, afternoon, and evening. Jesus also prayed at meals. He learned to pray at home from Mary and Joseph. They taught Jesus the **psalms**, the songs of prayer from the Old Testament. Mary, Joseph, and Jesus prayed as a family.

On Saturdays, Jesus went to the **synagogue** to pray with his family, friends, and neighbors. In Jerusalem, he liked to pray in the great Temple.

Jesus sometimes prayed when he was with crowds of people in busy towns. He also liked to go off by himself at times to pray in the hills and desert or along the shores of the Jordan River or the Sea of Galilee. Jesus experienced prayer as both talking to and listening to God.

His disciples noticed how much Jesus liked to pray. By his words and example, Jesus taught his disciples to pray as he did.

Based on many Gospel stories

114 Scripture

 **Cultural Awareness**

Emphasize that Jesus was reared in the Jewish faith and that, like Jewish people today, he worshiped God in a synagogue. Both Christians and Jews pray the psalms when they worship today. Help the students appreciate that many traditions of our Catholic faith are rooted in the traditions of the Jewish faith.

Focus on

Prayer of Jesus The *Cathechism of the Catholic Church* states that "When Jesus prays he is already teaching us how to pray. His prayer to his Father is the theolagal path (the path of faith, hope, and charity) of our prayer to God. But the Gospel also gives us Jesus' explicit teaching on prayer. Like a wise teacher he takes hold of us where we are and leads us progressively toward the Father." (#2607)

114

Psalm Prayers

Some of Jesus' favorite prayers were the psalms. He prayed them alone and sang them with others. Here are some psalms you can learn by heart.

Of Faith
"O LORD, my God, in you I trust."
Psalm 25:1b–2a

Of Hope
"For you are my hope, O Lord."
Psalm 71:5a

Of Love
"I love you, O LORD, my strength."
Psalm 18:2

Of Petition
"O LORD, be my helper."
Psalm 30:11b

Of Thanksgiving
"I will give thanks to you, O LORD, with all my heart."
Psalm 9:2a

Of Sorrow
"Have mercy on me, O God, in your goodness."
Psalm 51:3a

Of Praise
"O LORD, my God, you are great and good!"
Based on Psalm 104:1b

Activity

The psalms show us how to pray to God in many ways. Write your own words for each kind of prayer in the box below.

My Prayer of Thanks _____

_____

My Prayer of Praise _____

_____

My Prayer of Sorrow _____

_____

My Prayer of Love _____

_____

Vocabulary

psalms: songs of prayer from the Old Testament

synagogue: a special place where Jewish people pray and study God's word

---

Point out the prayers on page 115. Explain that Jesus learned these psalms as he grew up in Nazareth, and he prayed them throughout his life. Call on several members of the class to read these verses from the psalms.

Step 3/CONCLUSION

Learning How to Live Our Faith

Writing a Psalm

Read aloud the introduction to the activity. Stress that through prayer we respond to the different ways in which God shows love and care for us. Then explain the activity and have the students work on their own to complete it. Afterward, invite sharing.

Teaching Tips

Distribute Bibles to the students and help them locate the Book of Psalms. Explain that there are 150 psalms and that many of them may have been written by King David, an ancestor of Jesus. Allow the students to look through the psalms to get an idea of what they look like. You might have them locate some of the verses they studied on page 115.

115

Objective

This lesson helps the students learn about the Church's official prayers.

Step 1/INTRODUCTION

Learning About Our Lives

Writing Daily Prayers

Discuss with the students the question at the top of page 116. Have them identify when they feel called to pray or times when they think praying would be a good thing to do. (*Responses might include: on a sunny day; when they are feeling worried, lonely, or sad; when they have received good news; and so forth.*) Help the students appreciate that any emotion or experience can be shared with God in prayer.

Explain the directions for the activity. Encourage the students to think quietly about prayers they might pray in the morning, afternoon, and evening and to write them down. When all have finished, call on volunteers to read aloud their prayers.

or...

Explain to the class that people often recite traditional memorized prayers at certain times of the day. These may include beginning the day with the Morning Offering, praying the Angelus at noon, or making an Act of Contrition in the evening. Distribute copies of these prayers to the class and pray them at appropriate times over the next several weeks.

Activity

On a typical day, how many times do you stop to pray? _____
    Think back to yesterday. What was happening? What were you feeling? Then write a short prayer for each of these times.

Morning Prayer: <u>Possible responses may include: asking for guidance</u>
<u>throughout the day, telling God about a specific concern or need, and giving</u>
<u>thanks to God for a beautiful morning.</u>

Afternoon Prayer: <u>Possible responses may include: thanking God for helping</u>
<u>in a specific way, asking for help to remember that God is always with us, and</u>
<u>giving praise for answered prayers.</u>

Evening Prayer: <u>Possible responses may</u>
<u>include: thanking God for home and family,</u>
<u>asking for forgiveness, and praying for a</u>
<u>restful night of sleep.</u>

116 Prayer

🍎 Teaching Tips

A wonderfully practical resource for classroom prayer is *Children's Daily Prayer*, Elizabeth McMahon Jeep, Liturgy Training Publications, Chicago, Illinois. This resource is published yearly and offers suggestions and instructions for daily and weekly prayer throughout the school year.

Christian Daily Prayer

Throughout the history of the Church, Christians have believed that praying often is important. The Scriptures tell us to "pray always, without stopping!" (based on 1 Thessalonians 5:17). Like the early Christians, some men and women in religious communities today continue the long tradition of praying together every morning and evening. Other Christians also gather together for prayer every day.

When we celebrate Mass in our parishes, we sometimes say we are celebrating **liturgy**, which means the official public prayers of the Church. The prayers that some Christians use to pray together every morning and evening are called the **Liturgy of the Hours**. These are also official public prayers of the Church. These prayers express our faith that God is with us always, from sunrise to sunset, every hour of the day. The Liturgy of the Hours includes singing or reading psalms from the Scriptures, reciting The Lord's Prayer, and praying petitions that express our concern for the needs of the Church.

Vocabulary

liturgy: the official public prayers of the Church

Liturgy of the Hours: the official prayers of the Church that some Christians pray together every morning and every evening

Prayer 117

Learning About Our Faith

Reading About the Church's Prayer

Read with the class "Christian Daily Prayer" on page 117. Use the following questions to guide discussion.

- What is liturgy? (*The official public prayers of the Church*)
- What is the Liturgy of the Hours? (*The official prayers of the Church that some Christians pray together every morning and every evening*)
- What does the Liturgy of the Hours help us remember? (*That God is with us always*)

Learning the Vocabulary

Have volunteers read aloud the words and definitions in the Vocabulary box. Check the students' understanding by having them use each term in a sentence.

Step 3/CONCLUSION

Learning How to Live Our Faith

Praying with Light

Have the students gather in an area you have prepared for prayer. Begin the prayer experience by lighting a candle and praying, "God, you are with us always. You created light to give us warmth and to remind us of your constant presence. You gave us the gift of your Son, Jesus, the Light of the World. We praise you, Lord, our Light and Life." Encourage the students to offer spontaneous prayers of praise to God. Conclude by praying together The Lord's Prayer.

Focus on

Scripture Many formal prayers and devotions used by Catholics are based on passages from Scripture or events depicted in Scripture. With few exceptions the mysteries of the Rosary refer to events described in the Gospels. The Hail Mary quotes from the account of the Annunciation in the Gospel of Luke. The Lord's Prayer is a direct quote of Jesus' words in the sixth chapter of Matthew. Among other prayers taken directly from Scripture are the Nunc Dimittis and the Magnificat, both taken from the Gospel of Luke.

Enriching the Lesson

Explain that in addition to the official prayers of the Church many Catholics also pray *devotions*. Devotions are special prayers that honor God, Jesus, Mary, or the saints in word and ritual. You may want to teach or review common devotions, such as the Stations of the Cross, found on pages 349–352. Emphasize that devotions can be prayed alone or with a group.

Objective

This lesson helps the students appreciate that prayer brings us closer to God.

Step 1/INTRODUCTION

Learning About Our Lives

Naming Ways of Communicating

Have the students identify the important people in their lives, such as relatives and friends to whom they feel especially close. Ask them to think about what kinds of things they talk about and share with these people. Then ask them to think of what they might talk about with a casual friend or someone they do not know well. Elicit responses from several students. Note that we are most likely to share our true selves with those who know us best and the people we love and trust.

Step 2/DEVELOPMENT

Learning About Our Faith

Reading the Text

Call on volunteers to take turns reading aloud "Prayer and Friendship" on page 118. Then discuss the following questions.

- What do we show God when we pray often? (*That our friendship with God is important to us*)

- Who can help us when we are not sure about what to say to God in prayer? (*The Holy Spirit can help us find the words to say.*)

- What does prayer help us do? (*It helps us grow closer to God and to all those with whom we pray.*)

Prayer and Friendship

When we are good friends with someone, we usually spend time talking to them, listening to them, and playing with them. Whenever we can, we include them in our family activities and celebrations, too. The more time we spend with our friends, the closer we become.

On the other hand, we may have a friend who seems too busy to talk to us or to do things with us. When this happens, we may start to think that this friend does not want to be our friend anymore. This can make us feel angry or sad.

We know that God is always with us and that we can pray at any time. But it is only when we take the time to talk to and listen to God in prayer that we can say we have a friendship with God. The more often we pray, the more we show God that our friendship is very important. We can do this by spending some quiet time listening to God. God likes spending quiet time with us as much as hearing us pray aloud. When we do use words to pray, we can use prayers we have learned at Mass or in Religion class. Or we can use our own words. We can talk to God in the same way that we would talk to a close friend. When we are not sure what to say to God in prayer, we can just be still or we can ask the Holy Spirit to help us find the words to say.

We have learned that we can pray in many ways and at any hour of the day. The most important thing is to take the time to pray. The more time we spend in prayer, the closer our relationship with God can become. Whether we are praying alone, with our family, or with our parish community, we believe that prayer can bring us closer to God and to all those with whom we pray.

118 Prayer

Focus on

Prayer The *Catechism of the Catholic Church* tells us that Scripture identifies, more than a thousand times, the *heart* as the source of prayer. The Catechism says: "It is the *heart* that prays. If our heart is far from God, the words of prayer are in vain" (# 2562).

Activity

The sentences below describe some of the ways Catholics pray. For each sentence that describes a way that you have spent time with God, write an **X** on the line. For each sentence that describes a way to spend time with God that you will try sometime soon, write an **S** on the line. Then complete the last sentence to tell about one more way you can spend time with God. Be sure to try some new ways to pray sometime SOON!

_____ I listen to God in quiet before Mass begins.

_____ I talk to God early in the morning.

_____ I pray with my friends in Religion class.

_____ I say a prayer before I go to bed at night.

_____ I pray to God in my own words.

_____ God speaks to me through the Scriptures at Mass.

_____ I pray at meals with my family.

_____ God speaks to me when I read the Scriptures at home.

One more way that I can pray is _____
_____
_____
_____
_____
_____ .

We Believe

God calls believers to pray. The Scriptures tell many stories of Jesus praying, both alone and with others. Jesus gives us the Holy Spirit to help us pray.

Doctrine 119

Learning the Doctrine

Direct attention to the We Believe box on page 119 and have the students read the statement aloud. Encourage the students to remember this central part of the lesson.

Step 3/CONCLUSION

Learning How to Live Our Faith

Completing a Checklist

Ask one of the students to read the directions for the activity on page 119. When students have finished the exercise, have them count the number of *X*'s and *S*'s they have listed. Poll the class to determine whether they have more *X*'s or *S*'s. Tell the students that the sentences that they have marked with an *S* are opportunities for them to improve in their prayer life and are a means of growing closer to God. Suggest they incorporate these new ways of praying into their daily lives.

Point out the incomplete sentence at the bottom of the page and have the students write in the space provided another way that they can pray. Allow time for volunteers to read aloud their written responses.

CURRICULUM CONNECTION

Language Arts As a way of helping students focus on the meaning of their expressions of prayer, try having each member of the class write a short prayer in prose or poetic form. Have the students exchange papers and edit each other's prayers, so that they sound or read better. Then have the students explain to the original authors why they made the changes they did. Have the students then transfer their prayers to decorated cards. Encourage them to pray their prayers each day for a week.

Enriching the Lesson

Write the adage "The family that prays together stays together" on the chalkboard. Discuss with the students how praying together helps their families grow closer to God and to one another. Then have the students suggest how prayer helps the Catholic community grow closer to God and become more caring and loving.

Objective

This lesson helps the students celebrate by praying with the psalms.

Identifying the Wonders of Creation

Call on a student to read aloud the first paragraph of "Praying with the Psalms" on page 120. Encourage each class member to name a wonder of creation for which they want to praise God. List the students' responses on the chalkboard. Remind the students that all of creation is a gift from God.

Preparing for Prayer

Work with the students to develop gestures or actions to accompany the words of Psalm 148. Allow time for the students to practice these gestures several times.

Have the class form two groups for the proclamation of the psalm. Select a volunteer to act as the leader or take this role yourself. Allow time for all students to read through their parts silently.

Praying with the Psalms

Psalm 148 is often used in the Liturgy of the Hours for morning prayer. It is a psalm of praise for all that God has created. Before you begin this prayer, share with your class some of the wonders of creation for which you want to praise God.

The next time you pray in the morning, try to pray your own prayer of praise. Your voice will be heard by God along with the voices of many other Christians around the world who are praising God in the morning!

Leader: Look around the world!
See how many wonderful things there are!
LET THE HEAVENS AND THE EARTH PRAISE GOD!

All: LET THE HEAVENS AND THE EARTH PRAISE GOD!

Side 1: Even the sun and the moon join in praising God;
the shining stars adore the Lord of all creation!
Fire, rain, and wind are all in God's command.

Side 2: All the creatures of the sea and all birds of the sky,
all the animals of the earth, both wild and tame,
praise God!
Every living creature lifts up a song of praise!

All: LET THE HEAVENS AND THE EARTH PRAISE GOD!

Side 1: The mountains and the hills praise God,
the trees, the deserts, and the swamplands,
the seashores and all that is between them
praise the Lord!

Side 2: Let leaders and peoples from all nations praise God!
Let the young and the old, the women and the men,
families and loved ones all join in praising the Lord
of all creation!

All: LET THE HEAVENS AND THE EARTH PRAISE GOD!
AMEN!

Based on Psalm 148

120 Prayer

Teaching Tips

As part of your prayer experience, you may want to read aloud to the class the story of the creation of the world, found in Genesis 1:1–2:4. Do this before having the students pray together Psalm 148.

CURRICULUM CONNECTION

Art Have the students make a mural in praise of the wonders of creation. Use a length of butcher paper or white shelf paper cut to match the width of the bulletin board panel above the front chalkboard in your classroom. You will also need crayons or markers for this activity. Suggest that the students use images and words from Psalm 148 or ideas from the list on the board to create the mural. Divide the paper into panels and have small groups of students work on different portions of the mural.

Chapter Review

Write the code letter(s) that tells which type of prayer each psalm below is an example of.

CODE

PE = Prayer of Petition   F = Prayer of Faith
T = Prayer of Thanksgiving
S = Prayer of Sorrow   PR = Prayer of Praise

---

1. __PR__ "O LORD, my God, you are great and good!"

2. __S__ "Have mercy on me, O God, in your goodness."

3. __PE__ "O LORD, be my helper."

4. __F__ "O LORD, my God, in you I trust."

5. __T__ "I will give thanks to you, O LORD, with all my heart."

Fill in the answers to the first two questions.

1. What is prayer? listening and talking to God
through our words, our songs, and our gestures

2. What are some ways the Church prays? in the
sacraments; in the Liturgy of the Hours; using
words, songs, and gestures

Pray often in the Spirit.
Based on Ephesians 6:18

3. Talk about some reasons prayer is so important in our relationship with God.

★ ★ ★ Enriching the Lesson ★ ★

Give the students six sheets of paper each and have them make prayer booklets that illustrate the five types of prayer. Instruct them to title the first page "My Prayer Booklet." Have them copy the names of the types of prayer at the top of each page, one per page. Invite them to use their own words to write an example of each prayer. After they have finished, encourage the students to decorate their booklets.

Identifying Prayer Types

Explain the directions for the first activity on page 121 and have the students complete it independently. When all have finished, check the students' answers. Note: Students' answers may vary. The red annotated answers shown match the psalm prayers on page 115 of the student text.

Completing the Review

Have the students write answers to the next two review questions on the lines provided in the text. Afterward, check their responses and answer any questions they may have. Encourage all to participate in the discussion of the third question. Be supportive of each student who responds.

Praying with the Scriptural Verse

Read aloud with the group the verse from Scripture at the bottom of page 121. Comment that Saint Paul encourages us to pray often and in a variety of ways. Remind the students that the Holy Spirit helps us pray. Conclude the lesson by inviting the students to present prayers of petition, beginning with the words *Spirit of God . . . .*

10 Our Church Celebrates Initiation

Objectives

To help the students

■ Learn that the Church welcomes new members through the three sacraments of initiation.

■ Understand how the early Christians initiated new members.

■ Appreciate how the sacraments of initiation are celebrated today.

■ Recognize that symbols help us pray.

■ Pray a rite from the Order of Christian Initiation and review the chapter.

Chapter Outline

	Step 1 Learning About Our Lives	Step 2 Learning About Our Faith	Step 3 Learning How to Live Our Faith
Day 1	■ Welcome the students. ■ Introduce the chapter. ■ Discuss the illustrations. *ABOUT 13 MINUTES*	■ Read about Church initiations. ■ Learn the vocabulary and doctrine. *ABOUT 9 MINUTES*	■ Discuss the questions. *ABOUT 8 MINUTES*
Day 2	■ Talk about membership. *ABOUT 5 MINUTES*	■ Read about Christian initiation. ■ Identify sacramental actions. ■ Complete an activity. *ABOUT 13 MINUTES*	■ Research Scripture. ■ Pray a litany. *ABOUT 12 MINUTES*
Day 3	■ Discuss Christian initiation. *ABOUT 8 MINUTES*	■ Read the story. ■ Learn about the sacraments of initiation. ■ Read about the Easter Vigil. *ABOUT 17 MINUTES*	■ Name ways of sharing Jesus' light. *ABOUT 5 MINUTES*
Day 4	■ Write about differences. *ABOUT 7 MINUTES*	■ Read the text. ■ Complete a chart. ■ Read about symbols. ■ Review the vocabulary. *ABOUT 12 MINUTES*	■ Name welcoming words. ■ Share the Sign of Peace. *ABOUT 11 MINUTES*
Day 5	**Prayer** Prepare to pray; pray the Ephphetha Rite. **Review** Match words and phrases; complete the chapter review; pray with the scriptural verse.		

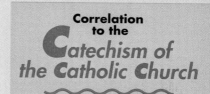

Plan Ahead

	Preparing Your Class	Materials Needed	Additional Resources
Day 1	Read through the lesson plan for this class session. Plan how you will welcome the students.	■ small personal gift for each student	As you plan this chapter, consider using the following materials from The Resourceful Teacher Package.
Day 2	Read through the lesson plan for this class session.	■ Bibles (one for each student) ■ pencils or pens	■ *Classroom Activity Sheets 10* and *10a*
Day 3	Read through the lesson plan. Post around the room some pictures of people receiving the sacraments of Baptism, Confirmation, and Eucharist.	■ pictures of people receiving the sacraments of Baptism, Confirmation, and Eucharist	■ *Family Activity Sheets 10* and *10a*
Day 4	Read through the lesson plan for this class session. Consider the similarities and differences you notice between your parish and others.	■ pencils or pens	■ *Chapter 10 Test* ■ *Prayers for Every Day* ■ *Projects: Grade 3*
Day 5	Prepare an environment for prayer in the classroom. Review this week's sessions to prepare for the chapter review.	■ candle and matches ■ pencils or pens	

Additional Resources (continued)

You may also wish to refer to the following Big Books.

■ *We Celebrate the Sacraments,* pages 2–12

■ *We Celebrate God's Word,* pages 7 and 21

■ *We Celebrate the Mass,* pages 12–15 and 19–21

In preparing the students for the Sunday readings, you may wish to use Silver Burdett Ginn's *Getting Ready for Sunday* student and teacher materials.

BOOKS FOR THE JOURNEY

Papa Panov's Special Day. Leo Tolstoy. Lion USA, 1988. A shoemaker learns that, in welcoming a roadsweeper and a poor woman, he had welcomed Jesus.

Stuffer. Peter Parnall. Macmillan, 1992. A story of a horse that is welcomed by a little girl, sold to other owners when the child goes off to school, and finally welcomed by another little girl.

MORE BOOKS FOR THE JOURNEY

Our Church. Graham English. The Liturgical Press, 1992. "I'm Mary, I'm Ten Years Old and I'm a Catholic," PP. 1–2. A child refers to her baptism in the Catholic Church as her reason for being Catholic.

REDUCED CLASSROOM ACTIVITIES

NAME _____

OUR CHURCH CELEBRATES INITIATION

Think of a new friend you've made. Write his or her name here.

_____

1. What words did you say when you first met?

_____
_____

2. What did you do together when you first met?

_____
_____
_____

How did you help this person make friends with you?

_____
_____

4. What did you learn about each other?

_____
_____
_____

To the Teacher: This activity follows "A Ceremony of Welcome" and draws on the students' personal experiences of welcoming friends.

Chapter 10 Our Church Celebrates Initiation   THIS IS OUR FAITH 3   **10**

NAME _____

SIGNS OF WELCOME

Think about the story "Barbara's Big Day." Underline the correct answer to finish each sentence. Then use these words to fill in the puzzle. You will find the name of a special ceremony.

1. The priest poured water over Barbara's head when he (confirmed, baptized) her.
2. Her (friends, godparents) stood beside her.
3. The priest prayed that the (Holy Spirit, Blessed Mother) would be her helper and guide.
4. Barbara received the sacraments of initiation at the (Easter, peace) Vigil.
5. Barbara's godparents gave her a (or) an (unlit, lighted) candle.
6. Barbara prayed the (Apostles' Creed, Hail Mary) during Baptism.
7. A (parent, priest) confirmed Barbara.
8. He used (oil, wax) to make the Sign of the Cross on Barbara's forehead.
9. Barbara received the Eucharist for the first time at (Communion, offertory) time.
10. The whole (earth, community) rejoiced because Barbara was a new member of the Church.

1. b a p t i z e d
2. g o d p a r e n t s
3. H o l y   S p i r i t
4. E a s t e r
5. l i g h t e d
6. A p o s t l e s '   C r e e d
7. p r i e s t
8. o i l
9. C o m m u n i o n
10. c o m m u n i t y

To the Teacher: This activity follows the story "Barbara's Big Day."

10a THIS IS OUR FAITH 3   **Chapter 10** Our Church Celebrates Initiation

RITUALS OF LIFE

Students in the third grade are familiar with various forms of initiation. They have joined teams and clubs of various kinds. Many have some experience of how it feels to be welcomed into a group. These occasions enhance a child's sense of belonging and self-worth.

Third-grade students also have had the experience of ritual. There have been birthday parties, holiday celebrations, and introductions to new groups. Ritual is a common experience that is at the base of our celebration of the sacraments. Ritual helps us express what is in our hearts.

These experiences of initiation and ritual provide the foundation in a child's life for grasping the meanings of the sacraments of initiation: Baptism, Confirmation, and Eucharist. While the children will eventually grasp the meaning of each of these three sacraments, what is most important at this age is for them to gain a sense of initiation as a ritual and a process of welcome.

THE ORDER OF CHRISTIAN INITIATION

The Order of Christian Initiation provides the model for teaching and for experiencing the sacraments of initiation. It is a process of welcoming and initiating people into the Christian life. This involves learning about the Catholic faith and experiencing the faith that others give witness to in their daily lives. It also involves celebrating the three sacraments of Baptism, Confirmation, and Eucharist as moments of entering into the Christian life. This chapter reviews these three sacraments.

The children in your class may have received the sacraments of initiation at different times. Some students, those from Greek Orthodox and other Eastern Churches, may have received the sacrament of Confirmation at the time of their Baptism. Other students may have been baptized into other Christian denominations. You should realize as well that there may be some children who have not been baptized nor received the Eucharist. It is important to be aware of and sensitive to these different situations.

DAY 1
DOCTRINE

Objective

This lesson helps the students learn that the Church welcomes new members through the three sacraments of initiation.

Step 1/INTRODUCTION

Learning About Our Lives

Welcoming the Students

Give the students an experience of being welcomed. Have them go out into the hall. Stand at the door of the classroom and greet the students as they enter the room. Give them each small personalized gifts, such as a pencil with a colorful tag bearing the student's name or a folder with the student's name. Note that the gift is a sign of welcome.

Introducing the Chapter

Invite the students to turn to page 122 in the text and read aloud the chapter title. Work with the class to define the word *initiation* as "how new members learn more about and are welcomed into a group." Encourage the students to respond to the chapter-focus questions by sharing their experiences of belonging to groups.

Discussing the Illustrations

Direct attention to the illustrations on page 122. Help the students see that the pictures show people of their own age being welcomed or initiated into a group. Have volunteers read aloud "A Ceremony of Welcome." Discuss the questions at the bottom of the page. Help the students identify the words (*ballet and football terminology*), actions (*ballet positions*), and signs or symbols (*ballet slippers, football uniforms*) that are part of these welcomes.

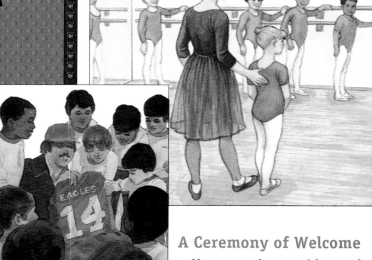

Our Church Celebrates Initiation

To what groups, clubs, or teams do you belong? What did you have to do to become a member?

122 Doctrine

A Ceremony of Welcome

Many groups have special ways of preparing and welcoming new members. People who want to become members of certain groups go through an **initiation** that includes learning about the group and being welcomed into the group. New members are welcomed into the group in a special ceremony.

Initiation ceremonies usually use special *words* and special *actions*. They may also include special *signs* or *symbols* as well.

Look at the pictures above. What do you think is happening in each picture? How can you tell that the new members are being welcomed? What do the words, actions, and signs or symbols in the pictures tell you?

★ ★★★ ★
★ Enriching ★
★ the Lesson ★

If your parish has a welcome or hospitality ministry, invite one of the members to visit your class and explain to the students how this group welcomes new families to the parish. Work with the class beforehand to develop a list of questions to ask your visitor.

122

Signs of Welcome at Church

When Jesus invites us to believe that he loves us and to follow in his ways, he calls us to live as members of the Christian community. The Church uses special words, symbols, and actions to welcome new members and to remind the people in parish communities that they belong to the family of Jesus' followers. The Church welcomes new members through the three sacraments of initiation: Baptism, Confirmation, and Eucharist.

In Baptism, we are united with Jesus and the Church and are welcomed into the Church for the first time. In Confirmation, the Holy Spirit helps us grow as Christians. And in the Eucharist, we deepen our unity with Jesus and with other Catholics in our parishes and around the world.

Discuss

1. What words, symbols, or actions would you use to welcome a new member to your family or a guest to your home?

2. What words, symbols, and actions help you to feel welcome in your parish?

3. What could you say about the sacraments of initiation that you have celebrated if you were talking to someone who is not a member of the Catholic Church?

Vocabulary

initiation: how new members learn more about and are welcomed into a group

We Believe

The Church celebrates three sacraments of initiation: Baptism, Confirmation, and Eucharist. The Church welcomes new members through these sacraments.

Doctrine 123

Focus on

Initiation Help students appreciate that the sacraments of initiation join people to Jesus as well as to the Church. As is true in all the sacraments, the community and the person receiving the sacrament experience the presence of Christ in a unique way. Through the grace of the sacraments, we can share more deeply in God's life and participate more fully in the saving work of Jesus Christ. The parish Church that celebrates initiation grows in faith as new members are welcomed.

Step 2/DEVELOPMENT

Learning About Our Faith

Reading About Church Initiations

Call on students to take turns reading aloud "Signs of Welcome at Church" on page 123. Use the questions below to guide discussion.

■ How does the Church welcome new members? (*Through the three sacraments of initiation*)

■ What are the sacraments of initiation? (*Baptism, Confirmation, and Eucharist*)

■ What happens in the sacrament of Baptism? (*We are united with Jesus and the Church, and we are welcomed into the Church.*)

■ What does Confirmation celebrate? (*The Holy Spirit's help in our growth as Christians*)

■ What does receiving the Eucharist help us do? (*Deepen our unity with Jesus and other Catholics*)

Learning the Vocabulary and Doctrine

Review with the class the definition in the Vocabulary box on page 123. Then have a student read the We Believe statement. Encourage the students to memorize these two sections.

Step 3/CONCLUSION

Learning How to Live Our Faith

Discussing the Questions

Engage the students in a discussion of the questions on page 123. For the last question, have the students tell how these sacraments help give them a sense of belonging.

or...

Have the students work in pairs to role-play family and Church welcoming experiences. Examples of family welcoming experiences might include those of welcoming a newborn or adopted baby, a foster child, a grandparent who is moving in, or a stepsister or stepbrother.

DAY 2
SCRIPTURE

Objective

This lesson helps the students understand how the early Christians initiated new members.

Step 1/INTRODUCTION

Learning About Our Lives

Talking About Membership

Invite the students to discuss how they feel about being members of their school and parish communities. What gives them a sense of belonging and identity? What are the privileges and responsibilities they associate with belonging to these communities? Tell the class that celebrating the sacraments and remaining faithful to the teachings of Scripture have been traditionally associated with membership in the Church. Emphasize that one of our responsibilities is to welcome others to our school and parish.

Step 2/DEVELOPMENT

Learning About Our Faith

Reading About Christian Initiation

Introduce the Scripture stories on initiation by reading aloud the first paragraph of "Early Christian Initiation" on page 124. Emphasize that the Scriptures help give us a sense of identity.

Identifying Sacramental Actions

Call on volunteers to read aloud each of the three sections on the individual sacraments of initiation. Direct the students' attention to the accompanying illustrations on pages 124 and 125. Have the students identify the action in each illustration (*Baptism: the pouring of the water; Confirmation: signing with oil; Eucharist: the sharing of the body and blood of Christ*).

Early Christian Initiation

Whenever the Church welcomes new members through the sacraments of initiation, we are reminded of who we are, who we are called to be, and how we have promised to live. In the Gospels, we read how Jesus teaches his followers to live. In the Acts of the Apostles and the letters of Paul, we read how the early Christians followed what Jesus taught.

Jesus told his apostles, "Baptize all people in the name of the Father, and of the Son, and of the Holy Spirit" (based on Matthew 28:19). And the apostles did just that. People who wanted to become Christians were baptized to show that they wanted to change their lives and follow Jesus.

"You will receive the gift of the Holy Spirit" (based on Acts 2:38c). The Acts of the Apostles is the book in the Bible where we learn about Pentecost and where we read about the apostolic Church.

Focus on

Mass The word *Mass* comes from the Latin phrase *Ite missa est* that was prayed at the end of eucharistic celebrations. These words mean "Go, you are sent." Today we say "Go in peace to love and serve the Lord." The words remind us of our responsibility to serve Jesus by loving and serving others. We are called to become like the one we have received: Jesus Christ.

"The bread we share is the body of Christ. The cup of wine we share is the blood of Christ" (based on 1 Corinthians 10:16–17). In his letters to the early Christian communities, Paul reminds them how important it is to share the body and blood of Christ. Today, the Mass is the most important prayer of the Catholic Christian community.

Activity

Write the answers on the lines provided.

1. In which sacrament today do people promise to live as Christians or to help their children live as Christians?

   Baptism

2. In which sacrament today do we celebrate the gift of the Holy Spirit?

   Confirmation

3. In which sacrament do we share the body and blood of Christ as we remember what Jesus has done for us?

   Eucharist

★ ★ ★ ★
Enriching the Lesson
★

Bring to class a variety of breads, including if possible kinds that may not be familiar to many of the students, such as barley bread, matzoh, soda bread, or corn bread. After they have had a chance to sample the different kinds of bread, have a discussion about the part that bread plays in people's lives. Explain that bread is often used as a symbolic food in many blessings and rituals in different cultures. Distribute bread recipes for the children to try at home with their families.

Completing an Activity

Explain to the students the activity at the bottom of page 125. After they have completed the activity, have them check their answers with a partner.

Step 3/CONCLUSION

Learning How to Live Our Faith

Researching Scripture

Distribute Bibles to the students. Tell them that before Jesus gave his followers the gift of himself in the Eucharist at the Last Supper he told them about a special bread. Help the students locate John 6:35 and John 6:51 in their Bibles. Read these verses aloud and ask the following questions.

- What did Jesus call himself? (*The bread of life*)

- What did Jesus say would happen to those who ate the bread of life? (*That anyone who ate the bread of life would never hunger and would live forever*)

Help the students understand that in Baptism we begin to share in Jesus' new life. In Confirmation the Holy Spirit helps us follow Jesus. Through the Eucharist, Jesus nourishes us with his body and blood.

Praying a Litany

Compose a litany prayer with the class, thanking Jesus for each of the sacraments of initiation. For example: "We thank you, Jesus, for the sacrament of Baptism. Help us to live as faithful Christians always." Have the students respond to each prayer by saying, "Amen."

125

DAY 3

DOCTRINE

Objective

This lesson helps the students appreciate how the sacraments of initiation are celebrated today.

Step 1/INTRODUCTION

Learning About Our Lives

Discussing Christian Initiation

Direct attention to the pictures of Baptism, Confirmation, and Eucharist you have posted around the room. Invite the students to tell stories about times they have attended a Baptism, a Confirmation, or a First Eucharist. Encourage them to tell what happened at these celebrations. Then have the students recall the sacraments they have received and tell their favorite family stories about them.

Step 2/DEVELOPMENT

Learning About Our Faith

Reading the Story

Ask for volunteers to read aloud "Barbara's Big Day" on pages 126 and 127. Afterward, ask the students to name the sacraments that Barbara received (*Baptism, Confirmation, and Eucharist*). Review the following points with the class.

At Baptism, our lives are joined to Jesus, and the Church welcomes us as new members. We receive new life through the Holy Spirit. Those being baptized are cleansed from original sin. Baptism also cleanses the person from any actual sins for which he or she is sorry.

At Confirmation, God sends the Holy Spirit to give us renewed strength and courage to live and share our faith in Jesus.

The Eucharist celebrates the presence of Jesus. During the Eucharist we praise and thank God. We remember that Jesus sacrificed his life and rose to new life for us. At Eucharist, we receive the body and blood of Christ.

Barbara's Big Day

It is the night before Easter. Barbara's parish is celebrating a very special Mass. Tonight, at the **Easter Vigil**, she will be initiated as a full member of the Church. Barbara is one of several people who will become a Catholic. Her family and friends are happy to be with her at the initiation celebration.

When she says the Apostles' Creed, her parents and godparents stand behind her.

The priest pours water on Barbara's head. He says, "I baptize you, Barbara, in the name of the Father, and of the Son, and of the Holy Spirit."

Her godparents give her a lighted candle. Her parents and godparents pray that Barbara will live according to the teachings and example of Jesus. Her friends join in that prayer.

The priest places his hands on Barbara's head. He prays that the Holy Spirit will be her helper and guide.

126 Doctrine

Focus on

RCIA Ask the students if they know of anyone who will be receiving the sacraments of initiation in their parish at this coming Easter Vigil. You may get this information from the pastor or parish director of religious education. Invite the students to compose prayers for each of the catechumens and candidates. You may want to send these prayers to the RCIA program coordinator to be used at a meeting of the catechumens and candidates.

126

Then the priest confirms her. He makes the Sign of the Cross with oil on her forehead. He says, "Barbara, be sealed with the Gift of the Holy Spirit."

Barbara answers, "Amen."

The Mass continues. At Communion time, Barbara receives the Eucharist for the first time.

Later, the whole community has a party for Barbara. Everyone expresses their welcome and their love.

The Easter Vigil

As Barbara did, adults and older children often celebrate all three sacraments of initiation at the Easter Vigil. The Easter Vigil, the greatest feast of the Church year, is celebrated the night before Easter. At this Mass, the Church celebrates the resurrection of Jesus, the Light of the World, and his victory over darkness, sin, and death. We celebrate new life in Christ for both lifelong members of the Church and the new members who are being welcomed.

Vocabulary

Easter Vigil: the night before Easter, when the Church celebrates new life in Christ and the resurrection of Jesus, the Light of the World

❧❧❧❧❧❧❧❧❧❧❧❧

Doctrine **127**

Learning About the Sacraments of Initiation

List on the chalkboard the three sacraments that Barbara received. For each sacrament, ask the following questions: *What sign or symbol was used? What words were spoken? What action took place?* Write the students' responses next to each sacrament. Note that, although each sacrament has its own name and its own words, symbols, and actions, the three sacraments together are called sacraments of initiation.

Reading About the Easter Vigil

Read aloud "The Easter Vigil" on page 127. Explain that when the Vigil begins, the church is dark. A fire, sometimes called the Easter fire, is lit. Then the Easter candle is lit from the fire as the priest prays, "Christ our Light." Everyone lights candles from the Easter candle. Jesus' light fills the church.

Step 3/CONCLUSION

Learning How to Live Our Faith

Naming Ways of Sharing Jesus' Light

Explain that at the Easter Vigil we remember that through Baptism we are called to be the light of Christ for others. Have the students name specific ways in which they can share Jesus' light with others through their words and actions.

Teaching Tips

Take your class on a visit to your church sanctuary to view the Easter candle. Note that the five grains of incense on the cross represent Jesus' wounds. Explain the Greek letters as a sign that Jesus is the beginning (Alpha) and end (Omega) of all life. Point to the numbers of the current year. Explain that the candle is lit at Mass during the Easter season and at every Baptism during the year.

Enriching the Lesson

Distribute drawing paper and crayons. Invite students to draw a picture of the Easter candle. On the candles, have the students draw a cross with the marks of Jesus' wounds, the Alpha and Omega symbols, and the numbers of the current year. Ask the students to write a prayer at the bottom of the page asking Jesus to help them be a light to others.

DAY 4
DOCTRINE/PRAYER

Objective

This lesson helps the students recognize that symbols help us pray.

Step 1/INTRODUCTION

Learning About Our Lives

Writing About Differences

Explain to the students that in every parish community and every church building, we can see and experience things that are similar to other parishes. We can sometimes see differences as well. Have the students work together in small groups to make lists of the similarities and differences they are aware of between other parishes and their own. After giving the students sufficient time to work, encourage the groups to share their lists with the class. Tell the students that in this lesson they will learn about the similarities and differences between Baptism in the early Church and today.

Step 2/DEVELOPMENT

Learning About Our Faith

Reading the Text

Call on volunteers to read aloud "Baptism: Yesterday and Today." Ask these questions:

■ What do we call the place where people are baptized? (*A baptismal font or a baptismal pool*)

■ What is immersion? (*Baptizing a new Christian by placing his or her whole body under water*)

Invite the students to answer the last two questions in this section.

Completing a Chart

Direct the students' attention to the illustrations on page 128. Point out that one shows a scene from the early Church and the other shows a Baptism from the Church today. Ask the students to examine the illustrations for things that are the same and things that are different. Have them work independently to complete the chart on page 128. Afterward, review their responses. (*Possible answers of similarities*

128

Baptism: Yesterday and Today

In every Catholic Church, you will find a place where a person can be baptized. We call this place a **baptismal font** or a **baptismal pool**. Both the pool and the font contain water that is blessed and used to baptize. The pool usually has running water flowing into it. Often times, a priest may pour the water over the person's head. Barbara was baptized in this way. Sometimes, the person is baptized by **immersion**, which means the person's whole body is placed under water. In the early Church, people were usually baptized by immersion in a river or lake. A baby can be immersed in a large font or a pool. Adults and older children being baptized can stand or kneel

in a pool if the water is not deep enough for immersion. Does your parish have a baptismal font or a baptismal pool? Where in your church is it located?

Activity

Look at the two illustrations of Baptism on this page. Complete the chart below to indicate what is the same about the two illustrations and what is different.

Same: _____

_____

Different: _____

_____

128   Doctrine

Focus on

Baptismal Garments   Note that a white garment is also a part of the Baptismal rite. The new Christian receives it after being anointed. Infants are given a bib-like cloth; adults and older children usually put on a white robe. It is a sign that the new Christians have become a new creation and have "clothed themselves in Christ."

Symbols of Initiation

When we celebrate the sacraments, we use many symbols to help us pray. Symbols help us to see the things we pray about or that we read about in the Scriptures.

In Baptism, water reminds us that we are celebrating new life. Water helps all living things to grow.

The light of the Paschal, or Easter, candle reminds us that Jesus is the Light of the World and that as Christians, we too can bring light to the world.

In both Baptism and Confirmation, we are anointed with oil to show that we have been chosen by God for a special way of life as followers of Jesus.

In the Eucharist, we receive the body and blood of Jesus to remind us of Jesus' love for us.

Vocabulary

baptismal font: a container for water that is used in Baptism

baptismal pool: a larger baptismal font in which a person can kneel, stand, or be immersed

immersion: baptizing a new Christian by placing his or her whole body under water

Prayer   129

Reading About Symbols

Read through "Symbols of Initiation" on page 129 and have the students underline the symbols used in each sacrament of initiation (*water, light, oil, bread and wine*). Discuss what each of the symbols represents.

Reviewing the Vocabulary

Review the definitions found in the Vocabulary box on page 129. Answer any questions the students may have about these words and their meanings.

Step 3/CONCLUSION

Learning How to Live Our Faith

Naming Welcoming Words

Explain that the words and actions in our celebrations help us pray, as in the action of pouring water in Baptism, and to feel united, as in the sharing of the cup in Communion. Ask the students to name other ways they feel welcomed during the Eucharist. (*Responses may include: being greeted by an usher, the words of the priest ["The Lord be with you"], and the Sign of Peace.*)

Sharing the Sign of Peace

Ask the students to stand as you pray, "Lord Jesus, you call us to share your light with one another. Help us be signs of your love by welcoming others." Then share a sign of peace with one another.

CURRICULUM CONNECTION

Language Arts   Invite the students to imagine that they have been asked to decide on another symbol for the sacraments of initiation, one that would be appropriate for the Church of today. Ask them to name that symbol and write a paragraph explaining the reason for their choice, and where in the rites of Christian initiation they would use the symbol.

Enriching the Lesson

Have the students use self-adhesive paper, scissors, and crayons to make initiation badges. Have them cut a 3" paper circle and draw lines to divide it into three parts. Ask them to write the name of one of the sacraments of initiation in each area and write or draw one thing they learned about each sacrament. Remove the backing to wear the badge.

DAY 5
PRAYER/REVIEW

Objective

This lesson helps the students pray a rite from the Order of Christian Initiation.

Preparing to Pray

Explain to the class that when adults and older children are preparing to receive the sacraments of initiation at the Easter Vigil, they sometimes come together to pray earlier in the day on Holy Saturday, the day before Easter. One of their prayers is called the Ephphetha Rite. This is a special way of praying that they will open their ears to hear God's word and that they will open their mouths to tell others about their new life as Christians.

Tell the students that they will be praying the Ephphetha Rite today. You may want to ask a volunteer to help you demonstrate what the students will do during the rite.

Have the class form two groups and ask the students within each group to find a partner. Encourage the students to practice reading the words they will pray in the rite.

Praying the Ephphetha Rite

Gather the students in the area you have prepared for prayer. Light a candle and make the Sign of the Cross. Then proceed with the reading and Ephphetha Rite from the text on page 130.

Praying a Rite of Christian Initiation

Reader: A reading from the Gospel of Mark (based on Mark 7:31–37). A man who could not hear and could not speak very well was brought to Jesus. The crowd begged Jesus to lay his hands on the man. Jesus took him away from the crowd and placed his fingers in the man's ears. Then he touched the man's tongue. Jesus looked up to heaven and said, "Ephphetha! Be opened." Immediately, the man could hear and speak clearly. When the crowd of people learned what had happened, they were very excited and told everyone about what Jesus had done. The gospel of the Lord.

All: Praise to you, Lord Jesus Christ.

Leader: I now invite those of you chosen to be *Group 1* to turn to your partners. Make the Sign of the Cross on your partner's right ear, on the left ear, and on your partner's mouth. Say to your partner:

Group 1: Ephphetha! Be opened! Hear the word, believe it, and share it.

Leader: I now invite each of you in *Group 2* to make the Sign of the Cross on your partner's right ear, on the left ear, and on your partner's mouth. Say to your partner:

Group 2: Ephphetha! Be opened! Hear the word, believe it, and share it.

Leader: Let us pray.

All: Jesus, we thank you for inviting us to be members of your family, the Church. Thank you, too, for all the people who are preparing to join the Church. Help us to welcome them, love them, and grow with them as Catholics who are faithful to your word. Amen.

Cultural Awareness

The sacraments of initiation are celebrated in many Protestant communities. All Christians are baptized. Many also celebrate Confirmation, although Confirmation is not considered a sacrament in some traditions. Communion services and eucharistic celebrations are also common in most Christian communities. Invite ministers from other denominations to describe the process of initiation in their churches. If you have any non-Catholic students in your class who belong to other churches, invite them to share their own traditions of initiation.

Chapter Review

For each phrase in Column 1, write the letter of the matching word(s) from Column 2.

Column 1

__b__ container for water that is blessed and used to baptize

__e__ helps all living things to grow

__f__ baptizing someone by placing them under water

__c__ welcoming new members into a group

__a__ the sacraments of initiation

__d__ symbol used to show that we have been chosen to follow Jesus

Column 2

a. Baptism, Confirmation, Eucharist

b. baptismal pool or font

c. initiation

d. oil

e. water

f. immersion

Fill in the answers to the first two questions.

1. What is the *Easter Vigil?* the night before Easter, when the Church celebrates new life in Christ and the resurrection of Jesus, the Light of the World

2. What are the three sacraments of initiation and their symbols? Baptism—water, oil, and light; Confirmation—oil; Eucharist—bread and wine

3. Talk about some of the ways you can show people that you are a Catholic.

You are now members of the household of God.
Based on Ephesians 2:19

Review 131

Matching Words and Phrases

Explain the directions for the matching activity at the top of page 131. Have the students work independently to complete it. When all have finished, check the students' responses.

Completing the Chapter Review

Take time to go through the review questions at the bottom of page 131. Direct the students to write answers to the first two questions on the lines provided in the text. Afterward, ask volunteers to read aloud their responses. Encourage all to participate in the discussion question. Be supportive of each student who responds.

Praying with the Scriptural Verse

Have a student read the verse from Ephesians aloud. Lead the students in the following prayer. After each line, ask the students to respond, "Be with us, Lord." Conclude by saying "Amen."

Help us continue to live as followers of Jesus.

Help us continue to grow in our faith.

Help us continue to care about others.

Focus on

The Elect On the first Sunday of Lent, those who are to receive the sacraments of initiation come to a special Mass with their sponsors, families, and catechists to be affirmed by the community and to sign their names in the Book of the Elect. This is a sign that they have been called and chosen by God to become members of the Church. From this point on, until the Easter Vigil, they are called the elect. The Rite of Election is usually celebrated with the bishop presiding. People from all over the diocese are joined together.

Enriching the Lesson

Have the students make cards for those in your parish who will soon be baptized. Suggest that the students paraphrase the scriptural verse, writing instead, "Soon you will become members of the household of God." Have them write personal messages of welcome and decorate the cards. Make arrangements to deliver the cards at the appropriate time.

Our Church Celebrates Healing

Objectives ~~~~~~

To help the students
- Realize that Jesus healed the sick.
- Learn that the Anointing of the Sick is a sacrament of healing.
- Understand that we can seek forgiveness in the sacrament of Reconciliation.
- Appreciate that we are called to be healers.
- Pray for healing and forgiveness and review the chapter.

Chapter Outline ~~~~~~

	Step 1 **Learning About Our Lives**	Step 2 **Learning About Our Faith**	Step 3 **Learning How to Live Our Faith**
Day 1	■ Introduce the chapter. ■ Write about praying. ■ Recall the General Intercessions. ■ List healing actions and words. *ABOUT 15 MINUTES*	■ Read a Scripture story. *ABOUT 8 MINUTES*	■ Identify qualities. *ABOUT 7 MINUTES*
Day 2	■ Introduce the lesson. *ABOUT 3 MINUTES*	■ Read the story. ■ Listen to a Scripture story. ■ Understand how Jesus heals us. ■ Learn vocabulary and doctrine. *ABOUT 20 MINUTES*	■ Write about the sacrament. ■ Pray together. *ABOUT 7 MINUTES*
Day 3	■ Review days 1 and 2. ■ Read and discuss the story. *ABOUT 12 MINUTES*	■ Read about forgiveness and sin. ■ Learn the vocabulary. *ABOUT 10 MINUTES*	■ Complete a checklist. *ABOUT 8 MINUTES*
Day 4	■ Work in groups. *ABOUT 8 MINUTES*	■ Read the text. ■ Study the photograph. ■ Review Reconciliation. ■ Learn to be healers. *ABOUT 14 MINUTES*	■ Complete the drawings. *ABOUT 8 MINUTES*
Day 5	**Prayer** Prepare for prayer; write prayer requests. **Review** Fill in correct words; complete the chapter review; pray with the Scripture verse.		

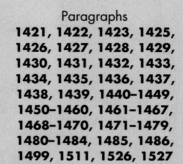

Correlation to the Catechism of the Catholic Church

Paragraphs
1421, 1422, 1423, 1425,
1426, 1427, 1428, 1429,
1430, 1431, 1432, 1433,
1434, 1435, 1436, 1437,
1438, 1439, 1440–1449,
1450–1460, 1461–1467,
1468–1470, 1471–1479,
1480–1484, 1485, 1486,
1499, 1511, 1526, 1527

Plan Ahead

	Preparing Your Class	Materials Needed
Day 1	Read through the lesson plan for this class session.	■ lined paper ■ pencils or pens
Day 2	Read through the lesson plan for this class session.	■ Bible ■ chalkboard ■ lined paper ■ pencils or pens
Day 3	Read through the lesson plan for this class session. Review the vocabulary words and definitions from Days 1 and 2.	■ pencils or pens
Day 4	Read through the lesson plan for this class session. Review the process for celebrating Reconciliation as suggested in Step 2.	■ notebook paper ■ crayons or markers ■ pencils or pens
Day 5	Prepare an environment for prayer in the classroom. Choose a reading for the prayer service. Review this week's sessions to prepare for the chapter review.	■ prayer table with Bible ■ slips of paper ■ basket ■ small bowl ■ olive oil

Additional Resources

As you plan this chapter, consider using the following materials from The Resourceful Teacher Package.

■ *Classroom Activity Sheets 11 and 11a*

■ *Family Activity Sheets 11 and 11a*

■ *Chapter 11 Test*

■ *Prayers for Every Day*

■ *Projects: Grade 3*

You may also wish to refer to the following Big Books.

■ *We Celebrate the Sacraments*, pages 2, 3, and 13–18

■ *We Celebrate God's Word*, page 13

In preparing the students for the Sunday readings, you may wish to use Silver Burdett Ginn's *Getting Ready for Sunday* student and teacher materials.

BOOKS FOR THE JOURNEY

The Hundred Penny Box. Sharon Bell Mathis. Puffin, 1986. A remarkable story of a young boy's love for his great-great-aunt.

I Can't Talk About It. Doris Sanford and Graci Evans. Questar Pubs, 1986. This story deals with a child's mixed emotions in dealing with sexual abuse and with the courage it takes to tell and forgive.

MORE BOOKS FOR THE JOURNEY

Journey to Jo'burg. Beverly Naidoo. HarperCollins, 1988. Two children's courageous story of their journey to get their mother back.

Mustard. Charlotte Graber. Bantam, 1988. When it comes time to face the death of Mustard, the family's pet cat, it is especially difficult for Alex.

REDUCED CLASSROOM ACTIVITIES

NAME _____

OUR CHURCH CELEBRATES HEALING

Someone has hurt your feelings and has apologized. Reconciliation means that you forgive this person. On the jigsaw puzzle, write a message about your forgiveness. Then draw a picture that illustrates your message. Cut the puzzle apart. Give the pieces to the person and celebrate your healing once the pieces have been rejoined.

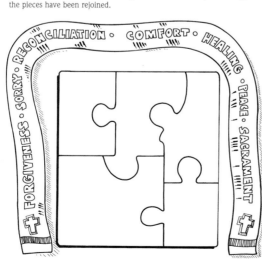

FORGIVENESS • SORRY • RECONCILIATION • COMFORT • HEALING • PEACE • SACRAMENT

To the Teacher: This activity will encourage students to forgive others, which parallels God's forgiveness of us in Reconciliation.

Chapter 11 Our Church Celebrates Healing   THIS IS OUR FAITH 3   **11**

NAME _____

ANOINTING OF THE SICK

Recall the story of Ellie and her grandma. Imagine how the story would differ if you were in Ellie's place and someone you knew was being anointed.

Name the people in your story: _____

Which priest will you ask to come to anoint the sick? _____

What do you see and hear? _____

How do you think the person will feel after being anointed? _____

How would you feel? _____

To the Teacher: This activity will help students enter into the experience of the Anointing of the Sick.

11a THIS IS OUR FAITH 3   **Chapter 11** Our Church Celebrates Healing

THE EXPERIENCE OF PAIN

Experiences of sickness or injury are part of life for students in the third grade. They have known cuts and bruises, scrapes and scratches, as part of growing up. Some young people of this age may have been seriously sick at one time. Other students may have seen family members or friends become seriously ill or injured.

At this age, children are also aware of other ways of hurting. They may have experienced the emotional pain that accompanies a family argument or a divorce. They may have felt the emotional hurt that comes from being rejected or laughed at by their peers. They may have felt the pain of loneliness most acutely. Children themselves can also be the source of pain when they act selfishly in ways that hurt others and lead others to strike back. From this, they know the experience of sin.

THE HEALING POWER OF JESUS

In the experience of physical and emotional pain, the healing power of Jesus can be introduced. Jesus healed those who were sick or disabled and forgave those who were in sin. This chapter helps the students get a sense that it is the risen Christ who forgives and heals today through the Church and through the sacraments of healing: Reconciliation and the Anointing of the Sick. In this chapter we seek to increase the students' awareness of the healing power of Christ that is present in our lives.

The chapter aims to deepen the students' awareness in two areas. First, it emphasizes that there is forgiveness and healing, comfort and strength, for life's hurts and for the children's own sins. This is vital to their growth in faith. No matter how great the hurt, God's presence and strength are always with us to help us overcome evil and bear whatever physical and emotional pain we are experiencing.

Second, through the chapter, each student may sense his or her personal call—which is the call to all Christians—to become healers, peacemakers, and reconcilers. The sacraments celebrate the healing and forgiveness experienced in daily living. They call us to keep alive and known to all the compassion, mercy, and healing of Christ.

PRAYER/SCRIPTURE

Objective

This lesson helps the students realize that Jesus healed the sick.

Step 1/INTRODUCTION

Learning About Our Lives

Introducing the Chapter

Direct attention to the chapter-focus question on page 132. As the students share experiences of helping someone who has been hurt, encourage them to focus on the specific actions and words they have used to help heal the hurts of others.

Writing About Praying

Explain the directions for the activity at the top of page 132 and have the students work on their own to write answers to the questions. Afterward, invite sharing. (*Possible responses to the second question may include: leaders of the church, people who are sick or who have died, people who are poor or homeless, and people who are lonely.*)

Recalling the General Intercessions

Remind the students that we pray for others communally during the General Intercessions or Prayers of the Faithful and that we often pray for others privately after Communion. Then read "Praying for Healing" on page 132 with the class. As the word *healing* is introduced, direct attention to the Vocabulary box on page 133 and have students read and learn the definition.

Listing Healing Actions and Words

Distribute lined paper. Have the students work in pairs to make lists of actions and lists of words that can heal people. Allow time for the students to share their lists with the rest of the class. (*Possible answers for actions might include: a mother cleans a scraped knee; a doctor's care. Possible responses for words might include: I hope you feel better soon; I forgive you.*)

11

Our Church Celebrates Healing

Activity

When you go to Mass, who are some of the people for whom you pray?

_____

Who are some of the people for whom the Church prays during Mass?

_____

_____

What have you said or done to help someone who is hurting to feel better?

Praying for Healing

When we go to Mass, we often pray for people who are sick or who have died. We also pray for people who are alone, sad, or lonely. And we pray that people can forgive one another and live together in peace. In all of these prayers, we ask for **healing**. Healing takes place through the actions, words, and prayers that help people who are hurting to become well. When healing takes place, people who have been hurt feel better, and people who need forgiveness are forgiven.

132   Prayer

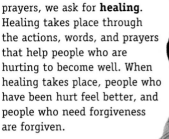

🍎 Teaching Tips

In discussing the students' use of healing words and actions, affirm their efforts to help those who are hurting. Reassure the students that they are living as Jesus taught when they reach out to others. Emphasize that our words and actions may not solve a problem, but they help to show our support and care for those who are hurting.

132

The Healing of the Sick Woman

One day, Jesus went to visit his friends Peter and Andrew. As Jesus arrived, Peter ran to Jesus. He said, "Jesus, my mother-in-law has a very high fever. Can you help her?"

Jesus went over to the woman. He took her hand and helped her to sit up. At once the fever went away.

The woman looked at Jesus and thanked him. Then she got up and prepared a meal for all the people who were there.

Based on Mark 1:29–31

Vocabulary

healing: the actions, words, and prayers that help people who are hurting to become well, to feel better, or to be forgiven

Scripture **133**

Learning About Our Faith

Reading a Scripture Story

Call on volunteers to read aloud "The Healing of the Sick Woman" on page 133. Discuss the questions below.

- What did Peter ask Jesus to do? (*Help his sick mother-in-law*)
- What did Jesus do? (*He took the woman's hand and helped her sit up.*)
- What happened to the woman? (*She was healed at once and felt well enough to prepare a meal for Jesus and the others.*)

Help the students appreciate that the woman was healed by Jesus' touch. Christ's touch was so powerful that the woman was completely cured of her illness and eager to be a hostess to her guests.

Step 3/CONCLUSION

Learning How to Live Our Faith

Identifying Qualities

Point out the phrase *at once* in the story and ask the students what it means. Elicit that the woman was cured instantly. Have the students recall times when they have prayed for someone who is sick. Ask: *Do you expect God to instantly cure you or the people you pray for?* Lead them to recognize that people usually need time, rest, and medicine to get well. Have the students name attitudes they need to develop when they turn to God in prayer. Help them appreciate that we are called to be patient with God and to trust in his care for us.

Focus on

Scripture Choose several alternate passages from the Gospels where there are stories of Jesus' healing power. Divide the class into groups. Have each group read and prepare to act out one of the stories. After each group has presented its story, ask members of the class to tell how the person was healed and what the reaction to the healing was.

Enriching the Lesson

Distribute lined paper and have the students make two columns, labeled *physical pain* and *emotional pain*. Have the students list examples of these two different kinds of pain in the correct columns. Emphasize that emotional pain can result from disappointment, frustration, or being excluded. Explain that both kinds of pain hurt us.

Objective

This lesson helps the students learn that the Anointing of the Sick is a sacrament of healing.

Step 1/INTRODUCTION

Learning About Our Lives

Introducing the Lesson

Explain to the students that at the end of Mass, the priest sometimes calls people from the community, blesses them, and sends them forth to bring the Eucharist to parishioners who are sick in the hospital or at home. Ask the students if they have ever been present at Mass when this ritual was taking place and if they understood what was happening. Tell the class that in this lesson, they will learn how the Church shows care and concern for the sick.

Step 2/DEVELOPMENT

Learning About Our Faith

Reading the Story

Have volunteers take turns reading aloud the story "Anointing of the Sick." Explain to the students that the priest in the story represents all of us in the Church as we pray that the ill person will be stronger and regain health. We all pray as well that God will grant the person relief, peace, and salvation.

Listening to a Scripture Story

Invite the students to listen as you read aloud Mark 2:1–12. Explain that this is the Scripture story that Ellie's father read during Grandma's anointing. Help the students recognize the great faith and trust the people had in Jesus' power to heal.

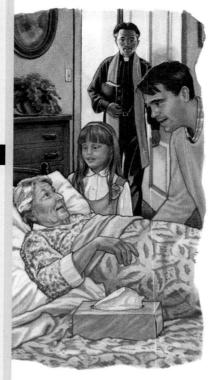

Anointing of the Sick

Ellie had been playing her radio very loudly again. Grandma screamed at her to turn it down. Grandma had been sick for a long time. Her pain was getting worse, and she was trying to get some rest. Ellie's father decided to ask Father Ezaki to come to bless Grandma and pray for her healing.

Father Ezaki began the **Anointing of the Sick** by saying, "Peace to this house and to all who live in it. Let us pray that the Lord will bring healing and peace to your grandmother." Grandma asked Father Ezaki to take a moment to celebrate the sacrament of Reconciliation with her as well. Sometimes when people pray for physical healing, they also pray to be healed in other ways, such as being forgiven for any wrong they may have done. So Ellie and her father left the room. Grandma confessed that she had been yelling at Ellie. Grandma was sorry. She knew that she probably hurt Ellie's feelings. Father Ezaki suggested a penance. "Maybe you can give Ellie a kiss to let her know that you are sorry and that you really love her." Grandma asked God to forgive her. Father Ezaki absolved her in the name of Jesus and the Church.

134 Doctrine

Teaching Tips

Show the students a pyx and explain to them that it is a container used to carry the Eucharist to the sick. The word *pyx* is taken from a Greek word that means "box." If you are unable to show the students this vessel for the Blessed Sacrament, describe it as a small, round metal case. Tell the students that the eucharistic bread in church is kept in a covered cup called a ciborium.

Cultural Awareness

Point out the pictures of Father Ezaki and explain that he is a real Catholic priest whose father was Japanese and a member of the Buddhist faith. Emphasize that, like us, the priests who celebrate the sacraments with us come from various cultural and racial backgrounds. Stress that God calls us to be one family and to respect and learn from one another.

Ellie and her father came back into the room. The Anointing of the Sick continued. Ellie's father read from one of the Gospels about Jesus' forgiving and healing a paralyzed man.

Then Father Ezaki placed his hands on Grandma's head. He prayed in silence for her to be healed. They all prayed that Grandma would become well and feel better.

Father Ezaki dipped his thumb in blessed oil and traced the Sign of the Cross on her forehead. He prayed, "Through this holy **anointing** may the Lord in his love and mercy help you with the grace of the Holy Spirit." He then traced the Sign of the Cross on her hands. "May the Lord who frees you from sin save you and raise you up," he prayed.

They all prayed The Lord's Prayer together. Ellie hugged her Grandma and told her how sorry she was for playing her music so loudly. Grandma hugged her back and said, "I'm very sorry I shouted at you. And don't ever forget how much I love you." Father Ezaki blessed them all. They were all grateful for God's gift of peace.

Two Sacraments of Healing

There are two special ways that Jesus heals our hurts, forgives us, and helps us make up with friends whom we've hurt. They are the Church's two sacraments of healing: Anointing of the Sick and Reconciliation. Sometimes they are celebrated together, but they are usually celebrated at different times.

Vocabulary

Anointing of the Sick: the sacrament of comfort and strength, of forgiveness, healing, and peace

anointing: putting blessed oil on a person's body as a sign of love, respect, or honor

We Believe

The Church brings Jesus' forgiveness and healing through the sacraments of healing. These sacraments are Anointing of the Sick and Reconciliation.

Doctrine 135

Focus on

Anointing Anointing with oil (usually a mixture of olive oil and perfume) is one of the oldest rituals in many cultures. Along with its use for healing, oil is used as a sign in the sacraments of Baptism and Confirmation. It is also a traditional sign of commissioning priests and kings, conveying the fact that a person has been chosen by the community for leadership. It is also a symbol of strength and power. The name Christ means "anointed one."

Understanding How Jesus Heals Us

Read through "Two Sacraments of Healing" on page 135 with the class. Emphasize that in the Anointing of the Sick, we may not be cured, but we receive God's comfort, strength, healing, forgiveness, and peace.

Learning the Vocabulary and Doctrine

Print the word *sacrament* on the chalkboard. Help the students recall that sacraments are defined as "special celebrations of the Church that show Jesus' love for us and signs of his presence with us now." Ask a volunteer to read the We Believe statement aloud. Then have the class read the definitions of *Anointing of the Sick* and *anointing* found in the Vocabulary box. Encourage the students to remember the doctrinal summary as well as the new words.

Step 3/CONCLUSION

Learning How to Live Our Faith

Writing About the Sacrament

Distribute lined paper to the students. Direct them to recall what they have learned about the Anointing of the Sick by writing a caption for each illustration on pages 134 and 135.

Praying Together

Work with the class to make a list on the chalkboard of people the students are aware of who are sick. This list might include classmates, students from other grades, and relatives. It might also include groups of people who suffer from cancer, AIDS, or other serious diseases. Invite the students to offer spontaneous prayers for the people they name.

DAY 3
MORALITY

Objective

This lesson helps the students understand that we can seek forgiveness in the sacrament of Reconciliation.

Step 1/INTRODUCTION

Learning About Our Lives

Reviewing Days 1 and 2

Have the students recall the definitions for each of the Vocabulary words learned thus far in Chapter 11: *healing, Anointing of the Sick,* and *anointing.* You can have the students do this orally or you may want to take the time to have them write out the definitions on notebook paper. Tell the students that in this lesson they will learn about another sacrament of healing.

Reading and Discussing the Story

Direct attention to "Seeking Forgiveness" on page 136 and invite the students to read the story silently. Afterward, go through each of the Discuss questions with the class. As you do this, ask the students to put themselves in the place of Marc, Derek, and Steve. In discussing the third question, encourage different pairs of students to role-play Marc's apology to Derek and Derek's response.

or . . .

Ask the students if they have ever been falsely accused of doing something, as Derek was, or if they have ever accused someone else of doing something they did not do. Have the students write about their experiences on a separate sheet of paper, describing what happened and how the situation was resolved.

136

Seeking Forgiveness

One day after school, Derek and Marc were showing each other their baseball card collections. They both had several cards that were the same. Suddenly Marc remembered that his brother Steve had one special card that was very valuable. He decided to show it to Derek without asking Steve's permission.

Derek and Marc were both excited as they talked about the valuable card. When Marc's mother came home, she brought some freshly baked cookies and invited them into the kitchen.

Later, when Derek went home, Marc noticed that Steve's most valuable card was missing. He looked for it everywhere. Steve would be very angry. Finally, Marc called Derek and accused him of stealing the card. Derek said that he did not take it, but Marc was sure he had.

When Marc went to school the next day, he told his friends what had happened. No one spoke to Derek or invited him to visit for the rest of the week.

The next Saturday, when Marc came home for dinner after baseball practice, Marc's father said, "By the way, Marc, while we were cleaning today we found that baseball card you've been looking for. It was under the sofa in the living room."

Discuss

1. How do you think Marc felt when he discovered Steve's card was missing?

2. How do you think Derek felt when Marc accused him of taking the card?

3. What could Marc do, now that he found out what really happened?

Focus on

Sacrament of Penance According to the *Catechism of the Catholic Church,* "Those who approach the sacrament of Penance obtain pardon from God's mercy for the offense committed against him, and are, at the same time, reconciled with the Church which they have wounded by their sins and which by charity, by example, and by prayer labors for their conversion." (#1422)

Forgiveness and Sin

Sometimes we say or do something that we do not know will end up hurting someone. For example, you might borrow your older sister's drawing pencils without her permission. She may have been happy to let you use them before, but this time she gets angry. Other times we know that what we will say or do is wrong and may hurt someone, and we do it anyway. This is what we call a **sin**. Sin always hurts our relationship with another person and with God.

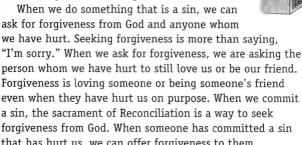

When we do something that is a sin, we can ask for forgiveness from God and anyone whom we have hurt. Seeking forgiveness is more than saying, "I'm sorry." When we ask for forgiveness, we are asking the person whom we have hurt to still love us or be our friend. Forgiveness is loving someone or being someone's friend even when they have hurt us on purpose. When we commit a sin, the sacrament of Reconciliation is a way to seek forgiveness from God. When someone has committed a sin that has hurt us, we can offer forgiveness to them.

Activity

Put a check in front of the situations below in which someone is hurting another person on purpose. Then talk about some ways they may want to ask for forgiveness.

_____ Breaking a window accidentally

_____ Telling lies about a friend or classmate, when you know what you are saying is not true

_____ Taking money out of your mother's wallet to buy something you want

_____ Calling people names

Vocabulary

sin: anything we do or say that we know is wrong and will hurt others and our relationship with God

Learning About Our Faith

Reading About Forgiveness and Sin

Call on volunteers to take turns reading aloud "Forgiveness and Sin" on page 137. Use the following questions to guide discussion.

- What is sin? (*Anything we do or say that we know is wrong and may hurt others and our relationship with God*)
- What is forgiveness? (*Loving someone or being their friend even when they have hurt us on purpose*)
- What can we do when we commit a sin? (*Seek forgiveness in the sacrament of Reconciliation*)

Learning the Vocabulary

Refer the students to the Vocabulary box on page 137. Review the definition for *sin* with the class. Check the students' understanding of this word by having them use it in a sentence.

Step 3/CONCLUSION

Learning How to Live Our Faith

Completing a Checklist

Explain the directions for the activity at the bottom of the page and have the students work on their own to complete it. As you review the students' responses, have them identify which of the situations involve a sin (*telling lies, taking money, and calling people names*). Help the students recognize that these actions are wrong and that committing these sins hurts our relationship with others and with God. Invite them to discuss ways they might ask for forgiveness in each situation.

Teaching Tips

It is important that students be able to distinguish between consequences and intentionality. Not every action that has bad consequences is sinful. Mistakes, no matter what the consequences, are not to be considered sinful actions. The intention to do harm must be present for a sin to exist. An effective way to explain this difference to students is to discuss several examples of mistakes or accidents that have harmful consequences and several examples of situations in which harm is intentionally done.

Enriching the Lesson

Invite the students to describe their feelings in the following situations: 1) recognizing that they have committed a sin; 2) being forgiven by someone they have hurt; 3) being forgiven in the sacrament of Reconciliation. Lead the students to realize that when we sin, we feel separated from those we have hurt. Reconciliation heals our relationships.

137

Objective

This lesson helps the students appreciate that we are called to be healers.

Step 1/INTRODUCTION

Learning About Our Lives

Working in Groups

Have the class form cooperative groups of three or four students each. Instruct each group to work together to think of a specific situation in which healing or forgiveness is needed. Have them describe the situation on notebook paper. Then ask them to suggest ways in which healing or forgiveness can help resolve the problem. Allow time for each group to present its work to the class.

Step 2/DEVELOPMENT

Learning About Our Faith

Reading the Text

Read "Healing Our Hearts" with the class. Explain in your own words how God calls each of us to be a peacemaker. We are called to forgive others. We are all called to heal people in the world around us.

Studying the Photograph

Direct the students to look at the photograph on page 138. Explain that the photograph shows a missionary priest talking to a woman at an outdoor confessional in Mexico. He is assuring her of God's forgiveness and healing. This is a good opportunity to assure the students that God's forgiveness, especially in the sacrament of Reconciliation, is available to them throughout their lives, anywhere they may go.

Reviewing Reconciliation

Recall with the students the steps of the sacrament of Reconciliation by instructing them to turn to "About Reconciliation" on pages 340–341 of their texts. Read through this section with the class, answering any questions the students might have. If time permits, you might have the students role-play receiving the sacrament of Reconciliation.

Healing Our Hearts

We are called to accept God's healing and forgiveness and to bring healing and forgiveness to others. We are called to share God's peace. Before receiving the Eucharist, we all say, "Lord, I am not worthy to receive you, but only say the word and I shall be healed." What do you think this means?

When we hurt from sickness or sin, God does not forget us. Jesus reaches out to us. The Holy Spirit is with us. The Church gathers around us to comfort and forgive us.

The sacrament of Anointing of the Sick is for anyone who is sick and for those who are weakened in their old age. When the priest anoints us, it is Jesus Christ who strengthens us, heals us, and gives us peace.

The sacrament of Reconciliation celebrates God's forgiveness and our reconciliation with the Church community, whom the priest represents. When the priest absolves us, it is Jesus Christ who forgives us. Normally we celebrate the sacrament of Reconciliation by itself, but it may also be celebrated along with the Anointing of the Sick.

CURRICULUM CONNECTION

Art Invite the students to make a "Healing Our Hearts" montage using magazines, newspapers, and old religion texts. Have the students look through these materials to find pictures of people bringing healing and forgiveness to others. Instruct them to glue the pictures to a heart-shaped poster. Hang the poster in the main hallway of the school.

We Are All Healers

When God forgives us or makes us well, he is a healer. Each time we offer forgiveness to someone who has hurt us, we are healers. Each time we help take care of someone who is sick, we are healers. And each time we pray for someone to be healed or forgiven, we are healers.

Jesus calls us to love one another in all that we do and say. Sometimes this can be difficult. But we are called to forgive one another, be patient with one another, and be united with one another. So even when we Christians hurt one another, we can know the power of healing words and actions that show that we can continue to love one another and be friends.

Activity

Look at the people in the pictures. What could you do to help heal their hurts? Draw yourself doing something to help them.

Morality   139

Teaching Tips

Some of the students may have painful memories of praying for the recovery of someone, such as a grandparent, who later died. Be sensitive to the students' reactions to these experiences. Help them understand that we cannot always understand God's plan for us. Emphasize that God does hear and respond to our prayers, even though his response is sometimes different from what we hope it will be.

Learning to Be Healers

Read with the class "We Are All Healers" on page 139. Help the students understand that, like Jesus, they are called to be healers. Emphasize that when we become aware of the pain, sadness, or sorrow of others, we can make a choice to follow Jesus' example of healing.

Step 3/CONCLUSION

Learning How to Live Our Faith

Completing the Drawings

Explain the directions for the drawing activity. Allow time for the students to complete this activity. Then ask for volunteers to share how they would respond to the needs of others in word and deed.

DAY 5
PRAYER/REVIEW

Objective

This lesson helps the students pray for healing and forgiveness.

Preparing for Prayer

Explain to the students that the oil used during the Anointing of the Sick is called the oil of the sick. It is blessed by the bishop during Holy Week each year. Tell the class that during the prayer service you will be making the Sign of the Cross on the students' foreheads with olive oil that you have brought from home.

Choose a reading for the prayer service. You might select one of the following passages: Matthew 11:28–30, which describes Jesus as bringing the "rest" and comfort of God; Mark 6:53–56, which describes believers bringing sick people to Jesus to heal them; or Mark 2:1–12, which the students listened to on Day 2. Select a student to proclaim the reading during the prayer service, and provide him or her with a Bible.

Writing Prayer Requests

Give out small slips of paper to the students. Instruct them to write on the slips of paper the name of someone who needs healing or something for which they are sorry and want to be forgiven. Tell the students that these prayer requests will remain confidential. After the students have completed them, have the students place their requests in a small basket on the prayer table.

Pour lightly scented olive oil into a small bowl. Place it on the prayer table for use during the prayer service.

You may want to pray the Prayer of Sorrow together to conclude your prayer. If the students do not know this prayer by heart, have them turn to page 5 and read it aloud.

Praying for Healing and Forgiveness

Leader: As we pray today, we remember how important it is to have faith that Jesus has the power to heal. In the Gospel stories about Jesus' healing and miracles, Jesus very often tells the person who has been healed that it is his or her faith that makes the healing possible. At Mass, just before the priest receives the Eucharist, we all say, "Lord, I am not worthy to receive you, but only say the word and I shall be healed." We can know the healing power of Jesus in the Eucharist, too. Today, you will be anointed with oil. As an expression of your faith in Jesus' power to heal, you can say "Amen," which means "I believe it is so." Let us pray.

Leader: Lord God, we thank you for your Son, Jesus Christ, who brings us healing and forgiveness. May your blessing be upon each of us now, as we are anointed with oil. In Jesus' name we pray.

All: Amen.

Leader: I invite you all to be anointed with this oil today. As you are anointed, know that Jesus is the great healer who can bring you comfort and strength when you are not well, forgiveness and peace when you have hurt someone. Receive Jesus' healing and forgiveness.

Leader: (The Leader anoints each student by making the Sign of the Cross on his or her forehead and says to each student:) Be well. Receive the peace of Jesus.

Student: Amen.

🍎 Teaching Tips

Be sure to have the students understand that the prayer service in this lesson is not the celebration of the sacrament of Anointing of the Sick. The celebration of the sacrament is presided over by a priest, and the blessed oil of the sick is used. The purpose of the prayer service is to give the students the opportunity to pray for healing and reconciliation, for themselves and for those close to them.

Focus on

Chrism Mass Explain that the oils used in the sacraments are blessed at a liturgy called the Chrism Mass. This Mass is usually held on Holy Thursday morning in the cathedral of the diocese—the bishop's parish. A priest from every parish in the diocese attends this Mass. After the oils are blessed, they are given to the priests to bring back to their parishes for use throughout the year.

Chapter Review

Fill in the correct word(s) to complete each sentence. Then use the letters from the words you wrote to find the answer to the question below.

1. When a priest puts the blessed oil of the sick on someone's body, the priest is celebrating the sacrament of

   <u>A</u> <u>n</u> <u>o</u> <u>i</u> <u>n</u> <u>t</u> <u>i</u> <u>n</u> <u>g</u> of the <u>S</u> <u>i</u> <u>c</u> <u>k</u> .

1   2

2. A <u>s</u> <u>i</u> <u>n</u> is anything we say or do that we know is wrong and will

            3

   hurt another person or God.

3. When we have sinned, we ask for God's forgiveness and peace in the sacrament of

   <u>R</u> <u>e</u> <u>c</u> <u>o</u> <u>n</u> <u>c</u> <u>i</u> <u>l</u> <u>i</u> <u>a</u> <u>t</u> <u>i</u> <u>o</u> <u>n</u> .

                        4

4. We know the <u>f</u> <u>o</u> <u>r</u> <u>g</u> <u>i</u> <u>v</u> <u>e</u> <u>n</u> <u>e</u> <u>s</u> <u>s</u> of

                    5   6

   God and others when they still love us even though we have hurt them on purpose.

What do we call the actions, words, and prayers that help people who are hurting to

become well, to feel better, or to be forgiven? <u>H</u> <u>e</u> <u>a</u> <u>l</u> <u>i</u> <u>n</u> <u>g</u>

                                       6 1 4 2 3 5

Fill in the answers to the first two questions.

1. What are the two sacraments of healing? _____

   <u>Anointing of the Sick</u>

   <u>and Reconciliation</u>

2. What does Jesus Christ do for us through the

   sacraments of healing? <u>brings us comfort,</u>

   <u>strength, forgiveness, healing, and peace</u>

3. Talk about how we can be healers and peacemakers.

> **God says,**
> **"I, the LORD, am**
> **your healer."**
> **Exodus 15:26c**

CHAPTER REVIEW

Filling in Correct Words

Read aloud the directions for the first exercise on page 141 and have the students work independently to complete it. When everyone has finished, call on volunteers to read aloud each statement and to answer the question.

Completing the Chapter Review

Direct the students to write answers to the next two questions on the lines provided in the text. Encourage all to participate in the discussion of the third question. Be supportive of each student who responds.

Praying with the Scripture Verse

Point out the verse from Scripture at the bottom of the page. Ask: *How is God our healer?* Elicit from the students that God forgives us in the sacrament of Reconciliation and gives us peace. God also comforts and strengthens us in the Anointing of the Sick.

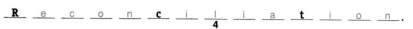

Enriching the Lesson

Ask one of your parish priests to visit your class to explain the sacraments of healing to the students. He might ask for a volunteer to play the part of the sick person and then act out the steps of the sacrament. Encourage him to share some personal experiences of visiting with and anointing people who are sick.

12 Our Church Celebrates Vocations

Objectives

To help the students

- Explore how Christians use their talents.
- Understand the meaning of a vocation.
- Learn about the sacrament of Holy Orders.
- Recognize that Matrimony celebrates the lifelong love between a man and a woman.
- Pray a litany prayer and review the chapter.

Chapter Outline

	Step 1 Learning About Our Lives	**Step 2** Learning About Our Faith	**Step 3**  Learning How to Live Our Faith
Day 1	■ Review the sacraments. ■ Introduce the chapter. ■ Identify careers. *ABOUT 12 MINUTES*	■ Learn how Christians use talents. *ABOUT 5 MINUTES*	■ Consider how to use talents. ■ Pray together. *ABOUT 13 MINUTES*
Day 2	■ Discuss career opportunities. *ABOUT 5 MINUTES*	■ Read about special talents. ■ Read and discuss the text. ■ Learn about choosing vocations. *ABOUT 20 MINUTES*	■ Listen for God's call. *ABOUT 5 MINUTES*
Day 3	■ Introduce the lesson. *ABOUT 7 MINUTES*	■ Read about Holy Orders. ■ Read about religious vocations. ■ Learn the vocabulary and doctrine. *ABOUT 15 MINUTES*	■ Write about commitments. ■ Pray together. *ABOUT 8 MINUTES*
Day 4	■ Write about weddings. *ABOUT 5 MINUTES*	■ Read the text. ■ Review the vocabulary and doctrine. *ABOUT 10 MINUTES*	■ Think about the poem. ■ Recognize God's call. *ABOUT 15 MINUTES*
Day 5	**Prayer** Prepare for prayer; pray for vocations. **Review** Fill in the blanks; complete the chapter review; pray with the scriptural verse.		

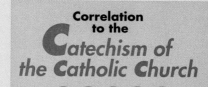

Plan Ahead

	Preparing Your Class	**Materials Needed**
Day 1	Read through the lesson plan for this class session. Take time to think about the talents you have noticed in your students.	■ pencils or pens ■ writing paper
Day 2	Read through the lesson plan for this class session. Practice leading the guided meditation in Step 3.	■ pencils or pens
Day 3	Read through the lesson plan for this class session. Be prepared to share about someone you know who has dedicated themselves to serving the Church.	■ pencils or pens
Day 4	Read through the lesson plan for this class session.	■ pencils or pens
Day 5	Prepare an environment for prayer in the classroom. Review this week's sessions to prepare for the chapter review.	■ symbol(s) to represent the sacraments of vocation ■ pencils or pens

Additional Resources

As you plan this chapter, consider using the following materials from The Resourceful Teacher Package.

■ *Classroom Activity Sheets 12 and 12a*

■ *Family Activity Sheets 12 and 12a*

■ *Chapter 12 Test*

■ *Prayers for Every Day*

■ *Projects: Grade 3*

You may also wish to refer to the following Big Books.

■ *We Celebrate the Sacraments,* pages 2, 3, and 19–24

■ *We Celebrate the Mass,* pages 9 and 11

In preparing the students for the Sunday readings, you may wish to use Silver Burdett Ginn's *Getting Ready for Sunday* student and teacher materials.

BOOKS FOR THE JOURNEY

Peppe the Lamplighter. Elisa Bartone. Lothrop, Lee & Shepard, 1993. A young boy who becomes a lamplighter helps his father appreciate that no one job is better than another.

A Very Young Musician. Jil Krementz. Simon & Schuster, 1991. This story of a young musician who questions what his life's work will be can help readers appreciate their own talents and abilities.

MORE BOOKS FOR THE JOURNEY

The Amazing Felix. Emily Arnold McCully. G.P. Putnam's Sons, 1993. A child, the son of a world famous pianist, is not good at the piano but surprisingly discovers he is gifted at another way of entertaining.

The Random House Book of Poetry for Children. Selected and introduced by Jack Prelutsky. Random House, Inc., 1983. "Me," by Karla Kuskin and "I Can Fly," by Felice Holman. Poems in which children are cherished, appreciated, and enjoyed for who they are.

REDUCED CLASSROOM ACTIVITIES

NAME _____

OUR CHURCH CELEBRATES VOCATIONS

Decode the missing word in each sentence by using the numbers and letters on the telephone. Fill in the correct word on the line provided.

1. A vocation is a call from _God_ to use our
   (5-10-3)
   gifts for our own good and the good of others.

2. All bishops, priests, and deacons are ordained in the sacrament
   of Holy _Orders_.
   (10-12-3-4-12-13)

3. The sacrament that celebrates the lifelong and life-giving love
   between a man and a _woman_ is Matrimony.
   (15-10-8-1-9)

4. The bride and _groom_ stand before the priest
   (5-12-10-10-8)
   and community and promise to love each other as long as they live.

5. Bishops, _priests_, and deacons are called to
   (11-12-7-4-13-14-13)
   be leaders and servants.

To the Teacher: This activity follows "Praying for Vocations."

Chapter 12 Our Church Celebrates Vocations

THIS IS OUR FAITH 3 **12**

NAME _____

A SPECIAL MESSAGE

Decode the message by crossing out the following words from the list of letters.

artist   musician   scientist   plumber   builder

Write the message on the lines provided.

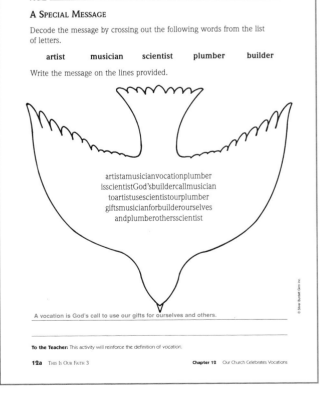

artistamusicianvocationplumber
isscientistGod'sbuildercallmusician
toartistusescientistourplumber
giftsmusicianforbuilderourselves
andplumberothersscientist

A vocation is God's call to use our gifts for ourselves and others.

To the Teacher: This activity will reinforce the definition of *vocation*.

12a THIS IS OUR FAITH 3

Chapter 12 Our Church Celebrates Vocations

VOCATIONS IN LIFE

In the Christian community, some people are married, while others are living as single people. Some have been called by God to be ordained as priests or deacons; others are religious brothers or sisters. Each one of us has a vocation, or a special calling from God.

As a Church, we celebrate two of these vocations as sacraments: Matrimony and Holy Orders. In this chapter, we consider Matrimony the sacrament that celebrates the promise of lifelong and life-giving love between a man and a woman. We speak of Holy Orders as the sacrament in which bishops, priests, and deacons are ordained to proclaim and give witness to God's love and to serve his people.

The perspective for looking at these sacraments should not be lost. Both are vocations, or calls from God. We are all called by God to use our talents and abilities for our own good and for the good of others. In the sacrament of Matrimony, the bride and groom promise to use all that God has given as they share faithful and life-giving love. Throughout their life together as a married couple, they will face the challenge of expressing their love for each other. In the sacrament of Holy Orders, those who are ordained are called especially to the threefold service of teaching, sanctifying, and leading.

GOD'S PLAN FOR US

Students at this level are years away from being married, ordained, or living as single adults. The whole notion of a vocation may be vague to them. The lessons on the sacraments of Matrimony and Holy Orders, however, aim at awakening within these young people a sense that God has something special and important for them to do and that God wants to see them grow and develop as happy and capable Christians.

The focus of this awakening is the call that God extends to all of us to use our talents and abilities for the good of ourselves and others. Third graders can already identify some of their own abilities and desires. We can help them see how they can use these God-given gifts for their own happiness and for the welfare of others. We can help them look at adults in various states of life who use their own talents to help others. In so doing, we nurture the seeds of a vocation, which will bear fruit in the students' adult years.

Objective

This lesson helps the students explore how Christians use their talents.

Step 1/INTRODUCTION

Learning About Our Lives

Reviewing the Sacraments

Review what the students have studied previously about the sacraments. Ask the following questions and print the answers in list form on the chalkboard.

- What do we call celebrations of Jesus' love for us and our love for him? (*Sacraments*)

- Which sacrament is a celebration of welcome into the Church? (*Baptism*)

- Which sacrament celebrates a special meal with Jesus? (*Eucharist*)

- Which sacrament is sometimes referred to as the sacrament of the Holy Spirit? (*Confirmation*)

- What are these three sacraments called together? (*Sacraments of initiation*)

- Which sacrament involves making up through sorrow and forgiveness? (*Reconciliation*)

- Which sacrament offers comfort, forgiveness, and healing to the ill? (*Anointing of the Sick*)

- What are these two sacraments called together? (*Sacraments of healing*)

Introducing the Chapter

Discuss the chapter-focus questions with the students. Encourage each student to participate. Take the time to affirm the talents you have noticed in your students.

Identifying Careers

Direct attention to the art collage on page 142 and read the paragraph at the top of the page. As you guide the discussion, stress that we are often good at the things we enjoy most. Note that the things we enjoy doing often develop into talents.

Our Church Celebrates Vocations

Activity

Each picture below shows someone doing something he or she enjoys. For each picture, talk about a career that you think this person might enjoy when he or she grows up.

What are three things that you do very well? Which of these do you enjoy the most?

142 Scripture

★ Enriching the Lesson ★

Distribute lined paper. Invite the students to write a paragraph about someone they know who uses his or her talents and gifts for the good of others. Instruct them to describe the person they chose and explain what is special about how the talents are used to help others. Encourage them to write specific ways this person shares his or her talents with others.

Teaching Tips

In your class discussions of talents, be sure to emphasize to students that it is important to not only recognize and use our talents, but also to develop them throughout our lives. Share examples of how people can develop talents in particular fields through education and practice.

How Christians Use Their Talents

In the Bible, we can read about our special talents and gifts. We can also learn how we are to use these gifts to help others.

"Each of us has received God's gifts. Some are apostles. Some are pastors and teachers. All are given gifts by God. These are to be used in ways of service to build up the body of Christ in love."

Based on Ephesians 4:7, 11–12, 16

"Put your gifts at the service of one another. The one who serves is to do it with the strength given by God."

Based on 1 Peter 4:10–11

"Whoever wants to be first must serve the needs of all."

Mark 10:44

Learning About Our Faith

Learning How Christians Use Talents

Tell the students that they all have talents and, like all Christians, they must use their talents for others. Call on volunteers to read "How Christians Use Their Talents." Have the students underline the words in each verse that tell how Christians can use their talents.

Step 3/CONCLUSION

Learning How to Live Our Faith

Considering How to Use Talents

Ask the students to name some of the problems and needs in the world. List their responses on the chalkboard. Then have them select one situation they would like to improve. Distribute writing paper and ask the students to write about using their talents to improve the situation they chose. Encourage volunteers to read aloud their ideas.

Praying Together

Invite the students to say spontaneous prayers asking God to help them serve others.

★ ★★★ ★ Enriching the Lesson ★

Invite the students to talk about any special talents they may have, such as juggling, gymnastics, playing a musical instrument, performing magic tricks, and so on. Invite the students to bring to class on one particular day the props they will need to demonstrate these talents and to teach them to others in the class. Impress upon them that using one's talents for others often involves helping them develop the same abilities.

143

DAY 2
MORALITY

Objective

This lesson helps the students understand the meaning of a vocation.

Step 1/INTRODUCTION

Learning About Our Lives

Discussing Career Opportunities

Engage the students in a discussion about what they hope for in the careers they will choose in later life or why they are interested in a certain field. (*Responses may include: money, enjoyment, success, the opportunity to serve others, fame, and the chance to use their talents or gifts.*) Tell the students that in this lesson they will learn about God's personal call to each of them.

Step 2/DEVELOPMENT

Learning About Our Faith

Reading About Special Talents

Read the first paragraph of "Many People, Many Talents" on page 144. You may want to explain that the word *cherish* means "to treat with special care." Emphasize that we can develop our talents and use them to help others. Call on four volunteers to read the four examples of people who made the best use of their talents and abilities. Then ask the students to look back over the examples they have just read. Ask them to describe how these people used their talents for their own good and the good of others.

Many People, Many Talents

Each of us has special abilities and talents. When we cherish and develop our talents, we enrich our lives and bring joy to others.

144 Morality

- Mary liked to write and draw. She became an artist. She met Luke, who was also an artist. They fell in love and were married. They now have three children. They help their parish by making special Mass booklets and bulletins.

- Gary is single. He always liked music. He learned to play the guitar and the piano and became a professional musician. He also gives free music lessons to children who want to learn to play but are unable to pay for lessons.

- Joan liked science. She also enjoyed taking care of people. She wanted to be like the Sisters who taught her. So Joan joined a special religious community of women. Sister Joan also became a nurse. She now cares for the sick in a country called Bolivia.

- Juan liked to read poetry and stories. Like Sister Joan, he felt a special need to serve God and to help people. So he became a priest. Father Juan likes to tell people stories about Jesus.

Cultural Awareness

Point out the story about Sister Joan on page 144. Ask: *Why do you think Sister Joan chose to work in Bolivia rather than in the United States?* Help the students recognize that Sister Joan may have felt that she was needed more in Bolivia. Note that Sister Joan's work is one way of building bridges between our country and our neighbors around the world. Have the students name other ways we can build bridges between countries.

Focus on

Christian Vocation According to the *Catechism of the Catholic Church* "Those who with God's help have welcomed Christ's call and freely responded to it are urged on by love of Christ to proclaim the Good News everywhere in the world. This treasure, received from the apostles, has been faithfully guarded by their successors. All Christ's faithful are called to hand it on from generation to generation, by professing the faith, by living it in fraternal sharing, and by celebrating it in liturgy and prayer." (#3)

God Calls Us

When we are baptized, God calls us to live as Christians. Our parents and godparents promised to help us do this. God also has a specific purpose for each of our lives that makes us very special. God's call to cherish, develop, and use our own unique gifts for our own good and the good of others is known as a **vocation**.

There are vocations to many ways of living and of serving God. God calls some people to be parents. God calls some to be bishops, priests, or deacons. God calls others to be nuns, religious sisters, or brothers, who live in community with others who have the same calling, or vocation. God calls some people to marry and others to be single. All of these vocations are important.

Choosing a Vocation

As we grow up, we begin to recognize some of our own special gifts and talents. We can learn how to use some of our gifts to help others right now. At the same time, we also begin to think about what we will be when we grow up. When our parents, teachers, and other adults we admire live their vocations, they help us see the many choices we have. Someday, with God's help, we will choose our own vocation. We will make a promise, or a commitment, to answer God's call to use our talents for our own good and the good of others.

Vocabulary

vocation: God's call to develop and use our own unique gifts for our own good and the good of others

Teaching Tips

Help the students recognize that they will become more aware of God's call as they grow. Encourage them to trust in God's guidance and to be open to trying new things and pursuing their interests. Emphasize that they needn't be anxious about God's plan for them. Assure the students that God is with them, helping them develop their gifts.

Reading and Discussing the Text

Have the students silently read "God Calls Us" on page 145. Ask the following questions.

■ Who helps us live as Christians? (*Parents and godparents*)
■ What is God's call to cherish, develop, and use our own unique gifts for our own good and the good of others known as? (*A vocation*)

Have the students name some of the vocations to which people are called. Emphasize that God has a plan and purpose for each of us.

Learning About Choosing Vocations

Read "Choosing a Vocation" with the class. Help the students understand that when they discover what God is leading them to do with their talents, they will be called to make a commitment to use these talents to serve others. Emphasize that we can more easily answer God's call if we are listening to what God says to us in prayer and through other people or when we read the Scriptures.

Step 3/CONCLUSION

Learning How to Live Our Faith

Listening for God's Call

Invite the students to sit comfortably and close their eyes. Ask them to listen to God's voice within their hearts as you lead them in the following meditation. Pause for a few moments after each sentence.

Picture God calling your name. Listen as God tells you about the many talents you have been blessed with. Take a moment to ask God how you can use your talents now for your own good and the good of others. Tell God that you want to make the best use of your talents. Ask God to help you listen to and respond to his plan for you.

DAY 3

DOCTRINE

Objective

This lesson helps the students learn about the sacrament of Holy Orders.

Step 1/INTRODUCTION

Learning About Our Lives

Introducing the Lesson

Encourage the students to think about the leaders who serve your parish and your school. Ask them to name some of the people they know, or their parents knew growing up, who have made a commitment to serve God as nuns, religious sisters or brothers, priests, deacons, lay leaders, or as a bishop. Write the following questions on the chalkboard and distribute lined paper.

Name one parish or school leader you especially admire.

What kind of commitment has this person made to serve God and the Church?

How does this person show God's love?

Have the students work on their own to answer the questions. Afterward, invite the students to share their responses with the class. Be sure to tell the students about someone you admire because he or she has lived a life dedicated to serving God and the Church.

Step 2/DEVELOPMENT

Learning About Our Faith

Reading About Holy Orders

Call on volunteers to read aloud "The Sacrament of Holy Orders" as the rest of the students follow along in their texts. Discuss the following questions.

■ What do we call our ordained Church leaders? (*Bishops, priests, and deacons*)

■ How do these Church leaders serve the Church? (*They preach God's word, celebrate the sacraments, and help others live their vocations.*)

■ What sacrament do bishops, priests, and deacons receive when they are ordained? (*Holy Orders*)

146

The Sacrament of Holy Orders

God calls some people to serve the Church as leaders in preaching God's word, in leading celebrations of the sacraments, and in helping others to live their own vocations. These leaders are called bishops, priests, and deacons. They are ordained in the sacrament of **Holy Orders** during a special Mass. Holy Orders is one of two vocations that the Church celebrates as a sacrament of commitment.

During the Mass of Ordination, the bishop places his hands on the head of each person being ordained. He prays that God will help them carry out their new roles. Those being ordained promise to spend their lives serving the Church as leaders and servants. The bishop then gives the newly ordained priests or deacons special signs of their service to the Church.

New bishops receive a ring, a shepherd's staff, and a stiff folded cap called a *miter*. New priests put on a special robe called a *chasuble* and a long strip of cloth called a *stole*. New deacons receive a stole and the *Book of Gospels*.

146 Doctrine

Teaching Tips

Bring to class a chasuble and stole to show the students. Allow them to examine the vestments. You might also invite a priest or deacon to visit your class to talk to the students about being ordained and how he came to know that God was calling him to a religious vocation.

Enriching the Lesson

Point out that bishops receive a shepherd's staff when they are ordained. Remind the students that Jesus called himself the Good Shepherd (John 10:11–15). Have the students look through back issues of your diocesan newspaper for pictures of your bishop. Discuss with the class how your bishop acts as a shepherd to the people of your diocese.

Religious Vocations

Throughout the history of the Church, many people have chosen to follow Jesus in a special way. Some have chosen the religious life of a priest, brother, or sister to help the Church spread the good news and grow in love.

Today, many parts of the world do not have enough priests and sisters or other leaders to help them. As Catholics, we need to pray for more people to dedicate their lives to continuing the work of Jesus in the world. Each year the Church sets aside a special Sunday as Vocations Awareness Sunday. On this day, we pray especially for vocations to the priesthood, sisterhood, and brotherhood.

We often learn about the possibilities for our own vocations from the good examples set by the priests, sisters, brothers, and lay leaders in our parishes and schools. Our families help us live the kind of life Jesus wants us to live so that someday we may also be open to the call to serve God in these same ways.

Activity

Complete the sentences below to tell about a leader in your parish Church or in the worldwide Catholic Church whom you admire.

A Catholic leader I admire is _____

_____ .

I admire this person because _____

_____

_____

_____

_____

_____

_____ .

Vocabulary

Holy Orders: the sacrament in which bishops, priests, and deacons are ordained to special service in the Church

We Believe

Everyone has a God-given vocation. All vocations are important. The Church celebrates two vocations with sacraments: Holy Orders and Matrimony. We call these sacraments of commitment.

Doctrine 147

Focus on

Lay Ministries Help your students understand that many leadership positions in the Church are sometimes filled by people who are not ordained. Ask the students to think of examples of leaders in your parish or diocese who are not priests, deacons, nuns, or religious sisters or brothers. Examples might include Director of Religious Education, Pastoral Associate, Youth Minister, or Music Minister.

- What promises do those being ordained make? (*To serve the Church as leaders and servants*)
- What special signs do those being ordained receive? (*Bishops receive a ring, shepherd's staff, and a miter. Priests receive a chasuble and a stole. Deacons receive a stole and the Book of Gospels.*)

Reading About Religious Vocations

Read through "Religious Vocations" on page 147 with the students. Emphasize the need for religious vocations and our responsibility to pray that people will respond to God's call to serve the Church in this special way. You may wish to tell the students when your parish celebrates Vocations Awareness Sunday and how this day is observed in the parish.

Learning the Vocabulary and Doctrine

Point out the Vocabulary box on page 147 and ask a student to read aloud the definition for *Holy Orders.* Have the class recite the definition together. Then read the We Believe statement to the class. Tell the students that they will be learning about the sacrament of Matrimony in the next lesson.

Step 3/CONCLUSION

Learning How to Live Our Faith

Writing About Commitments

After reading aloud the directions for the activity on page 147, encourage the students to consider someone they admire. Allow sufficient time for the students to complete the activity. Then ask for volunteers to read aloud what they have written.

Praying Together

Conclude by asking the Holy Spirit to continue to guide you and your students and to help all people be open to God's call to serve the Church as leaders and servants.

DAY 4
DOCTRINE/MORALITY

Objective

This lesson helps the students recognize that Matrimony celebrates the lifelong love between a man and a woman.

Step 1/INTRODUCTION

Learning About Our Lives

Writing About Weddings

Use the activity questions on page 148 to engage the students in a discussion about their experiences of attending weddings. Then direct the students' attention to the writing activity and have the students complete it independently. When they have finished, invite the students to share their responses with the class. Tell the students that in this lesson they will learn about the vocation of married people.

or...

Invite the students to bring photographs of a family wedding to class and talk about the people and things that are shown in the pictures. You may also wish to bring family wedding photographs to share with the class.

Step 2/DEVELOPMENT

Learning About Our Faith

Reading the Text

Call on volunteers to read aloud "The Sacrament of Matrimony" on page 146. Use the following questions to guide discussion.

- What do we call the sacrament that celebrates the love and commitment between a man and a woman? (*Matrimony*)

- What do the bride and groom promise? (*To always love and care for each other in sickness and health; to welcome children and to bring them up according to the teachings of Jesus*)

- What is the wedding ring a sign of? (*The bride and groom's love for each other and their promises*)

- What does the priest pray for? (*That the couple will grow in their love and share their love with others*)

148

Activity

Have you ever been invited to a wedding or seen one on TV? Maybe you have been a ring bearer or a flower girl in a wedding. What do you remember most about that special celebration? What symbols do you remember seeing that were part of this sacrament? Write down some of the things you remember about the last wedding you saw.

_____

_____

_____

The Sacrament of Matrimony

God calls some people to share their lives in marriage. The sacrament that celebrates the love and commitment between a man and a woman is called **Matrimony**. Like Holy Orders, it is also called a sacrament of commitment. Matrimony is usually celebrated at a Mass. The Bible readings and homily are about love and marriage.

The bride and groom promise to always love and care for each other, to always stand by each other, and to love each other in sickness and in health. They promise to welcome children lovingly and to bring them up according to the ways of Christ.

The bride and groom place a wedding ring on each other's fingers as a symbol of their love. The priest blesses them and prays that they will grow in their love and share it with others.

Teaching Tips

During the discussion of Matrimony, be especially sensitive to those students whose parents are divorced or separated. Emphasize that marriage is not always easy and that sometimes a couple is unable to resolve their differences and remain together. Help the students understand that God still loves and cares about each member of the family.

I Wonder

Inside myself I wonder,
What is it I will be?
My teachers and my parents say,
For now, I should be me.

Sometimes my *me*'s an artist,
Sometimes an Olympic star.
And sometimes a mechanic
Who fixes up a car.

Sometimes my *me* is single,
Sometimes a missionary.
And when I go to weddings,
I think that I will marry.

Inside myself I wonder,
What is it I will be?
Someday I will have grown to learn
What God has planned for me.

God Calls Me

Jesus promised that the Holy Spirit would help us in the decisions we make every day. The Holy Spirit will also guide each of us as we listen for God's special call. Some of us may receive the call to be priests, deacons, sisters, or brothers. Some may choose to marry and raise families or to remain single. Some of us will serve our parishes as professionals and others will serve as volunteers. When we pray for God's help—and take the time to listen in prayer as well—we can have faith that we are making good decisions and commitments to serve in the ways that God has planned for us.

Vocabulary

Matrimony: the sacrament that celebrates the lifelong and life-giving love between a man and a woman, who promise to love each other as husband and wife

Morality 149

Reviewing the Vocabulary and Doctrine

Read the definition in the Vocabulary box on page 149. Then review the We Believe statement from page 147. Solicit the students' questions. Tell the students that the sacraments of vocation are sometimes called sacraments of commitment. Explain that the word *commitment* means "promise." Have the students name the promises that are made in Matrimony and Holy Orders.

Step 3/CONCLUSION

Learning How to Live Our Faith

Thinking About the Poem

Give the students a few moments to silently read the poem on page 149. Then have the class form two groups and read the poem aloud, alternating groups. Ask Group 1 what stanza 1 of the poem is saying. Ask Group 2 what stanza 2 is saying. Continue this questioning for stanzas 3 and 4.

Recognizing God's Call

Help the students understand that the kind of people they are now is just as important as the kind of work they will make a commitment to someday. Point out that they may change their minds many times between now and the time they are ready to graduate from high school about what they will be when they grow up.

Read "God Calls Me" with the class. Have the students discuss some ways in which people can develop their talents and abilities. Remind the students that God's call first comes to us in Baptism. Conclude by praying this prayer.

Jesus, help us be what you want us to be. Help us listen to the Holy Spirit, who guides us. Help us use our talents to improve ourselves and care for others. Above all, Lord, help us love you and do your will always. Amen.

Objective

This lesson helps the students pray a litany prayer.

Preparing for Prayer

Read the first paragraph of "Praying for Vocations" on page 150 with the class. Explain that after each petition in the Prayer of the Faithful, which is usually read by one person, everyone else responds with "Lord, hear our prayer." Direct attention to the lines provided in the text for the students to write their invocations for married couples, men and women in religious communities, all Christians who remain single, and ordained ministers. Invite the students to complete the petitions to use in the litany.

As the students write their prayers, move about the room, offering suggestions and assistance. Help students understand the connection between the people they are praying for and their own futures. Invite them to write their own prayer response accordingly. An example might be: *Lord, guide us to our futures.*

Praying for Vocations

Give each student an opportunity to participate in the reading of the invocations during the prayer experience. Ask them to read either their first, second, third, or fourth invocation. Arrange for approximately one-fourth of the class to read each of the four prayers.

Place one or more symbols that represent our baptismal call and both of the sacraments of vocation on the prayer table before beginning the service. These symbols might include a candle or a small bowl of water, a chasuble or stole, and a ring or wedding album. As the invocations are prayed, have a volunteer hold the appropriate symbol up for all to see.

Praying for Vocations

When we pray a litany, we sometimes use petitions to tell God our needs and concerns. A familiar example of this are the General Intercessions at Mass, which are sometimes called the Prayer of the Faithful. Today, we ask for God's blessing on people who have been faithful in the special commitments they have made.

Teacher: The Scriptures tell us, "There are different gifts but the same Spirit; there are different ministries but the same Lord; there are different works but the same God who produces them in everyone. The Spirit produces all these gifts and gives them to each of us according to God's plan" (based on 1 Corinthians 12:4–7). Let us pray.

Students: For all married couples, especially _____.
All: Lord, hear our prayer.
Students: For all people in religious communities, especially _____.
All: Lord, hear our prayer.
Students: For all Christians who choose the single life, especially

_____

All: Lord, hear our prayer.
Students: For all priests, deacons, and bishops, especially

_____

All: Lord, hear our prayer. Help us to listen and follow. Amen.

Chapter Review

Complete the sentences by filling in the blanks.

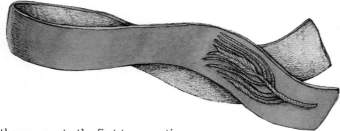

1. God's call to use our gifts according to his plan

   for each of us is called a _____vocation_____.

2. The two sacraments of commitment are _____Holy Orders_____

   and _____Matrimony_____.

3. When priests are ordained, they receive a chasuble and a _____stole_____.

4. Newly ordained bishops receive a ring, a shepherd's staff, and a _____miter_____.

5. Newly ordained deacons receive a stole and the _____Book of Gospels_____.

6. A symbol of everlasting love is the wedding _____ring_____.

Fill in the answers to the first two questions.

1. What does *vocation* mean? God's call to develop

   and use our own unique gifts for our own good and

   the good of others

2. What are the two sacraments of commitment?

   Holy Orders and Matrimony

3. Talk about some ways a person can discover
   and respond to his or her vocation.

> **Live up to the calling you have received.**
> **Based on Ephesians 4:1**

CHAPTER REVIEW

Filling in the Blanks

Have the students work independently to complete the first exercise on page 151. Give the students permission to look through the chapter to find any answers they cannot remember. When all have finished, ask volunteers to read aloud the completed statements.

Completing the Chapter Review

Take time to go through the review questions. Direct the students to write answers to the first two questions on the lines provided in the text. Encourage all to participate in discussing how people can discover and respond to their vocations. Be supportive of the students' ideas.

Praying with the Scriptural Verse

Have one of the students read the verse from Scripture at the bottom of the page. Ask the students what the verse means in light of what they have studied about vocations. Reiterate that all of us are called by God to use our talents for ourselves and for others. Encourage the students to take more time to listen to God when they pray so that they can hear and be open to God's special call to them.

Completing the Activity

Explain the directions for the Unit Organizer activity. You may want to complete the Prayer box with the class to make sure that they understand the assignment. Encourage the students to refer to the Vocabulary boxes and the We Believe statements in Chapters 9 through 12 to help them complete each box. When finished, call on volunteers to read aloud their responses.

(*Possible responses for Prayer may include: listening and talking to God; using words, songs, and gestures; using psalm prayers; in the sacraments; Liturgy of the Hours; at Mass; when we are alone; with our families at home. Possible responses for Initiation may include: that new members will feel welcome. Possible responses for Healing may include: that people will become well and that people will be forgiven. Possible responses for Vocation may include: that God will help those being ordained and those who marry to be good and faithful servants of the Church.*)

Looking Back: Self-Assessment

The critical–reflection questions below give the students an opportunity to sharpen their thinking skills. The questions can be used as a class discussion or an independent writing activity.

- What did you learn in this unit that you think you will always remember?
- Which was your favorite Scripture story in this unit?
- What did you like most about it?
- Which activity in this unit did you most enjoy? Why?

UNIT 3 ORGANIZER

Prayer expresses our faith in God. In the *Prayer* box, write a sentence about the ways in which Catholics pray. Then for each of the *Initiation, Healing,* and *Commitment* boxes, write one thing the Church prays for in the sacraments. You may use any of the vocabulary words listed to complete this activity.

Prayer
prayer, psalms, synagogue, sacraments, liturgy, Liturgy of the Hours

_____
_____
_____
_____ .

Initiation
initiation, Easter Vigil, baptismal font, baptismal pool, immersion
The Church prays for

_____
_____
_____ .

Healing
healing, Anointing of the Sick, anointing, sin
The Church prays for

_____
_____
_____ .

Vocation
vocation, Holy Orders, Matrimony
The Church prays for

_____
_____
_____ .

UNIT 3 REVIEW

Place an X before each true statement.

1. _____ God calls us to use our talents only for our own good.

2. __X__ The sacrament of lifelong and life-giving love between a man and a woman is called Matrimony.

3. __X__ The psalms are from the Old Testament.

4. __X__ In Reconciliation, we celebrate God's forgiveness.

5. _____ Baptism is never celebrated at the Easter Vigil.

6. __X__ Holy Orders is celebrated at a special Mass.

Fill in the blanks with the correct words.

forgives	synagogue	talents
followers	Temple	prayed

Jesus ___prayed___ every morning, afternoon, and evening. He prayed at home, in the ___synagogue___, and in the great ___Temple___. As members of the Church, we are called to live as Jesus' friends and ___followers___. Jesus ___forgives___ us when we hurt others. Jesus wants us to use the ___talents___ that God gives us.

Reviewing the Unit

The purpose of the Unit Review is to reinforce concepts presented in the preceding four chapters and to check the students' understanding. After explaining the directions, give the students sufficient time to complete the two-page review. Answer any questions they may have.

Testing

After the students have completed the Unit Review, you may wish to distribute copies of the Unit 3 Test from the Tests booklet in The Resourceful Teacher Package.

Optional Unit Project

Have the students form groups of two or three to create prayer posters. Print the five kinds of prayer on the chalkboard: adoration, thanksgiving, petition, faith, and contrition. Then ask the students for a definition of each. Have each small group select on its own one of the kinds of prayer. Have each group write a prayer of at least three sentences, writing it on a large sheet of poster paper and decorating it appropriately. The lettering on the posters should be large enough to be read when held up for the whole group to see. Have all the groups share their prayer posters with the rest of the students.

Match the words in Column A with the definitions in Column B.

Column A

1. __c__ psalms

2. __b__ Holy Orders

3. __f__ vocation

4. __h__ prayer

5. __g__ Liturgy of the Hours

6. __a__ Easter Vigil

7. __d__ sin

8. __e__ initiation

9. __j__ forgiveness

10. __i__ healing

Column B

a. special celebration of the resurrection of Jesus and new life in Christ

b. the sacrament in which bishops, priests, and deacons are ordained

c. songs of prayer from the Old Testament

d. something that we know is wrong and hurtful to others and to our relationship with God

e. the ways we welcome new members into the Church

f. God's call to make a commitment to use our gifts and talents well

g. official prayers that some Christians pray every morning and evening

h. using words, songs, and gestures to listen or talk to God

i. helping people to become well or to be forgiven

j. loving someone even when they have hurt us on purpose

IDENTIFYING PROBLEM-SOLVING TERMS

Let's identify what we have learned about how Catholic Christians solve problems. Write the number for each term about solving problems next to the definition that best describes it.

1. Problem

2. Solution

3. Goal

4. Consequence

5. Stop and Think

__3__ what the person with the problem wants to have happen

__1__ a disagreement between people

__2__ a way to solve a problem

__5__ the first problem-solving step

__4__ what happens as a result of a solution

Identifying Consequences

The game of tag has already started when Alice arrives outside for recess. Alice really wants to play, but the others say, "No, you're too late." Alice feels both sad and angry. She decides to stop and think of different ways to cope with the situation.

▼▼▼▼▼

Day to Day 155

Day to Day ~

Objective

This lesson helps the students evaluate possible solutions to a problem by considering the consequences of each solution.

Introducing the Lesson

Ask the students to recall the steps for problem solving. If necessary, refer to page 55 in the student text. Then have the students turn to page 155. Read aloud the directions for the matching activity and ask the students to complete it. Review their responses when they have finished.

Reading and Discussing a Story

Ask a volunteer to read aloud "Identifying Consequences" at the bottom of page 155. Use the following questions to facilitate discussion.

■ What is Alice's problem? (*She has been left out of the game of tag.*)

■ How does Alice feel? (*Sad and angry*)

■ Does Alice stop and think? (*Yes*)

■ What is Alice's goal? (*She wants to be included in a game of tag.*)

Evaluating Solutions

Read aloud the directions for the activity at the top of page 156. Ask the students to work in pairs to list possible consequences of the solutions given. Explain that a consequence might happen immediately after a solution is tried or it could happen later. For example, a short-term consequence of watching television after school is that homework doesn't get finished. A long-term consequence might be a low grade on the test at the end of the week. Also, emphasize that part of thinking about consequences is asking "What might happen if I try this solution?" and "Is this solution something that fits with the kind of person Jesus calls me to be as his follower?"

When the students have finished their lists, have them share their responses with the class. Read aloud "What Makes a Good Solution?" Help students evaluate the acceptability of their different solutions using the criteria described.

Lesson continues on page 156.

155

Have them circle what they think is the best solution for Alice's problem. Then discuss their choices.

Considering Solutions and Consequences

Use the following activity as another opportunity for the students to identify possible solutions and their consequences. Tell the following story.

Maria and John are running to the only unoccupied swing on the playground. They both get there at the same time, but Maria jumps on the swing. Feeling mad, John pulls Maria off the swing and gets on it himself.

Ask these questions to guide discussion.

- What is the problem? (*Both Maria and John want to use the swing.*)
- What is the goal? (*The goal is for both of them to have a chance to swing.*)
- Did either Maria or John remember to stop and think? (*No.*)
- What solution is tried? (*Maria jumps on right away. John pulls Maria off.*)
- What might be the consequence of John pulling Maria off the swing? (*Maria might tell the teacher and John would be in trouble; Maria might pull John off the swing and get into a physical fight.*)
- Does this solution fit with being a follower of Jesus? (*Jesus calls us to be kind and considerate of others. This solution causes hurt feelings.*)

Invite the students to brainstorm other possible solutions to John and Maria's problem. List these on the chalkboard. For each solution, ask the students to name two or more possible consequences. Then help the students evaluate the solutions and choose the best one. You might also wish to have them act out several of the solutions.

Concluding the Lesson

Read with the students "Following Jesus" at the bottom page 156. Remind them that, as followers of Jesus, we are called to choose solutions to problems that are helpful, not hurtful, to others. Conclude the lesson by reading the prayer together.

156

Activity Choosing the Best Solution

For each possible solution, list some possible consequences. Then circle the best solution.

SOLUTION A	SOLUTION B	SOLUTION C
Alice could call members of the group names and tell them she doesn't really want to play anyway.	Alice could tell them she'll be "it" if they let her join.	Alice could ask some other kids who aren't playing tag if they would like to start a new game of tag.
Possible Consequences:	Possible Consequences:	Possible Consequences:

What Makes a Good Solution?

A good solution helps the person with a problem reach his or her goal. A good solution shows care for others. A good solution keeps a problem from getting worse. A good solution has positive consequences. A good solution shows Christian friendship.

Following Jesus

Jesus cares about us. Jesus knows that it is sometimes hard to figure out which solution is best. If our feelings have been hurt, we may find it difficult to choose solutions that treat others fairly and with kindness. Jesus gives us the Holy Spirit to help us choose solutions that show we care about others.

PRAYER

Jesus, I love you. Help me to solve my problems in ways that bring me closer to you, to others, and to truly living as a Christian. Thank you for giving me the Holy Spirit to help me choose what is good and loving. Amen.

OPENING DOORS
A Take-Home Magazine™

THIS IS OUR FAITH

© Silver Burdett Ginn Inc.

Growing Closer

WHO HAS TIME to pray? *You do* when you're...

grocery shopping

taking a walk

driving the car

doing chores

Try it!

PRAYING MEMORIZED PRAYERS can be a good thing. These prayers provide prayer words when we cannot seem to pray in our own words. These memorized prayers also keep us united with other Catholics by allowing us to practice something we share in common. Write out the words of your favorite prayer and hang it in a place where you can see it—and pray it—often!

Looking Ahead

Unit 4 will center on the traditional moral principles of the Church. These principles find their roots in the life and teachings of Jesus, who drew upon the moral heritage contained in the Old Testament. Your child will learn that for Jesus and the Church, the basic law is that we love and care. Jesus and the Church stress that love of neighbor is the most basic sign of our love for God.

Opening Doors

Sending the Magazine Home

As you complete Unit 3 with your class, assist the students in carefully removing *Opening Doors: A Take-Home Magazine* (two pages) from their texts by separating the pages from the book along the perforations. Demonstrate how to fold the two pages to form an eight-page booklet.

When the magazines are folded, take time to explain each section of the magazine to the students. Allow the students to ask any questions they may have. Ask the students to take the magazine home and encourage their families to read it with them and to participate in the suggested activities. You may wish to attach a letter of your own, encouraging the family to use the magazine each time their child brings it home.

People of Prayer

Prayer is at the heart of Christian faith. And integral to Catholic life and faith is worship, or public prayer. Like Jesus, who worshiped in the Jewish temple, we value and pray the traditional prayers of our faith community. And like Jesus, who often went off to pray alone, we too are growing in our personal awareness of God's presence and activity in and through our lives. We believe that praying together supports the development of our prayerfulness as individuals.

The best and perhaps only way to learn to pray is by simply doing it. Growing up in a worshiping community, our children are learning to pray. Being in the presence of praying people, especially in our own families, and praying with them is the best way for our children to learn to pray.

2

Among the more commonly known styles of black sacred song are the *spirituals.* Some spirituals that are becoming more and more familiar to American Catholic worshiping communities are "There Is a Balm in Gilead," "Let Us Break Bread Together," "Every Time I Feel the Spirit," and "Were You There." *European hymns* have been embellished with distinctively black rhythms and gestures. And a wealth of *new music* has been composed in recent years with the particular needs of the black faith community in mind.

Black Catholic worshiping communities throughout the United States have been deeply affected by the introduction of black sacred music into Catholic liturgy, an introduction first attempted by Father Clarence Joseph Rivers in the late 1960s. For with black sacred song comes the artful use of music "to teach, comfort, inspire, persuade, convince, and motivate." It moves us to the depths of our being. It powerfully connects body and spirit, the sacred and the secular, the individual and the community.

All sacred music cultivates in us a deeper awareness of the presence of God. Black sacred music calls us to that awareness in a unique and engaging way.

7

BLACK
SACRED MUSIC

When we think about the sacred music most familiar to us, traditional songs such as "Now Thank We All Our God" and more modern songs such as "One Bread, One Body" may come to mind. In addition to these two styles of sacred song there is another type known as *black sacred music.*

Sister Thea Bowman, writing in the preface to the African American Catholic Hymnal *Lead Me, Guide Me* (G.I.A. Publications, Inc. 1987), tells us much about the origins of black sacred music, its unique characteristics, and its introduction into Catholic worship.

According to Sister Thea, "African men and women brought [to America] sacred songs and chants that reminded them of their homelands and that sustained them in separation and in captivity, songs to respond to all life situations, and the ability to create new songs to answer new needs." Sister goes on to tell us that "Black sacred song celebrates our God, His goodness, His promise, our faith and hope, our journey toward the promise." From the unique styles of African-American musical expression and a rich heritage of common stories and experiences, a new tradition of sacred song has emerged.

6

An *ancient insight* in the Church is that *what we believe* is evident from *how we pray.* In other words, the way we worship reveals what we really believe as a community. In praying as individuals and as a parish community, we praise God, give thanks, express sorrow, and petition for specific needs. In all of this, we express our faith in our God who loves and sustains us.

By using *familiar words* and gestures and by designating a specific time and place for prayer, we can turn to God with great ease. Called to pray both together and alone, we take time to think about God, to talk to and listen to God, and to rest in God's presence. In all of our prayer experiences, we express and deepen the faith that calls us to live as one.

3

Prayers at Mass

Jesus taught us how important prayer is in our lives by showing us how important it was in his life. The Scriptures tell us that he sometimes went off to pray alone and that he also prayed in the temple. Spending time with God, telling God our needs, and listening to God speak to us is is praying as Jesus prayed. Read the following with your child.

At Mass we pray together in many different ways. We pray together aloud and we pray together silently. We sing and sometimes dance. And sometimes the priest prays a prayer of the whole community and we answer, "Amen."

Some of the Mass prayers are listed here for you. Match each prayer line in Column 1 with a prayer line in Column 2 that is taken from the same Mass prayer.

1. ... through Christ our Lord.
2. Our Father,
3. The Word of the Lord.
4. Lord our God.
5. It will become for us the bread of life.
6. Lamb of God, you take away the sins of the world:
7. Let us give thanks to the
8. We pray to the Lord:

A. who art in heaven...
B. have mercy on us.
C. Amen.
D. Thanks be to God.
E. Lord, hear our prayer.
F. It is right to give him thanks and praise.
G. Blessed be God for ever.
H. Christ is risen, Christ will come again.

Join in praying the many different kinds of prayers we pray at Mass. Remember to listen to God whenever you pray.

4

5

160

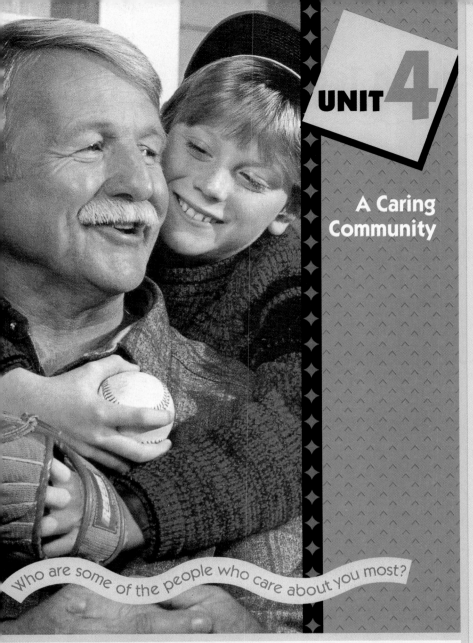

Who are some of the people who care about you most?

UNIT 4

A Caring Community

Unit Aim

To help the students understand and appreciate the Church's moral principles, which include Jesus' commandment to love, the Ten Commandments, the corporal works of mercy, and the spiritual works of mercy.

Doctrinal Summaries

CHAPTER 13

Jesus teaches that what is most important is that we love God, others, and ourselves.

CHAPTER 14

God gives us the Ten Commandments to help us live good and happy lives. The commandments show us ways of loving God, ourselves, other people, and all of creation.

CHAPTER 15

We best show our love for Jesus when we help people in need. Jesus teaches that whatever we do for people in need, we do for him. Catholics identify the corporal works of mercy as seven ways we can care for people in need.

CHAPTER 16

Jesus teaches us by word and example to care for people who are unhappy, who have problems, or who need help. In the spiritual works of mercy, the Church tells us some ways we can show care and concern.

Note:
As you prepare this unit, you may wish to refer to the reference section, *Our Catholic Heritage*, beginning on page 327.

Additional resources for Unit 4 include a Unit Test and a Family Letter as well as a video and selections from the THIS IS OUR FAITH Music Program. You might also find it helpful to preview *Saints and Other Holy People* and *Prayer Celebrations* for possibilities to enhance the unit.

Introducing the UNIT

Direct attention to the unit-focus question and ask the students to suggest ways that the grandfather and the child are caring for one another. Then elicit responses to the unit-focus question. Tell the students that in Unit 4 they will learn how Catholics are called to show care for God, other people, themselves, and creation.

Vocabulary

Pharisees
Sabbath
scribes
commandments
reverence
parables
corporal
mercy
spiritual

161

13 Our Church Teaches Us to Love

Objectives

To help the students

- Appreciate the value of rules.
- Learn about Jesus' commandment to love.
- Recognize whom Jesus calls us to love.
- Understand that Father Damien showed love for God by helping others.
- Celebrate their love for God and others by praying with sign language and review the chapter.

Chapter Outline

	Step 1 Learning About Our Lives	**Step 2** Learning About Our Faith	**Step 3** Learning How to Live Our Faith
Day 1	■ Introduce the chapter. ■ Read the story. ■ Discuss the story. *ABOUT 15 MINUTES*	■ Read a Scripture story. ■ Discuss the text. ■ Learn the vocabulary. *ABOUT 10 MINUTES*	■ Talk about making choices. *ABOUT 5 MINUTES*
Day 2	■ Discuss favorite teachers. *ABOUT 6 MINUTES*	■ Learn the vocabulary words. ■ Dramatize the story. ■ Discuss the story. ■ Memorize the doctrine. *ABOUT 16 MINUTES*	■ Complete a checklist. ■ Pray together. *ABOUT 8 MINUTES*
Day 3	■ Talk about the experience of being loved. *ABOUT 5 MINUTES*	■ Read the text. ■ Research Scripture. *ABOUT 13 MINUTES*	■ Study photographs. ■ Make a banner about love. *ABOUT 12 MINUTES*
Day 4	■ Recall saint stories. *ABOUT 4 MINUTES*	■ Read a biography. *ABOUT 6 MINUTES*	■ Learn how to give all. ■ Complete an activity. ■ Review the chapter. *ABOUT 20 MINUTES*
Day 5	**Prayer** Prepare for the prayer service; pray together. **Review** Complete the sentences; complete the chapter review; pray with the scriptural verse.		

Plan Ahead ~~~~~~~~~~~~

	Preparing Your Class	**Materials Needed**
Day 1	Read through the lesson plan for this class session.	■ chalkboard or posterboard ■ pencils or pens
Day 2	Read through the lesson plan for this class session. In Step 1, be prepared to discuss a favorite teacher with the students.	■ chalkboard ■ pencils or pens
Day 3	Read through the lesson plan for this class session. Prepare the art materials needed for the banner-making activity in Step 3.	■ colorful magazines ■ butcher paper ■ crayons, scissors, and pencils ■ paste, glue, or tape ■ Bibles
Day 4	Read through the lesson plan for this class session. You may want to have books about the saints available for the students to look through in Step 1.	■ pencils or pens
Day 5	Have ready the banner from Day 3 for the celebration. Prepare an environment for prayer in the classroom. Practice the sign-language responses.	■ crayons or markers ■ pencils or pens

Additional Resources

As you plan this chapter, consider using the following materials from The Resourceful Teacher Package.

■ *Classroom Activity Sheets 13 and 13a*

■ *Family Activity Sheets 13 and 13a*

■ *Chapter 13 Test*

■ *Prayers for Every Day*

■ *Projects: Grade 3*

You may also wish to refer to the following Big Book.

■ *We Celebrate God's Word,* page 3

In preparing the students for the Sunday readings, you may wish to use Silver Burdett Ginn's *Getting Ready for Sunday* student and teacher materials.

BOOKS FOR THE JOURNEY

Frederick's Fables. Leo Lionni. Knopf, 1993. "Geraldine, the Music Mouse," pp. 41–50. Geraldine gradually is able to share her cheese with her hungry friends.

The Legend of the Persian Carpet. Tomie dePaola. G.P. Putnam's Sons, 1993. A young apprentice lovingly creates something that brings back the light and beauty the king needs.

MORE BOOKS FOR THE JOURNEY

A Child's Book of Prayers. Edited by Linda Yeatman. Workman Publishing, 1992. "Love God with All Your Soul and Strength," by Isaac Watts, p. 70; "Dear Lord, In Your Word You Teach Us to Love One Another," by Leonard H. Dengeinge, p. 63.

The Story of Jumping Mouse. John Steptoe. Morrow, 1989. A Native American legend of a mouse with a genuinely unselfish spirit.

REDUCED CLASSROOM ACTIVITIES

NAME _____

OUR CHURCH TEACHES US TO LOVE

Read the two great commandments in the hearts below. After each sentence below the hearts, write **1** if the sentence makes you think of the first great commandment, or write **2** if it makes you think of the second great commandment.

"You shall love the Lord your God with all your heart, with all your soul, with all your mind, and with all your strength."
1
Mark 12:30

"You shall love your neighbor as yourself."
2
Mark 12:31

1. I have received the sacrament of Baptism.   1
2. I go to the store for my mother.   2
3. I do not make fun of other boys and girls.   2
4. I say prayers before I go to bed.   1
5. I respect the property of my neighbors.   2
6. I go to church on Sunday.   1
7. I gladly help my father clean the yard.   2
8. I receive Eucharist at Mass.   1
9. I say grace before I eat my meals.   1
10. I share my lunch with another person.   2

© Silver Burdett Ginn Inc.

To the Teacher: This activity follows the Scripture story "Jesus Teaches About Love."

Chapter 13 Our Church Teaches Us to Love   THIS IS OUR FAITH 3   **13**

NAME _____

REMEMBERING GOD'S LAW

Complete the crossword puzzle. Fill in the puzzle by writing the correct word to complete each sentence.

Across

1. The _____ are rules given to us by God to help us live good lives.
2. We show our love for _____ when we love other people.

Down

3. The second great commandment tells us to love our _____ as ourselves.
4. _____ had lived a life of love and service to God and helping lepers.
5. The two great commandments were told to us by _____.

© Silver Burdett Ginn Inc.

To the Teacher: This activity will reinforce the concepts presented in Chapter 13.

13a THIS IS OUR FAITH 3   **Chapter 13** Our Church Teaches Us to Love

Background for the Teacher

THE EXPERIENCE OF SELFISHNESS

Students at this level know well the pull between selfishness and caring about others. They know from experience how hard it can be at times to give up some pleasure or preference in order to do something for someone else. They want to do what is right, yet they often feel pulled toward choosing what is immediately satisfying.

It is this experience that provides the opportunity for the students to learn about Jesus' commandment to love. God calls us to love God first and secondly to love other people as we love ourselves. These commandments make up the most important instructions from Jesus on how we are to live.

To love God above all has always been central to Israel's covenant with their creator. Devout Jews remind themselves daily of God's primacy in their lives. They know well the words from Deuteronomy 6:5, which Jesus recited to the scribe in Mark's Gospel: "You shall love the Lord your God with all your heart, with all your soul, with all your mind, and with all your strength" (Mark 12:30). Jesus drew his second commandment about loving one's neighbor as oneself from Leviticus 19:18.

JESUS' COMMANDMENT TO LOVE

Jesus' commandment to love reflects the theme of all the great prophets before him: You cannot love God without loving the people around you. Jesus' teaching stresses the primacy of love for God but points out that the surest sign of this love is caring about one's neighbor. Jesus repeated this theme often.

The first letter of John expresses this even more forcefully: "If anyone says, 'I love God,' but hates his brother, he is a liar; for whoever does not love a brother whom he has seen cannot love God whom he has not seen. This is the commandment we have from him: whoever loves God must also love his brother" (1 John 4:20–21).

DAY 1
MORALITY/SCRIPTURE

Objective
This lesson helps the students appreciate the value of rules.

Step 1/INTRODUCTION

Learning About Our Lives

Introducing the Chapter
Discuss the chapter-focus questions with the group. Have the students identify the positive effects of rules in their various communities. Help them appreciate that rules protect us, guide us in making good decisions, and help us to live happier lives. List on the chalkboard these three reasons for having rules and refer to them throughout the week.

or . . .

Have the students imagine what it would be like if there were no rules. Have them describe what would happen if we did not have rules at home, at school, or in our communities. Emphasize that rules guide us in knowing how to live together and how to act lovingly toward one another.

Reading the Story
Direct attention to the story, "To Call or Not to Call" on pages 162 and 163. Tell the students that they are about to read a story in which someone has to decide whether to follow a rule. Ask the students to listen as you read the story and to think about what they would do if they were Samantha.

Discussing the Story
Discuss the story, using these questions: *What would you have done if you were Samantha? Why didn't Samantha's dad punish her?* Take a poll to determine how many students would have done what Samantha did. Have them explain why they might do the same. Lead them to understand that Samantha's dad recognized that she had broken the rule in order to help Mrs. Green. Clarify that Samantha had used good judgment and common sense in realizing that Mrs. Green's emergency was more important than keeping the rule.

162

What are some good things about the rules that we live by at home, in school, in cities and towns? How do they help us and others?

162 Morality

Our Church Teaches Us to Love

To Call or Not to Call
Samantha loved talking to her friends on the telephone. Whenever the phone rang, she was the first to answer. She was always sure it was for her.

One day, Samantha's teacher sent a note home, telling Samantha's dad that she had not completed her homework for two weeks. Samantha and her dad agreed that taking away Samantha's phone privileges might help the situation. "If you even pick up that phone without asking, you'll be grounded for a month," her dad said. "And no playing outside after school!"

Samantha was sad, but she always obeyed her father. It was hard not to use the phone whenever she wanted. But she kept the rule for two days.

Then one afternoon when she was the only one inside the house, Samantha was looking out her window. The snow was falling. It was so pretty. The last thing Samantha wanted to do was her homework. She loved to daydream.

A few minutes passed. Suddenly, Samantha was startled. She saw her neighbor, Mrs. Green, slip and fall on the icy sidewalk. She couldn't get up. It looked as if her leg might be badly hurt.

Samantha ran to the front door of her house. Then she stopped. Samantha reached for the phone, then put it down. She thought of Dad's rules. Then she picked up the phone and dialed 911.

 **CURRICULUM CONNECTION**

Language Arts Explain to the students that in the story, Samantha was faced with a *dilemma*, a situation in which there seems to be more than one right choice. Invite them to brainstorm in teams of three or four students other situations in which there is a dilemma. Have one member of each team tell the class about the dilemma the team came up with.

When Samantha's dad came home, she told him what happened. She expected her dad to be angry about her using the phone. To her surprise, he hugged her proudly and said, "You did the right thing."

Breaking the Sabbath Laws

One day, Jesus and some of his disciples were walking through a grainfield. The disciples were hungry and so began picking the grain to eat. Some **Pharisees** saw this and questioned Jesus about why the disciples were breaking the laws of the **Sabbath**, a day for rest and prayer. The Pharisees were very religious and based their entire lives on living according to God's laws. Jesus reminded them about a story from the Scriptures that tells about a time when David and his friends were also breaking the Sabbath laws.

Jesus left the grainfield and then entered a synagogue. He met a man there who had a broken hand. The Pharisees asked Jesus if it was lawful to cure this man on the Sabbath. Jesus asked them, "Would you not on the Sabbath lift out a sheep of yours that has fallen into a pit? And is not a human being more valuable than a sheep? Certainly, it is lawful to do good on the Sabbath."

Based on Matthew 12:1–12

Discuss

1. What did Samantha's dad mean when he told her that she did the right thing?

2. What did Jesus mean when he said "it is lawful to do good on the Sabbath"?

3. What might you have said or done in each story?

Vocabulary

Pharisees: very religious Jews who based their entire lives on living according to God's laws

Sabbath: a day for rest and prayer

◆ ◆ ◆ ◆ ◆ ◆ ◆ ◆ ◆ ◆ ◆

Scripture 163

Cultural Awareness

Explain to the students that in the Jewish faith, the Sabbath celebration begins at sundown on Friday and ends on Saturday evening. On Friday night the family gathers and lights two candles. A prayer of blessing is said over the bread and wine that will be shared at the Sabbath meal. Encourage the students to respect the religious traditions of the Jewish people, from whom we have inherited many of our Catholic traditions. Invite them to talk about the prayers they pray with their families before eating.

Teaching Tips

Ask the students: *Which day do Christians set aside for prayer and rest?* Explain that we honor Sunday as a special day because Jesus rose from the dead on a Sunday—Easter Sunday. Invite the students to share a personal experience or draw a picture story about how their family can make Sunday a special day of prayer, rest, and family unity.

Learning About Our Faith

Reading a Scripture Story

Read with the class "Breaking the Sabbath Laws" on page 163. Use the following questions to guide discussion.

■ What did the disciples do when they were walking through the grainfield? (*They began picking the grain to eat because they were hungry.*)

■ What did the Pharisees accuse Jesus and his disciples of? (*Breaking the law that forbade work on the Sabbath*)

■ What did the Pharisees ask Jesus in the synagogue? (*If it was lawful to cure a person on the Sabbath*)

■ How did Jesus respond? (*By telling the Pharisees that it is lawful to do good on the Sabbath*)

Discussing the Text

Direct attention to the discussion questions at the bottom of page 163. Guide the students to understand that Samantha realized that helping Mrs. Green was more important than obeying a rule that seemed unimportant at the time. Likewise, Jesus recognized that disobeying the law in the given circumstances would result in something good.

Learning the Vocabulary

Direct attention to the Vocabulary box on page 163 and ask volunteers to read aloud the definitions for *Pharisees* and *Sabbath*.

Step 3/CONCLUSION

Learning How to Live Our Faith

Talking About Making Choices

Ask the students to discuss what guides them when they are faced with a choice and are not sure what to do. Help them appreciate that we must use good judgment in following rules. Tell students that the most important factor in deciding how to live and act is listening to what Jesus says.

DAY 2

Objective

This lesson helps the students learn about Jesus' commandment to love.

Step 1/INTRODUCTION

Learning About Our Lives

Discussing Favorite Teachers

Engage the students in a discussion about their favorite teachers. Encourage all of the students to participate by naming a teacher they enjoyed or a teacher who really helped them to learn. Explain that not all teachers work in schools and that we can also learn from parents, grandparents, priests, Scout leaders, coaches, siblings, and friends. If time permits, you might have the students talk about something they have learned from someone other than a classroom teacher or a parent. Then ask the students to name the person that we, as Catholics, regard as our greatest teacher. Lead the students to recognize that Jesus is our most important teacher. Tell the students that in this lesson they will learn that Jesus teaches us about what is most important in life.

Step 2/DEVELOPMENT

Learning About Our Faith

Learning the Vocabulary Words

Write the words *scribes* and *commandments* on the chalkboard. Point out their definitions in the Vocabulary box on page 165. Ask the students to read to themselves what the words mean. Explain that these new words will appear in the Scripture story they are about to hear.

Dramatizing the Story

Ask for volunteers to dramatize the story "Jesus Teaches About Love" on pages 164 and 165. Have the students take the parts of the narrator, the scribe, and Jesus. The rest of the group can serve as the crowd in the story. Allow the students a few moments to look over what they are to act out. Then have them act out the story.

164

Jesus Teaches About Love

One day, Jesus was talking to some well-educated men called **scribes**. One of them had been listening very carefully. He was impressed by what Jesus was saying. So he decided to ask Jesus a question.

"Which is the most important of all the **commandments**?" the scribe asked. Everyone listened to hear the answer.

"The first and greatest commandment of all is this," Jesus told them. "You shall love the Lord your God with all your heart, with all your soul, with all your mind, and with all your strength."

People in the crowd nodded their heads in agreement. Then they listened as Jesus continued.

"This is the second commandment," Jesus added. "You shall love your neighbor as yourself. There are no other commandments greater than these two."

164   Scripture

Focus on

Scribes   The Hebrew meaning of the word *scribe* was "writer." But in the New Testament, the word refers to the learned class among the Jews. The scribes were authorities on the written law and oral tradition. They often worked alongside the Pharisees. They interpreted the Scriptures and made additions in places that they felt needed explanation or elaboration. Jesus condemned them for this (Matthew 23), citing their hypocrisy and pride. But there were also sincere scribes and Pharisees who sought the truth, such as Nicodemus (John 3) and Gamaliel (Acts 5:34).

The scribe was pleased with Jesus' answer. "You are right," said the scribe. "To love God with all our heart, with all our thoughts, and with all our strength, and to love our neighbor as ourselves is worth more than anything."

Based on Mark 12:28–33

Activity

Read the list below and place an **X** on the line before each sentence that tells one way that we can show our love for God and others.

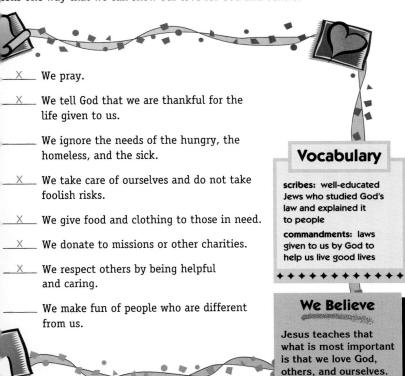

__X__ We pray.

__X__ We tell God that we are thankful for the life given to us.

_____ We ignore the needs of the hungry, the homeless, and the sick.

__X__ We take care of ourselves and do not take foolish risks.

__X__ We give food and clothing to those in need.

__X__ We donate to missions or other charities.

__X__ We respect others by being helpful and caring.

_____ We make fun of people who are different from us.

Vocabulary

scribes: well-educated Jews who studied God's law and explained it to people

commandments: laws given to us by God to help us live good lives

✦ ✦ ✦ ✦ ✦ ✦ ✦ ✦ ✦ ✦

We Believe

Jesus teaches that what is most important is that we love God, others, and ourselves.

Doctrine **165**

Enriching the Lesson

Have the students use paper, rulers, and pencils to make "commandments charts." Show them how to make a chart with seven rows and two columns. Label each row on the far left with the days of the week in consecutive order, beginning with today. Label the first column "Loving God" and the second "Loving Others." Tell the students that each time they show love for God or their neighbor, they may place a star on the chart for that day. Have stars available for the students' use. Check progress over the next week.

CURRICULUM CONNECTION

Social Studies Discuss with the students their ideas about rules for their community and for the country. Ask if there are general principles or ideals that we strive to live up to as a community and a nation. List on the chalkboard as many of their suggestions as time permits. Then ask whether there are any similarities between these social rules and Jesus' teachings about love.

Discussing the Story

Review the story, using these questions.

- What did Jesus say was the first of all the commandments? (*To love God with all your heart, soul, mind, and strength*)
- What did Jesus say was the second greatest commandment? (*To love your neighbor as yourself*)
- Are there any more important commandments? (*No*)
- How are these commandments related? (*To love God is to love others; to love others is to love God.*)

Memorizing the Doctrine

Read through the We Believe statement on page 165 with the class. Encourage the students to learn this important faith summary by heart. Emphasize that we can show our love for God in many ways but that we cannot love God without loving other people.

Step 3/CONCLUSION

Learning How to Live Our Faith

Completing a Checklist

Direct attention to the activity on page 165 and explain the directions. Have the students work independently to determine different ways in which they can show love for God and others. Afterward, check the students' responses. Point out the two items in the list that were not checked by the students (*ignoring the needs of the hungry, the homeless, and the sick and making fun of those who are different from us*). Help the students recognize that when we ignore or make fun of people we are not showing love for them.

Praying Together

Use the items the students checked in the previous activity to pray a class litany. Direct the students to make the Sign of the Cross and bow their heads as you pray, "Loving Jesus, you teach us that what is most important is that we love God, our neighbor, and ourselves. Help us to keep your commandments...." Have volunteers read each of the checked items from the list, one at a time. After each item is read, have the students respond in prayer, "Jesus, we will keep your commandments."

165

DAY 3
SCRIPTURE

Objective

This lesson helps the students recognize whom Jesus calls us to love.

Step 1/INTRODUCTION

Learning About Our Lives

Talking About the Experience of Being Loved

Invite the students to name some of the people in their lives who love them. After giving each student an opportunity to identify at least one person, ask them to explain how they know they are loved and how the people they named show love for them. You may want to list their responses on the chalkboard. (*Possible answers may include people who love us take care of us, help us, make meals for us, read to us, take us to special places, give us medicine when we are sick, buy us clothes and presents, hug and kiss us, teach us about God and Jesus, pray for us, and teach us to pray.*) Then ask the students to talk about how it makes them feel to know that they are loved. Tell the class that in this lesson they will learn how important love is for all people.

Step 2/DEVELOPMENT

Learning About Our Faith

Reading the Text

Call on volunteers to read aloud "The Importance of Love" on page 166. Then discuss the following questions.

- What do we learn about love from Jesus' words in the Bible? (*Whom we are to love and the ways we are to love*)

- What does Jesus teach that is especially important for us to do? (*To love those who are difficult to love*)

- Have the students discuss what kinds of people are difficult to love. (*Possible answers are: people who have hurt us, people who are crabby or mean, people we don't understand, and people we do not know.*)

166

The Importance of Love

Love is very important to Jesus. When we read the Scriptures, we learn that Jesus often talks about whom we are to love and the ways we are to love. Jesus teaches us that it is especially important to love those whom it is difficult to love. These may be people who have hurt us in some way. Can you think of some of the people whom Jesus tells us to love?

Activity

Look up the following Scripture verses in your Bibles.

Whom does Jesus tell us to love?

Matthew 5:43–44 ——— our enemies

John 13:34–35 ——— one another

What else does Jesus say about the ways we can love others?

Matthew 5:43–44 We can pray for people who persecute us.

Luke 6:27–31 We can pray for those who hurt us, we can give to others generously, and we can treat others as we would like them to treat us.

John 14:15 We can love Jesus by keeping God's commandments.

166 Scripture

Teaching Tips

The Scripture activity on page 166 is an opportunity for the students to sharpen their research skills. Instead of having the students turn immediately to the New Testament, you may want to invite them first to study the Bible's table of contents. Have the students note the number of books in the Old Testament and recall that these books tell about God's people before the time of Jesus. Remind them that the New Testament tells about Jesus and the early Church. Then help them locate the Gospels of Matthew, Luke, and John.

Enriching the Lesson

Invite the students to make cards for one person in their lives who is an example of Jesus' teachings on love. Give the students 9" × 12" sheets of construction paper and crayons or markers. Instruct them to fold the paper in half. You might suggest that the students copy one of Jesus' sayings about love on their cards and decorate them with signs of love. Encourage the students to write a personal message on the cards, thanking the person for being a sign of love.

Activity

Next to each caption below, write the number of the teaching of Jesus that best fits.

1. Give to others generously; the greatest love you can show is to give up everything for your friends.

2. Pray for those who act mean toward you.

3. We can forgive those who hurt us.

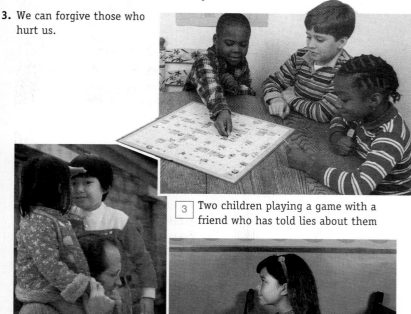

3 Two children playing a game with a friend who has told lies about them

1 A man who has left his high-paying job to share God's love with children in Southeast Asia

2 A new girl in school praying for the students who make fun of her

Scripture 167

Focus on

The Early Church Explain to the students that the first Christians tried very hard to live up to Jesus' law of love. They set up communities that were based on love, respect, and care for everyone. Invite the students to give you suggestions for rules that would help us set up such communities today. Write their suggestions on the chalkboard. Ask them if they are willing to apply these same rules to their classroom community.

Researching Scripture

Before the students begin the Scripture search activity, you may wish to have them read "About the Bible" on page 328 of their books. Distribute Bibles to the students and explain the directions for the activity on page 166. Work with the class to locate and read the first two verses. Then have the students work independently to complete the rest of the Scripture research activity. As the students locate and read the verses listed at the bottom of the page, have them write what Jesus is telling us about how we can love others. As the students work, move about the room, helping them find the passages in their Bibles and assisting them in understanding what each passage means. When everyone has finished, invite the students to share their responses with the group. It may be necessary for you to explain to the class that the word *persecute* means "to treat cruelly."

Step 3/CONCLUSION

Learning How to Live Our Faith

Studying Photographs

Point out the photographs on page 167 and have the students tell what is happening in each picture. Ask volunteers to read aloud the captions beneath each one. Then explain the directions for the activity. Have the students match the numbers of Jesus' teaching about love to the correct photographs. Afterward, check the students' answers. Help the students recognize that the people in each picture are putting one of Jesus' teachings into practice.

Making a Banner About Love

Provide the students with a long sheet of butcher paper for a commandments-of-love banner. Have available crayons or markers; scissors; paste, glue or tape; and a supply of colorful magazines that show pictures of people. Encourage the students to write on the banner Jesus' two great commandments of love: "You shall love the Lord your God with all your heart, with all your soul, with all your mind, and with all your strength. You shall love your neighbor as yourself." Invite the students to surround these words with magazine pictures and their own drawings of people showing love and care for one another.

167

Objective

This lesson helps the students understand that Father Damien showed love for God by helping others.

Step 1/INTRODUCTION

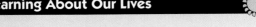

Learning About Our Lives

Recalling Saint Stories

Ask the students to recall what we mean when we call someone a saint. Help them remember that they learned in Chapter 2 that saints are holy men and women who showed in extraordinary ways that they loved God and others. Invite the students to name some of the saints they are aware of and to give examples of what makes those people special. You might wish to list on the board the names of saints that the students may have studied in previous grades: Mary, Joseph, Nicholas, Rose of Lima, Francis of Assisi, Thérèse of Lisieux (The Little Flower), Frances Cabrini, John the Baptizer, and John Bosco. Then tell the students that in this lesson they will read about another holy person who showed that he loved God and others.

Step 2/DEVELOPMENT

Learning About Our Faith

Reading a Biography

Introduce "Father Damien's Life of Love" on page 168 by reading aloud the first two paragraphs. Explain that Father Damien is an example of someone who showed his love for God in a very special way. Have volunteers read the rest of the story aloud. Point out that Father Damien was a happy person because he lived Jesus' commandment to love. Jesus also wants us to be happy and to love God and others in our own special ways. Ask the students to identify the different roles Father Damien took on to reach out to the people of Molokai (*doctor, nurse, priest, teacher, and friend*).

168

Father Damien's Life of Love

We are called to show our love for God and for others every day of our lives. Some people show their love for God and for others in very special ways. They do all they can to reach out to love people who have nobody else to love them.

Father Damien knew about the people on Molokai, one of the islands of Hawaii. Molokai was a place where people who had a terrible skin disease called leprosy were sent.

Damien freely went to care for these suffering people, knowing he would probably get leprosy. For sixteen years he reached out to these people with love. He built houses for them. He taught them. He cared for children on the island who had no parents. He was doctor, nurse, priest, and friend to all the people on the island.

Eventually, Father Damien did get leprosy. He was sick for five years before he died in 1889. Damien lived a life of great love and service to God as he cared for these people who had nobody else to love them.

In 1995, during a visit to Belgium, where Father Damien was born, Pope John Paul II honored Father Damien by calling him Blessed Father Damien. He did this because Father Damien is a good example of a person who lived a very holy life and who suffered for the sake of helping others.

168 Morality

Cultural Awareness

Display pictures from all parts of the world of people who need care, such as those affected by famine, the AIDS epidemic, war, or lack of affordable housing. Help the students understand that these people are our neighbors and that Jesus calls us to love them. Have the students suggest ways they can love these people. Perhaps they can contribute food, money, or clothing to the Red Cross or Catholic Charities. Emphasize that another important way they can show their love is by praying for these people and situations.

CURRICULUM CONNECTION

Social Studies Show the students a globe. Find Hawaii on the globe and point it out to the students. If the island of Molokai is visible, show it to the students and remind them that this is where Blessed Father Damien lived out his life of love and service. Then find Belgium in northwestern Europe and explain that Father Damien came from this small country. Note how far Damien traveled to share his love with the people of Molokai.

Giving Our All

There are many ways to show love for God and for others. Some of them are easy to do. But some things are hard to do. We are called to show our love for one another every day of our lives. We can love in big ways and in small ways. Every effort we make to show love is important to God. Like Damien, we can live a life of great love and service to God.

Activity

Underline the number of each action that shows love for God or for others. Circle the numbers of the things that are sometimes difficult for you to do.

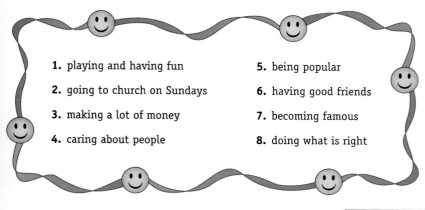

1. playing and having fun
2. going to church on Sundays
3. making a lot of money
4. caring about people

5. being popular
6. having good friends
7. becoming famous
8. doing what is right

Learning How to Live Our Faith

Learning How to Give All

Call on a volunteer to read "Giving Our All" on page 169. Discuss this paragraph with the students, helping them appreciate that they too are called to a life of service and love.

Completing an Activity

Have a student read the directions for the activity on page 169. Encourage the students to underline the number of each action they will do as they lead a life of love. Invite them to circle the numbers of the things on the list that are sometimes difficult for them to do. Afterward, invite sharing. Allow time for the students to explain why some of the things on the list are difficult for them to do.

Reviewing the Chapter

Divide the class into four groups. Assign Group 1 pages 162–163; Group 2 pages 164–165; Group 3 pages 166–167; and Group 4 pages 168–169. Invite each group to make a poster to review the pages they have been assigned or to find some other means—such as pantomiming, role-playing, or questioning—to present a review. Provide time for the students to present their reviews of these activities.

Enriching the Lesson

Through your diocesan vocations office, contact a community of missionary priests, sisters, or brothers to arrange for a speaker to address the students about his or her experiences in overseas missions. Be sure that the students have prepared questions beforehand. Ask the speaker to mention things that the students can do to assist in mission work.

Objective

This lesson helps the students celebrate their love for God and others by praying with sign language.

Preparing for the Prayer Service

Tell the students that this week's prayer service focuses on prayer as one way in which we can demonstrate our love for God and others. Direct attention to the sign-language diagrams on page 170. Explain that these diagrams will help the students learn three different responses that they will pray during the celebration. Practice each of the signs with the students until they are able to do them with ease. Instruct them to recite the responses as they sign them.

Place the banner the students made on Day 3 on a table in the area you have set aside for prayer. Begin the prayer service by saying, "God, we want to lead a life of love. We have made a banner that shows many people living the life of love to which you call us. We need your help in loving others. To show that we want to love, we are going to sign our banner in a special way." Then invite the students to come to the banner one by one and to use markers to sign their names in a special way. For example, they might draw a heart around their names.

Select a student to read aloud during the prayer celebration the Scripture story "Jesus Teaches About Love" on pages 164 and 165 of the text. Allow time for the student to practice the reading several times. Explain to the student that he or she will read this story after everyone has signed the banner.

Praying Together

Lead the students in praying the sign-language prayer on page 170. You may want to sign and recite the responses and then ask the students to repeat them after you.

Praying with Sign Language

Jesus teaches us that to love God and others is more important than anything. We have learned that prayer is one way we can show love for others. Prayer also shows our love for God. As we pray today, let us remember that all our prayers can be beautiful expressions of our love for God and for one another. Let us pray.

Leader: For all the times that you listen to our prayers,
All: We love you, God.

We   love   you,   God.

Leader: For loving us no matter what and for giving us Jesus to show us how great your love for us is,
All: We thank you, God.

We   thank you,   God.

Leader: As we learn to love everyone, even our enemies; as we learn to forgive those who have hurt us; and as we learn to love others as generously and completely as Jesus did, we pray,
All: Help us, God.

Help   us,   God.

Leader: God, we pray for those whom we find it most difficult to love. Help us always to remember that it is important to you that we find a way to love and forgive others. We pray all these things in Jesus' name.
All: Amen.

Enriching the Lesson

Prior to teaching this lesson, obtain from the school files or the first-grade and second-grade teachers the pictures from earlier grades that your students had taken as a class. Show the pictures to the students and discuss with them how many loving people were involved in getting them to their present stage of growth. Have each student name all those responsible for keeping him or her safe and healthy over the years.

Chapter Review

neighbor	Jesus	love	commandments
Pharisees	Damien	scribes	Sabbath

Write the words that best complete the sentences in the paragraphs below.

In the choices that he made, _____Jesus_____ showed us that

_____love_____ is more important than anything.

The _____Pharisees_____ lived according to God's law. The laws of the

_____Sabbath_____ helped Jewish people to set aside a day for rest and prayer.

The _____scribes_____ studied and helped explain God's law to people. They

knew that the _____commandments_____ were part of God's law. Jesus taught

that the two most important commandments were to love God and to love our

_____neighbor_____ as ourselves. Father _____Damien_____ is a good

example of someone who loved God and others generously.

Fill in the answers to the first two questions.

1. What is a commandment? _A commandment is a_

   law given to us by God to help us live good lives.

2. What does Jesus say are the two greatest

   commandments? _to love God completely and to_

   love our neighbors as ourselves

3. Talk about what you can learn from Father
   Damien's example of love.

> **Let us love one another because love comes from God.**
> Based on 1 John 4:7

Review 171

CURRICULUM CONNECTION

Music Obtain a recording of "Day by Day" from the musical play *Godspell*. Have the students listen carefully to the words and compare these words to those of Jesus about loving God completely. If time permits, teach the students how to sing this simple melody.

Enriching the Lesson

Prepare a special bulletin board or display area in the classroom and place on it a picture of Father Damien and a brief biography. Explain to the students that this space will be reserved for pictures of people who, like Father Damien, have shown love for others in an extraordinary way. Tell students that you will be periodically featuring the lives of different people and inviting them to bring in pictures of people who have shown heroic love for others. Invite the students to create a title for this special area in the classroom.

Completing the Sentences

Point out the words at the top of page 171 and explain the directions for the first review exercise. Allow the students ample time to fill in the words that correctly complete each sentence. When the students have finished writing, check their responses by having volunteers read each sentence aloud.

Completing the Chapter Review

Instruct the students to work independently to write answers to the next two review questions. Afterward, encourage the students to share their responses with the class. In discussing the third question, help the students recognize that Father Damien's example of love can inspire us to be more loving toward the people in our lives.

Praying with the Scriptural Verse

With the group, read aloud 1 John 4:7 at the bottom of the page. Explain that God is the source of all love.

Conclude the lesson by inviting the students to stand in a circle. Ask that they use this quiet prayer time to listen for new ways to show their love for God. After each part of the following prayer, invite the students to respond, "Let us love one another."

Jesus, sometimes we do not love the way you showed us to love. Help us to keep trying.

Jesus, Blessed Father Damien heard and followed your commandment to love others. Help us to follow you, too.

Jesus, sometimes it is hard to love some people. Help us to love those people especially well.

Jesus, when we love others, we show that we love you. Help us to remember this each time we show our love.

14 Our Church Teaches the Commandments

Objectives ~~~~~

To help the students

- Recognize that Jesus taught that all of God's commandments are important.
- Learn the Ten Commandments.
- Appreciate that we are called to lead good lives by keeping God's laws.
- Understand that we can turn to many people to help us make good decisions.
- Promise obedience to God's commandments and review the chapter.

Chapter Outline ~~~~~~~~

	Step 1 Learning About Our Lives	**Step 2** Learning About Our Faith	**Step 3** Learning How to Live Our Faith 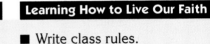
Day 1	■ Introduce the chapter. ■ Read the text. ■ Write about rules. *ABOUT 11 MINUTES*	■ Read about Jesus' teachings. *ABOUT 5 MINUTES*	■ Write class rules. ■ Pray together. *ABOUT 14 MINUTES*
Day 2	■ Learn the background. *ABOUT 7 MINUTES*	■ Read the Ten Commandments. ■ Understand the commandments. ■ Review the vocabulary and doctrine. *ABOUT 20 MINUTES*	■ Find ways to grow in love. *ABOUT 3 MINUTES*
Day 3	■ Discuss the value of rules. *ABOUT 4 MINUTES*	■ Label pictures. *ABOUT 7 MINUTES*	■ Consider a dilemma. ■ Write story endings. ■ Pray together. *ABOUT 19 MINUTES*
Day 4	■ Introduce the lesson. *ABOUT 5 MINUTES*	■ Read the text. *ABOUT 7 MINUTES*	■ Complete an activity. ■ Make clay hearts. *ABOUT 18 MINUTES*
Day 5	**Prayer** Prepare for the celebration; pray with Scripture.		
	Review Label statements; complete the chapter review; memorize the commandments; pray with the scriptural verse.		

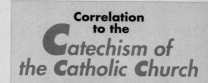

Plan Ahead

	Preparing Your Class	**Materials Needed**
Day 1	Read through the lesson plan for this class session. Think about the importance of obeying rules.	■ pencils or pens ■ scissors ■ chalkboard ■ posterboard ■ lined paper
Day 2	Read through the lesson plan for this session. Review the Ten Commandments chart on page 343.	■ pencils or pens
Day 3	Read through the lesson plan for this class session. Consider how the commandments help you to care about God and others.	■ pencils or pens ■ notebook paper
Day 4	Read through the lesson plan for this class session. Think about whom you rely on to help you make good decisions.	■ pencils or pens ■ self-drying clay
Day 5	Prepare an environment for prayer in the classroom. Review this week's sessions to prepare for the chapter review.	■ commandment posters from Day 2 ■ pencils or pens

Additional Resources

As you plan this chapter, consider using the following materials from The Resourceful Teacher Package.

■ *Classroom Activity Sheets 14 and 14a*

■ *Family Activity Sheets 14 and 14a*

■ *Chapter 14 Test*

■ *Prayers for Every Day*

■ *Projects: Grade 3*

You may also wish to refer to the following Big Book.

■ *We Celebrate God's Word,* page 3

In preparing the students for the Sunday readings, you may wish to use Silver Burdett Ginn's *Getting Ready for Sunday* student and teacher materials.

BOOKS FOR THE JOURNEY

The Butter Battle Book. Dr. Seuss. Random House, 1984. A story of plotting revenge and getting back at one another.

The Stories of Hans Andersen. Retold by Robert Mathias. Silver Burdett Ginn, 1985. "The Emperor's New Clothes," pp. 72–76. Everyone in the kingdom lies about the Emperor's nakedness except one small boy.

MORE BOOKS FOR THE JOURNEY

Lily and the Wooden Bowl. Alan Schroeder. Doubleday, 1994. This is a Japanese folk tale in which a young girl promises to live by a rule her dying grandmother asks her to keep.

Shiloh. Phyllis Reynolds Naylor. Atheneum Macmillan, 1991. A story of a boy who cares so much about a dog that is being abused that he goes against the rules in one way yet lives by them in another.

REDUCED CLASSROOM ACTIVITIES

NAME _____

OUR CHURCH TEACHES THE COMMANDMENTS

God gave us the Ten Commandments to help us love and care for God, ourselves, other people, and all of creation.

We all need rules to help us love and care. Imagine that you and your friends are starting a club in your neighborhood. Think of four rules for your club. Write them on the sign outside the clubhouse. Then draw the club members and decorate the clubhouse.

To the Teacher: This activity follows the We Believe box in Chapter 14.

Chapter 14 Our Church Teaches the Commandments — THIS IS OUR FAITH 3 **14**

NAME _____

A ROAD MAZE

Look at the four commandments at the bottom of the page. Using different colored crayons, trace each of the four roads to the proper road sign at the top.

7th   4th   2nd   1st

| other people's houses to take their property. | and always obey your parents. | using God's name disrespectfully. | away from God. God should be first in our lives. |

To the Teacher: This activity will help students recall four of the commandments.

14a THIS IS OUR FAITH 3 — **Chapter 14** Our Church Teaches the Commandments

171c Chapter Organizer

THE TEN COMMANDMENTS

Third-grade students tend to take rules seriously. They may not like certain rules that seem to keep them from doing things they want to do, but they can appreciate that rules are an important part of life. One can see this in how seriously they take the rules of the games they play.

The students at this level are able to learn some of the more basic rules of life, even though they may not have had enough experience to grasp the deeper reasons behind some of those important rules. One of the most important sets of rules is the Decalogue, or the Ten Commandments. Some of the commandments are beyond the students' grasp. Others are well within their experience and ability to understand.

Jesus built his moral teachings on the foundation of the Jewish tradition. He did not frame his moral teachings in terms of the Ten Commandments, but he obviously asserted their validity and importance. They were a vital part of the morality of the Jewish people of his day.

CHRISTIAN MORAL TEACHINGS

Christian moral teachings have consistently valued the Ten Commandments. However, the commandments have not been the sole or even the most important element in framing Christian moral teachings. In the Gospels, Jesus' emphasis on the commandments to love God and neighbor set the tone for the moral teachings of the Church. In later years the Church centered Christian moral teachings on the acquisition of virtue. There was a stress on the theological virtues of faith, hope, and charity and the cardinal virtues of prudence, justice, fortitude, and temperance.

What is important for us today is that the students view the Ten Commandments positively as guides for sustaining a happy life. The commandments are practical ways of living out the teachings of Jesus to love God and to love our neighbor. The code of the Ten Commandments is designed to help us learn to care about God, about ourselves, and about other people in the world that God created for us.

DAY 1
MORALITY

Objective

This lesson helps the students recognize that Jesus taught that all of God's commandments are important.

Step 1/INTRODUCTION

Learning About Our Lives

Introducing the Chapter

Have the students turn to page 172 in their text and read to themselves the chapter-focus questions. Then elicit their responses by asking them to discuss whether they always obey school and home rules. Invite them to name rules that they always obey and to give their reasons for choosing to disobey other rules. Tell the class that in this chapter they will learn that Jesus taught his friends to follow all of God's commandments.

Reading the Text

Call on a volunteer to read aloud "Obeying the Rules" on page 172. Help the students value the importance of "good rules" by discussing the following examples.

Why is not running in the school hallways a good rule? *(Answers may include: we might trip and fall, we might run into another student or a wall and hurt ourselves or someone else, or we might disturb another class.)*

Why is not fighting with our brothers and sisters a good rule at home? *(Answers may include: we might get hurt or hurt our brother or sister, we should learn to solve our problems peacefully, or we should treat our brothers and sisters with love.)*

Help the students appreciate that good rules make sense and they help us to live safely and happily.

Writing About Rules

Read aloud the instructions for the writing activity at the bottom of the page. Allow time for the students to complete this activity. Afterward, invite the students to share their answers. Then have the students discuss the value of the rules they named. Help them to articulate why these rules are helpful.

172

14

Our Church Teaches the Commandments

Obeying the Rules

There are many rules to follow in our schools. Our families have rules, too. These rules are important. When our teachers or parents teach us rules, they may tell us some good reasons to follow rules. We are sometimes told that rules are "for our own good." The people who set the rules are those who love us and those who have concern for our safety and well-being.

Do you always obey the rules at home and at school? Why or why not?

Activity

On the lines below, write two rules that you are expected to live by at home and two rules that you are expected to live by at school. Then tell the class why it is a good idea to obey each rule.

Home: _____

_____

School: _____

_____

172   Morality

Enriching the Lesson

Bring pictures of different traffic signs to the class and display them. You may be able to borrow copies of cardboard signs from your local police department, which uses them for traffic school. Show the students the pictures and ask the students to explain what the rule on each sign means. Discuss with the class how the signs help people and what would happen if we didn't have traffic signs.

Teaching Tips

Instead of having the students complete individually the writing activity on page 172, you may wish to brainstorm as a class rules that the students are expected to live by at home and rules that they are expected to live by at school. Write the two lists on separate parts of the chalkboard or on different pieces of poster board. Then have the students choose rules to write on page 172. This gives everyone a chance to participate in the activity and to be successful.

Other Rules That Matter

We have learned about Jesus' commandment to love. We have learned that we should love God with our whole heart and mind and that we should love others as ourselves. These are the commandments that Jesus says are most important. He has told us this because he knows that when we obey these rules, we will be happy.

When Jesus talked about how important love is, some listeners thought that none of the other laws of God's people mattered anymore. One day, while Jesus was preaching on a hillside, he explained that *all* of God's laws are important. As a child, Jesus had learned many more of God's commandments. And when Jesus taught his followers, he often reminded them about these commandments and how important it is to obey them.

Morality   173

Focus on

God's Law   In reassuring his followers that it was important to remain faithful to God's commandments, Jesus said, "Do not think that I have come to abolish the law or the prophets. I have come not to abolish but to fulfill. Amen, I say to you, until heaven and earth pass away, not the smallest letter or the smallest part of a letter will pass from the law, until all things have taken place" (Matthew 5:17–18). Jesus is telling his followers that all of the commandments would be important until the kingdom that Jesus came to bring is completed.

Learning About Our Faith

Reading About Jesus' Teachings

Have students take turns reading aloud "Other Rules That Matter" on page 173. Then ask the following questions.

- What is Jesus' commandment to love? (*You shall love the Lord your God with all your heart, with all your soul, with all your mind, and with all your strength, and you shall love your neighbor as yourself.*)
- Why did Jesus say that these commandments are the most important? (*Because Jesus knows that if we obey these rules, we will be happy*)
- What did some people think when Jesus said that loving God and others was the most important way to act? (*They thought that Jesus was telling them that God's other laws no longer mattered.*)
- What did Jesus say about this? (*He said that obeying all of God's laws was important.*)

Step 3/CONCLUSION

Learning How to Live Our Faith

Writing Class Rules

Divide the class into small cooperative groups and distribute lined paper to each group. Direct the groups to compose a list of five class rules that are important for everyone to follow and that will help to make your classroom a happier and safer place for everyone in the class. Allow the groups sufficient time to complete this activity. Afterward, call on a representative from each group to share his or her list with the class. Record the responses on the chalkboard. Call attention to any rules that two or more of the groups have in common. Then work with the class to combine the different lists to create a master list of class rules to which all the students agree. Copy this list onto a posterboard and post it in a prominent place.

Praying Together

Allow the students the opportunity to offer spontaneous prayers thanking Jesus for teaching about the importance of God's laws and asking Jesus to help them live according to God's laws.

DAY 2

SCRIPTURE/DOCTRINE

Objective

This lesson helps the students learn the Ten Commandments.

Step 1/INTRODUCTION

Learning About Our Lives

Learning the Background

Tell the students that in today's lesson they are going to learn about a special set of rules called the Ten Commandments. Ask the students if they have ever heard of the Ten Commandments or if they know any of the individual commandments. Then give the students the following background: Hundreds of years before Jesus was born, God called a man named Moses to lead the Hebrew people out of the land of Egypt, where they lived as slaves. Moses led the people through the desert until they came to a mountain. God told Moses, "Tell the people how much I love them. Remind them that I saved them from slavery. Tell them that I will make an agreement with them. If they listen to me and follow my laws, they will be my special people, and I will be their God." The Hebrew people agreed to do everything God asked of them. Then God gave Moses and the Hebrew people the Ten Commandments. Jesus learned the Ten Commandments as a young boy and followed them in his own life. He taught others to follow the commandments. Today, as Catholic people following the teachings of Jesus, we also value the Ten Commandments, which guide us in loving God and other people.

Step 2/DEVELOPMENT

Learning About Our Faith +

Reading the Ten Commandments

Ask a volunteer to read "Words to Live By" on page 174. Then assign each row of students in your classroom one or more of the Ten Commandments and ask the students to read aloud the commandments sequentially. Ask for volunteers from each row to explain what that row's commandment is about. Provide help as needed. Have the students keep their explanations simple and brief.

174

Words to Live By

For a long time, God's people have been guided by the Ten Commandments. Jews and Christians use these commandments as guides to living good and happy lives.

The Ten Commandments

1. I, the Lord, am your God. You shall not have other gods besides me.
2. You shall not take the name of the Lord, your God, in vain.
3. Remember to keep holy the Sabbath day.
4. Honor your father and mother.
5. You shall not kill.
6. You shall not commit adultery.
7. You shall not steal.
8. You shall not bear false witness against your neighbor.
9. You shall not covet your neighbor's wife.
10. You shall not covet anything that belongs to your neighbor.

Based on Exodus 20:2–17

Focus on

The Jewish People Three names are often used to refer to the Jewish people: Israelites, Hebrews, and Jews. To clarify, the descendants of Abraham received the name *Israel* when God changed Jacob's name to Israel. *Israel* is a Hebrew word that means "to wrestle with God." They were also called Hebrews. The name *Jew* is taken from the Hebrew word for "Judah," the name of one of the original twelve tribes of Israel and one of the two kingdoms that was formed after the original kingdom was divided following Solomon's reign as king.

Focus on

The Ten Commandments The Decalogue, or Ten Commandments, was the law of the Jewish people as they wandered in the desert in search of the promised land. Modern Scripture scholars see the Ten Commandments as early laws that helped these nomadic people learn to live together as a community. The worship of one God helped the Israelites to focus on their identity as God's chosen people at a time when all the nations around them were worshiping a variety of deities.

Ways of Loving

God gave us the Ten Commandments to teach us how to love and care. The first three commandments show us ways to love God.

- We have faith in and trust God. God is the center of our lives. (1)

- We use God's name only with **reverence**. (2)

- We take time to pray, to celebrate the Eucharist, and to rest, especially on Sunday. (3)

The other seven commandments show us ways to love and care for others, ourselves, and the things that God has given us.

- We obey and respect our parents and others who take care of us. (4)

- We care for our health and treat others kindly. We don't hurt others. (5)

- We respect our own bodies and others' bodies. Husbands and wives love, respect, and are faithful to each other. (6 and 9)

- We do not steal or waste things. We are not greedy or careless. We do not cheat. We share what we have with others. (7 and 10)

- We always tell the truth. We are honest. (8)

Vocabulary

reverence: an attitude of respect, care, and honor

◆ ◆ ◆ ◆ ◆ ◆ ◆ ◆ ◆ ◆ ◆

We Believe

God gives us the Ten Commandments to help us live good and happy lives. The commandments show us ways of loving God, ourselves, other people, and all of creation.

Doctrine 175

Understanding the Commandments

In this section each of the commandments is explained in a way that is appropriate for the students at this grade level. As you read this section with the students, you may want to refer to the Ten Commandments chart on page 343 in the Our Catholic Heritage section. Remind the students that they have already learned Jesus' two great commandments, which teach us to love God, others, and ourselves. Explain that the Ten Commandments give us more specific ways to show our love.

Read the introductory paragraph on page 175 and the explanation of the first three commandments. When discussing the second commandment, refer the students to the definition of *reverence* in the Vocabulary box.

Ask for volunteers to read aloud the explanations of the other seven commandments. Then ask the students to look at the illustrations on this page and state which commandment is being followed in each picture.

Reviewing the Vocabulary and Doctrine

Point out the We Believe box on page 175, which contains a statement of the central doctrine of the lesson. Ask for a volunteer to read the statement. Explain that the Ten Commandments are like signs, or markers, on our path. They point the way to how God wants us to live and to eternal happiness with God.

Step 3/CONCLUSION

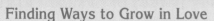
Learning How to Live Our Faith

Finding Ways to Grow in Love

Invite the students to look over the list of the Ten Commandments and their explanations. Ask the students to choose the commandment they most want to better understand and obey at this time of their lives. You might ask them questions like the following: *Do you need to have more faith in God? Do you need to grow in honesty? Can you be more respectful to your parents? Can you take better care of your body?* Encourage the students to offer silent prayers asking God to help them grow in the commandments they chose.

DAY 3
MORALITY

Objective

This lesson helps the students appreciate that we are called to lead good lives by keeping God's laws.

Step 1/INTRODUCTION

Learning About Our Lives

Discussing the Value of Rules

Engage the students in a discussion of how rules help us to care. Ask them to name one of the Ten Commandments and explain how it helps them to care about God, others, themselves, or things.

Distribute writing paper and pencils to the students. Invite them to rewrite the Ten Commandments in their own words, telling what each one means to them. Stress to the students that they should try to write the commandments in a positive rather than negative way. For example: *You shall not have other gods beside me* might become *You shall put God first in your life; You shall not kill* can become *You shall care for all living things.* Afterward, invite the students to share their paraphrased commandments with the class.

Step 2/DEVELOPMENT

Learning About Our Faith

Labeling the Pictures

Ask a student to read the directions for the labeling activity on page 176. Point out the four stories about caring listed on the page: Caring About God, Caring About Others, Caring About Ourselves, and Caring About Things. Have the students label each story with the number of each commandment that is being followed in the story. Answer any questions about how the activity is to be done and then have the students proceed with the assignment. Check their answers when they have finished.

Activity

We are called to lead good and happy lives by keeping God's laws. Read these four stories. Decide which commandment is being followed in each story. Write the number of the commandment in the box next to each story.

Caring About God

3   It is a cold, rainy Sunday morning. Kim would like to stay in her warm bed, but she gets up and goes with her family to Sunday Mass.

Caring About Others

4   Max is excited when Joe invites him to go fishing for the day. But then Max remembers that his parents had asked him to help Grandpa clean out his garage. So Max tells Joe he cannot go fishing this time.

Caring About Ourselves

5   Carlos jumps on his bicycle and rushes to soccer practice. A block away from home, he stops, hesitates, and then rides back to get his helmet. He puts it on and then rides quickly to soccer practice.

Caring About Things

7   Nicole did not do her homework. She watched TV instead. During recess, Nicole takes Emilie's math homework. She copies it and then slips it back into Emilie's desk. But during lunch, Nicole tears up the copied homework and does it herself.

Teaching Tips

Ask the students if they think it is selfish to love and care for themselves. Help them appreciate that God created each of them as a special and unique individual and that God wants them to love, respect, and care about themselves. Explain that it is only selfish to love yourself when, in doing so, you turn away from God and fail to show love for him and for others.

CURRICULUM CONNECTION

Language Arts   After students have completed the activity on page 176, have them form groups of four. Ask the members of each group to come up with four situations similar to those in the activity. You might have the group members work together on creating the content of each scenario and then have each student write one of the pieces. Invite the groups to share these written pieces with the class. Have the rest of the class identify the appropriate commandment as they did in the original activity.

Sally's Decision

On her way to school, Sally was thinking about a new video she wanted. Her birthday was still three months away, and she could hardly wait. Only a few blocks from home, Sally noticed a wallet lying on the sidewalk in front of her. She bent down, picked it up, and looked inside. She found pictures of a family from her neighborhood, along with some credit cards and $25 in cash. Sally looked around to see if anyone was watching. Then she decided to put the wallet into her backpack without saying a word to anyone. Sally continued on her way to school, still thinking about that new video.

Discuss

1. If you found a neighbor's wallet with money inside, what would you do?

2. If you stopped to think about the rules and commandments you have been taught, how might your response be different?

3. If Sally told you what she had done, what could you say to help her decide to return the wallet and the money?

Focus on

Responding to God's Law The *Catechism of the Catholic Church* states that "God has loved us first. The love of the One God is recalled in the first of the 'ten words.' The commandments then make explicit the response of love that man is called to give to his God." (#2083)

Enriching the Lesson

Have the students work with their role-play partners to create original dilemmas. Ask the students to think about some of the decisions that third graders must make about following the Ten Commandments. You might first discuss this with the entire class and then record the students' responses on the chalkboard. Invite each pair of students to choose one of the decisions listed on the chalkboard and write a story or create a skit showing how we are called to live the commandments.

Learning How to Live Our Faith

Considering a Dilemma

Call on a volunteer to read aloud "Sally's Decision" on page 177. After the students have heard the story, direct attention to the three Discuss questions. Invite the students to talk about what their immediate reaction would be to finding a neighbor's wallet. Ask the students what they might be tempted to do. Then ask them what commandments or rules would guide them in making a decision. Help them recognize that the seventh commandment, *You shall not steal*, teaches us that we are called to try our best to return the things we find to their owners. Also help the students understand that Jesus' commandment to love helps them know what is the right thing to do in this situation. Emphasize that if we truly love our neighbor as we love ourselves, we will want to return the wallet. We will make this decision because if we had lost our wallet or some other valuable possession, we would want anyone who found it to return it to us.

In discussing the third question, you may want to have the students pair up and role-play the situation. Have one student in each pair take the part of Sally. Give the other students the option of role-playing the part of a trusted friend, a sibling, a parent, or a teacher. After allowing time for the students to rehearse their role-plays, invite volunteers to come to the front of the room and act them out.

Writing Story Endings

Invite the students to use notebook paper to write an ending to the story "Sally's Decision." Ask them to write what they think Sally did later that day with the wallet in her backpack. Direct them to write a paragraph of no more than three or four sentences. When everyone has finished, encourage the students to read their paragraphs aloud to the class.

Praying Together

Explain to the students that when we are faced with a decision, we can turn to what we have learned about the commandments and Jesus' teachings to help us make good choices. Encourage the students to offer spontaneous prayers asking for Jesus' help in making good choices.

DOCTRINE / MORALITY

Objective

This lesson helps the students understand that we can turn to many people to help us make good decisions.

Step 1/INTRODUCTION

Learning About Our Lives

Introducing the Lesson

Begin the lesson by inviting the students to name the people they rely on to help them make good and caring choices. (*Possible answers may include: mothers, fathers, teachers, friends, older siblings, grandparents, priests, and so on.*) Encourage volunteers to share an experience of seeking advice from another person about a decision they had to make. Discuss with the students their reasons for choosing the person they shared their problem with and what kind of advice they received from this person. Then ask the students whether they followed the advice they were given or made a different choice. Tell the class that in this lesson they will learn about how we can be guided in making good decisions.

Step 2/DEVELOPMENT

Learning About Our Faith

Reading the Text

Call on volunteers to read aloud "What Would *Jesus* Do or Say?" on page 178 as the rest of the students follow along in their texts. Then discuss the reading with these questions.

- What are we, as Catholics, committed to? (*Living according to the rules that Jesus taught*)

- What can we do if rules seem difficult or confusing? (*Remember Gospel stories to help us think about what Jesus would do in the same situation*)

- What guided Jesus in making decisions when he was young? (*God's commandments as written in the Scriptures and Mary and Joseph's guidance*)

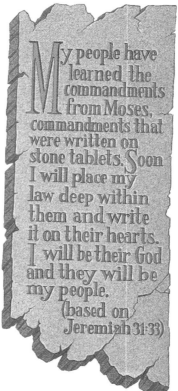

My people have learned the commandments from Moses, commandments that were written on stone tablets. Soon I will place my law deep within them and write it on their hearts. I will be their God and they will be my people.
(based on Jeremiah 31:33)

What Would *Jesus* Do or Say?

As Catholics, we are committed to living according to the rules that Jesus taught. If those rules ever seem difficult or confusing, we can recall stories from the Gospels to help us think about what Jesus would do or say in the same situation. We can even pray to Jesus, asking, "Jesus, what would *you* do?" or "What would *you* say if you were in my shoes, Jesus?"

When Jesus was a young child and made decisions, he may have taken time to think about God's commandments in the Scriptures. And he may have asked Mary or Joseph to guide him. But as he grew, he knew God's law so well that it became a part of everything he said and did. Jesus learned many things from the Scriptures.

When we know and understand God's law and believe that it is good, then we know that God's law is written on our hearts. And when we believe in the importance of love, as Jesus did, we pray for our hearts to be filled with love for God and others. We also pray that all the decisions we make will show that we are people of God.

178 Doctrine

Teaching Tips

Write the word *consequence* on the board and help the students define it as "a result." Explain that every decision we make has a consequence. Recall the story "Sally's Decision" from Day 3. Discuss the choices Sally could make (visit the neighbor to return the wallet, put the wallet back where she found it, or take the money and throw the wallet away). Invite the students to explore the consequences of each choice. Stress that we must always consider what will happen as a result of our decisions.

Activity

As Catholics who are still growing in faith and love, we have many people and places to which we can turn for help as we make decisions.

For each question in Column A, write the number of the person or place from Column B that shows where you might find the answer to the question. A hint is given for the first one.

Column A

___4___ Would Jesus use kinder words than this?
(Hint: Where do we read stories about Jesus?)

___2___ Is it okay to steal something I really want?

___5___ Do I believe in my heart that this is right?

___1___ Will eating too much of this make me sick?

___3___ What rules can help make the playground safe for everyone?

Column B

1. mother or father

2. the commandments

3. teachers

4. the Gospels

5. myself

■ What happened because Jesus knew God's law so well? (*It became a part of everything he said and did.*)

■ What did the prophet Jeremiah say that God would do? (*Write God's law on the hearts of his people*)

■ How do we know that God's law is written on our hearts? (*Because we know and understand God's law and believe that it is good*)

Step 3/CONCLUSION

Learning How to Live Our Faith

Completing an Activity

Read aloud the introduction for the activity on page 179. Help the students understand that making good decisions is something that they will learn more about as they grow in faith and learn more about the teachings of Jesus and the Church. Remind them that Jesus has given us the Holy Spirit to help us make good choices. Assure them that as they learn more about their faith, God's law will become written on their hearts and become an important part of their daily lives.

Then read aloud the instructions to the activity. Explain to the students that the people and places listed in Column B are sources where they might go to find the answers to the questions in Column A. Tell the students that they are to match the questions with the sources where they most likely would find an answer. Have the students work independently to complete the activity. Afterward, check the students' answers. Encourage the students to seek advice and guidance whenever they are confused about a difficult choice.

Making Clay Hearts

Have the students cover their desks with newspaper and then distribute a fist-sized piece of self-drying clay to each student. Invite the students to shape their clay pieces into a heart. Then have the students use the eraser side of a pencil to press a message into the clay heart. This message should help them recall that God has promised to write the law on our hearts or that their hearts are filled with love for God and others. Allow time for the students to share their messages with the class. Set the clay hearts aside to dry.

CURRICULUM CONNECTION

Reading   This would be a good time to introduce the award-winning book *Shiloh*, by Phyllis Reynolds Naylor. It is the story of a young boy who cares about a dog that is being abused. See page 171c for more information.

Focus on

The Covenants   The reading taken from the Book of Jeremiah on page 178 was a message of hope to the Hebrew people who were living in exile in Babylon. Through Jeremiah, God was inviting the people into a new agreement or covenant. This agreement would be written in their hearts, not merely on stone as the Ten Commandments were, and will last forever. As Catholics, we believe that such a covenant was established through the life, death, and resurrection of Jesus.

DAY 5

PRAYER/REVIEW

Objective

This lesson helps the students promise obedience to God's commandments.

Preparing for the Celebration

If you have not already done so in this chapter, you may want to have students make posters illustrating the Ten Commandments. Use the students' work to decorate the prayer area and to help them recall the theme of this week's lessons. As an alternative, plan a procession, using the commandment posters to begin your celebration.

Teach the students the response for the prayer on page 180. Tell the class that this response is taken from Book of Exodus, in the Old Testament. Explain to the students that after Moses explained God's laws to the people, he asked them if they were willing to live as God asked. The people answered together, as if they were one voice, "We will do as the Lord has told us." Practice the response several times so that during the celebration, the students are able to respond as "one voice" like their Hebrew brothers and sisters did long ago.

Praying with Scripture

Use the reading of the Ten Commandments (Exodus 20:2–17) from Day 2 as the Scripture for your celebration.

Incorporate the clay hearts the students made on Day 4 into the celebration. At the conclusion of the prayer service, during the closing prayer, invite the students to hold their clay hearts in both hands and raise them above their heads. Explain that this is a sign that they are asking Jesus to make God's law grow deeper within their hearts.

Praying with Scripture

When God gave the commandments, God's people agreed to live by them. And Jesus promised that whoever obeys and teaches these commandments will be called greatest in the kingdom of heaven. Today we pray for God's guidance and grace as we promise to be obedient to the commandments. Let us pray.

Leader: Lord God, your laws show us the way of Jesus' love. You have promised much happiness to all those who keep your commandments. Hear our promises today to live as Catholics who are faithful and obedient to the ways that lead to eternal happiness.

All: We will do as the Lord has told us.

Leader: Lord, you teach us to love and respect you, to place our trust completely in you, and to take time to pray.

All: We will do as the Lord has told us.

Leader: Lord, you teach us to love and respect our parents, to do our best to stay healthy and safe, and to treat others kindly.

All: We will do as the Lord has told us.

Leader: Lord, you teach us to respect and care for our bodies.

All: We will do as the Lord has told us.

Leader: Lord, you teach us to be responsible, fair, and honest in all that we do and say.

All: We will do as the Lord has told us.

Leader: Gracious God, we thank you for your gift of eternal life. And we thank you for being with us each day as your law grows deeper and deeper within our hearts. We pray in the name of Jesus Christ, our Lord, who leads us in the way of love.

All: Amen.

180   Prayer

Teaching Tips

Before leading the prayer experience on page 180, you might have the students reflect on what it means to make a promise. In the prayer, the students will say the words of promise, "We will do as the Lord has told us," that the Israelites said upon receiving the law of Moses. Have the students define what a promise is and describe what it means to keep one's promises. Invite them to reflect on times when a promise was made to them and the promise was kept. Assure the students that God hears the promises that they make in their prayer today.

Chapter Review

Next to each phrase below, write the letter **G** if the phrase mostly shows a way to love God. Write the letter **O** if the phrase mostly shows a way to love and care for others, for ourselves, and for all the gifts that God has given us.

- **G** Saying God's name with respect
- **O** Telling our parents the truth
- **O** Playing safely
- **G** Trusting God to help us
- **O** Being careful not to be wasteful
- **O** Obeying our parents
- **G** Taking time to pray, especially on Sunday
- **O** Speaking kindly about our neighbors
- **O** Making peace with people who would rather fight us
- **O** Being grateful for what we have and not being jealous of what someone else has

Fill in the answers to the first two questions.

1. What is the meaning of *reverence*? __an attitude of__
   __respect, care, and honor__

2. What do the Ten Commandments help us to do?
   __to live good and happy lives by loving God, others,__
   __ourselves, and all of creation__

3. Talk about how you can live according to the Ten Commandments each day.

> **Love one another by living according to the commandments.**
> Based on 2 John 1:5–6

Enriching the Lesson

On the chalkboard, make a classroom chart for the five school days of next week. Brainstorm with the students five actions they could perform as a class to show love for God, others, and creation. For example, they might read storybooks to the students in kindergarten, pick up litter on the playground, assist in readying the parish community for Sunday liturgy, and so forth. Post the chart in the classroom and work with the students next week in completing the activities.

Labeling Statements

Explain the directions for the first activity on page 181 and have the students work on their own to read the statements and mark them with a *G* or an *O*. Afterward, check the students' responses. Answer any questions they may have about living the Ten Commandments.

Completing the Chapter Review

Take time to go through the next two questions on page 181. Direct the students to write the answer to each question on the lines provided in the text. Encourage all to participate in the discussion question. Be supportive of each student who responds.

Memorizing the Commandments

To help the students memorize the Ten Commandments, have the students form pairs. Assign each pair a number from one to ten. Then have the students turn to page 174 of their books and commit to memory the corresponding commandment. Then call out a number from one to ten at random so that each pair can recite the commandment they memorized. Each pair may be assigned more than one commandment if necessary.

Praying with the Scriptural Verse

Ask for a volunteer to read the scriptural verse at the bottom of the page. Remind the students that by keeping God's commandments we show love for God, ourselves, others, and all of creation. Ask the students to each think of one way they can be more loving and caring during the coming week. Invite them to share these resolutions with the class. Use the scriptural verse as a response after each student shares his or her resolution.

15 Christians Help Others

Objectives ~~~~~

To help the students
- Learn the parable of the Good Samaritan.
- Learn the corporal works of mercy.
- Understand that Jesus calls us to work together to help others.
- Appreciate that Dorothy Day lived the corporal works of mercy.
- Pray original prayers of petition based on current news stories and review the chapter.

Chapter Outline ~~~~~

	Step 1 Learning About Our Lives	**Step 2** Learning About Our Faith	**Step 3** Learning How to Live Our Faith
Day 1	■ Introduce the chapter. ■ Write a dialogue. ■ Conduct interviews. *ABOUT 14 MINUTES*	■ Read a Scripture story. ■ Put the story in order. *ABOUT 12 MINUTES*	■ Identify ways to be good Samaritans. *ABOUT 4 MINUTES*
Day 2	■ Remember experiences of care. *ABOUT 6 MINUTES*	■ Learn the new vocabulary. ■ Read and discuss the story. ■ Learn about the works of mercy. ■ Review the doctrine. *ABOUT 13 MINUTES*	■ Pray together. *ABOUT 11 MINUTES*
Day 3	■ Solve a word puzzle. *ABOUT 8 MINUTES*	■ Read about Jesus' mercy. ■ Discuss questions. *ABOUT 14 MINUTES*	■ Personalize the works of mercy. *ABOUT 8 MINUTES*
Day 4	■ Remember people who help others. *ABOUT 4 MINUTES*	■ Read a biography. *ABOUT 8 MINUTES*	■ Read and discuss the text. ■ Write about people in need. ■ Review the chapter. *ABOUT 18 MINUTES*
Day 5	**Prayer** Look at newspapers and magazines; read the text; write petitions; pray together. **Review** Fill in the blanks; complete the chapter review; pray with the scriptural verse.		

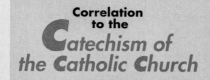

Correlation to the

Catechism of the **C**atholic **C**hurch

Paragraphs
**678, 1822, 1823, 1826,
1932, 2443, 2447, 2449,
2463**

Plan Ahead ~~~~~~~~

	Preparing Your Class	**Materials Needed**
Day 1	Read through the lesson plan for this class session. Become familiar with the picture story on page 182.	■ Bibles ■ pencils or pens ■ chalkboard
Day 2	Read through the lesson plan for this class session. Prepare to tell the students a personal story about an experience of being shown love and care.	■ chalkboard
Day 3	Read through the five Bible stories told in Step 2. Prepare to share a personal experience of helping someone in need.	■ pencils or pens ■ Bibles ■ half-sheets of lined paper
Day 4	Read through the lesson plan for this class session.	■ chalkboard ■ pencils or pens
Day 5	Prepare an environment for prayer in the classroom. Review this week's sessions to prepare for the chapter review.	■ current newspapers and news magazines ■ pencils or pens

Additional Resources

As you plan this chapter, consider using the following materials from The Resourceful Teacher Package.

■ *Classroom Activity Sheets 15* and *15a*

■ *Family Activity Sheets 15* and *15a*

■ *Chapter 15 Test*

■ *Prayers for Every Day*

■ *Projects: Grade 3*

You may also wish to refer to the following Big Book.

■ *We Celebrate God's Word,* pages 9 and 13

In preparing the students for the Sunday readings, you may wish to use Silver Burdett Ginn's *Getting Ready for Sunday* student and teacher materials.

Books for the Journey

Casey's Revenge. Joy Berry. Kids Media Group, 1991. This book teaches children that friends should be chosen for who they are, not for what they have.

The Lean Mean Machine. Joy Berry. Kids Media Group, 1991. Maggie learns how to deal with strong emotions when she misinterprets events with her friends.

More Books for the Journey

Experience Jesus Today. Charles Singer and Albert Hari. OCP Publications, 1993. "The Last Judgment," pp. 170–171. A reflection describing people who need help and a prayer asking for help in being open to those in need.

The President Builds a House. Tom Schachtman. Simon & Schuster, 1989. This book is filled with photographs and simple explanations of the work of Habitat for Humanity and gives a very practical application of Jesus' commandment to love.

Reduced Classroom Activities

NAME _____

Christians Help Others

Cut along the outside lines on this page and page 15a to make a board game. Tape the two pieces together and glue the game to stiff paper. Find a marker for you and your partner. Take turns flipping a coin to see how many spaces you should move your marker:

heads = 1 space
tails = 2 spaces

To the Teacher: This activity will help students focus on corporal works of mercy that are relevant to their lives.

Chapter 15 Christians Help Others   This Is Our Faith 3   **15**

NAME _____

15a This Is Our Faith 3   **Chapter 15** Christians Help Others

CHRISTIAN MERCY AND COMPASSION

As Christians we are called to act with compassion and mercy. Such action is at the very heart of what it means to be a committed follower of Christ. The Church has traditionally referred to certain acts of compassion as the corporal works of mercy and spiritual works of mercy.

The imperative for acting in a compassionate way is evident in the Old Testament. The major prophets of Israel repeatedly called God's people to respond to the problems of those in need: orphans, widows, debtors, slaves, the hungry, the oppressed, the homeless. For the people of Israel, to act with mercy has been an important part of loving and serving God.

Jesus expressed this compassion in his public ministry. His life was one of compassion both for those who had physical needs and for those who had spiritual needs. He gave food and drink to the hungry. He gave sight to the blind and the gifts of speech and hearing to those who did not have these faculties. Jesus comforted widows and healed the sick and disabled. His life was one of compassion for all.

Jesus promised to reward acts of mercy and compassion. He said that those who will inherit the kingdom of God are those who show compassion to the hungry, the thirsty, the stranger, the naked, the ill, and the prisoner.

THE CORPORAL WORKS OF MERCY

The Church has continuously placed the corporal works of mercy before us as an ideal. Throughout history and in today's world, we have marvelous examples of men and women who have lived these works of mercy. In this chapter the students will read about Dorothy Day, who dedicated her life to helping the poor.

Catholics have a long and admirable history of compassion and mercy. In the name of Jesus, people perform merciful acts daily in hospitals, homes for the aged, children's homes, treatment centers for drug and alcohol addiction, and in various other social service programs. Missionaries not only bring the gospel of Christ to others but also work to alleviate physical suffering. Catholic Relief Services and Catholic Charities are two major Church agencies that help those in the world who are poor, hungry, and homeless.

Objective

This lesson helps the students learn the parable of the Good Samaritan.

Step 1/INTRODUCTION

Learning About Our Lives

Introducing the Chapter

Have the students turn to page 182 in their texts. Ask for a volunteer to read aloud the chapter title. Invite the students to respond to the chapter-focus question by naming people they have cared for or helped. Encourage them to describe the kinds of things they did to help the people they named. Tell the students that in this chapter they will learn how Catholic Christians are called to help others.

Writing a Dialogue

Familiarize yourself with the picture story on page 182. The four frames represent a sequence of events in the life of John, an eight-year-old boy. He has fallen off his bicycle and waits for someone to help him. Three children of the same age ride by on their own bicycles. One of them comes back and helps the fallen boy. This is a modern version of the Scripture story of the Good Samaritan (Luke 10:29–37), which the students will read in Step 2.

Ask the students to look at the illustrations on page 182. Do not tell them what is happening in the pictures. Allow the students time to study the pictures and figure out what the story is about. Have the students write in the balloons what they believe the characters are saying or feeling. Afterward, ask volunteers to share what they have written.

Conducting Interviews

Have the class form cooperative groups of five students each. Ask each group to decide among themselves who will take the parts of a reporter, John, and the two girls and boy who rode by on their bicycles. Ask the reporter to interview the group about what happened and question each child about what he or she did. Encourage the children to give their reasons for helping or not helping and to express their feelings about the incident. Allow five minutes

Christians Help Others

Write a Dialogue

Write your own words in the story below to tell what you think the children are thinking or saying.

Who are some of the people you help and care for?

182 Morality

Focus on

Levites The students may be curious about the Levite mentioned in the parable of the Good Samaritan. Explain to them that the Levites were one of the ancient tribes, or families, of the Jewish people. Some of the Levites were priests, while others served in different Temple ministries as musicians, singers, sacristans, and doorkeepers. The Levites were considered to be a holy people dedicated to serving the Lord.

The Good Samaritan

Jesus taught many people during his lifetime. He often spoke to them in **parables**, which were brief stories that helped them understand what he was teaching. He once told a parable about a man who helped another man who had been beaten up and left for dead. Read the parable of the Good Samaritan in Luke 10:29–37.

Activity

Write the numbers 1 through 7 on the lines below to show the correct sequence of events in the parable of the Good Samaritan. The first one is done for you.

__2__ The robbers left the man, whom they thought was probably dead.

__6__ After bandaging the injured man's sores, the Samaritan took him to an inn.

__3__ Later, a priest who was walking on the same road saw the man and crossed to the other side of the road to continue his own journey to Jericho.

__1__ After Jesus taught about loving our neighbor as our ourselves, a lawyer asked Jesus, "Who is my neighbor?" Jesus began to tell the story about a man who was beaten and robbed while walking along the road from Jerusalem to Jericho.

__7__ The next day, the Samaritan paid the innkeeper and told him that he would pay for anything more the man needed.

__4__ A Levite also saw the man and passed him by on the opposite side of the road.

__5__ A Samaritan stopped when he saw the man and knelt down to see if he could help.

Vocabulary

parables: brief stories that helped people understand what Jesus taught

✦ ✦ ✦ ✦ ✦ ✦ ✦ ✦ ✦ ✦ ✦

Scripture 183

Step 2/DEVELOPMENT

Learning About Our Faith

Reading a Scripture Story

Call on a student to read aloud the first paragraph on page 183. As the word *parables* is introduced, direct the students' attention to the Vocabulary box and have them learn the definition. Distribute Bibles to the students and help them locate the parable of the Good Samaritan (Luke 10:29–37). Have the students read the parable silently to themselves.

Putting the Story in Order

Instruct the students to review what they read by completing the activity on page 183. Have them put the story in correct order by numbering each of the seven sentences in their texts. Afterward, check the students' answers. Then have the students discuss how this parable compares with the picture story on page 182. Ask the students to state the message of the parable. Guide them to understand that in this parable, Jesus is teaching us that anyone who needs our help is our neighbor and that we are called to help anyone in need.

Step 3/CONCLUSION

Learning How to Live Our Faith

Identifying Ways to Be Good Samaritans

Have the students discuss whether they have ever acted like the Good Samaritan by unselfishly helping another person. Encourage them to share their experiences. Ask them how this experience made them feel. Write on the chalkboard a list of the words they use to describe how they feel. These may include: *proud, happy, kind,* and *loving.* Then invite the students to identify realistic opportunities for them to act as good Samaritans at home or at school. Point out that the situations need not be as dramatic as helping someone who was beaten and robbed. Emphasize that each day presents us with opportunities to help and to show care for others. Urge the students to look for the many different ways they can reach out to others in their daily lives.

Enriching the Lesson

Divide the students into small groups and randomly assign to each person the role of one of the characters in the story of the Good Samaritan. Have the groups act out the story as you slowly read aloud the Biblical account. Repeat this reading several times with the students switching roles each time. After each student has had the chance to be the robbed person, the Levite, and the Samaritan, talk about what it felt like to play each of the roles. This approach will help the students remember the story and identify more with each of the characters.

Teaching Tips

Ask: *Why do we sometimes fail to care about what happens to others?* Point out the actions of the boy and the girl in the picture story and the actions of the priest and the Levite in the parable and discuss why these individuals did not stop to help the injured person. (*Possible responses may include: they were too busy, they did not care about a stranger, they didn't think the person needed help, or they did not know what to do.*) Then ask the students to discuss their own reasons for failing to care for or help another person.

183

DAY 2
SCRIPTURE / DOCTRINE

Objective
This lesson helps the students learn the corporal works of mercy.

Step 1/INTRODUCTION

Learning About Our Lives

Remembering Experiences of Care
Invite the students to tell personal stories about times when someone showed care or love for them. These stories might focus on being cared for when they were ill or when they were confused, worried, or scared. Allow time for each of the students to participate in this discussion. Talk with them about how it feels to be taken care of or helped. (*Possible responses might include: safe, peaceful, loved, valued, special, and happy.*) Then talk with the students about how they would feel if they needed help or care and no one responded to them. (*Possible responses are: sad, alone, ignored, and angry.*) Help the students recall that they have learned that Jesus teaches us to love our neighbor as much as we love ourselves. Prepare the students for the Scripture story by explaining to them that Jesus also taught his followers specific ways in which they could show love and care for their neighbors.

Step 2/DEVELOPMENT

Learning About Our Faith

Learning the New Vocabulary
Print the words *Corporal Works of Mercy* on the chalkboard and then underline the words *Corporal* and *Mercy*. Have the students look at the Vocabulary box on page 185 and read the definitions. Explain that the corporal works of mercy are loving ways that help us care for others just as the Good Samaritan did.

Reading and Discussing the Story
Ask a volunteer to read the story "For Those Who Care" on pages 184 and 185. This is a story that Jesus told about the many ways we can show that we care. Ask the following questions to guide discussion.

184

For Those Who Care

One day, Jesus was talking to a group of people. He told them how he would reward those who cared about others.

"To those people I will say, 'Come into my Father's house. You will be happy forever because when I was hungry, you gave me food. When I was thirsty, you gave me a drink. When I was a stranger, you welcomed me. When I had nothing to wear, you gave me some clothes. When I was sick, you cared for me. When I was in prison, you came to visit me.'"

184 Scripture

Cultural Awareness

When Jesus spoke about feeding the hungry, giving drink to the thirsty, and clothing the naked, he made no reference to any particular group in society. He included all people who were in need of help. Point out to the students that Jesus included people of every culture, race, and ethnic background in his command to love. In a world troubled with racism, we have a clear and forceful command from Jesus to love all people as our brothers and sisters. In so doing, we show our love for Jesus Christ.

Teaching Tips

Invite students to think of how they might pantomime a situation that calls for someone to perform a corporal work of mercy. Explain to the students that they can involve other classmates in their pantomimes. Then encourage the students to present their pantomimes while the class guesses which corporal work of mercy is being acted out.

"Then the people will ask me, 'Lord, when did we see you hungry and feed you? When did we see you thirsty and give you drink? When did we welcome you as a stranger or clothe you? And when did we visit you when you were sick or in prison?'"

"And I will answer, 'As often as you did those things for one of the least of my brothers or sisters, you did them for me.'"

Based on Matthew 25:34–40

Caring for Others

Jesus teaches us that when we care for or help people in need, we do it for him. We are asked to see Jesus' face in the face of each person we meet. The Church helps us remember what we are called to do for Jesus through people who are in need. We call these caring actions the **corporal** works of **mercy**. These actions are specific ways that we can help people who have physical needs. As followers of Jesus, we are called to bring the love of Jesus to all people and to love and care for each person as Jesus would. For just as we see Jesus in others, others can also see Jesus in us when we help them and care for them.

Vocabulary

corporal: affecting our bodies and the needs of our bodies

mercy: loving care or compassion

✦ ✦ ✦ ✦ ✦ ✦ ✦ ✦ ✦ ✦ ✦

Corporal Works of Mercy

1. Feed the hungry.
2. Give drink to the thirsty.
3. Clothe the naked.
4. Visit those in prison.
5. Shelter the homeless.
6. Visit the sick.
7. Bury the dead.

We Believe

We best show our love for Jesus when we help people in need. Jesus teaches that whatever we do for people in need, we do for him. Catholics identify the corporal works of mercy as seven ways we can care for people in need.

Doctrine **185**

- Whom did Jesus say he would reward? (*Those who cared about others*)
- Who did Jesus say would be welcomed into his Father's house? (*Those who feed the hungry, give drink to the thirsty, welcome strangers, clothe others, and visit the sick and imprisoned*)
- When we do these things, for whom are we caring? (*Jesus*)

Learning About the Works of Mercy

Read "Caring for Others" with the students. Help them appreciate that when we live the corporal works of mercy, we are showing our love for Jesus and, at the same time, we are signs of Jesus' love and care.

Have a volunteer read aloud the list of the seven corporal works of mercy. Take the time to clarify what each one means. Ask the students to give their own examples of each one. For example, contributing clothing that is in good condition to the Salvation Army or the St. Vincent de Paul Society is one way of clothing the naked.

Reviewing the Doctrine

Ask one of the students to read the We Believe statement on page 185. Emphasize that Christians do not care for others simply to be nice. We help and care for others because of our belief in and love for Jesus. Our relationship with Jesus inspires, or motivates, us to act in caring ways. Ask the students if they have any questions about the vocabulary or doctrine. Encourage the students to remember this central part of the lesson.

Step 3/CONCLUSION

Learning How to Live Our Faith

Praying Together

Have the students name the one thing that makes Christians helping others so important. Write the word *Christian* on the chalkboard as a clue. Underline the word *Christ* and elicit from the students that when we help others we do so in Jesus' name and out of our love for Jesus. Invite the students to offer silent prayers expressing their faith in Jesus and their desire to show others a sign of Jesus' love through their loving and caring actions.

Focus on

The Least Jesus identified himself with sinners and outcasts, those who were least likely to be treated with care and respect by others in that society. In what Matthew presents as Jesus' last words of instruction to his apostles, we learn that we will be judged on how well we fulfill this clear command of Jesus to feed, clothe, and shelter those in need. Ask the students to identify who the "least of people" might be in our modern society.

Enriching the Lesson

Invite the students to draw pictures to illustrate the seven corporal works of mercy. Provide drawing paper and crayons or markers. Make sure that the students draw at least one picture for each of the seven works. Encourage the students to label their drawings and to explain them to the class. Collect the pictures to use in the review on Day 4.

DAY 3
SCRIPTURE

Objective

This lesson helps the students understand that Jesus calls us to work together to help others.

Step 1/INTRODUCTION

Learning About Our Lives

Solving a Word Puzzle

Introduce the activity on page 186 by reading aloud the paragraph at the top of the page. Help the students recognize that we are called to see Jesus in one another. Have the students trace the path through the maze. Then ask them to complete the scriptural verse by filling in the blanks using words from the maze. When everyone has finished, ask the students to read the solution aloud together.

Ask: *Whom does Jesus mean when he talks about "my sisters and brothers?"* Lead the students to the recognition that since all people were created by God and Jesus is God's Son, every human being is Jesus' brother and sister. As children of God and Jesus' followers, we are all one human family. Tell the students that in this lesson, they will learn how Jesus showed care for the people of his time.

Step 2/DEVELOPMENT

Learning About Our Faith

Reading About Jesus' Mercy

Call for volunteers to read aloud "Jesus' Works of Mercy" on page 187. Or list the five references on the board (Mark 1:40–45; Mark 2:1–12; Mark 6:34–44; Mark 7:31–37; Mark 8:22–26), have the class form groups, and assign one reading to each group. In discussing these readings, help the students understand the following points.

■ People recognized Jesus' compassion and came to him for help and healing.

■ People believed in Jesus' ability to heal.

■ Although we cannot perform miracles as Jesus did, we can help others in many ways. We can do this alone or by working with others.

186

Activity

God cares for each of us. We should also care for one another. Showing that you care about others is the same as showing that you love Jesus.

Follow the maze on the hiking trip below to find a special message from Jesus about caring for one another.

Whenever __y__ __o__ __u__ cared for one of __m__ __y__ sisters or __b__ __r__ __o__ __t__ __h__ __e__ __r__ __s__, you __c__ __a__ __r__ __e__ __d__ for __m__ __e__.

Based on Matthew 25:40

Jesus' Works of Mercy

In the Gospel of Mark, we can read many stories about Jesus performing works of mercy. In Mark 1:40–45, we read about Jesus healing a leper. In this story, the leper is told by Jesus not to tell anyone that he has cured the man. But the leper is so excited that he tells everyone he sees. Then so many people want Jesus to help them that they come to him from everywhere. And even when Jesus tries to find quiet places to pray, people find him and ask for his help.

In Mark 2:1–12, we read about how Jesus heals a paralyzed man. The crowds that come to the house where Jesus is preaching are so large that nobody can even get near the door. The four men who bring the paralyzed man to Jesus have to open up the roof to get inside. They lower the mat that the man is lying on through the roof, right above Jesus. Amazed by their faith, Jesus heals the man while everyone watches.

People came to Jesus again and again because they believed he could do great things for them. In Mark 6:34–44, we read that Jesus feeds five thousand hungry people with only five loaves of bread and two fish. In Mark 7:31–37, Jesus heals a deaf person. And in Mark 8:22–26, Jesus heals a blind person.

Christians today may not be able to heal the sick as Jesus did, but they can help the sick by visiting them. Christians today may not be able to feed five thousand hungry people with only five loaves of bread and two fish, but they can share food with those who have little or none. Jesus calls Christians today to work together to help others in many ways.

Scripture 187

★ Enriching the Lesson ★

You may wish to invite to class people from your parish or local community who minister to the corporal needs of people. This might include people who work in soup kitchens or who prepare meals for the hungry. It might include those who minister to the homeless in society or people who visit prisoners. Ask them to describe the work that they do and to explain what motivates them to do such actions for the welfare of others. Have the students prepare beforehand a list of questions to ask.

Focus on

The Gospel of Mark The readings on page 187 are all taken from the Gospel of Mark. Mark's Gospel is believed to be the first of the four Gospels to be written. It was probably written in approximately A.D. 70. It is also the shortest Gospel. Mark's Gospel focuses on Jesus as the Son of God, who gave his life so that we might have eternal life. Mark also placed great emphasis on Jesus' miracles as a sign of God's coming kingdom.

Discussing Questions

Discuss with the students the following questions.

- How do you think people today feel about asking for help when they need food, clothing, or shelter?

- How do you feel when you see someone in need? Is it sometimes difficult for you to know what to do to help?

In discussing the first question, encourage the students to think about how they would feel if they were in the position of needing to ask for help. Discuss with them why it might be hard for someone to ask for help. As the students respond to the second and third questions, point out that when we are deciding whether to help someone, we can ask ourselves *What would Jesus say or do?* Emphasize that when the students perform even the most basic acts of kindness for others (opening a door for someone, setting the table at home, being friends with someone who doesn't have many friends, calling grandparents just to say hello, and so forth), they are doing what Jesus taught us to do.

Step 3/CONCLUSION

Learning How to Live Our Faith

Personalizing the Works of Mercy

Distribute half-sheets of lined paper. Invite the students to think of someone they know who needs a sign of Jesus' care, mercy, and love. Then have the students think of one positive way they can reach out to that person. Give the students an example from your own life experience. For instance, *I can visit Mrs. Jones, my neighbor who just had twins, to help her with the babies.* Invite the students to write a statement about how they can be a sign of Jesus' love for others.

DAY 4
MORALITY

Objective

This lesson helps the students appreciate that Dorothy Day lived the corporal works of mercy.

Step 1/INTRODUCTION

Learning About Our Lives

Remembering People Who Help Others

Ask the students to think of people they know or people they have heard about who live the corporal works of mercy by helping others. Provide time for the students to share stories about these people. Tell the students that in today's lesson they will read about a woman who helped others.

Step 2/DEVELOPMENT

Learning About Our Faith

Reading a Biography

Explain to the students that some people have shown us in especially powerful ways how to live the corporal works of mercy. When we look at these people's lives, we learn even more about how we can follow Jesus more closely. One such person was Dorothy Day. Have volunteers read aloud "Making a Big Difference" on page 188. After the reading, ask the students to circle all the corporal works of mercy that Dorothy Day practiced. Then discuss the following questions.

- What are some things that upset Dorothy and made her sad? (*Reading about and seeing people who were poor, hungry, and unemployed; seeing people who lived in poor conditions*)

- How did Dorothy's newspaper work help others? (*It made the readers aware of the poor.*)

- In what other ways did Dorothy help the poor and needy? (*She and Peter Maurin opened a house in New York City to offer food, clothing, and shelter to the poor. Word of Dorothy's work spread, and soon other people began to serve the poor in other cities.*)

188

Making a Big Difference

We are called to show our love for Jesus by doing good works for people who are hurting and in need. We are called to live the corporal works of mercy. Dorothy Day faithfully did just that!

Dorothy grew up in a large, happy family. She lived in Chicago with her mother, her father, and eight brothers and sisters.

Dorothy loved to read. But she was sad when she read about people who were poor and hungry. She was even sadder when she saw people who had worn-out clothes or little food, lived in broken-down houses and apartment buildings, and were out of work.

Dorothy became a newspaper reporter. She wrote about the poor. With a friend named Peter Maurin, she started a newspaper called *The Catholic Worker.* The two hoped their paper would bring help for the poor.

But Dorothy Day wanted to do even more. She saw people in New York City who needed food, clothes, and a place to sleep. She and Peter opened a house where these people could come for food, clothing, and shelter. Dorothy spent the rest of her life living with the poor and helping them in every way she could.

Dorothy Day died in 1980. She had truly lived the corporal works of mercy. Some people who saw and experienced what Dorothy was doing for the poor started Catholic Worker houses in other towns and cities. Dorothy Day planted a seed. Catholic Worker volunteers have helped that seed grow. They are making a difference as they continue to serve the poor today.

188   Morality

Teaching Tips

The justice and peace bumper sticker "Think Globally, Act Locally" has application for helping the students understand how they are called to live the works of mercy. Explain that although we are all called to care about the needs of the worldwide community, we should also concentrate our efforts on doing what we can to change situations in our own communities. Have the students create a slogan promoting living out the corporal works of mercy at home and at school. Have them print their slogans on tagboard strips.

188

In Simple Ways

Like Dorothy Day, some Christians live the corporal works of mercy in extraordinary ways. Others live them in very simple ways. Jesus calls each of us to live the works of mercy in our own ways, wherever we are. We can do this at home, at school, at work, or at play.

Some of us may see people in need every day. Some of us may only read or hear about people in need. We can *all* take more time to look and listen for opportunities to help others. People sometimes will come to us for help. Sometimes people find it difficult to ask for help.

Activity

Think about some people in need. These can be individuals or entire countries. Perhaps you know these people or you have heard about them on the news. On the lines below, write about one thing you saw, heard, or read. Then describe one thing you can do to help the person or group that needs help.

What I saw, heard, or read: _____

_____

_____

_____

_____

What I can do: _____

_____

_____

_____

_____

Morality 189

Learning How to Live Our Faith

Reading and Discussing the Text

Direct the students' attention to the photograph at the top of page 189. Discuss with the students what is happening in the picture. Call on a volunteer to read aloud the first paragraph in "In Simple Ways." On the chalkboard, make a chart with four sections. Label the sections *home, school, work,* and *play*. Ask the students to brainstorm ways they can live the corporal works in each of these places. Fill the chart with their responses. Save the students' answers for them to use as a reference for the writing activity at the bottom of the page.

Read through the next paragraph with the class. Emphasize that each of us can be more alert to the needs of others. Explain that one way we can learn about the needs of others is by watching the news, reading newspapers and the parish bulletin, and trying to notice what's happening in the lives of the people around us.

Writing About People in Need

Explain the instructions for the activity on page 189. Have the students work in small groups to complete the activity. The students' responses to this activity will vary. In geographic areas where larger social needs may not be so obvious, you may want to point out the needs that can be seen or heard in your community. Reassure the students that while larger social problems, such as poverty and famine, cannot be solved through their own individual efforts, their care, concern, and prayers do have an impact.

Reviewing the Chapter

If you had the students do the enrichment activity on Day 2, use their drawings to review the seven corporal works of mercy. Or have them do this orally. Also have the students recite the definitions for the new vocabulary words *parables, corporal,* and *mercy* as well as the We Believe statement.

Enriching the Lesson

Have the students work in small groups to create skits about living the corporal works of mercy. Suggest that the students draw on the ideas they listed in the brainstorming activity or the people they identified in the writing activity on page 189. Allow time for the groups to practice their skits and then invite each group to perform its skit for the class. Praise the students for their creativity in acting out their works of mercy and compliment them for their willingness to participate.

Focus on

Interfaith Hospitality Network A present-day example of how people work together to take care of the corporal needs of others is the Interfaith Hospitality Network. This nationwide organization consists of volunteers from various churches and synagogues who join together to provide temporary shelter, food, and clothing to homeless families. Some people prepare meals while others provide hospitality to the homeless at a central shelter. The goal of the network is to get people back on their feet and into living places that they can call home.

Objective

This lesson helps the students pray original prayers of petition based on current news stories.

Looking at Newspapers and Magazines

Have the students form small groups and distribute current newspapers and news magazines to each group. Ask the students to look through the headlines and news stories to find examples of real people in need. Tell the students that in today's celebration they will have the opportunity to pray for people around the world who need help and care.

Reading the Text

Call on a volunteer to read aloud "Praying with Today's Headlines" on page 190. Invite the students to identify the burdens that are being experienced by the people described in the news stories they discussed in their small groups.

Writing Petitions

Review the procedure for writing petitions by explaining the example in the text. In addition to this example, you might wish to suggest to the students other examples of petitions, such as "For those people who suffer from AIDS, cancer, or other life-threatening diseases, that we may offer them words of comfort, hope, and healing." Then have the students work in their groups to write three petitions. Tell the students that they will have the opportunity to pray their petitions during the celebration.

Praying Together

Practice with the students the class response to the petitions.

During the celebration, allow a few moments of silent reflection following the praying of the petitions. During this time, invite the students to silently offer to God some of the burdens that they themselves carry.

Praying with Today's Headlines

In Galatians 6:2, Paul tells the early Christians that they are to help carry one another's burdens. A *burden* is something that weighs us down. The corporal works of mercy help us identify some of the burdens that many people experience.

Today, we will offer prayers of petition for the needs we identify from current newspapers or magazines. We will begin each petition by saying the name of the person or group for whom we are praying. Then we will include some action that can help that person or group. We will conclude each petition by responding together, "Help us to carry one another's burdens." One example is given for you.

Petition: For the families who were left homeless after last week's hurricane, that our government, our churches, and all of us will be generous in providing food, clothing, and shelter to them for as long as they need our help.

Response: Help us to carry one another's burdens.

190 Prayer

Teaching Tips

For the prayer celebration, collect enough small, flat rocks for all the students. Encourage the students to use water colors and paint brushes to write on the rocks a burden that people may be carrying. Some examples are loneliness, cancer, poverty, homelessness, drug addiction, divorce, fear, and sadness. During the celebration, invite the students to place their rocks on the prayer table as a sign that they are asking Jesus to help them respond to the needs of God's family.

Enriching the Lesson

Have the students choose either the parable of the Good Samaritan (Luke 10:29–37), which the students read on Day 1, or the story "For Those Who Care" on pages 184 and 185 to read during the celebration. If the Good Samaritan story is chosen, you may want to have the students act it out. Select ten volunteers to take the parts of the narrator, the lawyer, Jesus, the man traveling from Jerusalem to Jericho, the two robbers, the priest, the Levite, the Good Samaritan, and the innkeeper. Practice with the group prior to the prayer service.

Chapter Review

Find words from the chapter to complete the sentences below.

1. Jesus told _____parables_____ to help people understand what he was teaching.

2. The good _____Samaritan_____ was the only one who stopped on the road to Jericho to help the injured man.

3. The Church gives us the _____corporal_____ works of mercy to teach us some of the ways we can help others.

4. We best show our love for _____Jesus_____ when we help people in need.

5. In the _____Gospel_____ of Mark, we read many stories about Jesus' helping people.

6. _____Dorothy Day_____ made a big difference for many people when she began the first Catholic Worker house.

7. One way we can help to carry another's _____burdens_____ is to pray for one another.

Fill in the answers to the first two questions.

1. What is the meaning of *corporal*? _Corporal_ means "affecting our bodies and the needs of our bodies."

2. What do the corporal works of mercy teach us?
   ways that we can show loving care or compassion for people in need

3. Talk about some reasons the corporal works of mercy are so important.

Help carry one another's burdens.
Based on Galatians 6:2

Enriching the Lesson

Divide the students into groups of three or four. Distribute contemporary news magazines to the groups. Ask the students to cut out pictures that show people in need and to mount the pictures on drawing paper. Direct the students to write under each mounted picture what they would do to help the person or persons in need. Afterward, collect the students' work and use it to create a contemporary montage on living the works of mercy. Post this on a bulletin board or on a wall outside your classroom.

Filling in the Blanks

Have the students read to themselves the directions for the first review exercise on page 191. Tell the students that they may look back at the pages in this chapter to help them locate answers they cannot recall on their own. When everyone has finished, call on volunteers to read aloud the completed sentences. Have the students correct any mistakes they may have made.

Completing the Chapter Review

Direct attention to the next two questions. Ask the students to write the answer to each question on the line provided in the text. In discussing the third question, help the students recall that the corporal works of mercy are seven ways of helping people who have physical needs. Through these works of mercy, we bring Jesus' love and care to people in need.

Praying with the Scriptural Verse

Read together the verse from Galatians at the bottom of the page and note that this verse was the response spoken by the students in the prayer celebration. Talk with the students about the burdens that Jesus carried for others and how Dorothy Day followed Jesus' example in helping ease the burdens of the poor. Have the students recall from memory the corporal works of mercy. Emphasize that responding to the physical needs of others is an example of helping to carry one another's burdens.

16 Christians Comfort Others

Objectives

To help the students

- Understand the meaning of the parable of the Unforgiving Servant.
- Learn the spiritual works of mercy.
- Recognize that the spiritual works of mercy help us care for others.
- Want to live the spiritual works of mercy as Saint Angela Merici did.
- Thank God for people who have encouraged them to live good lives and review the chapter.

Chapter Outline

	Step 1 Learning About Our Lives	**Step 2** Learning About Our Faith	**Step 3** Learning How to Live Our Faith
Day 1	■ Talk about feelings. ■ Read and finish a story. *ABOUT 7 MINUTES*	■ Read a parable. ■ Explore the meaning of the story. *ABOUT 12 MINUTES*	■ Respond to needs. *ABOUT 11 MINUTES*
Day 2	■ Recall key words. *ABOUT 3 MINUTES*	■ Present the vocabulary. ■ Read the text. ■ Learn spiritual works of mercy. ■ Identify spiritual works of mercy. *ABOUT 20 MINUTES*	■ Complete an activity. ■ Pray a litany together. *ABOUT 7 MINUTES*
Day 3	■ Remember stories about Jesus. *ABOUT 7 MINUTES*	■ Read and discuss a Scripture story. ■ Understand the message. ■ Learn the doctrine. *ABOUT 14 MINUTES*	■ Identify caring expressions. *ABOUT 9 MINUTES*
Day 4	■ Name people who live the works of mercy. *ABOUT 10 MINUTES*	■ Read a biography. *ABOUT 10 MINUTES*	■ Write thank-you letters. *ABOUT 10 MINUTES*
Day 5	**Prayer** Read the text; prepare for prayer; pray together. **Review** Choose words and actions; complete the chapter review; discuss the chapter; pray with the scriptural verse.		

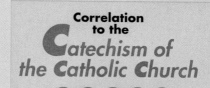

Correlation
to the
**Catechism of
the Catholic Church**

Paragraphs
1822, 1823, 1969, 2447

Plan Ahead

	Preparing Your Class	**Materials Needed**
Day 1	Read through the lesson plan for this class session. Decide how you will present the Step 3 activity.	■ chalkboard ■ pencils or pens
Day 2	Read through the lesson plan for this class session.	■ chalkboard ■ pencils or pens
Day 3	Read through the lesson plan for this class session. Think about various Gospel stories that show Jesus living the spiritual works of mercy.	■ pencils or pens
Day 4	Read through the lesson plan for this class session. Think of names to offer as examples for Step 1.	■ pencils or pens
Day 5	Prepare an environment for prayer in the classroom. Review this week's sessions to prepare for the chapter review.	■ Bible ■ pencils or pens

Additional Resources

As you plan this chapter, consider using the following materials from The Resourceful Teacher Package.

■ *Classroom Activity Sheets 16* and *16a*

■ *Family Activity Sheets 16* and *16a*

■ *Chapter 16 Test*

■ *Prayers for Every Day*

■ *Projects: Grade 3*

You may also wish to refer to the following Big Book.

■ *We Celebrate the Mass,* page 11

In preparing the students for the Sunday readings, you may wish to use Silver Burdett Ginn's *Getting Ready for Sunday* student and teacher materials.

Books for the Journey

Jennie's Hat. Ezra Jack Keats. HarperCollins, 1985. A story of a girl who is very disappointed when an anticipated hat turns out to be plain.

My Rotten Redheaded Older Brother. Patricia Polacco. Simon & Schuster, 1994. The author's own story of how annoying her older brother was and how an event changed their relationship for the better.

More Books for the Journey

A Child's First Catholic Dictionary. Richard W. Dyches and Thomas Mustachio. Ave Maria Press, 1994. "Works of Mercy," p. 110. A definition of the works of mercy and mini-pictures showing people performing each work.

I Never Told and Other Poems. Myra Cohn Livingston. Margaret K. McElderry Books, 1992. "I Would Have Come," p. 12. A poem to help children imagine why someone might need to phone a friend.

Reduced Classroom Activities

Christians Comfort Others

NAME _____

As mayor of God's Love Village, you are responsible for upkeep of the roads. There are two main roads that lead into the village from anywhere in the United States: Corporal Works of Mercy Highway and Spiritual Works of Mercy Highway. The problem is, someone took down all the signs on both roads and mixed them together.

Use what you know about the Spiritual and Corporal Works of Mercy to find the right signs for each road. Cut out the signs on page 16a and paste them back onto the correct posts.

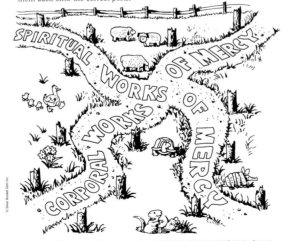

To the Teacher: This two-page activity allows students to classify the Works of Mercy as either Spiritual or Corporal.

NAME _____

Be patient with others.

Give drink to the thirsty.

Clothe the naked.

Feed the hungry.

Bury the dead.

Forgive injuries.

Give advice to those who are confused.

Visit those in prison.

Visit the sick.

Help others make good choices.

Shelter the homeless.

Comfort those who are hurting.

Teach those who lack knowledge.

Pray for the living and the dead.

SPIRITUAL SUFFERING

The corporal works of mercy, examined in the previous chapter, dealt with more evident bodily suffering: hunger, lack of adequate housing or clothing, sickness, and so on. There is another whole range of suffering that may be even more painful and debilitating. This is suffering that undermines the human spirit, such as fear, guilt, weakness, loneliness, a sense of emptiness, depression, and hopelessness. These spiritual hurts permeate our society and our world.

Jesus witnessed spiritual suffering in the lives of many of the people he met. His gentleness and strength brought peace, comfort, and encouragement to many. Even as he walked to his own death at Calvary, he stopped to comfort the weeping women. On the cross he expressed loving care for his mother, and he prayed for the forgiveness of his executioners.

THE SPIRITUAL WORKS OF MERCY

Today we are called as followers of Jesus to be sensitive people. The Church describes the actions of sensitive and caring people in the spiritual works of mercy. These works include correcting sinners (helping people make good choices), teaching the ignorant (helping those who lack knowledge), giving advice to those who are confused, comforting those who suffer, being patient with others, forgiving injuries, and praying for the living and the dead. The students will learn about these works of mercy in this chapter.

It is important that the students do more than simply memorize the spiritual works of mercy. As their catechist, you should help them examine their own attitudes of concern and compassion. The students should reflect on what motivates them to act with mercy. You should help them understand their own sensitivities in such a way that they will grow in empathy. These are the first steps toward becoming compassionate persons.

We all need to learn how to offer guidance and encouragement to others. We need to develop a more patient attitude and a willingness to forgive. This sharing of ourselves is at the very heart of the spiritual works of mercy. In a world where people don't want to get involved, the spiritual works of mercy challenge us to reach deep within ourselves and to reflect on our own faith and principles. Helping the students to do the same kind of inner searching contributes to an essential part of their moral development.

DAY 1
MORALITY/SCRIPTURE

Objective

This lesson helps the students understand the meaning of the parable of the Unforgiving Servant.

Step 1/INTRODUCTION

Learning About Our Lives

Talking About Feelings

Direct attention to page 192 and read aloud the chapter-focus statement. After the students share their responses, explain that being patient and forgiving are two ways of showing care for others. Tell the students that in this chapter they will learn about specific ways that Catholics are called to show care for others.

Reading and Finishing a Story

Ask for volunteers to read "Redfeather's Response." Then ask the students to share ideas about possible endings to the story. Discuss some options that Redfeather has in responding to the boys' request. Help the students appreciate that if Redfeather helped with the poster, it might result in better understanding, friendship, and acceptance.

Invite the students to discuss how Gerry and Joe's feelings about Redfeather changed. Help them appreciate that Redfeather must overcome his feelings of hurt and anger in order to respond to Gerry and Joe's request and to begin a friendship.

Step 2/DEVELOPMENT

Learning About Our Faith

Reading a Parable

Call on volunteers to take turns reading aloud "The Unforgiving Servant" on page 193. Ask the following questions.

■ How were the king and the first servant alike? (*They were both owed money.*)

■ What did the first servant ask the king to do? (*To give him more time to pay back the money he owed*)

■ What did the king do? (*He forgave, or canceled, the servant's debt.*)

192

16

Tell about a time when someone hurt you and you forgave them or a time when someone was annoying you and you were patient with them.

192 Morality

Christians Comfort Others

Redfeather's Response

In school, everyone called him Matthew. At home, on the reservation, his real name was Redfeather.

Redfeather's first months in the new school were hard. He was shy. His classmates made fun of him. They laughed at him when he spoke because he always spoke very softly and politely.

Redfeather often ate alone. He spent his free time drawing in a notebook he never showed to anyone. One day, Joe and Gerry took the small notebook from Redfeather's backpack during recess. They wanted to see what was in it.

When they opened it they were amazed. On page after page were beautiful drawings of hawks, eagles, rabbits, wolves, horses, rolling hills, houses, and people. There were several drawings of Redfeather's grandfather.

Gerry and Joe felt guilty. So during lunch they slipped the notebook back in Redfeather's backpack. They did not know that he saw them. Redfeather felt hurt and angry.

The next day they asked Redfeather to draw a hawk for them. They were making a poster for their soccer team, the Hawks. Redfeather did not say or do anything right away. He was not sure how to respond.

Cultural Awareness

Judging others from first impressions may prevent us from making new friends or seeing another person's gifts. The boys in the story might have thought that Redfeather was strange because he was quiet and stayed by himself while he was, in fact, shy. Offer the group other examples: thinking someone is stupid because he or she does not speak English well; concluding that you wouldn't have fun with someone who uses a wheelchair; or deciding that you have nothing in common with a person whose skin is a different color.

The Unforgiving Servant

Peter asked Jesus, "How often do you expect me to forgive someone who has hurt me? Should I forgive him seven times?"

Jesus said to Peter, "You need to forgive him seventy-seven times. Let me tell you a story to help you understand what I am teaching about forgiveness.

"A king wished to settle his accounts with his servants. The first servant, who owed the king a very large sum of money, could not pay. So the king ordered that the servant, his family, and all that he owned, be sold to pay the debt. The servant fell down on his knees and begged the king to be patient with him. 'Please give me more time. I will pay you back in full.' The king felt sorry for the servant and so released him and forgave his debt.

"Later, this same servant met another servant who owed money to him. He demanded that he be paid. The other servant begged for his debtor to be patient. 'Please give me more time. I will pay you back in full.' But the servant who could not pay his debt was thrown in jail. Others who saw what had happened told the king. The king was very angry that the first servant did not show the same compassion that had been shown to him. So the king had the first servant, who showed no mercy to his fellow servant, thrown into jail."

Based on Matthew 18:21–35

Discuss

1. Do you think the king's decision to be patient and forgive the first servant was a good one? Why or why not?

2. Why do you think the first servant would not forgive the second servant?

3. Why did the people and the king become angry?

Teaching Tips

Peter's question to Jesus and Jesus' response focus on God's limitless mercy and forgiveness. As Christians, we are called to forgive in the same way anyone who has hurt us—without limit. Help the students understand that forgiveness is not to be offered grudgingly or with conditions. Like God, we must forgive others completely and begin again to live in love and peace.

- Why was the second servant thrown in jail? (*Because he could not pay his debt to the first servant*)

- What did the king do when he heard about what the first servant had done? (*The king had the first servant jailed.*)

Exploring the Meaning of the Story

Direct attention to the Discuss questions on page 193 and invite the students' responses. In answering the first question, help the students recognize that the king's decision was good because it showed that being patient and forgiving was more important than money. Emphasize that the first servant was not as merciful as the king. As you discuss the third question, point out that the first servant did not treat the second servant the way he had been treated. Explain that in this parable, Jesus is teaching us that people who fail to show compassion, forgiveness, patience, and mercy to others may have none of these qualities shown to them.

Step 3/CONCLUSION

Learning How to Live Our Faith

Responding to Needs

Tell the students that, like Redfeather, we all have the need to be accepted and respected for who we are. Like the first servant, we need to be treated with compassion, forgiveness, and patience. Write the following sentences on the chalkboard or dictate them to the students, one at a time. Instruct them to copy each sentence and complete it according to how they would like people to respond to them when they are experiencing each feeling described. Afterward, have students share their responses. Call attention to the universality of their answers, noting that while every one of us is unique we all have common needs.

- When I am hurting inside, I wish someone would....

- When it takes me a long time to understand something, I wish people would....

- When I don't know something I need to know, I would like someone to....

- When I am confused, I want someone to....

193

DAY 2
DOCTRINE/MORALITY

Objective

This lesson helps the students learn the spiritual works of mercy.

Step 1/INTRODUCTION

Learning About Our Lives

Recalling Key Words

Encourage the students to identify the important words and ideas they discussed on Day 1. These would include: *helping, teaching, being patient,* and *forgiving others.* Have the students tell how these actions or qualities were used in the parable of the Unforgiving Servant. For instance, the king helped the first servant by forgiving his debt. Remind the students that in Chapter 15 they learned about the seven ways they can help others by practicing the corporal works of mercy. Explain that in this lesson they will learn about seven other works of mercy.

Step 2/DEVELOPMENT

Learning About Our Faith

Presenting the Vocabulary

Write the words *spiritual works of mercy* on the chalkboard and underline the word *spiritual.* Have the students recite this word after you. Direct attention to the Vocabulary box on page 195 and ask a volunteer to read aloud the definition. Help students understand that the corporal works of mercy are loving actions that help us care for the physical needs of others, whereas the spiritual works of mercy are loving actions that help us care for the needs of others' minds, hearts, and spirits.

Reading the Text

Call on a volunteer to read aloud "More Ways to Help" on page 194. Help the students recognize that the characters in the story "Redfeather's Response" and the parable of the Unforgiving Servant did not have physical needs, they had spiritual needs. Emphasize that Jesus cared greatly about people's spiritual needs and that the Church carries on Jesus' example through the spiritual works of mercy.

194

More Ways to Help

The corporal works of mercy that we learned about in Chapter 15 are all important ways to help others. But we can help others by caring for them and comforting them in many other ways, too. In the story about Redfeather and in the parable of the Unforgiving Servant, the people who needed help did not need food or clothing. And they were not sick or in prison.

Redfeather's feelings were hurt. He needed *comfort*. He also needed *advice* about how to respond to Gerry and Joe. He wanted to make a *good choice* about *forgiving* them.

The first servant needed the *forgiveness* and *patience* of his king. And he could have used some *advice* about how to respond to the other servant who asked for his *forgiveness* and *patience*.

By describing some specific ways in which we can be caring, the Church helps us remember Jesus' example and teachings of the many ways we can show love. These ways of helping people and caring for them are called the **spiritual** works of mercy. These works of mercy help others in very important ways, too.

Spiritual Works of Mercy

1. Help others make good choices.
2. Teach those who lack knowledge.
3. Give advice to those who are confused.
4. Comfort those who are hurting.
5. Be patient with others.
6. Forgive injuries.
7. Pray for the living and the dead.

★ Enriching the Lesson ★

Prepare a box with a small slip of paper in it for each student. On each slip, write a brief story that illustrates one of the spiritual works. For example, one slip could describe a situation in which a child is lonely because his or her best friend has moved away. Another slip might describe a student who is having trouble learning how to multiply. Have each student pick a slip of paper and read the story to the class. Encourage the students to name the particular work of mercy involved.

Focus on

Counseling Help the students be aware of the broad range of counseling that takes place daily in their community. There are counselors who help people with their personal and family relationships. Other counselors console and give advice to those who grieve the loss of a loved one. Such counseling is an expression of the spiritual works of mercy—helping people make good choices, giving advice to the confused, comforting those who are hurting, and praying for the living and the dead.

194

Activity

Sometimes we can show concern by talking with others. Complete the sentences using the words below. Then talk about the spiritual work of mercy that each sentence shows.

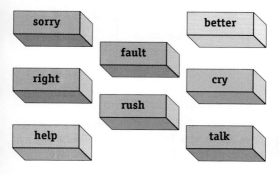

sorry

better

fault

right

cry

rush

help

talk

1. That's okay! It wasn't your _____fault_____.

2. Can I _____help_____ you figure it out?

3. I'm _____sorry_____ that you feel lonely.

4. I don't mean to _____rush_____ you. Take your time.

5. It's okay to _____cry_____. We are praying for you and your family.

6. I believe you are certainly doing the _____right_____ thing.

7. I think you should _____talk_____ to your Mom about this, too.

Vocabulary

spiritual: affecting the mind, heart, or spirit

✦ ✦ ✦ ✦ ✦ ✦ ✦ ✦ ✦ ✦ ✦

Morality **195**

Learning the Spiritual Works of Mercy

Read aloud the seven spiritual works of mercy. Discuss the meaning of each work with the students, encouraging them to think of a practical example of each. Also have the students match the italicized words in the first two paragraphs on page 194 with specific works of mercy from the list. When you think the students understand the spiritual works of mercy, invite them to work in small groups to role-play a situation in which they are called to perform one of the spiritual works. Allowing sufficient time for them to prepare, encourage them to act out their roles. Have the students watching the performances identify which spiritual work is being acted out.

Identifying Spiritual Works of Mercy

Invite the students to study the photographs on pages 194 and 195 and to identify the spiritual work that is being demonstrated in each picture. Help the students understand that in the picture on page 194, the priest is teaching the children and therefore practicing the second spiritual work. In the picture on page 195, the woman is comforting the little boy and therefore performing the fourth spiritual work.

Step 3/CONCLUSION

Learning How to Live Our Faith

Completing an Activity

Have a volunteer read aloud the directions for the activity on page 195. Provide time for the students to complete the activity by filling in the blanks with words they could say. Afterward, invite sharing by having the students read aloud the completed statements and identify the work of mercy that each statement reflects.

Praying a Litany Together

Invite the students to choose one of the spiritual works of mercy in which they would most like to grow. Perhaps they are not as patient with a younger sibling as they could be or they hold a grudge against someone who has hurt them. Encourage the students to offer brief spontaneous prayers asking God to help them be more caring.

Objective

This lesson helps the students recognize that the spiritual works of mercy help us care for others.

Step 1/INTRODUCTION

Learning About Our Lives

Remembering Stories About Jesus

Invite the students to recall from the Gospels stories about Jesus in which Jesus is shown as living the spiritual works of mercy, such as Jesus' post-resurrection appearance on the road to Emmaus (Luke 24:13–35), when he taught his followers about the prophets foretelling the coming of the Savior (*the second spiritual work*); the story of Zacchaeus (Luke 19:1–10), in which Jesus' acceptance led to Zacchaeus making a good choice (*the first spiritual work*); and Jesus forgiving the soldiers who crucified him (*the sixth spiritual work*).

Step 2/DEVELOPMENT

Learning About Our Faith

Reading and Discussing a Scripture Story

Introduce the reading on page 196 "Jesus Forgives Peter." Explain to the students that this is one of the appearances of Jesus to his disciples after his resurrection. The students will learn in the story that Peter once denied knowing Jesus. Peter spoke his denial three times during Jesus' imprisonment. This was a period when the followers of Jesus, including Peter, were fearful that, like Jesus, they would be arrested. Peter's denials must have weighed heavily on his mind during Jesus' trial and crucifixion and in the days that followed. Ask for volunteers to read the story aloud. Use the following questions to guide discussion.

- What had Peter done that made him feel sad? (*He denied knowing Jesus.*)

- What words does Jesus say to Peter? (*"Peter, do you love me?"*)

- How do you think the words Jesus spoke made Peter feel? (*Happy and forgiven*) Why?

Jesus Forgives Peter

Soon after his resurrection, Jesus had a special conversation with Peter. As they walked along the water's edge, Jesus asked, "Do you love me, Peter?"

Peter answered, "Yes, Lord, you know that I love you."

They walked in silence together until Jesus asked again, "Peter, do you love me?"

Peter must have been puzzled. "Why is Jesus asking me again?" Peter wondered. But he answered, "Yes, Lord, you know I love you."

As Jesus was questioning him, Peter must have remembered how, after Jesus was arrested, he had three times denied being a friend of Jesus. He had been afraid of being hurt by Jesus' enemies. "Now Jesus is giving me another chance," Peter thought to himself.

In a moment, Jesus asked him a third time, "Do you love me?"

Peter answered, "Lord, you know everything. You know well that I love you."

"Then feed my sheep," Jesus said to him.

Based on John 21:15–17

196 Scripture

Teaching Tips

Help the students appreciate the power of their words. Have them give examples of times when someone's words have hurt their feelings. Their examples may include instances of name-calling, teasing, yelling, or being lied about. Discuss with the students how they felt when hurtful things were said to them or about them. Then ask the students to share experiences of hearing encouraging, caring, forgiving, or supportive words. Remind the students to think before they speak. Emphasize that words can hurt or help.

Enriching the Lesson

Distribute drawing paper and crayons or markers. Invite the students to draw a picture of a third grader living out one of the spiritual works of mercy. You might assign a work to each one of the students or allow them to make their own choice. Encourage the students to draw a realistic and practical situation. Afterward, encourage volunteers to display their work and explain it.

Encouraging Others

Peter knew that Jesus forgave him for the weakness and fear that led Peter to pretend he didn't know Jesus. Now Jesus was telling Peter to support, forgive, and encourage others. This is what Jesus meant when he said, "Feed my sheep."

Whenever we help and care for one another by performing any of the spiritual works of mercy, we encourage others. When we do not take time to comfort someone whose feelings have been hurt or to perform whatever work of mercy may be needed, that person may think that nobody cares. We all need to do our part to show that Catholics are caring and loving people.

Activity

Place an **X** before each sentence that says something a caring and loving Catholic might say.

_____ "Don't bother me! You should be able to do that on your own by now!"

__X__ "We're all here for you. How can we help?"

__X__ "It's okay. I know you didn't mean to hurt her."

_____ "I really don't have time to listen. I have enough problems of my own."

__X__ "I know someone who can help you make the right decision."

> ### We Believe
>
> Jesus teaches us by word and example to care for people who are unhappy, who have problems, or who need help. In the spiritual works of mercy, the Church tells us some ways we can show care and concern.

Doctrine 197

Focus on

Priests The parish priest is someone whose ministry involves daily practice of the spiritual works of mercy. Invite the students to look at the list of the spiritual works and think about what a priest does in the community. Stress that long before modern counseling, the parish priest was an advice giver to people in need, someone who was willing to listen, a comforter to those who hurt, and a shoulder for those in mourning. You might invite a priest to speak to the class about his ministry to others.

Understanding the Message

Read with the students "Encouraging Others" on page 197. You may want to explain to the students that Jesus had chosen Peter to lead the Church after Jesus returned to his Father in heaven. Note that Jesus encouraged, supported, and forgave Peter and then asked him to treat others as Jesus had treated him. Emphasize that Jesus knew that the leaders of the Church would need the qualities of encouragement, support, and forgiveness in order to lead the Church community as Jesus wanted them to.

or...

Tell the following Scripture stories about Peter in your own words: Matthew 4:18–22; 8:14–15; 16:13–19; 26:69–75 and Luke 24:1–12. Have the class form six groups. Assign each group one of the Scripture stories to act out. Provide time for the students to practice and make up additional dialogue. After each group gives its presentation, ask the students how they think Peter felt. If the students say that they think Peter felt worried, ashamed, puzzled, sad, or confused, ask them what words he needed to hear to make him feel better.

Learning the Doctrine

Call on a volunteer to read aloud the We Believe statement on page 197. Ask the students if they have any questions about the meaning of what has been read. Encourage the students to memorize the statement once they understand its meaning.

Step 3/CONCLUSION

Learning How to Live Our Faith

Identifying Caring Expressions

Explain the directions for the activity on page 197 and have the students work independently to complete it. When everyone has finished marking the caring and loving statements, invite the students to read them aloud together. Ask the students to give an example of a time when they expressed Christian love and care in words to someone else. Have them explain whom they spoke to, what the situation was, and what they said.

DAY 4
MORALITY

Objective

This lesson helps the students want to live the spiritual works of mercy as Saint Angela Merici did.

Step 1/INTRODUCTION

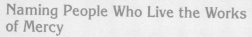

Learning About Our Lives

Naming People Who Live the Works of Mercy

Encourage the students to identify people in their lives who are living examples of the works of mercy. Explain that the people they name should be people who encourage, comfort, forgive, and are patient with other people and those who pray for them, help them make good choices, teach them with love, and give them good advice. Invite each student to participate in this discussion by naming at least one person and explaining how this person lives the spiritual works of mercy.

Step 2/DEVELOPMENT

Learning About Our Faith

Reading a Biography

Direct attention to the story "Spiritual Helpers" on page 198. Discuss Saint Angela Merici's life using the following questions.

- What led Angela to care for others? (*She knew what it felt like to be sad and lonely because her parents and sister had died when she was young.*)

- What did Angela do for the poor children in her village? (*She took care of them and taught them about Jesus and the Church.*)

- Why did other women join Angela in her work? (*They wanted to help her do her good works.*)

- What was Angela's community called? (*The Ursulines*)

- How did the Ursulines spend their time? (*By praying and helping people*)

- What were the Ursuline Sisters the first to do? (*They were the first Sisters to teach young girls. Explain to the students that poor children rarely were able to go to school*

198

Spiritual Helpers

We are called to forgive, comfort, encourage, support, and pray for others. We can follow the example of people like Angela Merici. Angela Merici, a saint, is someone who lived the spiritual works of mercy in an interesting and unique way.

As a young girl, Angela reached out to people who were hurting inside. Her father, mother, and sister died when Angela was very young. She knew what it felt like to be sad and lonely. This helped her care for others.

Angela loved children. Many of the children in her village in Italy were very poor. She wanted them to know about Jesus and the Church. She spent much of her time teaching them and taking care of them. She also brought comfort and hope to their families.

Many young women were inspired by Angela and her good works. They wanted to join her and help her with her work. So she organized them into a community of sisters called the Ursulines. They spent their time praying and helping people.

The Ursulines were the first community of sisters formed to teach young girls. The sisters still teach. They also spend their lives caring for people and helping them by living all the spiritual and corporal works of mercy.

Focus on

Saint Angela Merici Saint Angela Merici lived from 1474 to 1540. She was born in northern Italy, in the small town of Brescia. We celebrate Saint Angela's feast day on January 27. In the Opening Prayer on this day, we pray, "Lord, may Saint Angela commend us to your mercy; may her charity and wisdom help us to be faithful to your teaching and to follow it in our lives." Angela chose to name her order after Saint Ursula, who as the patron saint of medieval universities was viewed as a leader of women.

Teaching Tips

Contact your diocesan vocations office to obtain the address of the Ursuline Provincial House or the central office. Work with the class to write a letter to the Ursulines requesting additional information on Saint Angela's life, the history of the Ursulines, and the Ursuline community today. Use these materials to create a bulletin board in your classroom.

Activity

Write a thank-you letter to a student in your class, to someone on your school's staff, or to a family member. Thank the person for showing you how their performing a spiritual work of mercy has made a big difference to you.

Spiritual work of mercy performed: _____

_____

Dear _____,

★ ★ ★ ★ ★
Enriching
the Lesson

You may wish to extend the activity on page 199 by suggesting that the students keep a journal over the next month on the corporal works of mercy and spiritual works of mercy. They might record in their journal the actions of people who treat them in ways that express these works of mercy. They could also record things that they do for others that show that the works of mercy are becoming a part of their lives.

---

during the time Angela lived. As a result, these children were illiterate when they grew up, and those who wanted to improve their lives were often unable to do so.)

■ Which of the spiritual works of mercy did Angela live? (*All of the spiritual works of mercy are possible answers.*)

Step 3/CONCLUSION

Learning How to Live Our Faith

Writing Thank-You Letters

Direct attention to the writing activity on page 199 and read aloud the instructions. Explain to the students that they might want to write their letters to the persons they named in Step 1 of this lesson. Tell the students to explain in their letters that they have learned about the spiritual works of mercy and why they think that the person to whom they are writing the letter is an example of one or more of these works of mercy. Allow the students quiet time to work on their own to complete the letters. Afterward, invite students to share their letters out loud. Be careful not to insist on this, as these letters may be very personal.

At the end of the week, if possible, allow the students to carefully tear out their letters and supply envelopes for them to mail the letters. If it is not feasible for the students to tear a page from their books, you may want to have them write the letters onto theme paper, decorate the letters, and then mail them.

or...

As an alternative to having the students mail their letters, you might work with the class to design a "Spiritual Worker of Mercy" award. This might be a certificate, a ribbon, or a badge of some sort. If possible, encourage the students to invite to the prayer celebration for Day 5 the persons to whom they wrote their letters. At the celebration, the students can read aloud or present their letters and then present the awards.

Objective

This lesson helps the students thank God for people who have encouraged them to live good lives.

Reading the Text

Read with the class "Praying in Our Own Words" on page 200. Remind the students that praying for the living and the dead is one of the spiritual works of mercy. Invite the students to think of the persons they want to offer thanks for in the prayer celebration. Tell the students that they will use their own words to pray. Decide with the class whether they would prefer to write out their prayers before the celebration or if they want to offer spontaneous prayers. If they choose the written format, allow time for them to compose their prayers.

Preparing for Prayer

Have the class form seven groups. Assign each group one of the seven spiritual works of mercy. Invite each group to prepare one of the following for the prayer celebration: a symbol, skit, banner, or poster that represents the assigned work of mercy; a TV interview of someone who has witnessed a work of mercy; or anything else they can think of to teach others their spiritual work of mercy.

Choose a volunteer to read the parable of the Unforgiving Servant (Matthew 18:21–35) during your celebration.

Praying Together

Begin the prayer service by praying words similar to these: "God, you call us to care about others. We offer our prayers today for our brothers and sisters in faith, who have encouraged us to live as faithful Catholics by caring for the needs of others' minds, hearts, and spirits." Then encourage the students to offer their written or verbal prayers. When they have finished, recite together the prayer on page 200.

Next, invite each group to come forward to present its work of mercy. Then listen to the reading of the parable. Share a sign of peace or encouragement with them to conclude.

Praying in Our Own Words

Today, we will each thank God for someone who has encouraged us to live as faithful Catholics. The person may be someone who has helped us make a good decision or someone who has helped us understand something better. It may be someone who has given us advice or has comforted us. It may be someone who has shown us patience or forgiveness. It may be someone who has prayed with us. Maybe someone right here in our classroom has performed one of these spiritual works of mercy in our lives.

God, we thank you for the love and encouragement that our friends and families give us. Help us to be ready and willing always to encourage anyone who needs our help or our prayers. Amen.

200   Prayer

★ ★ ★ ★ Enriching the Lesson ★

To encourage the students to continue praying for the living and the dead, make a prayer box with an opening at the top. Place it in a prominent spot in the classroom. Have the students write on a slip of paper the name of someone for whom they wish to pray. Tell them that the prayer box will be a part of the class prayer once a week for the rest of the year. Encourage the students to drop a name into the box at any time. Assure them that the class will then pray for these written petitions.

Chapter Review

Choose words or actions from the "billboard" below that will help you along the road to becoming a loving and caring Christian. Write the words on the road.

Write the answers to the first two questions.

1. What does *spiritual* mean? _*Spiritual* means "affecting the mind, heart, or spirit."_

2. Name the spiritual works of mercy. _Help others make good choices. Teach_
   those who lack knowledge. Give advice to those
   who are confused. Comfort those who are hurting.
   Be patient with others. Forgive injuries. Pray for the
   living and the dead.

Cheer the
fainthearted;
support the weak;
be patient toward all.
**Based on
1 Thessalonians 5:14**

3. Talk about what your life would be like without people who live out the spiritual works of mercy.

Review 201

★ ★ ★ ★ ★
Enriching
the Lesson

Have the students create a review activity for the spiritual works of mercy. Divide the class into groups and have each group come up with examples of people displaying each of the spiritual works of mercy. Place each example on an index card with the spiritual work identified on the reverse side. Have the students challenge each other to correctly identify the work of mercy that is portrayed on the card. Save the cards from year to year as a way of reviewing the works of mercy.

Choosing Words and Actions

Ask a volunteer to read aloud the directions for the first exercise on page 201 and then have the students work independently to complete it. Afterward, have the students read aloud the words they chose from the list.

Completing the Chapter Review

Instruct the students to write answers to the next two review questions on page 201. Then ask for volunteers to read their responses aloud to the class. Encourage all to participate in the discussion of the final question. Help the students appreciate that without the spiritual works of mercy, the world would be a less caring, helpful, and loving place.

Discussing the Chapter

Provide time for the students to talk about what they learned in the past two chapters. Answer any questions they might have about the spiritual works of mercy and the corporal works of mercy. Recall all the good work the students have done during the past two weeks in learning how to care for the physical and spiritual needs of others. Take a poll about which activity or Scripture story they liked best.

Praying with the Scriptural Verse

Call on a student to read the scriptural verse at the bottom of the page. Explain that *fainthearted* means "timid or lacking courage." Explain that the scriptural verse tells the students three things they can do for others. Invite each student to offer a brief, spontaneous prayer about living the challenges of this verse; for example, "Lord, help me to give good advice to my friends when they share a problem with me."

Completing the Chart

Explain the directions for completing the chart on page 202. Direct the students to first write on the lines provided in the text what they remember learning about the greatest commandments, the Ten Commandments, the Corporal Works of Mercy, and the Spiritual Works of Mercy. Then have students list in the next column what they will do or how they will respond as a result of what they have learned about these important teachings. Allow sufficient time for the students to work on their own to complete the chart. Afterward, check the students' responses. Answer any questions the students may have about the Church's moral teachings.

Looking Back: Self-assessment

The critical reflection questions below give the students an opportunity to sharpen their thinking skills. The questions can be used for a class discussion or for an independent writing activity.

■ Which idea in this unit did you find the most challenging? Why?

■ Which picture in this unit did you like best?

■ What did you like about it?

■ Which person in this unit would you like to learn more about?

UNIT 4 ORGANIZER

In each heart below, write one thing you remember from the chapter and one caring action you will take because of what you learned.

Our Church teaches us to love

Our Church teaches us the Commandments

Christians comfort others

Christians help others

202 Organizer

202

UNIT 4 REVIEW

Place an X before each true sentence.

1. __X__ Scribes were well-educated Jews who studied and explained God's law.

2. _____ The commandments are seven signs of God's presence.

3. __X__ To value a law is to believe it is important.

4. _____ We can love God without loving other people.

5. __X__ To love God is the greatest commandment.

6. __X__ Reverence is an attitude of respect, care, and honor.

7. _____ Jesus said we should love ourselves more than anybody else.

8. __X__ The Sabbath is a day for rest and prayer.

9. _____ Pharisees did not think God's laws were important.

10. __X__ Mercy is loving concern or compassion.

Write one of the Ten Commandments that shows our love for God.

_____

_____

Write two of the Ten Commandments that show our love for others.

1. _____

_____

2. _____

_____

Reviewing the Unit

The purpose of the Unit Review is to reinforce concepts presented in the preceding four chapters and to check the students' understanding. After explaining the directions, give the students sufficient time to complete the two-page review. Answer any questions they may have.

You may wish to extend the review activity on page 203 by having the students rewrite the statements that are false to make them into true statements. (*Possible responses include: 2. The commandments are ten signs of God's presence; 4. We cannot love God without loving other people; 7. Jesus said we should love others as much as we love ourselves; and 9. Pharisees based their entire lives on living according to God's laws.*)

Testing

After the students have completed the Unit Review, you may wish to distribute copies of the Unit 4 Test from the Unit Tests booklet in The Resourceful Teacher Package.

Optional Unit Project

Review with the students Jesus' commandments to love and the Ten Commandments. Remind them again that God's commandments are guides to loving God and caring for others. They are guides to happiness. Then invite the students to make on poster-size paper advertisements that seek to convince people to keep the commandments of God. The students should select Jesus' commandments to love or one of the Ten Commandments and create eye-catching, convincing ads. Allow time and ample art supplies for the students to complete the assignment. After the posters have been completed, let the students display their ads.

Complete each sentence by writing the correct word. Then circle the number of each corporal work of mercy and underline the number of each spiritual work of mercy.

1. Forgive _____injuries_____ .

(2.) Visit those in _____prison_____ .

(3.) _____Visit_____ the sick.

4. Be _____patient_____ with others.

(5.) Shelter the _____homeless_____ .

(6.) Give _____drink_____ to the thirsty.

7. _____Comfort_____ those who are hurting.

8. Pray for the _____living_____ and the dead.

Match the people listed in Column A with their achievements listed in Column B.

Column A	Column B
A. Angela Merici	__C__ worked among lepers on an island called Molokai
B. Dorothy Day	__B__ started *The Catholic Worker* newspaper and Catholic Worker houses for the poor
C. Father Damien	__D__ taught about the importance of love
D. Jesus	__A__ taught young girls and brought comfort and hope to their families

COMMUNICATION SKILLS for PROBLEM SOLVERS

To *communicate* with someone means to give him or her information. Being able to give someone information about how you feel and what you need is an important part of problem solving. It is important to be aware that your tone of voice, your body posture, and your words all work together to send information about how you feel. Sometimes your tone of voice gives a message that is different from the message your body posture gives. And it is always important to choose your words carefully. This could help avoid confusion.

Activity Communication Choices

Look at the two illustrations below. Circle the number of the illustration that you think better communicates what the person with the problem is trying to say.

I'D LIKE MY HAT BACK.

STOP! I'M MAD! AND I WANT MY HAT BACK **NOW**!

Everyone knows that **IGNORING SOMEONE** can be a helpful solution when that person is teasing you. Look at the following illustrations. Circle the number of the picture that shows the person who is doing the best job of ignoring.

THAT'S NOT TRUE!
LISA L-I-K-E-S DAVID.

LISA L-I-K-E-S DAVID.

Asking for help is sometimes the best solution to a problem. We cannot always solve our problems all by ourselves. But knowing *when* to ask for help and when to try to solve the problem on our own is sometimes hard to figure out. For example, nobody wants to be called a tattletale, but sometimes telling an adult about a problem is very important or may even be necessary.

Day to Day   205

Day to Day

Objective

This lesson helps the students understand that how we communicate is an important aspect of problem solving.

Introducing the Lesson

Have the students open their books to page 205. Ask one or more volunteers to read aloud "Communication Skills for Problem Solvers." Call on students to demonstrate different tones of voice and body postures; for example, a pleasant tone of voice versus an angry one, or a shy body posture versus an assertive one. Emphasize that, in addition to the words a person says, important messages are conveyed by the sound of the person's voice and by his or her body posture.

Completing the Activity

Direct the students' attention to the first pair of illustrations on page 205. Read aloud the first paragraph under "Communication Choices." Have the students study the two pictures and read the captions. Then ask them to circle the number of the picture that they think shows the best response. Use the following questions to facilitate discussion.

■ How are the two pictures different from each other? (*One picture shows someone feeling shy and uncomfortable about letting the other boys know what he wants. The other picture shows an assertive response, or one that communicates how the sender of the message is feeling without being aggressive or offensive to the other boys.*)

■ What tone of voice would the boy use in the first picture? In the second picture? (*The tone of voice in the first picture would probably be quiet and rather meek. The tone of the voice in the second picture would probably be strong and assertive.*)

■ What does the boy's body posture communicate in the second picture? (*It communicates anger and assertiveness.*)

Ask for a volunteer to read aloud the paragraph above the second pair of pictures on page 205 and have the students complete the activity.

Lesson continues on page 206.

Invite the students' responses to the following questions.

■ Have you ever had an experience of trying to ignore someone who is teasing you? What was that like?

■ Have you ever tried to tease someone who was good at ignoring? What was that like?

Explain to the students that another way to deal with teasing is to try agreeing with the other person. For example, in the illustration shown, Lisa could reply, "Well, I guess you're right. So what's the big deal?" Agreeing often catches the other person off guard and he or she has no further reason to tease.

Ask for a volunteer to read aloud the paragraph in the box at the bottom of page 205. Then direct the students' attention to the pair of illustrations at the top of page 206. Ask the students to read the directions and complete the activity. Then ask the following questions.

■ Which picture suggests a situation in which it is most important to ask for help? (*The second one*)

■ What is the difference between being a tattle-tale and asking for help? (*Usually we think of a tattle-tale as someone who tells on others as his or her main way of trying to solve problems. Although it is important to try to solve problems for ourselves by using our problem-solving skills, telling an adult about a problem is sometimes the best solution, especially if safety is an issue.*)

Concluding the Lesson

Read with the class "Problem Solving Reminders." Then ask the students to read silently "Following Jesus" at the bottom of page 206. If time permits, you may wish to distribute Bibles and have the students read Luke 6:27–36. Emphasize that, as followers of Jesus, we are called to love our enemies as well as our friends.

Read aloud the directions in the prayer box. Invite the students to complete the sentences and then allow time for them to reflect silently on their prayers.

206

Activity When to Ask for Help

Look at the pictures below. Circle the number of the picture that shows a problem that requires asking for help.

Problem Solving Reminders

1. Remember to stop and think.
2. Think of as many solutions as you can.
3. Think about the consequences of a solution before trying the solution.
4. If the first solution does not work, try another.
5. If you cannot get any solutions to work, have trouble thinking of any solutions, or the problem is dangerous for you or others, seek help from an adult.
6. Remember that Jesus is always with you. Pray to Jesus, and ask him for his help.

Following Jesus

In Luke 6:27–36, Jesus tells us that we are to love our enemies. If we love only those who love us, we are not doing all that we can do as Christians. So even when people treat us in ways that make us angry or uncomfortable, we should try to communicate with them in a loving way.

PRAYER

Write a prayer to Jesus and ask for his help with a problem you are having a hard time solving. Use one of the following sentences to help you begin.

Jesus, I wish I could _____ .

Jesus, please help me with _____ .

Jesus, my biggest problem is _____ .

Jesus, I'm sad. Please help me figure out what

to do about _____ .

Opening Doors
A Take-Home Magazine™

THIS IS OUR FAITH

© Silver Burdett Ginn Inc.

Growing Closer

YOUR FAMILY PROBABLY HAS SOME WONDERFUL STORIES to tell! Keep these stories alive by telling them often to one another. Reminisce about a favorite relative or friend. By telling the story over and over again, your family will remember that special person or event and keep the memory alive from one generation to the next.

WRITE A FAMILY LETTER or telephone a relative or friend who has moved away. Allow everyone to contribute a few lines of news, a local newspaper article of interest, or a drawing. Tell the person receiving the letter or phone call how your family remembers him or her even though you may not often be together.

Looking Ahead

Four major categories of ministry were evident in the earliest Christian communities. They are extensions of Jesus' own ministry. Unit 5 will deal with these four categories: ministries of the word, ministries of building community, ministries of worship or liturgy, and ministries of service.

8

Opening Doors ~~

Sending the Magazine Home

As you complete Unit 4 with your class, assist the students in carefully removing *Opening Doors: A Take-Home Magazine* (two pages) from their texts by separating the pages from the book along the perforations. Demonstrate how to fold the two pages to form an eight-page booklet.

When the magazines are folded, take time to explain each section of the magazine to the students. Allow the students to ask any questions they may have. Ask the students to take the magazine home and encourage their families to read it with them and to participate in the suggested activities. You may wish to attach a letter of your own, encouraging the family to use the magazine each time their child brings it home.

Our Memory, Faith, and Vision

For nearly twenty centuries, Christians have shared a memory, faith, and vision. We have been called to *remember* what Jesus did for us, to *celebrate* his presence with us now, and to *believe* and trust that we share in the resurrection of Jesus.

In the Memorial Acclamation at Mass, we proclaim the mystery of Jesus' passion, death, and resurrection, and of his coming again in glory. Called not only to remember but also to make present this mystery, the Church unites herself with Jesus in the eucharistic celebration.

In Judaism and Christianity, remembering is more than nostalgic recollection. It is a reenactment of the event recalled. The Jewish people remember in this way when they share the Passover Seder. In this ritual meal, special foods help Jews remember in a vivid manner some of the most important events in Jewish history. They eat unleavened bread as a reminder of their hurried flight from their captors. They eat a claylike mixture of apples, nuts, and wine to remind them of the mortar their ancestors used to build bricks while they were slaves to the Egyptians.

After Alice's many persistent visits with officials, Monmouth County had its first shelter for the homeless.

A short time later, when Alice saw abandoned houses being bought by developers and leveled to makes space for luxury condos and other businesses, she sought to secure some of those abandoned houses for the poor. Alice Kelsey is still pursuing her goal to have every community along the Jersey shore donate one abandoned house to be suitably repaired and then purchased at an affordable rate by a low-income family. Working just enough hours to support herself, she reserves plenty of time to devote to the poor.

Poverty and pain respect no age or geographic boundaries. In northeastern Wisconsin, Father "Marty" Carr operates a shelter called *The Place 2B*. Centered in a repossessed motel in Oshkosh, this ministry serves runaway teenagers, mothers and children from abusive families, transients, and many other homeless persons. The hospitality includes not only shelter and food but also counseling services and recreation. An ongoing food pantry, daily meals, and special holiday meals serve hundreds of area residents.

Among the many volunteers at *The Place 2B* are area teenagers who want to do their part. They might cook or serve meals, run errands, or simply listen to the concerns of those teens seeking help or companionship. The recreational facility also meets the needs of these teens to simply come together with their friends. With the support of many churches, the facility for Father Carr's ministry has truly become "The Place To Be!" Like Alice Kelsey, he and his helpers show us that a heritage of caring continues when the followers of Jesus work together to make a difference!

A Heritage of Caring Continues

Belgian Father Damien de Veuster sacrificed his health and life to work among the lepers at Molokai, Hawaii. Saint Francis of Assisi gave to the poor even the clothes he was wearing. Saint Elizabeth of Hungary was forced to give up living as a princess in a castle because she persisted in helping the poor people in the hospitals she had built at the edge of her castle property.

In today's society, it still takes a real commitment to help the poor and forgotten. How can such difficult situations be helped? The opportunities to do so are often very close to home. Two remarkable individuals who have spent the better part of their lives generously meeting the challenge to serve others in this way are Alice Kelsey and Father Martin P. Carr.

Alice Kelsey is an advocate for the homeless who believes in getting things done. After learning that the homeless in affluent Monmouth County, New Jersey, did not have a place of refuge, Alice moved quickly to find help. She discovered that two years earlier a U.S. Army post had offered the county a barracks for the homeless.

6

When Catholics remember Jesus in the eucharistic liturgy, we do much more than just recall the first time Jesus gave his body and blood to his disciples. We believe that Jesus gives himself to us again each time we share the Eucharist.

"Christ has died, Christ is risen, Christ will come again."

Through the eyes of faith, we recognize Jesus' living presence in the Eucharist and celebrate the life-giving strength we receive. We believe that because Jesus rose from the dead, our lives, too, will be transformed by God.

Like the Eucharist, hope is a gift that we not only receive but also make present "as we wait in joyful hope for the coming of our Savior, Jesus Christ." And like Jesus, we proclaim the promise of the kingdom not only with words but also with our lives. When we gather to *remember* and *celebrate*, and when we love and serve one another, we keep alive the vision of new and eternal life that we *believe* we have already begun to share!

3

A Gift to Remember

4

Jesus asks us to remember him when we gather together to share the meal he has provided for us. Work through these pages with your child. Help your child appreciate Jesus' request that we remember him by sharing in the Eucharist and by being Christ for one another.

Imagine that your best friend has moved away. You feel sad, lonely, and discouraged. All of those favorite games you played together and all of those special places where you spent time together no longer feel or look the same. "I'll never forget you" and "Write to me" become very important words at this disappointing time.

Jesus and his friends may have felt the same kind of sadness when the time came for him to leave them. Before he died, Jesus gave his friends a very special way to

remember him. He blessed, broke, and shared bread with them. And they shared a cup of wine. After telling them that this food and drink were his body and blood which would be broken and given for them, Jesus told his friends to remember him whenever they shared this food and drink. He also promised to be with them always, even after he died. Whenever Jesus' friends gathered together to remember and to celebrate, Jesus was with them. As Jesus' friends we, too, remember Jesus when we share this special gift, this holy food. We, too, remember that Jesus is with us in a special way in the Eucharist.

Sharing in the Eucharist is one very important way we remember Jesus. But there are many other ways, too. Fill in the activity below with ways you can remember Jesus. The first one is done for you.

I remember Jesus when I *am kind to others.*

I remember Jesus when I _____.

I remember Jesus when I _____.

I remember Jesus when I _____.

I remember Jesus when I _____.

I remember Jesus when I _____.

When you go to Mass, listen for the words of Jesus that ask us to remember him whenever we gather for Eucharist.

5

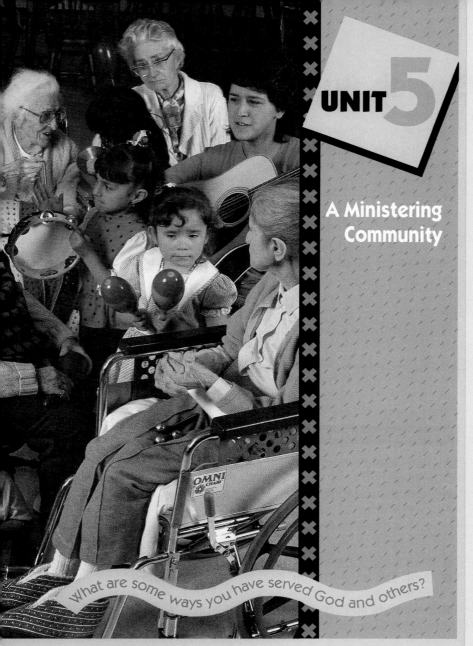

UNIT 5

A Ministering Community

What are some ways you have served God and others?

To help the students understand and appreciate the Church's ministries of community building, of the word, of worship, and of service.

Doctrinal Summaries

CHAPTER 17
Jesus is with us to unite us as a community of his followers. He calls us all through Baptism to share in his ministry of building community.

CHAPTER 18
The Church today continues Jesus' ministry of the word. Each of us is called to share God's word with others and to live its message.

CHAPTER 19
Jesus prayed both alone and with others. Paul encouraged the first Christians to worship God together. We are all called to take an active part in the Church's worship today.

CHAPTER 20
Jesus spent his life serving people in need. He calls us to share in his ministry of love, justice, and peace.

Note:
As you prepare this unit, you may wish to refer to the reference section, *Our Catholic Heritage,* beginning on page 327.

Additional resources for Unit 5 include a Unit Test and a Family Letter as well as a video and selections from the THIS IS OUR FAITH Music Program. You might also find it helpful to preview *Saints and Other Holy People* and *Prayer Celebrations* for possibilities to enhance the unit.

Introducing the UNIT

Ask the students what they think is happening in the photograph on page 211. Suggest that the young people can be ministering to the older people by sharing their music, by cheering them, or by just keeping them company. It is also possible that the young students are being ministered to by the older people in the photograph. Emphasize that ministry can be a two-way street. Elicit responses to the unit-focus question.

Vocabulary

ministry
ministry of
  community
  building
pastor
deacon
diocese
bishop
pope
ministry of the
  word

prophet
lector
epistles
praise
worship
ministry of
  worship
justice
ministry of
  service

17 Our Church Builds Community

Objectives　～～～～～

To help the students

■ Recognize that the Church continues Jesus' ministry of building community.
■ Identify leaders in the Church.
■ Name gifts and talents that can be used to build community.
■ Learn that Jesus wants us to cooperate with him in building unity.
■ Pray for community builders in our families, school, and parish and review the chapter.

Chapter Outline　～～～～～～

	Step 1 **Learning About Our Lives**	**Step 2** **Learning About Our Faith**	**Step 3** **Learning How to Live Our Faith**
Day 1	■ Introduce the chapter. ■ Read and discuss the story. *ABOUT 15 MINUTES*	■ Learn about community building. ■ Learn the vocabulary. *ABOUT 10 MINUTES*	■ Identify talents and gifts. *ABOUT 5 MINUTES*
Day 2	■ Consider the human body. *ABOUT 3 MINUTES*	■ Read a scriptural story. ■ Learn about the Church community. ■ Review vocabulary and doctrine. *ABOUT 22 MINUTES*	■ Name community builders. *ABOUT 5 MINUTES*
Day 3	■ Complete a name activity. *ABOUT 7 MINUTES*	■ Identify qualities of Church leaders. *ABOUT 10 MINUTES*	■ Complete an activity. ■ Write a prayer. *ABOUT 13 MINUTES*
Day 4	■ Discuss experiences and feelings. *ABOUT 6 MINUTES*	■ Discuss a picture. ■ Read the Scripture story. ■ Remember the Church's call to be catholic. *ABOUT 14 MINUTES*	■ Discuss the questions. *ABOUT 10 MINUTES*
Day 5	**Prayer** Prepare for prayer; pray together. **Review** Complete a matching activity; fill in review answers; reflect on a scriptural verse.		

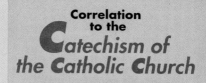

Correlation
to the
**Catechism of
the Catholic Church**

Paragraphs
**543, 791, 801, 806, 871,
873, 951, 2045**

Plan Ahead ∼∼∼∼∼∼

	Preparing Your Class	**Materials Needed**	**Additional Resources**
Day 1	Read through the lesson plan for this session. Consider your students' gifts and talents that can be used to help build community.	■ chalkboard or posterboard ■ pencils or pens	As you plan this chapter, consider using the following materials from The Resourceful Teacher Package. ■ *Classroom Activity Sheets 17 and 17a* ■ *Family Activity Sheets 17 and 17a* ■ *Chapter 17 Test* ■ *Prayers for Every Day* ■ *Projects: Grade 3* You may also wish to refer to the following Big Book. ■ *We Celebrate the Sacraments,* page 19 In preparing the students for the Sunday readings, you may wish to use Silver Burdett Ginn's *Getting Ready for Sunday* student and teacher materials.
Day 2	Read through the lesson plan for this session. Bring to class pictures of Pope John Paul II and your local bishop.	■ copies of diocesan newspapers ■ pencils or pens	
Day 3	Read through the lesson plan for this session.	■ pencils or pens	
Day 4	Read through the lesson plan for this session.	■ pencils or pens	
Day 5	Read through the lesson plan for this session. Prepare an environment for prayer in the classroom.	■ construction paper ■ glue or paste ■ pencils or pens	

BOOKS FOR THE JOURNEY

The Children's Illustrated Bible. Stories retold by Selina Hastings. Dorling Kindersley, 1994. "Paul's Letters," pp. 306–307. The letter of Paul to the people of Corinth describing the Church as one body with many members.

Just One Wish. Arcadio Lobato. Picture Book Studio, 1989. A simple shepherd's *unselfishness* convinces the local townspeople that their selfishness had destroyed their community.

MORE BOOKS FOR THE JOURNEY

Mrs. Katz and Tush. Patricia Polacco. Bantam, 1992. The friendship between an old woman and a young boy makes life happier and more worthwhile for both of them.

Praise for the Singing. Collected by Madelaine Gill. Little, Brown & Co., 1993. "We Gather Together" by Edwin T. Buehrer and Adrian Valerius, pp. 60–61. A song that rejoices in community and the making of it.

REDUCED CLASSROOM ACTIVITIES

NAME _____

OUR CHURCH BUILDS COMMUNITY

Unscramble the underlined word in each sentence. Then write the word correctly on the line provided.

1. Paul was a <u>aredel</u> of the early Church. leader
2. Paul helped begin the first <u>nihsrtCia</u> communities. Christian
3. Many of Paul's <u>stltree</u> became part of the Bible. letters
4. Today the Church continues Jesus' <u>ynimsirt</u> of community building. ministry
5. The Holy Spirit gives each <u>orepsn</u> special talents. person
6. Paul said, "There are many ways to serve <u>dGo</u>." God
7. The <u>eopp</u> is the leader of the Catholic Church. pope
8. Jesus prayed that all people would live in unity and <u>aecpe</u>. peace
9. Paul became an <u>tspaloe</u> after Jesus' resurrection. apostle
10. Paul said, "We are all part of one <u>ybod</u>." body

The Holy Spirit gives each person special gifts and talents to use for the good of all.

To the Teacher: This activity follows the Scripture story "One Body, Many Members."

Chapter 17 Our Church Builds Community   THIS IS OUR FAITH 3 **17**

NAME _____

WE HELP BUILD COMMUNITY

You play a very important part in building community. So do all your classmates. On the quilt below, draw a picture that shows how you helped build community in your class this year. Then draw how your class helped build community in your school. Write your name, the name of your classroom community, and the name of your school community in the circles. Use your school colors to decorate the quilt.

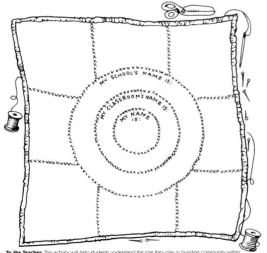

To the Teacher: This activity will help students understand the role they play in building community within the Church. Make a class "community quilt" by arranging finished squares on a bulletin board.

17a THIS IS OUR FAITH 3   **Chapter 17** Our Church Builds Community

THE EXPERIENCE OF COMMUNITY

Third-grade students come to class with a variety of experiences of community. Each person has been a member of a class at school. Each student has lived with other people at home. Most students have been members of various clubs, teams, and other parish, school, or community organizations.

The students have probably been part of a group where at some point the individuals did not work well together. They are aware of how easily a group can be pulled apart into various cliques. On the other hand they probably know that an individual can also pull a group together, from a position of authority or by leadership ability. The students tend to admire and follow someone who helps them become closer members of a family, team, club, or group.

THE BODY OF CHRIST

In this chapter the students will be introduced to the image of the Body of Christ so vividly described by Saint Paul in his letter to the Corinthians, a community that he established. Paul had become aware of problems, disputes, and questions that had surfaced in the young Christian community as the members tried to live out their baptismal calling.

Paul exhorts the new Christians at Corinth to put aside their differences and recognize that their diversity does not militate against unity and can even be a source of unity. He emphasizes that despite their differences they share a common name, Christian, which means "Christ-like." Paul calls them to fight against the things that divide them and to be one body, Christ's Church. Paul's letter is a graphic reminder that Jesus wants people to live as one community of love and to care for one another.

Throughout the letters of the New Testament, we are made aware of how Jesus' followers built community through the guidance of the Holy Spirit. In the Acts of the Apostles, we read about the community in the early Church. The people shared all that they had and often celebrated their faith in Jesus at eucharistic meals. Each follower of Christ came to realize his or her responsibility for fostering unity in the Church.

The same striving for community exists today. Each baptized and confirmed Christian shares in the community-building ministry of Christ. Everyone in the Church has the responsibility to pray for the guidance of the Holy Spirit in fostering community in the Church.

DAY 1
MORALITY

Objective

This lesson helps the students recognize that the Church continues Jesus' ministry of building community.

Step 1/INTRODUCTION

Learning About Our Lives

Introducing the Chapter

Discuss the chapter-focus question with the students. Have them name positive attitudes and actions that create unity among different groups of people. Then direct attention to the chapter title. Write the word *community* on the chalkboard or on posterboard and ask the students to recall the definition, which they may have already learned in Unit 1 of Grade 2. Elicit from the students that a community is a group of people who share something important. Ask the students to circle the word *community* within the chapter title in their student texts. Help them understand that in this chapter they will learn how Catholics are called to work as one to build community.

Reading and Discussing the Story

Call on volunteers to read aloud the story "Pulling Together" on pages 212 and 213. As the other students read along silently, ask them to focus on how well the Kowalski family works together. Then use the following questions to discuss the story.

■ What contributions did each family member make to their family outing? (*Grandpa prepared snacks and food for dinner; Jane, Michael, and Tony gathered firewood; Mom and Dad set up the tent.*)

■ Who took the lead in helping all the family members pull together? (*Mom and Jane*)

■ What turned out to be the best thing about the camping trip? (*Answers may vary.*)

Help the students appreciate that the best part of the camping trip was that the Kowalskis were working together as a family.

Our Church Builds Community

What are some things that help people live, play, study, and work together in unity?

Pulling Together

The Kowalski family had never gone camping before. All six family members—Mom, Dad, Grandpa, Jane, Tony, and Michael—climbed out of their minivan at the campsite in the hills. Everyone but Grandpa began exploring the area.

They walked into the woods, and they soon discovered a stream. Within a few minutes, they saw a deer, three squirrels, and six kinds of birds. Tony and Jane tripped over fallen branches. After half an hour in the woods, Mom, Dad, Jane, Tony, and Michael were hungry. They went back to their campsite.

Grandpa had snacks set out for them. While they ate, they planned how they would set up the tent, prepare dinner, and tell stories around the campfire after dark.

"Dad and I can set up the tent if Grandpa will start organizing everything for dinner," Mom suggested. "Then we can all cook the food together."

CURRICULUM CONNECTION

Social Studies *Community* is a traditional concept that appears in Social Studies textbooks and educational materials. Have the students explore how *community* is presented in their Social Studies program. Or have them explore how *community* is defined in reference material. Ask the students to compare what they find with what they have learned about *community* in their Religion book. How are the treatments similar and how are they different?

"The boys and I can get wood for a fire," Jane volunteered.

All agreed and set to work. Everything went almost as planned. Dad and Mom got the tent up, but it took longer than they thought. Grandpa set the table and prepared the corn, hot dogs, and hamburgers for cooking. Jane, Tony, and Michael found plenty of logs and branches for the fire, but only a few dry ones.

Together they cooked the food and enjoyed their dinner. The campfire sputtered and smoked more than it burned, but the stories were wonderful, as each person took a turn speaking.

Soon it was time for the Kowalskis to start thinking about getting settled into their sleeping bags in the tent. As Jane poured water on the fire, she said, "We haven't had this much fun together as a family for a long time." They all agreed!

Jesus Builds Community

Jesus had worked hard to bring people together. So much of his **ministry** was aimed at building community, especially among people who had faith in God.

Today the Church continues Jesus' **ministry of community building**. Communities grow when people use their gifts and talents for the good of the communities to which they belong. We are each called to use our gifts to help the Church community and other groups, such as our families, to grow in unity. We also welcome and encourage the gifts that other people bring to the Church and to these groups.

Vocabulary

ministry: the ways we serve God and all people according to God's special call

ministry of community building: ways in which we help the Church to grow in unity

✖ ✖ ✖ ✖ ✖ ✖ ✖ ✖ ✖ ✖ ✖

Morality   213

Learning About Our Faith

Learning About Community Building

Read through "Jesus Builds Community" on page 213 with the class. Ask the students to give examples of the different ways in which Jesus built community. (*Possible responses may include: inviting people to follow him; calling people to love God and one another; sharing meals with his followers; and treating everyone with respect, love, and caring.*) Emphasize that communities grow when people use their gifts and talents for the good of all.

Learning the Vocabulary

Point out the Vocabulary box on page 213. Call on volunteers to read aloud the words and definitions and have the students repeat them. Reinforce that we continue Christ's work in the world by participating in the ministry of community building.

Step 3/CONCLUSION

Learning How to Live Our Faith

Identifying Talents and Gifts

Invite the students to name some of the gifts and talents they share and use with their families that can be used to help build community in the Church. For example, students who like to sing or play the piano for the enjoyment of their family members might one day be part of the parish music ministry or participate in parish or school talent shows or musicals. Youngsters who like to cook may see that their culinary talents could one day contribute to a parish bake sale to raise money for a new parish building or another worthy cause.

or...

Write the following list on the chalkboard and have the students copy it on notebook paper, leaving a blank line after each group: a family; a team or class; a school or neighborhood; a club or troop; a band or chorus. Ask the students to write in the space what they can do or suggest to help each group work better together.

Enriching the Lesson

Work together to create a word gram by first brainstorming the word *community* with the students, asking them to think of all the things that are necessary to build communities (sharing, caring, work, help, teamwork, and so on). Next, print the word *community* vertically on the chalkboard and have the students find a word for each letter of the word *community*. (For example, for the *c* in community, you could use the word *caring*, since it has a *c* in it; for the *o*, *work*; for the *m*, *me*; and so on.

Teaching Tips

Explore with the students the different ways they have worked to build community in their class during the school year. What activities have they participated in since September that have helped them grow in unity? Have the students name the various ways they, as a community, have tried to serve God and one another by responding to Jesus' call to become a community.

213

SCRIPTURE/DOCTRINE

Objective

This lesson helps the students identify leaders in the Church.

Step 1/INTRODUCTION

Learning About Our Lives

Considering the Human Body

Ask the students to stand. Lead them through the following exercise by having them repeat the verse below as they touch each part of their bodies as it is named.

> Head and shoulders, knees and toes, knees and toes;
>
> Head and shoulders, knees and toes, knees and toes.
>
> And eyes and ears, and mouth, and nose;
>
> Head and shoulders, knees and toes, knees and toes.

Afterward, invite the students to comment on the miracle of the human body and how all the parts of our bodies work together. Tell the class that in this lesson they will learn how a leader of the Christian community in the first century used the example of the human body to help people understand how Jesus wanted Christians to work together.

Step 2/DEVELOPMENT

Learning About Our Faith

Reading a Scriptural Story

Have volunteers take turns reading aloud the story "One Body, Many Members" on page 214. Ask the following questions.

- Who was Paul? (*A leader in the early Church and an apostle*)
- What did Paul do? (*He helped begin the first Christian communities in many cities.*)
- To what did Paul compare the Church? (*The human body*)
- What did Paul say about the many members of the body? (*That we need each member*)
- What do we call Christ's body? (*The Church*)

One Body, Many Members

Paul was one of the leaders of the early Church. He was called to be an apostle after Jesus' death and resurrection. He helped begin the first Christian communities in many cities. And like Jesus, Paul worked hard to bring people of faith together as God's children.

Later, Paul and his partners wrote letters to those churches. Many of the letters became part of the Bible. Here is what one letter says about the Church and our part in it.

"There are many ways to serve God. There are many things to do. The Holy Spirit gives each person special gifts and talents to use for the good of all.

"We have all been baptized into one body. The Church is like a single body made up of many members. We need them all—hands, feet, eyes, and ears. The parts are many and different, but the body is one. The eye cannot say to the hand, 'I don't need you.' The head can't say to the feet, 'I have no need of you.'

"God made the body so that all its parts have concern for one another. If one part is hurt, the whole body shares the pain. If one part is honored, the whole body shares the joy.

"Now you are part of Christ's body, the Church. Each one of you has a part to play in the whole."

Based on 1 Corinthians 12

214   Scripture

(globe icon)	***Cultural Awareness***

Recall that we become Christians at Baptism. Discuss other things that Christians have in common, such as belief in Jesus, love of God and neighbor, and a willingness to care for others. Explain that Christians are, first of all, human beings and that as humans, we are independent and unique, yet we are also dependent on one another. Stress that Paul calls us to recognize how much we need one another and to work together in building community. Explore with the students how they can be partners with other Christians around the world.

The Church Builds Community

Jesus worked to build community wherever he went. Today the Church continues Jesus' ministry of community building. In the sacrament of Baptism, we are all made members of Christ's body, the Church. As we grow in faith, we come to understand that all members of the Church are called to share in the ministry of community building.

Some people are called through the sacrament of Holy Orders to be leaders in this important ministry. A **pastor** is a priest who leads a parish community. He is often assisted by other priests and professional lay ministers as well as lay volunteers in the task of building unity in the parish. A parish may also have a **deacon**, who is ordained to help the priest in serving the parish community in many different ways.

A parish community is part of a **diocese**, which is a larger community of many parishes that are located near one another. As pastoral leader of a diocese, a **bishop** works to build community among many parishes and between his diocese and the worldwide community of Catholics. The **pope**, bishop of Rome and leader of the Catholic Church all over the world, helps the worldwide Catholic community to grow in peace and harmony. The Catholic Church builds community not only among its own members but also with other Christian churches throughout the world.

Vocabulary

pastor: a priest who leads a parish community

deacon: a person ordained to help the priest in serving the parish community in many different ways

diocese: a community of many parishes that are located near one another

bishop: pastoral leader of a diocese

pope: bishop of Rome and leader of the Catholic Church all over the world

✗ ✗ ✗ ✗ ✗ ✗ ✗ ✗ ✗ ✗ ✗ ✗

Activity

Each member of the Church is called to help people live in harmony with one another.

Our **pastor** is _____ .

Our **bishop** is _____ .

Our **pope** is _____ .

We Believe

Jesus is with us to unite us as a community of his followers. He calls us all through Baptism to share in his ministry of building community.

Doctrine 215

Emphasize that each of us has been baptized into Christ's body, the Church, and that we each have special gifts that we are called to use.

Learning About the Church Community

Direct the students to read to themselves "The Church Builds Community" on page 215. Afterward, discuss the questions below.

- What are some of the barriers that Jesus broke down by his words and actions? (*Answers will vary.*)
- How are we called to share in the ministry of community building? (*Through Baptism*)
- What sacrament celebrates the call to ordained leadership in the Church? (*Holy Orders*)
- What is a pastor? (*A priest who leads a parish community*)
- What does a deacon do? (*Helps the priest in serving a parish community*)
- What is a diocese? (*A community of many parishes that are located near one another*)
- Who leads a diocese? (*A bishop*)
- What does the pope do? (*Leads the Catholic Church and helps the Catholic community to grow in peace and harmony*)
- What is one of the pope's titles? (*Bishop of Rome*)

Reviewing the Vocabulary and Doctrine

Call attention to the Vocabulary words on page 215. Encourage the students to memorize the definitions once they have understood what they mean. Point out the We Believe statement. Ask the students if they have any questions about this doctrinal summary.

Step 3/CONCLUSION

Learning How to Live Our Faith

Naming Community Builders

Have the students complete the activity at the bottom of page 215. If necessary, assist the students in spelling the names correctly. Then call on volunteers to read their answers aloud.

Focus on

Cardinals Some bishops are the leaders of very important dioceses or have the special responsibility of advising the pope. These bishops and archbishops are called cardinals. Together they are part of a group known as the College of Cardinals. One of their duties is to elect a new pope. The word *cardinal* comes from a word that means "hinge." The continuity of Church leadership depends, or hinges on, the College of Cardinals. Cardinals are appointed by the pope.

Enriching the Lesson

This is a good opportunity to consider with the students the roles of the pope and your bishop. Show photographs of the pope, especially pictures of his visits to the United States. Use copies of your diocesan newspaper to help the students appreciate how your bishop or bishops serve your diocese. Discuss with the class the different occasions on which the bishop has visited your parish.

215

Objective

This lesson helps the students name gifts and talents that can be used to build community.

Step 1/INTRODUCTION

Learning About Our Lives

Completing a Name Activity

Ask a volunteer to read aloud the first paragraph on page 216. Invite students to share their responses. Then have the students write their first names vertically on the lines provided or on another sheet of paper. Read and explain the directions for the activity. As the students work independently, move about the room and offer assistance. Allow time for the students to share with the group the words they have written. Praise them for their creativity in completing this activity.

Step 2/DEVELOPMENT

Learning About Our Faith

Identifying Qualities of Church Leaders

Call on volunteers to read aloud "Ministries in Scripture" on page 216 as the rest of the students follow along in their texts. Instruct the students to underline in the first paragraph the qualities that Paul said Church leaders must exhibit. (*They must be worthy of respect, sincere, gentle, peaceful, responsible, have the ability to bring people together as a community and help them be united.*) You may want to clarify that the word *sincere* means "honest" or "truthful."

Discuss Paul's letter to the Philippians by asking the following questions.

■ For whom did Paul thank God? (*All people who shared in the ministries of the Church and those who supported Church leaders*)

■ What did Paul call the Philippians? (*Partners in sharing the gospel with others*)

■ What did Paul pray for in his letter to the Philippians? (*That their faith and love would increase*)

Activity

Consider the groups or teams you belong to and the things that you enjoy doing. Think about the qualities you have that can help you show teamwork and support for these groups or teams.

Use the letters that spell your first name as the first letters of words that describe some qualities you have. Follow the examples for *Sam* and *Pat*.

Strong	**P**eaceful
Athletic	**A**rtistic
Musical	**T**alented

216   Scripture

Ministries in Scripture

In Paul's letters to the early Christian churches, he often gave instructions to the Church leaders. He wrote about the qualities that Church leaders should have. They were to be people whom others could respect; they were to be sincere, gentle, peaceful, and responsible. They were to be people who could bring people together as a community of believers and help them to be united. To learn more of what Paul wrote about Church leadership, read 1 Timothy 3:1–13.

In one part of his letter to the Philippians (Philippians 1:3–11), Paul gave thanks to God for all the people who shared in the ministries of the Church and who supported Paul, Timothy, and other Church leaders. He told them that they were all partners in sharing the gospel with others. And he prayed that their faith and their love would increase.

Focus on

Paul   Explain that Paul's name in Hebrew was "Saul." He was a Jew who had persecuted Christians. One day, while traveling to Damascus, a bright light blinded Saul. The voice of Jesus spoke to him. Soon after that, Saul began preaching about Jesus to many people. He began using the Greek form of his name, "Paul." Paul spent the rest of his life working as a missionary. He wrote many letters, or epistles, to the churches he established during his travels.

Activity

Complete the paragraph below to describe some of the gifts of people in your parish who share in the ministry of community building. Then write a prayer for these community builders and share this prayer aloud. Know that your prayer is also part of this ministry.

One Church leader whom I admire as a good community builder is _____ because

_____ .

I believe that one way I can help bring together the people at _____ *name of parish* _____ parish is to

_____ .

I can also help build community in my own family by

_____ .

My Prayer for the Community Builders in My Parish and My Family

_____

_____

_____

_____

_____

Morality 217

Completing an Activity

Read with the class the directions for the first activity on page 217 and have the students work independently to complete it. When everyone has finished writing, encourage volunteers to read aloud their responses. You may want to choose as a class project one or more of the students' ideas for building community in the parish. This might include inviting parents to a social during the school day to help them get to know one another, putting on a play for another class, or acting as greeters at a Sunday Mass. Encourage the students to follow through on their plans for building community with their families.

or...

Distribute drawing paper and crayons or markers. Encourage the students to draw pictures showing how they can help their families or parish grow in unity, peace, and love and become a stronger community. Suggest that the students depict in their drawings practical actions that they, as third graders, can realistically do. Afterward, allow time for volunteers to share their work with the class.

Writing a Prayer

Invite the students to write a prayer for building community in the parish and family on the lines provided in the text. Then have the students bring their books to the area you have designated for prayer. Encourage each of the students to share with the class the prayers they wrote by reading them aloud.

Objective

This lesson helps the students learn that Jesus wants us to cooperate with him in building unity.

Step 1/INTRODUCTION

Learning About Our Lives

Discussing Experiences and Feelings

Begin the lesson by asking the students to recall times when they have refused to cooperate with something another person wanted them to do or an experience of cooperating reluctantly or grudgingly with another person's request. These experiences may range from not wanting to write a thank-you note to a grandparent who sent a birthday gift to refusing to do something that they knew was wrong. Encourage each of the students to participate in this discussion. Ask them to give their reasons for not wanting to cooperate with what they were being asked to do. Then ask the students how they feel when they cooperate in good efforts and how it makes them feel to refuse to cooperate. Tell the class that in this lesson they will learn how Jesus wants us to cooperate with him in building unity among the Church community.

Step 2/DEVELOPMENT

Learning About Our Faith

Discussing a Picture

Note the illustration on page 218. Ask the following questions.

■ What job is the person in the picture doing? (*Taking care of sheep*)

■ What are the responsibilities of a shepherd? (*Tending the flock, gathering it together, making sure that the sheep are safe and secure*)

■ What would happen if the shepherd did not take care of the flock? (*The sheep would wander away, get lost, and possibly be hurt.*)

Explain that the job of a shepherd was an important one at the time of Jesus and that some people still work as shepherds today.

218

One Flock, One Shepherd

One day, Jesus was talking to a large group of people. They were confused and upset. They wanted to follow Jesus, but some people had said bad things about him.

Jesus wanted to build this community. So he told them a story about himself and about themselves.

"Sheep gather around their shepherds," Jesus said. "When the shepherd calls the sheep by name, they follow him. They know who he is because they recognize his voice."

Everyone knew how sheep flocked together around their shepherds. There were shepherds all over their country.

"I am the good shepherd," Jesus told them. "I know my sheep and they know me. I protect them from the dangers that scatter them. I keep my sheep together as a flock."

Focus on

Shepherds The image of the shepherd is very important in the Bible. Two of the greatest leaders from the Old Testament, Moses and King David, were both shepherds. The image of the Church's pastoral leaders as shepherds continues today. The bishop of every diocese carries a staff shaped like a shepherd's crook. This symbol of leadership is called a crosier.

Teaching Tips

In ancient Palestine, it was common to keep the town's flocks of sheep together at night for safety. In the morning, each shepherd simply had to call to his own sheep and they would depart from the other sheep and follow the shepherd. The shepherd knew his sheep and the sheep knew the shepherd's voice. In John 10:1–18, Jesus describes himself as the Good Shepherd. Followers of Jesus interpret this to mean that Jesus knows us individually, calls us by name, and wants us to know his voice, too.

Jesus paused for a moment. Then he continued. "There are other sheep who are not yet part of my flock. I will call them and lead them together. Then there will be one flock and one shepherd."

Based on John 10:1–18

Discuss

1. How would you respond to someone who made fun of your beliefs, your Church, or your family?

2. What are some of the things that we say or do that could cause us to become separated from our brothers and sisters in Christ?

3. What things could we say or do to bring people back together once they have been separated from one another?

Morality 219

★★★★
Enriching the Lesson

Ask the students to bring to class empty shoeboxes. Supply art paper, crayons, scissors, paste, clear plastic wrap, and rubber bands and have students make dioramas for the Scripture story. First cut out a window at one end of the box. Draw and cut figures for Jesus, the sheep, and scenery. Leave a tab at the bottom of each to bend back and paste down. Color the inside of the box for background and paste the figures facing the window. Secure the lid with a rubber band and cover the window with clear plastic wrap.

Reading the Scripture Story

Ask volunteers to read "One Flock, One Shepherd" on pages 218 and 219. In discussing the story, bring out that Jesus is like a shepherd looking after his sheep (the Church). Stress that Jesus still takes care of all of us in the Church.

Remembering the Church's Call to Be Catholic

Direct attention to the last sentence in the Scripture story: *Then there will be one flock and one shepherd.* Ask the students to recall that the third mark of the Church is that the Church is catholic. Ask the students to recall the definition of the word *catholic*, "open to and accepting of people everywhere." Help the students appreciate that Jesus wants us, as individuals and as the Church, to welcome all people into his flock. Emphasize that Jesus wants to be the shepherd of all people.

Step 3/CONCLUSION

Learning How to Live Our Faith

Discussing the Questions

Direct attention to the questions on page 219 and engage the students in a discussion about each of them. In discussing the first question, urge the students to be positive, rather than defensive, when responding to those who might make fun of their beliefs or families. Help them appreciate that they can talk with others about how important their life with Jesus is and how much they love their family and the Lord. Emphasize that fighting with others, insulting them, or arguing with them will only make the situation worse.

As you discuss the second question, help the students understand that sin separates us from Jesus and the Christian community. We can also become separated from the Church community when we do not participate in the sacraments, especially the Eucharist, with our brothers and sisters in Christ. In discussing the third question, remind the students that the virtue of hospitality or welcoming is one of the important aspects of community. By being open to others, we can help them be reunited with the community and reconciled with their sisters and brothers.

219

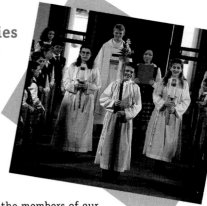

Day 5
PRAYER/REVIEW

Objective

This lesson helps the students pray for community builders in our families, school, and parish.

Preparing for Prayer

Tell the students that in today's prayer service they will have the opportunity to offer prayers for the communities to which they belong. Ask a volunteer to read aloud the first paragraph on page 220. Then point out the first of the students' prayer petitions and read aloud the sentence. Invite the students to identify the different ways their families build community and family togetherness. (*Possible responses may include: eating together; attending Sunday Mass and praying together; going on vacations as a family; working through problems together; taking the time to visit museums, parks, sporting events, and other special places; and talking with one another frequently.*)

Then read aloud the second of the students' prayer petitions, in which the students have the opportunity to pray for parish and school leaders. Elicit responses from the students as to specific things that they can name in praying for each individual. For example, "For Sister Catherine, our principal, who helps us have pride in our school; for Father Garcia, our pastor, who leads us in prayer and helps us remember God's love always; for Mrs. McGrath, our school secretary, who helps us whenever we have a problem," and so on.

Praying Together

Select a volunteer to begin the prayer service by reading the Scripture story on page 214 of the text. Conclude the prayer service by having the students join hands and pray the Our Father.

Praying for Our Communities

Leader: As we pray today, we remember that we belong to many communities—the communities of our families, our school, our parish, our diocese, our cities and towns, our nation, and the world. We pray today especially for the community builders in our own families, our school, and our parish. Let us pray.

Leader: Holy Spirit, you call us to serve the members of our own families.

All: Help us to respect our parents as they bring our families together to share all the good things that families can share.

Leader: Holy Spirit, you call us to serve one another in our school and in our parish community.

All: Help us to support our parish leaders, our pastor, our principal, and our teachers in their ministry of building community.

Leader: Holy Spirit, you call us to make every effort to be united. May our prayers today be a sign of all the efforts that we will continue to make to help build unity in all the communities in which we live. Guide us in our prayer each day so that we might remember to pray for one another always.

All: Lord God, help us to serve you and all your people by using the gifts you have given us. Help us to use these gifts to build up the community of Christ's body, the Church. Amen.

220 Prayer

★ ★★★ ★
Enriching the Lesson

Remind the students that the end of the year is not far off. Ask them how they want to celebrate the community they have built during this year. Work with them to plan an end-of-the-year unity celebration. This might be a class Mass, a picnic, a field trip, or a classroom party. Help the students plan how each of them will contribute to the celebration.

Focus on

Church Community According to the *Catechism of the Catholic Church*, "Because they are members of the Body whose Head is Christ, Christians contribute to *building up the Church* by the constancy of their convictions and their moral lives. The Church increases, grows, and develops through the holiness of her faithful..." (#2045)

Chapter Review

For each word in Column A, write the letter for its definition from Column B.

Column A

<u>b</u> **1.** bishop

<u>c</u> **2.** ministry

<u>f</u> **3.** pastor

<u>d</u> **4.** diocese

<u>a</u> **5.** pope

<u>g</u> **6.** deacon

<u>e</u> **7.** ministry of community building

Column B

a. leader of the whole Catholic Church

b. pastoral leader of a diocese

c. ways we serve God and all people

d. community made up of many parishes

e. helping the church to grow in unity

f. priest who leads a parish community

g. a person ordained to assist in serving a parish community

Fill in the answers to the first two questions.

1. What is the *ministry of community building?*

<u>ways in which we help the Church to grow in unity</u>

2. What special role does the pope have in the Church? <u>helping the Catholic Church all over the</u>

<u>world to grow in unity</u>

3. Talk about where, how, and with whom you can help build community.

Do everything you can to be united in the Spirit.
Based on Ephesians 4:3

Review 221

Teaching Tips

You may wish to participate in this activity with the students. Distribute paper and have the students put their names at the top of the page. Have them pass the papers around the room. Encourage the students to write on each page something special about the person whose name is written at the top. Stress that they write about a gift that the person gives to the community (for example, good ideas, a sense of humor, and so on). Collect the sheets. Later, recopy each list. Distribute them on Day 1 of Chapter 18.

Completing a Matching Activity

Explain the directions for the first activity on page 221. Have the students work independently to match the words in Column A with the definitions in Column B. When everyone has finished, call on volunteers to read aloud the correct answers. Answer any questions the students may have about the words they have learned in Chapter 17.

Filling in Review Answers

Direct attention to the next two questions on page 221. Have the students read the questions to themselves and write their responses on the lines provided in the text. Afterward, allow time for sharing. Then invite responses to the last question on page 221. Help the students appreciate that one of the best ways they can help build community is to be generous in sharing their gifts and talents.

Reflecting on a Scriptural Verse

Have students read aloud the verse from Ephesians at the bottom of the page. Encourage the students to work for unity by being open to others and looking for ways to bring people together. Help them appreciate that they can ask the Holy Spirit to help them grow in their love of the community. They can also pray that they might be like Jesus, breaking down barriers and building bridges in which people feel united at home, school, and in their other important communities.

18 Our Church Preaches God's Word

Objectives ～～～

To help the students

■ Understand that Jesus continues to bring us God's word through the ministry of the word.

■ Learn that Jesus *is* God's Word.

■ Identify ministers of the word in the parish.

■ Understand Paul's role in spreading God's word in the early Church.

■ Pray with the Lectionary and review the chapter.

Chapter Outline ～～～～～～

	Step 1 **Learning About Our Lives**	**Step 2** **Learning About Our Faith**	**Step 3** **Learning How to Live Our Faith**
Day 1	■ Introduce the chapter. ■ Read a letter. ■ Discuss the questions. *ABOUT 14 MINUTES*	■ Read about God's word. ■ Learn the doctrine. *ABOUT 8 MINUTES*	■ Complete an activity. *ABOUT 8 MINUTES*
Day 2	■ Look for good news. *ABOUT 6 MINUTES*	■ Introduce the reading. ■ Read a Scripture story. ■ Understand the message. *ABOUT 15 MINUTES*	■ Make good-news scrolls. *ABOUT 9 MINUTES*
Day 3	■ Complete an activity. *ABOUT 11 MINUTES*	■ Read the text. ■ Identify parish ministers. *ABOUT 9 MINUTES*	■ Pray together. *ABOUT 10 MINUTES*
Day 4	■ Discuss letter writing. *ABOUT 8 MINUTES*	■ Read and discuss the text. *ABOUT 10 MINUTES*	■ Write a note of care. *ABOUT 12 MINUTES*

Day 5 **Prayer** Learn about the *Lectionary for Masses with Children*; prepare for prayer; pray with the Lectionary.
Review Complete a crossword puzzle; complete the chapter review; pray with the scriptural verse.

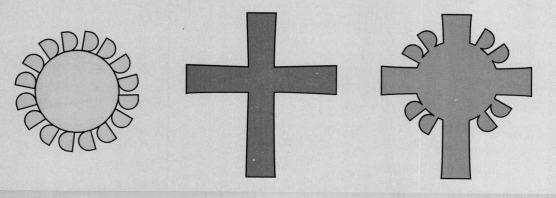

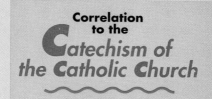
Plan Ahead

	Preparing Your Class	**Materials Needed**
Day 1	Read through the lesson plan for this session.	■ pencils or pens
Day 2	Read through the lesson plan for this session. Find a good-news story in the newspaper to use as an example in Step 1.	■ newspapers ■ news magazines ■ drawing paper ■ crayons
Day 3	Read through the lesson plan for this session. Be prepared to supply the students with the names of parish ministers of the word in Step 2.	■ chalkboard ■ pencils or pens
Day 4	Read through the lesson plan for this session. Be prepared to discuss some of your own letter-writing experiences in Step 1.	■ pencils or pens
Day 5	Read through the lesson plan for this session. Prepare an environment for prayer in the classroom.	■ *Lectionary for Masses with Children* (if available) ■ Bible ■ prayer table ■ scrolls from Day 3

Additional Resources

As you plan this chapter, consider using the following materials from The Resourceful Teacher Package.

■ *Classroom Activity Sheets 18 and 18a*

■ *Family Activity Sheets 18 and 18a*

■ *Chapter 18 Test*

■ *Prayers for Every Day*

■ *Projects: Grade 3*

You may also wish to refer to the following Big Book.

■ *We Celebrate the Mass,* pages 5–9

In preparing the students for the Sunday readings, you may wish to use Silver Burdett Ginn's *Getting Ready for Sunday* student and teacher materials.

Books for the Journey

Baby. Patricia MacLachlan. Delacorte Press, 1993. This story reveals how words are so powerful that when they are left unspoken an entire family can suffer.

Da Vinci—The Painter Who Spoke with Birds. Yves Pinguilly. Chelsea House Publishers, 1993. In this story a lively and healing exchange of letters takes place between a child hospitalized with two broken legs and a learned and loving uncle.

More Books for the Journey

Best Friends. Selected by Lee Bennett Hopkins. HarperCollins, 1986. "The Telephone" by Jack Prelutsky, p. 42. A poem about words making a friend feel better.

The Magic Purse. Yoshio Uchida. Margaret K. McElderry Books, 1993. A story about the delivery by a poor young farmer of a girl's letter to her parents and the difference the farmer's kindness and courage make.

Reduced Classroom Activities

NAME _____

Our Church Preaches God's Word

God's words are winning words. To play the "winning words" card game, cut out the cards on this page and page 18a. Then follow the directions below. Both you and your partner will need a set of cards.

Directions:

1. Choose a partner and combine both sets of cards into one deck.
2. Take out one "loser" card from the deck.
3. Shuffle the remaining cards and deal them.
4. You and your partner find the matching pairs in your hands. Read these cards aloud to each other.
5. Take turns drawing one card from your partner's hand.
6. If the card matches a card in your hand, put both cards on the table and announce, "I have a card that says . . ."

The object of the game is to be the first player out of cards. The person who ends up with the "loser" card must read it aloud.

1	2	3
I know how you feel.	You're cool!	Don't feel bad, it's OK.

To the Teacher: By engaging in this game, students will verbalize their own and God's encouraging words and recognize the contrast between loving words and unloving words. If possible, duplicate the cards on sturdy paper.

© Silver Burdett Ginn Inc.

Chapter 18 *Our Church Preaches God's Word*   THIS IS OUR FAITH 3 **18**

NAME _____

4	5	6
You can do it!	I think you're great.	I'll be your good friend.

7	8	9
"I am with you always." *Matthew 28:20*	"I will forgive you." *Based on Jeremiah 31:34*	"I will never forget you." *Isaiah 49:15*

10	11	A LOSER says:
"Do not be afraid." *Matthew 14:27*	"Take courage and be strong." *Daniel 10:19*	"You're not my friend." "I don't like you anymore!"

© Silver Burdett Ginn Inc.

18a THIS IS OUR FAITH 3   Chapter 18 *Our Church Preaches God's Word*

THE MIRACLE OF WORDS

This chapter uses our everyday experience of words to help the students understand and appreciate God's word. From the beginning of our lives, we learn the power of language and the richness of the spoken word. As we grow, we experience new words and new ways of using these words. We learn that we can create with words, harm with words, and use words to influence the feelings of others.

Our Judeo-Christian tradition is rooted in words. The people of ancient Israel passed down beliefs and stories to new generations through an oral tradition. Jesus began his public ministry with words. He spoke in the synagogue at Nazareth and explained that his role was to bring words of healing, freedom, new life, love, justice, and peace. Jesus is the Word of God. When Jesus speaks, God speaks.

The followers of Jesus began to preach Christ's message after the experience of Pentecost. They continued to preach the word of God and to teach his message for some thirty-five years without using a written account of what Jesus had said and done. With the deaths of the apostles who personally knew Jesus, many Christian teachings began to be put down in writing in what we now call the Gospels. The writers of the Gospels, the evangelists, used the written word to pass on to others the mystery, hope, and joy of the Word made flesh.

THE PROPHETIC MINISTRY

As Catholics today, we share in the prophetic ministry of the Church. We are called to share the good news as Jesus did. We are called to be ministers of God's word by sharing the message that his love is without limits.

The pope, bishops, priests, and deacons have a special calling to preach God's word. Some people are called to be lectors (readers) who proclaim the word of God at Mass. Other people are called to be catechists and to teach God's word as they help younger and older people alike grow as Christians. Parents are also part of this teaching ministry as they share God's word with their children at home.

Tell the students that they will learn about the ministry of the word in this chapter. They will begin to understand how they themselves can participate in this ministry.

Our Church Preaches God's Word

Objective

This lesson helps the students understand that Jesus continues to bring us God's word through the ministry of the word.

Step 1/INTRODUCTION

Learning About Our Lives

Introducing the Chapter

Direct attention to the chapter-focus statement on page 222. Invite the students to share their experiences with the class. Help the students appreciate that it is not always easy to find the right things to say to someone who is hurting but that when we take the time to find the right words, they do have the power to help others.

or...

If you had the students do the Teaching Tips activity on page 221, distribute the recopied students' lists now. Allow time for the students to read them quietly to themselves. Comment on how much you enjoyed reading all the positive things the students had to say about one another and yourself. Invite the students to each name one thing on their lists that surprised or pleased them. Emphasize that words have the ability to empower, encourage, and affirm.

Reading a Letter

Have volunteers read aloud the letter on page 222. Then ask the students why Katie wrote to Patty. Help them recognize that Patty is spending the summer away from her friends because she is visiting her dad.

Discussing the Questions

Consider with the students the Discuss questions at the top of page 223. In answering the first question, have the students circle the words in their texts that they think will help Patty feel better. Allow time for the students to think about the last question before answering. Encourage everyone to offer a response.

Share a story about a time when something you said helped someone feel better.

Dear Patty,

Thank you for writing back so soon. All the kids in the neighborhood miss you very much. You are so much fun! We wish you could be here with us for the <u>whole</u> summer!

Are you having a good time? What kinds of things are you doing? Does your dad have a piano for you to play? You did such a great job at your recital last month!

Sorry to hear you got the chicken pox from your little brother. We hope you feel better soon! Please write back soon. We can't wait to see you at school this Fall.

> *Your friend,*
> *Katie*

P.S. Nicole has two new kittens. I hope you like the picture her Mom took of all of us. Do you have any pictures you could send us?

CURRICULUM CONNECTION

Language Arts   Have students pick names of the other students in the class out of a hat or basket and write letters to the people whose names they have chosen. The letter should be in the spirit of the one on page 222. Have them mention what they like or admire about the other person. Suggest that they share something that has happened to them recently.

Discuss

1. What words in Katie's letter might Patty have especially appreciated?

2. How do you think Patty will respond?

3. What words would mean the most to you if you got a letter like this?

Jesus Brings Us God's Word

Jesus often used words to help people. He began his ministry using God's word. He said he was going to bring God's message to all people. He was planning to teach and preach. He was sent to be a minister of God's word.

Christ continues to bring us God's word through the Church's **ministry of the word**. As members of the Church, we all share in this ministry. But we can only share what we ourselves have received.

Activity

Circle the two verses that you would most like to share with someone.

"I will be with you always."
Based on Matthew 28:20

"Do not be worried or afraid. I give you my peace."
Based on John 14:27

"I will never forget you."
Based on Isaiah 49:15

"You can do anything with God's help."
Based on Mark 10:27

With whom would you share these messages?

Vocabulary

ministry of the word: serving others by sharing God's word with them

✖ ✖ ✖ ✖ ✖ ✖ ✖ ✖ ✖ ✖ ✖ ✖

We Believe

The Church today continues Jesus' ministry of the word. Each of us is called to share God's word with others and to live its message.

Doctrine 223

Learning About Our Faith

Reading About God's Word

Ask volunteers to read "Jesus Brings Us God's Word" on page 223. Note the illustration of the open Bible on this page. Remind the students that God's word is found in the Bible. As the phrase *ministry of the word* is introduced, refer to the Vocabulary box and read the definition with the class. Then discuss these questions.

■ What did Jesus say when he began his ministry? (*That he was going to bring God's message to all people by teaching and preaching; that he was sent to be a minister of God's word*)

■ How does Christ continue to bring God's word to us? (*Through the Church's ministry of the word*)

■ What is the ministry of the word? (*Serving others by sharing God's word with them*)

Learning the Doctrine

Look at the We Believe statement on page 223. Recall that *to minister* means "to help." Ask the students what they think God's word is in their lives. Stress that the good things that people say to them, which help them feel good about themselves, are the words of God in their lives. Emphasize that we share God's word not just by what we say but also by what we do.

Step 3/CONCLUSION

Learning How to Live Our Faith

Completing an Activity

Explain the directions for the activity on page 223. Allow time for the students to work on their own to complete it. Afterward, poll the group to determine which Bible verses they would most like to share with others. Ask the students to explain why they made these selections. Then invite them to share the names of the people with whom they want to share the messages. Encourage them to offer their ideas on how the messages would help others.

Enriching the Lesson

Divide the class into groups of three. Give each group a slip of paper on which you have written a very simple retelling of one of the following Gospel stories: Matthew 9:9–13; 9:35–38; 11:25–30; 12:46–50; 18:1–5; 19:13–15; and 26:26–30; Mark 1:35–39 and 12:41–44; Luke 15:1–7; 19:1–10; and 23:32–34; or any story you would like the students to know. Have them read their slips of paper and share how Jesus ministered to others through his words. If time permits, have the students act out the stories.

Teaching Tips

Remind the students that Jesus planned to carry out his ministry of God's word by teaching and preaching. Clarify the difference between these two ways of sharing God's message. Help the students understand that the word *preaching* means "to proclaim" or "to announce" God's word to people. The word *teaching* means "to instruct." We can teach others about God's word by both our words and actions.

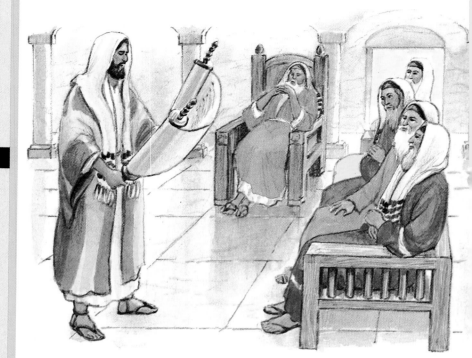

DAY 2
SCRIPTURE

Objective

This lesson helps the students learn that Jesus *is* God's Word.

Step 1/INTRODUCTION

Learning About Our Lives

Looking for Good News

Have the class form cooperative groups and distribute current newspapers and news magazines to each group. Ask the students to look through these resources to find stories or headlines that are good news for one or more persons. After allowing time for the students to work together to complete the activity, invite a representative from each group to share the group's story with the class. Have the students discuss why the story they chose is good news and who received the good news.

Step 2/DEVELOPMENT

Learning About Our Faith

Introducing the Reading

Remind the students that in Jesus' time there were few written works for the ordinary person to read. Most people memorized and passed on to each other the stories and poems they heard from other people. They understood and appreciated the importance and power of the spoken word, and they listened well to the words that were spoken. Point to the illustration on page 224 and have the students note how everyone is listening attentively to Jesus.

Reading a Scripture Story

Before reading the Scripture story "Jesus Speaks God's Word," introduce the word *prophet* to the students by pointing out the definition in the Vocabulary box on page 225. Also explain the meaning of the words *synagogue* and *scroll,* which appear in the reading. These words may be unfamiliar to the students. Help them recall that a synagogue is a place of prayer and learning for the Jewish people. Tell them that in the synagogue, God's word is read from a scroll, or a piece of parchment. Take a sheet of drawing paper and roll it up in the form of a scroll to demonstrate

224

Jesus Speaks God's Word

Jesus grew up in a Jewish family, who often prayed together and talked about the Scriptures they heard at the synagogue and Temple. Jesus' hometown was Nazareth. He sometimes read the Scriptures in the synagogue there.

One Sabbath day, Jesus was in the synagogue at Nazareth. He unrolled the scroll of the **prophet** Isaiah until he came to a special passage. He read the following words out loud.

224 Scripture

CURRICULUM CONNECTION

Social Studies During Jesus' time, people wrote on papyrus, a material made from thin strips taken from a papyrus plant, or on specially prepared leather. Sacred documents were often written on leather because it did not tear or wear out as quickly as papyrus. Ink made from soot was used for writing. It was applied with a brush made from the frayed end of a hollow reed that was sharpened with a knife.

Focus on

Prophets Before Jesus, there was a long tradition of prophets in Israel going back through the centuries. A few of the prophets were seers, or people who were able to foretell the future. But the most common and important type of prophet was a person who used words and actions to call people back to God. The prophets of Israel stressed believing in one God and being a moral people. They looked forward to a day when a messianic figure would come to deliver Israel from its captors and redeem its people.

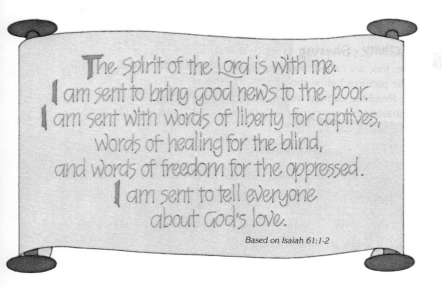

The Spirit of the Lord is with me.
I am sent to bring good news to the poor.
I am sent with words of liberty for captives,
words of healing for the blind,
and words of freedom for the oppressed.
I am sent to tell everyone
about God's love.

Based on Isaiah 61:1-2

Then Jesus said, "Today, these words of the Scriptures have come true in me." The people in the synagogue were amazed at Jesus' words. They could not believe that this man was the boy who had grown up right there in Nazareth.

Based on Luke 4:16–22

Jesus *Is* God's Word

Jesus said that he was sent by the Father to bring God's word to all people. Jesus' ministry of teaching and preaching helped the people understand how much God loved them. They came to know Jesus as a great storyteller, teacher, and prophet. They also came to know Jesus as God. Jesus said to them, "Now that you know me, you also know and see the Father" (based on John 14:7).

Vocabulary

prophet: someone called by God to speak in his name

✗ ✗ ✗ ✗ ✗ ✗ ✗ ✗ ✗ ✗ ✗ ✗

Scripture 225

---

what a scroll looks like. Explain that in Jesus' time, God's word was written by hand on the scroll. Then ask one of the students to read the Scripture story on pages 224 and 225. Be sure to include the words written on the scroll as part of the reading.

Ask the students to identify the ways in which Jesus said he would be a minister of God's word (*by bringing words of good news to poor people, to those who are not free, and to blind people*). Help the students understand that Jesus came to share with everyone the good news about God's love. Have the students note the reactions of the people in the synagogue to Jesus' words. Ask the students how they would react if someone stood up in church after the words from Isaiah were read and said, "These words in the Scriptures are about me. This is what I have been called by God to do." Lead the students to the recognition that some people would be amazed, but others would be shocked or confused. Emphasize that this event occurred at the beginning of Jesus' ministry, when people did not yet understand that Jesus had been sent by God.

Understanding the Message

Read through "Jesus *Is* God's Word" on page 225 with the students. Emphasize that as a storyteller, teacher, and prophet, Jesus brought God's word to people. In these ways, people came to know that Jesus had not just been sent by God, but Jesus *is* God. Jesus taught that if we know him, we know God, because Jesus is God.

Step 3/CONCLUSION

Learning How to Live Our Faith

Making Good-News Scrolls

Tell the students that the best way we can help other people understand how much God loves *them* is to witness to the fact that he loves *us* and that his word has been good news for us. Clarify that to witness means "to tell." We witness when we tell others, in words or actions, about our relationship with God and Jesus. Provide the students with drawing paper to roll into scrolls. Invite them to use crayons to write on their scroll a short paragraph witnessing about a time when they experienced God's love. Afterward, invite the students to read their witness paragraphs aloud to the class.

DAY 3
MORALITY/PRAYER

Objective

This lesson helps the students identify ministers of the word in the parish.

Step 1/INTRODUCTION

Learning About Our Lives

Completing an Activity

Read aloud the instructions for the activity on page 226. Have the students work independently to complete it. When they have finished, invite them to share their responses with the group. Discuss how their answers might help someone change how he or she is feeling or acting. Ask the students to recall that they have learned that we are called to continue Jesus' ministry of the word, and ask them to share ways in which we can do so. Answers should reflect the understanding that we share God's word with others by our words and actions and by putting God's message into practice in our lives.

or...

Have the students pair off and act out the situations in the activity above or create new role-plays that show how words can help others feel better. Encourage the students to use examples from their own lives. Invite volunteers to perform their role-plays for the class.

226

Activity

Read each sentence. Write words that a friend or another person might say to help someone in each situation. Use your own words or select words from the word wall below.

1. "I keep trying, but I can't do these math problems."

_____

2. "I'm sorry I called you names."

_____

3. "It seems as if nobody likes me."

_____

4. "I'm afraid I'll make a mistake if I try."

_____

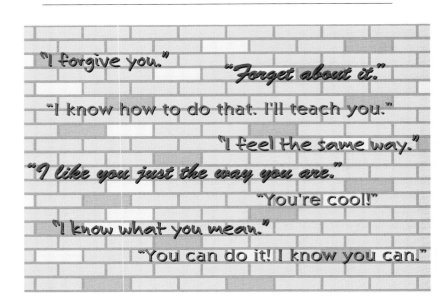

"I forgive you."   "Forget about it."
"I know how to do that. I'll teach you."
"I feel the same way."
"I like you just the way you are."
"You're cool!"
"I know what you mean."
"You can do it! I know you can."

Focus on

Catechists   The word *catechist* comes from a word that means "to echo." Anyone who echoes God's word by teaching Religion is a catechist. As a catechist, you echo the word of God through your teaching, your example, and your witness to the students.

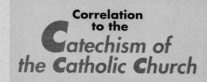

Correlation to the Catechism of the Catholic Church

Paragraphs
2623, 2624, 2625, 2633, 2639, 2641, 2701, 2742

Plan Ahead

	Preparing Your Class	**Materials Needed**
Day 1	Read through the lesson plan for this session. Be prepared to share some of your own experiences of praising God.	■ chalkboard
Day 2	Read through the lesson plan for this session. To prepare for the discussion in Step 3, consider whether your actions and attitudes help or hinder the prayer of others.	■ chalkboard ■ pencils or pens ■ writing paper
Day 3	Read through the lesson plan for this session. Try to discover the names of people in your parish who perform the various ministries listed on page 237.	■ chalkboard ■ pencils or pens ■ Bibles ■ paper
Day 4	Think of an example of discouragement in your own life to share with the students in Step 1. Practice the sign-language gestures.	■ pencils or pens ■ colored construction paper ■ scissors, tape, yarn ■ crayons or markers
Day 5	Read through the lesson plan for this session. Prepare an environment for prayer in the classroom. Decide how you will carry out the blessing ritual.	■ colored paper streamers ■ pencils or pens

Additional Resources

As you plan this chapter, consider using the following materials from The Resourceful Teacher Package.

■ *Classroom Activity Sheets 19* and *19a*

■ *Family Activity Sheets 19* and *19a*

■ *Chapter 19 Test*

■ *Prayers for Every Day*

■ *Projects: Grade 3*

You may also wish to refer to the following Big Books.

■ *We Celebrate the Sacraments,* page 7

■ *We Celebrate the Mass,* pages 2, 3, and 21

In preparing the students for the Sunday readings, you may wish to use Silver Burdett Ginn's *Getting Ready for Sunday* student and teacher materials.

BOOKS FOR THE JOURNEY

A Child's Book of Prayers. Edited by Linda Yeatman. Workman Publishing, 1992. "Saying Thank You to God" by Matthias Claudius, pp. 22–23. A prayer about God's goodness to us.

Our Church. Graham English. The Liturgical Press, 1992. "Hello, I'm Emma and I'm a Catholic," pp. 21–22. A child identifies going to Mass as one of the signs of being Catholic.

MORE BOOKS FOR THE JOURNEY

Praise for the Singing. Collected by Madelaine Gill. Little, Brown & Co., 1993. "Praise God, From Whom All Blessings Flow" by Michael Kuhn and Thomas Ken, p. 20. A song that calls all creatures here on earth below to praise God.

Praise God. Gunvor Edwards and Joan Brown. The Liturgical Press, 1994. A book that could be a companion to a child in worshiping with the faith community at Mass.

REDUCED CLASSROOM ACTIVITIES

NAME _____

OUR CHURCH WORSHIPS GOD

Use the words in the window to complete the sentences below.

As each word is used, choose a different colored crayon to color that window. Press hard.

Next, color the entire window with black crayon, being careful not to press too hard. Then use a pencil tip or other pointed object to scratch designs on the "church window."

1. _Worship_ means to give praise and honor to God.

2. The _priest_ is a minister of worship.

3. The _Church_ continues Jesus' ministry of worship.

4. The _Holy Spirit_ is with us to help us to pray.

5. We can worship God in our _parish church_.

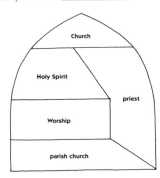

To the Teacher: This activity follows the Scripture story "Praying Together."

Chapter 19 Our Church Worships God   THIS IS OUR FAITH 3   **19**

NAME _____

A PRAYER OF PRAISE

Write a prayer of praise on the computer screen. List things that you would like to praise God for.

19a THIS IS OUR FAITH 3   **Chapter 19** Our Church Worships God

THE EXPERIENCE OF PRAYER

Some of the students in your group have a rich experience of prayer. Their families pray together often and they participate weekly in the Sunday liturgy. Other students may have little experience with prayer. Their families may not pray and may seldom attend Mass. Most of the students' experience is probably somewhere between these two extremes.

This chapter explores with the students the experience of prayer. It is important for them to share something of their own prayer experiences. This sharing provides an opportunity for the students to become more aware of what they think and feel about God in their lives.

FOLLOWING JESUS' EXAMPLE

Against the backdrop of the students' own experiences of prayer, this chapter considers how all Catholics are called to take an active part in the Church's worship. We have seen earlier in the year that Jesus prayed often. He offers us a model of prayer. In this chapter, students will learn that after Jesus' resurrection his followers continued to pray together. They worshiped God in the Temple and in their homes. Their experiences were communal and private, formal and informal. Recognizing Jesus' closeness to God in prayer and his dedication to people in need led the early Church to

describe him as a priest, that is, as a mediator between God and humanity. Jesus' life was one of building bridges between people and God. Jesus was an intercessor for humankind with God. This came to be seen as Christ's priesthood.

All Christians share in the priesthood of Christ by reason of their Baptism and Confirmation. Some members of the Church share in the priesthood of Christ in a special way through ordination. They are the bishops, priests, and deacons of the Church. Ordained priestly service is meant to encourage and support the priesthood of all the baptized, many of whom serve the Catholic community in the ministry of worship.

We hope the students will come to understand that worship is at the center of the Church's life of faith. They will come to understand that as members of the Church, we are all called to pray and to participate in Catholic worship.

DAY 1
PRAYER

Objective
This lesson helps the students understand what it means to praise God.

Step 1/INTRODUCTION

Learning About Our Lives

Introducing the Chapter
Have the students form small groups of three or four. Direct attention to the chapter-focus questions on page 232 and have each group discuss them. Appoint someone in each group to record the answers. After about five minutes, have the students report back on their feelings about prayer. Remind the students that earlier in the year, in Chapter 9, they learned about various times, places, and ways to pray and they explored reasons for praying. Tell them that in this lesson they will examine how the Church helps people pray together.

or . . .

Review with the students what they already know about prayer. Ask the following questions.

■ How would you define prayer? (*Talking to and listening to God through our words, our songs, and our gestures*)

■ What are the five basic types of prayer? (*Prayers of thanksgiving, petition, sorrow, faith, and praise*)

■ When can you pray? (*Any time*)

List the students' responses to the third question on the chalkboard. Help the students recall that they can pray at any time of the day when they are moved to do so. Help them understand that one of the most important times for them to pray is at Mass, when the Church community gathers together.

Identifying Reasons for Praising God
Call on volunteers to read aloud "Praising God." Help the students understand the difference between a prayer of thanks and a prayer of praise. Then explain the directions for the activity and have the students work independently to complete their lists. When everyone has finished, invite sharing.

232

19

Our Church Worships God

What are some things you like about praying with others at home? In class? In church?

Praising God
Jesus prayed many kinds of prayers. We have already learned about the psalms Jesus prayed from the Scriptures. When Jesus wanted to say how wonderful his Father is and how grateful he was, Jesus said a prayer of **praise**. When we say a prayer of thanks, we usually thank God for something or someone very specific. We might say, "Thank you, God, for beautiful flowers!" When we say a prayer of praise, we may just want to say, "God, you are so wonderful!" And then we may want to tell God all the reasons we believe this!

Activity

On the lines below, make a list of some events, people, places, or things for which you would like to praise God. Put a check next to one that is especially important to you right now.

_____

_____

_____

232 Prayer

 **Teaching Tips**

As you lead the students in the opening activity for this lesson, you may wish to review in your own mind the guidelines for cooperative learning groups. As the teacher, you should always ask for a product from students involved in cooperative group work, such as a list of items, a written definition, or something they have built together. Always set a time limit on the group work and assign roles to groups members. Walk around from group to group to observe.

Focus on

Praise The *Catechism of the Catholic Church* states that "Praise is the form of prayer which recognizes most immediately that God is God. It lauds God for his own sake and gives him glory, quite beyond what he does, but simply because HE IS. It shares in the blessed happiness of the pure of heart who love God in faith before seeing him in glory." (#2639)

Discuss

1. What are some ways to praise God?

2. Have you ever praised God when you were by yourself? When?

3. What are some times and places you have praised God together with others?

Praising God in Song

Long before the time of Jesus, Jewish people entered their Temple singing a short psalm or hymn. In Psalm 100, the people of Israel call upon all the nations of the world to join with them in praising God. Psalm 100 also praises God who created us and who remains faithful to us forever.

A Processional Psalm

Everyone, come and sing to the Lord!
Serve the Lord happily!
Praise the Lord with happy songs!

May we never forget that we belong to God.
We can say to the Lord,
"We are your people, we are your flock!"
We enter the temple gates with thanksgiving
   and praise.

Bless the name of the Lord, who is so good to us!
Our Lord's kindness and faithfulness last forever!

Based on Psalm 100

Vocabulary

praise: a way to show or tell God how wonderful we believe he is and how grateful we are to him

✖ ✖ ✖ ✖ ✖ ✖ ✖ ✖ ✖ ✖ ✖

Discussing Questions

Discuss with the class the questions on page 233. Encourage the students to respond to the first two questions by sharing their personal experiences of praising God. In discussing the third question, ask students what they have enjoyed most about praying with others.

Step 2/DEVELOPMENT

Learning About Our Faith

Reading a Psalm of Praise

Ask a volunteer to read aloud "Praising God in Song." Discuss the following questions.

- What did Jewish people do when they entered their Temple? (*Sang a psalm or hymn*)

- What do the people of Israel call on the people of the world to do in Psalm 100? (*To join them in praising God*)

Read "A Processional Psalm" with the class in a lively and spirited manner. Help the students appreciate the joy and gratitude expressed in this psalm.

Memorizing the Vocabulary

Direct attention to the Vocabulary box and have the students memorize the definition of the word *praise.* Have each student use the new word in a sentence.

Step 3/CONCLUSION

Learning How to Live Our Faith

Examining Our Actions and Attitudes

Ask the students what they do as individuals when they enter church. (*Responses may include: signing themselves with holy water, genuflecting, kneeling in the pew and offering a silent prayer, greeting the people around them, sitting in silence while waiting for the Mass to begin, reading the parish bulletin, and so on.*) Then discuss with the students what we do as a community at the beginning of our celebrations. (*Stand for the entrance processional, sing together, pray the Sign of the Cross together, and respond, "And also with you!" to the priest's greeting*) Ask the students what they think about as they perform these actions. Do they take the time to praise God? Why or why not?

233

Objective

This lesson helps the students recognize how the Church continues Jesus' ministry of worship.

Step 1/INTRODUCTION

Learning About Our Lives

Writing About Prayer

Write the following questions on the chalkboard.

- What is one gift for which you are especially thankful?
- How can you thank God for that gift?
- When and where can you thank God?

Distribute writing paper to the students. Instruct the students to copy the sentences onto their papers, leaving three blank lines after each question. Then have the students write answers to each question. When everyone has finished writing, invite volunteers to share their work.

Learning the Vocabulary

Point out the Vocabulary box on page 235, and ask the students to read the definition of the word *worship*. Encourage them to learn this important word. Help them understand that Catholics believe that all prayer is worship because each time we turn to God in prayer, we are recognizing his greatness.

Step 2/DEVELOPMENT

Learning About Our Faith

Reading the Story

Ask for a volunteer to read the story "Praying Together," which begins on page 234. Review the story by asking the following questions.

- What did Jesus' friends and followers continue to do after his resurrection? (*Pray together*)
- What did Jesus' followers do together in the Temple? (*They worshiped together, giving honor and praise to God.*)
- What did Paul's letters encourage Jesus' followers to do? (*To praise and thank God in worship together*)

234

Praying Together

Jesus prayed regularly with his friends in their homes, in synagogues, and in the Temple in Jerusalem. After his death and resurrection, Jesus' friends and followers continued to pray together. They gathered regularly in the Temple to **worship**, or to give honor and praise to God. They often prayed together in their homes, too.

Paul, an important leader among the first Christians, wrote letters to Jesus' followers in many cities. He often encouraged them to praise and thank God in worship together. These are his words to two early Christian communities.

234   Scripture

Dear faithful ones in Ephesus,

Sing psalms and hymns and spiritual songs among yourselves, singing and playing music to the Lord in your hearts. Give thanks always and for everything in the name of our Lord Jesus Christ to God the Father...

Based on Ephesians 5:20

Dear friends in Philippi,

Don't worry about anything, but ask God for what you need and want. Pray to God with thankful hearts. Then God's peace will be with you...

Based on Philippians 4:4–9

Vocabulary

worship: to give honor and praise to God, especially as a community

ministry of worship: helping people to pray and take part in community worship

✖ ✖ ✖ ✖ ✖ ✖ ✖ ✖ ✖ ✖ ✖ ✖

We Believe

Jesus prayed both alone and with others. Paul encouraged the first Christians to worship God together. We are all called to take an active part in the Church's worship today.

Doctrine 235

The Ministry of Worship

The Church today continues to worship God. We gather together to give praise and thanks, to ask for God's help, to ask for forgiveness of our sins, and to pray for others. We pray together in devotions and in the liturgy, the Church's official community prayer. Every baptized Catholic is called to take an active part in the Church's worship, especially the Eucharist. We can help others to pray, too. There are many ways we can serve our parish communities through the **ministry of worship**.

Teaching Tips

Take this opportunity to review the proper way to perform some of the actions we participate in during Mass. For example, when we make the Sign of the Cross, we should consciously touch the forehead, chest, and shoulders while saying the words, rather than making a vague sweeping motion over the upper body. Help the students understand that our reverence shows that we believe in what we are praying. Do the same with genuflecting, sharing the Sign of Peace, and receiving the Eucharist.

Enriching the Lesson

Have the students identify some of the devotional prayer experiences they have participated in over the past several years. These may include a school May crowning, Advent and Lent prayer services, the Stations of the Cross, and the like. Discuss with the class what made these experiences special and how the experiences helped them worship God or honor Mary or one of the saints.

As you read through Paul's letters on page 235, review with the students the specific ways in which Paul encouraged the first Christians to worship God. (*By singing psalms and hymns; by giving thanks always for everything; and by asking God for what they needed and wanted*)

Learning About the Ministry of Worship

Ask one of the students to read through "The Ministry of Worship" on page 235 as the rest of the students follow along in their texts. Have the students underline the four reasons that Catholics gather together for public prayer (*to praise and thank God, to ask for God's help, to tell God we are sorry for our sins, and to pray for others.*) You may want to clarify the difference between devotional prayer and liturgy by explaining that devotions are prayers we pray alone or with others in honor of Jesus, the Blessed Trinity (Father, Son, and Holy Spirit), Mary, and the saints. Give the students examples of devotional prayer they may be aware of, such as the Way of the Cross, Benediction, and the Rosary. Emphasize that liturgy is the Church's official community, or public, prayer. Explain that we usually celebrate the sacraments at public liturgy, and that the Eucharist is our greatest liturgy and the most important way in which Catholics worship God.

Reviewing the Vocabulary and Doctrine

Direct attention to the Vocabulary box and have the students learn the definition of *ministry of worship*. Stress that many people serve in this ministry, which helps us pray and participate more fully in the liturgy. Then read aloud the doctrinal summary in the We Believe box on page 235.

Step 3/CONCLUSION

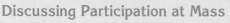

Learning How to Live Our Faith

Discussing Participation at Mass

Invite the students to discuss how they act at Mass when they attend with the class or their families by asking these questions: Do you join in on the responses and singing? Do you listen attentively to the readings and the homily? Do you receive Eucharist reverently? How do your actions at liturgy help or hinder the prayer of others? Help the students recognize that their actions can have a positive or negative effect on the worship experiences of others.

235

DAY 3
PRAYER

Objective

This lesson helps the students identify different forms of the ministry of worship.

Step 1/INTRODUCTION

Learning About Our Lives

Discussing Liturgical Roles

Invite the students to name the special opportunities that they, as Catholic school students, have to take special roles at school Masses and prayer services. (*These may include: serving at Masses; acting as lectors; reading the petitions, or General Intercessions; singing in the school choir; helping to plan Masses and prayer services; participating in processionals; bringing up the offertory gifts; and so forth.*) Encourage the students to discuss how it makes them feel to participate in liturgies in these special ways. Help the students appreciate that these experiences involve people we know and are planned especially for children, so they help us participate more fully in the liturgies.

Step 2/DEVELOPMENT

Learning About Our Faith

Identifying Ministers of Worship

Explain to the students that the Church continues Jesus' ministry of worship. Read "Our Worship Experience" with the students. Then point out the photographs on page 236. Ask the students to identify the ministerial role shown in each picture. (*Counterclockwise, beginning at the top: students playing together in a children's ensemble; two students serving at Mass; a student reading from the Lectionary; a eucharistic minister offering the consecrated host to a child; a banner displayed in church.*)

Ask the students if they have ever participated in any of the ministries shown on this page, either by being altar servers, playing or singing music, reading lessons, or making a banner. Encourage them to talk about these experiences.

236

Our Worship Experience

We are called to give honor and praise to God, both alone and with others. Catholics all over the world gather in communities to worship God. The pictures below show some familiar ways we can share in the ministry of worship.

236 Prayer

 **CURRICULUM CONNECTION**

Language Arts Invite the person in charge of the altar servers to visit your class to talk about this ministry. In advance of the interview, have the students sharpen their writing and listening skills by working in small groups to write a list of questions to ask the guest speaker. As the speaker answers the questions, have students take notes, then write a story about altar servers in your parish. If a speaker cannot come to class, ask him or her to respond to the questions on an audiocassette.

Activity

Write the names of people who serve in these ministries at your school or parish Masses.

A *priest* leads the worshiping community.

_____

_____

Eucharistic ministers distribute Communion.

_____

_____

Altar servers assist the priest during Mass.

_____

_____

Music ministers play instruments and lead the community in singing hymns and psalms.

_____

_____

Ushers greet people when they come to Mass and as they leave.

_____

_____

★ Enriching the Lesson ★

Invite the students to develop a bulletin board showing "who's who" in the planning and celebrating of the Eucharist in your school or parish. Encourage the students to use the categories in the activity on page 237. Challenge them to find out about the people who plan and carry out the worship for the community. Suggest that they interview various people and, if possible, obtain their photos. Have the students prepare beforehand a list of relevant questions to ask each person.

🌐 *Cultural Awareness*

Explain that parishes try to create a special "worship mood" through music. Parishes with large numbers of Spanish- or Polish-speaking parishioners will often sing hymns in those languages. Music in an African-American parish might include spirituals. Parishes with many senior citizens may have traditional music. Some parishes always have organ music; others use the guitar. Ask students to describe the kind of music they most enjoy singing at Mass. Have them name their favorite hymns or songs.

Step 3/CONCLUSION

Learning How to Live Our Faith

Completing a Writing Activity

Explain the directions for the writing activity on page 237. First ask the students if they know the names of people who fill the various roles in the ministry of worship. As they suggest names, write them on the chalkboard for all to see. You may need to have a list available as the students may not know the names of all the parish leaders. The students should then complete the activity in their own books.

Researching Scripture

Invite the students to compare some of the actions of the first Christians with the things we do at liturgy. Have the class form small groups for this activity. Ask each group to choose one person to act as the recorder to write down the group's observations. Distribute Bibles and instruct the students to look up the following Scriptures. Have the recorder write one sentence beginning with the words *The people in the early Church* for each verse and then write the action mentioned in the verse.

- Acts 2:46 (*The people in the early Church broke bread together. This is what the early Church called the Eucharist.*)
- Ephesians 5:19–20 (*The people in the early Church sang psalms and hymns.*)
- Philippians 4:6 (*The people in the early Church prayed with petitions.*)

Remind the students that the people in the early Church did everything according to the teachings of the apostles. Recall that in Chapter 4 they learned that the Church is apostolic. That is why we continue many of the same actions the first Christians learned from the apostles.

Praying Together

Invite the students to offer spontaneous prayers for all the people in your parish and school who serve in a special way in the ministry of worship. Be sure to include the choir director, ushers, leaders of song, and deacons, along with the names the students listed on page 237.

Day 4

SCRIPTURE

Objective

This lesson helps the students develop an attitude of praise.

Step 1/INTRODUCTION

Learning About Our Lives

Reviewing the Chapter

Have volunteers recite the definitions for the Vocabulary terms *praise, worship,* and *ministry of the word.* Then read aloud the We Believe statement from page 235, eliminating key words. Ask the students to supply the missing words. Discuss with the students how people share in the ministry of worship today. Finally, have the students name ways they give honor and praise to God when they are alone and with others.

Step 2/DEVELOPMENT

Learning About Our Faith

Reading a Scripture Story

Ask volunteers to read "Jesus Gives Praise to the Father" on pages 238 and 239. Explain to the students that in this story, Jesus sounds discouraged. Discuss this word with the students. Help them understand that *discouraged* means "to feel a little down in the dumps, to feel that things are not going so well." Give the students an example from your own life to show them what the word means. Then ask the following questions.

■ Why was Jesus discouraged? (*Because of the lack of results after all his preaching and teaching*)

■ What did Jesus do even though he was discouraged? (*Jesus trusted in God and prayed.*)

■ When have you been discouraged?

■ What have you done when you were discouraged?

■ What did you say to God when you were discouraged?

Jesus Gives Praise to the Father

One day, Jesus went off by himself to think and to pray. For months he had been telling people about God's love. For months he had been reaching out to people who were sick or poor or troubled.

But it seemed that only a few people really listened to Jesus. Not many people seemed to be changing their lives and opening their hearts to God and others in response to Jesus.

Some educated and powerful people were turning away from him. The leaders of the Temple were

238 Scripture

Focus on

Believing in Jesus According to John's Gospel, Jesus performed many wonderful signs—healing the sick, feeding the hungry, and exorcising demons. When Jesus raised Lazarus from the dead, many people believed in Jesus. But signs were not enough to make some people believe. Many people did not admit that they believed in Jesus for fear that they would lose their land and nation to the power of Rome. They felt that if too many people started believing in Jesus and following him, the Roman authorities would surely crush the movement.

238

actually against him. Jesus wondered if all his work was for nothing.

The only people who seemed to change their lives because of Jesus were some of the poorest and least educated people. These simple people seemed to sense that God was actively working through Jesus.

As Jesus thought about this, he felt sad and discouraged. He wished that more people would listen to him and understand his words and actions. Then his thoughts turned to God.

Jesus knew that God was with him. He believed God was part of what was happening. So he prayed, "Father, Lord of heaven and earth, I praise you. I thank you for showing to the simple people what the educated and powerful refuse to understand. Father, in your goodness, you have a reason for it to be this way" (based on Matthew 11:25–26).

An Attitude of Praise

Jesus teaches us that we can always have an attitude of praise because God is always wonderful to us and blesses us. When we show that our hearts are always ready to praise God, we can encourage our friends and our families to have faith, even when they may feel sad or discouraged. This kind of encouragement can help people to pray during times when they may not feel like praying.

Scripture 239

Read through "An Attitude of Praise" on page 239 with the students. You may want to clarify that the word *attitude* means "mood" or "way of thinking or acting." Help the students understand that Jesus calls us to have an attitude of praise, that is, a glad heart that trusts in God's goodness. Sharing these positive feelings can help those who are in need of encouragement, peace, or comfort.

Step 3/CONCLUSION

Learning How to Live Our Faith

Making a Bulletin Board

Provide the students with colored construction paper, scissors, tape, yarn, and crayons or markers. Point out the bulletin board on which you have posted the words *GOD WITH US*. Invite each of the students to make a kite to display on the bulletin board. Encourage them to write on their kites one way that God is part of their lives. Have them add decorations that show how they praise God. Show the students how to add yarn tails to the kites.

Learning a Sign-Language Prayer

Use the diagrams below to teach the students the first line of Jesus' prayer on page 239, "Father, Lord of heaven and earth, I praise you."

★★★★ Enriching the Lesson ★★★★

Distribute lined paper to the students. Ask them to spend a moment thinking about someone they know who needs encouragement because of some situation in his or her life. Invite the students to write letters to these people, assuring them of God's presence and care. The students should also tell the people to whom they are writing how much they care for them and want to help them. Afterward, talk with the students about how they will give the letters to the people to whom they wrote.

DAY 5

PRAYER/REVIEW

Objective

This lesson helps the students pray a prayer of praise for the ministry of worship.

Preparing for Prayer

Rehearse the reading of Psalm 149:1–2 in the student text on page 240. As an alternative, you may want to have the students read Psalm 100, from Day 1. Either of these psalms can be part of a processional or recessional. The students can carry a variety of colored paper streamers as they process.

The highlight of this celebration is a blessing rite. If your celebration is part of an all-school Mass, you might bless all the ministers of worship. Those with special roles, such as those of server, choir member, and other roles discussed in this chapter can be given a sign of their ministry, such as badges or ribbons the students make. Others can be signed with oil or with a symbolic laying on of hands.

Decide on how you will carry out the blessing rite and assemble any materials you may need, such as oil or water, if you plan on signing the students individually.

Select a volunteer to act as leader of prayer and another student to be a reader. Supply the leader of prayer with a list of the students' names for the blessing rite. Have the reader practice proclaiming the reading from Ephesians on page 235.

You may want to incorporate the sign-language prayer the students learned on Day 4 into your celebration. If you choose to do so, have the students pray it together after the reading.

Praying for the Ministers of Worship

You might also incorporate petitions into your celebration. Ask the students to each write a petition praising God; asking God to give encouragement, comfort, or peace to someone who is hurting; or asking God to help them develop an attitude of praise. Invite the students to pray the petitions after the leader of prayer says "Let us pray" following the commissioning.

Praying for a Blessing on the Ministers

Leader: Our prayer today is a prayer of praise to God for the ministers of worship in our school. Let us begin our prayer with Psalm 149:1–2.

Group 1: Sing to the Lord a new song of praise!

Group 2: Come, all you faithful children of God!

All: God, you are so wonderful to us! We praise you now and always!

Group 1: Be happy because God is good!

Group 2: Come, rejoice in your king and Lord!

All: God, you are so wonderful to us! We praise you now and always! Amen!

Based on Psalm 149:1–2

Reader: A reading from Paul's letter to the Ephesians. (Student reads Ephesians 5:20 from page 235 of the student text.)

Leader: As your name is read, please come forward to receive a special blessing on your ministry of worship.

Teacher: (to each minister of worship) I praise God for you, ___person's name___. May God bless you and guide you to always serve the Lord with gladness! (Please respond: Amen.)

Leader: Let us pray.
Lord, we thank you for the gifts and talents that all of these special people use to serve you in this school community. As they help us to pray, fill them with hearts of praise to lead us in celebrating your unending love for us.

Ministers: We thank you for calling us each by name. We thank you for the gifts you have given us. Help us to use them to encourage others in their faith. And keep our faith strong always. Through Jesus Christ our Lord.

All: Amen.

240 Prayer

★ Enriching the Lesson ★

Plan a class prayer service. With the students, choose a theme or focus. Then select readings, readers, and songs and decide on a prayer you can pray together. This may be a creed, a traditional prayer, or a prayer written by the class. Discuss preparations that need to be made and the materials you will need. You might also wish to invite parents to attend this special event.

240

Chapter Review

Unscramble the word(s) to complete each statement. The words appear in order.

1. To _____praise_____ God is to show or tell him how wonderful we believe he is.

| ispare |

2. _____Paul_____ encouraged the first Christians to worship God together.

| uaPl |

3. To give honor and praise to God, especially as a community, is to _____worship_____ .

| psworih |

4. To help people to pray and take part in community worship is a _____ministry_____ of worship.

| ystiminr |

5. Two ways we can share in the ministry of worship are as a _____music_____ minister and as an _____altar_____ server.

| smiuc |

| atarl |

Fill in the answers to the first two questions.

1. What does *worship* mean? _to give honor and_
praise to God

2. What are some forms of the ministry of worship? _leading the community, distributing_
Communion, assisting the priest, singing or playing
an instrument, welcoming people at Mass

3. Talk about your own experiences of worship.

> **Come, let us worship the Lord who made us.**
> Based on Psalm 95:6

CURRICULUM CONNECTION

Art Consider having the students make individual booklets or posters on the four ministries they are learning about in Unit 5. You can have them begin their projects now and complete them after they have finished Chapter 20. Have the students decide whether they want to make booklets or posters. Then give them the necessary materials to get started. Encourage the students to look back through Chapters 17, 18, and 19 for ideas to include in their project.

Unscrambling Words

Read aloud the directions for the first activity on page 241. Allow sufficient time for the students to complete the assignment. When everyone has finished, call on volunteers to read aloud the completed sentences.

Reviewing the Chapter

Take time to go through the review questions. Direct the students to write on the lines provided in the text the answers to the first two questions. Then check the students' work. Encourage each student to participate in the discussion of the third question.

Praying with the Scriptural Verse

Have the students recite the verse at the bottom of the page. Explain that this verse is from Psalm 95, which is a Hebrew song of praise to God. Read aloud the first seven verses of Psalm 95 from a Bible. After each verse, have the students repeat the scriptural verse in their books as a refrain. Allow a time of quiet and invite them to offer silent prayers of honor and praise to God.

20 Our Church Serves

Objectives

To help the students

- Recognize that Jesus brought a message of love, justice, and peace to victims of injustice.
- Understand that the Church continues Jesus' ministry of service.
- Learn the biography of Saint Martin of Tours.
- Identify ways of reaching out to others.
- Pray for God's help in reaching out to people and review the chapter.

Chapter Outline

	Step 1 Learning About Our Lives	**Step 2** Learning About Our Faith	**Step 3** Learning How to Live Our Faith
Day 1	■ Introduce the chapter. ■ Discuss the photograph. ■ Read the text. *ABOUT 9 MINUTES*	■ Discuss suffering. ■ Complete an activity. ■ Read the text. *ABOUT 14 MINUTES*	■ Write prayers. *ABOUT 7 MINUTES*
Day 2	■ Identify people. *ABOUT 5 MINUTES*	■ Learn about John the Baptizer. ■ Read a Scripture story. ■ Learn about a Church ministry. *ABOUT 17 MINUTES*	■ Discuss ways of reaching out to others. *ABOUT 8 MINUTES*
Day 3	■ Examine attitudes about people in need. *ABOUT 10 MINUTES*	■ Read a saint's biography. ■ Learn about the ministry of service. *ABOUT 10 MINUTES*	■ Complete an activity. ■ Pray together. *ABOUT 10 MINUTES*
Day 4	■ Complete a writing activity. *ABOUT 5 MINUTES*	■ Read about a service organization. ■ Recall the works of mercy. *ABOUT 12 MINUTES*	■ Create a photo essay. ■ Pantomime ministry of service actions. *ABOUT 13 MINUTES*
Day 5	**Prayer** Complete the petitions; prepare for prayer. **Review** Complete sentences; review the chapter; pray with the scriptural verse.		

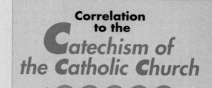

Correlation
to the
**Catechism of
the Catholic Church**

Paragraphs
**544, 1822, 1823, 1826,
2443, 2444, 2546**

Plan Ahead ～～～～～

	Preparing Your Class	**Materials Needed**
Day 1	Read through the lesson plan for this session.	■ chalkboard ■ colored chalk ■ pencils or pens ■ construction paper, scissors, and crayons
Day 2	Read through the lesson plan for this session. Prepare for the Step 1 discussion by thinking about whom you go to when you are feeling discouraged.	■ pencils or pens
Day 3	Read through the lesson plan for this session. Be prepared to share a story or information about people who are in need.	■ chalkboard ■ newspapers and magazines ■ scissors ■ pencils or pens
Day 4	Read through the lesson plan for this session. Review the spiritual and corporal works of mercy.	■ pencils or pens ■ chalkboard ■ newspapers and news magazines ■ scissors and paste
Day 5	Read through the lesson plan for this session. Prepare an environment for prayer in the classroom. Plan how you will conduct the prayer service.	■ lined paper ■ crayons ■ white sheet ■ fabric crayons ■ prayer table

Additional Resources

As you plan this chapter, consider using the following materials from The Resourceful Teacher Package.

■ *Classroom Activity Sheets 20 and 20a*

■ *Family Activity Sheets 20 and 20a*

■ *Chapter 20 Test*

■ *Prayers for Every Day*

■ *Projects: Grade 3*

You may also wish to refer to the following Big Book.

■ *We Celebrate God's Word,* page 13

In preparing the students for the Sunday readings, you may wish to use Silver Burdett Ginn's *Getting Ready for Sunday* student and teacher materials.

BOOKS FOR THE JOURNEY

Charlotte's Web. E.B. White. HarperCollins, 1990. The story of a special spider who befriends and saves the life of a pig.

A Grandmother's Story. Glenn Halak. Simon & Schuster, 1992. The love and compassion of a grandmother for her grandson leads her to an unusual trip.

MORE BOOKS FOR THE JOURNEY

The Llama's Secret. Argentina Polacios. Troll Associates, 1993. A llama helps the family who depends on him realize they are in danger and saves them from drowning.

Revenge of the Small Small. Jean Little. Viking, 1992. The youngest child in the family hurts from the unkindness of her brothers and sisters and does something that helps them stop hurting her.

REDUCED CLASSROOM ACTIVITIES

NAME _____

OUR CHURCH SERVES

Pretend you and a friend are starting a "free service" business. With your partner, create a flier that you might pass out to your neighbors, advertising your free services. Fill in the missing information. Then decorate your flier.

FREE SERVICE

_____ and _____
(name)   (name)
will help you with these tasks:

_____
_____
_____
_____

We have experience. Just ask

_____
(names of people you've worked for)

To the Teacher: This activity will foster students' awareness of service possibilities close to home.

Chapter 20 Our Church Serves   THIS IS OUR FAITH 3 **20**

NAME _____

A MINISTRY OF SERVICE

Louis Braille was born in France in 1809. When he was three years old, an accident blinded him. He didn't give up but became a very good student at the National Institute for the Blind.

After Louis graduated, he became a teacher at the Institute. He invented a system of printing and writing that helped blind people to read. In the Braille alphabet, each letter is represented by a different pattern of raised dots.

Study the Braille alphabet. Then decode the message of God's love.

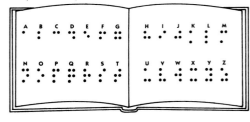

A B C D E F G   H I J K L M
N O P Q R S T   U V W X Y Z

" H a p p y   a r e   t h o s e

w h o   p l a c e   t h e i r

f a i t h   i n   m e ."

Based on Luke 7:23

To the Teacher: This activity follows the Scripture story "Jesus' Life of Service."

20a THIS IS OUR FAITH 3   Chapter 20 Our Church Serves

THE COMPASSION OF JESUS

The students at this level are aware of people who are in need. Some students may have more experience and personal contact with suffering than others. Some may be more aware than others of poverty, hunger, unemployment, prejudice, and injustice. Whatever their differing experiences, it is important that the students be brought to look at the suffering of people in need.

Jesus was very sensitive to the suffering people of his day. He looked into the hearts of individuals and into the causes of pain that were part of the world of his time. Jesus was compassionate to the victims of injustice. He was also understanding and merciful to sinners.

Jesus identified himself with the victims of injustice and spoke up against those whose selfishness caused so much suffering. Jesus was not a revolutionary in the contemporary sense. He was not even a social activist in the way that many people are today. However, his message of justice and love had powerful social and political implications. His example of justice and compassion strongly influenced people, literally changing their lives.

THE MINISTRY OF SERVICE

The Church continues Jesus' ministry of compassion and justice. The early followers of Jesus took seriously his concern for suffering people. Throughout the Church's history many exemplary Christians have devoted their lives to the service of those who suffer.

Today, many Catholics are rediscovering our tradition of working for justice and peace. They are actively involved in the Church's ministry of service. The ministry of service involves compassionate action toward victims of injustice as well as more organized efforts to remove the causes of injustice from within society's institutions.

We hope the students will hear this same call to serve. This chapter will help them consider the call to be a person of justice and peace. This is a difficult task in a society where competition is more valued than cooperation and where winning at any cost is often held as an ideal. Jesus teaches us that we are worthy of love and recognition simply because we have been created by God. In fully recognizing God's love for us, we can better live as peaceful and compassionate people.

Day 1
Morality

Objective

This lesson helps the students recognize that Jesus brought a message of love, justice, and peace to victims of injustice.

Step 1/Introduction

Learning About Our Lives

Introducing the Chapter

Ask a volunteer to read aloud the chapter-focus question. Encourage all the students to respond by identifying a person or group that is in need or is experiencing sorrow or hurt. Then discuss the following questions with the students.

- What do the people you named need most?
- What can you or other members of your parish do to help them?

Help the students understand that it is not always possible for them to meet all the needs of others. Point out that one thing they can always do is bring these painful situations to the attention of someone who is in a position to help. Have the students suggest people they could turn to with a problem. Stress that sharing another person's problem with someone who might be able to help is not tattling or disloyalty. Rather, it is a way of showing love and care for others.

Discussing the Photograph

Direct attention to the photograph on page 243 and have the students describe what they see. Help the students understand that the boy represents the millions of people throughout the world who lack many of the things we take for granted, such as proper clothing, food, shelter, and education.

Reading the Text

Read "People in Need" with the students. Help them recognize that people throughout the world suffer in many different ways. Emphasize that we can work as individuals and as a community to meet the needs of people who suffer.

242

20

Our Church Serves

Who in your community seems to be sad, hurting, or in need?

People in Need

There are people in need all around us. Sometimes friends, neighbors, or members of our own families are hurting. Sometimes those in need may be strangers.

There are sick people without medicine or doctors. There are women and men who want to work but cannot get jobs. There are people who are treated badly because of how they look or what they believe. There are people who have no family, too little to eat, or nowhere to live. Some people have needs so great that it takes the work and love of many people to help meet those needs.

Focus on

Love of the Poor According to the *Catechism of the Catholic Church,* "'The Church's love for the poor . . . is a part of her constant tradition.' This love is inspired by the Gospel of the Beatitudes, of the poverty of Jesus, and of his concern for the poor." (#2444).

Activity

Listed in this puzzle are five ways that people suffer. The words read across and down. Circle each word. On the lines next to the puzzle, write about some other ways that people suffer in the world today.

M	I	O	X	P	R	A
I	K	I	M	S	P	B
G	Y	N	O	U	O	D
E	V	J	Q	W	V	F
C	H	U	N	G	E	R
B	L	S	W	A	R	H
H	A	T	E	X	T	J
Y	Z	I	Q	Z	Y	L
M	O	C	N	A	P	V
N	P	E	R	B	T	X
O	F	X	I	D	A	L

Possible answers include: being homeless, lacking clothes, having a terminal illness such as cancer, or having family problems.

Jesus' Message of Service

Throughout history, there have been people in need. Jesus knew that much suffering was caused by selfishness and greed. So he not only helped people who were suffering but also spoke out against those who caused the suffering. Jesus brought a message of love, **justice**, and peace to victims of injustice. He taught us to treat everyone fairly and with respect.

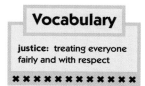

Vocabulary

justice: treating everyone fairly and with respect

✗ ✗ ✗ ✗ ✗ ✗ ✗ ✗ ✗ ✗ ✗ ✗

Morality 243

Focus on

Greed In speaking of greed, the *Catechism of the Catholic Church* says, "The tenth commandment forbids greed and the desire to amass earthly goods without limit. When the Law says, 'You shall not covet,' these words mean that we should banish our desires for whatever does not belong to us. Our thirst for another's goods is immense, infinite, never quenched. Thus it is written: 'He who loves money never has money enough' " (#2536). The Catechism says that greed comes from envy.

Enriching the Lesson

The puzzle on page 243 contains five words that name ways that people suffer. Have the students work in small groups to come up with five words that name ways we serve others who are in need. Examples might include love, justice, peace, fairness, and respect. Ask each group to use their words to create a word search puzzle similar to the one on page 243. Then have the groups exchange puzzles and search for the hidden words.

Learning About Our Faith

Discussing Suffering

Draw a large teardrop on the chalkboard. Ask the students to name some things that cause them to cry. Write their answers in the teardrop, using many colors of chalk. Draw a second teardrop on the chalkboard and tell the students that some things cause most people to cry. Within the second teardrop write the following words: *injustice, poverty, hunger, war,* and *hate.* Discuss each of these words with the students, asking them why these tragedies often cause many people to cry, even people who are not among those who suffer.

Completing an Activity

Explain the directions for the hidden-word puzzle and have the students solve it. Set a time limit for finishing the puzzle. Brainstorm other reasons that people suffer and list the students' ideas on the chalkboard. Have them choose several of the reasons listed and copy them on the lines provided in their texts.

Reading the Text

Call on a volunteer to read aloud "Jesus' Message of Service" on page 243. As the word *justice* is introduced, have the students read and memorize the definition in the Vocabulary box. Then ask the following questions.

- What did Jesus believe were two reasons for suffering? (*Selfishness and greed*)
- How did Jesus respond to those who suffered? (*He helped them and spoke out against people who caused suffering.*)

Step 3/CONCLUSION

Learning How to Live Our Faith

Writing Prayers

Distribute construction paper, scissors, and crayons. Direct the students to cut a fist-sized teardrop from the paper. Then ask each student to choose one of the reasons for suffering that the class considered in the previous activities. Invite each student to write on his or her teardrop a prayer for people who experience this form of suffering. When the students have finished, allow time for sharing. Suggest that they pray their prayers daily on their own for the remainder of the week.

243

DAY 2
SCRIPTURE/DOCTRINE

Objective

This lesson helps the students understand that the Church continues Jesus' ministry of service.

Step 1/INTRODUCTION

Learning About Our Lives

Identifying People

Begin the lesson by asking the students to think about whom they turn to when they are feeling confused or overwhelmed or when they are troubled about something. Encourage each of the students to participate in this discussion. Then ask the students how the people they go to help them. Point out that people can help us by listening to us, supporting us, showing care for us, comforting us, as well as by offering us advice about a problem or helping us solve the problem. Remind the students that they have already learned that ministry is serving God and all people according to God's special call. Tell the class that in this lesson, they will learn about another special ministry to which we are called by Jesus.

Step 2/DEVELOPMENT

Learning About Our Faith

Learning About John the Baptizer

Ask the students if anyone has ever heard of John the Baptizer. Explain that John was a relative of Jesus. Their mothers, Elizabeth and Mary, were cousins. John was a famous preacher. Tell the students that during his life, John called people to repent for their sins and to turn their attention to God. Point out that John was called the Baptizer because he baptized many people.

Tell the students how John the Baptizer looked forward to the coming of a messiah, a chosen agent of God who would bring peace and justice. He preached his message of repentance while keeping in mind that there was another to come after him whose sandals he felt unworthy to touch.

244

Jesus' Life of Service

John the Baptizer was in prison. He had bravely stood up and criticized a powerful ruler.

John was a well-known preacher who had baptized Jesus. While in prison, John kept hearing reports about what Jesus was doing and saying.

"Go to Jesus," John told two of his friends. "Ask him if he is the one whom God promised to send to help us in our need."

So the two went to look for Jesus. They found him surrounded by a crowd of people.

"John the Baptizer sent us to ask you a question," they told Jesus. "Are you the one God promised to send to help us? Or should we look for someone else?"

Jesus answered by pointing to some of the many needy people he had helped. Some had been blind, deaf, or lame. Most were poor. Jesus said, "Just look around you. Go back and tell John what you have seen and heard."

Messiah The word *messiah* was originally a Hebrew word that meant "one who has been anointed." It was used in the Old Testament to designate a "future king who would make all things new." The term *messiah* was translated into Greek as *Christos* from which we get the name *Christ*. In the story on page 244, John the Baptizer longs to know if Jesus is the one God promised to send. Jesus seeks to prove that he is indeed the promised one by pointing to the ways he helps those in need—people who are blind, deaf, lame, and poor.

Then Jesus recalled words from the Scriptures to show that he was the one whom God had promised to send: "The blind are able to see. Crippled people can walk straight again. Deaf people can now hear. People who were dead have new life. And the poor have received the good news of God's love." Then Jesus said, "Happy are those who place their faith in me."

Based on Luke 7:18–23

The Church's Ministry

Jesus spent his life serving others. He reached out especially to those who were poor, weak, sick, hungry, and homeless.

The Church today continues Jesus' works of love, justice, and peace among all God's people. All Catholics are called to the **ministry of service**—reaching out to people in need and working to change situations and attitudes that cause pain and suffering.

Vocabulary

ministry of service: reaching out to people in need and working to change situations and attitudes that cause people's pain and suffering

✗ ✗ ✗ ✗ ✗ ✗ ✗ ✗ ✗ ✗ ✗ ✗

We Believe

Jesus spent his life serving people in need. He calls us to share in his ministry of love, justice, and peace.

Doctrine 245

Reading a Scripture Story

Have a volunteer read aloud the story "Jesus' Life of Service" beginning on page 244. Discuss the following questions with the students.

■ Why did John the Baptizer send his friends to see Jesus? (*To ask if Jesus was the one whom God had promised to send to help his people*)

■ What did Jesus tell John's friends to do? (*Tell John about the people they had seen Jesus help*)

■ Who did Jesus say would be happy? (*Those who place their faith in him*)

Emphasize that the message Jesus preached and the miracles he performed were signs to John the Baptizer and others that he was the one whom God had promised to send.

Learning About a Church Ministry

Have one of the students read aloud "The Church's Ministry" on page 245. Help the students recall that Jesus sought to eliminate suffering from the lives of individuals by directly healing their pain and by speaking out against conditions that kept people in fear, ignorance, and hunger. Point out the definition for the term *ministry of service*. Then read aloud the We Believe statement. Answer any questions the students may have about this central teaching of the lesson.

Step 3/CONCLUSION

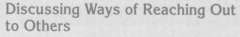

Learning How to Live Our Faith

Discussing Ways of Reaching Out to Others

Invite the students to share personal experiences of their reaching out to people in need. Have them share whom they reached out to, what the situation was, and how they tried to help the person. Also encourage the students to discuss reaching out to others through various service projects in which they have participated. These may include fund-raisers for a charity or a national or worldwide relief effort, food or clothing drives, or Advent or Lenten projects. You might also call attention to causes promoted by celebrities and the work those people do to help raise awareness about the suffering of others.

Cultural Awareness

Discuss what might keep people from reaching out to others. Stress that fear and ignorance sometimes keep us from helping others. Explore how fear or ignorance may prevent someone from helping a person with AIDS, such as fear of catching the disease or ignorance of how the disease is transmitted. Note that those who are suffering are sometimes afraid of, or suspicious of, the people who are trying to help them. Emphasize that this is a two-way barrier. Recall that Jesus tried to break down the barriers that divided people.

Enriching the Lesson

Have the students form pairs. Direct each pair to think of a case in which they have all the power they need to change a situation that is causing pain or suffering to an individual or a group of people. Ask the students to use their imaginations to decide what they will do to change the situation. Then have the students work together to draw "Before" and "After" pictures showing the situation and how it was resolved. Then have each pair of students explain their work.

245

DAY 3
MORALITY

Objective

This lesson helps the students learn the biography of Saint Martin of Tours.

Step 1/INTRODUCTION

Learning About Our Lives

Examining Attitudes About People in Need

Direct attention to the Discuss questions at the top of page 246 and lead the students in a discussion of each of them in turn. In response to the first question, allow the students to share the stories or information they are aware of about people in your community or in the world who are in need. Make a list on the chalkboard of all the different feelings the students express in answering the second question. These may include: sadness (about the people); anger (at the unjust conditions that cause poverty); fear (that they, too, might one day be in need or that needy people might commit crimes to get money for food and other needs); or helplessness (because they do not know what they can do to solve the problem). In discussing the last question, affirm the students' ideas for helping those who are in need. Tell them that in this lesson they will meet someone who showed us how to reach out to the poor.

Step 2/DEVELOPMENT

Learning About Our Faith

Reading a Saint's Biography

Call on volunteers to read aloud "A Friend of the Poor." Then use the following questions to guide discussion.

■ What did Martin notice as he rode his horse through town? (*He saw a beggar with no warm clothes.*)

■ What did Martin do? (*He cut his cloak in half and gave one half to the man.*)

■ What did Martin dream about that night? (*That Jesus was wearing the part of the cloak that Martin had given to the beggar*)

■ What did this dream help Martin to decide to do? (*To spend the rest of his life serving and caring for the poor*)

246

Discuss

1. What stories have you read about people in the world who are in need?

2. How do these stories make you feel?

3. How could you use your gifts to help carry someone else's burden?

A Friend of the Poor

One cold, snowy evening a young soldier named Martin was riding his horse through a town in France. He pulled his warm cloak around himself as the wind whistled and whirled.

At the city gate, Martin saw a man begging. The man had no warm clothes. He looked as if he were freezing.

Martin drew his sword, took off his warm cloak, and cut his cloak in half. He gave half the cloak to the beggar and wrapped the other half around himself.

That night, Martin dreamed that he saw Jesus Christ wearing the half of his cloak that he had given to the beggar. Soon after, Martin decided to spend the rest of his life serving and caring for people who were poor.

Years later, Martin became the bishop of Tours. Each year on November 11, the Church honors Saint Martin of Tours as a friend of the poor and a model for those who help people in need.

246 Morality

Teaching Tips

As a teacher, you are well aware of the effect and influence you have on the attitudes of your students. The questions on the top of page 246 offer you the opportunity to share your faith with your students. Think about people in your own life who have been in need and how you used your own gifts to carry someone's burden, perhaps for a child who was sick or a friend who was in need. Share not only the story, but also your feelings about what happened.

Our Ministry of Service

We are called through Baptism to share in Jesus' ministry of love, justice, and peace. When we use the special gifts and talents we have been given to serve our brothers and sisters who are in need, we are answering God's call.

Many people help or serve people who are poor or in need. People help others for many different reasons. When we help others because we are following God's call, what we do is a ministry of service. When we share in this ministry, we recognize the many needs that people have. People who are homeless, for example, need more than shelter. They also need the love and care of people who will listen to their stories, who will not judge them, and who will treat them with respect.

Activity

Look through some newspapers or magazines. Cut out a picture that shows someone in need.

Write about one way you can reach out to this person. Show the picture to your group as you share what you wrote.

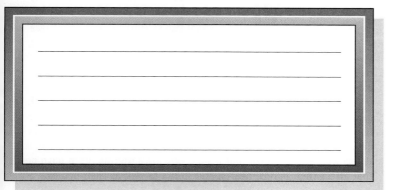

Help the students recall the Scripture story "For Those Who Care" from Chapter 15, pages 184 and 185. Remind them that Jesus said that whenever we cared for, helped, or served the "least of my brothers and sisters," we were serving him. Emphasize that we can serve others in very basic ways, and point out that Martin's ministry of service began with the simple act of sharing. Encourage the students to follow Martin's example of sharing not only talents and gifts, but also possessions.

Learning About the Ministry of Service

Read through "Our Ministry of Service" on page 247 with the class. Remind them that God has blessed each one of us with special gifts that are to be used for our own good and the good of others. Explain that we best use these gifts when we serve others.

Step 3/CONCLUSION

Learning How to Live Our Faith

Completing an Activity

Distribute magazines, newspapers, and scissors to the students and explain the directions for the activity at the bottom of the page. Or you may want to have the students work in cooperative groups to complete the activity. When everyone has finished writing one way in which they can reach out to people like those in the pictures they chose, encourage volunteers to display their photographs and read their ideas to the class. You may want to have the students use the pictures they chose to make a collage. Invite them to suggest a title to print on the collage.

Praying Together

Conclude today's lesson by having the students pray again the teardrop prayers they wrote on Day 1. Help the students understand that by praying for others on a consistent basis, we become "partners" with them and that our prayers are one concrete way of bearing one another's burdens.

Enriching the Lesson

List on the chalkboard the different kinds of suffering that were identified in the students' lists on page 243. Have the students match these with a person who can alleviate the suffering by using his or her gifts. For example, illness can be eased by a doctor or nurse. Assist the students in understanding that we are motivated to serve others because of our love for Jesus.

Teaching Tips

As the class did with the ministry of worship, find out who the people are in the parish who are part of its ministry of service. Have the students check the weekly bulletin for a listing of service programs and people to contact. You might obtain a list of parish programs from the parish secretary for people who are poor, hungry, or homeless. Or invite someone to speak to the class about what the parish does to minister to people in need.

Objective

This lesson helps the students identify ways of reaching out to others.

Step 1/INTRODUCTION

Learning About Our Lives

Completing a Writing Activity

Direct attention to the writing activity at the top of page 248 and allow ample time for the students to work on their own to write about whom they can help and how they can help the people they named. Afterward, encourage volunteers to read their responses aloud. Comment on the students' ideas for helping others and emphasize that the ideas we hear from others help us discover new and different ways for reaching out to people. Point out how valuable it is that, as ministers of service, we share our ideas with one another.

Step 2/DEVELOPMENT

Learning About Our Faith

Reading About a Service Organization

Have volunteers take turns reading aloud "Covenant House" on page 248. Use the questions below to discuss the story.

- Whom does Covenant House minister to? (*Homeless teenagers in large cities all over the United States*)

- Which of the teenagers' needs do the Covenant House workers first deal with? (*Their need for food, clothing, shelter, and medical care*)

- What are some other ways that Covenant House workers help teenagers? (*By talking with them to help them deal with their problems and by helping them find jobs or finish school*)

- What do the Covenant House workers recognize about people who are suffering? (*That they all have needs that affect their minds, hearts, and spirits as well as their bodies*)

248

Activity

Look at the list of people below. Next to each category, write someone's name and describe one way you can reach out to and care for that person.

Family member: _____

Neighbor: _____

Friend: _____

Classmate: _____

Covenant House

Covenant House is one of many organizations in the United States today that share in the Church's ministry of service. Located in many large cities throughout the United States, Covenant House helps America's homeless teenagers. Covenant House workers first help these teenagers by giving them food, clothing, shelter, and medical care. Covenant House workers also minister to the teenagers by teaching them to trust in the love and care that the community offers.

Covenant House workers talk to the runaway teenagers to help them deal with all kinds of problems. The ministers of service at Covenant House show by their actions that God loves each and every person in need. They help the teenagers to find jobs or to finish school. Covenant House workers recognize that people who are suffering often have needs that affect their minds, hearts, and spirits as well as their bodies.

CURRICULUM CONNECTION

Social Studies Help the students understand that many Catholics work in community groups and organizations that serve people in need of assistance. These may include hospitals, counseling centers, and shelters. Other churches and synagogues are active in their own ministry of service. Also explain that there are various civic groups that devote their time and resources to helping people in need.

Activity

Look through a newspaper or magazine. Find a story or picture about people serving others. Paste it in the space below. On the lines provided, write about the many ways that these people are being helped.

Your Local News Source   Page 1

~~~ Neighborhood News ~~~

Vol. 21-No. 12   Daily Edition

PEOPLE SERVING OTHERS

_____

_____

_____

_____

_____

_____

_____

Review with the students the corporal and spiritual works of mercy studied in Chapters 15 and 16. Make a list of the works of mercy on the chalkboard. Next to each work of mercy, define the human need being met. For example, feeding the hungry meets the human need for food and proper diet. Stress that performing works of mercy is a continuation of Jesus' ministry of service. Then have the students look back at the story about Covenant House. Ask the students to identify all the different works of mercy the workers perform for and with the homeless teens. For example, in counseling, the Covenant House workers comfort those who suffer; they are patient with the teens as they help them learn to trust again; and they undoubtedly pray for the teens who come to them. (The students should be able to connect with Covenant House all of the corporal works of mercy except visiting those in prison and burying the dead.)

Step 3/CONCLUSION ~~~~~

Learning How to Live Our Faith

Creating a Photo Essay

Introduce the activity on page 249 by stressing that God wants all of us to serve others in need and to address the causes of suffering. Read the instructions and have the students complete the activity. Have an adequate supply of newspapers and news magazines available for the students to use to complete the first part of the activity. Allow time for the students to show the other students what they have produced.

Pantomiming Ministry of Service Actions

Write the words _minister, serve,_ and _help_ on the chalkboard. Brainstorm with the students all the actions they can do as they live these three words. Invite volunteers to secretly choose a word from the chalkboard list and to pantomime the action for the class. Encourage the class to guess what is being pantomimed.

★ Enriching the Lesson ★

Make four columns on the chalkboard. Above each, write one of the following labels: _Someone is hungry. I can...; Someone is being treated unjustly. I can...; Someone is sick. I can...; Someone is angry. I can...;_ Then discuss with the students what they can do in each of the situations. Help the students be realistic with the possibilities. Lead the students to appreciate that the possibilities are many when we focus on what _can_ be done rather than on the greatness of the challenge. No step taken to help someone is too small.

🍎 Teaching Tips

To help the students learn about another organization that responds to the call to serve others, see In the Spirit of Jesus, Lesson Two, on "Catholic Relief Services," pages 324 and 325 in the Amen section.

PRAYER/REVIEW

Objective

This lesson helps the students pray for God's help in reaching out to people.

Completing the Petitions

Tell the students that in today's celebration the class will offer prayers for the Church's ministry of service. Note that there are three places on page 250 in which the students have the opportunity to add to the prayers. Go through each of these petitions one at a time with the students. For the first petition, each of the students can mention their own families by surname or they might simply pray for "the families of our classmates" or "the families of _____ school."

For the second petition you can fill in either the name of your town or your diocese. Then ask the students to identify local situations and people in need of the ministry of service. For the third petition, help students name people who can be encouraged by the students' prayers. You might wish to have the students write these petitions on lined paper, or you could create a list on the chalkboard.

Preparing for Prayer

Choose a leader of prayer. Then decide with the students whether or not they would like to include the Scripture story from pages 244 and 245 in the prayer celebration.

If you had the students do the "Enriching the Lesson" activity on Day 4, this can be used as the basis of a communal prayer at some point during your celebration.

The students also might work together to make a "Love, Peace, and Justice" table cover for the prayer table. Use a white sheet cut to size. Spread the sheet out on the floor or a large table at which the students can work. Distribute fabric crayons and invite the students to draw symbols for these words, or they could draw pictures that represent the ministry of service.

Praying for the Church's Ministry of Service

Leader: As Catholics who share in Jesus' ministry of service, let us pray for the courage and the wisdom to do all we can to work for justice as we help people who are in need.

Leader: Lord, give your Church wisdom to see and courage to meet the needs of our own families, especially _____.

All: Lord, we are the Church! We are the ones you call to this service.

Leader: Lord, guide your Church in its efforts to meet the needs of people and situations in our community, especially

_____.

All: Lord, we are the Church! We are the ones you call to this service.

Leader: Lord, lead your Church to bring the good news of your love to all the corners of the earth, using the many gifts, talents, and resources with which you have blessed us.

Help others, especially _____, to hear and be encouraged by the prayers of your faithful servants.

All: Lord, we are the Church! We are the ones you call to this service.

Leader: Lord, guide us in all our efforts to serve others with loving compassion and respect. And Lord, when we are the ones who are suffering or in need, give us the grace to accept the love of those who minister to us. Amen.

250 Prayer

🍎 Teaching Tips

If the students are making ministry booklets or posters about the ministries they have learned about in Unit 5, have them complete the project after finishing Chapter 20. You might display the completed projects on a table in the vestibule of the church on Sunday morning or hang them in the parish hall.

Chapter Review

Complete the sentences by writing word(s) from the border.

justice   injustice   needs   war   hate

1. Five ways people suffer are <u>hunger, injustice, hate, war, and poverty</u>
   _____ .

2. <u>Justice</u> is treating others fairly and with respect.

3. Reaching out to people in need and working to change situations that cause people's suffering are ways of sharing in the ministry of <u>service</u>.

4. <u>Saint Martin of Tours</u> was a friend of the poor.

5. Covenant House workers meet many different <u>needs</u> of America's homeless teenagers.

hunger   poverty   service   Saint Martin of Tours

Fill in the answers to the first two questions.

1. What is *justice?* <u>treating everyone fairly and</u>
   <u>with respect</u>

2. Who were some of the people in need whom Jesus helped? <u>people who were blind, crippled,</u>
   <u>deaf, poor, weak, sick, outcasts, hungry, or homeless</u>

3. Talk about what you can do to help someone in need or to work for justice and peace.

Put your gifts at the service of one another.
Based on 1 Peter 4:10

Review 251

Completing Sentences

Ask a volunteer to read aloud the directions for the first exercise on page 251. Then have the students work independently to complete the sentences, using the words from the borders. When everyone has finished, read the completed sentences aloud together.

Reviewing the Chapter

Take time to go through the questions at the bottom of the page. Direct the students to write answers to the first two questions on the lines provided in the text. Check that everyone has answered the questions correctly by having volunteers share their answers with the class. Be supportive of each student who participates in the discussion of the third question.

Praying with the Scriptural Verse

Read to the students the verse from Scripture at the bottom of the page. Ask the students to think about how God is calling them to the ministry of service. Then read aloud this prayer.

"Lord, help us see the hurts of other people. Help us see the ways they are suffering from physical hurts. Help us see the ways they are suffering from hurt feelings. Guide us in our efforts to be of service to them. We want to treat others with love and compassion. Help us be like you, O Lord." Invite the students to respond, "Amen."

★ Enriching the Lesson ★

Stress the idea that working with others at home and doing one's share of tasks at home is also a matter of justice. It is only right that everyone does his or her fair share. Have the students brainstorm a list of practical ways they can help at home.

Completing the Organizer

Explain the directions for the organizer activity on page 252 to the students. You may want to do the Community Building box together to make sure the students understand the assignment. Then direct them to work independently to complete the activity. Afterward, have volunteers read their answers aloud to the class.

(Possible answers for Community Building include: The pope *unites the Catholic Church all over the whole world. A* bishop *helps unite the many parishes of a diocese. A* pastor *encourages people within a parish to share their gifts with one another. A* parent *helps unite a family.*

Possible answers for Word include: A lector *proclaims God's word at Mass. A* religion teacher *helps us understand God's word. A* priest *or a* deacon *invites us to live God's word. A* parent *encourages us to live God's word.*

Possible answers for Worship include: The priest *leads the worshiping community.* Eucharistic ministers *distribute Communion.* Altar servers *assist the priest during Mass.* Music ministers *play instruments and lead the community in singing hymns and psalms.* Ushers *welcome people when they come to Mass. Answers could also include those listed under Word.*

Possible answers for Service include: Covenant House workers *help homeless teenagers.* Students *pray for people in need.* Jesus *healed people who were blind, deaf, and lame.* Saint Martin of Tours *shared his cloak with a beggar who was cold.)*

Looking Back: Self-Assessment

The critical-reflection questions below give the students an opportunity to sharpen their thinking skills. The questions can be used as a class discussion or independent writing activity.

- Which chapter in this unit did you find the most interesting? Why?
- What was your favorite part of this year's journey with your group?

252

UNIT 5 ORGANIZER

In each box below, identify some people who share in this ministry and describe what each person does.

Ministry: ways we serve God and all people according to God's call

252 Organizer

UNIT 5 REVIEW

Match the words in Column A to the definitions in Column B.

Column A

1. ministry
2. pope
3. prophet
4. praise

Column B

___3___ someone called by God to speak in his name

___4___ thanking God for being wonderful

___1___ the ways we serve God and all people according to God's special call

___2___ the leader of the Catholic Church all over the world

Circle the letter of each correct answer.

1. Today, the _____ continues Jesus' ministry of the word.

   (a) scribes   (b) Church   (c) government

2. The Holy Spirit helps us work to live in _____ and harmony.

   (a) wealth   (b) anger   (c) unity

3. Jesus taught his friends and followers to _____ God.

   (a) find   (b) forget   (c) worship

4. Jesus spent his whole life _____ people in need.

   (a) serving   (b) needing   (c) ignoring

5. Jesus calls us to share his ministry of love, justice, and _____.

   (a) power   (b) peace   (c) preaching

Review   253

Reviewing the Unit

The purpose of the Unit Review is to reinforce concepts presented in the preceding four chapters and to check the students' understanding. After explaining the directions, give the students sufficient time to complete the two-page review. Answer any questions they may have.

Testing

After the students have completed the Unit Review, you may wish to distribute copies of the Unit 5 Test from the Unit Tests booklet in The Resourceful Teacher Package.

Optional Unit Project

Invite the students to make mobiles representing the four ministries of the Church to which all Catholics are called to participate. Give each student two wooden dowels. Also supply the students with yarn, construction paper, scissors, hole punchers, and crayons or markers. Have the students choose a shape for the four mobile pieces. They might draw the outline of a church with a steeple, a heart, or a shape of their own choosing. Ask the students to list on each piece of the mobile the different ways we can live out the ministries of the Church. Then have them wrap yarn around the two dowels to secure them into the shape of an X. Direct them to punch a hole in each of the four mobile pieces and string yarn through the holes. Show them how to tie each stringed piece to one of the four ends of the dowels. Finally, tie in the center of the dowel a string for hanging the mobile.

253

UNIT 5 REVIEW

Name the four ministries of the Church.

building community   worshiping God

sharing God's word   serving others

Find the hidden words in the puzzle that Jesus spoke about. The first letter of each word is given. Write the words on the answer lines.

```
L   I   F   V   L   I   N   E
F   O   R   G   I   V   E   A
N   H   E   A   L   I   N   G
P   E   R   H   O   P   E   X
E   X   D   O   R   A   L   R
A   L   O   V   E   H   A   S
C   O   M   F   O   R   T   T
E   M   S   T   R   A   N   G
```

F O R G I V E   L O V E

H E A L I N G   H O P E

C O M F O R T   P E A C E

Name four ways to serve in the ministry of worship.

Lead the worshiping community.   Distribute communion.

Assist the priest.   Sing or play an instrument.

254 Review

Day to Day
Skills for Christian Living

FEELING LEFT OUT

Fitting in and belonging to a group is not always easy. Some of us may feel that we have no close friends. Some of us may feel that the friends we were once close to no longer care about us. The person who is our best friend today may be best friends with someone else tomorrow. We are beginning to learn that friendships sometimes change.

When we experience changes in friendships, we have many different feelings and often react in a variety of ways. If we feel angry and resentful, we may want to get back at those who have hurt us. Some of us may be good at pretending everything is fine, yet on the inside we feel sad and lonely.

Some of us may try to keep our hurt from showing by being silly or acting tough. Sometimes when we feel left out, we can easily forget that we were created by a loving God who never forgets us or leaves us.

Karen's Problem

Karen is a new student in the third grade. She is having a hard time making friends and is feeling very lonely. Part of the reason things are so difficult for her is that she is shy and unsure about how to make friends. The other kids are not unkind. They just do not seem to notice her. She is never picked to be someone's partner and is usually alone at recess. Some of the kids spend time on the weekend at each other's houses, but Karen is never invited. Karen wishes she could go back to her old school. When her mother asks her how things are going, she pretends to like her new school so that her mother will not worry.

Day to Day **255**

Day to Day

Objective

This lesson helps the students develop their ability to cope when feeling lonely or left out.

Introducing the Lesson

Tell the students that today's lesson is about what to do when feeling left out or lonely. Read together "Feeling Left Out" at the top of page 255. Ask the students if they can remember times when they felt left out of something. Invite them to tell about their feelings and what they did to feel better.

Completing the Activity

Ask for one or more volunteers to read aloud "Karen's Problem." Direct the students' attention to the activity at the top of page 256 and have them work in groups of four or five to complete it. Challenge them to think creatively about possible solutions for Karen. When they have finished, invite each group to share its responses. Use the following questions to help the students evaluate each group's solutions.

■ Does the solution help Karen reach her goal?

■ Does the solution show care for others?

■ Does the solution keep the problem from getting worse?

■ Does the solution show Christian friendship?

Lesson continues on page 256.

255

Read aloud "Reminders When Feeling Left Out." Encourage the students to consider each item mentioned in terms of Karen's experience by asking the following questions.

- With whom might Karen share her feelings?
- What are some activities she could try if she was a new student in our school?
- How might she reach out and let others know she would like to be their friend?
- How could she let others know she would be a good friend?
- How might remembering Jesus' love help Karen?

Concluding the Lesson

Close the lesson by reading aloud "Following Jesus." Remind the students that feeling lonely or excluded is an experience common to everyone and that helping others feel accepted is something each of us can do as part of being a Christian friend. Then invite the students to form a large circle, join hands, and say the prayer together.

256

Activity Finding a Solution

Use your problem-solving skills to complete the chart below and find the best solution for Karen.

Karen's problem: _____

Karen's goal: _____

Possible solutions	Possible consequences
_____	_____
_____	_____
_____	_____

REMINDERS WHEN FEELING LEFT OUT

1. Share your feelings with someone who will listen.
2. Use your problem-solving skills to think of some good solutions.
3. Participate in activities that give you a chance to meet new friends and also keep you busy with something fun to do.
4. Reach out to others and let them know that you are interested in being their friend.
5. Be a good friend. Remember to listen. Be willing to share and take turns.
6. Remember that Jesus cares about you and loves you, especially when you are feeling unloved by others.

Following Jesus

Jesus always looked out for people who were feeling left out. We know that he looks out for us, too, when we feel this way. Jesus wants us all to care for one another in the same ways that he cares so that nobody feels left out.

PRAYER

Jesus, help us to choose the best words and actions that show our care for others, especially for those who are lonely. Amen.

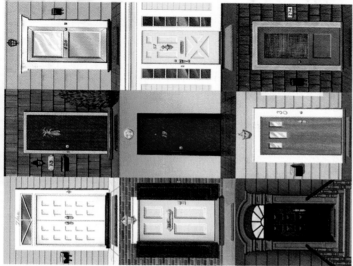

Opening Doors ～
A Take-Home Magazine™

Growing Closer

TRY TO FIND a few minutes each week to read the Scriptures, either alone or with your family. Rediscover how the word of God challenges you to bring the message of Jesus to others.

MAKE IT A FAMILY PRACTICE to discuss Sunday's gospel together. Allow the gospel message to speak personally to you. Encourage one another to live out the challenge of Jesus' words and example.

Answers for pp. 4–5: Mass, Church, or Eucharist • sabbath • Sunday • God or Jesus • Scriptures or Eucharist • pray • sing • praise • God or Jesus

listen • Scriptures • lector • Old Testament • New Testament • psalm • priest or deacon • priest or deacon • gospel

homily • message

ministry • love, healing, guidance, forgiveness, peace, strength, comfort • Church • people

Looking Ahead

As the summer approaches, take time to recognize God in your midst. Each time your family is gathered together and each time you join the family of Jesus to celebrate together, remember that "where two or three are gathered together in my name, there am I in the midst of them" (Matthew 18:20).

Opening Doors ～

Sending the Magazine Home

As you complete Unit 5 with your class, assist the students in carefully removing *Opening Doors: A Take-Home Magazine* (two pages) from their texts by separating the pages from the book along the perforations. Demonstrate how to fold the two pages to form an eight-page booklet.

When the magazines are folded, take time to explain each section of the magazine to the students. Allow the students to ask any questions they may have. Ask the students to take the magazine home and encourage their families to read it with them and to participate in the suggested activities. You may wish to attach a letter of your own, encouraging the family to use the magazine each time their child brings it home.

The Book of Psalms

"The precepts of the Lord give joy to the heart."
adapted from Psalm 19:9

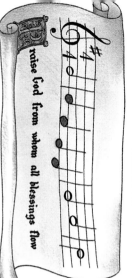

praise God from whom all blessings flow

Helping us to take the word of God to heart, the psalms, a book of 150 songs from the Old Testament, have become an important part of the Liturgy of the Word. Sung or recited after the First Reading, the psalm is related to the other readings proclaimed at Mass. The psalm, however, serves a more meditative purpose. It gives the worshiping community an opportunity to think about and respond to God's word by helping to maintain a prayerful pace, or flow, in the liturgy.

Because of the range of sentiments found in them, the psalms are often the point where our life stories connect with the story of God's salvation. For the Hebrew psalm writers, the events of their lives were very much a part of this story of the whole people of God. Even though written from a personal perspective, they have long been prayers of the whole community.

Paul himself became a hunted and persecuted man—someone seen as a traitor by some Jewish leaders.

Called to preach the good news wherever it had not yet been proclaimed, Paul was constantly on the move. He would stop in a town or city for a short while, preach the gospel, baptize converts, and leave behind trained disciples to lead the new community as he traveled on. Because Paul cared deeply about each of the churches he founded, he was dedicated to writing letters of encouragement to them. In addition, whenever Paul heard of one of the new Christian communities experiencing a problem, he would attempt to correct the situation by reminding the people of who they were called to be as followers of Jesus.

Paul's first epistle was addressed to the Thessalonians, urging them to continue growing in patience, faith, and love until Jesus came again in glory.

At Galatia, there was a major argument about whether or not Gentile converts had to become Jews before they could become Christians. Paul tried to settle the issue in his letter to this community by emphasizing that salvation was by faith in Jesus and not determined by circumcision or any other law.

The illicit lifestyle of many Christians in Corinth and the lack of unity among members of the worshiping community were among the concerns of the Corinthians which came to Paul's attention. Thus, in his letter to the Corinthians, Paul dealt with proper Christian conduct and described the Church as the body of Christ whose members needed to work together.

When we read the letters of Paul today, it is important to keep in mind the historical reasons why they were written. As in all Scripture, however, the truths revealed in Paul's letters are as timeless as the God who inspired them!

While about one third of the Psalms are lamentations, or cries of distress, many more are festive hymns of praise or thanksgiving to the God of salvation. The Hebrew word for psalms is *tehillim*, which means "praises." Written over a period of 1,000 years, the psalms tell the praises of the people of God and of their faith in God's presence and power in all aspects of life.

"Come before the Lord with joyful song!"

adapted from Psalm 100:2

The Psalter, or Book of Psalms, was probably the hymn book used in Jewish worship as early as the sixth century B.C. So we should not be surprised to see many references to the psalms in the New Testament. Jesus sometimes alluded to the psalms when he was teaching or praying. In the reading of the passion at the Palm Sunday liturgy, we hear Jesus reciting from a psalm about trusting God (Psalm 22:2): "My God, my God, why have you abandoned me?" In the parable of the tenants recorded in Mark 12:1–12, we find Jesus comparing the "beloved son" (verse 6, probably indicating himself) to "the stone which the builders rejected" which became "the cornerstone" (Psalm 118:22). Psalm 118 is the Responsorial Psalm used in the Easter Sunday liturgy.

So a tradition of nearly 3,000 years of worship continues. In fact, it is believed that most of the psalms were written specifically for the purpose of prayer and worship. The Hebrew *tehillim* have been used effectively in both Jewish and Christian liturgy for many centuries!

Being Catholic

The Letters of Paul

Do you still take the time to write letters to long-time friends? If so, then you know that letters often can have more impact than a phone call. Letters can be read again and again. They can be saved and savored.

One of the most famous of all letter writers in the Scriptures is Saint Paul. Before his conversion, Paul was a religious bigot. He persecuted Christians as traitors to Judaism. After his conversion,

... LET US NOT GROW TIRED OF DOING GOOD, FOR IN DUE TIME WE SHALL REAP OUR HARVEST .... LET US DO GOOD TO ALL

Sharing the Message

The Liturgy of the Word is an important part of the Mass. God speaks to us through the Scriptures, telling us of God's love and of our responsibility to each other as children of the same Father. As you work through these pages with your child, rediscover both the gift and the challenge the word of God is to us as Christians.

We go to —— on the Christian —— day,
which is ——. We ——, we ——
in the ——. We —— shares himself with us
songs, and we —— God for all the wonderful things
—— has done for us.

We also —— to the ——. A person
called a —— usually reads a story from the
—— part of the Bible and a story from
one of the letters found in the ——. In
between these two readings, we say or sing a ——.
Now it is time to stand and welcome Jesus among us as the
—— or —— reads a —— story
to us. Sometimes the gospel story is difficult to understand.
The priest or deacon gives a special talk called a ——.

4

the gospel story. Just as Jesus' —— was to bring
God's word to everyone he met, we too share in the
ministry of the word. God's word brings
people ——, ——, ——,
——. Through us, the ——,
God's word is brought to all of God's ——.

Some of these words can be used more than once.

Church	praise	Jesus	Eucharist
forgiveness	sabbath	Mass	guidance
healing	pray	Old Testament	lector
listen	sing	New Testament	message
ministry	Sunday	priest	peace
people	deacon	Scriptures	
psalm	gospel		
strength			
comfort			
God			
homily			
love			

Listen carefully to the Scripture readings the next time you go to Mass. Try to share the message of God's word with others this week.

5

Celebrating the Journey

Leader: We are the Church! We believe that by worshiping together, we keep faith alive in our hearts. We believe that by serving together, we keep Jesus Christ alive in the world.

Reader: A reading from Paul's letter to the Ephesians.

Leader: Our journey together has led us to this peaceful moment where we can rest, pause to remember, and be refreshed and strengthened for the journey ahead. Let us bless one another now with this water, which reminds us of the life of Jesus born in each of us at Baptism.

Leader: Our faith has been renewed as we have seen Jesus in one another and in all the people of

parish. Let us profess our faith together now as we join hands and recite the Apostles' Creed.

Leader: Let us pray.

All: God, we thank you for the Holy Spirit who came to give life to us, your Church. We thank you for each other and for another year of growing and learning together. Keep us close to you and to one another. We ask this in Jesus' name. Amen.

261

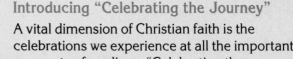

Introducing "Celebrating the Journey"

A vital dimension of Christian faith is the celebrations we experience at all the important moments of our lives. "Celebrating the Journey" is a special feature designed to help celebrate the completion of another important phase of the faith journey.

Using "Celebrating the Journey"

Plan a special time at the end of the year to use this celebration with your class. Select a student to read the suggested story from Scripture. Choose a few of the students' favorite songs to sing at various times during the celebration. Allow the students to participate as fully as possible. You may wish to invite other people, such as the director of religious education, the principal, the pastor, or members of the students' families, to the celebration. End the celebration with a simple snack.

Special Preparations/Instructions

Have a large bowl of water available. Begin and end with a song about Christian unity.

Suggested reading is Ephesians 2:19–22.

During the baptismal blessing, play gentle background music. The leader dips his or her right thumb in the water and blesses the first student on the forehead. Both say, "We do believe." The first student blesses the next student and both say, "We do believe." The process continues until the last student blesses the leader.

The Apostles' Creed can be found in the Prayers section of the student text and the teacher guide.

262

263

Our Church Celebrates Advent

Lesson Outlines ～～～～

	Step 1 — Learning About Our Lives	Step 2 — Learning About Our Faith	Step 3 — Learning How to Live Our Faith
Lesson 1	■ Discuss some photographs. ■ Make a family tree. *ABOUT 15 MINUTES*	■ Read about the Jesse Tree. ■ Study the Jesse Tree banners. *ABOUT 5 MINUTES*	■ Complete an activity. *ABOUT 10 MINUTES*
Lesson 2	■ Review Lesson 1. ■ Recall family stories. *ABOUT 10 MINUTES*	■ Learn about Jesus' ancestors. *ABOUT 5 MINUTES*	■ Make Jesse Tree symbols. ■ Complete an activity. *ABOUT 15 MINUTES*
Lesson 3	■ Talk about preparing for events. *ABOUT 6 MINUTES*	■ Read about John the Baptizer. ■ Talk about good news. *ABOUT 15 MINUTES*	■ Learn a sign-language prayer. *ABOUT 9 MINUTES*
Lesson 4	**Project** Review the Jesse Tree; make a Jesse Tree. **Prayer** Discuss the students' Jesse Trees; discuss the Jesse Tree symbol; prepare for a prayer service; participate in a prayer service.		

Plan Ahead

	Preparing Your Class	**Materials Needed**
Lesson 1	Read through the lesson plan for this session. Select pictures of yourself and your family to share with the class. Think of symbols for your ancestors.	■ pictures of your family and deceased relatives ■ chalkboard ■ colored chalk ■ pencils or pens
Lesson 2	Read through the lesson plan for this session. Before class, read Genesis 15:1–6 and 28:10–22 and Exodus 24:12–18 and 31:18. Be prepared to share these stories with the students.	■ colored chalk ■ construction paper or drawing paper ■ crayons or markers ■ scissors ■ large envelopes
Lesson 3	Read the entire plan for this lesson. Practice the sign-language gestures for the Advent prayer.	■ drawing paper ■ crayons
Lesson 4	Gather the materials for the class Jesse Tree and assemble it. Have ready the envelopes containing the students' Jesse Tree symbols, which they made in Lesson 2.	■ chalkboard ■ construction paper or drawing paper ■ crayons or markers ■ scissors ■ yarn or thread

Additional Resources

As you plan this chapter, consider using the following materials from The Resourceful Teacher Package.

■ *Classroom Activity Sheets for Advent*

■ *Family Activity Sheets for Advent*

■ *Prayers for Every Day*

You may also wish to refer to the following Big Book.

■ *We Celebrate God's Word*, page 4

In preparing the students for the Sunday readings, you may wish to use Silver Burdett Ginn's *Getting Ready for Sunday* student and teacher materials.

REDUCED CLASSROOM ACTIVITIES

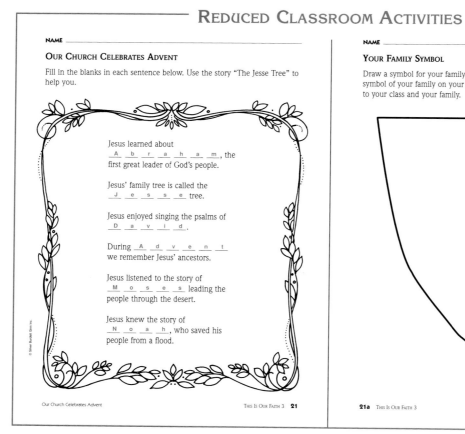

NAME _____

OUR CHURCH CELEBRATES ADVENT

Fill in the blanks in each sentence below. Use the story "The Jesse Tree" to help you.

Jesus learned about
A b r a h a m , the
first great leader of God's people.

Jesus' family tree is called the
J e s s e tree.

Jesus enjoyed singing the psalms of
D a v i d .

During A d v e n t
we remember Jesus' ancestors.

Jesus listened to the story of
M o s e s leading the
people through the desert.

Jesus knew the story of
N o a h , who saved his
people from a flood.

Our Church Celebrates Advent

THIS IS OUR FAITH 3 **21**

NAME _____

YOUR FAMILY SYMBOL

Draw a symbol for your family. Cut along the heavy black lines. Place this symbol of your family on your family Christmas tree. Explain your symbol to your class and your family.

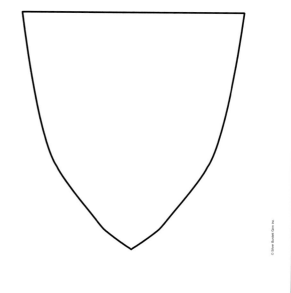

21a THIS IS OUR FAITH 3

Our Church Celebrates Advent

263c Organizer

Background for the Teacher

THE THREEFOLD COMING OF THE LORD

Each year the Church celebrates the four weeks of the season of Advent. The word *advent* is derived from the Latin word *adventus,* which means "coming." During this time, we reflect on the coming of the Lord. Although at Christmas, Jesus' birth in the little town of Bethlehem may be uppermost in our minds, the season of Advent invites us to reflect on the threefold coming of the Lord.

First, there is the coming of the Lord as a baby in Bethlehem nearly two thousand years ago. This historical event happened once and is commemorated each year at the Christmas holiday. Secondly, there is the mystery of the coming of the Lord in the Eucharist and in the celebration of all the sacraments. We celebrate the coming of Jesus to us through the Scriptures and in the many grace-filled events of our lives. The Church recognizes the Lord's coming in the sacramental moments of each day. Thirdly, there is the coming of Jesus when he returns in glory.

THE FOCUS OF OUR ATTENTION

In these lessons, we focus our attention on the celebration of the first coming of the Lord—the birth of Jesus. We invite the third-grade students to expand their understanding of Jesus' coming by introducing them to some of Jesus' ancestors and relatives, who prepared the way for the coming of Jesus. They represent branches of Jesus' family tree. The custom of the Jesse Tree provides a way to learn about these early ancestors of Jesus.

Jesus came into a family that had prepared for his coming and that influenced his growth and development as a human being. Jesus was born to a people with a long history of a relationship with God. Jesus was influenced by the important people and the major events of his Jewish heritage. The Jesse Tree provides a way to focus on these people and events.

Lesson 1

Objective
This lesson helps the students learn about the Jesse Tree.

Step 1/INTRODUCTION

Learning About Our Lives

Discussing Some Photographs
Show the students pictures of members of your family. If possible, show some pictures of relatives who are now deceased.

Making a Family Tree
Draw a large tree on the chalkboard. Write your name at the top of the tree. Using the photographs, fill in the names of other relatives in your family tree. Tell the students a short story about each family member you add to your family tree. Ask the students what would be a good symbol for each family member. Using colored chalk, draw the suggested symbols next to the family names. Finally, ask the students what would be a good symbol for you. Draw their suggested symbol next to your name. Write on the chalkboard the following words: *This is the family tree of (your name). On it are the ancestors of (your name).* Explain the word *ancestors* to the students.

Step 2/DEVELOPMENT

Learning About Our Faith

Reading About the Jesse Tree
Tell the students that Jesus had a family tree, too. Explain that during the liturgical season of Advent we think about Jesus' family tree. Ask a volunteer to read aloud "The Jesse Tree" on pages 264–265. Ask the following questions.

- What do we call Jesus' family tree? (*The Jesse Tree*)

- Who were some ancestors of Jesus? (*Abraham, Moses, Noah, David*)

- Why do you think that a symbol for Noah might be a boat? (*Answers may vary*)

Explain to the students that we call Jesus' family tree "the Jesse Tree" because Jesse was the father of David, who was an ancestor of Jesus.

264

Our Church Celebrates Advent

The Jesse Tree

When Jesus was a little boy, he learned about people who lived long ago. He loved to hear his mother, Mary, tell the stories of his ancestors.

He learned about Abraham, the first great leader of God's people. He listened to the story of Moses leading God's people through the desert. He heard the story of Noah, who saved his family from a great flood. And he enjoyed singing the psalms of King David.

During the season of Advent, we remember some of the people on Jesus' family tree. Each of them helped to make things ready for Jesus to come into the world at Christmas time. Jesus' family tree is called the **Jesse Tree**.

Teaching Tips

Read aloud several stories about Jesus' ancestors. Gather the students around you. Using an appropriate children's Bible, read the story of Noah and the Great Flood (Genesis 6:1–9:17), the story of David and Goliath (1 Samuel 17:1–49), or a story from Moses' life, such as The Call of Moses (Exodus 3:1–15) or The Crossing of the Red Sea (Exodus 14:5–31). Some of the students may already be familiar with the details of these stories from Vacation Bible School experiences or from their own families sharing them.

To help us remember the ancestors of Jesus, we draw a symbol for each person and hang it on a tree branch. Noah's symbol might be a boat, and David's symbol might be a musical instrument.

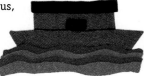

Activity

Choose four members of *your* family. In the boxes below, draw a different symbol for each person. Then write the name of the person beneath his or her symbol.

Direct the students' attention to the two banners on page 264. Give them time to look at the symbols on the banners. Discuss the symbols and see whether the students can come up with any ancestors of Jesus. (Do not expect too much from this discussion, since the students may not know much about the Old Testament.)

Step 3/CONCLUSION

Learning How to Live Our Faith

Completing an Activity

Read the directions for the activity on page 265. Ask each student to choose four members of his or her family and to draw a symbol for each person. Afterward, invite the students to tell brief stories about their family members to illustrate why they chose the four symbols that they drew on page 265. Encourage the students to ask their families about their ancestors. Tell the students that they will have time during Lesson 2 to tell these stories.

🍎 Teaching Tips

Avoid the impression that a family must include only blood relatives. In the activity on page 265, suggest that the students may want to include significant adults and other close family friends who have played an important role in their lives. Help the students feel pride in the ways in which these individuals have helped them feel a sense of community and belonging.

265

LESSON 2

Objective

This lesson helps the students become acquainted with some of the ancestors of Jesus.

Step 1/INTRODUCTION

Learning About Our Lives

Reviewing Lesson 1

Review what the students have learned about the Jesse Tree.

Recall your own family tree, which you drew on the chalkboard during Lesson 1. Discuss what a symbol means. Help the students understand that the symbols you drew on the chalkboard and the symbols on the banners on page 264 stand for characteristics of the people on the family tree or for events in their lives.

Recalling Family Stories

Provide time for a few volunteers to tell stories about their ancestors. Discuss symbols the students might put on a family tree for these ancestors. Draw some of these symbols on the chalkboard and invite the students to use colored chalk to color the symbols.

Step 2/DEVELOPMENT

Learning About Our Faith

Learning About Jesus' Ancestors

Ask volunteers to read aloud "Jesus' Ancestors" on page 266. Look at the chart at the bottom of page 266. Provide time for the students to discuss the ancestors of Jesus and their symbols and to tell any stories they can remember about Abraham, Moses, Jacob, Mary, and Joseph. To help the students understand the symbols, tell the students the stories from the Old Testament that you read before class.

Jesus' Ancestors

The Bible told people that a great leader would come from the family of Jesse. Jesse lived a long time before Jesus. He was the father of King David. Both Jesse and King David were Jesus' ancestors.

Jesus had many ancestors. Some of them are listed below. Read the list and look at the symbols. Then look at the Jesse Tree banners on page 264. Find the symbols for these ancestors and talk about them with your class.

	Abraham: God said his children and grandchildren would be as many as the stars.
	Jacob: He dreamed about angels going up and down a ladder to heaven.
	Moses: He was a great leader of God's people. God gave him stone tablets on which the Ten Commandments were listed.
	Mary: She was the mother of Jesus.
	Joseph: He was a carpenter. He loved and cared for Mary and Jesus.

The Lineage of Jesus Isaiah prophesied that the Messiah would come from the house, or family, of King David by saying, "But a shoot shall sprout from the stump of Jesse, and from his roots a bud shall blossom. The spirit of the Lord shall rest upon him" (Isaiah 11:1–2). Joseph, Jesus' foster father, was a direct descendant of King David. By accepting Jesus as his own son, Joseph made it possible for God's plan for the world, as prophesied by Isaiah, to be fulfilled.

Activity

Fill in the blanks to complete the missing words. Then use these words to fill in the puzzle below. When you have completed the puzzle, you will find the name of a special Advent activity.

1. <u>J</u> <u>e</u> <u>s</u> <u>u</u> <u>s</u> is our Savior.

2. Moses was a <u>l</u> <u>e</u> <u>a</u> <u>d</u> <u>e</u> <u>r</u> of God's people.

3. <u>J</u> <u>o</u> <u>s</u> <u>e</u> <u>p</u> <u>h</u> was a carpenter.

4. We celebrate Jesus' birth on
   <u>C</u> <u>h</u> <u>r</u> <u>i</u> <u>s</u> <u>t</u> <u>m</u> <u>a</u> <u>s</u>.

5. We <u>p</u> <u>r</u> <u>e</u> <u>p</u> <u>a</u> <u>r</u> <u>e</u> for Christmas
   during <u>A</u> <u>d</u> <u>v</u> <u>e</u> <u>n</u> <u>t</u>.

6. There are <u>f</u> <u>o</u> <u>u</u> <u>r</u> weeks in the Advent season.

7. Noah and King David were
   <u>a</u> <u>n</u> <u>c</u> <u>e</u> <u>s</u> <u>t</u> <u>o</u> <u>r</u> <u>s</u> of Jesus.

8. <u>J</u> <u>e</u> <u>s</u> <u>s</u> <u>e</u> was the father of King David.

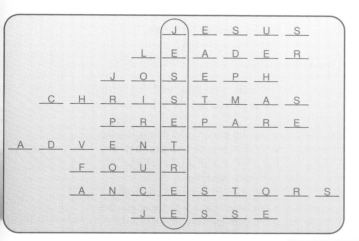

Learning How to Live Our Faith

Making Jesse Tree Symbols

Provide each student with construction paper or drawing paper, crayons or markers, scissors, and a large envelope. Invite the students to make the five symbols pictured on page 266. Tell the students that in Lesson 4 they will make more symbols for a Jesse Tree. After the students have made and cut out the symbols, have them write their names on the envelopes and put the Jesse Tree symbols inside the envelopes. Collect these envelopes for use in Lesson 4. If some students finish their symbols early, invite them to make one of the symbols for a class Jesse Tree for Lesson 4.

Completing an Activity

Read the directions at the top of page 267. Check to be sure that the students understand the activity. When the puzzle at the bottom of the page is completed, note that the highlighted letters spell out *JESSE TREE*.

Teaching Tips

Offer a spontaneous prayer thanking God for Jesus' ancestors and the people who have gone before us in faith. Then encourage the students to offer their own prayers for the people in their lives who have helped them to grow in their love for God.

LESSON 3

Objective

This lesson helps the students recognize that John the Baptizer prepared the way for Jesus.

Step 1/INTRODUCTION

Learning About Our Lives

Talking About Preparing for Events

Ask the students to name events that they look forward to and that require preparation beforehand. List these events on the chalkboard. *(Responses may include: birthday parties, vacations, Christmas, or other holiday celebrations.)* Lead a class discussion, using the following questions.

- How do you and others get ready for these special events?

- Do you tell other people about what's going to happen?

- Are there any special preparations that you have to make for these events?

Guide the students to understand that when we know something important is about to happen, we spend time preparing for it. Tell the class that in this lesson they will learn about someone who helped prepare the way for Jesus' coming.

Step 2/DEVELOPMENT

Learning About Our Faith

Reading About John the Baptizer

Direct attention to page 268 and invite volunteers to read aloud "John the Baptizer." Then ask the following questions.

- Who were John's parents? (*Elizabeth and Zechariah*)

- Why were Elizabeth and Zechariah sad before John was born? (*Because they did not have a child with whom to share their love*)

- How did Zechariah learn that Elizabeth was going to have a baby boy? (*God sent an angel to tell him.*)

- What else did the angel tell Zechariah? (*To name the baby John; that John would prepare the way for Jesus*)

- What did God call John to be? (*A prophet*)

268

John the Baptizer

John the Baptizer was an important part of Jesus' family tree. John's parents, Elizabeth and Zechariah, were kind and loving people who wanted to have a child. But for many years, they were sad because they did not have a child.

One day, God sent an angel to Zechariah. The angel said, "Elizabeth is going to have a son. Name him John. He will prepare the way for God's Son, Jesus."

Elizabeth and Zechariah were filled with joy when John was born. They taught John to love God and to follow God's ways.

When John grew up, he went to the desert to pray and study. Then God called him to be a **prophet**, a messenger who speaks for God. God told John to tell people to prepare for Jesus' coming.

John traveled from town to town. He baptized many people and told them, "Change the way you are living. Be baptized. Prepare the way for the Lord."

Teaching Tips

Help the students prepare for the coming of Jesus by bringing in an Advent calendar to use in your classroom. Or you may wish to have the students work in four groups to make a class Advent calendar. Ask each group to create artwork and suggest an activity for each day in one of the weeks of Advent. Tape or glue the finished art and activity suggestion for each day onto a large calendar grid. Allow a different student each day to read the suggested activity from the calendar.

John told everyone how to get ready for Jesus. He said, "Share your food and clothes with the poor. Be sorry for your sins. Tell the truth. Be happy with what you have. Believe in the good news!"   *Based on Luke 1:5–17; 3:1–14*

Activity

During Advent, we prepare the way for Jesus by doing kind things for others. We try to treat everyone with love and care. Learn the signs that tell us what God wants us to do during Advent.

Prepare   the way

for   the Lord.

- What did John tell people when he went from town to town? (*Change the way you are living; be baptized; prepare the way for the Lord.*)

- What did John say that the people should do to get ready for Jesus? (*He said they should share their clothes and food with the poor; be sorry for their sins; tell the truth; be happy with what they have; believe in the good news.*)

Talking About Good News

Ask the students how Jesus is good news. (*Responses may include: Jesus loves us, Jesus taught us how to live, and Jesus died and rose for us.*) Tell the students that, like John, they can be prophets by telling others the good news about Jesus. Distribute drawing paper and crayons. Invite the students to draw cartoons of themselves as prophets, with a conversation bubble over their heads. Have them write a message in the bubble about preparing for Jesus during Advent.

Step 3/CONCLUSION

Learning How to Live Our Faith

Learning a Sign-Language Prayer

Use the diagrams on page 269 to teach the sign-language gestures for the Advent prayer. Practice each sign several times. When all are comfortable with the signs, pray the prayer together.

⭐ ⭐ ⭐ ⭐
Enriching the Lesson

On a poster, draw a large tree with bare branches. Cut green leaves from construction paper. Tell the students that each time they show kindness to others or treat others with love and care during Advent, they may write their good deed on a leaf and paste it on the tree. Explain that the tree is a sign of Jesus' good news growing in the world.

269

LESSON 4

Objective

This lesson helps the students make a Jesse Tree.

Reviewing the Jesse Tree

Distribute the envelopes containing the Jesse Tree symbols that the students made in Lesson 2. Discuss the meaning of the symbols.

Making a Jesse Tree

Have volunteers read the top of page 270. Show the students the Jesse Tree you have assembled. Explain that this is the class Jesse Tree but that each of them can also make a Jesse Tree at home. Carefully read the directions on page 270.

On the chalkboard, write the following names: Adam and Eve, Noah, Abraham and Sarah, Jacob, Joseph, Moses, Miriam (Moses' sister), David, Isaiah, John the Baptizer, Joseph (Jesus' foster father), and Mary. Invite five students to come to the chalkboard and draw the five symbols from Lesson 2 next to the appropriate names. Ask the students if they can think of any symbols for the remaining names. Help the students by telling them brief stories about these figures. Suggest that some symbols might be the following: Adam and Eve (apple), Noah (boat), Joseph (a coat of many colors), Miriam (cymbals or tambourine), David (a harp), Isaiah (a scroll), John the Baptizer (a wrap of fur). Draw these symbols on the chalkboard.

Provide construction paper or drawing paper, crayons or colored markers, and scissors. Invite the students to complete their Jesse Tree symbols and put them in their envelopes to take home. Have the students who finish early make symbols for the class Jesse Tree. Keep these in an envelope. During each week of Advent, put a symbol on the Jesse Tree each day and say a prayer.

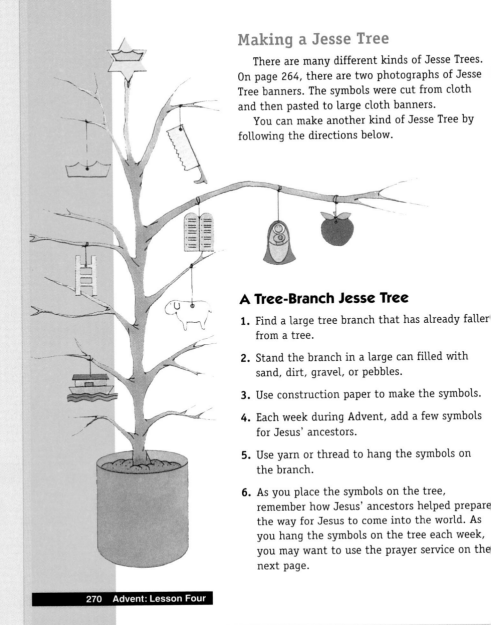

270 Advent: Lesson Four

Making a Jesse Tree

There are many different kinds of Jesse Trees. On page 264, there are two photographs of Jesse Tree banners. The symbols were cut from cloth and then pasted to large cloth banners.

You can make another kind of Jesse Tree by following the directions below.

A Tree-Branch Jesse Tree

1. Find a large tree branch that has already fallen from a tree.

2. Stand the branch in a large can filled with sand, dirt, gravel, or pebbles.

3. Use construction paper to make the symbols.

4. Each week during Advent, add a few symbols for Jesus' ancestors.

5. Use yarn or thread to hang the symbols on the branch.

6. As you place the symbols on the tree, remember how Jesus' ancestors helped prepare the way for Jesus to come into the world. As you hang the symbols on the tree each week, you may want to use the prayer service on the next page.

Cultural Awareness

Trees are a symbol of life for many cultures. Palestinian, Swiss, and Mexican families often celebrate the birth of a child by planting a tree. In certain cultures, one type of tree is planted for a girl, and another is planted for a boy. The tradition of Jesse Trees and Christmas trees helps us remember that through Jesus we receive new life.

Focus on

Advent/Christmas Trees During the Middle Ages, mystery plays were popular in most large churches. Mystery plays presented stories of the events in the Bible, especially stories about Jesus' life. The traditional Advent plays began with Adam and Eve in the garden, with an apple tree as a central prop. When the mystery plays were no longer popular, the common culture retained the tree with bright red ornaments and Old Testament symbols as part of the seasonal celebration.

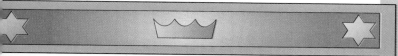

Advent Prayer Service

Teacher: As our ancestors did long ago, let us prepare the way of the Lord. Listen carefully to these readings from the Bible.

Reader 1: The Lord says, "The time is coming when I will keep my promise to send a great ruler. He will do what is right and just. When he comes, everyone will be safe."

Based on Jeremiah 33:14–16

Reader 2: When the great king comes, he will be from Jesse's family. He will be wise and strong. He will know and do God's will. He will stand up for the poor and bring peace and justice to all the nations.

Based on Isaiah 11

Reader 3: Shout for joy, O children of God! Sing a glad song in your hearts. Your king is already among you. God will make you new in his love.

Based on Zephaniah 3:14–17

Reader 4: The Lord says, "City of Bethlehem, listen! Everyone thinks you are too small. But the ruler of Israel will be born within you. He will be like a good shepherd. He will bring peace to the whole world."

Based on Micah 5:1–3

All: Loving Father, we remember that your Son, Jesus, was born on Christmas. We need Jesus in our world today. Help us to get ready for him to come to us again. Amen.

CURRICULUM CONNECTION

Science Help the students understand what it means to wait and hope, as Jesus' ancestors did, by having them grow narcissus bulbs. Each student will need a bulb, pebbles, and a clear plastic bowl. Have each student put a pebble in the bottom of the bowl and place the bulb in the middle. Fill the bowl with water until the bottom half of the bulb is covered. Maintain this level of water throughout the growing period. Place the bowls in a dark place. Watch for signs of growth during the next four weeks.

Discussing the Students' Jesse Trees

Ask the students if any of them made a Jesse Tree at home. Discuss any problems they encountered. Tell students that they will have a prayer service and that one of them will put the first symbol on the class Jesse Tree. Encourage the students to do this with their families at home.

Discussing the Jesse Tree Symbol

From the class Jesse Tree envelope, take out the symbol for Adam and Eve (an apple). Discuss with the students why this symbol represents Adam and Eve.

Show the students how to add yarn or thread to the top of the symbol so that it can be hung from the Jesse Tree.

Preparing for a Prayer Service

Select a volunteer to add the Jesse Tree symbol to the tree during the prayer service. Ask for volunteers to read the parts on page 271 labeled *Reader 1, Reader 2, Reader 3,* and *Reader 4*. As the readers practice their parts, work with the remainder of the students on the prayer labeled *All*. Discuss what this prayer means. Emphasize that during Advent we get ready to celebrate the birth of Jesus.

Participating in a Prayer Service

Gather the students around the class Jesse Tree. Begin the prayer service on page 271 by reading the part labeled *Teacher.* Invite the four readers to read their Scripture readings. After the class has responded to the readings by saying the prayer at the bottom of page 271, invite the student who is holding the Adam and Eve symbol to put it on the Jesse Tree branch that is closest to the base. Afterward, invite volunteers to tell what they remember about Adam and Eve. Close with a spontaneous prayer of thanksgiving for the ancestors of Jesus.

Our Church Celebrates Christmas

Objectives ～～～

- **LESSON 1:** To help the students understand the story of the first Christmas.
- **LESSON 2:** To help the students learn that gifts tell us something about the person to whom they are given.
- **LESSON 3:** To help the students recognize that the gifts given to Jesus by the wise men help to reveal who Jesus is.
- **LESSON 4:** To help the students learn about the Holy Family and celebrate their learning about gift giving.

Lesson Outlines ～～～～～

	Step 1 Learning About Our Lives	**Step 2** Learning About Our Faith	**Step 3** Learning How to Live Our Faith
Lesson 1	■ Recall the Christmas story. *ABOUT 6 MINUTES*	■ Read a Christmas play. *ABOUT 12 MINUTES*	■ Write a message of praise. ■ Pray together. *ABOUT 12 MINUTES*
Lesson 2	■ Think about Christmas gifts. *ABOUT 5 MINUTES*	■ Read a story. ■ Act out the story. *ABOUT 18 MINUTES*	■ Match two columns. *ABOUT 7 MINUTES*
Lesson 3	■ Review Lesson 2. *ABOUT 5 MINUTES*	■ Read about gifts. *ABOUT 7 MINUTES*	■ Complete an activity. ■ Make a mobile. *ABOUT 18 MINUTES*
Lesson 4	**Project** Review Lesson 3; talk about the Holy Family; make a family gift. **Prayer** Make gifts for the prayer service; participate in a prayer service.		

Plan Ahead

	Preparing Your Class	**Materials Needed**
Lesson 1	Read through the lesson plan for this session. Choose a carol to sing in Step 3.	■ pencils or pens
Lesson 2	Read through the lesson plan for this session. Think about gifts you have given that seem especially appropriate.	■ pencils or pens
Lesson 3	Read the lesson plan. Have ready an item of gold, some incense, and a jar of perfumed ointment. Make a Christmas mobile to show the students in Step 3.	■ matches and colored chalk ■ construction paper or drawing paper ■ crayons or markers ■ scissors and yarn or string ■ dowels or hangers
Lesson 4	Make your own gift ornament to show the students as a sample. Be prepared to teach the song "We Three Kings." Prepare a bulletin board as described in the lesson.	■ a selection of Christmas cards ■ drawing paper ■ crayons or markers ■ scissors and yarn ■ yellow, gray or black, and blue construction paper

Additional Resources

As you plan this chapter, consider using the following materials from The Resourceful Teacher Package.

■ *Classroom Activity Sheets for Christmas*

■ *Family Activity Sheets for Christmas*

■ *Prayers for Every Day*

You may also wish to refer to the following Big Book.

■ *We Celebrate God's Word*, page 5

In preparing the students for the Sunday readings, you may wish to use Silver Burdett Ginn's *Getting Ready for Sunday* student and teacher materials.

REDUCED CLASSROOM ACTIVITIES

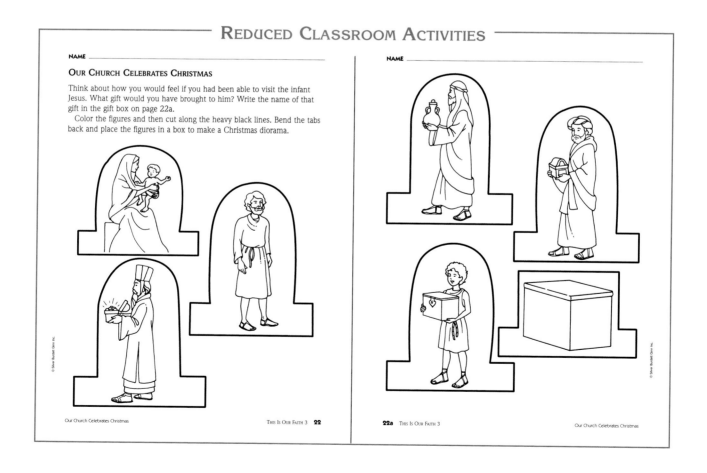

NAME

OUR CHURCH CELEBRATES CHRISTMAS

Think about how you would feel if you had been able to visit the infant Jesus. What gift would you have brought to him? Write the name of that gift in the gift box on page 22a.

Color the figures and then cut along the heavy black lines. Bend the tabs back and place the figures in a box to make a Christmas diorama.

NAME

Our Church Celebrates Christmas

THIS IS OUR FAITH 3 **22**

22a THIS IS OUR FAITH 3

Our Church Celebrates Christmas

Background for the Teacher

THE FIRST CHRISTMAS

Each year in the Church's liturgy, we hear the Christmas story proclaimed. This marvelous event—God becoming one of us in the infant Jesus—is so familiar that it hardly needs retelling. The story of Mary and Joseph's journey to Bethlehem, the over-crowded inn, the simple stable where the Savior was born, the angel-filled night sky, and the announcement to lowly shepherds evoke memories, feelings, and images of Christmases past. Yet, in the retelling of this ancient story, it becomes ever new.

In Lesson 1, the students have the opportunity to put on a Christmas play. This will enable them to enter into and experience the story of Jesus' birth in a special way. At their own level, they are able to wonder at and celebrate the reality of God becoming one of us in Jesus.

THE STORY OF THE MAGI

The Church calls our attention to the visit of the magi on the Sunday closest to January 6th. The Feast of the Epiphany celebrates the manifestation of God in the newborn king. The story of the visit of the wise men to the manger in the town of Bethlehem, taken from the Gospel of Matthew (2:1–12), is the focus of Lesson 2. This passage highlights the importance of the birth of Jesus. Having such noble visitors from the East illustrates the specialness of the birth of Jesus.

The Scriptures describe the visitors to Bethlehem as astrologers. These men believed that the appearance of a new star in the sky was a sign of the birth of a new king. These strangers to the land of Israel came and bowed down in recognition of the newborn king. This extraordinary occurrence illustrates a message that is basic to the entire New Testament and especially to the Gospel of Matthew: Jesus, God's Son, was accepted by the Gentiles as well as many of the Jewish people. Jesus is the Savior of *all*. He welcomes *all* people into his kingdom.

THE GIFTS OF THE MAGI

Third graders are able to grasp the significance of the gifts given by the magi to Jesus. Tradition has assigned meaning to the gifts. The gold is a gift fit for a king. The frankincense is the incense regularly used in worship ceremonies in the Jewish Temple. It is a gift appropriate for the Son of God. The myrrh, used in burial, is a foreshadowing of the death that Jesus would suffer as a human being. Encourage the students to explore why they themselves give things to other people.

LESSON 1

Objective

This lesson helps the students understand the story of the first Christmas.

Step 1/INTRODUCTION

Learning About Our Lives

Recalling the Christmas Story

Ask the students to recall what we prepare for during Advent. Elicit that during Advent we prepare to celebrate Jesus' birth on Christmas. Then invite the students to discuss how and when they first heard the story of Jesus' birth. Ask them if they have ever seen the Christmas story acted out or been part of a Christmas pageant. Allow time for them to share these experiences with the class. Tell the class that in today's lesson they will put on a play about the first Christmas.

Step 2/DEVELOPMENT

Learning About Our Faith

Reading a Christmas Play

Direct attention to "A Christmas Play" on pages 272 and 273. Before reading, assign the following parts: six readers, Joseph, the innkeeper, and the angel. Instruct the rest of the class to act as the chorus of angels. Have the students mark their parts in their books and practice reading them silently. Then read the play as a class. Use the following questions to guide discussion.

- Why did Mary and Joseph go to Bethlehem? (*They went to be counted. Explain to the students that the counting of a country's citizens is called a census.*)
- Why couldn't Mary and Joseph stay in the inn? (*It was too crowded.*)
- Where did Mary and Joseph stay? (*In a stable*)
- What happened during the night? (*Jesus was born.*)
- Why were the shepherds frightened? (*The sky was filled with light, and an angel appeared to them.*)
- What did the angel tell the shepherds to do? (*To go see the newborn Savior in the stable in Bethlehem*)

272

Our Church Celebrates Christmas

A Christmas Play

Reader 1: Long ago, the Emperor sent out a letter ordering everyone in the whole world to be counted. So Joseph, who was a descendant of King David, went to Bethlehem, the hometown of David. Joseph's wife, Mary, went with him.

Reader 2: While they were in Bethlehem, the time came for Mary to have her baby. Joseph looked for a place for Mary to rest. He went to talk to the innkeeper.

Joseph: My wife is going to have her baby. Can we stay in your inn?

Innkeeper: There is no room here. My inn is filled with travelers who came to be counted. You and your wife may stay in the stable.

Reader 3: So Joseph and Mary stayed the night in the stable. And on that night, Mary's son was born. She wrapped him in soft clothes and put him in an animal's feeding tray to sleep.

Focus on

Nativity Scenes Christmas nativity scenes or creches have been popular since the Middle Ages. In Italy in 1223, Saint Francis of Assisi began the custom of presenting live nativity scenes, with people portraying Mary, Joseph, the angels, the shepherds, and the magi. A wax figure was used for Jesus. These scenes may have been the forerunner of Christmas pageants.

Enriching the Lesson

Distribute drawing paper and crayons. Show the students how to fold the paper to form four rectangles. Invite them to draw one of the following scenes in each rectangle: Mary and Joseph traveling to Bethlehem; Joseph and Mary looking for shelter in Bethlehem; Mary, Joseph, and Jesus in the stable; and the shepherds finding the Holy Family.

eader 4: Out in the fields, shepherds were guarding their sheep. Suddenly, the sky was filled with bright light, and an angel of the Lord appeared to the shepherds. They were frightened. The angel said:

Angel: Don't be afraid! I have good news! Your Savior has been born today. You will know who he is because you will find him in the stable in Bethlehem.

eader 5: Suddenly many other angels from heaven appeared and began praising God. They said:

Angels: Glory to God in heaven! And peace to God's people on earth!

eader 6: The shepherds hurried to Bethlehem and found Mary and Joseph in the stable with Jesus. Then they returned to the fields, praising and thanking God for all they had seen and heard.

Based on Luke 2:1–20

ctivity

ike the shepherds, we can thank God for sending Jesus to be with us. 'se the lines below to write a Christmas message of praise and thanks o God.

■ What did the shepherds do after they saw Jesus? (*They returned to the fields, praising and thanking God for all they had seen and heard.*)

Step 3/CONCLUSION

Learning How to Live Our Faith

Writing a Message of Praise

Explain the directions for the activity on page 273. Allow sufficient time for the students to write their messages of praise and thanks to God in the space provided in the text.

Praying Together

Instruct the students to bring their books to the prayer area. Introduce the prayer by praying, "Loving God, we thank you for the gift of your Son and our Savior, Jesus. We praise and thank you with these words." Encourage the students to read aloud the greetings they wrote in the previous activity. Conclude by singing together a carol such as "Angels We Have Heard on High" or "Away in a Manger."

Focus on

The Stable In Jesus' time, it was common for travelers to stay at inns that had one large room in which paying guests would eat and sleep and one area, usually sheltered by a cave or lean-to, in which the servants and animals were lodged. It was most probably in one of these areas that Joseph and Mary settled down on the night that Jesus was born.

273

LESSON 2

Objective

This lesson helps the students learn that gifts tell us something about the person to whom they are given.

Step 1/INTRODUCTION

Learning About Our Lives

Thinking About Christmas Gifts

To key into the students' excitement about the coming of Christmas, ask the following questions.

- What do you think about when you hear the word *Christmas?*
- Of all the gifts you have ever received, which is your favorite?
- Who are the people to whom you give presents at Christmas?
- What gifts do you like to give these people at Christmas?
- Why do you give these people Christmas gifts?

Step 2/DEVELOPMENT

Learning About Our Faith

Reading a Story

Call on volunteers to read "The Wise Men" on pages 274–275. Afterward, discuss the story to make sure that the students understand all that happened. Explain that the wise men had traveled a long distance to see Jesus. Ask the following questions.

- How do you think the wise men felt as they journeyed?
- How did they feel when they saw Jesus?
- Why did they bring gifts?

Adoration of the Magi (oil), Johann Overbe

The Wise Men

Shortly after Jesus was born, some travelers arrived in the city of Jerusalem. They were wise men who studied the stars. They had followed a bright star. They knew it would lead them to the newborn king of God's people.

The wise men had special gifts for Jesus. They had brought gold and rare spices fit for a king.

In Jerusalem the wise men talked to King Herod. They asked him where Jesus was. Herod asked the chief priests and other leaders about the new king.

"According to the prophets, he was to be born in Bethlehem," they said.

The Magi Throughout time, the wise men in the story of the Epiphany have been called astrologers, magi, or the three kings. To a certain extent, all of these descriptions are true. In the Old Testament, Psalm 72:10 prophesies that kings will offer gifts to the Messiah. *Magi* is a Greek word that means "sages" or "wise men." The wise men were called astrologers because they were guided by a star to Bethlehem.

Cultural Awareness

Folk legends about the wise men have always been popular. One of these legends describes the wise men by both name and race. Melchior is often depicted as a bearded, elderly White man who brought the gift of gold; Caspar, as a Hispanic man who brought frankincense; and Balthazar, as a Black man who presented Jesus with myrrh. Help the students appreciate that these legends about the wise men are often used to teach that Jesus came for people of all races.

Herod sent the wise men to Bethlehem. They followed the star again until they came to the place where Mary and Joseph and the baby Jesus were. The visitors were so pleased to find Jesus. They bowed down before him. Then they gave him their special gifts. Giving Jesus these gifts made the wise men very happy.

Based on Matthew 2:1–12

Activity

During the season of Christmas, we enjoy giving gifts. The gifts are a sign of our love. When we choose a gift, we try to find something the person needs or will enjoy. We look for a gift that will be just right.

Draw a line to match each gift with an appropriate person. Be sure each person gets a gift.

bookmark

ecorated box

game of checkers

high-school girl

third-grade boy

mother

father

friend

aunt

baby

pencil cup

key ring

vase

pull toy

Acting Out the Story

Divide the class into groups of eight (three wise men, a servant leading a camel, Herod, a chief priest, Mary holding a doll to represent the baby Jesus, and Joseph). Invite each group to plan a skit for the story of the wise men. Encourage students to use their own words in the skit. Suggest that they have at least four scenes: coming to Jerusalem on camels; meeting King Herod; leaving King Herod and traveling to Bethlehem; and meeting Jesus, Mary, and Joseph. Provide time for the groups to present their skits. Afterward, discuss the new learning that came out of the dramatizations.

Step 3/CONCLUSION

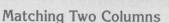

Learning How to Live Our Faith

Matching Two Columns

Read the directions for the activity on page 275. Check to be sure that the students understand the directions. After they have completed the activity, invite sharing. Discuss why the students made their choices. Emphasize that in selecting a gift, a person tries to choose something appropriate for the receiver. Note that each gift tells us something about the person to whom it is given. Ask the students to give examples of purchasing a Christmas gift that is just right for a person. If the students have difficulty with this activity, use your own experiences to explain that we give certain gifts to certain people because of who they are and what they like.

LESSON 3

Objective

This lesson helps the students recognize that the gifts given to Jesus by the wise men help to reveal who Jesus is.

Step 1/INTRODUCTION

Learning About Our Lives

Reviewing Lesson 2

Review with the students what they learned from the story of the wise men and from their group dramatizations. Discuss gift giving. Stress once again that each gift tells us something about the person to whom it is given. Ask the students what they would choose to give to an aunt who likes to work in the garden and raise flowers, to a friend who likes computers, to a baby, and to a father who travels a lot. Use other examples until you are sure that the students understand that we pick gifts that the person will truly appreciate.

Step 2/DEVELOPMENT

Learning About Our Faith +

Reading About Gifts

Show the gold, incense, and ointment. Call on a volunteer to read each of the three sections of "The Gifts of the Wise Men" on page 276. As the article is read, pass around the three items. After the first paragraph is read, ask the students what is in the illustrated box to the left of the text. On the chalkboard, write *gold for a king*. Next to this, write *Jesus is a king*. After the second paragraph is read, ask what is in the illustrated censer. On the chalkboard, write *incense rises to God*. Next to this, write *Jesus is God's Son*. If fire laws permit, light the incense you brought to class so that the students can see it ascend upward. After the third paragraph is read, ask what is in the decorated vase on page 276. On the chalkboard, write *myrrh for a person like us*. Next to this, write *Jesus is one of us*. Afterward, help the students realize that the gifts given to Jesus are appropriate because they show that he is both fully divine and fully human. Invite three students to come to the chalkboard and use colored chalk to draw the three gifts.

276

The Gifts of the Wise Men

In the Bible we read that the wise men brought gifts for Jesus. One gift was gold. This was a sign that the wise men considered Jesus a king. They were honoring Jesus, their king, with a precious and valuable gift.

Another gift the wise men brought was incense. This gift showed that Jesus is God's Son. We use incense when we pray to and worship God. When the smoke of the burning incense rises up, it reminds us of our love and prayers rising up to God.

The third gift the wise men brought was unusual. In Jesus' time, when a person died, the body would be washed and covered with special perfumes and ointments. One such fragrance was called **myrrh**. The gift of myrrh was a sign that Jesus was human and that someday he would die.

Remembering the Wise Men's Visit

On the Feast of Epiphany, we celebrate the wise men's visit to Jesus and his family. In some countries, people celebrate this day by blessing their homes or asking a priest to do so.

Activity

One of the prayers of blessing is written below. Say the prayer together. Then write your own prayer of blessing for your home. Share your prayer with your family.

May Christ bless our home and stay with us throughout the new year.

Teaching Tips

The word *epiphany* means "showing." Explain to the students that Epiphany is the first day that Jesus was shown to people from other lands. This is another sign that Jesus was to be the Savior of all the people of the world.

Cultural Awareness

Explain to the students that in many cultures, especially in Latin America, gifts are given on Epiphany rather than on Christmas Day. This is a way of remembering the gifts that the wise men gave to Jesus. In remembrance of the Feast of Epiphany, give each student a small bag of gold-wrapped chocolate coins. You might hide these in their desks at some point when they are out of the room and let them "discover" the treats as the wise men discovered Jesus in Bethlehem.

Step 3/CONCLUSION

Learning How to Live Our Faith

Completing an Activity

Ask a volunteer to read "Remembering the Wise Men's Visit" on page 277. Then read the directions for the activity. Brainstorm ideas for blessings the students might want for their homes and families. List these on the chalkboard. Then encourage the students to write in the space provided their own prayers of blessing for their homes. Afterward, invite volunteers to share their prayers.

Making a Mobile

Provide construction paper or drawing paper, crayons or markers, scissors, yarn or string, and a dowel or hanger. Invite the students to make Christmas mobiles. Suggest that they draw and decorate three containers like the ones shown on page 276. Encourage them to write or draw on each container one gift they would like to give a person they love. Or, if the students prefer, have them cut out the shapes of gifts they would like to give. Suggest that they cut out one shape for the house blessing they wrote on page 277 and write this prayer on the shape. Then show them how to attach the shapes to the dowel or hanger. Encourage them to take their mobiles home.

LESSON 4

Objective

This lesson helps the students learn about the Holy Family.

Reviewing Lesson 3

Recall with the students the blessings they wrote in Lesson 3. Discuss some of the "gifts" the students made for their mobiles. Talk about the appropriateness of each gift.

Talking About the Holy Family

Read Luke 2:40 to the students. Discuss what the Scripture passage means. In your discussion, ask questions like the following to help students understand that Mary, Joseph, and Jesus lived a very human life.

- What are some things Jesus had to learn as he grew from a baby into a young child?

- What are some things that you think Mary did in their house?

- What are some things that you think Joseph did to take care of his family?

- Would you have liked to visit Jesus' family and spend the night? Why or why not?

- Would you have liked to play with Jesus? Why or why not?

Making a Family Gift

Read the directions on page 278 for making a gift ornament. With the students, read aloud the prayer. To help the students understand the prayer, recall for them their discussion of the Holy Family. Then provide the students with the following supplies: a selection of Christmas cards, drawing paper, crayons or markers, scissors, and yarn. As the students make their gift ornaments, go around the room and provide help as needed.

A Gift for Your Family

1. On a separate sheet of paper, copy the family prayer below.

   Loving God,
   Help us to live like the Holy Family, united in respect and love. Bring us to the joy and peace of your eternal home. We ask this through Jesus, our brother. Amen.

2. Find a Christmas card with a picture of the Holy Family, or draw your own picture.

3. On a sheet of construction paper, paste your copy of the family prayer and the Holy Family picture.

4. Punch a hole at the top of the construction paper. Then use yarn to hang your gift on your Christmas tree.

5. Say the prayer with your family during the Christmas season.

Loving God,
Help us to live like the
Holy Family, united in respect
and love. Bring us to the joy
and peace of your eternal home.
We ask this through Jesus,
our brother, Amen.

Enriching the Lesson

Invite the students to name ways they can help their families become more united in love and respect through their actions and words. List their ideas and comments on the board. Emphasize that we must do more than just pray that our families become more loving. Each of us must also work to make our prayers a reality. Help the students appreciate that our individual efforts help family love to grow and make our families happier and more peaceful.

Prayer Service for the Christmas Season

All: We three kings of Orient are,
Bearing gifts we travel afar.
Field and fountain, moor and mountain,
Following yonder star.
O star of wonder, star of night,
Star with royal beauty bright,
Westward leading, still proceeding,
Guide us to the perfect Light.

Reader 1: The wise men brought gold because,
Jesus, you are a king.

All: Jesus, be our king always.

Reader 2: The wise men brought incense because,
Jesus, you are God's Son.

All: Jesus, bring our prayers to God the Father.

Reader 3: The wise men brought myrrh because,
Jesus, you are one of us.

All: Jesus, be our brother forever.

Reader 4: The wise men followed the star,
and they found Christ,
who is the Light of the World.
May we, too, find Jesus in our lives.

All: Amen.

 **Teaching Tips**

During your prayer service, light a handful of incense grains or a stick of incense in a heatproof bowl. Call students' attention to the smoke created by the incense. This will help them visualize their prayers rising to God.

Making Gifts for the Prayer Service

Provide each student with the following materials: pieces of yellow, gray or black, and blue construction paper, scissors, and crayons or markers. Ask the students to cut out from the yellow sheet of paper a coin and a star. Encourage them to decorate these shapes. Then have them cut out and decorate a wisp of smoke from the gray or black paper. Ask them to cut out and decorate a drop of oil from the blue paper. Tell them that they will use these symbols in their prayer service. Encourage them to write on the backs of the four shapes the names of people they love and want to pray for. Or suggest that they write short prayers on the shapes.

Participating in a Prayer Service

Teach the students the song "We Three Kings." Ask for volunteers to read the four reader parts on page 279. Provide time for them to practice. Give the students a few moments to look over the prayer service. Gather the students around a prepared bulletin board and point out the sections labeled *Jesus, you are king; Jesus, you are the Son of God;* and *Jesus, you are one of us.* Begin the prayer service by having the students process around the room, carrying their symbols and singing "We Three Kings." Then process to the bulletin board. After each of the first three readings, have the students bring the appropriate symbol to the bulletin board and pin it under the correct label. After the last reading, students can pin the stars across the top of the bulletin board.

279

Our Church Celebrates Lent

Objectives ～～～～

- LESSON 1: To help the students understand the Stations of the Cross.
- LESSON 2: To help the students recognize Lent as a time of reconciliation.
- LESSON 3: To help the students understand that Jesus calls us to make sacrifices for others.
- LESSON 4: To help the students learn that Lent is a time to grow and change.
- LESSON 5: To help the students remember Jesus' great love for them.

Lesson Outlines ～～～～～～～

	Step 1 Learning About Our Lives	**Step 2** Learning About Our Faith	**Step 3** Learning How to Live Our Faith
Lesson 1	■ Think about the dead. *ABOUT 5 MINUTES*	■ Read and learn about the Stations of the Cross. *ABOUT 12 MINUTES*	■ Remember Jesus. ■ Decide how to help others. ■ Pray together. *ABOUT 13 MINUTES*
Lesson 2	■ Talk about making up. *ABOUT 7 MINUTES*	■ Read about reconciliation. ■ Examine our consciences. *ABOUT 15 MINUTES*	■ Write a prayer. *ABOUT 8 MINUTES*
Lesson 3	■ Discuss membership requirements. *ABOUT 6 MINUTES*	■ Read about discipleship. ■ Listen to a Scripture story. *ABOUT 12 MINUTES*	■ Complete an activity. *ABOUT 12 MINUTES*
Lesson 4	■ Review Lesson 1. *ABOUT 5 MINUTES*	■ Read about the cross. *ABOUT 8 MINUTES*	■ Pantomime change. ■ Complete an activity. ■ Pray together. *ABOUT 17 MINUTES*
Lesson 5	**Project** Look at crosses; make a cross; pray together. **Prayer** Make a Stations of the Cross booklet; say the Stations of the Cross.		

Plan Ahead ～～～～～

	Preparing Your Class	**Materials Needed**
Lesson 1	Bring to class a picture or momento of someone important to you who has died. Be prepared to tell the students about each of the Stations of the Cross.	■ parish booklet on the Stations of the Cross (optional) ■ chalkboard ■ pencils or pens
Lesson 2	Read through the lesson plan for this session. Think about the different ways you make up after a quarrel.	■ pencils or pens
Lesson 3	Read through the lesson plan for this session. Practice telling the Scripture story in Step 2.	■ pencils or pens
Lesson 4	Have ready a pantomime of change you might show the students to help them prepare their own pantomimes. Have a crucifix for the concluding prayer.	■ chalkboard ■ crayons or colored pencils ■ a crucifix
Lesson 5	Locate pictures of different types of crosses. Make a sample of each of the three crosses explained on page 288. Make a Stations of the Cross booklet to show the students.	■ twigs or sticks ■ purple yarn ■ construction paper ■ crayons, scissors, stapler ■ 15 large sheets of drawing paper

Additional Resources

As you plan this chapter, consider using the following materials from The Resourceful Teacher Package.

■ *Classroom Activity Sheets for Lent*

■ *Family Activity Sheets for Lent*

■ *Prayers for Every Day*

You may also wish to refer to the following Big Book.

■ *We Celebrate the Sacraments,* pages 13–15

In preparing the students for the Sunday readings, you may wish to use Silver Burdett Ginn's *Getting Ready for Sunday* student and teacher materials.

REDUCED CLASSROOM ACTIVITIES

OUR CHURCH CELEBRATES LENT

Imagine that you are Simon, the person who helped Jesus carry the cross. Write your answer to each question below.

1. What did Jesus say to you when you took the cross from him?
   _____
   _____
   _____

2. How did you feel as you carried the cross?
   _____
   _____
   _____

3. What were most of the people in the crowd yelling?
   _____
   _____
   _____

4. What did Jesus say to you when you were finished helping him?
   _____
   _____
   _____

HELPING OTHERS DURING LENT

Color the card. Cut along the heavy black lines, and fold along the broken line. Write a message inside. Send your card to someone who is sick or lonely.

Hope you feel better soon

THE WAY OF THE CROSS

The practice of the Stations of the Cross probably got its start in the Holy Land in the Middle Ages, when pilgrims went to visit the sites of Christ's passion and death. On returning home, they continued to commemorate the events of Jesus' sacrifice on the cross. This devotion developed over the centuries and became known as the Way of the Cross.

The Stations of the Cross consist of fourteen wooden crosses placed on the walls of a church. These may be accompanied by pictures or sculptured scenes. A person making the Way of the Cross visits each of the fourteen stations. At each station the person reflects on some particular aspect of the sacrifice of Jesus and recites a traditional prayer.

Here is a list of the Stations of the Cross.
1. Jesus Is Condemned to Death.
2. Jesus Accepts His Cross.
3. Jesus Falls.
4. Jesus Meets His Mother.
5. Simon Takes the Cross.
6. Veronica Wipes the Face of Jesus.
7. Jesus Falls Again.
8. Jesus Meets the Women.
9. Jesus Falls the Third and Last Time.
10. Jesus Is Stripped of His Clothes.
11. Jesus Is Nailed to the Cross.
12. Jesus Dies.
13. Jesus Is Removed from the Cross.
14. Jesus Is Buried.

In recent years a fifteenth station—Jesus Is Raised from the Dead—has been informally added by many churches to the Way of the Cross. The fifteenth station brings to fullness the sacrifice of Jesus on the cross.

A CALL TO RECONCILIATION AND DISCIPLESHIP

Lesson 2 focuses on our need for repentance and forgiveness. We hear this call each year on Ash Wednesday as we are signed with ashes: "Turn away from sin and be faithful to the gospel." In response to Jesus' command, we are called to reflect on our lives as Catholic Christians and to recognize our personal sinfulness. During Lent we can take advantage of the many opportunities to celebrate the sacrament of Reconciliation. As you teach this lesson, you can challenge your third graders to examine their words and actions to determine how well they are following Christ. The remainder of the Lenten lessons highlight Christ's call to discipleship and our recognition of the cross as a symbol of victory. These lessons afford you with the opportunity to help the students become more aware of Jesus' sacrifice and his great love for them.

LESSON 1

Objective

This lesson helps the students understand the Stations of the Cross.

Step 1/INTRODUCTION

Learning About Our Lives

Thinking About the Dead

Bring to class a picture or a memento of someone important to you who has died. Share with the students something about why the person is important to you. Tell briefly how the memento helps you remember and feel close to the person who has died. Do not dwell on the sadness of death but rather on how the memory of people is kept alive by thinking about them and by sharing memories of them.

Step 2/DEVELOPMENT

Learning About Our Faith

Reading About the Stations of the Cross

Have a volunteer read aloud "Stations of the Cross" on page 280. Explain to the students that the Stations of the Cross are a series of pictures that tell the story of Jesus' crucifixion and death on the cross. Stress that, just as photographs or mementos of a deceased family member remind us of that person, the stations remind us of how much we love Jesus.

Learning About the Stations of the Cross

Tell the story of the Way of the Cross to the students. Refer to the list of the Stations of the Cross provided in the Background for the Teacher section of this chapter. You might want to use one of the Stations of the Cross booklets that are frequently used by parishes during Lent, or you can use the booklet on pages 349–352 of the student text.

Our Church Celebrates Lent

Jesus Falls a Third Time (oil), Guilio Vespaziani

Stations of the Cross

Many people want to remember the good things that Jesus did. They want to remember that Jesus died on the cross for them. Every year during the season of Lent, Christians from many parts of the world gather at a place near Jerusalem called **Calvary**, where Jesus was crucified. They gather to remember the way Jesus carried the heavy cross up the hill. They remember how he died.

People who cannot travel to Calvary want to remember Jesus, too. So they go to church and stand before pictures of Jesus carrying the cross. They say a prayer at each picture and remember how much Jesus loves them. The crosses that mark the stops in this procession are called the **Stations of the Cross**.

Focus on

Stations of the Cross The word *stations* comes from a word which means "halting place" or "stopping place." The first stations of the Cross, located outside of the Holy Land, were built out-of-doors in imitation of the places that Jesus stopped at on his journey to Calvary. Eventually, smaller images of the stations were displayed along the walls of church interiors so that people could pray the Way of the Cross in any kind of weather.

CURRICULUM CONNECTION

Fine Art Bring to class contemporary books that contain pictures of sites in the Holy Land. Show the students pictures of the *Via Dolorosa,* the street known as the Way of Sorrows. Explain that this street retraces Jesus' actual steps to Calvary. Tell the students that each year on Good Friday thousands of visitors walk along this street, remembering Jesus' last hours. The street leads to the Church of the Holy Sepulcher, built over the place where Jesus was buried.

Activity

During Lent we can remember Jesus in many ways. List three ways you can remember Jesus.

1. _____
   _____

2. _____
   _____

3. _____
   _____

Now travel with Jesus up to Calvary by writing on each line one thing you will do for others during Lent.

Learning How to Live Our Faith

Remembering Jesus

Read the directions for the activity at the top of page 281. Ask the class to suggest ways of remembering Jesus. To help them get started in compiling a list, use this sentence: "I will remember Jesus by (helping others, caring for others, picking up my room, and so on)." Write their suggestions on the chalkboard. After compiling a list, have the students select three ways they will remember Jesus. Have them write their selections in the space provided on page 281.

Deciding How to Help Others

Have the students complete on their own the activity at the bottom of page 281. Invite them to write three things they will do for others during Lent. Encourage the students to be realistic and to write things they really can do. After they have written their intentions in the space provided, ask for volunteers to share some of the things they plan to do for others during Lent.

Praying Together

Invite the students to say spontaneous prayers in which they mention one thing they remember about Jesus and thank God for the gift of Jesus.

LESSON 2

Objective

This lesson helps the students recognize Lent as a time of reconciliation.

Step 1/INTRODUCTION

Learning About Our Lives

Talking About Making Up

Invite the students to discuss their experiences of making up with friends after a quarrel. Ask the following questions: How do you tell friends that you are sorry for what you have done? How do your actions show that you are sorry? How do your friends show that they are sorry after an argument? How do you show your friends that you are willing to forgive them? Then ask the students what the Catholic Church calls the process of forgiveness or making up. (*Reconciliation*) Tell the students that in this lesson they will learn why Lent is a time of reconciliation.

Step 2/DEVELOPMENT

Learning About Our Faith

Reading About Reconciliation

Call on volunteers to read aloud "A Time of Reconciliation" on pages 282 and 283. Then discuss the questions below.

- What was Jesus' mission? (*To tell people the good news about God's love for them*)

- What does the priest say on Ash Wednesday when he traces the cross on our foreheads? (*"Turn away from sin and believe in the good news!" or "Remember, you are dust, and to dust you shall return."*)

- What is a sin? (*Choosing to do something we know is wrong; turning away from God's love*)

- What does God want us to think about during Lent? (*Our words and actions*)

- What can we do if we have sinned? (*Celebrate God's forgiveness in the sacrament of Reconciliation*)

Help the students appreciate that God will always forgive us when we express our sorrow for our sins. Emphasize that reconciliation helps prepare us to celebrate Easter.

282

A Time of Reconciliation

After praying and fasting in the desert for forty days, Jesus began his **mission**. A mission is the work God calls us to do. Jesus'

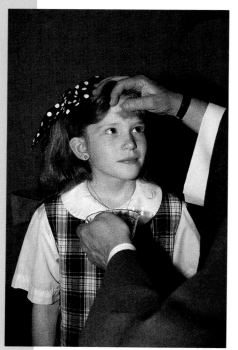

mission was to tell people the good news about God's love for them. When Jesus announced his mission, he said, "Turn away from sin and believe in the good news" (based on Mark 1:15).

On **Ash Wednesday**, the first day of the season of Lent, we receive ashes on our foreheads. As the priest uses ashes to trace the Sign of the Cross on our foreheads, he may repeat Jesus' words from Mark 1:15. Or the priest may say, "Remember, you are dust, and to dust you shall return" (based on Genesis 3:19). The ashes remind us that Lent is a time to change our lives. It is a time to tell God that we are sorry for our **sins**. A sin is choosing to do something we know is wrong. When we sin, we turn away from God's love.

During Lent, God wants us to think about our words and actions. We can think about how we have shown our love for God, Jesus, and others. We can ask ourselves if we have tried to follow God's commandments every day. When we think about all these things, we call this an examination of conscience. Many parishes have special opportunities throughout the season of Lent to think about the ways we may have sinned.

If we have sinned, we can celebrate God's forgiveness in the sacrament of Reconciliation. God will forgive us if we are sorry for our sins.

Lent is a special time to celebrate Reconciliation. In Reconciliation we promise to follow Jesus more closely. As we turn away from our sins and try to grow closer to Jesus, we get ready to share in Jesus' new life, which we celebrate at Easter.

Activity

Think about your words and actions. Then write a prayer to Jesus. In your prayer, tell Jesus one thing you want to change about how you are living and what you will do to try to grow as a follower of Jesus.

Examining Our Consciences

Invite the students to sit quietly and answer each of the following questions silently in their hearts.

- Do I listen and talk to God?
- Do I use the names of God and Jesus with respect and love?
- Do I love, respect, and obey my parents and all adults who care for me?
- Do I show care for everything God has created? Do I fight or hurt others?
- Do I respect my body and the bodies of others?
- Do I take things that don't belong to me?
- Do I tell the truth?
- Am I satisfied with what I have?

Step 3/CONCLUSION

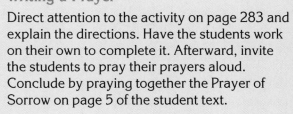

Learning How to Live Our Faith

Writing a Prayer

Direct attention to the activity on page 283 and explain the directions. Have the students work on their own to complete it. Afterward, invite the students to pray their prayers aloud. Conclude by praying together the Prayer of Sorrow on page 5 of the student text.

Teaching Tips

If the students will have the opportunity to celebrate the sacrament of Reconciliation individually during Lent, prepare them by reviewing together "About Reconciliation" on page 340. Go through each of the steps with the students, helping them understand the process. Answer any questions they may have about the sacrament.

Enriching the Lesson

Plan a reconciliation prayer service together. Have a group of students choose and prepare to read a Gospel story about forgiveness, such as the Lost Sheep (Luke 15:3–7), the Forgiving Father (Luke 15:11–32), or the Great Commandment (Luke 10:28). Another group of students can plan to act out a skit about making up. Ask a third group to choose music for the prayer service.

283

LESSON 3

Objective

This lesson helps the students understand that Jesus calls us to make sacrifices for others.

Step 1/INTRODUCTION

Learning About Our Lives

Discussing Membership Requirements

Invite the students to name organizations or groups they are a part of and list their responses on the chalkboard. Then ask the students to identify the advantages of belonging to the groups they named. Finally, have them explain what they must do to be a part of the groups or what is required for membership. Note that belonging to different groups brings both privileges and responsibilities. Tell the students that in this lesson they will learn what Jesus told his disciples they must do if they wanted to be his followers.

Step 2/DEVELOPMENT

Learning About Our Faith

Reading About Discipleship

Have students open their books to page 284 and silently read "Take Up Your Cross and Follow Me." Afterward, discuss the questions below.

■ What did Jesus tell his friends they must do to be his disciples? (*"Forget about yourself, take up your cross, and follow me."*)

■ What do we remember during Lent? (*Jesus' sacrifice on the cross*)

■ Why did Jesus die and rise? (*To save us from sin and to share his new life with us*)

■ What does Jesus mean when he tells us to take up our cross? (*That we must be willing to make sacrifices for others*)

284

Take Up Your Cross and Follow Me

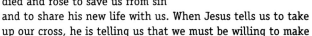

During Lent, we remember that Jesus told his friends what they must do if they wanted to be his disciples. Jesus said, "If you want to come with me, you must forget about yourself, take up your cross, and follow me" (based on Matthew 16:24).

Lent is a time to remember Jesus' sacrifice on the cross. Jesus died and rose to save us from sin and to share his new life with us. When Jesus tells us to take up our cross, he is telling us that we must be willing to make sacrifices for others.

Jesus wants us to think about the needs of other people. He asks us to look for ways to show care for others in special ways during Lent. It is not always easy to make sacrifices, but Jesus promises that he will always help us to follow his example.

During Lent, there are three ways we can follow Jesus. We can pray, fast, and do good works. When we pray, we can ask Jesus to help us be less selfish. We can fast by giving up a favorite snack to remember the people in our world who are hungry. The good works we do are a sign that Jesus is alive in the world today. People can see this through our words and actions.

Activity

Here are some ways you can take up your cross during Lent. Choose three things you will do to show that you are a follower of Jesus.

_____ Share my toys with my brother or sister.

_____ Give up candy or ice cream.

_____ Pray the Stations of the Cross.

_____ Make friends with someone new at school.

_____ Give money to the missions.

_____ Forgive someone who has hurt me.

_____ Do my chores without being asked.

_____ Write a letter to my grandparents.

_____ Watch less television.

_____ Treat everyone with love and kindness.

_____ Collect food for the hungry.

_____ Watch less television.

_____ Celebrate Reconciliation.

_____ Students write their own suggestions.

_____

Listening to a Scripture Story

Gather the students around you in a circle and use your own words to tell the following Scripture story. "Jesus said to his disciples: 'When you do good deeds, don't try to show off. If you do show off, you won't get a reward from your Father in heaven. When you give to the poor, don't blow a loud horn. That's what showoffs do. When you give to the poor, don't let anyone know about it. Then your gift will be given in secret. Your Father knows what is done in secret, and your Father will reward you'" (based on Matthew 6:1–4).

Discuss with the class the meaning of Jesus' words. Help the students understand that Jesus does not want us to brag about the ways in which we try to follow him during Lent. Emphasize that our Lenten sacrifices should be made out of love rather than out of a desire to look good or to get a reward.

Step 3/CONCLUSION

Learning How to Live Our Faith

Completing an Activity

Have a volunteer read aloud the directions for the activity on page 285. When the students have finished, invite them to share what they decided on with the class by saying, "Jesus, I have decided to follow you by . . ." and adding their choices.

Enriching the Lesson

Take a walk with the students around the school playground or to a nearby park. Tell them to each find two twigs of similar size. Back in the classroom, show the students how to wrap yarn diagonally around the twigs to form a cross. Suggest to the students that they keep their twig crosses as reminders of their promise to take up their cross and follow Jesus during Lent.

Focus on

Lent The word *Lent* comes from a word which means "to lengthen." It refers to the lengthening of the days as springtime approaches. We celebrate the forty days of Lent in remembrance of the forty days that Jesus spent in the desert fasting and praying as he prepared for his ministry.

285

LESSON 4

Objective
This lesson helps the students learn that Lent is a time to grow and change.

Step 1/INTRODUCTION

Learning About Our Lives

Reviewing Lesson 1
Review with the students what they learned about the Stations of the Cross. Ask the following questions.

- What are some things that happened to Jesus on the day that he died on the cross?
- Why is the cross important to us?
- What does the cross remind us of?

Step 2/DEVELOPMENT

Learning About Our Faith

Reading About the Cross
Have volunteers read "The Symbol of the Cross" on page 286. Direct the students' attention to the photographs. Note the crucifix on the wall and the priest making the Sign of the Cross. Write on the chalkboard the word *Lent.* Ask the students to share with the class what they know about Lent. Write their responses on the chalkboard. Have the students read aloud the last sentence on page 286. Ask them to circle this sentence while you write it on the chalkboard next to the word *Lent.* Ask the following questions.

- What does "to grow and change" mean?
- In what ways can we change so that we can be a happier class and have happier and more peace-filled families?
- How would we act if we changed?
- How might other people act if we changed?

The Symbol of the Cross

Lent is a special season for the Church. During this season, we remember that Jesus suffered and died on the cross. The cross is a Lenten symbol that reminds us of Jesus' great love for us. When we make the Sign of the Cross or when we see a cross, we think of Jesus.

Lent is also a time to remember our Baptism. At Baptism, we are signed with the cross of Jesus. As we remember our Baptism, we should try to be more like Jesus. Lent is a time to grow and to change our selfish ways.

Focus on

The Cross   In speaking of the cross, the *Catechism of the Catholic Church* quotes Saint Rose of Lima as saying, "Apart from the cross, there is no other ladder by which we may get to heaven" (#618). Help the students understand that the cross is a great symbol for Christians because by Jesus' sacrifice and death on the cross, Jesus made it possible for us to share in his victory over death and live happily forever with God in heaven.

Signs of Victory

The early Christians believed that the cross was a sign of Jesus' victory over death. To them, the cross was a reminder of Jesus' great love.

Many times the early Christians used precious stones, or jewels, to decorate their crosses. Such a cross was called a ***crux gemmata***, or jeweled cross.

Activity

Follow the code to color the *crux gemmata*. Write a motto beside the cross to help you remember Jesus' great love for you.

| 1 gold | 2 orange | 3 red | 4 blue | 5 green | 6 purple |

★ ★ ★ ★
Enriching the Lesson
★   ★

Teach the students to sing a simple melody to accompany the following memorial acclamation: "Lord, by your cross and resurrection you have set us free. You are the Savior of the world." Throughout the season of Lent, you might include this memorial acclamation in your daily prayers with the students.

Learning How to Live Our Faith

Pantomiming Change

Divide the class into pairs. Then invite the pairs to decide on something they would like to change in the way they act toward others. Suggest that one partner pantomime the way they act now. Have the second partner pantomime the way they would act if they changed. Invite the class to guess what change is being pantomimed.

Completing an Activity

Have volunteers read aloud "Signs of Victory" on page 287. Then provide the students with crayons or colored pencils and invite them to color the cross on the bottom of page 287 by following the color code. Afterward, invite the students to share their work.

Praying Together

Gather the students around you. Show them a crucifix. Holding the crucifix in your hand, begin a spontaneous prayer in which you thank Jesus for something he has done. For example, "Jesus, I thank you for showing me how to treat others." Pass the crucifix to the student next to you and invite him or her to say a spontaneous prayer of thanksgiving to Jesus. After each student has had the opportunity to pray with the crucifix, conclude the prayer by saying, "God, we thank you for the gift of Jesus. He has shown us how to love you. He has shown us how to love others. Amen."

LESSON 5

Objective

This lesson helps the students remember Jesus' great love for them.

Looking at Crosses

Show the students as many pictures of crosses as you can find. If possible, show the following crosses that are used in the Christian world: Celtic or Irish, Greek, Maltese, Jerusalem, tau, and Saint Andrew's. Discuss the differences among these crosses. Show a crucifix to the class. Clarify the difference between a cross and a crucifix (the addition of the corpus to the crucifix). Again, talk about what a cross reminds us of (Jesus' love for us).

Making a Cross

Call on volunteers to read the four paragraphs on page 288. Then provide the necessary supplies for making the three types of crosses: twigs or sticks, purple yarn, construction paper, and crayons. Depending on your time, invite the students to make one cross or to make all three crosses. Encourage them to take their cross(es) home. Suggest that they look at their crosses each day to help them remember Jesus' great love for them.

Praying Together

Have each student bring one of his or her crosses as the class gathers around you. Hold up the cross *you* made before class and tell the students what it helps you remember about Jesus. Then invite volunteers to hold up their crosses and explain what the crosses help them remember about Jesus. When all the volunteers have shared their crosses, close by saying, "God, we thank you for your Son, Jesus, who has taught us how much you love us. Amen."

288

Making Crosses

Make one of the three crosses described below and place it in your room at home. Look at your cross often and remember Jesus' great love for you.

1. Find two twigs or sticks. Place one across the other. Wrap purple yarn around the sticks where they cross to hold them together.

2. Cut out a cross from heavy construction paper or cardboard. Glue toothpicks in rows to decorate your cross.

3. Draw a cross on white paper. Use brightly colored crayons to color it. Press hard. Then use a black crayon to cover the entire colored cross. Use a key or pencil tip to scrape off the black to make different designs. The bright colors will shine like a *crux gemmata*.

Prayer Service for Lent

During Lent, Catholics throughout the world pray the Stations of the Cross. They say a special prayer for each station.

After you have finished making the Stations of the Cross booklet on pages 349–352, pray the Stations of the Cross with your class. You may do this in church or in your classroom. Take turns reading the title of each station and talking about what is happening in each picture. Then say together the prayer for each station.

Lent: Lesson Five   289

Direct the students to the booklet on pages 349–352 of their texts. Explain that this booklet will help them pray the Stations of the Cross. Give out scissors. Then, following the directions on page 349 in the Teacher Edition, explain how to make the booklet. Assist the students with the stapling of the booklet.

Saying the Stations of the Cross

Call on volunteers to read "Prayer Service for Lent" on page 289. Then decide which of the following ways you will help the students learn how to pray the Stations of the Cross: (1) Provide fifteen students with large sheets of drawing paper and invite the students to draw the fifteen pictures that are illustrated in the booklet on pages 349–352. Post these pictures in the classroom and use them for the Way of the Cross. Have the students take turns reading the title of each station and talking about what is happening in each picture. Then say together the prayer provided in the booklet for each station. (2) Take a trip to the parish church and walk through the actual Stations of the Cross with the students. Have the students use their booklets. Discuss what each station depicts. (3) Have the students make and number fifteen large crosses and space these around the room on the floor. Together, walk from cross to cross and recite the prayers. (Note: If saying the Way of the Cross is unfamiliar to your class, you may wish to recite prayers at a few stations each day for several days, taking time to discuss the events. Then, when the students are familiar with this devotion, you might pray at all fifteen stations at one time.)

★ Enriching the Lesson ★

If at all possible, visit other Catholic parishes in your area, especially those that may have outdoor Stations of the Cross. On this field trip, call special attention to the way in which the events of Jesus' last hours are depicted. Also give the students the opportunity to see and examine the baptismal font. Help them remember that in Lesson 4 they learned that Lent is a time to recall our Baptism. Invite the students to reverently sign themselves with water from the font.

Teaching Tips

As you pray the Way of the Cross with the students, have them genuflect at each station. Traditionally, this is done after the words "We adore you, O Christ, and we bless you" are prayed. Teach the students to respond with the following prayer as they genuflect: "Because by your cross you have redeemed the world." Explain to the students that genuflecting is a sign of reverence and respect and a way of praying with our bodies.

Our Church Celebrates Holy Week

Objectives ~~~~~

- **LESSON 1:** To help the students understand how the Church celebrates the Triduum.
- **LESSON 2:** To help the students learn what happens during the days of Holy Week.

Lesson Outlines ~~~~~~~

	Step 1 Learning About Our Lives	**Step 2** Learning About Our Faith	**Step 3** Learning How to Live Our Faith
Lesson 1	■ Brainstorm. *ABOUT 6 MINUTES*	■ Read about the Triduum. *ABOUT 10 MINUTES*	■ Fill in missing letters. ■ Compose a litany prayer. *ABOUT 14 MINUTES*
Lesson 2	■ Identify important events in life. *ABOUT 3 MINUTES*	■ Identify events in Jesus' life. ■ Read about Holy Week. ■ Learn about Holy Week. *ABOUT 13 MINUTES*	■ Complete an activity. ■ Make a mural of Holy Week. *ABOUT 14 MINUTES*

Plan Ahead

	Preparing Your Class	Materials Needed
Lesson 1	Read through the lesson plan for this session.	■ chalkboard ■ pencils or pens
Lesson 2	Read and prepare to tell the students about the following Scripture passages: Luke 19:28–38; 22:7–20; 22:39–71; 23:1–56; and 24:1–12.	■ posterboard ■ crayons or markers

Additional Resources

As you plan this chapter, consider using the following materials from The Resourceful Teacher Package.

■ *Classroom Activity Sheets for Holy Week*

■ *Family Activity Sheets for Holy Week*

■ *Prayers for Every Day*

You may also wish to refer to the following Big Book.

■ *We Celebrate God's Word,* pages 15, 16, 17, and 18

In preparing the students for the Sunday readings, you may wish to use Silver Burdett Ginn's *Getting Ready for Sunday* student and teacher materials.

REDUCED CLASSROOM ACTIVITIES

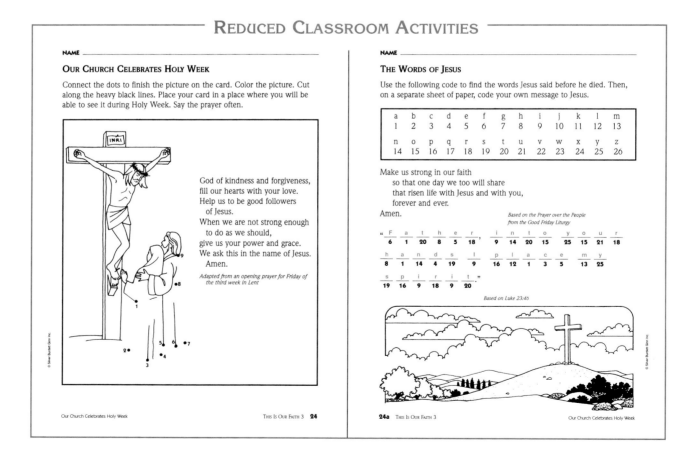

NAME _____

OUR CHURCH CELEBRATES HOLY WEEK

Connect the dots to finish the picture on the card. Color the picture. Cut along the heavy black lines. Place your card in a place where you will be able to see it during Holy Week. Say the prayer often.

God of kindness and forgiveness,
fill our hearts with your love.
Help us to be good followers
    of Jesus.
When we are not strong enough
    to do as we should,
give us your power and grace.
We ask this in the name of Jesus.
    Amen.

*Adapted from an opening prayer for Friday of
the third week in Lent*

Our Church Celebrates Holy Week   THIS IS OUR FAITH 3   **24**

NAME _____

THE WORDS OF JESUS

Use the following code to find the words Jesus said before he died. Then, on a separate sheet of paper, code your own message to Jesus.

a	b	c	d	e	f	g	h	i	j	k	l	m
1	2	3	4	5	6	7	8	9	10	11	12	13
n	o	p	q	r	s	t	u	v	w	x	y	z
14	15	16	17	18	19	20	21	22	23	24	25	26

Make us strong in our faith
    so that one day we too will share
    that risen life with Jesus and with you,
    forever and ever.
Amen.

*Based on the Prayer over the People
from the Good Friday Liturgy*

" F   a   t   h   e   r , i   n   t   o   y   o   u   r
   6   1   20   8   5   18   9   14   20   15   25   15   21   18

   h   a   n   d   s   l   p   l   a   c   e   m   y
   8   1   14   4   19   9   16   12   1   3   5   13   25

   s   p   i   r   i   t ."
   19   16   9   18   9   20

Based on Luke 23:46

24a   THIS IS OUR FAITH 3   Our Church Celebrates Holy Week

Background for the Teacher

HOLY WEEK

The most sacred and solemn time for Catholics during the year is Holy Week and Easter. During this time, we enter into the events of the central mystery of our faith: the death and resurrection of Jesus. We remember Jesus' entry into Jerusalem and his Last Supper with his apostles. We recall the passion and the death of Jesus on Good Friday. We celebrate his triumphant rising from the dead on Easter. Through the liturgy of each of these days—Palm Sunday, Holy Thursday, Good Friday, Holy Saturday, and Easter Sunday—we participate symbolically in these events.

On Passion or Palm Sunday, we see the crowd welcoming Jesus into Jerusalem with shouts of praise. Later, we hear this same crowd before Pilate calling for the death of Jesus. On Holy Thursday, we recall the institution of the Eucharist. We once again take to heart the example of Jesus as he washed the feet of his apostles. We renew our intention to follow Jesus' command to love others through dedicated service.

On Good Friday, we solemnly commemorate the death of Jesus on the cross. The death of Jesus must always be seen in connection with his triumphant resurrection after three days in the tomb. Otherwise, we would not be able to call this day of his suffering and death "good." We know that through apparent defeat came victory, that through death came life. We know that Jesus overcame sin and death for our sake.

TEACHING ABOUT GOOD FRIDAY

In the past there has been reference to Jesus opening the gates of hell and paying a price for our sins. It is best to avoid talking about these concepts with the third grader. Present Jesus as the obedient Son of God who trusted in God and followed his will, even to death on the cross.

Encourage the students to participate in the Holy Week services that are part of the life of the parish. Suggest that they look carefully for crosses and crucifixes that might serve as reminders of what happened to Jesus on Good Friday. Tell the students to think about Good Friday always in connection with the resurrection of Jesus. This is the central mystery of our faith.

LESSON 1

Objective

This lesson helps the students understand how the Church celebrates the Triduum.

Step 1/INTRODUCTION

Learning About Our Lives

Brainstorming

Write the word *holy* on the chalkboard and invite the students to suggest all the words, objects, people, and days they think of when they hear the word *holy*. Accept any reasonable responses. Then remind the students that they learned in Chapter 2 that the word *holy* means "being close to God, loving God and others, and doing God's work in the world." Tell the class that this lesson will focus on three holy days that the Church community celebrates each year.

Step 2/DEVELOPMENT

Learning About Our Faith

Reading About the Triduum

Call on volunteers to take turns reading aloud "The Triduum" on pages 290 and 291. Use the questions below to guide discussion.

- When do we celebrate the Triduum? (*Holy Thursday evening through Easter Sunday evening*)

- What do we remember on Holy Thursday? (*Jesus' gift of the Eucharist*)

- What does the washing of the feet remind us to do? (*To serve others as Jesus did*)

- How do we show our love for Jesus on Good Friday? (*By kissing the cross, kneeling before it, or touching it gently*)

- What do we call the Holy Saturday celebration? (*The Easter Vigil*)

- Why do we hold lighted candles at the Easter Vigil? (*As a sign that Jesus has risen and that Jesus' new life shines throughout the world*)

Our Church Celebrates Holy Week

The Triduum

The **Triduum**, the three holiest days of the Church year, is from Holy Thursday evening through Easter Sunday evening. The word *Triduum* means "three days."

On Holy Thursday we remember the Last Supper, when Jesus gave us the Eucharist. During this meal, Jesus took bread into his hands, gave thanks to God, broke the bread, and said, "This is my body, which is given for you. Do this in memory of me." Then Jesus took a cup of wine and said, "This is my blood. Do this in memory of me" (based on 1 Corinthians 11:23–25).

During Mass on Holy Thursday, the priest and other ministers may wash the feet of people in the parish community. In this **ritual**, we remember that Jesus washed the feet of his apostles. And we remember that Jesus calls us to serve others as he did. In a ritual, we use words, actions, and gestures to remember or celebrate something very meaningful.

On Good Friday, we remember the day Jesus died. There are no Masses on Good Friday. Instead, we go to church to hear the story of Jesus' death on the cross.

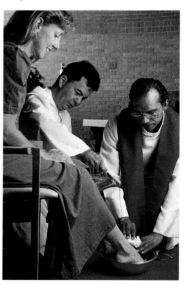

Focus on

The Triduum Coming from the Latin, *triduum* means "three days." In fact, what it refers to are three celebrations, beginning with the remembrance of the Lord's Supper on Holy Thursday evening, then the feast of the Passion and Death of the Lord on Good Friday, and the celebration of the Lord's resurrection at the Easter Vigil and on Easter Sunday.

290

Later, we show our love for Jesus by kissing a special cross. We can also kneel before the cross or touch it gently. Then we all receive the Eucharist.

On Holy Saturday, we remember Jesus' promise to rise from the dead. At night, we go to church for the celebration of the Easter Vigil, when we welcome new members into the Church. Everyone holds a lighted candle. This is a sign that Jesus has risen and that Jesus' new life shines throughout the world.

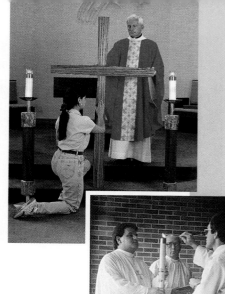

Activity

Fill in the missing letters in the sentences below.

1. The **T** r i d u u m includes the three holiest

   d a y s of the Church year.

2. On **H** o l y Thursday

   we remember the

   L o r d 's Supper.

3. On Good **F** r i d a y we remember that

   Jesus died on the **c** r o s s .

4. On Holy Saturday, at the **E** a s t e r

   Vigil, we celebrate new **l** i f e

   with **J** e s u s .

Learning How to Live Our Faith

Filling in the Missing Letters

Direct attention to the activity on page 291 and explain the directions. Have the students work independently to fill in the blanks with the correct letters. Give them permission to look back at the text on pages 290 and 291 to assist them in recalling the answers or to help them with spelling. When everyone has finished, check the students' work by selecting volunteers to read the completed sentences aloud.

Composing a Litany Prayer

Work with the students to compose a litany prayer on the chalkboard, based on the celebration of the Triduum. Write three petitions with the class, one for each celebration or observance of the Triduum. For example, "On Holy Thursday, we thank you, Jesus, for giving us your Body and Blood in the Eucharist." After the petitions have been written, ask the students to suggest an appropriate response to pray after each petition, such as "We celebrate your love in the Triduum" or "Help us to love and serve you always."

Teaching Tips

Reinforce that there are no Masses at all on Good Friday and no Masses during the day on Holy Saturday. Explain that these are the only two days of the entire Church year when parishes are not allowed to celebrate the Mass. Help the students understand that not celebrating Mass on these days helps us remember Jesus' sacrifice on the cross, his death and burial, and his resurrection.

Enriching the Lesson

Invite the students to think of a gesture to accompany each of the petitions in the prayer in Step 3. The gestures could reflect one of Jesus' actions or a ritual taken from the Triduum. For example, the students might genuflect for the Good Friday petition.

LESSON 2

Objective

To help the students learn what happens during the days of Holy Week.

Step 1/INTRODUCTION

Learning About Our Lives

Identifying Important Events in Life

Ask the students to identify important events in their own lives that they celebrated with their friends and relatives. (These events might include their births, Baptisms, First Communions, first days at school, and so on.) Help the students understand that in the future their friends and families will celebrate other special days that occur in their lives. (These days might include their Confirmations, graduations from high school and college, wedding days, and so on.) Ask the students which of these days is remembered every year. (These days might include birthdays, wedding anniversaries, and other extra-special days.)

Step 2/DEVELOPMENT

Learning About Our Faith

Identifying Events in Jesus' Life

Tell the students that Christians remember many special events in Jesus' life. Ask the following questions.

- What special event in Jesus' life do we celebrate on December 25th? (*His birth*)
- What special event in Jesus' life do we celebrate every spring after Lent? (*His resurrection*)

Explain to the students that today they will learn about some other special events in Jesus' life that took place during the week that Christians call Holy Week.

Reading About Holy Week

Ask volunteers to read aloud "Good Friday" on page 292 and the prayer on page 293. Answer any questions the students have about the reading or the prayer.

292

The Crucifixion (oil), Hendrick Krock, 18th century

Good Friday

During **Holy Week**, the week before Easter, we remember the important events of the last week of Jesus' life on earth.

The day that Jesus was crucified on the cross is called Good Friday. That is the day that Jesus carried his cross up the hill to the place known as Calvary. Ever since that time, the cross has been a special symbol to all Christians. It reminds us of Jesus, the Son of God, who died on Good Friday and rose to new life at Easter.

We celebrate Christ's Passion on Good Friday. We hear a reading from the Gospels that we call the Passion of our Lord Jesus Christ. *Passion* means "suffering."

Focus on

Good Friday   The students may be curious about the fact that we call the day on which Jesus died "good." Help the students appreciate that if Jesus had not died on Good Friday he could not have risen on Easter Sunday. Jesus' sacrifice and death on the cross are good because they were an important part of God's plan for the world.

On Good Friday we pray this prayer.

Lord,
Send your blessing on us,
    for we remember that Jesus died on the cross
    and rose to new life on Easter Sunday.
Forgive us and help us.
Make us strong in our faith
    so that one day we, too, will share
    that risen life with Jesus and with you,
    forever and ever.
Amen.   *Based on the Prayer over the People*
                   from the Good Friday Liturgy

Activity

What do you know about Holy Week, the week that begins with Palm Sunday and ends with Easter? Write your answer to each question below.

1. **What happens on Palm Sunday?** We remember Jesus entering Jerusalem and the people greeting him by cheering and waving palms.

2. **Why is Holy Thursday important?** Holy Thursday is the day when we remember and celebrate the Last Supper and Jesus' washing his apostles' feet.

3. **What are some ways we can remember the events of Good Friday?** by praying the Stations of the Cross, by going to church and listening to the story of Jesus' death, and by kissing a special cross at church

Teaching Tips

Recall that in Lesson 1 the students learned that on Good Friday they are invited to show love for Jesus by kissing the cross, kneeling before it, or touching it prayerfully. To prepare the students for this solemn ritual, you may want to practice it with them. Using a large crucifix, demonstrate how to reverence the cross by kissing it. Then invite the students to do the same. Wipe the crucifix clean with a linen cloth after each student has kissed it.

Learning About Holy Week

On the chalkboard, write the following words: *Passion Sunday, Holy Thursday, Good Friday, Holy Saturday,* and *Easter Sunday.* Then tell the students the events that took place on these days. (You will want to have read Luke 19:28–38, 22:7–20, 22:39–71, 23:1–56, and 24:1–12.) After you tell the story for each day, invite a student to come to the chalkboard and write the events you related next to or below that day. Discuss any questions the students have about the stories.

Step 3/CONCLUSION

Learning How to Live Our Faith

Completing an Activity

Read the directions for the activity on page 293. Invite the students to look at the list of events on the chalkboard as they complete the activity. Then call on volunteers to share their work.

Making a Mural of Holy Week

Divide the class into five groups. Provide each group with a long sheet of posterboard or paper and crayons or markers. Assign each group one of the five days listed on the chalkboard. Then invite the students to label their murals and to draw all the events that took place on their assigned days. After the groups have completed their work, have the students come to the front of the room and explain their murals. Then post the murals in one long strip around the classroom.

293

Our Church Celebrates Easter

Objectives

- **LESSON 1:** To help the students learn the story of the first Easter.
- **LESSON 2:** To help the students become familiar with the Emmaus story.
- **LESSON 3:** To help the students recognize ways in which Jesus is present to them.
- **LESSON 4:** To help the students illustrate ways in which Jesus is present to them today and celebrate their understanding of that presence.

Lesson Outlines

	Step 1 Learning About Our Lives	**Step 2** Learning About Our Faith	**Step 3** Learning How to Live Our Faith
Lesson 1	■ Recall the Easter Vigil. *ABOUT 4 MINUTES*	■ Read a Scripture story. ■ Understand the message. *ABOUT 14 MINUTES*	■ Announce Jesus' resurrection. *ABOUT 12 MINUTES*
Lesson 2	■ Share stories. *ABOUT 5 MINUTES*	■ Read and discuss a story. *ABOUT 5 MINUTES*	■ Color a puzzle. ■ Dramatize the Scripture story. ■ Write a letter. *ABOUT 20 MINUTES*
Lesson 3	■ Review Lesson 2. ■ Talk about people being close. *ABOUT 8 MINUTES*	■ Read about signs of Jesus' love. ■ Use the Discuss questions. *ABOUT 7 MINUTES*	■ Complete an activity. ■ Make a butterfly. *ABOUT 15 MINUTES*
Lesson 4	**Project** Review Lesson 3; make an Easter poster.		
	Prayer Discuss the Easter posters; prepare for the prayer service; participate in the prayer service.		

Plan Ahead

	Preparing Your Class	**Materials Needed**
Lesson 1	Read through the lesson plan for this session. Be prepared to offer headline suggestions to the students in Step 3.	■ pencils or pens
Lesson 2	Read through the lesson plan for this session. Think about a time when something almost too good to be true happened to you. Practice reading Luke 24:13–35 with expression.	■ pencils or pens ■ crayons
Lesson 3	Have ready to show the students a picture, letter, or gift from someone about whom you care who lives far away. Following the directions in Step 3, make a sample butterfly to show the students.	■ clothespins ■ a box of white facial tissue ■ pipe cleaners ■ tape ■ water colors and brushes, tempera, or markers
Lesson 4	Gather a selection of Catholic magazines, diocesan or parish newsletters and newspapers, and old Religion textbooks. Consider what songs you might sing during the prayer service.	■ printed material with photographs to cut out ■ posterboard or shelf paper ■ paste or glue ■ crayons or markers and scissors ■ a candle for the prayer service

Additional Resources

As you plan this chapter, consider using the following materials from The Resourceful Teacher Package.

■ *Classroom Activity Sheets for Easter*

■ *Family Activity Sheets for Easter*

■ *Prayers for Every Day*

You may also wish to refer to the following Big Book.

■ *We Celebrate God's Word,* pages 19 and 20

In preparing the students for the Sunday readings, you may wish to use Silver Burdett Ginn's *Getting Ready for Sunday* student and teacher materials.

NAME _____

OUR CHURCH CELEBRATES EASTER

Use each letter in the word *Alleluia* to write one way that we can be signs of Jesus' love.

_____ A _____

_____ L _____

_____ L _____

_____ E _____

_____ L _____

_____ U _____

_____ I _____

_____ A _____

Our Church Celebrates Easter

THIS IS OUR FAITH 3 **25**

NAME _____

THE JOY OF EASTER

On the cross below, write the names of people who bring you Jesus' message of joy. Remember to thank them and pray for them throughout the fifty days of the Easter season.

25a THIS IS OUR FAITH 3

Our Church Celebrates Easter

293c Organizer

THE RESURRECTION

All four Gospels reflect the fact that there were no eyewitnesses to Jesus' resurrection. Instead, the Gospels announce, or reveal, the undisputed fact of Jesus' resurrection and appearance to his disciples. Matthew's Gospel, the focal point of Lesson 1, allows us to see the reaction of Mary Magdalene and another believer to this startling news. Matthew's announcement is filled with divine signs—an earthquake, the appearance of an angel, a dazzling white garment in a dusty and dry land, the appearance of the risen Lord—all pointing to the fact that God intervened in nature and raised Jesus.

As you teach this lesson, your students may want to know *how* Jesus was raised or *how* Jesus looked after his resurrection. These are questions we cannot answer. It is more important for you to focus on *why*. Help your students recognize the depth of God's love for us in giving us his only Son and the promise of everlasting life.

THE EMMAUS STORY

Lesson 2 tells the story of two of Jesus' disciples who were traveling to Emmaus in the days following Calvary. They talked of the things that had happened to Jesus in Jerusalem. They tried to make sense of the loss of this person in whom they had placed their faith and future.

We know from the account in the Gospel of Luke that Jesus joined these disciples as they walked and that he explained why he had to die. The disciples came to recognize their risen Lord as he shared a meal with them. They recognized him in the breaking of the bread. For these disciples this appearance of Jesus was something too good to be true. What joy they must have experienced in learning that Jesus was not dead, but alive!

THE PRESENCE OF JESUS TODAY

Knowing that Christ is alive as the risen Lord is not an experience reserved for those who witnessed his appearances after the resurrection. Today we can experience the risen Lord in our life of prayer and worship. Jesus is present to us in a special way in the Eucharist. He is present through the Holy Spirit in the deepest level of our lives. This presence of Jesus is every bit as real as his physical presence was to those who ate and drank with him. This should cause us great happiness as the modern-day disciples of Jesus.

In these lessons the students will reflect on how we have great joy when something unexpectedly wonderful happens to us. They will learn that the resurrection of Jesus was such an event for the Emmaus disciples. It is for us today as well. Just as the early disciples saw Jesus in the breaking of the bread, so we also see Jesus present for us in the Eucharist today.

LESSON 1

Objective

This lesson helps the students learn the story of the first Easter.

Step 1/INTRODUCTION

Learning About Our Lives

Recalling the Easter Vigil

Have the students review what they learned about the Easter Vigil in previous lessons by asking the following questions.

- When do we celebrate the Easter Vigil? (*On Holy Saturday evening*)

- What do we celebrate at the Easter Vigil? (*Jesus' rising to new life*)

Tell the students that the early Christians celebrated Jesus' resurrection in an all-night celebration that ended at dawn on Easter Sunday. Explain that the early Church did this because on the first Easter Sunday, Jesus' friends and followers discovered that he had risen when they went to the tomb very early on Sunday morning.

Step 2/DEVELOPMENT

Learning About Our Faith

Reading a Scripture Story

Read with the class "Jesus Is Risen" on pages 294 and 295. Then discuss these questions.

- What happened when the women got to Jesus' tomb? (*An earthquake shook the ground and an angel appeared.*)

- What did the angel tell the women about Jesus? (*That he had risen*)

- What did the angel tell the women to do? (*To tell the disciples that Jesus had risen*)

- What happened when the women left the tomb? (*Jesus appeared to them and told them to tell the disciples to go to Galilee, where they would see him.*)

Our Church Celebrates Easter

Jesus Is Risen

Early on the first day of the week, Mary Magdalene and another woman went to visit Jesus' **tomb**, where his body had been placed when he died. Suddenly an earthquake shook the ground, and an angel of the Lord appeared. The angel rolled back the stone from the front of the tomb and sat on it. The men guarding the tomb were so afraid that they began to shake.

The angel said to the women: "Do not be afraid! I know that you are looking for Jesus who was crucified. He is not here. He has risen, just as he promised. Come and see the place where they put his body. Then go quickly to tell his disciples that he has been raised."

294   Easter: Lesson One

Enriching the Lesson

Have the students dramatize the story "Jesus Is Risen." You might use a large empty appliance carton to represent the tomb. Explain to the students that Jesus' tomb was carved out of a rocky hill and that people had to bend down to enter or to look into the tomb. The opening to the tomb was covered by a large stone.

294

The women hurried away from the tomb to tell the disciples the good news. They were filled with joy and fear. Suddenly Jesus stood before them and greeted them. The women fell down in front of him, touched his feet, and worshiped him. Jesus said, "Do not be afraid. Go and tell my disciples to go to Galilee, where they will see me."

Based on Matthew 28:1–10

On Easter we celebrate Jesus' resurrection. The empty tomb is a sign that God's love is even more powerful than death. God promises that those who love and follow Jesus will share his new life forever.

Activity

Just as Jesus asked Mary to tell the other disciples the good news of his resurrection, Jesus calls us to be his messengers of good news today. Write a heading announcing Jesus' resurrection. Then write how you feel about Jesus' rising to new life.

The Good News Times

Congratulations

Easter: Lesson One **295**

CURRICULUM CONNECTION

Geography Use a map of the Holy Land to point out Jerusalem, where Jesus was crucified and buried. Note that Jerusalem is in the district known as Judea. Recall for the students that Jesus told the women to tell the other disciples that he would see them in Galilee. Have the students find the district of Galilee on the map and calculate the distance between the city of Jerusalem and the district of Galilee (approximately 70 miles).

Understanding the Message

Read aloud to the class the paragraph that follows the story. Help the students understand that by rising from the dead, Jesus won a victory over death. We too will rise to new life if we live as followers of Jesus.

Step 3/CONCLUSION

Learning How to Live Our Faith

Announcing Jesus' Resurrection

Point out the activity on page 295 and explain the directions. Give the students sufficient time to write their headlines and their feelings about Jesus' resurrection. Afterward, invite the students to share their work with the class.

or...

Have the students use crayons or markers to transfer their resurrection headlines to 2" × 12" tagboard strips. Use these strips to make an Easter bulletin board or to decorate the hallway wall outside your classroom.

LESSON 2

Objective

This lesson helps the students become familiar with the Emmaus story.

Step 1/INTRODUCTION

Learning About Our Lives

Sharing Stories

Introduce the lesson by sharing with the students a time in your life when something seemed too good to be true. Invite the students to share their own experiences. Help them to see that there are times when we experience something so wonderful that it is hard to believe it is real.

Step 2/DEVELOPMENT

Learning About Our Faith

Reading and Discussing a Story

Tell the students that the story they are about to read is about two people who had a wonderful experience that seemed too good to be true. Ask volunteers to read aloud "The Road to Emmaus" on pages 296–297. If you wish, read aloud from the Bible Luke 24:13–35, emphasizing what the disciples did after they recognized Jesus. (Although the passage is long, reading the story slowly and with expression will keep the class interested.) Afterward, ask the following questions.

■ How were the two disciples feeling at the beginning of their journey? Why? (*They were sad because they thought Jesus was gone forever.*)

■ Who joined the disciples? (*Jesus*)

■ When did the disciples recognize Jesus? (*When he broke bread as he had done at the Last Supper*)

The Road to Emmaus

After Jesus died, his family and friends were sad. They thought Jesus was gone forever. Jesus had promised to be with them again, but that seemed too good to be true.

On Sunday, two of his friends were walking on the road to a town called Emmaus. As they walked along, another man began to walk with them. They did not know who he was.

"What are you talking about?" the man asked the two friends.

They stopped walking. One of the friends of Jesus said, "Are you the only person who does not know what has happened these past few days?"

The man who had joined them began to talk about Jesus. He helped them understand why Jesus had died.

When they arrived at Emmaus, the friends of Jesus invited the man to stay for supper. After they sat down, the man took a loaf of bread, blessed it, broke it, and gave them each a piece. Suddenly they knew who the man was.

Based on Luke 24:13–35

Activity

Who was the man who joined the apostles on the road to Emmaus? Find and color the hidden words to discover the answer. Hint: Look for two words.

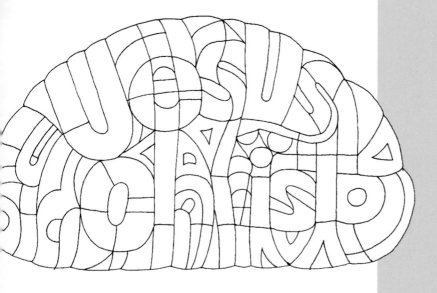

Enriching the Lesson

Help the students understand that in the Emmaus story, the disciples were so excited by the news that Jesus was alive and had appeared to them that they returned to Jerusalem to share the news with all the other disciples. Distribute drawing paper and crayons. Invite the students to draw pictures of the disciples from Emmaus sharing with the people in Jerusalem the news of Jesus' resurrection.

CURRICULUM CONNECTION

Mathematics Explain that Emmaus was located seven miles west of Jerusalem and that the disciples walked from Jerusalem to Emmaus and then returned to Jerusalem. Have them calculate the total number of miles the disciples walked (*14*). Then explain that the average person usually can walk one mile in fifteen to twenty minutes. Tell the students that the disciples walked for a total of three to five hours that day.

Learning How to Live Our Faith

Coloring a Puzzle

Invite the students to complete the coloring activity at the bottom of page 297. Distribute crayons and encourage the students to find the hidden words (*Jesus Christ*). Use the activity to reinforce the idea that the disciples on the road to Emmaus recognized Jesus, their risen Lord.

Dramatizing the Scripture Story

If you did not read or tell the students the ending to the Emmaus story (Luke 24:33–35), explain to the students that the disciples hurried back to Jerusalem and told the apostles and the women that they had seen the risen Lord. Talk to the students about how the apostles and the women in Jerusalem may have been feeling. Then divide the class into groups of eight to ten. Ask the groups to prepare a dramatization about the Emmaus event. Suggest that they have at least four scenes: the two disciples walking by themselves, the two disciples meeting Jesus and walking with him, Jesus breaking bread with the two disciples, and the disciples telling the apostles and the women in Jerusalem about meeting the risen Lord. Encourage the students to be creative with their dialogue and their actions. Then invite each group to present its dramatization. Compliment the students on the outstanding features of each presentation.

Writing a Letter

Ask the students to pretend that they are disciples of Jesus. Tell them that they can choose to be the disciples who went to Emmaus or the people waiting in Jerusalem. Encourage them to write a letter to a friend and tell the friend about the events of the day and about how they are feeling. Afterward, invite volunteers to share their letters.

LESSON 3

Objective
This lesson helps the students recognize ways in which Jesus is present to them.

Step 1/INTRODUCTION
Learning About Our Lives

Reviewing Lesson 2
Recall with the students the Emmaus story, which they read in Lesson 2. Help the students understand that the appearance of Jesus to the two disciples on the road to Emmaus was one of the events that took place soon after the resurrection of Jesus.

Talking About People Being Close
Talk with the students about ways that people who are important to them can be close even when they are far away. Share a picture, a letter, or a gift from someone about whom you care who lives far away. Point out how these things and other things, such as phone calls and flowers, make that person present to you. Invite the students to share similar experiences.

Step 2/DEVELOPMENT
Learning About Our Faith

Reading About Signs of Jesus' Love
Tell the students that this lesson will help them identify ways that Jesus is present in their lives today. Call on a volunteer to read the first two paragraphs of "Signs of Jesus' Love" on page 298. Discuss the reading. Then have the students read the third paragraph silently to find four ways that the risen Jesus is close to them. Instruct them to number or underline the four ways. Afterward, discuss the four ways by noting the corresponding photographs at the top of page 298.

Signs of Jesus' Love

While walking to Emmaus, Jesus' friends did not know that the man they met was Jesus. But when the man broke bread and shared it with them, they recognized Jesus.

We are friends of Jesus. We want to recognize Jesus in our lives, too. The risen Jesus comes to us in many ways.

When we pray, Jesus is close to us. When we celebrate the Eucharist at Mass, Jesus comes to us in a special way. When we read the Bible or study our religion, the words of Jesus and his teachings become part of us. At home, at school, and with our friends, the love and care of parents, teachers, and other good people are signs of Jesus' love for us.

Discuss

1. During the past week, who were the people who helped you?

2. Who were the people who were kind to you?

3. Who were signs that Jesus was with you?

Activity

Unscramble the letters on each butterfly to find a way that we can bring Jesus' love to others. Write each word on the line provided.

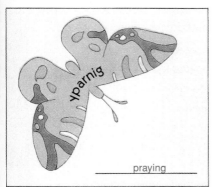

praying

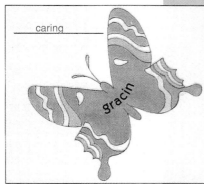

caring

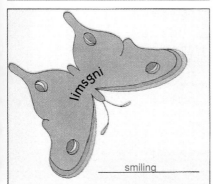

smiling

helping

CURRICULUM CONNECTION

Science Study with the students the life cycle and development of a butterfly. You may want to order a Butterfly Garden or Butterfly Culture from Insect Lore, P.O. Box 1535, Shafter, CA 93263 (1-800-LIVE BUG). These kits also include instructions on caring for butterflies and interesting facts. They are guaranteed to produce three to five live "painted lady" butterflies.

Cultural Awareness

Discuss with the students what prevents us from seeing Jesus in others. Emphasize that fear and ignorance often keep us from recognizing Jesus in others. Explore the following questions with the class. How can we be a sign of Jesus to someone who needs a wheelchair? (*By remembering that Jesus showed care and compassion for people with injuries*) How can we be a sign of Jesus to someone who speaks another language? (*By remembering that Jesus came for all people*)

Using the Discuss Questions

Discuss the questions at the top of page 299. Help the students see that many people care for them—everyone from their own parents to the lunchroom personnel, playground helpers, and safety patrols.

Step 3/CONCLUSION

Learning How to Live Our Faith

Completing an Activity

Read the directions for the activity on page 299. Provide time for the students to unscramble the four words on the butterflies.

Making a Butterfly

Tell the students that a butterfly is a symbol of the risen Lord. Talk about how a caterpillar lives in a chrysalis and how the caterpillar becomes a butterfly and breaks out of the chrysalis. Discuss this in relationship to Jesus' death and resurrection.

Provide the materials for the students to make clothespin butterflies. Show the students the butterfly you made by following the directions given below. Give each student a clothespin for the butterfly's body, a facial tissue for its wings, and a pipe cleaner for its antennae. Have available tape and coloring materials, such as a set of watercolors and several brushes, tempera, or markers. Tell the students to do the following: Make the wings by gathering the facial tissue at the center and taping it; decorate the tissue wings by using one of the coloring materials; paint the clothespin; insert the wings between the clothespin prongs; wind the pipe cleaner around the clothespin head to form the antennae. Encourage the students to take their butterflies home to remind them that the risen Lord is always with them.

LESSON 4

Objective

This lesson helps the students illustrate ways in which Jesus is present to them today.

Reviewing Lesson 3

Have the students look at pages 298–299, which they studied in Lesson 3. Reread the third paragraph on page 298 and discuss the four ways that the risen Jesus is present to us. To help the students understand these four ways, look once again at the photographs on page 298.

Making an Easter Poster

Read the directions on page 300 for making Easter posters. Divide the class into four groups and assign each group one of the posters detailed on page 300. Provide the students with the following materials: a wide selection of Catholic magazines, mission magazines, diocesan or parish newsletters and newspapers, old Religion textbooks, posterboard or shelf paper, paste or glue, crayons or markers, and scissors. Provide time for the students to complete their posters by pasting the pictures they have found and by titling the posters. Invite each group to explain its poster to the class. Display the posters in your classroom for use with the prayer service.

Easter Posters

To make the posters, you will need magazines and newspapers, posterboard or shelf paper, paste or glue, and felt-tip markers.

1. Your teacher will divide the class into four groups.

2. Read and follow the directions for your group.

   Group 1: Find pictures of people who are praying.

   Group 2: Look for pictures of people who are sharing meals and celebrating Mass together.

   Group 3: Find pictures of people who are sharing God's word with others.

   Group 4: Look for pictures of people of all ages who are showing love and concern for others.

3. Cut out the pictures and paste them on your group's poster. Print a title at the top of the poster.

4. Share your finished poster with the other groups. Tell your classmates about some of the ways the risen Jesus is with us now.

5. Later, display your posters in your school hallway, in the back of church, or in the parish hall.

Prayer Service for the Easter Season

Before your prayer service, gather around the Easter candle in church or around a candle in your classroom. Choose a joyful Easter song to sing. Also choose a leader and readers.

Leader: At Easter time, we are joyful. We sing happy songs. Our brother, Jesus, who died, now lives a new life. He is in heaven with God the Father, and he lives in us. Today we remember that the risen Jesus is still with us in many ways. Let us thank Jesus and give him praise.

Reader 1: Jesus, when we pray, you are close to us.

All: Thank you, Jesus. Alleluia!

Reader 2: Jesus, when we receive the Eucharist at Mass, you come to us in a very special way.

All: Thank you, Jesus. Alleluia!

Reader 3: Jesus, when we read the Bible and study about you in religion class, your words become part of us.

All: Thank you, Jesus. Alleluia!

Reader 4: Jesus, when other people love and care for us, we see your love.

All: Thank you, Jesus. Alleluia! Amen.

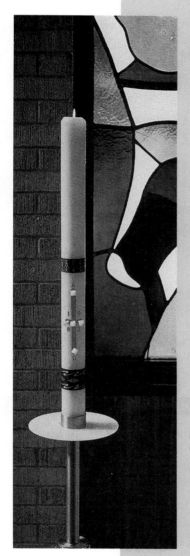

CURRICULUM CONNECTION

Language Arts Challenge each group to create an Easter poem about Jesus' presence among us today. Instruct each group to write two couplets for their poem. Explain that a couplet is composed of two lines with the same number of syllables and that the last word in each line rhymes. An example is found below.

Jesus is with us today,
When we share
    and when we pray.

Teaching Tips

Call attention to the picture of the Easter candle on page 301 and explain the markings. Note that the five grains of incense are a sign of Jesus' wounds. Point out the symbols that represent the words *Alpha* and *Omega*. Explain that these are the first and last letters of the Greek alphabet and that they are a sign that our life begins and ends with Jesus. Also call attention to the date of the year and tell the students that a new Easter candle is lighted each year at the Easter Vigil. If possible, take the students to see the Easter candle in the church.

Discussing the Easter Posters

Gather the students around the four posters. Discuss how these posters show ways in which Jesus is present to them today. Tell the students that during the prayer service they will add their names to the posters.

Preparing for the Prayer Service

Assign four readers for the prayer service on page 301 and provide time for them to practice their parts. Suggest that the students compose a simple melody to sing the response: "Thank you, Jesus. Alleluia!" Practice singing the response. Note the photograph on page 301. Talk with the students about the Easter candle.

Participating in a Prayer Service

Gather the students near the posters they made. Have available markers or crayons for the students to use during the prayer service. Hold a lighted candle in your hand if this is permitted in your school. Begin the prayer service by reading the part for the Leader. After Reader 1 has read and the students have responded, invite the students from the group who made the first poster (the one on people praying) to come to the poster. Invite each student to draw a simple butterfly on the poster and to print his or her name on the butterfly. While these students are completing their work, sing an Easter song with the rest of the class. After each reading and response, invite the appropriate group to add butterflies and names to their poster while the rest of the class sings. To conclude the prayer service, hold your lighted candle high and pray, "God, today we pray in Jesus' name. He is with us today and always. May the light of his presence help us live as good Christians. Amen. Alleluia!"

Our Church Honors Saints

Objectives ～～～～

- LESSON 1: To help the students learn about the life of Saint Francis.
- LESSON 2: To help the students learn about Saint Peter.
- LESSON 3: To help the students learn about the life of Blessed Kateri Tekakwitha.
- LESSON 4: To help the students learn about the life of Saint Teresa of Avila and celebrate all they have learned about the saints.

Lesson Outlines ～～～～～～

	Step 1 Learning About Our Lives	**Step 2** Learning About Our Faith	**Step 3** Learning How to Live Our Faith
Lesson 1	■ Choose what is important. *ABOUT 10 MINUTES*	■ Read a story. ■ Recite a prayer. *ABOUT 12 MINUTES*	■ Complete a crossword puzzle. ■ Pray together. *ABOUT 8 MINUTES*
Lesson 2	■ Review Lesson 1. *ABOUT 5 MINUTES*	■ Decide who was important to Jesus. ■ Read about Peter. *ABOUT 10 MINUTES*	■ Complete an activity. ■ Choose leadership qualities. ■ Pray together. *ABOUT 15 MINUTES*
Lesson 3	■ Discuss names. *ABOUT 6 MINUTES*	■ Read and discuss the story. ■ Role-playing Kateri's way of life. *ABOUT 12 MINUTES*	■ Complete an activity. ■ Pray together. *ABOUT 12 MINUTES*
Lesson 4	**Project** Learn about Saint Teresa. **Prayer** Talk about saints; prepare for the prayer service; participate in the prayer service.		

Plan Ahead

	Preparing Your Class	Materials Needed
Lesson 1	Read through the lesson plan for this session. Learn what you can about Saint Francis of Assisi. Be prepared to tell the students about this saint.	■ chalkboard ■ writing paper ■ crayons or markers ■ drawing paper (optional) ■ pencils
Lesson 2	For Step 2 of the plan, think of some people, animals, and things that might have been especially important to Jesus. Think of a leadership quality for each student.	■ chalkboard ■ pencils or pens ■ drawing paper ■ crayons or markers ■ scissors
Lesson 3	Read through the lesson plan for this session. Assemble the bags and objects needed for Step 2. Bring to class the name books needed for Step 1.	■ name books ■ plastic or cloth bags ■ an orange, a spoon, a book, chalk, a roll of tape, an onion, a can of soda
Lesson 4	Consider some things that Saint Teresa might have said to her sisters about loving God and neighbor. Find some easy-to-read booklets about the saints.	■ chalkboard ■ pencils ■ props to use in portraying saints

Additional Resources

As you plan this chapter, consider using the following materials from The Resourceful Teacher Package.

■ *Classroom Activity Sheets for Saints*

■ *Family Activity Sheets for Saints*

■ *Prayers for Every Day*

You may also wish to refer to the following Big Book.

■ *We Celebrate God's Word*, page 21

In preparing the students for the Sunday readings, you may wish to use Silver Burdett Ginn's *Getting Ready for Sunday* student and teacher materials.

REDUCED CLASSROOM ACTIVITIES

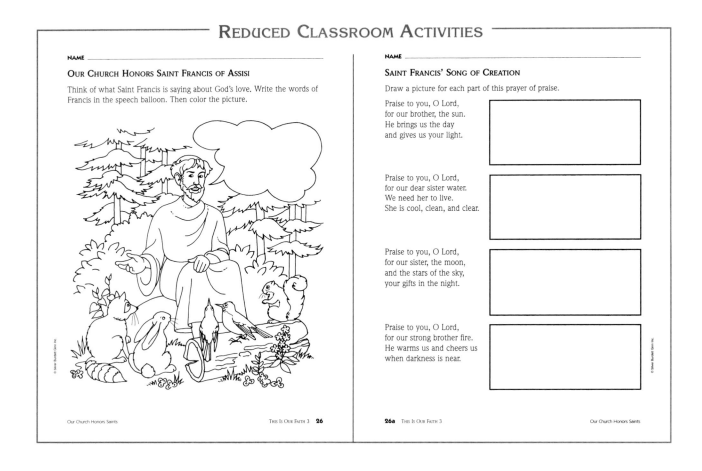

NAME _____

OUR CHURCH HONORS SAINT FRANCIS OF ASSISI

Think of what Saint Francis is saying about God's love. Write the words of Francis in the speech balloon. Then color the picture.

Our Church Honors Saints

THIS IS OUR FAITH 3 **26**

NAME _____

SAINT FRANCIS' SONG OF CREATION

Draw a picture for each part of this prayer of praise.

Praise to you, O Lord,
for our brother, the sun.
He brings us the day
and gives us your light.

Praise to you, O Lord,
for our dear sister water.
We need her to live.
She is cool, clean, and clear.

Praise to you, O Lord,
for our sister, the moon,
and the stars of the sky,
your gifts in the night.

Praise to you, O Lord,
for our strong brother fire.
He warms us and cheers us
when darkness is near.

26a THIS IS OUR FAITH 3

Our Church Honors Saints

THE LIFE OF SAINT FRANCIS

Saint Francis of Assisi is one of the most well known and popular saints of the Church. Thousands of men and women live in Franciscan communities as religious brothers, priests, and sisters. Many laymen and laywomen find inspiration for their daily living in the philosophy and simple lifestyle of Saint Francis.

Francis came from a wealthy family in Assisi. He had money to spend and a taste for worldly goods. A series of experiences, including an encounter with a poor and sickly leper, turned his life around. He sought to imitate the life of Jesus in the most exact way he could.

THE LIFE OF SAINT PETER

Saint Peter was a man who followed Jesus with energy and commitment. He is the best known of any of the twelve apostles because there are more stories told about him in Scripture than about any of the other apostles. We know that he was married and earned his living by fishing with his brother, Andrew. We know that Jesus ate at his house and cured his mother-in-law. In Scripture we see Peter at the Transfiguration, caught up in the glory that surrounded Jesus; and then we see him in the courtyard of the high priest where he denied knowing Jesus. Tradition tells us that Peter went to Rome, became Rome's first bishop, and was crucified there at the foot of Vatican Hill, during the reign of the Emperor Nero.

THE LIFE OF BLESSED KATERI TEKAKWITHA

Kateri Tekakwitha is the first Native American to be proposed for canonization. Known for her purity and good works, she became a Christian on Easter Sunday in 1676. Her conversion, the result of the missionary efforts of traveling Jesuits, was a great controversy in Kateri's village. Her deep faith was scorned by the people of her own village. Despite being almost completely blind, she traveled from Auriesville, New York, to a Native American Christian community near Montreal to practice her faith. More than 500 Native Americans from thirty tribes danced at her beatification ceremony in Rome in 1980.

THE LIFE OF SAINT TERESA OF AVILA

Teresa was a dynamic woman highly regarded in her own times as well as today. She founded convents for nuns who wished to live a reclusive spiritual life rather than the relaxed style prevalent in convents of the sixteenth century. She also wrote letters and books that are regarded as classics of spiritual literature and was known for her sense of humor.

LESSON 1

Objective

This lesson helps the students learn about the life of Saint Francis.

Step 1/INTRODUCTION

Learning About Our Lives

Choosing What Is Important

Brainstorm with the students a list of people, animals, and things that are important to them. On the chalkboard write their responses. Give each student a sheet of writing paper and provide crayons or markers. Ask each student to write between five and ten people, animals, and things that are important to him or her and to draw next to each item a picture of that person, animal, or thing. Afterward, invite sharing. Discuss the students' choices and put special emphasis on the people, animals, and "created" things that the students mention.

Step 2/DEVELOPMENT

Learning About Our Faith

Reading a Story

Tell the students that today they are going to read about a man who loved all of God's creation. Call on volunteers to read aloud "Saint Francis of Assisi" on page 302. Enhance the story with your own knowledge of Saint Francis. Emphasize Francis' special love of animals. Answer any questions that the students may have about Saint Francis or about the meaning of the reading.

302

Our Church Honors Saints

Preaching to the Birds (oil on panel), Bonaventura Berlinghieri, 13th century, Church of San Francesco, Pescia, Italy

Saint Francis of Assisi

Many years ago in Italy, there lived a man named Francis. The town he came from was called Assisi, and so people called him Francis of Assisi.

As a young man, Francis went from town to town telling everyone about God. He told people how much God loved them. Francis loved people, too, and he helped them whenever he could. He told them how much God loved animals. Francis loved animals, too. He took such good care of the birds that they would sit on his shoulder.

Francis said that people and animals and all living things are created and loved by God. Francis called all created things his brothers and sisters.

Focus on

Saint Francis of Assisi   Saint Francis of Assisi lived from 1181–1226. He had such a remarkable reputation as a holy man that he was canonized a saint only two years after he died. We celebrate the feast of Saint Francis of Assisi each year on October 4. During the Opening Prayer on this day, we ask God to help us follow Jesus by "walking in the footsteps of Francis of Assisi and by imitating his joyful love" (*The Sacramentary*, October 4).

This is part of a poem that Francis wrote to thank God for all the gifts of creation.

Song of Creation

Praise to you, O Lord,
for our brother, the sun.
He brings us the day
and gives us your light.

Praise to you, O Lord,
for our sister, the moon,
and the stars of the sky,
your gifts in the night.

Praise to you, O Lord,
for our dear sister water.
We need her to live.
She is cool, clean, and clear.

Praise to you, O Lord,
for our strong brother fire.
He warms us and cheers us
when darkness is near.

Activity

Use the clues below to fill in the crossword puzzle.

Down

1. This is a gift from God that we need to live.

2. This is the name of the town from which Francis came.

4. These twinkle in the night sky.

7. This gift gives us light at night. Francis called it sister _____.

Across

3. This gift gives us the light of day. Francis called it brother _____.

5. We need this gift when the earth is dry.

6. Francis made friends with the _____.

8. Francis thanked and praised _____ for all the gifts of God's creation.

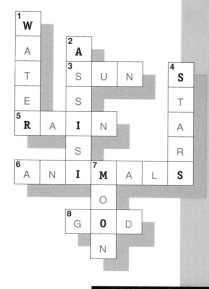

Ask the students to look at the prayer on page 303. Explain that Saint Francis wrote this prayer in praise of creation. Divide the class into four groups. Assign each group one of the stanzas of the prayer. Provide time for each group to get together and decide on gestures and movements it might use to accompany its stanza. If time permits, provide drawing paper and crayons or markers and invite each group to make a picture or a series of pictures to illustrate its stanza. Gather the groups around you and read "Song of Creation" with each group using its gestures as its stanza is said. Encourage each group to teach the remainder of the class the gestures for its stanza. Then say the entire prayer and invite the students to use all the gestures. If the students drew pictures, post these around the classroom.

Step 3/CONCLUSION

Learning How to Live Our Faith

Completing a Crossword Puzzle

Have the students complete the crossword puzzle on page 303. After the students have completed the puzzle, ask for volunteers to give their answers to each of the clues in the activity.

Praying Together

Using the lists the students made in Step 1, invite the students to say a spontaneous prayer to thank God for the important people, animals, and things in their lives. After each student shares one person, pet, or thing that is important to him or her, invite the class to respond, "Thank you, God, for this gift."

Enriching the Lesson

Saint Francis was famous for his love of animals, and on his feast day it is customary in rural areas for farm animals to be blessed. Some parishes and schools have outdoor prayer services in which the pets of parishioners are blessed. Work with the class to compose a simple blessing prayer for pets. Include in the prayer a sentence asking God to help the students care for their pets with the same love and devotion that Francis showed for all of God's creatures.

LESSON 2

Objective

This lesson helps the students learn about Saint Peter.

Step 1/INTRODUCTION

Learning About Our Lives

Reviewing Lesson 1

Review with the students what they learned about Saint Francis in Lesson 1. Have them turn to the prayer on page 303 and recite it, using the gestures they decided on during Step 2 of Lesson 1. Recall with the students the people, animals, and things they said were important to them. Write all the people's names on the chalkboard.

Step 2/DEVELOPMENT

Learning About Our Faith

Deciding Who Was Important to Jesus

Invite the students to brainstorm people, animals, and things that might have been important to Jesus when he lived in Palestine. Write their responses on the chalkboard. If they do not say *Peter*, add this name to the chalkboard at the end of the brainstorming. Tell the students that Peter was very important to Jesus and that today they will learn more about this apostle.

Reading About Peter

Call on volunteers to read "Saint Peter, Leader of the Church" on page 304. Ask the following questions.

- What question did Jesus ask the apostles? (*"Who do you say that I am?"*)

- What did Simon answer? (*"You are the redeemer, God's Son."*)

- What was the new name that Jesus gave to Simon? (*Peter*)

- What does the name *Peter* mean? (*Rock*)

- In what way is a leader like a rock? (*Accept all reasonable answers.*)

304

Saint Peter, Leader of the Church

The apostles had been with Jesus for three years. When Jesus healed the sick, they were there. When he told the people about God's love, they were there. When he taught the people how to pray, the apostles listened carefully.

Jesus wanted his work to go on. He wanted the good news of God's love to be shared with everyone.

Jesus had chosen his apostles with care. Soon he would go back to his Father. Now it was time to choose a leader.

One time, Jesus asked, "Who do people say that I am?"

"Some people say that you are John the Baptizer come back to life or one of the other great prophets," the apostles answered.

"Who do *you* say that I am?" Jesus continued.

Simon answered, "You are the Redeemer, God's Son."

After this, Jesus changed Simon's name to *Peter*, a name that means "rock." Then Jesus said that Peter would be the leader of the Church.

At Pentecost, Peter became the leader Jesus called him to be. He led the early Church in continuing Jesus' ministries of preaching and healing.

Based on Matthew 16:13–18 and Acts 2 and 3

Focus on

Saint Peter   There are three days honoring Peter each year. On February 22 we celebrate the Chair of Saint Peter. This title represents the authority Jesus gave Peter to lead the Church. In the early Church, Church leaders were given a chair as a sign of their role. Popes and bishops taught from their chairs. On June 29 we honor Saints Peter and Paul as two of our greatest teachers. On November 18 we celebrate the Dedication of the Churches of Saints Peter and Paul. This day celebrates the churches that were built over their tombs.

Activity

Leaders are important. Good leaders need to have talents and qualities that will help those who follow them.

Look at the list of qualities below. Choose the four that you think are the most important for good leadership. Write the name of a quality within each footstep. Tell the class why you feel each of your choices is important.

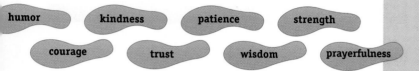

humor   kindness   patience   strength

courage   trust   wisdom   prayerfulness

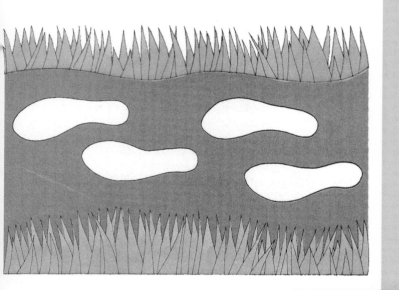

Enriching the Lesson

Have the students each bring to class a fist-sized rock. Empty one or more boxes of alphabet pasta on a large work area and have the students find the letters that spell out their first and last names. Instruct them to glue the letters onto their rocks. Encourage the students to use the rocks as paperweights at home or at school. Help them appreciate that the rocks are a sign that God has a special plan in mind for each of them.

Learning How to Live Our Faith

Completing an Activity

Call on a volunteer to read the directions for the activity on page 305. After each student has picked out four qualities of good leadership and written them in the footprints at the bottom of the page, discuss the choices the students made. Be sure to ask the students why they made these choices.

Choosing Leadership Qualities

Invite the students to think of their own leadership qualities. If some students cannot think of any quality they have that would make them a good leader, name a quality that you have recognized in each student. Provide the students with drawing paper, crayons or markers, and scissors. Ask each student to make a footprint or a shoe print. Encourage the students to write on their footprints or shoe prints their leadership qualities and brief prayers thanking God for these qualities. Make a footprint or shoe print for yourself and one for Saint Peter.

Praying Together

Gather the students around you. Using the footprint you made for Saint Peter, begin a spontaneous prayer by saying something like the following: "God, we thank you that Saint Peter had the quality of _____." Then invite each student to thank God for his or her leadership quality. Encourage the students to respond to each prayer with the refrain, "May (student's name) use this quality to help and love others." Encourage the students to take their footprints or shoe prints home and post them in a special place.

Objective

This lesson helps the students learn about the life of Blessed Kateri Tekakwitha.

Step 1/INTRODUCTION

Learning About Our Lives

Discussing Names

Ask the students if they know how they got their names. If possible, distribute books that give the meanings of names and have the students work in small groups to discover what their own names mean. Tell the class that in today's lesson they will read about someone with two very unusual names.

Step 2/DEVELOPMENT

Learning About Our Faith

Reading and Discussing the Story

Ask volunteers to take turns reading aloud "Kateri Tekakwitha" on pages 306 and 307. Then ask the following questions.

- Where was Tekakwitha born? (*In a Mohawk village in the woodlands of upper New York State*)

- How did Tekakwitha get her name? What does *Tekakwitha* mean? (*She was blind and had to touch the things around her to move from place to place.*)

- Why did the Blackrobes visit the village? (*To share the gospel*)

- What did Tekakwitha want to do? (*Become a Christian*)

- What was Tekakwitha's baptismal name? (*Kateri*)

- Why did Kateri leave her village? (*The villagers made fun of her and made it hard for her to live her faith.*)

- What does Kateri teach us? (*She teaches us that Jesus welcomes all people and the Church is open to everyone.*)

Kateri Tekakwitha

Kateri Tekakwitha was born in a Mohawk village in the woodlands of upper New York State in 1656. When she was three, a disease spread through Tekakwitha's village. Her parents died. She was left almost blind. She had to walk slowly, touching things with her hands. That is why she came to be called *Tekakwitha*, which means "She who feels her way along."

One day, a group of **Blackrobes** came to visit. Blackrobes was the name Native Americans gave to the priests who shared the gospel with them. Tekakwitha asked the priests many questions. She saw that they treated everyone with love and respect. She wanted to follow their example and become a Christian.

Tekakwitha had to wait many years for a priest to return to her village. Finally, ten years later, she was baptized and given the Christian name *Kateri*.

After her Baptism, Kateri's people made fun of her. They made it hard for her to live her faith.

Kateri heard about a Native American Christian community in Canada. It was called a "praying village." Kateri did not mind that she had to walk two hundred miles to the village. She was happy to be with people who shared her belief in Jesus.

When Kateri died, she was respected as a holy woman who cared for others. Her example led many other Native Americans to join the Catholic Church. Kateri's life teaches us that Jesus welcomes all people and that the Church is open to everyone.

Activity

The Church honors Blessed Kateri Tekakwitha on July 14th. To discover the prayer we pray on this day, unscramble the words below.

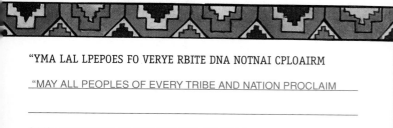

"YMA LAL LPEPOES FO VERYE RBITE DNA NOTNAI CPLOAIRM

"MAY ALL PEOPLES OF EVERY TRIBE AND NATION PROCLAIM

OGS'D TRENGASES NI EON GOSN FO SPARIE."

GOD'S GREATNESS IN ONE SONG OF PRAISE."

Based on the Opening Prayer from the Memorial of Blessed Kateri Tekakwitha

Role-Playing Kateri's Way of Life

Remind the students how difficult it was for Kateri to see. Explain to them that people who are visually impaired have to rely on their other senses to help them "see." Before class, put a number of objects in nontransparent plastic or cloth bags. These objects may include an orange, a spoon, a book, a piece of chalk, a roll of tape, an onion, a can of soda, and so on. Invite volunteers to close their eyes and identify the objects, using their senses of touch and smell. Note that Kateri had to depend on others to help her live. Emphasize her trust in God's care for her in leaving her home to travel to the praying village.

Step 3/CONCLUSION

Learning How to Live Our Faith

Completing an Activity

Direct attention to the scramble activity on page 307 and have the students work independently to complete it. When they have finished, have them read the prayer aloud together. Help the class understand that we are all one family in God.

Praying Together

Explain that God calls us to welcome all people to the Church. Invite the students to offer prayers asking God to help them be more open to others. Conclude by praying, "Loving God, be with us on our journey of faith. Help us to treat all others as our brothers and sisters."

CURRICULUM CONNECTION

Geography Using a large map of North America, have the students trace Kateri's journey from Auriesville, New York to Montreal, Canada. Kateri lived in a village located on the Mohawk River, west of Amsterdam, New York. Explain that Kateri's journey, made on foot, covered more than 200 miles through unsettled land.

Enriching the Lesson

Explain that making jewelry from colorful beads is a Native American craft. Have the students make wristbands by stringing colorful beads on braided threads or strings. These supplies are available at craft stores. Encourage the students to wear their wristbands as a reminder to praise God by living their faith as Kateri did.

LESSON 4

Objective

This lesson helps the students learn about the life of Saint Teresa of Avila.

Learning About Saint Teresa

Have the students turn to the story of Saint Francis on page 302. Point out the line in the second paragraph that says that Francis went from town to town telling everyone about God. Tell the students that today they are going to learn about a woman who did a lot of traveling to tell people about God.

Call on volunteers to read "Saint Teresa of Avila" on page 308. Check to be sure the students understand what they have read. Then draw on the chalkboard six houses (convents), each with a cross about one foot by one foot. Use colored chalk to draw between the houses a road with trees, rocks, and bushes. Invite the students to add other features to the scene on the chalkboard. Invite six volunteers to come to the chalkboard and to write in the houses (convents) what Saint Teresa might have said to the sisters in the houses when she told them about God and about how to live a good Christian life.

Using your fingers, walk down the road from one convent to the next. When you get to a convent, knock on the chalkboard and ask to enter. Invite the students to respond to your request. Then read to the students what is written in the convent. Ask them to pretend that they are the sisters that Saint Teresa was speaking to and to respond to what she is saying. Continue across the chalkboard until you have entered all six convents.

Saint Teresa of Avila

Saint Teresa was born in Spain in 1515. When her mother died, Teresa's father placed her in a convent to live with the sisters. As she grew up, Teresa wanted to be a sister, too. She became a Carmelite sister at a convent near the city of Avila.

As the years went by, Sister Teresa became worried about the way she and the other sisters were living. She knew that God would want them to try harder. So Sister Teresa went from convent to convent. She showed the sisters how to pray better and reminded them to care more about one another.

Sister Teresa also wrote many books about God. Through prayer and meditation, Teresa grew very close to God. She came to understand God's ways better than many other people did. Her books became so famous that Pope Paul VI gave Teresa the title of **Doctor**, or Teacher, of the Church.

Teaching Tips

We honor Saint Teresa of Avila on October 15 each year. Her religious name in the Carmelite Order was Sister Teresa of Jesus. Saint Teresa is one of only two female Doctors of the Church. The other is Saint Catherine of Siena. On October 15 we pray that Saint Teresa's example and teaching will help us desire to become truly holy, as she was.

Prayer Service to Honor Saints

Teacher: There are many wonderful people in God's family. Some of them lived long ago. By learning about them, we understand better what it means for us to live as God's children. Let us ask these saints to help us to be holy as they were holy.

Reader 1: Saint Francis, you called all created things your brothers and sisters.

All: Help us to care for our world.

Reader 2: Saint Peter, Jesus chose you to be the leader of his Church.

All: Help us to be good leaders.

Reader 3: Blessed Kateri, you walked two hundred miles to be with other Christans.

All: Help us to appreciate our own Christian communities.

Reader 4: Saint Teresa, you asked the sisters to try harder to do God's will.

All: Help us to try harder.

Teacher: Let us pray.

All: Lord, you have given us many friends in heaven. Through their prayers we know that you will watch over us always and fill our hearts with your love. Amen.

Enriching the Lesson

Have the students form four cooperative groups. Assign one of the holy men or women studied in this unit to each group: Francis of Assisi, Peter, Kateri Tekakwitha, and Teresa of Avila. Direct each group to use construction paper, crayons, scissors, glue, and other art materials to create a symbol representing the person they have been assigned. During the prayer service, as each holy person is presented, have a student from each group display and explain the symbol for that person.

Talking About Saints

Recall what the students have learned about Saint Francis, Saint Peter, Blessed Kateri, and Saint Teresa of Avila. Ask the students if they know about any other saints who lived long ago. Provide time for the students to share any stories they know about saints. Ask the students if they know about any other people living today who do good things for people and live as children of God. Encourage the students to share stories about these people.

Preparing for the Prayer Service

Ask four volunteers to be Saint Francis, Saint Peter, Blessed Kateri, and Saint Teresa for the prayer service. Tell these students to reread the stories in the textbook about these saints. If possible, provide the students with some books, written for the third-grade level, to read more about these four people. Provide simple props for the four students and encourage them to prepare to tell the class about the saints they represent. Select four readers for the prayer service on page 309 and provide time for them to practice what they will say. Practice the part labeled *All* with the students.

Participating in a Prayer Service

Gather the students around you. Begin the prayer service by reading the *Teacher* part on page 309. Then invite the student who is portraying Saint Francis to talk to the students about this saint. Afterward, have Reader 1 read and invite the students' response. Continue in this manner throughout the prayer service.

Our Church Honors Mary

Objectives

- **LESSON 1:** To help the students learn about the Presentation of Mary.
- **LESSON 2:** To help the students recognize Mary as the mother of all Christians.
- **LESSON 3:** To help the students learn about Our Lady of Fatima.

Lesson Outlines

	Step 1 Learning About Our Lives	Step 2 Learning About Our Faith	Step 3 Learning How to Live Our Faith
Lesson 1	■ Think about going to church. *ABOUT 8 MINUTES*	■ Learn about Mary. *ABOUT 5 MINUTES*	■ Find the way through a maze. ■ Discuss Mary's days. *ABOUT 17 MINUTES*
Lesson 2	■ Review Lesson 1. *ABOUT 5 MINUTES*	■ Read a Scripture story. ■ Learn about Mary and the Church. *ABOUT 11 MINUTES*	■ Solve a puzzle. *ABOUT 14 MINUTES*
Lesson 3	■ Picturing Mary. *ABOUT 5 MINUTES*	■ Reading the text. *ABOUT 13 MINUTES*	■ Identifying prayer needs. *ABOUT 12 MINUTES*

Plan Ahead

	Preparing Your Class	Materials Needed
Lesson 1	Read through the lesson plan for this session. Be ready to share your first memories of going to church.	■ writing paper ■ pencils or pens ■ crayons or markers
Lesson 2	Read through the lesson plan for this session. Review the story of the Visitation to be able to relate it to the students in Step 3.	■ pencils or pens
Lesson 3	Read through the lesson plan for this session. You may want to have statues and pictures available to use in Step 1.	■ pencils or pens

Additional Resources

As you plan this chapter, consider using the following materials from The Resourceful Teacher Package.

■ *Classroom Activity Sheets for Mary*

■ *Family Activity Sheets for Mary*

■ *Prayers for Every Day*

You may also wish to refer to the following Big Book.

■ *We Celebrate God's Word,* pages 4, 5, and 22

In preparing the students for the Sunday readings, you may wish to use Silver Burdett Ginn's *Getting Ready for Sunday* student and teacher materials.

REDUCED CLASSROOM ACTIVITIES

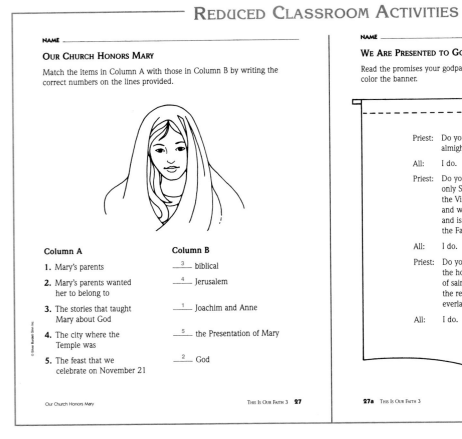

NAME _____

OUR CHURCH HONORS MARY

Match the items in Column A with those in Column B by writing the correct numbers on the lines provided.

Column A

1. Mary's parents

2. Mary's parents wanted her to belong to

3. The stories that taught Mary about God

4. The city where the Temple was

5. The feast that we celebrate on November 21

Column B

___3___ biblical

___4___ Jerusalem

___1___ Joachim and Anne

___5___ the Presentation of Mary

___2___ God

NAME _____

WE ARE PRESENTED TO GOD AT BAPTISM

Read the promises your godparents made for you at Baptism. Decorate and color the banner.

Priest: Do you believe in God, the Father almighty, creator of heaven and earth?

All: I do.

Priest: Do you believe in Jesus Christ, his only Son, our Lord, who was born of the Virgin Mary, was crucified, died, and was buried, rose from the dead, and is now seated at the right hand of the Father?

All: I do.

Priest: Do you believe in the Holy Spirit, the holy catholic Church, the communion of saints, the forgiveness of sins, the resurrection of the body, and life everlasting?

All: I do.

Background for the Teacher ~~~~~~~~

THE PRESENTATION OF MARY

The Feast of the Presentation of Mary is celebrated on November 21. This event is not found in the Scriptures but comes to us from tradition. According to tradition, Mary was presented in the Temple in Jerusalem at the age of three. She lived at the Temple with other girls. The Eastern Church celebrated this feast as early as the eighth century. In 1585, Sixtus V extended the feast to the universal Church.

The value of the Feast of the Presentation is that it reminds us that Mary was dedicated to the ways of God at an early age and that she was prepared for her unique role as the mother of Jesus.

Like many biblical figures before her (Abraham, Sarah, Moses, Elisha, Amos, and so on), Mary had a vocation, a "call" or an "election." We learn of this call when we read Luke 1:26–38 in which the Angel Gabriel tells Mary that the Lord is with her and that she is blessed among women. Mary's response to the angel's message that she will bear a son is the simple, faith-filled statement, "I am the servant of the Lord. Let it be done to me as you say" (based on Luke 1:38).

Throughout her life, Mary kept responding to this call from God. She supported Jesus in his ministry. She was seen at Cana, was present at the crucifixion, and heard her son tell the beloved disciple to take care of her. She also waited with the disciples for the coming of the Holy Spirit. Mary, mother of Jesus and model of faith, is considered to be the greatest of Christian saints.

THE CALL TO BE CARING CHRISTIANS

All of us baptized into Christ's death and resurrection have been called to be caring, faith-filled Christians. Like Mary, we wait on the Lord. In these lessons the students will learn about Mary's presentation in the Temple, her role as Mother of Christians, and her appearances in Fatima, Portugal in 1917. They will recognize that Mary's example is a source of faith and inspiration. They will also become aware that Mary is our mother, too. As our mother, Mary shows us how to follow God. She watches over us and guides us to Jesus. Mary acts as our intercessor, bringing our prayers and concerns to the Lord. As you teach these lessons, help your students recognize Mary's care for each of them as her children. Encourage them to turn to Mary in prayer, confident in her loving response and compassion.

LESSON 1

Objective

This lesson helps the students learn about the Presentation of Mary.

Step 1/INTRODUCTION

Learning About Our Lives

Thinking About Going to Church

Ask the students to recall, if they can, what it was like to go to church when they were younger. Discuss what they thought about as they looked around the church, what they said to their parents, and what they thought was happening during the Mass. After the students have shared their first memorable impressions of being at church, ask them what Scripture stories they can remember hearing at church since they first started going. Discuss the stories.

Step 2/DEVELOPMENT

Learning About Our Faith

Learning About Mary

Tell the students that Mary, the mother of Jesus, went to the Temple when she was a little girl, just as they went to church. Explain that the Temple was a special place of worship for the Jewish people. Ask volunteers to read aloud "Feast of the Presentation of Mary" on pages 310–311. Ask the following questions.

■ What were the names of Mary's parents? (*Joachim and Anne*)

■ Where did Mary's parents bring her when she was a little girl? (*To the Temple*)

■ What do we call the special day that commemorates this event? (*The Presentation of Mary*)

■ Why did Mary's parents bring her to the Temple? (*They wanted her to learn about God.*)

■ What did Mary do each day at the Temple? (*Listened to Bible stories, learned prayers and songs*)

Our Church Honors Mary

Feast of the Presentation of Mary

Mary is the mother of Jesus. This story is about Mary and her mother and father.

Joachim and Anne were holy people. They loved God very much and always tried to do God's will. Joachim and Anne loved each other very much, too. They wanted to have a child to care for and to love. They had been married for a long time when they finally had a little daughter, whom they called Mary. Joachim and Anne were very happy.

Mary's parents wanted her to belong to God. They wanted her to learn about God and follow the teachings of the Scriptures. When Mary was a little girl, Joachim and Anne brought her to the Temple in Jerusalem.

310 Mary: Lesson One

Focus on

Saying Yes to God In memory of Mary's willingness to always say yes to the Lord, it is traditional for the members of many religious communities—religious sisters, brothers, and priests—to renew their vows on the Feast of the Presentation of Mary. They ask God to help them hear God's word and keep it, as Mary did.

310

Each day, Mary listened to Bible stories about God and his people. She learned the prayers and songs of her people, including the **psalms**, and sang them with all her heart.

We remember the day that Joachim and Anne brought Mary to the Temple and presented her to God. We celebrate the Feast of the Presentation of Mary on November 21.

Activity

Help Mary and her parents find their way to the Temple.

Teaching Tips

Explain that we are presented to God at Baptism. Remind the class that at Baptism, our parents and godparents pray that we will follow Jesus' teachings and example. Have the students renew their baptismal promises by responding "I do" to these questions: *Do you believe in God, creator of heaven and earth? Do you believe in Jesus, God's Son and our Savior? Do you believe in the Holy Spirit, our helper and guide? Do you believe in the Catholic Church?* Then pray together The Lord's Prayer.

Step 3/CONCLUSION

Learning How to Live Our Faith

Finding the Way Through a Maze

Read the directions for the activity on page 311. Have the students complete the maze.

Discussing Mary's Days

Talk with the students about what Mary did each day. (She listened to Bible stories from the Old Testament, learned prayers and songs, and sang these songs.) Stress that the stories Mary heard were not about Jesus because Jesus hadn't been born yet. Note that these stories were about Abraham, Moses, and other leaders of the Hebrew people. Recall for the students any stories from the Old Testament they have heard. Discuss any religious songs the students know. Sing a verse from several songs.

Provide each student with a sheet of writing paper. Ask the students to pretend that they are Mary at the Temple. Invite each student to write and illustrate one diary entry for Mary in which she tells about her day at the Temple. Provide crayons or markers. Invite volunteers to share their diary entries. If a student mentions a Bible story that Mary may have studied, invite the student to tell a little about the story, to act out the story, or to say why he or she chose this story. When all the volunteers have shared their work, have the students write their names on the papers. Then bind the papers into a book about Mary. Invite a volunteer to make a cover for the booklet. Tell the students that during the days ahead they can each take the booklet home to share with their families.

LESSON 2

Objective

This lesson helps the students recognize Mary as the mother of all Christians.

Step 1/INTRODUCTION

Learning About Our Lives

Reviewing Lesson 1

Recall with the students what they learned about Mary in Lesson 1. Talk about what she might have been like as a little girl and what she might have done as she learned more about God. Then encourage the students to discuss what they think Mary was like as a parent. Ask the following questions: How did she treat Jesus? How was she like their own parents? Explain to the students that today they will learn about Mary's life after Jesus died and rose.

Step 2/DEVELOPMENT

Learning About Our Faith

Reading a Scripture Story

Direct the students to open their texts to page 312 and read the first two paragraphs silently. Then have them answer the following questions.

- How did the apostles, the other believers, and Mary act toward one another? (*They acted like a family.*)
- What happened because of the first Christians' example? (*New believers joined their group every day.*)

Have the students underline in their texts the different ways the first Christians were like a family.

Learning About Mary and the Church

Call on volunteers to read the next three paragraphs in the text. Emphasize that Mary must have been loved and honored by Jesus' disciples, who recognized that she was specially chosen by God to be Jesus' mother. They saw that she was an example of faith for them. Emphasize that Mary did not question God or get angry with God when Jesus died. Instead, she stood by Jesus. She trusted God's promises to her. Stress that Mary wants to help us grow closer to Jesus.

312

Mary, Mother of Christians

After Jesus returned to the Father in heaven, the apostles, other believers, and Mary—Jesus' mother—met together often. The first Christians were like a family.

They shared everything they had. They sold the things they owned and gave the money to anyone who needed it. They broke bread together in different homes. They shared their food happily and generously, always giving praise to God. They were such a great example to others that new believers joined their group every day.

Based on the Acts of the Apostles 2:42–47

Jesus' followers loved Mary and treated her with great respect. They knew that God chose Mary to be Jesus' mother. They saw that Mary was always faithful to God and that she was filled with God's life, which we call **grace**.

When he was dying on the cross, Jesus gave Mary to us as our mother. Jesus knew that we would need Mary's example to follow him and to build his Church.

We honor Mary as the mother of Christians. Mary shows her love and care for us by bringing our prayers and worries to Jesus.

Madonna and Child seated in a landscape (oil), Jan Sanders Van Hemesse 16th century, Rafael Valls Gallery, London, Englar

312 Mary: Lesson Two

Enriching the Lesson

Distribute posterboard and markers and have the students form five groups. Assign one of the following events to each group: Mary visiting Elizabeth; the Holy Family in the stable; Mary standing by Jesus' cross; Mary with the disciples after Jesus returned to God; and Mary in heaven. Ask the groups to illustrate their stories using pictures and words.

Activity

Solve the problems below. Find the letter that matches each correct answer. Copy the letters on the lines. Then read Mary's prayer (based on Luke 1:49).

8=A	13=S	14=N	15=G	16=D
17=E	18=M	19=H	20=R	21=O
23=Y	24=I	25=F	26=T	27=L

(9+6) (17+4) (9+7)　　(27-8) (7+1) (9+4)

_____God_____　　_____has_____

(8+8) (30-9) (9+5) (9+8)　　(8+7) (37-17) (6+11) (26-18) (9+17)

_____done_____　　_____great_____

(8+18) (7+12) (19+5) (8+6) (17-2) (29-16)

_____things_____

(19+6) (16+5) (8+12)　　(27-9) (6+11)

_____for_____　　_____me_____.

(8+7) (14+7) (21-5) ' (7+6)　　(23-9) (26-18) (6+12) (21-4)

_____God's_____　　_____name_____

(31-7) (5+8)　　(15+4) (12+9) (19+8) (19+4)

_____is_____　　_____holy_____.

Mary: Lesson Two   313

Learning How to Live Our Faith

Solving a Puzzle

Explain the activity on page 313. Make sure that the students are clear on what they are to do to solve the puzzle. Have them work on their own to complete the activity.

Before having the students read the prayer, explain the setting in which Mary prayed these words. Tell the students that when Mary was waiting for Jesus to be born, she went to visit her cousin Elizabeth. When Elizabeth saw Mary, she said, "Blessed is the fruit of your womb," words which we now pray in the Hail Mary. Elizabeth also asked, "Why should the mother of my Lord come to visit me? The Lord has blessed you." Mary responded to Elizabeth by praying a prayer of praise to God. After the students have grasped the context of the activity prayer, conclude by having them recite the prayer aloud together.

CURRICULUM CONNECTION

Mathematics Have the students work in pairs to construct their own "word problems." Ask each pair of students to write three words using the letters in the chart on page 313. Then have them create an addition and subtraction problem to arrive at the numbers for each of the letters in their words. Have the students trade problems with another pair to solve the puzzles.

Lesson 3

Objective

This lesson helps the students learn about Our Lady of Fatima.

Step 1/Introduction

Learning About Our Lives

Picturing Mary

Invite the students to close their eyes and picture Mary. Allow about one minute for them to get a clear mental image of Mary. Ask the students to open their eyes and describe what they noticed about Mary. Ask the following questions: What was she wearing? Where was she? What did she look like? What kind of a person did she seem to be? Then discuss with the students what their reaction would be if they had opened their eyes and saw Mary standing in the classroom. Encourage each student to express his or her opinion. Then explain to the students that today they will learn about Mary's visits to three children many years ago.

Step 2/Development

Learning About Our Faith

Reading the Text

Call on volunteers to take turns reading aloud "Our Lady of Fatima" on pages 314 and 315. Ask the following questions.

- What were the three children doing when they first saw the lady? (*Tending sheep*)

- What did the children call the lady? (*Our Lady*)

- What did Our Lady ask the children to do? (*To pray the Rosary for peace in the world*)

- What happened when other people went to the field with the children? (*Only the children could see the lady.*)

- What did Lucia ask? (*For a sign so that everyone would believe in the lady*)

- On her last visit, what did the lady tell the children? (*That she was Our Lady of the Rosary; that she wanted them to build a church for her*)

- What sign did Our Lady give everyone? (*The sun changed colors and seemed to dance in the sky for ten minutes.*)

Our Lady of Fatima, artist unknown

Our Lady of Fatima

On May 13, 1917, three children named Lucia, Jacinta, and Francisco were tending sheep in the fields near the small town of Fatima, Portugal. Suddenly they saw a lady dressed in shining white clothes. The lady told the children she was from heaven and they should not be afraid. She said that if they returned to the field each month, she would tell them who she was.

Every month, for six months, the children waited for the lady. They called her "Our Lady." She asked the children to pray the Rosary for peace in the world. She reminded them that God wanted everyone to turn away from sin and to live good lives.

Teaching Tips

Review with the students how to pray the Rosary. Show the class a large rosary or draw one on the board with colored chalk, indicating the five decades and the introductory prayers. You might also take the time to review the mysteries of the Rosary, explaining that the mysteries help us think about the major events in the lives of Jesus and Mary.

Some people who heard about Our Lady's visits did not believe it. Others wanted to see if it were true. They went to the field and waited, but only the children could see her. Lucia asked Our Lady to show them a sign so that everyone would believe in her.

On Our Lady's last visit to Fatima, 100,000 people waited and prayed with the children. She said that she was Our Lady of the Rosary. She asked them to build a church for her. People reported that she then gave everyone the sign she had promised. They said that for ten minutes the sun changed colors and seemed to dance and spin in the sky and that Our Lady then appeared to the children once again—with Saint Joseph and Jesus beside her!

The next year, a church was built in honor of Our Lady of Fatima. Millions of people visit this holy place every year to pray and to remember the visits of Mary. We can remember Our Lady of Fatima each time we pray the Rosary. The message of Fatima is that Mary is always watching over us, guiding us to Jesus.

Activity

Mary asked Lucia, Jacinta, and Francisco to pray for peace. What do you think Mary wants us to pray for today? Write your ideas here.

_____

_____

_____

_____

_____

- When the children saw Our Lady again, whom was she with? (*Saint Joseph and Jesus*)

- What can we learn from the story of Mary's visits to Fatima? (*Mary is always watching over us, guiding us to Jesus.*)

Step 3/CONCLUSION

Learning How to Live Our Faith

Identifying Prayer Needs

Call attention to the activity on page 315 and explain the directions. Have the students work in cooperative groups to identify the things in today's world that Mary would ask us to pray for. Encourage the students to discuss different groups, people, and problems that need God's special attention and care. Then have them write the three things they think are most important on the lines provided in the text. Call on a representative from each group to read their list aloud.

Enriching the Lesson

The students will enjoy finger painting their vision of Our Lady of Fatima's sign to the people on her last visit. Prepare a large work area covered with newspaper for this project. Have bright colors available for the students to use in creating their pictures. Display the students' work during October (the month of the Rosary) or May (the month of Mary).

315

Our Church Celebrates Holy Days

Objectives

- **LESSON 1:** To help the students recognize that the Feast of All Saints is like a family gathering.
- **LESSON 2:** To help the students recognize that we show our love for the Trinity by serving others.
- **LESSON 3:** To help the students celebrate Christ as King of all people.

Lesson Outlines

	Step 1 **Learning About Our Lives**	**Step 2** **Learning About Our Faith**	**Step 3** **Learning How to Live Our Faith**
Lesson 1	■ Remember family gatherings. *ABOUT 7 MINUTES*	■ Read about the gathering of saints. *ABOUT 4 MINUTES*	■ Complete an activity. ■ Make a frieze of saints. ■ Pray together. *ABOUT 19 MINUTES*
Lesson 2	■ Study objects. *ABOUT 7 MINUTES*	■ Read the Scripture story. ■ Understand the message. *ABOUT 10 MINUTES*	■ Complete a prayer. *ABOUT 13 MINUTES*
Lesson 3	■ Play a word-association game. *ABOUT 6 MINUTES*	■ Read about Christ's kingship. ■ Introduce the Liturgical Calendar. *ABOUT 14 MINUTES*	■ Write about building the kingdom. *ABOUT 10 MINUTES*

Plan Ahead

	Preparing Your Class	Materials Needed
Lesson 1	Read through the lesson plan for this class session. Consider where you will put the frieze of saints. Find books of the lives of saints for the students to look at.	■ large sheets of paper, one for each student ■ crayons or markers ■ scraps of construction paper ■ glue or paste and scissors ■ pins or tape
Lesson 2	Read through the lesson plan for this class session. Gather the objects needed for Step 1.	■ triangle ■ picture of a shamrock ■ a pretzel twisted into the traditional "crossed arms" shape ■ pencils or pens
Lesson 3	Read through the lesson plan for this class session. Familiarize yourself with the cycle of the liturgical year for the activity in Step 2.	■ chalkboard and colored chalk ■ pencils or pens

Additional Resources

As you plan this chapter, consider using the following materials from The Resourceful Teacher Package.

■ *Classroom Activity Sheets for Holy Days*

■ *Family Activity Sheets for Holy Days*

■ *Prayers for Every Day*

In preparing the students for the Sunday readings, you may wish to use Silver Burdett Ginn's *Getting Ready for Sunday* student and teacher materials.

REDUCED CLASSROOM ACTIVITIES

OUR CHURCH CELEBRATES ALL SAINTS' DAY

Complete the paragraph by choosing the correct word for each sentence from the word box.

Mass	family	November 1	Church
Mary		heaven	saint

The Church celebrates the Feast of All Saints on November 1 . This feast reminds us of the union of God's family . Catholics celebrate the feast at Mass . Mary , the mother of Jesus, is called the Queen of Saints. Joseph is remembered as the saint of the universal Church. On this day the Church remembers holy people of all ages. We honor all the saints who live with God in heaven .

© Silver Burdett Ginn Inc.

November 1 is All Saints' Day.

MY FAVORITE SAINT

Think about some of the saints' lives you have read about. Choose one of these saints and write about him or her. Share what you have written with your class.

My Favorite Saint

_____
_____
_____
_____
_____
_____
_____
_____
_____
_____
_____
_____
_____
_____
_____

© Silver Burdett Ginn Inc.

315c Organizer

THE FEAST OF ALL SAINTS

The Feast of All Saints is a joyful celebration of the Church. On this special day we honor all those faithful departed who have died in the Lord. This includes the saints recognized by the Church, such as the apostles and the evangelists. It also includes our friends and relatives who are now saints in heaven.

The Feast of All Saints gives us an opportunity to reflect on the lives of our departed brothers and sisters in Christ. Third graders need believable examples of holy men and women. They need models of Christian living in whom they can find inspiration and encouragement for their daily lives. The students are apt to relegate the saints to books and plaster images unrelated to their own lives. We must focus instead on the saints as real people who loved God and cared for others in need.

HOLY TRINITY

After the Easter Season draws to a close, we celebrate the Solemnity of the Holy Trinity. On this day we pray: "Father, you sent your Word to bring us truth and your Spirit to make us holy. Through them we come to know the mystery of your life. Help us to worship you, one God in three Persons, by proclaiming and living our faith in you" (Opening Prayer for the Feast of the Holy Trinity).

The mystery of the Trinity cannot be fully explained. The fact that we know God as three distinct Persons helps us to begin to understand the breadth and depth of God's great love for us. God's love and care cannot be limited; it is revealed to us through the Father who created us, the Son who redeemed us, and the Spirit who sanctifies us. In this lesson, you can help your students express their gratitude and love to the Trinity of God by living as God desires.

CHRIST THE KING

The Solemnity of Christ the King is celebrated on the last Sunday in Ordinary Time, the last Sunday of the liturgical year. This feast was added to the Church calendar by Pope Pius XI in 1925 in order to help Catholics recognize the royal dignity of Jesus and our individual and collective dignity as Christians. Through Baptism, we too have been anointed, or set apart, to live and affirm the values of Christ's kingdom—justice, peace, and love.

In teaching this lesson, you have the opportunity to help your third graders acknowledge Jesus as their King and appreciate that we honor our King through service to others. You can also help them become more aware that we are called to recognize Jesus' presence in those who are hungry, sick, and poor. These are the people our King called "blessed."

LESSON 1

Objective

To help the students recognize that the Feast of All Saints is like a family gathering.

Step 1/INTRODUCTION

Learning About Our Lives

Remembering Family Gatherings

Have the students recall a family get-together they have experienced. Note that this gathering might have been a large get-together to which people came from miles away to visit relatives they had not seen in years or it might have been a small family party or picnic to celebrate a birthday or some other happy event. Ask the students to share stories of such gatherings. Discuss with the students what they did at these gatherings by asking the following questions.

- What games did you play at the family gathering?
- How did you feel when your family gathered together?
- What were some stories that were told?
- Which of your family members told jokes or stories?
- What did the children do?
- What favorite foods did you eat at the family gathering?
- Did you sing songs? What songs?
- Did you do any decorating?

Step 2/DEVELOPMENT

Learning About Our Faith

Reading About the Gathering of Saints

Introduce the reading by explaining to the students that each year the Church celebrates the gathering, or get-together, of all the saints in heaven. Ask volunteers to read aloud "Feast of All Saints" on page 316. Afterward, help the students understand that we are members of God's family here on earth. Stress that the people on earth who follow Jesus and serve others will become saints in heaven when they die. Note that someday the students will be with all the saints in heaven.

316

Our Church Celebrates Holy Days

Communion of Saints (fresco), Andrea da Firenze, 14th century, Spanish Chapel, Santa Maria Novella, Florence, Italy

Feast of All Saints

Each year the Church celebrates the union of the members of God's family. We celebrate this day on November 1, the Feast of All Saints.

On this day we celebrate what it means to belong to God's family. We come together at Mass to remember the great saints like Mary and Joseph and Francis and many, many more. We think of all the good people we have known who have died and gone to be with God in heaven. And we think about what it means to live as a member of God's family on earth today.

Cultural Awareness

On All Saints Day we read, "I saw before me a huge crowd which no one could count from every nation, race, people, and tongue . . . They cried out in a loud voice: 'Salvation comes from our God'" (based on Revelation 7:9–10). Explain that this reading reminds us that saints come from every ethnic group. Research the patron saints of different countries, such as Charles Lwanga (Africa), Rose of Lima (Peru), Brigid (Ireland), and others to help the students feel a sense of pride in their roots.

Focus on

The Saints The word *saint* comes from a Latin word which means "consecrated or dedicated to God." The saints dedicated themselves to serving God. We honor the saints as examples of how to serve God. We pray to them so that they will pray for us, encourage us, and inspire us to live according to God's plan for each of us.

On the Feast of All Saints we pray this prayer.

God, our Father,
You are all powerful and always alive.
Today we are happy as we remember
all the holy men, women, and children
of every time and place.
May their care for us help us to be
your holy sons and daughters, too,
so that one day we will celebrate with you
and with them in the happiness of heaven.
Amen.

Based on the Opening Prayer
from the Feast of All Saints

Activity

Match the name of each person with the words that tell something about that person.

1. Mary	_5_ someone living today who is trying to be a saint
2. Peter	_2_ one of the twelve apostles
3. Francis	_1_ the mother of Jesus
4. Joseph	_4_ a member of the Holy Family
5. _____ (Fill in your name.)	_3_ someone who lived long ago who loved all God's creation

Learning How to Live Our Faith

Completing an Activity

Read the directions for the matching activity at the bottom of page 317. Invite sharing.

Making a Frieze of Saints

Ask the students to think of people who are in heaven (people in Scripture stories, such as Mary, Joseph, and Peter; great saints, such as Saint Francis, Saint Thérèse of Lisieux, and Saint Nicholas; and the students' friends and relatives who have died). Ask each student to select one saint. Provide books about saints for the students who want to do more reading.

Tell the students that they are going to do a frieze of saints for the classroom. Provide a large sheet of paper for each student, crayons or markers, scraps of construction paper, scissors, and paste or glue. Invite each student to cut out a large figure of his or her saint and to color it, using crayons or markers. Suggest that each student draw a streamer across the chest of the saint and label that with the saint's name. Once the students have completed their figures, invite them to tell about their saints. After each student tells about his or her saint, pin or tape the saint to the wall to make a frieze of saints around the room.

Praying Together

Have the students listen as a volunteer reads the prayer on page 317. If time permits, have the students brainstorm movements and gestures to use with the prayer. Then say the prayer as a group, using the students' movements and gestures.

317

LESSON 2

Objective

This lesson helps the students recognize that we show our love for the Trinity by serving others.

Step 1/INTRODUCTION

Learning About Our Lives

Studying Objects

Bring to class a triangle (musical), a picture of a shamrock, and a pretzel twisted into the traditional "crossed arms" shape. Invite the students to study these objects and note the one thing these objects have in common. Elicit from the class that there are three parts to each object. Ask the class what these objects might have to do with God. Lead the class to recognize that we believe in one God, whom we know as three distinct Persons: God the Father, God the Son, and God the Holy Spirit. Have the students recall that we call the one God in three distinct Persons the Holy Trinity.

Step 2/DEVELOPMENT

Learning About Our Faith

Reading the Scripture Story

Have the students open their books to page 318 and invite a volunteer to read the Scripture story aloud. Explain that this story took place just before Jesus returned to the Father in heaven. Help the students understand that Jesus is giving the apostles the power to baptize believers in the name of the Trinity.

Holy Trinity

Jesus asked his apostles to go to a mountain in Galilee. When they saw the risen Jesus, they began to worship him. Jesus said, "All the power in heaven and on earth has been given to me. Go to the people of every nation and make them my disciples. Baptize them in the name of the Father, the Son, and the Holy Spirit. Teach them to do everything that I have commanded you. Remember, I am with you always, even until the end of the world."

Based on Matthew 28:16–20

318   Holy Days: Lesson Two

Teaching Tips

The photograph on page 318 is of a stained glass window in St. Joseph's Church in Hopkins, Minnesota. Explain to the students that the symbols inside each circle represent the three Persons of the Trinity: the six-pointed star is a symbol for God—the Father of Abraham, Isaac, and Jacob; the symbol in the bottom left circle is the first two letters of the Greek word for Christ; the flame in the bottom right circle stands for the Holy Spirit. The overlapping circles inside the triangle represent the unity of the Trinity.

318

The Church honors the Holy **Trinity** on the Sunday [af]ter Pentecost Sunday. We believe that there are [thr]ee Persons in the one God: God the Father, God the [So]n, and God the Holy Spirit. The three Persons in [Go]d each have an important place in our lives as [Ca]tholics. Each time we make the Sign of the Cross, [w]e say that we believe in the Holy Trinity. We believe [th]at God the Father created us. We believe that God [th]e Son, Jesus, saved us from sin and death and [sh]ares his new life with us. We believe that God the [Ho]ly Spirit helps and guides us as we grow in [ho]liness.

[A]ctivity

[W]e can honor the Holy Trinity when we pray. [Co]mplete the Glory Be by filling in the missing words. [Th]en pray it aloud with your class.

Glory be to the ____Father____,

and to the ____Son____,

and to the ____Holy Spirit____.

As it was in the ____beginning____,

is ____now____, *and ever shall be,*

____world____ *without* ____end____. *Amen.*

Understanding the Message

Direct the students to read silently the paragraph at the top of page 319. Then discuss the questions below.

■ When do we honor the Holy Trinity? (*On the Sunday after Pentecost*)

■ How can there be one God in three Persons? (*Answers should reflect that we cannot explain the mystery of the Trinity but that we believe in the Trinity because we trust in Jesus.*)

■ Why is God the Father important to us? (*God is our creator.*)

■ Why do we honor God the Son? (*Jesus saved us from sin and death and shares his new life with us.*)

■ Why do we honor the third Person of the Trinity? (*The Holy Spirit helps and guides us to grow in holiness.*)

Step 3/CONCLUSION

Learning How to Live Our Faith

Completing a Prayer

Point out the activity on page 319 and explain the directions. Have the students work independently to complete the prayer. When all have finished, have the students read the prayer aloud together.

★ Enriching the Lesson ★

Have the students make magnets honoring the Holy Trinity, using tagboard, markers, scissors, and 1" adhesive magnetic strips. Instruct them to create a symbol for the Trinity on tagboard, decorate it, and cut it out. Have them affix the magnetic strip to the back of the symbol and keep it in a place where they will see it often and remember to pray the Glory Be.

Focus on

The Glory Be   The Glory Be is called a *doxology*, or a prayer of praise to God. The trinitarian formula is used to praise each Person of the Trinity. The words "As it was in the beginning, is now, and ever shall be, world without end" were added in the fourth century. These words express our belief that God has no beginning and no end. God always was. God always will be.

LESSON 3

Objective

This lesson helps the students celebrate Christ as King of all people.

Step 1/INTRODUCTION

Learning About Our Lives

Playing a Word-Association Game

Challenge the students to name words, objects, colors, and images they associate with kings and royalty. (*Responses may include crown, throne, scepter, kingdom, palace, castle, purple, and so on.*) Encourage class members to explain why they associate these symbols with royalty. Then tell the class that at the end of every Church year the Church celebrates a feast honoring Christ the King.

Step 2/DEVELOPMENT

Learning About Our Faith

Reading About Christ's Kingship

Read with the class "Christ the King" on pages 320 and 321. Ask the following questions.

- When do we celebrate Christ as King? (*On the last Sunday of the Church year; the Sunday before Advent begins*)

- What is important in the kingdom that Jesus spoke about? (*Justice for everyone; treating people with respect and care; peace; welcoming people regardless of who they are; forgiveness*)

- What do the Scripture readings from the Feast of Christ the King remind us of? (*That Jesus leads his followers as a shepherd leads his sheep; that Jesus is a powerful and loving king*)

- What does the word *Christ* mean? (*The anointed one*)

- Who anointed Jesus? (*God*)

- How does Jesus save us? (*Through his life, death, and resurrection*)

320

Christ the King

On the last Sunday of the Church year, just before Advent begins, we celebrate the Feast of Christ the King. We read in the Gospels that

Christ Enthroned (icon, enamel on gold), 12th century, Russia

many people expected that God would send a great ruler to be their king. Jesus explained that he was not the kind of king they expected. He also told them that his kingdom would be much better than they imagined.

Jesus' kingdom is not a country or land. Jesus spoke about a kingdom in which there would be **justice** for everyone. All people would be treated with respect and care. He said that it would be a kingdom of peace. People would be welcomed regardless of who they are, and everyone would learn to be forgiving.

The Scripture readings that we sometimes hear on the Feast of Christ the King remind us that Jesus leads his followers as a shepherd leads his sheep. He loves them and cares for them. He guides them gently. The Scripture readings also remind us that Jesus is a powerful and loving king! Jesus taught that by acting in the ways that he taught us, we can help show others the way to the kingdom.

Focus on

Feasts That Honor Jesus The Solemnity of Christ the King is one of four feasts honoring Jesus during Ordinary Time. The others are Holy Trinity (the Sunday following Pentecost); the Body and Blood of Christ (the Sunday following Holy Trinity); and the Sacred Heart of Jesus (the Friday after the Body and Blood of Christ).

The word **Christ** means "the anointed one." In the time of Jesus, kings were anointed or blessed with oil. It was a sign that they had been called to special work. Jesus, God's Anointed One, was called by God to save us from sin and death. Jesus saves us by his life, death, and resurrection.

Activity

Think about how you can help make your family, school, and neighborhood more like the kingdom that Jesus taught about. Then complete the sentences below.

I will be a peacemaker. I will _____

_____

_____ .

I will show my love for Jesus by loving others. I will

_____

_____ .

I will treat people fairly. I will _____

_____

_____ .

Introducing the Liturgical Calendar

Draw a large circle on the chalkboard and, using colored chalk, work with the students to note the major Church feasts and seasons on the circle. You might do this by asking the following questions.

- What do we call the time before Christmas? *(Advent)*

- What do we call the time before Easter? *(Lent)*

Note the Christmas season from Christmas to the Baptism of the Lord and the Easter Season from Easter to Pentecost Sunday. Mark on the circle the three feasts covered in this unit (All Saints, Holy Trinity, and Christ the King). Help the students appreciate that during the Church year we celebrate the life, death, and resurrection of Jesus.

Step 3/CONCLUSION

Learning How to Live Our Faith

Writing About Building the Kingdom

Point out the activity on page 321 and explain the directions to the students. Give the students sufficient time to write their responses on the lines provided in the text. Afterward, encourage the students to share their ideas for helping to make the communities in which they live more like the kingdom of God.

Enriching the Lesson

Give each student two contrasting sheets of construction paper, markers, glue, and scissors to make Christ the King flags. Have them cut a triangle flag from one piece of paper and use the other paper to cut out words that praise Jesus. Direct them to decorate the flags with symbols of Jesus and attach the flags to drinking straws or dowels.

In the Spirit of Jesus

Objectives ～～～～～

- **LESSON 1:** To help the students appreciate Mother Teresa's work with the poorest of the poor.
- **LESSON 2:** To help the students learn about the work of Catholic Relief Services.

Lesson Outlines ～～～～～～

	Step 1 Learning About Our Lives	**Step 2** Learning About Our Faith ✝	**Step 3** Learning How to Live Our Faith ✳
Lesson 1	■ Study photographs. *ABOUT 10 MINUTES*	■ Introduce the story. ■ Read the story. *ABOUT 5 MINUTES*	■ Complete an activity. ■ Make a class helping button. ■ Pray together. *ABOUT 15 MINUTES*
Lesson 2	■ Discuss television news. *ABOUT 6 MINUTES*	■ Read the text. *ABOUT 7 MINUTES*	■ Unscramble a message. ■ Make cards of support. *ABOUT 17 MINUTES*

Plan Ahead ~~~~~~~~

Preparing Your Class

Lesson 1
Find photographs of people in need. Have enough so that there is one for each student. Read more about Mother Teresa and be prepared to tell the students any stories you know about her.

Lesson 2
Read through the entire lesson plan for this class session. Be prepared to discuss in Step 1 recent news stories about disasters that have affected a large number of people.

Materials Needed

- photographs of people in need
- drawing paper
- paste or glue and crayons or markers
- colored chalk and safety pins
- small slips of paper

- pencils or pens
- construction paper
- crayons or markers
- a large envelope for mailing

Additional Resources

As you plan this chapter, consider using the following materials from The Resourceful Teacher Package.

- *Classroom Activity Sheets for In the Spirit of Jesus*
- *Family Activity Sheets for In the Spirit of Jesus*
- *Prayers for Every Day*

You may also wish to refer to the following Big Book.

- *We Celebrate God's Word,* page 13

In preparing the students for the Sunday readings, you may wish to use Silver Burdett Ginn's *Getting Ready for Sunday* student and teacher materials.

REDUCED CLASSROOM ACTIVITIES

NAME _____

IN THE SPIRIT OF JESUS

Mother Teresa is one person who has dedicated her life to the service of the poor. Think of other people who live in the Spirit of Jesus. Choose one person to write a report about in the space provided.

_____

I first met _____ when _____

_____

_____

I will never forget _____

_____

_____

_____

One thing _____ said that I often remember

is _____

_____

_____

_____

_____

To the Teacher: Have students work in small groups to complete this activity. Suggest to students that they focus on school and parish leaders.

In the Spirit of Jesus   THIS IS OUR FAITH 3 **29**

NAME _____

WE LIVE IN THE SPIRIT OF JESUS

Write three ways that you can now show that you are living in the Spirit of Jesus.

1. _____

   _____

2. _____

   _____

3. _____

   _____

Write three ways that you can follow Jesus when you are older.

1. _____

2. _____

   _____

3. _____

   _____

29a THIS IS OUR FAITH 3   In the Spirit of Jesus

MOTHER TERESA OF CALCUTTA

Highlighting significant men and women of our day whose lives are examples of moral virtue is important. Such a person is Mother Teresa.

Mother Teresa was born in Yugoslavia in 1910. She felt the call to service early in her life and entered the religious community of the Loreto Sisters in Ireland at the age of eighteen. Sister Teresa journeyed to the city of Calcutta in India where the Loreto Sisters were missionaries. For about sixteen years, she taught school and served as the principal of St. Mary High School.

God, however, had other plans for Sister Teresa. In 1948, Calcutta was a city of abject poverty, as it is today. Hundreds of thousands of people lived without adequate food, water, or shelter. They simply died in the streets. Sister Teresa felt the call of God to share a special kind of love with these destitute people. In 1948, Pope Pius XII granted her request to be of service as a nun to the poorest of God's poor.

The approach of Mother Teresa to the poor of Calcutta has been simple, but effective. She approaches one person at a time, seeking to bind the person's wounds and offer whatever help and consolation she can. Mother Teresa and her religious sisters walk the streets of Calcutta, picking up people who are poor and dying. The religious community, Missionaries of Charity, maintains homes for people who are sick and dying, places for those who are destitute, and houses for unwanted children. In each person's face, Mother Teresa sees the face of Christ, who told us that when we feed and clothe those who are poor we feed and clothe him. Through the example of Mother Teresa, we too are challenged to discover Jesus in others.

CATHOLIC RELIEF SERVICES

Catholic Relief Services was founded in 1943 by the Catholic Bishops of the United States to assist poor and disadvantaged people outside our country. The motivating force of Catholic Relief Services is the gospel and Jesus' call to alleviate human suffering and to foster charity and justice in the world. Catholic Relief Services assists people on the basis of need—not creed, race, or nationality.

Catholic Relief Services works in the spirit of Jesus by helping us recognize the unity of the global community and our call to care for the least of our brothers and sisters. In this lesson, you have the opportunity to help your students appreciate that they are called to care for others through their individual efforts and by supporting the work of those who bring hope and tangible assistance in Jesus' name.

Lesson 1

Objective

To help the students appreciate Mother Teresa's work with the poorest of the poor.

Step 1/INTRODUCTION

Learning About Our Lives

Studying Photographs

Ask the students to look at the photographs you have collected of people in need. Talk about what these people need (food, shelter, clothing, love, understanding, bandages, medical help, someone to listen to them). Provide each student with two sheets of drawing paper. Ask each student to select one of the photographs. Have each student do the following: paste his or her photograph to one sheet of drawing paper, assign names to the people in the picture, and write on the second sheet of drawing paper a story about the picture. Afterward, invite the students to share their stories. Discuss how people might help the people in the photographs who are in need.

Step 2/DEVELOPMENT

Learning About Our Faith

Introducing the Story

Tell the students that there are many dedicated people who help the poor people of the world. Talk about how some people give food, clothing, and money to help poor and hungry people. Explain that other people devote their lives to helping those in need.

Reading the Story

Ask volunteers to read aloud "Mother Teresa" on pages 322–323. If you have a globe or a map, show the students their city and then show them the city of Calcutta. Afterward, ask the following questions.

- What did Agnes Boyaxhui do when she was eighteen? (*She joined a convent of sisters.*)
- What did Sister Teresa feel called by God to do in the city of Calcutta? (*She felt called by God to serve the poorest of the poor in the slums.*)

322

In the Spirit of Jesus

Mother Teresa

Many young girls in Yugoslavia wanted to be sisters. Agnes Gonxha Bojaxhiu was one of them. She wanted to serve God with her whole heart and soul. In 1928, when Agnes was eighteen, she joined a convent in India. The name that was given to her was Sister Teresa.

Sister Teresa was sent to teach at St. Mary's High School in Calcutta, a very large city in India. Each day when she prayed, Sister Teresa asked for help to know what God wanted her to do. "One day," she says, "I heard the call to give up all and to follow God into the slums to serve among the poorest of the poor."

Enriching the Lesson

Explain to the students that in 1979, Mother Teresa was awarded the Nobel Peace Prize for her work with poor people. People who are honored with this important award are given a cash prize of nearly $500,000. Tell the students that Mother Teresa used this money to continue serving those who are poor. Ask the students to work in small groups to decide how they would spend $500,000 serving others.

In 1948 she opened a school in the slums. At the same time, she was learning how to care for the many sick people of Calcutta. Most of them were too poor to go to a hospital. Every day, hundreds of poor people would die in the streets, with no one to help them.

Soon other young women came to help Teresa, who was now called Mother Teresa. They called their new group the Missionaries of Charity. Today, there are more than 3,000 of these sisters, in nearly sixty countries throughout the world, who help the poorest of the poor.

Activity

There are ten words hidden in the puzzle. The words tell what Mother Teresa and the women in her community share with people. Some words read across and others read down. Find each word and circle it.

A	C	L	O	T	H	I	N	G	E	H	S
H	T	E	I	S	Y	D	G	O	M	P	H
O	W	R	S	D	F	O	O	D	Y	X	E
P	E	A	C	E	L	U	W	A	C	O	L
E	M	R	U	V	G	M	E	B	E	F	T
Y	J	D	A	M	E	D	I	C	I	N	E
L	O	V	E	F	N	Z	O	W	Y	M	R
B	Y	X	F	U	D	C	A	R	E	P	O

Teaching Tips

Explore with the students their experiences of being sick. How do they feel? What do they want others to do to help them? What foods and actions help them to feel better? Then invite the students to talk about how they have helped family members and friends who have been ill. Ask them what they have done to cheer the people up or to let people know that they are loved. Help the students appreciate that when we try to help others we are serving God, just as Mother Teresa and the Missionaries of Charity do.

■ What did Sister Teresa do in the slums? (*She opened a school and cared for the many sick people of Calcutta.*)

■ Why did she do this? (*Because she wanted to serve God*)

Step 3/CONCLUSION

Learning How to Live Our Faith

Completing an Activity

Read the directions for the activity on page 323. After the students have completed the activity, discuss how they might share each of the ten words with people.

Making a Class Helping Button

Brainstorm with the students various signs and symbols that might show that a person is a caring helper (for example: a bandage, a bowl of soup, a heart, money, a pile of clothes). Write all their suggestions on the chalkboard and then vote on the best signs. Ask volunteers to come to the chalkboard and use colored chalk to design a class helping button. After all the drawings have been completed, number them. Give each student a slip of paper and invite the students to vote on the class helping button they like best. Tally the votes.

Once the class symbol is selected, provide the students with drawing paper, crayons or markers, and safety pins. Invite each student to make a class helping button and to pin it to his or her shirt or sleeve. Tell the students that this is a sign that they are helping and caring for people.

Praying Together

Say a spontaneous prayer of thanksgiving for the loving care that the students show to others.

LESSON 2

Objective

This lesson helps the students learn about the work of Catholic Relief Services.

Step 1/INTRODUCTION

Learning About Our Lives

Discussing Television News

Ask the students to discuss their experiences of watching news stories about people whose lives have been upset by wars, earthquakes, forest fires, floods, or other tragedies. Have them identify what they feel and think when they watch these reports. Ask them what news stories such as these make them want to do. Lead the students to the recognition that when we witness tragedies we often want to help. However, sometimes we do not know what to do or how to do it. Tell the students that this lesson will focus on an organization that helps people all over the world.

Step 2/DEVELOPMENT

Learning About Our Faith

Reading the Text

Call on volunteers to take turns reading aloud "Catholic Relief Services" on pages 324 and 325. Then discuss the questions below.

- Who started Catholic Relief Services? (*The Catholic Bishops of the United States*)

- Why did the bishops start CRS? (*To help people living overseas who had lost their homes in the war*)

- How many countries does CRS work in? (*In more than eighty countries*)

- How does CRS work in the spirit of Jesus? (*By caring for the poor, suffering, and forgotten people all over the world*)

324

Catholic Relief Services

Shanna was watching the news on television with her family. "We now turn to the problems in Bosnia," said the announcer. "Thousands of people have left their homes to escape from the war."

Shanna watched the long lines of people walking slowly along dirt roads. They carried their belongings in baskets and cardboard boxes. "Oh, those poor families," said Shanna. "Where can they go?"

The television showed a crowded camp. The announcer said, "Catholic Relief Services has set up centers to give food, water, and shelter to the villagers. When the war is over, the workers will stay in Bosnia to rebuild the villages. If you would like to help, copy the address that appears on your screen."

"Can *we* help the villagers?" asked Shanna.

Operation Rice Bowl   CRS sponsors a yearly Lenten program called Operation Rice Bowl. Materials include an Educator's Guide, a home calendar, posters, cardboard rice bowls for almsgiving, and a fact sheet. Write to Catholic Relief Services for more information if you would like your class to participate in the program. The address is: 209 W. Fayette St., Baltimore, MD 21201.

"Yes, Shanna," said her mother. "We will send a contribution tomorrow. Tonight, when we say our prayers, we will ask God to help them."

Catholic Relief Services was begun by the National Conference of Catholic Bishops of the United States in 1943. The bishops wanted to help people living overseas who had lost their homes during the Second World War.

Today, Catholic Relief Services works in over seventy-five countries. CRS helps in many ways. They find homes for orphans. They have built silos to help people in Haiti store grain. They have dug water wells in India. And they teach farmers in Africa to grow crops.

Catholic Relief Services works in the spirit of Jesus to care for poor, suffering, and forgotten people all over the world. Catholic Relief Services helps us to remember that all people are part of one big family—the family of God.

Activity

The scrambled words tell us the command that the workers of Catholic Relief Services live every day. Unscramble the words and write them on the lines below.

OYU SMTU VEOL OURY BRINGEHO SA LYORFSUE

YOU   MUST

LOVE   YOUR

NEIGHBOR   AS

YOURSELF .

Learning How to Live Our Faith

Unscrambling a Message

Direct attention to the activity on page 325 and explain the directions to the students. Have them work on their own to unscramble the words and copy the message on the lines provided in the text. When everyone has finished, read the message aloud together. Ask the students to identify the different ways that Catholic Relief Services workers show that they love their neighbors as much as themselves.

Making Cards of Support

Give the students construction paper and markers or crayons. Direct them to fold the paper to make a greeting card. Instruct the students to make cards that will be sent to CRS workers. Tell them that the cards should thank the workers for their efforts and offer support and prayers. Encourage the students to create colorful cards and to include in their cards information about themselves and how they learned about Catholic Relief Services. Send the completed cards to Catholic Relief Services, USCC, 209 West Fayette Street, Baltimore, MD 21201–3443.

Enriching the Lesson

Plan a service project with the class to help poor or suffering people in your community. You might have a canned food drive, collect puzzles and games for a shelter, gather winter clothing for the Saint Vincent de Paul Society, or carry out another idea generated by the students. Whatever you do, involve the students in this project as much as possible.

OUR CATHOLIC HERITAGE

Our Catholic Heritage

In June 1994, the *Catechism of the Catholic Church* was published in English and widely distributed throughout the United States. Bishops, pastors, and educators have used the *Catechism* as a basic resource in summarizing Catholic doctrine and for a better understanding of the theological background of the Church's teaching.

In this section, *Our Catholic Heritage,* there is a summary of Catholic belief, organized in the same way as the *Catechism.* It is meant as a ready reference for both you and your students to provide in summary fashion the basic teachings of the Catholic Church.

Over the course of the THIS IS OUR FAITH program, the *Our Catholic Heritage* section of each grade level is developmental in nature and planned to complement the information presented in the lesson plans. These pages are most effectively used in conjunction with the student book pages that cover the topics in question.

You may want to read the Apostolic Constitution *Fidei Depositum* and the *Prologue* (paragraphs 1–25). These introduce the *Catechism* and provide a better understanding of its purpose in religious education.

What Catholics Believe

The English translation of the *Catechism of the Catholic Church*, published in 1994, provides a clear and extensive statement of Catholic doctrine, divided into four parts, or pillars, of our faith. The first, "The Profession of Faith," develops the foundations of our creed, based on sacred Scripture and the tradition of the Church throughout the ages. As a Catholic Christian community, we renew our dedication to these beliefs each week at Sunday Mass, when we celebrate Baptism and Confirmation, and during the Easter Vigil. Our recitation of the creed reminds us of our unity in faith with Catholics throughout the world.

About the Bible

TEACHER REFLECTION

Sacred Scripture is a source of nourishment and strength for the Church. The Church has accepted throughout history that the books of both the Old and New Testaments were written under the inspiration of the Holy Spirit. The Church has recognized the importance of Biblical scholarship for understanding the Scriptures. We are encouraged to study the Bible continually to be able to more deeply appreciate the word of God.

You may want to review for yourself the teachings of the Church about the Bible in paragraphs 101–133 in the *Catechism*.

STUDENT REVIEW

Ask for volunteers to read "About the Bible" on page 328 in their books. This section describes the structure of the Bible, according to books, chapters, and verses. Distribute Bibles to the class. Check the students' understanding of what they have read by asking them to first locate the Old and New Testaments. Then have the students locate the verses given at the bottom of the page (Luke 7:18–23). Offer assistance to anyone who has difficulty finding the Scripture passage. If time permits, have the students begin with the Book of Genesis and name each book of the Old Testament. Then do the same for the New Testament.

We can know, live, and celebrate our faith. Catholics do this in special ways.

ABOUT The Bible

The Bible is divided into two parts: the Old Testament and the New Testament. Each part contains many books. There are 46 books in the Old Testament. These books tell us about God's people before Jesus was born.

There are 27 books in the New Testament. They tell us about the life of Jesus, the early Christians, and the beginnings of the Church.

Each book of the Bible has its own name. Each book is divided into chapters, which are numbered. And each chapter is divided into verses. The verses are also numbered.

Finding a story in the Bible is really very easy. Look, for example, at the story of John the Baptizer on pages 244 and 245 in your book. If you wanted to find this story in the Bible, you would need to look in the New Testament and find Luke 7:18–23. In other words, you would find the book called The Gospel According to Luke, chapter 7, verses 18 through 23.

Luke	7:	18–23
book of the Bible	chapter number	verse numbers

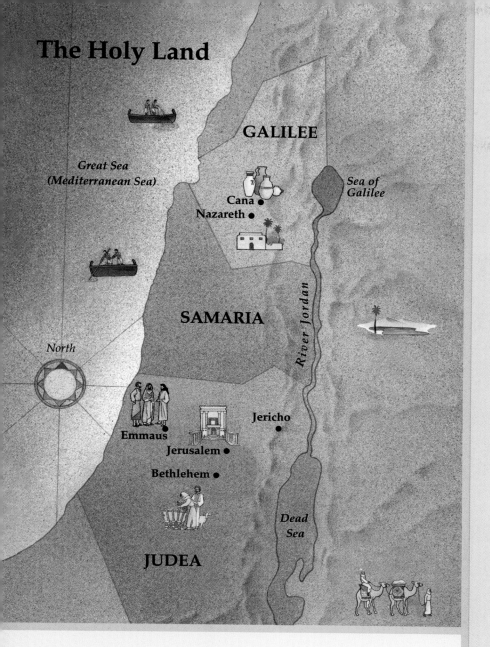

The Holy Land

Great Sea
(Mediterranean Sea)

GALILEE

Sea of
Galilee

Cana
Nazareth

North

SAMARIA

River Jordan

Emmaus
Jericho
Jerusalem
Bethlehem

Dead
Sea

JUDEA

Ask the students to look at the map on page 329. Ask a volunteer to identify the bodies of water on the map. Have another student read the names of the cities on the map. Recall with the students that Jesus was born in Bethlehem and grew up in Nazareth. Jesus went to Jerusalem with Joseph and Mary at special times, and Jesus traveled there with his apostles during his earthly ministry.

Have the students note the drawing on the left-hand side of the map. This is called a direction finder. Ask the students to explain its purpose. (It helps us locate the direction of one point on the map from another.) Help the students understand where east, south, and west are located in relation to north. You may wish to draw a direction finder on the chalkboard and label all four directions. Test the students' understanding of directions with the following three questions.

- Is Galilee north or south of Jerusalem? (*North*)

- In which direction is the Sea of Galilee from Nazareth? (*East*)

- If Jesus walked from Jerusalem to Bethlehem, in which direction would he have walked? (*South*)

About the Trinity

TEACHER REFLECTION

Over the centuries the Church has come to an "understanding" of the Trinity that comes from extensive reflection on the action of God in our lives. We have come to know God as love, both creative and redemptive. This revelation of God, in whose image we are made, helps us understand both the meaning of our humanity and our calling to be part of a loving community. We believe that God reveals the work of the Trinity in the mystery of creation.

You may want to review for yourself the Church's teachings about creation in paragraphs 279–412 of the *Catechism of the Catholic Church.*

STUDENT REVIEW

Ask for volunteers to read "About the Trinity" on pages 330–331 in their books. Ask the students the following questions.

- Who are the three Persons of the Blessed Trinity? (*God the Father, God the Son, and God the Holy Spirit*)

- When did the Holy Spirit come? (*On Pentecost*)

- Why did God send Jesus to us? (*To show us how to live*)

Refer to pages 62–91 in the student text for more information about the Blessed Trinity.

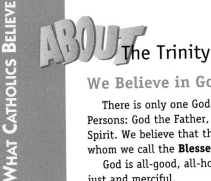

ABOUT The Trinity

We Believe in God

There is only one God. We know God as three distinct Persons: God the Father, God the Son, and God the Holy Spirit. We believe that there is one God in three Persons, whom we call the **Blessed Trinity**.

God is all-good, all-holy, and all-knowing. God is always just and merciful.

God the Father speaks to us in many ways. We know the Father especially through Jesus, the Scriptures, and the Church.

God created all things out of love. We share the gift of God's life and love. Catholics call this sharing in God's life **grace**. With grace, we help God care for the world.

We Believe in Jesus

Jesus, God's own Son, is the second Person of the Blessed Trinity. Jesus is both God and man. Jesus is human like us in all things but sin.

God sent Jesus to us to show us how to live. Jesus taught us about God's love. Jesus gave his life for us. Jesus died on the cross and rose from the dead. Jesus is our **Savior**. He saves us from sin and brings us new life. Jesus sent the Holy Spirit to help us live our new life.

We Believe in the Holy Spirit

The Holy Spirit is the third Person of the Blessed Trinity. The Holy Spirit is our helper and guide. The Spirit helps us live as followers of Jesus.

The Holy Spirit came on **Pentecost**. The Holy Spirit gave the disciples the courage to share Jesus' good news. The Holy Spirit is with the Church today, helping us to be a sign of Jesus. We receive the Holy Spirit at Baptism.

ABOUT The Catholic Church

Catholics are followers of Jesus who spread God's word, worship God, celebrate the sacraments, and serve those in need.

The Church has four marks, or signs: that it is one, holy, catholic, and apostolic.

We are one because we are united. Our belief in Jesus unites us.

We are holy because we love God and try to live the Gospel by caring for others.

We are catholic because the Church welcomes people of all kinds, as Jesus does.

We are apostolic because our teachings are true to the teachings of Jesus and his apostles.

The **pope** is the leader of the Catholic Church. We call the pope our Holy Father.

About the Catholic Church

TEACHER REFLECTION

It is our belief as Catholic Christians that Jesus established the Church and set its course by forming the apostles and disciples as evangelizers and missionaries. We believe that at Pentecost the Holy Spirit revealed the Church to the world and that the public mission of the Church began at that time. We profess in the creed that the Church is one, holy, catholic, and apostolic. These four marks describe essential features of the Church and its mission. We should be able to see and experience these characteristics of the Church in our parishes and in the work of the Church throughout the world.

You may want to review for yourself the teachings of the Church about the four marks of the Church in paragraphs 813–873 of the *Catechism of the Catholic Church.*

STUDENT REVIEW

Ask for volunteers to read "About the Catholic Church" on page 331 in their books. Then write the words *one, holy, catholic,* and *apostolic* on the chalkboard. Ask the students to tell how your local parish demonstrates these characteristics of the Church. Write their ideas under each of the terms on the chalkboard. Discuss how the students can participate in any of these activities or facets of parish life.

Refer to pages 12–54 in the student text for more information about the four marks of the Catholic Church.

About Mary and the Saints

TEACHER REFLECTION

Mary has always been a sign of God's special love for us. Mary's willingness to be God's servant—her saying yes to God—was the beginning of our salvation in Jesus Christ. We believe that Mary, from the first instant of her conception, was totally preserved from the state of original sin. The Church calls this doctrine the Immaculate Conception. The Church also teaches that at her death Mary was assumed, body and soul, into heaven. There she shares in the glory of her Son's resurrection. We honor Mary, the Mother of God, as Mother of the Church because she is the model of holiness for all of us.

You may want to review for yourself the Church's teachings about Mary in paragraphs 963–972 of the *Catechism*.

STUDENT REVIEW

Ask for volunteers to read "About Mary and the Saints" on page 332 in their books. Divide the class into four groups. Then have the students review pages 302–315 in the student text for more information about Mary and the saints. Together, plan a bulletin board display that will show what the students have discovered about Mary and the saints.

About Life Everlasting

TEACHER REFLECTION

Life everlasting, or new life forever, has traditionally been described as the "last things"—the particular judgment; the realities of heaven, purgatory, and hell; and the final judgment. We believe that at the second coming of Christ all people will be gathered in Christ's presence and that the truth of each one's relationship with God will be revealed. At the same time, the kingdom of God will come in its fullness.

You may want to review for yourself the Church's teachings about life everlasting in paragraphs 1020–1050 of the *Catechism*.

STUDENT REVIEW

Ask for volunteers to read "About Life Everlasting" on page 332 in their books. Read and discuss with the students Matthew 25:31–46.

ABOUT Mary and the Saints

Mary is the mother of Jesus. From the first moment of life, Mary was filled with grace. Mary is our mother, too. Mary loves and cares for us.

Mary is our greatest **saint**. Saints are special people who showed us how to follow Jesus. We honor the saints and ask them to pray for us.

Pieta (ivory), 15th century, Spain

ABOUT Life Everlasting

Jesus teaches us that if we follow his example we will be happy forever in **heaven**. Heaven is unending happiness with God and all who love God. If we show love for God, ourselves, and others, we will be happy together in heaven.

Even today, we are part of the **communion of saints**. The communion of saints is the community of all those, living and dead, who believe in Jesus Christ.

HOW CATHOLICS WORSHIP

Catholics have a sacred history of **worship**. Worship is giving honor and praise to God. Through the sacraments and prayer, we praise, thank, and adore God, and ask God's help.

 The Sacraments

The **sacraments** are sacred signs that celebrate God's love for us and Jesus' presence in our lives. There are seven sacraments. Through the sacraments, we are united with Jesus.

Each sacrament has special words and actions. The words and actions are signs that God is present.

The Sacraments of Initiation We become full members of the Church through the three sacraments of initiation. The sacraments of initiation are Baptism, Confirmation, and Eucharist.

> **Baptism** is a sacrament of welcome into the Church community. We receive the Holy Spirit and begin to share Jesus' new life.
>
> **In the celebration** the priest or deacon pours water over the head of the person being baptized and prays, "I baptize you in the name of the Father, and of the Son, and of the Holy Spirit."
>
> from the *Rite of Baptism*

How Catholics Worship

The liturgical life of the Church is the Catholic community's way of celebrating what we believe. Through the signs of the sacraments and our participation in the liturgical celebrations, we renew our faith and gain an even greater share in the life of grace, God's life in us. Through the sacraments we are challenged to follow ever more closely the way of Christ that leads to the realization of God's kingdom.

STUDENT REVIEW

Ask for a volunteer to read "How Catholics Worship" on page 333 in his or her book.

About the Sacraments

TEACHER REFLECTION

The whole life of the Church revolves around the Eucharist and the other sacraments. In the sacraments we encounter Christ and are enabled to live the life of faith more deeply. The sacraments of initiation—Baptism, Confirmation, and Eucharist—provide the building blocks for Christian life. Through them we are welcomed into the Church and are called to conversion and service.

The sacraments of healing—Reconciliation and Anointing of the Sick—recall the frailty of our human condition. The sacrament of Reconciliation provides us with an opportunity to acknowledge the reality of sin, to ask forgiveness, and to begin anew as disciples of Christ. Anointing of the Sick is a source of strength and consolation for those who are ill and for those who are caring for them.

The sacraments of commitment—Matrimony and Holy Orders—celebrate publicly the calling to family life and to ordained ministry in the Church. These vocations are sanctified in the sacramental rites in which we are called to build the Body of Christ through example and service.

You may want to review for yourself the teachings of the Church about the sacraments in Part Two of the *Catechism*.

STUDENT REVIEW

Ask for volunteers to read "About the Sacraments" on pages 333–335 in their books. As you review with the students their understanding of each sacrament, you can have them either draw a scene depicting the celebration of the sacrament or act out a part of the sacramental liturgy.

Refer to pages 123–130 in the student text for more information about the sacraments of initiation. Refer to pages 134–138 to help the students review the sacraments of healing. Refer to pages 145–149 for information about the sacraments of commitment.

Confirmation strengthens the new life we received at Baptism and helps us tell everyone the good news about Jesus.

In the celebration the bishop or priest lays his hand on the head of the one to be confirmed and anoints the forehead with holy oil as he prays, "Be sealed with the Gift of the Holy Spirit."

from the *Rite of Confirmation*

Eucharist celebrates the real presence of Jesus.

In the celebration the priest says the words of consecration over the bread and wine, which become the body and blood of Christ.

The Sacraments of Healing The sacraments of healing—Reconciliation and the Anointing of the Sick—celebrate God's forgiveness and healing.

Reconciliation celebrates God's healing and forgiveness of our sins.

In the celebration the priest prays the prayer of absolution, ending with the words, "I absolve you from your sins in the name of the Father, and of the Son, and of the Holy Spirit."

from the *Rite of Penance*

The Anointing of the Sick brings God's help and peace to sick people.

In the celebration the priest anoints the person with the oil of the sick as he prays, "Through this holy anointing may the Lord in his love and mercy help you with the grace of the Holy Spirit."

from the *Rite of Anointing*

The Sacraments of Commitment In the sacraments of commitment, the Church celebrates two special ways that people serve others by sharing their gifts. The sacraments of commitment are Matrimony and Holy Orders.

Matrimony celebrates the lifelong love of a man and a woman.

In the celebration the bride and groom make special promises to each other.

In **Holy Orders** bishops, priests, and deacons are ordained to serve the Church in a special way.

In the celebration the bishop lays his hands on the head of the person to be ordained. Afterward, he prays a special prayer of blessing.

About the Mass

TEACHER REFLECTION

Our celebration of the Mass is the primary source of renewal of our life in Christ. In the Mass we are once again welcomed into the community of the faithful, called to communion with others and service to others, and nourished by the Bread of Life. We are sent forth to exemplify the good news of the gospel in our everyday lives.

You may want to review for yourself the Church's teachings about the Mass in paragraphs 1322–1405 of the *Catechism*.

STUDENT REVIEW

Ask for volunteers to read "About the Mass" on pages 336–339 in their books. Review with the students each part of the Mass as it is pictured in the text. Once you are sure that the students understand the progress of the liturgy, invite the students to participate in planning a celebration of the Mass for your class.

You may wish to invite your parish priest to demonstrate and explain the various vestments and sacramentals used at Mass.

ABOUT The Mass

Introductory Rites

At Mass, we come together to pray and worship as the family of Jesus.

Entrance Procession and Gathering Song

As the priest and other ministers enter in procession, we stand and sing a gathering song.

Greeting

We make the Sign of the Cross. The priest welcomes us by saying, "The Lord be with you." We answer, "And also with you."

Penitential Rite

As a community, we admit that we have sinned and we thank God for the gift of forgiveness. We pray the opening prayer.

Gloria

We sing or say this hymn of praise to God.

336

Liturgy of the Word

First Reading

The lector reads a story about God's love for us, usually from the Old Testament.

Responsorial Psalm

The song leader sings a psalm from the Bible. We join in singing a response.

Second Reading

The lector reads from the New Testament, usually from one of the letters.

Gospel Acclamation

Before the Gospel is proclaimed by the priest or deacon, we sing, "Alleluia" or another acclamation.

Gospel

In honor of Jesus, who speaks to us in the Gospel reading, we stand as it is proclaimed.

Homily

The priest or deacon explains the readings, especially the Gospel, in a special talk called the homily.

Profession of Faith

We stand to declare our beliefs. We recite the Nicene Creed.

General Intercessions

We pray for the pope and the bishops, for our country, and for all God's people.

337

Liturgy of the Eucharist

Preparation of the Altar and the Gifts

As the table is prepared, we bring gifts of bread and wine to the altar. The priest offers our gifts to God.

Eucharistic Prayer

In this prayer of praise and thanksgiving, the priest addresses God our Creator in our name. Together we sing a song of praise for God's many blessings, especially Jesus.

We sing or say,

"Holy, holy, holy Lord, God of power and might. Heaven and earth are full of your glory. Hosanna in the highest. Blessed is he who comes in the name of the Lord. Hosanna in the highest."

The priest calls upon the Holy Spirit and asks that the bread and wine become Jesus' body and blood. The priest consecrates the bread and wine. We proclaim the mystery of faith. We sing or say these or other words,

"Christ has died,
Christ is risen,
Christ will come again."

As the Eucharistic Prayer ends, we say, "Amen."

Communion Rite

The Lord's Prayer

We pray together the prayer that Jesus taught us—The Lord's Prayer.

Sign of Peace

We offer each other a sign of peace to show that we are all brothers and sisters in Jesus.

Breaking of the Bread

While the priest breaks the bread, we sing or say, "Lamb of God, you take away the sins of the world: have mercy on us.

Lamb of God, you take away the sins of the world: have mercy on us.

Lamb of God, you take away the sins of the world: grant us peace."

Communion

Jesus invites us to share his body and blood in the Eucharist.

Concluding Rite

Blessing

The priest blesses us in the name of God the Father, God the Son, and God the Holy Spirit. We answer, "Amen."

Dismissal

The priest tells us to go in peace to love and serve God and others. We sing a song of thanks and praise.

About Reconciliation

TEACHER REFLECTION

The grace of the sacrament of Reconciliation, or Penance, gives us the courage to admit our failures and wrongdoing, to ask forgiveness, and to renew our dedication to the Christian life. The experience of celebrating this sacrament in community can give us a better appreciation of the social consequences of sin and the need for reconciliation as a whole people. Reconciliation makes visible the mercy of our loving God.

You may want to review for yourself the Church's teachings about Reconciliation in paragraphs 1422–1484 of the *Catechism*.

STUDENT REVIEW

Ask for volunteers to read "About Reconciliation" on pages 340–341 in their books. Plan a trip to the reconciliation room in the parish church. Ask the students to explain what they learned about the sacrament when they were preparing for their first celebration of reconciliation in the second grade. If the students have not already celebrated this sacrament, respond to any questions they may have about Reconciliation and how it is celebrated in their parish or school.

Refer to pages 134–138 in the student text for more information about the sacrament of Reconciliation.

ABOUT Reconciliation

In the sacrament of Penance, or Reconciliation, I celebrate God's forgiveness.

Preparation I think about my words and actions in my examination of conscience. I feel sorrow for my sins.

Rite of Reconciliation of Individuals

Priest's Welcome The priest welcomes me in the name of Jesus and the Church.

Reading from Scripture The priest may read a part of the Bible with me.

Confession I tell the priest my sins. The priest suggests ways that I might love God more.

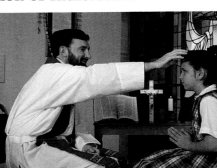

He asks me to say a prayer or do a kind act, called an act of penance, to show that I am sorry.

Prayer of Sorrow The priest asks me to tell God I am sorry for my sins. I say aloud a prayer of sorrow, called an act of contrition.

Absolution Acting in the name of the Church, the priest extends his hands over me and asks God to forgive me. The priest gives me absolution in the name of the Father, Son, and Holy Spirit.

Prayer of Praise and Dismissal With the priest, I praise God. The priest tells me to go in peace. I answer, "Amen."

Celebrating Reconciliation in Community

Introductory Rites We sing an opening song. The priest invites us to pray for God's forgiveness.

The Word of God We listen to readings from the Bible. The priest gives a homily.

Examination of Conscience The priest helps us to examine our conscience. We sing or say The Lord's Prayer.

Rite of Reconciliation Together we pray a prayer of sorrow. Then, one by one, we go to confession and receive absolution.

Proclamation of Praise for God's Mercy We praise and thank God for his mercy.

Concluding Rites The priest blesses us. We sing a song of praise and thanksgiving.

341

How Catholics Live

Morality can be described as the conduct of people who live according to a specific set of rules and principles. Christian morality is conduct that reflects faith in Jesus Christ and in his principles. To fully understand the demands of Christian morality, we need to recognize that it is based on the limitless love of God and the dignity of every human person as created by God. The focus of Christian morality is not rules, but relationships. The purpose of the Beatitudes and Commandments is to enable the relationship between God and ourselves to grow and to be expressed in our approach to our neighbor.

STUDENT REVIEW

Ask a volunteer to read the sentence under "How Catholics Live" on page 342 in his or her book.

About the Beatitudes

TEACHER REFLECTION

The Beatitudes speak to the attitudes and actions that are to be characteristic of our lives as followers of Jesus Christ. They challenge us to live life fully; they speak to authentic happiness. Happiness is not found in things, possessions, nor even in successes, but rather in developing right relationships with family, friends, and those with whom we work and associate.

You may want to review for yourself the Church's teachings about the Beatitudes in paragraphs 1716–1724 of the *Catechism*.

STUDENT REVIEW

Ask for volunteers to read the section "About the Beatitudes" on page 342 in the student text. Explain the meaning of each of the Beatitudes and encourage the students to mention examples of how each can be demonstrated in the way we live our daily lives.

The teachings of Jesus and the Church show us how Catholics live happy and loving lives.

ABOUT The Beatitudes

The Beatitudes are Jesus' teachings on how to find everlasting happiness. They teach us to love God and others. Christians believe that they are promised a place in the kingdom of heaven if they live the Beatitudes.

The Beatitudes	How We Live the Beatitudes
Happy are the poor in spirit. The reign of God is theirs.	We are poor in spirit when we know that we need God more than anything else in life.
Happy are the sorrowing. They will be comforted.	We obey God and trust in his goodness. We try to help those who are hurting. We know that God is with them.
Happy are the gentle. They will receive all that God has promised.	We are kind and loving. We use the gifts that God has given us to help others.
Happy are those who hunger and thirst for justice. They will be satisfied.	We work to lead others to God's kingdom. We share the things we have with those in need.
Happy are those who show mercy to others. They will receive mercy.	We forgive anyone who has hurt us. We accept others and are patient with them.
Happy are the single-hearted. They will see God.	We show our love for God by loving our neighbor.
Happy are the peacemakers. They will be called children of God.	We try to bring God's peace to the world. We help people make up after a fight.
Happy are those who are treated unfairly for doing what is right. The reign of God is theirs.	We carry on Jesus' work in the world. We stand up for what is right, even though it is not always easy.

About The Commandments

Jesus said it is important to obey the Ten Commandments. The commandments help us live as children of God.

The Ten Commandments	The Commandments Help Us to Live
1. I, the Lord, am your God. You shall not have other gods besides me.	We believe in and love God more than anyone or anything else in life. We remember God's gifts to us. We talk to and listen to God in prayer.
2. You shall not take the name of the Lord, your God, in vain.	We use the names of God, Jesus, and all holy persons, places, and things with respect and love. We never say God's or Jesus' name in anger.
3. Remember to keep holy the Sabbath day.	We worship God by celebrating the Eucharist together on Sunday. We relax and do special things on Sunday in honor of God.
4. Honor your father and mother.	We love, respect, and obey our parents and all adults who care for us.
5. You shall not kill.	We show respect for God's gift of life by caring for all human life. We never fight or hurt others.
6. You shall not commit adultery.	We respect our bodies and the bodies of others. We use our sexuality according to God's plan.
7. You shall not steal.	We never take things that belong to someone else. We are careful with other people's things. We do not cheat.
8. You shall not bear false witness against your neighbor.	We are truthful and honest. We never tell lies or hurt others by what we say.
9. You shall not covet your neighbor's wife.	We respect the promises that married people have made to each other.
10. You shall not covet anything that belongs to your neighbor.	We are satisfied with what we have. We are not jealous or greedy.

About the Commandments

TEACHER REFLECTION

As the commandments were first given to the Israelites, so they are proclaimed today to the new people of God and to all men and women of faith. The commandments challenge us to deepen our relationship with God and to see the world around us from God's loving and caring viewpoint. Observing God's commandments is the first step to becoming followers of Christ and thus being called to greater holiness.

You may want to review for yourself the Church's teachings about the commandments in paragraphs 2052–2557 of the *Catechism*.

STUDENT REVIEW

Ask for volunteers to read "About the Commandments" on pages 343–344 in their books. Have the students work in groups of two or three to make posters for each commandment. Each poster should have the words of the commandment written at the top, over an illustration of its meaning.

Refer to pages 164–165 and 172–178 in the student text for more information about the commandments.

About Sin and Grace

TEACHER REFLECTION

Sin is a conscious, deliberate choice not to do good; it is a rejection of a loving relationship with God and others. We are responsible for the consequences of our actions and our failure to act for the good. At the same time, we should remember the power of grace in our lives. Grace challenges us to live according to the dictates of conscience, which is informed by the word of God, the wisdom of the Church, and the advice of men and women of faith. With the help of the Holy Spirit, we are directed to lives of holiness and generosity.

You may want to review for yourself the Church's teachings about sin and grace, respectively, in paragraphs 1846–1876 and 1996–2005 of the *Catechism*.

STUDENT REVIEW

Ask for volunteers to read the section "About Sin and Grace" on page 344 in the student text. Have each student compose a prayer to the Holy Spirit to be said for guidance when we don't know the right thing to do. Pass the prayers out to different students to read in a prayer service.

The Great Commandment

"Love God with all your heart, all your thoughts, and all your strength, and love your neighbor as yourself" (based on Mark 12:28–31).

Jesus summed up the Ten Commandments in the **Great Commandment**, which teaches us that God's laws are based on love of God and love of neighbor.

The New Commandment

"This is my commandment: love one another as I love you" (John 15:12).

Jesus' love is the perfect example of how to live. We must love as Jesus loved. Our love for one another is a sign of Jesus' love.

 ## About Sin and Grace

Sin keeps us from living as Jesus' followers. Sin is a free choice to turn away from God's love. We sin by doing something we know is wrong, or we may sin by not doing what we know is right. By sharing in the gift of God's life and love, we have the grace to live as children of God, to be freed from our sins, and to be forgiven.

The Holy Spirit helps us turn away from sin and live as followers of Jesus. The Holy Spirit helps us make good choices. The Holy Spirit helps us know if something is right or wrong. We can pray to the Holy Spirit when we have a difficult choice to make.

Vocations

When we were baptized, we began our new life as Christians. Our parents and godparents wanted to share with us their Catholic faith. As we grow older, we will live more and more as Jesus taught us. We will be invited by God to choose many ways of helping others. God's call to each of us to help others in a special way is called our **vocation**.

Many Ways of Helping

Most Catholics are called by God to help others as members of their parish church. Some of the ways they help at Mass are by reading the Scriptures, leading music, or serving the Eucharist. Other ways to help include teaching others about God's love for them and working to help people who are poor.

345

About Vocations

TEACHER REFLECTION

Every member of the Christian community is called by God to a particular role in the service of the Church. Although our vocation may be to serve as priest, religious, or lay person; as teacher, missionary, or liturgical minister; we all derive our mission from our Baptism into the Church. Our vocation is strengthened by the Holy Spirit in Confirmation and encouraged by our participation in the Eucharist. Through prayer and our experience in the Christian community, we will be able to discern God's call to us and commit ourselves to our particular vocation in the Church.

You may want to review for yourself the Church's teachings about vocations in paragraphs 871–945 of the *Catechism*.

STUDENT REVIEW

Ask for volunteers to read "About Vocations" on pages 345–346 in their books. Work with the class to list on the chalkboard as many names as they can come up with of people in the parish, school, or community who have a vocation. Be sure to include your own name and the names of other teachers and administrators in your school.

Refer to pages 142–151 in the student text for more information about vocations.

Some vocations are celebrated as sacraments in the Church. **Bishops** and priests are called to lead the Catholic community in celebrating the sacraments and in teaching God's word. **Deacons** are also called to serve as leaders in the Church. Deacons often preach homilies, celebrate the sacraments of Baptism and Matrimony, and help direct the work of the parish among the poor.

Religious Sisters and Brothers, who dedicate their lives to serving others through the work of the Church, live in communities among other religious Sisters and Brothers. They make promises to God and to their communities that they will live simply and do the work that their communities help lead them to do.

Many other men and women, who do not belong to religious communities, also commit their lives to serving others full time through the work of the Church. These men and women serve as religious educators, musicians, Catholic school teachers, hospital workers, and lay missionaries. They all help the Catholic community to live as Jesus taught us to live.

ABOUT Missionaries

The Church reaches out to people who need to hear the good news of Jesus and invites them to join the Catholic Christian community. **Missionaries** are men and women, religious Brothers and Sisters, and priests who work in places where the Church needs to grow. Some of those places are here in our country. Others are in countries throughout the world. Missionaries often work among the poor and others who have needs that the Church can help meet. Some missionaries teach people how to grow crops for food. Others teach better health care methods or ways to organize schools.

Missionaries often build Catholic communities among the people with whom they work. They welcome the people into the Church. They celebrate Mass and the sacraments with their new communities. They teach others how to be leaders in the Church so that these communities can grow.

347

TEACHER REFLECTION

Missionaries are men and women, priests, religious brothers and sisters, laymen and laywomen, whose vocation it is to establish the Church in areas where there is no viable Catholic community. In many cases, the first step is caring for the physical needs of the people and promoting justice in places where there is great poverty or oppression. The ultimate goal is to build the Catholic Christian community so that eventually new leadership for the Church—the bishops, priests, religious and lay workers—evolves in that community. It may take many generations, but the work of missionaries has been successful all over the world.

You may want to review for yourself the Church's teachings about missionaries and other vocations in the Church in paragraphs 871–945 of the *Catechism*.

STUDENT REVIEW

Ask for volunteers to read the section "About Missionaries" on page 347 in the student text. Bring to class several magazines published by missionary societies of men and women. Read several accounts of life in the missions. Invite the students to write letters to the missions they have read about.

How Catholics Pray

Prayer is part of every believer's life and the life of the Church. Daily prayer and devotions, the liturgy of the hours, and the Sunday Eucharist all offer ways of celebrating and praising God. Growth in our life of prayer is nourished by taking every opportunity to listen to God and to speak with God as individual believers and as members of the Christian community.

STUDENT REVIEW

Ask a volunteer to read the paragraph under "How Catholics Pray" on page 348 in his or her book.

About Kinds of Prayer

TEACHER REFLECTION

There is no preferred way to pray. God leads each person according to his or her needs. In Christian tradition we find three major expressions or models of prayer—vocal prayer, meditation, and contemplation. Vocal prayer can be a recitation of formal prayers that are learned from others or that are part of the liturgy. We can also speak to God in our own words at any time. Meditation engages the mind, imagination, and emotions by focusing on a particular subject (a psalm, a Scripture passage, God's creation, the life of a saint). Contemplative prayer is attentiveness to God. Done in silence, it is active listening to God.

You may want to review for yourself the Church's teachings about kinds of prayer in paragraphs 2650–2758 of the *Catechism*.

STUDENT REVIEW

Ask for volunteers to read "About Kinds of Prayer" on page 348 in their books. Work with the students to assemble the booklet on pages 349–352.

Refer to pages 112–120 in the student text for more information about prayer.

Through prayer, Catholics express their faith and show their love for God and others. The Church is united through the celebration of the sacraments and the prayers of all of its members.

ABOUT Kinds of Prayer

Prayer is listening and talking to God. We can pray for the needs of others. We can make our whole life a prayer. We can greet God in the morning with prayer. We can pray before meals. We can thank God for our day before we go to sleep. God always hears our prayers.

Quiet Prayer is a way of praying without words. When we pray in silence, God speaks to us in our heart. We can pray quietly by remembering a Bible story or by using our imagination to think of God, Jesus, the Holy Spirit, or Mary. As we pray, we can think about our life with God.

The **Rosary** is a prayer honoring Mary. When we pray the Rosary, we repeat the Hail Mary over and over. We praise Mary and remember some of the most important times in the lives of Jesus and Mary. Praying the Rosary helps us grow closer to Mary and to her son, Jesus.

348

13 **Jesus Is Taken Down from the Cross**

Thank you, Jesus, for giving your life for us.

2 **Jesus Accepts the Cross**

Help me, Jesus, to always do the right thing.

13

STATIONS OF THE CROSS

Jesus Is Alive

Thank you, Jesus, for being with us always.

Making the Booklet

Assist the students in making the booklet "Stations of the Cross." Each student will need a pair of scissors, and the class will need a stapler. Direct the students to tear the pages along the perforated vertical line. Then show the students how to cut along the horizontal line in the middle of pages 349 and 351. The lines to be cut are indicated by a pair of scissors. Have the students place the cut pages on top of each other so that booklet page numbers 1, 3, 5, and 7 appear in the lower right-hand corners. Instruct the students to fold the booklet on the fold line so that the fold is to the left and booklet page 1 is in the lower right-hand corner. Have the students check to make sure that all pages are in proper sequence. Staple the books along the fold line.

You might want to use this booklet with the chapter "Our Church Celebrates Lent" on pages 280–289. It is ideal for use in making the Stations of the Cross. Encourage the students to read and reflect on the steps that Jesus took to the cross.

3 Jesus Falls the First Time
Help me, Jesus, to do my best.

4

12 Jesus Dies
Thank you, Jesus,
for loving us so much.

1 Jesus Is Condemned to Death
Help me, Jesus, when I am
all alone.

2

14 Jesus Is Buried
Thank you, Jesus,
for new life.

Jesus Falls the Third Time

Help me, Jesus, to help others
when they are sad.

6 **Veronica Wipes the Face
of Jesus**

Help me, Jesus, to share
with others.

7

Jesus Is Nailed to the Cross

Help me, Jesus,
when I am hurt.

4 **Jesus Meets His Mother**

Help me, Jesus, to obey
my parents and teachers.

5

7 Jesus Falls the Second Time

Help me, Jesus, to always
keep trying.

8

8 Jesus Meets the Women

Help me, Jesus, to love
all people.

5 Simon Takes the Cross

Help me, Jesus, to care
for others.

6

10 Jesus Is Stripped of His Cloth

Help me, Jesus, when I
am afraid.

ABOUT The Lord's Prayer

Jesus taught his friends The Lord's Prayer. In this special prayer, we honor God. We pray that what God wants will be done. We ask God for the things that we need.

Our Father, who art in heaven, hallowed be thy name.
God is our Father. We pray that everyone will remember how good God is.

Thy kingdom come.
Jesus told us about God's kingdom. We pray that everyone will live as Jesus taught us to live.

Thy will be done on earth as it is in heaven.
We pray that everyone will obey God's laws.

Praying with sign-language gestures

About The Lord's Prayer

TEACHER REFLECTION

The Lord's Prayer teaches us that when we pray we are to be inclusive and mindful of the fact that we are connected to one another. The Lord's Prayer is the prayer of the community. It also teaches us that first we are to praise and adore God and then petition for our needs for nourishment and healing to be met. Since apostolic times, this prayer has been considered the most important prayer for the Christian community.

You may want to review for yourself the Church's teachings about The Lord's Prayer in paragraphs 2759–2869 of the *Catechism*.

STUDENT REVIEW

Ask for volunteers to read "About The Lord's Prayer" on pages 353–354 in their books.

Give us this day our daily bread.

We know that God cares for us. We pray for our needs and the needs of the poor.

And forgive us our trespasses as we forgive those who trespass against us.

We ask God to forgive us for the wrong things we have done.

And lead us not into temptation.

We ask God to help us always to choose what is right.

But deliver us from evil.

We pray that God will protect us from things that may harm us.

Amen.

Our "Amen" says that this is our prayer, too.

Glossary

anointing

putting blessed oil on a person's body as a sign of love, respect, or honor *(page 135)*

Anointing of the Sick

the sacrament of comfort and strength, of forgiveness, healing, and peace *(pages 135, 335)*

Apostles' Creed

a summary of what Catholics and many other Christians believe *(page 95)*

apostolic

founded on and faithful to the teachings of Jesus and his apostles *(page 43)*

Ash Wednesday

the first day of the season of Lent *(page 282)*

Baptism

a sacrament of welcome into the Church community in which we receive the Holy Spirit and begin to share Jesus' new life *(page 333)*

baptismal font

a container for water that is used in Baptism *(page 129)*

baptismal pool

a larger baptismal font in which a person can kneel, stand, or be immersed *(page 129)*

bishop

pastoral leader of a diocese *(pages 215, 346)*

Blackrobes

a name for priests who shared the gospel with Native Americans *(page 306)*

Blessed Trinity

one God in three Persons *(page 330)*

Calvary

the hill where Jesus was crucified *(page 280)*

catholic

open to and accepting of people everywhere *(page 35)*

Catholic Church

the Christian community which celebrates the seven sacraments and recognizes the pope and bishops as its leaders *(page 17)*

Catholics

followers of Jesus who spread God's word, worship God, celebrate the sacraments, and serve those in need *(page 331)*

Christ

the anointed one *(page 321)*

355

Understanding What a Glossary Is

Direct the students' attention to the Glossary on page 355. Have the students choose a word from the Glossary and find the word in the text, using the page reference. Repeat this several times if necessary. Make sure that all the students realize that these are words that they study in the text throughout the year. Encourage them to remember the definitions of these important words of the Catholic faith.

Glossary

Christians

the worldwide community of people who believe that Jesus is the Son of God *(page 13)*

commandments

laws given to us by God to help us live good lives *(page 165)*

communion of saints

the community of all those, living and dead, who believe in Jesus Christ *(page 332)*

Confirmation

a sacrament of welcome which strengthens the new life we received at Baptism and helps us tell everyone the good news about Jesus *(page 334)*

corporal

affecting our bodies and the needs of our bodies *(page 185)*

crux gemmata

a cross decorated with precious stones or jewels *(page 287)*

deacon

a person ordained to help the priest in serving the parish community in many different ways *(pages 215, 346)*

diocese

a community of many parishes that are located near one another *(page 215)*

Doctor

Teacher of the Church *(page 308)*

Easter Vigil

the night before Easter, when the Church celebrates new life in Christ and the resurrection of Jesus, the Light of the World *(page 127)*

epistles

the letters, written mostly by Paul, that became part of the New Testament in the Bible *(page 229)*

Eucharist

a sacrament of welcome that celebrates the real presence of Jesus in the consecrated bread and wine we share *(page 334)*

faith

the belief that Jesus loves us and our response to God's call *(page 47)*

faithful

someone who is always with us and always caring; someone who is to be trusted and depended upon *(page 65)*

gospel

the good news of Jesus' love for all people *(page 43)*

grace

sharing in the gift of God's life and love *(pages 312, 330)*

356

Great Commandment

the commandment to love God and others and which teaches us that God's laws are based on love of God and love of neighbor *(page 344)*

healing

the actions, words, and prayers that help people who are hurting to become well, to feel better, or to be forgiven *(page 133)*

heaven

unending happiness with God and all who love God *(page 332)*

holy

being close to God, loving God and others, and doing his work in the world *(page 23)*

Holy Orders

the sacrament in which bishops, priests, and deacons are ordained to special service in the Church *(pages 147, 335)*

Holy Week

the week from Palm Sunday to Easter in which we remember the important events in the last week of Jesus' life on earth *(page 292)*

immersion

baptizing a new Christian by placing his or her whole body under water *(page 129)*

initiation

how new members learn more about and are welcomed into a group *(page 123)*

Jesse Tree

Jesus' family tree that has symbols of Jesus' ancestors on it *(page 264)*

justice

treating everyone fairly and with respect *(pages 243, 320)*

lector

a minister of the word who proclaims God's word at Mass *(page 227)*

liturgy

the official public prayers of the Church *(page 117)*

Liturgy of the Hours

the official prayers of the Church that some Christians pray together every morning and every evening *(page 117)*

marks of the Church

signs of the Church that show it is one, holy, catholic, and apostolic *(page 43)*

Matrimony

the sacrament that celebrates the lifelong and life-giving love between a man and a woman, who promise to love each other as husband and wife *(pages 149, 335)*

357

mercy
loving care or compassion *(page 185)*

ministry
the ways we serve God and all people according to God's special call *(page 213)*

ministry of community building
ways in which we help the Church to grow in unity *(page 213)*

ministry of service
reaching out to people in need and working to change situations and attitudes that cause people's pain and suffering *(page 245)*

ministry of the word
serving others by sharing God's word with them *(page 223)*

ministry of worship
helping people to pray and take part in community worship *(page 235)*

mission
the work God calls us to do *(page 282)*

missionaries
people who are sent out to spread the gospel throughout the world *(pages 49, 347)*

myrrh
a special perfume put on a person's body when he or she has died *(page 276)*

parables
brief stories that helped people understand what Jesus taught *(page 183)*

parish
a special community where followers of Jesus come together to pray and share stories of our faith *(page 17)*

pastor
a priest who leads a parish community *(page 215)*

Pentecost
the birthday of the Church; the day on which Jesus' first disciples received the gift of the Holy Spirit *(pages 85, 331)*

Pharisees
very religious Jews who based their entire lives on living according to God's laws *(page 163)*

pope
bishop of Rome and leader of the Catholic Church all over the world *(pages 215, 331)*

Glossary

praise

a way to show or tell God how wonderful he is and how grateful we are to him *(page 233)*

prayer

listening and talking to God through our words, our songs, and our gestures *(pages 113, 348)*

prophet

someone called by God to speak in his name *(pages 225, 268)*

psalms

songs of prayer from the Old Testament *(pages 115, 311)*

Reconciliation

sacrament of healing in which we celebrate God's healing and forgiveness of our sins *(page 334)*

respect

to act with care toward someone or something *(page 39)*

resurrection

Jesus' rising from death to new life *(page 75)*

reverence

an attitude of respect, care, and honor *(page 175)*

ritual

the words, actions, and gestures that we use to remember or celebrate something very meaningful *(page 290)*

Rosary

a prayer honoring Mary that recalls some of the most important times in the lives of Jesus and Mary *(page 348)*

Sabbath

a day for rest and prayer *(page 163)*

sacraments

special celebrations of the Church that show Jesus' love for us and are signs of his presence with us now *(pages 113, 333)*

saints

holy men and women who are honored by the Church because they showed in extraordinary ways that they loved God and others unselfishly *(pages 27, 332)*

Savior

a name for Jesus, who saves us from sin and brings us new life *(page 330)*

scribes

well-educated Jews who studied God's law and explained it to people *(page 165)*

Glossary

Scriptures

the written word of God *(page 15)*

sin

anything we do or say that we know is wrong and may hurt others and our relationship with God *(pages 137, 282, 344)*

spiritual

affecting the mind, heart, or spirit *(page 195)*

Stations of the Cross

a devotional prayer that helps us remember how much Jesus loves us and how he died for us *(page 280)*

synagogue

a special place where Jewish people pray and study God's word *(page 115)*

tomb

a place where a person's dead body is laid to rest *(page 294)*

Triduum

the three holiest days of the Church year; from Holy Thursday evening through Easter Sunday evening *(page 290)*

Trinity

the one God whom we know as three distinct Persons: God the Father, God the Son, and God the Holy Spirit *(pages 67, 319)*

trust

to have faith in God's love for us and to believe that God is always with us *(page 63)*

twelve apostles

those chosen by Jesus to teach and lead his friends and followers *(page 15)*

vocation

God's call to develop and use our own unique gifts for our own good and the good of others *(pages 145, 345)*

witness

one who shares what he or she knows about Jesus and lives in the ways that Jesus wants us to live *(page 49)*

worship

to give honor and praise to God, especially as a community *(pages 235, 333)*

Index

The Resourceful Teacher

INTRODUCTION

Welcome to The Resourceful Teacher section of your Teacher Edition. Like the many other features of THIS IS OUR FAITH, the material in this section is designed to help you be successful in preparing for and teaching your Religion class. Here you will find guidelines and practical ideas for your teaching and classroom management. This material expands on the instructions that accompany each chapter. Read through these pages thoughtfully as your year begins and turn to them often throughout the year as a source of ideas and for answers to questions that may arise.

The questions teachers of Religion ask—and we have sought them out and heard their inquiries—generally can be divided into three categories.

1. Questions about catechetics and the meaning of faith.

2. Questions about the psychological makeup of the child and the implications for teaching Religion.

3. Questions about preparing for and conducting a successful Religious Education class.

Answers to questions in these categories are in the Helps for the Teacher section. In some cases the question-and-answer format is used.

CATECHESIS

Catechesis refers to those actions that help people grow in their personal faith within a community of faith (*National Catechetical Directory*, 32–33).

As a teacher of Religion, you should have a clear idea of what you are trying to accomplish with the students in your class. All of us want faith for our students. This faith, we know, is a gift from God. However, we can do much to help our students grow in faith. We can help them grow in knowing, loving, and serving God.

As adult Catholics, we have grown in faith over the years by being part of a community of believers. The students in our Religious Education classes will grow through the same interaction with people of faith.

Our first community of faith consists of those people who nurture and care for us in our earliest years. We grow in age and wisdom in a home setting, just as Jesus did. We learn first from people at home about what it means to love others.

This growth in faith continues in the course of our lives as we expand our horizons beyond the home to the school and to the larger community, including the parish. In the parish community, students meet those people who best exemplify what it means to love God and serve the needs of all people. In the parish, children learn how to pray, worship, and practice the love that Jesus asks of all of us.

Part of the students' religious experience today is your Religion class. In fact, it may well be their most significant and meaningful experience in the Catholic Church. Here you have the opportunity to show the youngsters the joys of being a Christian. You have the God-given chance to help them learn about their Catholic faith. You can help them discover ways in their own lives in which they can make this faith their own and put it into daily practice. Most of this learning will be from your example as a faith-filled catechist.

Faith

In talking about catechesis, we use the term *growing in faith*. But what is faith? As a catechist, you must understand what we mean by *faith* so that you can help your students *grow* in their faith.

It is important to remember that the Church understands faith in a twofold way: (1) Faith is the body of sound doctrine, which teaches us about God and which has been passed down in the Church from age to age. (2) Faith is also a relationship with God. It is a relationship that we grow in over the years. This growing relationship involves a faith based on believing and trusting in the providential care of God. Faith gives meaning to life and directs our actions in love of God and neighbor.

A major aspect of our relationship with God involves the fact that our faith is the Catholic faith. Here we have the heritage and tradition of the Church as it has evolved under the inspiration and guidance of the Holy Spirit down through the centuries. Here are the doctrines and principles that have come down to us as our inheritance from past generations of Catholics. This inheritance includes Bible stories, practices of worship, definitive moral standards, and a wide variety of customs.

THIS IS OUR FAITH aims at helping the students grow in their relationship with God. It also seeks to help the students learn the traditional beliefs and practices of the Catholic Church. In these ways, THIS IS OUR FAITH aims at helping our children know, love, and serve God. It seeks to help the faith of children become "living, conscious, and active, through the light of instruction" (*National Catechetical Directory*, 32).

Catechist

The term *catechist* is the name given to those people in the parish community who seek to help others grow in their Catholic faith through preaching and teaching. Thus, parents are the first catechists a child meets in life. The parish priests act as catechists because they help people know and love God more fully. Teachers of Religion are catechists because they instruct students in the doctrines, principles, and customs of Catholicism. All catechists should have as their focus the desire to help people grow in their personal relationship with God.

CATECHISM OF THE CATHOLIC CHURCH

The *Catechism of the Catholic Church* is the document that contains the essential and fundamental beliefs of Catholic faith and morals.

It is organized into four parts: The Profession of Faith (what Catholics believe); The Celebration of the Christian Mystery (the Sacraments); Life in Christ (moral teachings); and Christian Prayer, with a concluding section on The Lord's Prayer.

The *Catechism* came about as a result of a recommendation of the bishops, recognizing the need for a compendium of the beliefs of the Church. The document, approved by Pope John Paul II in June 1992, is directed first and foremost to the bishops, who have the first responsibility for catechesis. It is directed also to those who prepare materials for catechesis, and through them, to all members of the faith.

The *Catechism of the Catholic Church* is the first such compendium of our faith since the Council of Trent and is therefore an important and historic document affecting future catechesis for generations to come.

A correlation of THIS IS OUR FAITH with the *Catechism of the Catholic Church* is available for teachers using the program.

National Catechetical Directory

The primary source for information about catechesis and your role as a Religion teacher is the document of the National Conference of Catholic Bishops, titled *Sharing the Light of Faith: National Catechetical Directory for Catholics of the United States*. Approved in the late 1970s by the Bishops of the United States and the Sacred Congregation for the Clergy in Rome, the directory defines the goals and characteristics of quality religious education. The NCD, as it is called, sets forth what should be taught in a comprehensive program and explains how the religious formation of children should be approached.

THIS IS OUR FAITH is built on the foundation of the *National Catechetical Directory*. The program's goals and methods are the same as those that are set forth in the pages of the directory. THIS IS OUR FAITH presents the authentic and complete message of Christ and his Church in a way that is adapted to the capacity of children at various grade levels.

PROFILE OF THE THIRD-GRADE CHILD

Karen could hardly wait for Saturday night. Her favorite girlfriends from school would be staying overnight for a slumber party. It had been so much fun planning the party with her mother. They had talked about the food they would prepare, including a great dessert that Karen had read about in a food magazine at school.

Karen also learned from her mother what she and her friends would not be allowed to do. Karen understood that she was responsible for taking care of her home and for respecting the privacy of other family members. She felt proud that her parents trusted her. Everything was going to be just great at her party—if only Saturday were not a whole day away!

This simple account of Karen's slumber party tells us about the concerns and needs of the eight-year-old child. The story illustrates the desire for the love of friends, the need to work with adults, and the increased ability to take responsibility. These are all parts of the psychology of the third grader.

As a teacher of eight-year-old children, you should allow room for the enthusiasm and activity of third graders, while setting boundaries of respect and responsibility. The following questions, which come from third-grade teachers, should help in defining more clearly how this can be done.

Q *How have the students in my third-grade class changed from the way they were in second grade?*

A The students are maturing in a number of different areas. They are mastering the ability to read, and they enjoy using this newly developed skill. They display the same curiosity about life, nature, and people, but they are able to learn more readily from their observations. Their reasoning ability has also grown. These features make teaching these students an exciting and challenging experience.

Q *What role do friends play at this age level?*

A Third graders have an increased social sense, and they place great emphasis on friendships with persons of the same sex. They dislike being embarrassed and criticized in front of their friends. They like being with their friends and doing things with them. On a broader scale, children at this age level display a general willingness to share with one another, more so than at an earlier age. This sometimes involves taking care of younger children.

What is the relationship of third graders to their parents and other significant adults?

There is a need among third graders for warm and supportive reinforcement from parents and other adults. Children of this age still need guidelines and rules to follow. They need to belong to a group, particularly a family group in which there is love and approval. At the same time, there is in the eight-year-old child the movement towards independence. This is sometimes expressed in talking back to adults and in outbursts of anger.

 What do the students need from me as a teacher to help them grow morally as the year goes by?

 Basically, they need to trust you as an adult who will accept them. They need to see you as someone who really cares for them. Here are a few specific ideas.

- Share in a positive way your thoughts and feelings about life and about God. You can be a significant influence on your students' lives when you share your own faith.

- Be patient, since children develop slowly.

- Allow for success, which enhances self-esteem, by assigning simple tasks that the children are able to accomplish well.

- When correcting a child or the class as a whole, react in proportion to the behavior. Be as gentle and patient as possible. Try to remember that the children are only eight years old.

- Realize that the children need to belong to the group and to feel secure. They grow best through being loved by you as their teacher and by being socially accepted by other children. Help them realize that you and God love them despite their errors and wrongdoings. Dwell on the children's good intentions, whenever possible.

- Discuss feelings of fear and anxiety, joy and happiness, sadness and anger as a part of the real experiences of the children's day-to-day lives. Accept their feelings.

- Help the children realize that Christians are happy people. Make humor and laughter a part of each class, whenever this is possible.

- Realize that despite all the common characteristics of eight-year-old children, each child is a unique person.

CLASSROOM ENVIRONMENT

Children learn best in an environment that is happy and secure. This environment will, of necessity, have the following characteristics.

First, there is reverence and respect for each individual in the group. The personal worth of each child is stressed when

- The teacher warmly welcomes each child to the session, calling each one by name.
- The teacher treats everyone fairly, showing no favoritism to particular children.
- The teacher praises a child for what he or she may have accomplished.
- The teacher sends home special notes to children who have missed a session because of sickness.
- The teacher enthusiastically responds to the children's ideas.

Second, a healthy environment is one in which there is a sense of caring among a cheerful community of people in the classroom. Such an environment is created when

- People share with one another.
- People cooperate as a group to get things done.
- People praise one another.
- Personal events such as birthdays and name days are remembered and celebrated.
- People are able to speak freely without fear of ridicule.
- People refrain from making judgments about one another.

Third, a healthy classroom environment is one in which there is a feeling that something of value is being accomplished. The children need to see that they have the opportunity to try new things and acquire new skills as part of the experience of religious education. This happens in a practical way when

- Children take part in activities that allow each individual to be successful.
- Children enjoy working together.
- Children have a clear understanding of what is being taught.
- Children have their questions answered in a way that is meaningful.
- Children are presented with a variety of activities.
- A prayer life is cultivated and the children experience quiet time for reflection.
- Audiovisual presentations are a regular part of the class sessions.

Finally, a healthy classroom environment has a physical setting that is pleasant. Some factors that contribute to a setting conducive to learning are

- A room large enough to accommodate members of the class comfortably, allowing plenty of room for activities.
- A room with windows.
- A room that is well lit and comfortably heated.
- A room that is made visually appealing through the use of pictures, posters, banners, flowers, and the children's art work.
- Chairs that are comfortable.
- Desks or tables that are roomy and the right height.
- Background music at appropriate times.

DEVELOPING SOCIAL SKILLS

Teacher Guidelines for Questioning

Students learn to ask questions in an appropriate way, first and foremost, from the modeling of their teacher. Here are some helpful guidelines for you to consider as you ask questions in the classroom.

- Actively encourage questions. Invite students to ask questions they may have about a particular subject or about directions for doing an activity.

- Avoid questions that start with the words *Would you like to.* Such wording makes it obvious that the teacher expects an affirmative answer.

- Avoid questions that can be answered with a simple *yes* or *no.* The best questions begin with the words *who, what, when, where, why,* and *how.*

- Give students time to think about their responses. Wait about fifteen to twenty seconds after asking a question before making additional comments or before calling on another student.

- Pose questions to the entire group of students before calling on any one member of the class to respond. Avoid going up and down the rows of students in seeking answers to questions. This way, students will pay attention to all the questions being asked and will not "tune out" questions until it is their turn.

- If a question is particularly difficult, give the class time to think about the question and the responses of individual students. Let questions become a puzzle that you and all the students work through together and complete satisfactorily.

- Once key ideas and objectives have been explored, do not continue to ask questions. Summarize the discussion by asking each student to tell one thing he or she is likely to remember about the lesson. In this way, teachers can gain insight into the real learning that has taken place during the session.

Student Guidelines for Questioning

Students should be taught how to get the attention of the teacher during the class and how to speak with other students in the class. In situations where the teacher is doing most of the talking, the students should learn to raise their hands in order to be recognized. This procedure should be the same when any adult talks to the class. Tell the students the reasons you are asking them to raise their hands. These include the right of each person in the class to the individual attention of the teacher. Also explain to the students that some members of the class may not feel comfortable in shouting for attention or in yelling out questions and answers.

There are other situations, such as in small groups, where the students should be allowed to enter the group conversation when appropriate. They should always allow the person speaking to finish what he or she has to say.

A successful method of teaching group discussion skills is to use a play microphone. Only the person with the microphone is allowed to speak. Everyone else in the group must listen to the person speaking. Once the person has finished, he or she will pass the microphone to someone in the group with a raised hand.

PLANNING

One of the keys to a successful Religion class is good planning. This involves taking the time to look ahead. It means being willing to put in work time before class. Such planning is one of the marks of a dedicated and concerned teacher.

There are three special planning times: before the year begins, before each unit, and before actual class time.

Before the Year Begins

Planning starts as soon as you receive copies of THIS IS OUR FAITH. Here are some suggestions for getting started.

- Open to the Contents pages in the student text, noting the major areas of Catholic faith that are being covered.

- Familiarize yourself with the organization of both the student and teacher editions of the text.

- Study the Teacher Edition. The beginning pages of the Teacher Edition provide valuable information on the organization of the program as well as the features of the student text and the Teacher Edition. There you will find a description of the three steps used in every lesson plan. You should become familiar with the features of the student text and this three-step plan.

- Study the Scope and Sequence Charts, which appear in the beginning pages of the Teacher Edition. This will familiarize you with the overall theme of the year as well as with the developmental strands that run through the grade levels.

- Make a program calendar for the year by first determining the number of Religion classes you will have. Other activities might include service projects, planning for liturgies, field trips, and so on. Isolate the days on which you will be able to conduct a class using one of the lessons in the student text.

Next, decide what lessons you will cover during the year and on what days these lessons will be taught. Examine the Contents page in the front of your Teacher Edition, noting that there is one introductory lesson; twenty core chapters; five unit review lessons; five Day to Day: Skills for Christian Living lessons;

thirty-one lessons in the Amen section; and the Our Catholic Heritage, a reference section based on the *Catechism of the Catholic Church*. Each of the sessions is designed to provide you with at least a half-hour's worth of material to use with the students.

Before the Unit Begins

Each of the units of THIS IS OUR FAITH has four chapters that have been placed together because they cover related areas of Catholic faith. Become familiar with the overall development of each unit that you are about to begin teaching.

- Notice that in the Teacher Edition there is a page of information that begins each unit. This unit opener contains the unit aim, a doctrinal summary of each chapter, and the vocabulary. Reading these will give you a preview of the unit.

- For a more detailed overview of the unit, read through the chapters themselves, noting what they are seeking to achieve and the kinds of activities that are suggested.

Before the Class Begins

Experienced teachers have found it valuable to begin their preparation for next week's classes soon after the completion of this week's classes. Here are some steps they recommend.

- After your Religion class is over and you have some time to sit and think, start asking yourself how the class went. What was successful? What did the students respond to most? What would you change if you could do the class over? Write down your observations on the pages of your Teacher Edition or in a separate notebook. You will find this valuable when you teach the same lesson next year.

- Look ahead to the next lesson by turning to its Chapter Organizer in your Teacher Edition. Note the Objectives for the lesson.

- Review the Chapter Outline. This gives you an overview of the major activities that make up the lesson plan that appears in the book. Read through the lesson plan notes on the pages that follow. Make notes to yourself about what will work with your students and what will need to be altered or supplemented. Make any changes you feel are necessary.

- Read the Background for the Teacher section of the Chapter Organizer. This will give you information about the theological content of the lesson as well as notes on the way the topic is approached in the lesson plan.

- Gather any supplies on the Materials Needed list that will not be readily available on the day of class. As you look through each lesson plan, you will find ideas for optional activities and additional information in the Teaching Tips, Cultural Awareness, Curriculum Connection, Focus on, and Enriching the Lesson boxes, which follow the basic lesson plan.

- During the days that follow this first preparation, review the lesson plan in your mind and in your heart. Ask yourself if you really understand what the lesson is trying to accomplish. Think about what you know about the topic and seek additional information if necessary. Pray to the Holy Spirit to guide you in your preparation.

- Finally, take time before class (one-half day to a full day) to review the lesson outline that you set down earlier in the week. Make any necessary changes. Make sure that you have all the materials you will need for the class. Assign an approximate time that you will spend on each of the activities in the lesson plan. Mentally rehearse how you will conduct the class.

Try to make this procedure a part of your routine.

 What does it mean to adapt the lesson plan to your needs?

 Experienced teachers know that the lesson plans that appear in teacher manuals are only suggested ways to teach the chapters. These teachers know their students and the kinds of activities they learn from best. They also know themselves and the kinds of things they do best in class. Experienced teachers take both of these into consideration when reviewing a lesson plan. They ask the following kinds of questions.

- What is really possible for me to accomplish in this lesson?

- What will the students be interested in?

- What is in this lesson that will work with my students?

- What do I have in my own experiences, interests, and talents that can complement or enrich this lesson plan?

Experienced teachers will make adjustments to the lesson plan that appears in the Teacher Edition, based on their answers to the questions above.

 Is there anything that I can read during the year that will help me be a better teacher?

 There are a variety of books and magazines available on becoming a better teacher. Two that should be read are *Sharing the Light of Faith: National Catechetical Directory for Catholics of the United States* and *The Creative Catechist* by Janaan Manternach and Carl J. Pfeifer, the authors of THIS IS OUR FAITH. Another helpful resource is the THIS IS OUR FAITH Program Director's Manual.

LEARNING ACTIVITIES

Storytelling

Children love stories. The sessions of THIS IS OUR FAITH contain many stories from the Bible and from contemporary life.

Be totally familiar with the story. While telling the story, look directly at the students. It is always a good idea to have visuals on hand to illustrate main points, attitudes, or feelings reflected in the story. Keep the storytelling short and simple, interrupting occasionally to ask the students how they would react in similar circumstances. Make sure that you distinguish Bible stories from other kinds of stories.

Drawing

Children do not always have the vocabulary or the experience to express themselves in words the way we do as adults. They are often able, however, to express themselves through drawing.

In order to use drawing effectively, maintain an atmosphere of order in the classroom. An art activity is not a play period. It helps to play appropriate background music. Explain clearly what the students are to do and have all materials ready.

Be sure that you do not make judgments about the artistic value of the students' drawings. Praise their work, allow them to show their work to others, and ensure that specific insights they have expressed are respected. Above all, do not interpret meanings. Leave that to the individual child.

Writing

Writing is a wonderful way for the students to gain insight into themselves and their faith. When we ask the students to write down their thoughts, they are forced to reflect on their ideas and feelings before putting their words on paper. Writing also brings up concerns and questions from the students' experiences that relate to your Religion lesson.

In the THIS IS OUR FAITH program, such writing activity varies in the student text for each grade level. Generally, the activities include writing responses to questions, creating a story or poem, or writing personal prayers.

You should seek to create an atmosphere that encourages the students to write with openness and spontaneity. Don't indicate beforehand what you would write or what you expect them to say in their writing. Do not criticize their grammar and spelling, as you might in a language arts class.

Reading

In all the grade levels of THIS IS OUR FAITH, there are both Biblical and contemporary stories in the student text. There is also poetry to be read by the students. Each lesson contains some explanation of the teaching of Jesus or of various beliefs of the Catholic Church. All of these readings are set at the appropriate reading level for the students of that particular grade.

Reading is important because it is the primary way the students gain new information in their Religious Education class. Through the reading of the lesson, they are introduced to the vocabulary of Catholicism. They learn what the Church believes. They become familiar with the Scriptures through the reading of Bible stories and passages.

Listening to the Teacher

Often, the notes in the Teacher Edition will call upon you to explain something to the students, to add information to materials in the student text, or to clarify concepts that may be confusing to the students. The key advice in making such explanations is to keep them short and simple and avoid moralizing. Remember that explaining something to students in the form of a lecture has been cited in research as one of the least effective ways of teaching.

Memorizing

Memorization is an essential part of all education, including religious education. Two things should always be kept in mind, however. First, the students should not be required to memorize something they do not first understand. Second, the material they memorize should be important or relevant.

In THIS IS OUR FAITH, the students are asked to remember the We Believe and Vocabulary boxes. These contain the key doctrinal concepts of the lesson as well as the new vocabulary.

You may also want the students to memorize the Scripture verse in particular lessons. Various traditional prayers that are valuable for the students to learn are introduced, and others will be found in the Amen section.

Keep in mind that students are usually able to memorize only small amounts of information at any one time. Repetition and the use of memory games are often helpful.

Discussing

Good discussion is an important part of religious education. The students should be able to consider their experience, understanding, and questions about life and about what they have learned.

In planning a discussion, make sure that there is sufficient time. Plan a seating arrangement that lends itself to good discussion. Involve everyone in the group. Keep the discussion moving by asking probing questions. It is important that the students experience a freedom of expression, not fearing censure or ridicule. Make positive comments about their contributions and never allow them to interrupt a child who is speaking.

Questioning

There are four kinds of questions that students will be answering in THIS IS OUR FAITH. They will be found on the pages of the student text or in the teacher notes for the lesson being taught.

Students will be asked *fact questions,* in which they are asked to recall information about the Catholic faith that has been presented.

After they have learned the given material they will be asked *meaning questions.* What does it mean and how will they put into practice a concept or principle they have learned?

The students will be asked *value questions.* How do they feel about what they have learned or what is their attitude about various aspects of the Catholic faith?

They will also be asked to answer *faith questions.* "Why is it sometimes hard for me to do the right thing?" "What does God want me to do?"

Evaluating

There is no form of evaluation that precisely assesses a student's growth in faith. That would be making judgments about the relationship of faith between God and the students. There is, however, an opportunity for the teacher to evaluate what the students have learned as a result of the class sessions.

THIS IS OUR FAITH offers the opportunity to review with the students the content of the lessons of each chapter. The Chapter Review page, which is part of the Day 5 lesson of each chapter, includes fact questions that ask the students to recall the key doctrinal concepts of the lessons and, often, new vocabulary in the chapter. The students are also asked to show how they will apply the teaching of the lessons to their daily lives.

At the end of every four chapters of THIS IS OUR FAITH, you will find a Unit Organizer and a two-page Unit Review. This review includes questions on the facts and concepts learned in the previous four chapters of the unit. It enables the teacher to evaluate what the students have learned and to give further clarification where needed. The suggested project allows for a practical application of the material taught in the unit.

Often, in the lessons themselves, the students are asked to examine their ideas and attitudes regarding some aspect of their life or faith. These are fine opportunities for the students to think critically, to reflect on the importance of possessing the Catholic faith, and to form the resolve to search always for deeper meaning in their relationship with God.

Prayer

Prayer is an important part of each Religious Education class in THIS IS OUR FAITH. The tasks of creating an environment for prayer in the classroom and of supplying various forms of prayer experience for the students are part of your role as a teacher. The students should have the opportunity to celebrate the Eucharist during the year. Those who are able to participate in the sacrament of Reconciliation should have the chance to do so. All the students should be able to experience the prayer services and informal prayers that are part of the lessons of THIS IS OUR FAITH. The students should learn firsthand as members of a community of faith and as persons of faith what it means to listen to and speak with God.

The Resourceful Teacher Package supplies you, the teacher, with a full prayer and liturgy supplement. This packet contains prayer services and ideas for prayer for the entire year. It also provides you with guidelines and helpful hints for planning celebrations with the students.

INVOLVING THE COMMUNITY

Parish Involvement

Earlier in these Helps for the Teacher pages, you read that your role as a teacher is set within the community of faith that is your parish. You have people around you who influence the faith development of the students in your class. Involving these people in a partnership with you will do much to help our children grow as Catholics. There are three groups of people to think about when speaking of this partnership: parents or guardians, priests, and other parishioners.

Involving Parents

■ At the beginning of the year, introduce yourself to the parents or guardians of each of the students in your class. You can do this by sending a letter home, making a friendly phone call, or inviting the parents or guardians to an open house. Explain what you are going to be studying with the students in Religious Education class. Help the parents feel that they are always welcome to talk to you about how their children are doing.

■ Make sure that parents or guardians are aware of *Opening Doors: A Take-Home Magazine,* which can be found at the end of each unit in the student text.

■ If a student misses a class, call the parents or guardians to let them know what they can do at home.

■ Try to keep parents informed about what is happening in the class. Send home assignments for the students to do. Ask that they be returned with their parents' or guardians' signatures.

■ Ask parents or guardians to help out with the class in a variety of ways. Try to have each parent do something for the class during the year.

■ If a progress report is sent home during the year, see it as an opportunity to communicate with the family. Be willing to answer any questions that parents may have.

Involving Priests

The priests of the parish have a powerful influence on the students in your class. Try to involve the priests in ways other than the usual celebration of the sacraments of Eucharist and Reconciliation. Invite them to visit your class to talk about specific topics. Make them feel welcome at all class events by always extending a personal invitation.

Involving Parishioners

Challenge yourself to think of ways you can involve parishioners in your class. Invite people to share their talents and interests with the students. Ask the parish musicians who play for liturgical celebrations to help you bring music to the classroom. Ask the social service people of the parish to show you ways of involving the young students in service activities.

TEACHER'S REFLECTIONS

Teacher's Reflections is a special resource for those who have the awesome responsibility of passing on the truths of our faith to young people. Its purpose is to provide a basis for reflection on the content of each chapter of THIS IS OUR FAITH.

This feature will give you the opportunity to grow in knowledge and faith so that you, in turn, can share that knowledge and faith with your students. As the *National Catechetical Directory* states, "Only men and women of faith can share faith with others, preparing the setting within which people can respond in faith to God's grace" (207).

Each reflection consists of a question for each chapter of the text. This question is intended to be answered after you teach. There is also space to note what really worked in the chapter or what you would change the next time you teach this chapter.

In addition to the chapter reflections, there are sections for beginning-of-the-year and end-of-the-year entries. You can write your thoughts and concerns as you begin a new year of teaching the good news. And when classes come to a close, you can report your general reactions of the entire year along with suggestions for the following year.

Here is a chance to record your thoughts, feelings, beliefs, successes, and setbacks during the year. From time to time, you can look back at your entries and see how much you have really grown in faith and understanding.

Finally, note the "Teacher's Prayer Before Class" below. Pray for guidance and support before teaching your class. Thus, you will acquire the grace necessary to fulfill the mission on which you are sent: to go and teach all nations.

Teacher's Prayer Before Class

Loving God, I am about to share your word with my students. Allow me to awaken in the hearts of my students an awareness of your presence in their lives today.

As I share my faith with these children, I ask you to help me

bring the good news to them;

proclaim your message of unconditional love to them;

envision ways in which to bring your word into their lives.

Help me listen to the needs of these children's hearts and respond to them with your gentle and compassionate spirit. I ask this in the name of Jesus, your great gift of love to us. Thank you, gracious God, for calling me to be a teacher and for helping me to share your good news this day. Amen.

BEGINNING OF THE YEAR

How do I feel about teaching the truths of our faith to others this year?

What are my greatest doubts and fears as I begin the year?

What are my greatest strengths as I begin the year?

What do I hope to accomplish by the end of the year?

How do I hope to help my students grow in faith?

CHAPTER 1

What did my students learn about the unity of the Church?

CHAPTER 2

How did I teach the meaning of the word *holy* to my students?

CHAPTER 3

How did my students understand and appreciate the catholic nature of the Church?

CHAPTER 4

How did I teach my students to be apostolic?

CHAPTER 5

What did my students learn about God the Father?

CHAPTER 6

How did I help my students deepen their understanding of the meaning that Jesus Christ has for their lives?

CHAPTER 7

What insights about the Holy Spirit did my students take with them?

CHAPTER 8

How did my students accept the beliefs expressed in the Apostles' Creed?

CHAPTER 9

What did my students learn about prayer?

CHAPTER 10

How did my students connect the concept of initiation into a group with the sacraments of initiation?

CHAPTER 11

How did my students respond to the belief that God heals us?

CHAPTER 12

How did I introduce my students to the sacraments of Matrimony and Holy Orders?

CHAPTER 13

How did my students accept the teaching that love of God and neighbor is worth more than anything?

CHAPTER 14

How did I help my students understand the Ten Commandments?

CHAPTER 15

What were my students' reactions to performing the corporal works of mercy?

CHAPTER 16

How did I help my students understand their responsibility to practice the spiritual works of mercy?

CHAPTER 17

How did my students learn to be builders of community?

ADVENT

How did my students relate the practice of making a Jesse Tree to their preparation for Christmas?

CHAPTER 18

How did I help my students see that they can be ministers of the word?

CHRISTMAS

What did my students learn from the story of the wise men?

CHAPTER 19

How did I teach my students about ministries of worship in the parish?

LENT

How did I help my students decide what to do for Lent?

CHAPTER 20

How did my students see that they can work for justice and peace?

EASTER

How real is Jesus to my students in the breaking of the bread each week?

END OF THE YEAR

How have I been changed by teaching the truths of our faith to others this year?

How did I improve my teaching skills this year?

What do I feel I have accomplished this year?

How did I help my students grow in faith?

What would I have done differently?

TEACHER'S REFLECTIONS

RESOURCE GUIDE: INTRODUCTION

This Resource Guide provides a list of recommended books, videos, and music recordings for use with the lessons in the student text. The guide follows the organization of the text into five units and the Amen section. The following is an explanation of the formats used in listing the different categories of resource material.

Books Books are listed by title, author or editor, publisher, copyright date, and description. The chapter number or section title in parentheses refers to the place in the student text where the material is recommended for use. For example:

I Got Community. Dale Gottlieb. Holt, 1995. A celebration of various individuals' contributions to the community in first person narration. **(1)**

Videos Videos are listed by video title, length, series title if applicable, company, copyright

date, description, and student text reference in parentheses. For example:

Zip Your Lip to Gossip. (25 min.) "Wooster Square" series. St. Anthony Messenger Press, 1990. Gossiping and telling things that are not true can hurt others and cause a lot of damage. **(14)**

Music Recordings Recordings are listed by title of the song or selection, title of the record album, company, copyright date, and student text reference in parentheses. For example:

"Easter Rise Up." *Come Meet Jesus!* Pauline Books & Media, 1990. **(Easter)**

The Resourceful Teacher section ends with a list of frequently used publishers and media companies. An introductory note to this list, on page 392, offers advice about sources and scheduling.

Unit 1

Books

Come a Tide. George Ella Lyon. Orchard, 1992. Each year when spring floods come, the families in the mountain communities work together to help one another. **(1)**

The Doorbell Rang. Pat Hutchins. Greenwillow, 1986. Two children with a dozen cookies learn the art of sharing. **(1)**

Snow Country. Marc Harchman. Lothrop, Lee & Shepard, 1990. When the worst snowstorm in twenty years hits, Teddy's mom takes in her neighbors who are stranded. **(1)**

The Little Crooked Christmas Tree. Michael Cutting. Scholastic, 1991. An evergreen tree shelters a stranded dove by crooking its branches, even though doing so makes the evergreen unsuitable for a Christmas tree. **(2)**

Mother Teresa, Sister of the Poor. Patricia Reilly Giff. Viking, 1986. An inspirational portrait of a holy woman who tends to the needs of the poor in India and around the world. **(2)**

The Rescue of Brown Bear and White Bear. Martine Beck. Little, Brown & Co., 1991. When an avalanche destroys the home of Brown and White Bear, a group of bears comes from town to help out. **(2)**

Amazing Grace. Mary Hoffman. Dial, 1991. Grace, who is an excellent dancer, is told she cannot play the role of Peter Pan in the school play because she is Black and a girl. Her grandmother helps her deal with the prejudice. **(3)**

What I Like. Lawrence Anholt. Putnam, 1991. In this simple, rhyming text, six children learn that differences in taste are the building blocks of good relationships. **(3)**

RESOURCE GUIDE

383

RESOURCE GUIDE

With the Wind. Liz Damrell. Orchard, 1991. The story of a young boy who enjoys horseback riding even though he is wheelchair-bound. **(3)**

On the Go. Ann Morris. Morrow, 1994. Photos showing how people move from one place to another in all parts of the world. **(4)**

Videos

Christian Corner. (10 min.) "Following Jesus Through the Church Year" series. Twenty-Third Publications, 1990. Story of Paul's conversion and his zeal to proclaim the gospel. **(1)**

Witness Way. (11 min.) "Following Jesus Through the Church Year" series. Twenty-Third Publications, 1990. Krispin travels with Paul to spread the news about Christ. **(1)**

Beauty in the Least. (30 min.) "McGee and Me" series. Family Entertainment Network, 1993. The whole Martin family discovers the importance of caring for others and loving one's neighbor as one's self. **(2)**

Loving My Neighbor. (30 min.) "Gerbert" series. Family Entertainment Video, 1988. Gerbert learns a deeper meaning of God's command to "love one another as yourself." **(2)**

Our Friends on Wooster Square, Vol. II. Franciscan, 1985. Important values and virtues based on Scripture are featured. **(2)**

Are You My Neighbor? (30 min.) "Veggie Tales" series. Oblate, 1994. Two fifteen-minute segments dealing with loving our neighbors and appreciating those who are different from us. **(3)**

Elephant's Picnic. (6 min.) "Stories and Parables" series. Our Sunday Visitor, 1993. The elephant plans a picnic and invites all the animals to join in the celebration, even those who try to stay aloof to it all. **(3)**

Learn to Follow Jesus. (50 min.) ECU, 1988. This video teaches children that putting faith into action is a vital part of spiritual growth. **(4)**

Martin the Cobbler. (27 min.) Billy Budd, 1980. Martin learns the true meaning of life in faith and learns to share this good news with others. **(4)**

Music Recordings

"Building the Kingdom." ***Hi God! 4.*** Oregon Catholic Press, 1995. **(1)**

"We Are the Church." ***Calling the Children.*** Oregon Catholic Press, 1992. **(1)**

"Let Us Sing." ***Hi God! 4.*** Oregon Catholic Press, 1995. **(2)**

"You Call Us to Live." ***Calling the Children.*** Oregon Catholic Press, 1992. **(2)**

"Children of God." ***Calling the Children.*** Oregon Catholic Press, 1992. **(3)**

"We Are Many Parts." ***Today's Missal.*** GIA Publications, 1980. **(3)**

"The Hoorah March." ***Hi God! 4.*** Oregon Catholic Press, 1995. **(4)**

"Make a Joyful Noise." ***Rise Up and Sing.*** Oregon Catholic Press, 1995. **(4)**

Unit 2

Books

Herbie Jones and the Dark Attic. Suzy Kline. Putnam, 1992. Herbie is not sure he can go through with it when he volunteers to sleep in the attic while Grandpa visits. **(5)**

Man Out at First. Matt Christopher. Little, 1993. After an accident, a young baseball player is afraid to go to bat. **(5)**

RESOURCE GUIDE

The Up and Down Spring. Johanna Hurwitz. Morrow, 1993. On a trip to Ithaca, New York, Roddy has trouble keeping his fear of flying a secret. **(5)**

Doodle Flute. Daniel Pinkwater. Macmillan, 1991. Spoiled Kevin Spoon wants Mason Mintz's doodle flute in this story about sharing and friendship. **(6)**

Josie's Troubles. Phyllis Reynolds Naylor. Macmillan, 1992. Josephine discovers that if a friendship is strong enough, there's room for other friends in it. **(6)**

Miss Tizzy. Libba M. Gray. Simon & Schuster, 1993. Miss Tizzy is the one person in the neighborhood people can count on for kind acts and expressions of love and concern. **(6)**

Molly the Brave and Me. Jane O'Connor. Random, 1990. Molly seems fearless, but in time of trouble Beth leads the way. **(7)**

One to Grow On. Jean Little. Puffin, 1991. The story of a girl who tells so many stories that no one knows when to believe her. **(7)**

Slinky Malinki. Lynley Dodd. Stevens, 1991. By day, Slinky Malinki is perfectly behaved, but at night she becomes a thief. **(7)**

The Good Fortunes Gang. Margaret Mahy. Delacorte, 1993. A young boy passes a bravery test set by relatives by sleeping one night in a graveyard. **(8)**

The Green Toenails Gang. Marjorie Sharmat and Mitchell Sharmat. Delacorte, 1991. Olivia Sharp tries to solve the mystery behind a secret club that her best friend wants to join. **(8)**

Ladies and Jellybeans. Candice Ransom. Macmillan, 1991. Wendy has a number of worries about third grade, including her concern about fitting in and making new friends. **(8)**

Videos

Breaking Through the Roof. (25 min.) "Ben and Eddie" series. Oblate, 1990. When Eddie doesn't

see any immediate change after praying for something, trusting God becomes difficult. **(5)**

Cling–The Greedy Fool. (11 min.) "Parables for Children" series. Twenty-Third Publications, 1994. Cling makes gallons of ice cream to store for himself in a warehouse instead of sharing it with his kingdom, but then is ordered to report to a faraway land. **(5)**

Where's God When I'm Scared? (30 min.) "Veggie Tales" series. Oblate, 1994. Junior learns that God is bigger than anything he might be afraid of. **(5)**

The Blunder Years. (40 min.) "McGee and Me" series. ECU, 1993. Nick learns that being true to the heart and treating friends well is more important than trying to fit in. **(6)**

Hey Kid, It's Jesus: He's Our Friend. (25 min.) Shepard, 1987. A variety of presentations illustrate how to find and share Jesus in everyday life. **(6)**

The Basketball Game. (30 min.) Brown-ROA, 1988. Mickey misses a foul shot and fouls one of the opponent's players. He then learns that every decision has a consequence. **(7)**

Do the Bright Thing. (30 min.) "McGee and Me" series. ECU, 1989. McGee leads viewers on an animated tour of Nick's head to explore how Nick makes decisions. **(7)**

Handle with Care. (10 min.) Twenty-Third Publications, 1989. Five open-ended stories in this video involve students in problem-solving and decision-making. **(7)**

Love's Bravest Choice. (27 min.) Oblate, 1991. Maria Goretti's life is witness to today's youth of her bravery, faith, and forgiveness. **(8)**

Saints: Timeless Heroes of Faith. (30 min.) Archdiocese of St. Paul, 1995. Elementary students dressed as their favorite saints tell about the saints' lives and how the saints made choices based on their faith. **(8)**

RESOURCE GUIDE

Waiting for the Wind. (30 min.) Family Films, 1990. A dying man spends his final days strengthening the faith of his wife and grandson, and sharing God's love with his skeptical son-in-law. (8)

Music Recordings

"I Know You Are God." *God Shines on You.* Oregon Catholic Press, 1995. (5)

"People Worry." *Stories and Songs of Jesus.* Oregon Catholic Press, 1994. (5)

"God Be with You." *Hi God! 4.* Oregon Catholic Press, 1995. (6)

"Jesus, You Love Us." *Calling the Children.* Oregon Catholic Press, 1988. (6)

"Come to Us, Spirit of Jesus." *God Shines on You.* Oregon Catholic Press, 1995. (7)

"Envía Tu Espíritu." *Pan de Vida.* Oregon Catholic Press, 1988. (7)

"We Believe." *Calling the Children.* Oregon Catholic Press, 1988. (8)

"We Believe, We Believe in God." *Hi God! 4.* Oregon Catholic Press, 1995. (8)

Unit 3

Books

Before I Go to Sleep: Bible Stories, Poems, and Prayers for Children. Ann Pilling. Crown, 1991. Religious poems and prayers and 22 stories from the Old and New Testaments. (9)

Give Us This Day: The Lord's Prayer. Tasha Tudor. Putnam, 1989. Children of turn-of-the-century New England highlight the paintings that illustrate this Christian prayer. (9)

Thanks Be to God. Pauline Baynes. Macmillan, 1990. This is a collection of prayers and thanksgiving. (9)

The Amish. Doris Faber. Doubleday, 1991. This study of the Amish stresses the strength of their beliefs, their diligence, their simple lifestyle, and their stewardship of the land. (10)

Kitty from the Start. Judy Delton. Houghton, 1987. The story of a Catholic girl growing up in the 1940s and her life in the third grade. (10)

My Brother's Bar Mitzvah. Janet Gallant. Kar-Ben, 1990. Eight-year-old Sarah worries about her brother Ben's bar mitzvah, because he is still acting like a kid when he is supposed to be becoming a man. (10)

Always Gramma. Vaunda Nelson. Putnam, 1988. A little girl talks about what she and her grandmother have shared. (11)

Blackberries in the Dark. Mavis Jukes. Knopf, 1993. Austin's first visit to his grandparents house after his grandfather's death feels lonely and strange until he and his grandmother express their sorrow together. (11)

A Quilt for Elizabeth. Benette W. Tiffault. Centering, 1992. After Elizabeth accepts her father's death, she and her grandmother begin a quilt using patches of his clothing. (11)

Anna the One and Only. Barbara M. Joose. Harper, 1988. Anna suffers from living in the shadow of her "flawless" sister. (12)

Justin and the Best Biscuits in the World. Mildred P. Walter. Lothrop, 1986. Justin thinks some things are "woman's work" until his grandfather shows him differently. (12)

Left and Right. Joanne Oppenheim. Harcourt, 1989. Two brothers who are shoemakers learn that they work best using each other's strength. (12)

Videos

Good and Perfect Gift. (24 min.) Franciscan, 1988. Manuelita has been praying for a special gift for Christmas: a dad who will spend Christmas Day with her family. **(9)**

Jesus in My Place. (30 min.) "Our Dwelling Place" series. Don Bosco, 1988. Stories of Jesus' death and resurrection including the Last Supper, Gethsemane, the crucifixion, and the Easter resurrection appearances. **(9)**

Kevin's Temptation. (9 min.) Twenty-Third Publications, 1994. Kevin relies on his inner strength to help him do the right thing. **(9)**

Baptism. (30 min.) "Sacred Heart Kids Club" series. Don Bosco, 1990. This program highlights aspects of belonging to God's family, genuine conversion experience, and the attractiveness of a joyful Christian community. **(10)**

Confirmation. (30 min.) "Sacred Heart Kids Club" series. Don Bosco, 1990. The sacrament of Confirmation brings to fullness our initiation in God's life and love. **(10)**

Eucharist. (30 min.) "Sacred Heart Kids Club" series. Don Bosco, 1990. Sharing in the Eucharist, we become one body in Christ. We respect and care for one another because of this union. **(10)**

Anointing of the Sick. (30 min.) "Sacred Heart Kids Club" series. Don Bosco, 1990. This program portrays the Church's care for those who are sick and the great love that Jesus has for those who are suffering. **(11)**

Miracles of Jesus. (30 min.) "Animated Stories from the New Testament." Tabor, 1991. Jesus heals the sick, raises the dead, casts out devils, and calms the elements. **(11)**

The Birdseed Blunder. (8 min.) "Parables for Children" series. Mass Media Ministries. King Bird has given Beaky, Fluff, and Squawk each a jar of birdseed. Will they use their gifts well or simply hide them away? **(12)**

Don Bosco. (16 min.) "Famous Men and Women of the Church." Don Bosco, 1988. The story of Don Bosco's early years as a farm boy, his struggling to become a priest, and his later years as a young priest helping abandoned boys. **(12)**

Music Recordings

"If Today You Hear God's Voice." **God Shines on You.** Oregon Catholic Press, 1995. **(9)**

"Our Father." **Rise Up and Sing.** Tape 12. Oregon Catholic Press, 1994. **(9)**

"God's Family." **Joyful Noises.** Brown-ROA, 1993. **(10)**

"We Are Family." **Sacred Heart Kids Club Music.** Franciscan, 1990. **(10)**

"O God, We Are Your Children." **God Shines on You.** Oregon Catholic Press, 1995. **(11)**

"Take My Hand." **Stories and Songs of Jesus.** Oregon Catholic Press, 1994. **(11)**

"These Are Our Gifts." **God Shines on You.** Oregon Catholic Press, 1995. **(12)**

"We Come to Share God's Special Gift." **Calling the Children.** Oregon Catholic Press, 1988. **(12)**

Unit 4

Books

Father Damien. Pam Brown. Stevens, 1988. Father Damien's ministry to people with leprosy is portrayed in this story. **(13)**

Now One Foot, Now the Other. Tomie dePaola. Putnam, 1981. Bobby helps his grandfather recover from a stroke. **(13)**

What Goes Around Comes Around. Sally Ward. Doubleday, 1991. Isabel accompanies her grandmother as she makes the rounds giving food to the needy. **(13)**

All Because I'm Older. Phyllis Reynolds Naylor. Dell, 1989. An eight-year-old gets blamed for his younger sibling's mistakes. **(14)**

RESOURCE GUIDE

The Girls' and Boys' Book about Good and Bad Behavior. Richard A. Gardner. Creative Therapeutics, 1990. This book talks about ethics and values. **(14)**

Teaching the Great Commandments. Anne DeGraaf. Standard, 1987. Excerpts from the Gospels, a mixture of parables, miracles, and other events from Jesus' life. **(14)**

Barry: The Bravest Saint Bernard. Lynn Hall. Random, 1992. The true story of a dog that saved 40 lives in Switzerland. **(15)**

The Gold Watch. Bernice Myers. Lothrop, 1991. When Joey's father loses his job, Joey pawns his bicycle to help out. **(15)**

Pinky and Rex and the Mean Old Witch. James Howe. Macmillan, 1991. Rex wants to get even with mean Mrs. Morgan, but Pinky thinks the old lady needs kindness. **(15)**

Grandfather's Day. Ingrid Tomey. Boyds Mills, 1992. Raydeen tries to mend her grandfather's broken heart when he comes to live with her family after the death of his wife. **(16)**

Kate Shelley and the Midnight Express. Margaret K. Wetterer. Carolrhoda, 1990. Based on a true story, the tale of a young girl who saves a train from disaster. **(16)**

White Owl and Blue Mouse. Jean Joubert. Zoland, 1990. A mouse who is responsible for an owl's capture tries to make amends. **(16)**

Videos

Legend of the Big Foot. (53 min.) "Last Chance Detectives" series. ECU, 1995. This story emphasizes that God wants us to do right and then trust God to do the rest. **(13)**

People of Hope. (15 min.) "Heroes and Heroines" series. Ikonographics, 1992.

Introduces students to Steven Biko, St. Elizabeth Seton, Gandhi, and Ignatius of Loyola. **(13)**

The Velveteen Rabbit. (25 min.) Vision Video, 1985. A little boy learns what it means to be a friend and his toy rabbit learns what it means to be real. **(13)**

The Commandments. (90 min.) Brown-ROA, 1995. This video details each of the Ten Commandments separately. **(14)**

The Ten Commandments. (20 min.) Paulist Press, 1992. This program examines each of the commandments in the context of a child's life. **(14)**

The Good Samaritan: A Story About Helping Others. (20 min.) "Adventures in Character Building" series. Oblate, 1990. The characters in this story learn the true meaning of being kind and helping others. **(15)**

Jesus' Concern for People. (30 min.) "Our Dwelling Place" series. Don Bosco, 1988. Several stories of Jesus' ministry of care and concern are told. **(15)**

The Kingdom of Heaven. (25 min.) "Animated Stories from the New Testament" series. Family Entertainment Video, 1987. A series of short stories and parables that help students learn what the "kingdom of Heaven" is like. **(15)**

Hurt Feelings. (25 min.) "Wooster Square" series. St. Anthony Messenger Press, 1990. Viewers explore what it feels like to be hurt when others are inconsiderate and what they can do to help. **(16)**

Magic Boy's Easter. (24 min.) ECU, 1989. When Josh is hospitalized with a degenerative disease, others try to comfort him to no avail. Then they are all transported to another time where Josh becomes a street magician's crippled servant. **(16)**

Pat on the Back. (25 min.) "Wooster Square" series. St. Anthony Messenger Press, 1990. Telling someone they did a great job or encouraging them to be the best they can be can be shown by a kind word or a pat on the back. **(16)**

Music Recordings

"The Good News of God's Salvation." *Calling the Children.* Oregon Catholic Press, 1988. **(13)**

"Jesus, You Are Bread for Us." *THIS IS OUR FAITH Music Program.* Silver Burdett & Ginn, 1990. **(13)**

"O God, We Are Your Children." *God Shines on You.* Oregon Catholic Press, 1995. **(14)**

"You Call Us to Live." *Calling the Children.* Oregon Catholic Press, 1988. **(14)**

"Lead Me, Lord." *THIS IS OUR FAITH Music Program.* Silver Burdett & Ginn, 1990. **(15)**

"Do You Really Love Me?" *Glory & Praise II.* Tape 1. NALR, 1979, available from Oregon Catholic Press. **(16)**

"Faithful Family." *Do Not Fear to Hope.* NALR, 1986, available from Oregon Catholic Press. **(16)**

Unit 5

Books

Communication. Aliki. Greenwillow, 1993. This cleverly composed picture book introduces ways by which we communicate with one another. **(17)**

My Stories, by Hildy Calpurnia Rose. Dale Gottlieb. Knopf, 1991. In her diary, Hildy Calpurnia Rose chronicles all the happenings in her Brooklyn apartment building. **(17)**

Read to Me Treasury. Sally Grindley. Doubleday, 1990. A collection of 14 stories by various authors that stress positive attitudes. **(17)**

Annie & Co. David McPhail. Holt, 1991. Six-year-old Annie decides to go out into the world and fix things. **(18)**

Busy People. Nick Butterworth. Candlewick, 1992. Many community helpers, such as doctors, farmers, and bakers, are introduced in this question-and-answer book. **(18)**

Family Celebrations. Diane Patrick. Silver Moon, 1993. Portrays a variety of family gatherings and occasions as they are observed in many cultures. **(19)**

Kids' Book of Prayers and All Sorts of Things. Elizabeth Heller and David Heller. Pauline Books & Media, 1995. Book of prayers about life issues and concerns, as well as prayers of thanksgiving in clear sensible language for children. **(19)**

Who Will Miss Me If I Don't Go to Church? Susan Heyboer O'Keefe. Paulist Press, 1993. A child discovers through inner dialogue the many reasons why he should go to church. **(19)**

Maniac Magee. Jerry Spinelli. Little, Brown & Co., 1990. Though his life circumstances get as low as they can go, Maniac Magee rises again and again when love is offered. **(20)**

The Memory Box. Mary Bahr. Whitman, 1992. In this sensitive story, Zach shares a "memory box" with his grandpa, who is fighting Alzheimer's disease. **(20)**

Sophie and the Sidewalk Man. Stephanie Tolan. Macmillan, 1992. Sophie saves money to buy an imported hedgehog and learns to share with a homeless man in the process. **(20)**

Videos

Let the Children Come to Me. (71 min.) Liguori, 1991. Twelve five-minute vignettes bring the word of God to life for children. **(17)**

Martin Luther King. (11 min.) Encyclopaedia Brittanica, 1989. Emphasizes the leadership of Dr. King, the strength of his convictions, and how he lost his life for his beliefs. **(17)**

Martin the Cobbler. (27 min.) Billy Budd, 1980. Martin is old, alone, and hurt. Reflecting on Scripture and meeting new friends help him discover again the meaning of life. (**17**)

Simon the Lamb. (25 min.) Oblate, 1993. Simon, shunned by the other lambs because he is different, rescues them from a winter storm in spite of their actions. (**18**)

Swim Team's Splash. (10 min.) "Doing the Right Thing" series. Twenty-Third Publications, 1994. Members of a swim team learn that hurting one team member hurts them all. (**18**)

Take Me Out of the Ball Game. (30 min.) "McGee and Me" series. ECU, 1990. Little League baseball teammates put too much trust and confidence in one powerful batter, instead of in one another and in God. (**18**)

The Rosary for Little Children. (35 min.) Oblate, 1995. Children will learn how to pray with their families and the Church in this music video about the Rosary. (**19**)

Sacred Heart. (30 min.) "Sacred Heart Kids Club" series. Don Bosco, 1986. Tina asks Sister Jane to help her plan a family prayer service. Mimie shows that the heart can speak through prayer. (**19**)

The Happy Prince. (30 min.) Oblate, 1993. A vain swallow's flight south for the winter is interrupted by the statue of a prince who wants to help the poor and needy. (**20**)

John the Baptist. (25 min.) "Animated Stories from the New Testament." Family Entertainment Video, 1987. A moving story of courage and conviction of John the Baptist. (**20**)

Selfish Giant. (30 min.) Oblate, 1993. A lonely ogre keeps his gates locked and forbids all to play in his beautiful garden. A perpetual winter seizes the garden, until a little boy shows the giant the joy of sharing. (**20**)

Music Recordings

"Take the Word of God with You as You Go." *Calling the Children.* Oregon Catholic Press, 1991. (**17**)

"We Hear God's Word." *Calling the Children.* Oregon Catholic Press, 1991. (**17**)

"The Good Shepherd." *Stories and Songs of Jesus.* Oregon Catholic Press, 1994. (**18**)

"Shepherd Song." *God Shines on You.* Oregon Catholic Press, 1995. (**18**)

"Welcome." *Hi God! 4.* Oregon Catholic Press, 1995. (**19**)

"God Shines on You." *God Shines on You.* Oregon Catholic Press, 1995. (**19**)

"Children of Tomorrow, Children of Today." *Hi God! 4.* Oregon Catholic Press, 1995 (**20**)

"Shalom." *God Shines on You.* Oregon Catholic Press, 1995. (**20**)

Amen

Books

Daniel's Gift. M.C. Helldorfer. Macmillan, 1987. A shepherd boy named Daniel is the focus of this Nativity story set in the Middle Ages. (**Advent/Christmas**)

The Donkey's Dream. Barbara Helen Berger. Putnam, 1985. The story of a donkey who at Christmastime carried "a lady full of heaven" to a stable. (**Advent/Christmas**)

While Shepherds Watched. Jenni Fleetwood. Lothrop, 1992. An eight-year-old shepherd boy is present when an angel tells of the birth of a special child in Bethlehem. (**Advent/Christmas**)

An Easter Celebration: Traditions and Customs from Around the World. Pamela Kennedy. Ideals, 1990. The pre-Christian background of spring festivals and goddesses; the symbolism of new birth and rebirth found in flowers, eggs, rabbits, and lambs; customs of Holy Week; Passover; and two Easter legends are discussed. **(Easter/Lent)**

Petook: An Easter Story. Caryll Houselander. Holiday House, 1988. The Easter themes of birth and resurrection are touched upon gently by Petook, a rooster living near Calvary. **(Easter/Lent)**

Brother Francis and the Friendly Beasts. Margaret Hodges. Scribner, 1991. Poetic text tells of Saint Francis' life, while emphasizing his deep love of animals. **(Saints)**

Mary of Nazareth. Cecil Bodker. Farrar, 1989. This story of Mary, mother of Jesus, incorporates what is known from the New Testament sources. **(Mary)**

Celebrate: A Book of Jewish Holidays. Judith Gross. Platt & Munk, 1992. This clear guide to the major Jewish Holy Days explains the days informally with brief retellings of associated Bible stories. **(Holy Days)**

Mother Teresa: Helping the Poor. William J. Jacobs. Gateway Biographies series. Millbrook, 1991. An admiring portrait of this woman of compassion and peace. **(In the Spirit of Jesus)**

Videos

Cosmic Christmas. (26 min.) Coronet, 1986. A young boy tries to explain to three visitors from outer space the true meaning of Christmas. **(Advent/Christmas)**

Star of Bethlehem. (13 min.) ECU, 1990. This video uses animated silhouettes to visualize the Christmas story. **(Advent/Christmas)**

Walking with Jesus. (8 min.) Twenty-Third Publications, 1987. Follow Jesus' journey to Calvary as each station is presented in language children can understand. **(Lent)**

Proud Tree. (25 min.) Liguori, 1990. The story of the crucifixion from the viewpoint of Rex, the tree that became the cross on which Jesus was crucified. **(Holy Week/Easter)**

Francis: The Knight of Assisi. (30 min.) "New Saints and Heroes" series. Don Bosco, 1986. A wonderfully animated story of the life of Saint Francis. **(Saints)**

Mary, Our Friend. (15 min.) Brown-ROA, 1987. This video explores the meaning of Mary's life in our lives as a model of Christian faith. **(Mary)**

Music Recordings

"Calling the Children." *Calling the Children.* Oregon Catholic Press, 1991. **(Christmas)**

"Jesus, I Will Stay with You." *Stories and Songs of Jesus.* Oregon Catholic Press, 1994. **(Easter)**

"Jesus, You Love Us." THIS IS OUR FAITH *Music Program.* Silver Burdett & Ginn, 1990. **(Lent/Easter)**

"Saints of God in Glory." *God, Beyond All Names.* Oregon Catholic Press, 1990. **(Saints)**

"An Angel Came from Heaven." *Stories and Songs of Jesus.* Oregon Catholic Press, 1994. **(Mary)**

PUBLISHERS AND MEDIA COMPANIES

Many of the resources listed, beginning on page 383, are available from your school, parish, diocesan, regional, college, or university media center. Inquire there first. If you must seek further, the following partial list of publishers/distributors will be helpful. In all cases where you plan to use free or rental materials, confirm availability and make arrangements several weeks in advance of your scheduled use. Be sure to preview your selection before showing it to your class.

Bantam Doubleday Dell
 Publishing Group, Inc.
1540 Broadway
New York, NY 10036
(800) 223-6834

Billy Budd Films
235 E. 57th St.
New York, NY 10022
(800) 772-0380

Boyds Mills Press
815 Church St.
Honesdale, PA 18431
(800) 949-7777

Brown-ROA
1665 Embassy West Dr.
Dubuque, IA 52002-2259
(800) 922-7696

Candlewick Press
(Div. of Walker Books)
2067 Massachusetts Ave.
Cambridge, MA 01240
(617) 661-3330

Carolrhoda Books
See The Lerner Group.

Centering Corporation
1531 N. Saddle Creek Rd.
Omaha, NE 68104-5074
(402) 553-1200

Coronet/MTI Film & Video
4350 Equity Dr.
P.O. Box 2649
Columbus, OH 43216-2649
(800) 321-3106

Creative Therapeutics, Inc.
155 County Rd.
P.O. Box 522
Cresskill, NJ 07626-0522
(201) 567-7295

Crown Books for Young Readers
See Random House, Inc.

Crown Ministries Internat'l
9 Winstone Ln.
Bella Vista, AR 72714
(800) 433-4685

Delacorte
See Bantam Doubleday Dell.

Dell Publishing Co.
See Bantam Doubleday Dell.

Dial Books for Young Readers
See Penguin USA.

Doubleday & Co., Inc.
See Bantam Doubleday Dell.

EcuFilm
810 12th Ave., S
Nashville, TN 37203
(800) 251-4091

Encyclopaedia Britannica
 Educational Corp.
310 S. Michigan Ave.
Chicago, IL 60604-9839
(800) 554-9862

Family Entertainment Network
See Nest Entertainment.

Family Films
(Div. of Concordia Publishing
 House)
3558 S. Jefferson Ave.
St. Louis, MO 63118-3968
(800) 325-3040

Farrar, Straus & Giroux
19 Union Square, W
New York, NY 10003
(800) 788-6262

Franciscan Communications
See St. Anthony Messenger
 Press.

Gateway
(Division Video Media)
2030 Wentz Church Road
P.O. Box 540
Worcester, PA 19490
(800) 523-0226

G.I.A. Publications, Inc.
7404 S. Mason Ave.
Chicago, IL 60638
(708) 496-3800
(800) 442-1358

Greenwillow Books
See William Morrow & Co.

Harcourt Brace & Co.
6277 Sea Harbor Dr.
Orlando, FL 32887
(800) 543-1918

Harper San Francisco
1160 Battery St., 3rd Floor
San Francisco, CA 94111
(415) 477-4444

Harper & Row
See HarperCollins.

HarperCollins Children's Books
See HarperCollins.

HarperCollins Publishers
100 Keystone Industrial Park
Scranton, PA 18512
(800) 242-7737

Holiday House, Inc.
425 Madison Ave.
New York, NY 10017
(212) 688-0085

Henry Holt & Co., Inc.
115 W. 18th St.
New York, NY 10011
(800) 488-5233

Houghton Mifflin Co.
222 Berkeley St.
Boston, MA 02116
(800) 225-3362

Ideals Publications
535 Metroplex Dr.
Nashville, TN 37211
(800) 558-4343

Ikonographics, Inc.
P.O. Box 801
Croton-on-Hudson, NY 10520
(800) 944-1505

Kar-Ben Copies, Inc.
6800 Tildenwood Ln.
Rockville, MD 20852
(800) 452-7236

Alfred A. Knopf, Inc.
See Random House, Inc.

The Lerner Group
241 First Ave., N
Minneapolis, MN 55401
(800) 328-4949

Liguori Publications
One Liguori Dr.
Liguori, MO 63057-9999
(800) 325-9521

Little, Brown & Co.
Time & Life Building
1271 Ave. of the Americas
New York, NY 10020
(800) 343-9204

Lothrop, Lee & Shepard Books
See William Morrow.

Macmillan Books for Young
   Readers
See Simon & Schuster Children's.

Mass Media Ministries
2116 North Charles St.
Baltimore, MD 21218
(800) 828-8825

Morehouse Publishing
871 Ethan Allen Hwy, Suite 204
Ridgefield, CT 06877-2801
(203) 431-3927
(800) 877-0012

William Morrow & Co., Inc.
1350 Ave. of the Americas
New York, NY 10019
(800) 843-9389

Nest Entertainment
(Family Entertainment Network)
6100 Colwell Blvd.
Irving, TX 75039-9833
(800) 452-4485

Nest Entertainment
(Family Entertainment Network)
6100 Colwell Blvd.
Irving, TX 75039-9833
(800) 452-4485

Oblate Media &
   Communications
7315 Manchester Rd.
Maplewood, MO 63143-9914
(800) 233-4629

Orchard Books
See Franklin Watts.

Oregon Catholic Press
5536 NE Hassalo
Portland, OR 97213
(800) 548-8739

Our Sunday Visitor Publishing,
   Inc.
200 Noll Plaza
Huntington, IN 46750
(800) 348-2440

Pauline Books & Media
50 St. Paul's Ave.
Boston, MA 02130
(800) 876-4463

Paulist Press
997 MacArthur Blvd.
Mahwah, NJ 07430
(201) 825-7300

Paulist Productions
17575 Pacific Coast Hwy.
Pacific Palisades, CA 90272
(800) 624-8613

Penguin USA
375 Hudson St.
New York, NY 10014
(800) 331-4624

Puffin Books
See Penguin USA.

G.P. Putnam & Sons
200 Madison Ave.
New York, NY 10016
(800) 631-8571

Random House, Inc.
201 E. 50th St., 22nd Floor
New York, NY 10022
(800) 733-3000

Scholastic, Inc.
555 Broadway
New York, NY 10012-3999
(800) 325-6149

Charles Scribner Sons Books
   for Young Readers
See Simon & Schuster Children's.

Shepard & Associates
P.O. Box 908
Estes Park, CO 80517
(800) 757-1877

Silver Burdett Ginn Inc.
See Simon & Schuster
   School Group.

Silver Moon Press
126 Fifth Ave., Suite 803
New York, NY 10011
(800) 874-3320

Simon & Schuster Children's
200 Old Tappan Rd.
Old Tappan, NJ 07675
(800) 223-2336

Simon & Schuster School Group
P.O. Box 2649
Columbus, OH 43216
(800) 848-9500

Simon & Schuster Trade
1230 Ave. of the Americas
New York, NY 10020
(212) 698-7000

St. Anthony Messenger Press
(also Franciscan
   Communications)
1615 Republic St.
Cincinnati, OH 45210
(800) 488-0488

Standard Publishing
8121 Hamilton Ave.
Cincinnati, OH 45231
(800) 543-1301

Stevens Publishing
3700IH35
Waco, TX 76706
(817) 776-9000

Gareth Stevens, Inc.
River Ctr. Bldg.
1555 N. River Center Dr.
   Suite 201
Milwaukee, WI 53212
(800) 341-3569

Tabor Publishing
200 E. Bethany Dr.
Allen, TX 75002
(800) 822-6701

Twenty-Third Publications
P.O. Box 180
Mystic, CT 06355
(800) 321-0411

Viking Press
See Penguin USA.

Franklin Watts
(Div. of Grolier Publishing Co.)
Sherman Tpk.
Danbury, CT 06813
(800) 672-6672

Whitman Pub.
(Devin-Adair Pubs.)
6 N. Water St.
Greenwich, CT 06830
(203) 531-7755

Zoland Books, Inc.
384 Huron Ave.
Cambridge, MA 02138
(800) 462-6420

For further information you may
wish to consult the following
publishers and/or distributors.

American Library Assoc.
50 East Huron St.
Chicago, IL 60611
(800) 545-2433

Child's World, Inc.
505 N. Highway 169
Suite 295
Plymouth, MN 55441
(612) 797-0155
(800) 599-7323

The Liturgical Press
St. John's Abbey
Collegeville, MN 56321
(800) 858-5450

Oxford Univ. Press
198 Madison Ave.
New York, NY 10016
(800) 334-4249
(212) 726-6000

United States Catholic
   Conference (USCC)
Publishing Services
3211 4th St., NE
Washington, DC 20017-1194
(800) 235-8722

Word Records & Music
3319 W. End Ave.
Nashville, TN 37203
(800) 876-9673